community health nursing
a canadian perspective

edited by
lynnette leeseberg stamler • lucia yiu

Toronto

National Library of Canada Cataloguing in Publication

Stamler, Lynnette Leeseberg, 1952-
Community health nursing : a Canadian perspective / Lynnette Leeseberg Stamler, Lucia Yiu.

Includes bibliographical references and index.
ISBN 0-13-076572-4

1. Community health nursing—Canada. 2. Community health nursing—Canada—Textbooks. I. Yiu, Lucia, 1951- II. Title.

RT98.S73 2005 610.73'43'0971 C2003-906790-4

ISBN 0-13-076572-4

Vice President, Editorial Director: Michael J. Young
Executive Acquisitions Editor: Samantha Scully
Executive Marketing Manager: Cas Shields
Developmental Editor: Toni Chahley
Production Editor: Joel Gladstone
Copy Editor: Rosemary Tanner
Production Coordinator: Andrea Falkenberg
Permissions Research: Nicola Winstanley
Photo Research: Marnie Lamb
Page Layout: Jansom
Art Director: Julia Hall
Interior and cover design: Gillian Tsintziras
Cover Image: Masterfile

9 09 08 07

CHNAC logo appears on the back cover by permission of the Community Health Nurses Association of Canada www.communityhealthnurses.org.

Statistics Canada information is used with permission of the Minister of Industry, as Minister responsible for Statistics Canada. Information on the availability of the wide range of data from Statistics Canada can be obtained from Statistics Canada's Regional Offices, its World Wide Web site at www.statcan.ca, and its toll-free access number 1-800-263-1136.

Printed and bound in Canada.

This book is dedicated to Allan for giving me love and courage, and to my entire family, who promote and support my efforts. It is further dedicated to students, colleagues, and clients, who regularly inspire me to be reminded of why I love nursing and teaching.

LLS

To my daughters, Tamara, Camillia, and Tiffany.

LY

Brief Contents

Contents

List of Canadian Research Boxes

1.1 Gleason, M. (2002). Race, class, and health: School medical inspection and "healthy" children in British Columbia, 1890–1930. *Canadian Bulletin of Medical History/Bulletin Canadien d'histoire de la médecine, 19*(1), 95–112.

1.2 Richardson, S. (1998). Political women, professional nurses, and the creation of Alberta's District Nursing Service, 1919–1925. *Nursing History Review, 6*, 25–50.

2.1 Romanow, R. J. (2002). Building on values: The future of health care in Canada. Final report of the Commission on the Future of Health Care in Canada.

2.2 Standing Senate Committee on Social Affairs. (2002). The health of Canadians—the federal role: Final report on the state of the health care system in Canada. [also known as the Kirby Report]

3.1 Committee to Advance Ethical Decision-Making in Community Health. (2001). *Final Report. March 2001–December 2001.* Toronto, ON.

3.2 Ward-Griffin, C., & McKeever, P. (2000). Relationships between nurses and family caregivers: Partners in care? *Advances in Nursing Science, 22*(3), 89–103.

3.3 Oberle, K., & Tenove, S. (2000). Ethical issues in public health nursing. *Nursing Ethics, 7*(5), 425–438.

4.1 O'Brien-Pallas, L., Doran, D. I., Murray, M., Cockerill, R., Sidani, S., Laurie-Shaw, B., and Lochhaas-Gerlach, J. (2001). Evaluation of a client care delivery model. Part 1: Variability in nursing utilization in community home nursing. *Nursing Economics, 19*, 267–276.

O'Brien-Pallas, L., Doran, D. I., Murray, M., Cockerill, R., Sidani, S., Laurie-Shaw, B., and Lochhaas-Gerlach, J. (2001). Evaluation of a client care delivery model. Part 2: Variability in client outcomes in community home nursing. *Nursing Economics, 20*, 13–21, 36.

4.2 Falk-Rafael, A. R. (2001). Empowerment as a process of evolving consciousness: A model of empowered caring. *Advances in Nursing Science, 24*, 1–16.

5.1 Clark, J. P., Feldberg, G. D., & Rochon, P. A. (2002). Representation of women's health in general medical versus women's health specialty journals: a content analysis. *BMC Womens Health, 20*(2), 5–10.

5.2 Young, L., Turner, L., Bruce, A., & Linden, W. (2001). Evaluation of a mindfulness-based stress reduction intervention. *Canadian Nurse, 97*(6), 23–26.

6.1 Valaitis, R. (2002). "They don't trust us; we're just kids." Views about community from predominantly female inner city youth. *Health Care for Women International, 23*, 243–266.

6.2 Hampton, M. J. (2001). *The Eskasoni story: Final report of the Eskasoni Primary Care Project.* Health Transition Fund, Health Canada.

Sims-Jones, N. (2003). The Eskasoni Primary Care Project. *Health Policy Research Bulletin, 5*, 14–15.

7.1 Friedenreich, C. M., Courneya, K. S., & Bryant, H. E. (2001). Influence of physical activity in different age and life periods on the risk of breast cancer. *Epidemiology, 12*(6), 604–612.

7.2 Siemiatycki, J., & Sharpe, C. R. (2001). Joint effects of smoking and body mass index on prostate cancer risk. *Epidemiology, 12*(5), 546–551.

7.3 Dryden, D. M., Francescutti, L. H., Rowe, B. H., Spence, J. C., & Voaklander, D. C. (2000). Epidemiology of women's recreational ice hockey injuries. *Medicine & Science in Sports & Exercise, 32*(8), 1378–1383.

7.4 Carabin, H., Gyorkos, T. W., Soto, J. C., Joseph, L., Payment, P., & Collet, J.P. (1999). Effectiveness of a training program in reducing infections in toddlers attending day care centres. *Epidemiology, 10*(3), 219–227.

8.1 Hogan, S. E. (2001). Overcoming barriers to breastfeeding: Suggested breastfeeding promotion programs for communities in eastern Nova Scotia. *Canadian Journal of Public Health, 92*(2), 105–108.

9.1 Coffman, S. (1997). Home-care nurses as strangers in the family. *Western Journal of Nursing Research, 19*(1), 82–96.

9.2 Dicicco-Bloom, B., & Cohen, D. (2003). Home care nurses: A study of the occurrence of culturally competent care. *Journal of Transcultural Nursing, 14*(1), 25–31.

10.1 McCallum, M. (1999). *Exploring the development of a comprehensive women's midlife health program.* Halifax, NS: Izaak Walton Killam-Grace Health Centre, Women's Health Program.

10.2 Wong, J., & Wong, S. (2003). Cardiovascular health of immigrant women: Implications for evidence-based practice. *Clinical Governance, 8*(2), 112–122.

10.3 O'Connor, R. (2002). *Report of the Walkerton Inquiry: The events of May 2000 and related issues.* Retrieved July 14, 2002 from www.walkertoninquiry.com/report1/index.html#summary

11.1 Duxbury, L., & Higgins, C. (2003). *Voices of Canadians: Seeking work-life balance.* Retrieved November 30, 2003 from http://labour-travail.hrdc-drhc.gc.ca/worklife/vcswlb-tcrctvp/ tm.cfm

11.2 Skillen, D. L., Anderson, M. C., Seglie, J., & Gilbert, J. (2002). Toward a model for effectiveness: What Alberta occupational health nurses think. *AAOHN Journal, 50*(2), 75–82.

12.1 O'Connor, D. R. (2002). *Report of the Walkerton inquiry: The events of May 2000 and related issues, part one.* Toronto, ON: Ministry of the Attorney General.

13.1 Herbert, R., & White, R. (1996). Healthy hearts at work: Prince Edward Island Heart Health Program: CSC worksite pilot project. *Canadian Journal of Cardiovascular Nursing, 7*(2), 12–18.

14.2 DiCenso, A., Guyatt, G., Willan, A., & Griffith, L. (2002). Interventions to reduce unintended pregnancies among adolescents: Systematic review of randomized controlled trials. *BMJ, 324*(7351), 1426–1434.

14.4 Arthur, H. M., Wright, D. M., & Smith, K. M. (2001a). Women and heart disease: The treatment may end but the suffering continues. *Canadian Journal of Nursing Research, 33,* 17–29.

15.1 Daniel, M., & Messer, L. C. (2002). Perception of disease severity and barriers to self-care predict glycemic control in Aboriginal persons with type 2 diabetes mellitus. *Chronic Diseases in Canada, 23*(4), 130–137.

16.1 Lynam, M. J., Gurm, B., & Dhari, R. (2000). Exploring perinatal health in Indo-Canadian women. *Canadian Nurse, 96*(4), 18–24.

17.1 Pejlert, A. (2001). Being a parent of an adult son or daughter with severe mental illness receiving professional care: Parents' narratives. *Health & Social Care in the Community, 9*(4), 194–204.

18.1 Schafer, P., & Peternelj-Taylor, C. (2003). Therapeutic relationships and boundary maintenance: The perspective of forensic patients enrolled in a treatment program for violent offenders. *Issues in Mental Health Nursing, 24,* 605–625.

19.1 Wolfe, D. A., & Jaffe, P. G. (1999). Emerging strategies in the prevention of domestic violence. The *Future of Children, 9*(3), 133.

20.1 Canadian Housing and Mortgage Corporation. (1999). Research report: Documentation of best practices addressing homelessness. Ottawa, ON: Author. Retrieved December 20, 2003 from www.cmhc-schl.gc.ca/publications/en/rh-pr/socio/socio041e.html

21.1 Maticka-Tyndale, E., Lewis, J., Clark, J. P., Zubrick, J., & Young, S. (1999). Social and cultural vulnerability to sexually transmitted infection: The work of exotic dancers. *Canadian Journal of Public Health, 90*(1), 19–22.

22.1 Chalmers, K., Sequire, M., & Brown, J. (2002). Tobacco use and baccalaureate nursing students: A study of their attitudes and personal behaviours. *Journal of Advanced Nursing, 40*(1), 17–24.

23.1 Malinowski, A., & Stamler, L. L. (2003). Adolescent girls' personal experience with *Baby Think It Over™. MCN: The American Journal of Maternal Child Nursing, 28*(3), 205–211.

24.1 Leenaars, A., Cantor, C., Connolly, C., EchoHawk, M., Gailiene, D., Ziong, A. S. et al. (2000). Controlling the environment to prevent suicide: International perspectives. *Canadian Journal of Psychiatry, 45*(9), 639–644.

25.1 Coristine, M., Crooks, D., Grunfeld, E., Stonebridge, C., & Christie, A. (2003). Caregiving for women with advanced breast cancer. *Psycho-Oncology, 12*(7), 709–719.

26.1 Roggenkamp, S. D., & White, K. R. (1998). Four nurse entrepreneurs: What motivated them to start their own business? *Health Care Management Review, 23*(3), 67–75.

26.2 Myers, M. E. (2000). *Parish nursing: A process of authenticating self through holistic theocentric interconnecting.* Unpublished doctoral dissertation, University of Toronto, Toronto, Ontario.

GLOBAL RESEARCH BOXES

14.1 Blue, L., Lang, E., McMurray, J. J. V., Davie, A. P., McDonagh, T. A., Murdoch, D. R. et al. (2001a). Randomized controlled trial of specialist nurse intervention in heart failure. *BMJ, 323,* 715–718.

14.3 Sandberg, J., Lundh, U., & Nolan, M. R. (2001a). Placing a spouse in a care home: The importance of keeping. *Journal of Clinical Nursing, 10,* 406–416.

Preface

Students and faculty have frequently asked for a community health nursing textbook that reflects the practice of community health nursing in Canada. This book was written in response to this need, incorporating the comments and suggestions of students and instructors across Canada.

The Community Health Nursing Association of Canada (2003) defines community health nursing/public health nursing as a practice specialty that "promotes the health of individuals, families, communities, and populations and an environment that supports their health. The practice of community health nursing combines nursing theory and knowledge, social sciences, and public health science with primary health care" (p. 7). Its goal is to promote, protect, and preserve the health of clients "wherever they live, learn, work, worship, and play in a continuous rather than episodic process" (p. 8).

One might argue that this definition could be applied to community health nursing in any country. Why, therefore, did we choose to write a community health nursing book from a Canadian perspective? We believe that there are historical, political, legislative, cultural, and social influences that are unique to Canadians. They have shaped the evolution of Canadians as a society, our definitions of health, and our expectations relative to health care delivery. Community health nurses are both a product of those influences and an influence themselves. It is not surprising that community health nursing has evolved differently in Canada than in other countries. We believe that new practitioners in community health nursing must understand these influences to continue to practise in and shape community health nursing.

Community Health Nursing: A Canadian Perspective has been written with the undergraduate student in mind. Each topic is explored with the understanding that this will be the student's first foray into the community nursing spectrum. Thus, this book can be used at multiple levels within a basic or post-RN curriculum. For example, students studying the historical and political forces that shaped nursing in Canada would benefit from several of the chapters at the beginning of the book (e.g., Chapters 1, 2, 4, and 5). Students taking a course on legal and ethical issues would find Chapter 3 very useful. Similarly, students in a senior trends and issues course might find the expanding roles in Chapter 26 a base for further exploration. We believe all the chapters would be helpful for a "family as client" or "community as client" course.

OUR APPROACH

Over time there has been much discourse on community health nursing versus public health nursing versus community-based nursing. A variety of authors have offered different definitions that attempt to discriminate amongst these terms. They base their conclusions on factors such as who is the client, what is the setting, what is the educational preparation of the nurse, and who is the employer. Historically, "community health nursing" was used to describe all nursing outside the hospital setting. In this book, community health nursing is defined as a specialty in nursing that encompasses a number of sub-specialties, such as public health nursing and home health nursing. The client may be an individual, group, community, or population, but care is rendered with an eye to the health of the population. The setting may be a home, institution, community, or an agency serving the population. The common academic preparation is the basic education leading to the designation Registered Nurse; however, it is clear that additional educational preparation is frequently required. The employer may be an individual, family, community, government, or non-governmental agency. Whether the chapter authors are addressing a specific health issue or a specific population or aggregate, it is clear that all are speaking about a segment within the larger whole of community health nursing.

It is our belief that community health nursing functions within a multiplicity of theories and understandings. Some theories are common to all facets of the nursing profession, such as ethical treatment of clients. Others come in various shapes and sizes, such as family assessment or the meaning of health. In some cases, nursing drove the development of the theory; in others, we have used the work of theorists in other disciplines. This text reflects that multiplicity, and the authors have described how the theories relate to community health nursing.

In response to feedback from across the country, this book is clearly designed as an overview text. Many texts have been written on some of the topics alone, especially those in the foundation chapters. This text was deliberately designed to introduce students to many of the elements and sub-specialties in community health nursing, but was not meant to be the definitive word on any of the content areas. Each chapter provides the basics of the content area and points the student to additional sources of information through the chapter features.

ABOUT THE CONTRIBUTORS

The contributors are as many and varied as the topics. Some hold academic positions, some are in management or policy positions, while others are front-line practitioners. All came with a desire to create a Canadian community health nursing text. Each brought expertise and knowledge to a particular chapter and topic. Each has presented the various historical, geographical, and theoretical perspectives that assist in explaining and describing community nursing practice. We believe that all have made a meaningful contribution to introducing nursing students to this specialty. You will find a list of the contributors, their affiliations, and the chapters they authored following the preface. To provide context on the varied experience and expertise of our contributors, we have also provided a short biographical sketch for each contributor immediately following the chapter(s) they wrote.

CHAPTER ORGANIZATION

The chapters in *Community Health Nursing: A Canadian Perspective* are organized into five parts:

- Part I: Perspectives on Community Health Nursing in Canada
- Part II: Foundations and Tools for Community Health Nursing Practice
- Part III: Community Clients with Special Health Issues
- Part IV: Common Community Health Issues
- Part V: Future Directions

Part I: Perspectives on Community Health Nursing in Canada introduces students to the general topic area. **Chapter 1** presents an historical perspective on Canadian community health nursing so that students may be enlightened by lessons from the past. **Chapter 2** presents the administration of community health from legislative, cultural, and political perspectives. The authors in **Chapter 3** have used the Standards of Practice for Community Health Nursing (found in Appendix 1) to frame a discussion on legal and ethical issues for CHNs. Finally, **Chapter 4** presents a discussion of the variety of settings, roles, and functions germane to community health nursing. These chapters form the underpinning for the subsequent sections.

Part II: Foundations and Tools for Community Health Nursing builds the base upon which the sub-specialties rest. It begins in **Chapter 5** with a discourse on health from various perspectives. **Chapter 6** provides an examination of primary health care as it was in the past and is in the present. **Chapter 7** describes the science of epidemiology and how it can inform community health nurses' practice. Health promotion is examined from a variety of theoretical frameworks in **Chapter 8**, demonstrating how the philosophy and framework can influence the decisions about interventions. In **Chapter 9** the authors explore individual and family care within the context of community, whereas in **Chapter 10** the community is defined as the client. Environmental and occupational health is explored in **Chapter 11**, followed by a discussion of communicable diseases and their control in **Chapter 12**. In **Chapter 13** community as client is once again the topic, but this chapter examines specifics around planning, monitoring, and evaluating community health programs. Part II concludes with **Chapter 14** on finding, using, and participating in community health nursing research. We believe the topics in Parts I and II are essential for an understanding of community health nursing.

Parts III and IV, composed of focus chapters, provide the details that make the picture of community health nursing more complete. In each focus chapter, a specific health issue or population is presented. In **Part III**, the focus in on **Community Clients with Special Needs**. As an overview text, we have chosen to focus on four specific client groups. They are Aboriginal Canadians (**Chapter 15**); multicultural clients, migrant workers, and newcomers (**Chapter 16**); clients with mental health issues (**Chapter 17**); and clients in the correctional system (**Chapter 18**). In each case the focus is on the populations, with a discussion on health issues frequently seen in each population. In contrast, **Part IV** focuses on **Common Community Health Issues** that may be seen in a variety of populations. Here we have chosen to focus on seven issues: family violence (**Chapter 19**), poverty and homelessness (**Chapter 20**), sexually transmitted infections (**Chapter 21**), substance abuse (**Chapter 22**), adolescent pregnancy (**Chapter 23**), suicide (**Chapter 24**), and hospice and respite care (**Chapter 25**). In these chapters, the authors have explored the issue first and then identified the populations most affected.

Part V: Future Directions contains two chapters. In **Chapter 26**, we present five examples of new and non-traditional areas of community health nursing. The authors outline how each sub-specialty arose out of practice, what nurses who practise in this sub-specialty do, and what additional education or certification is required. We conclude with **Chapter 27**, a brief summary of the opportunities and challenges facing community health nursing.

As you read through the book, you will notice that some concepts/items are mentioned in several of the chapters. This is because they are often seminal documents or definitions that may be viewed through the lenses of the various topics and authors. For instance, many of the chapters will talk about the Lalonde Report, the Epp Report, or the *Declaration of Alma Ata*. You will note that each author views the reports differently, depending on the chapter topic. For example, proponents of health promotion may view some of the reports from one perspective, while the author of the chapter on primary health care may discuss a slightly different perceived influence of the same report. Similarly, cross-cultural nursing is mentioned in the family chapter and the multicultural chapter, but may also be mentioned in the Aboriginal Canadians chapter and the family violence chapter. We anticipate that students and teachers will not see this as redundancy, but rather as an example of multiple perspectives and how and why a multiplicity of theory and practice exists in community health nursing.

A Note on Appendix—Canadian Community Health Nursing Standards of Practice

We are pleased to offer an excerpt from the Canadian Community Health Nursing Standards of Practices as an appendix to this textbook. Released in May 2003, this document explicitly reflects the current practice standards for Canadian community health nurses. In our appendix, we have included the Canadian Community Health Nursing Practice Model, along with a complete outline and description of the standards. In several chapters, contributors have made reference to the standards to enhance the discussion.

Chapter Features

A special effort has been made with this book to incorporate features that will facilitate learning and enhance an understanding of community health nursing in Canada.

- **Chapter Objectives** outline the salient points of the chapter and clarify the skills and knowledge to be learned in that chapter.
- **Canadian Research Boxes** present specific studies from the literature or the authors' knowledge to illustrate or augment the material covered in the chapter. Either the researchers themselves are nurses, or we have chosen health research that community health nurses can use in their practice. Each Research Box is followed by a few Discussion Questions to assist students in using the results.

Canadian Research Box 13.1

Herbert, R., & White, R. (1996). Healthy hearts at work: Prince Edward Island Heart Health Program: CSC worksite pilot project. *Canadian Journal of Cardiovascular Nursing, 7*(2), 12–18.

Based on the principles of community mobilization, this pilot project developed a multi-faceted risk-appraisal tool called Heart Check. The target population comprised 800 civil service employees working in Prince Edward Island. Two hundred and fifty-one persons participated during the six-day Heart Check in June 1992. Evaluation measures to examine process, short-term impact, and long-term out-

- **Case Studies** illustrate a practice application of the information presented in the chapter, followed by Discussion Questions. In Chapter 14 (Research), the case studies and the research boxes have been combined to illustrate a practice question, followed by a literature search and application of research found.

CASE STUDY

In Toronto, over 6000 people are homeless, twice the number in 1996. At that time, the Ontario government drastically cut spending on welfare and low-cost housing. The number of apartments that rent for less than $500 a month has decreased by about 70% since then. Toronto built almost 25 000 public housing units between 1984 and 1996, but fewer than 100 units between 1996 and 2001. Shelters now have 95% occupancy and six times the number of beds.

One result was a tent city, built and lived in by 80 people in downtown Toronto. They lived on five acres of

- **Key Terms** are boldfaced where they are introduced in the body of the text. For convenience, all of the key terms are listed at the end of each chapter in the order in which they appear.
- **Study Questions** test students' knowledge of the facts and concepts in the chapter. Answers to the study questions are included at the end of the book.

STUDY QUESTIONS

1. Name four community settings where CHNs work. Describe their role and functions.
2. What are the characteristics of a healthy community?
3. What nursing process skills will you use to promote the health of the community?
4. What assessment components are used when assessing community health?
5. What are the next steps following the collection of com-

- **Individual** and **Group Critical Thinking Exercises** challenge students to reflect on the content of the chapter and apply it in different situations.

INDIVIDUAL CRITICAL THINKING EXERCISES

1. What qualifications does a nurse need to become a nurse entrepreneur?
2. How should a nurse in independent practice manage client records?
3. Compare and contrast the role of a FCN with a nurse working in an acute care institution and in a government-funded community health agency.
4. Consider the knowledge, attitudes, and skills that are required for effective nursing practice within a faith community.

GROUP CRITICAL THINKING EXERCISES

1. What are the essential components of a business plan?
2. To whom is the nurse in independent practice accountable, and how is this accountability demonstrated?

- **References** cited in the chapter are presented in APA format. A complete list of the research box citations has been highlighted at the end of the book.
- **Additional Resources** direct students to further information on the chapter topic. These include references to books, journal articles, and websites. Students will also find references to specific government and non-governmental agencies relevant to the chapter topics.

Teaching Support

The following supplements are designed to aid instructors in presenting classes, fostering classroom discussion, and encouraging learning.

- An **Instructor's Manual** provides a chapter outline and discussion points for the Individual and Group Critical

Thinking Exercises and the Discussion Questions that accompany the Case Studies in the textbook.

- A **Pearson TestGen** provides over 800 questions. Each question is accompanied by the correct answer and is coded by the cognitive level and skill type tested, and a page reference in the textbook. The Pearson TestGen is a special computerized version of the Test Item File that enables instructors to view and edit the existing questions, add questions, generate tests, and print the tests in a variety of formats. Powerful search and sort functions make it easy to locate questions and arrange them in any order desired. TestGen also enables instructors to administer tests on a local area network, have the tests graded electronically, and have the results prepared in electronic or printed reports. Issued on a CD-ROM, the Pearson TestGen is compatible with IBM or Macintosh systems.
- Both the Instructor's Manual and the TestGen are provided in electronic format on an **Instructor's Resources CD-ROM**.

ACKNOWLEDGEMENTS

In the creation of a book such as this, there are so many people to thank. First, we need to thank colleagues for encouraging us to start the project. As the book moved from proposal to writing, we were thankful for the many authors who agreed to contribute to the book or suggested others who had the expertise we required. Many of our authors took time from other projects to add their knowledge to the book, making this book a priority. At Pearson Education Canada, Ms. Samantha Scully persuaded us to submit a proposal and guided us through the administrative areas, while Ms. Toni Chahley was always supportive as we developed the chapters and moved through the review process. Mr. Joel Gladstone and Ms. Rosemary Tanner provided expertise, ideas, and support, which were invaluable in moving through production. The reviewers, who were nameless to us at the time, contributed significant time and effort in assisting us to make this text strong and representative of Canadian community health nursing. Their names are listed below. We appreciate the assistance of Ms. Kathleen MacMillan at Health Canada in ensuring the accuracy of some of the policy information. Each of us had particular friends and family members who were supportive as we moved through the process of completing a major text. We are grateful to all of you. Finally, as teachers, we thank our students, who were guiding forces in considering the project at all.

We are very excited with this book and hope teachers and learners will be excited too. It has been a long journey, but the end is tremendous. Many nurses across the country have contributed countless hours to portray community health nursing with passion and pride. Come along with us and be amazed to learn what Canadian CHNs are doing today!

Lynnette Leeseberg Stamler and Lucia Yiu

REVIEWERS

Marie Dietrich Leurer, University of Saskatchewan
Sherry Bowman, St. Francis Xavier University
Donna Lynn Rosentreter, Langara College
Carolyn J. Rivard, Fanshawe College
Gail Pahwa, George Brown College
Dr. Frances Legault, University of Ottawa
Jean Langdon, University of Calgary
Alison Nelson, University of Calgary

Contributors

E. Merilyn Allison, RN, BA, BScN, MScN
Sessional Professor, St. Clair College of Applied Arts and Technology
Adjunct Assistant Professor, Faculty of Nursing, University of Windsor
Chapter 13 – Planning, Monitoring, and Evaluation

Lynn J. Anderson, RN, BScN, MN(c)
Faculty of Nursing, University of Alberta
Chapter 26 – Expanding Community Health Nursing Practice

Rhonda J. King Blood, RN, BScN, MA
Health Promotions Specialist, Urban Aboriginal Mental Health Program, Chinook Health Region, Lethbridge, AB
Chapter 15 – Aboriginal Canadians

Kathleen Carlin, RN, PhD
Philosophy Department, Ryerson University, Toronto
Chapter 3 – Ethical and Legal Considerations

Sharon L. Chadwick, RN, BScN, MSc, COHN(C), COHN-S
President, Canadian Occupational Health Nurses; Best Practices Specialist in Workplace Health and Safety, Alberta Human Resources and Employment
Chapter 11 – Environmental and Occupational Health

Donna Ciliska, RN, PhD
School of Nursing, McMaster University and Hamilton Public Health and Social Services, Public Health Research, Education and Development Program
Chapter 14 – Research

Sue Coffey, RN, DNSc
Assistant Professor, School of Nursing, York University, Toronto
Chapter 2 – Financing, Policy, and Politics of Health Care Delivery

Benita Cohen, RN, MScN, PhD (Community Health Sciences)
Assistant Professor, Faculty of Nursing, University of Manitoba
Chapter 8 – Health Promotion

Dauna Crooks, RN, BScN, MScN, DNSc
Associate Chief of Nursing, Education, Hospital for Sick Children, Toronto; Associate Professor, McMaster University, Faculty of Health Sciences; Associate Professor, Faculty of Nursing, University of Toronto
Chapter 25 – Hospice and Respite Care

Bernice Doyle, RN, COHN(c)
Manager, Workplace Health and Safety Policy and Standards Branch, Government of Alberta
Chapter 11 – Environmental and Occupational Health

Kathryn Edmunds, RN, MSN
Assistant Professor, Faculty of Nursing, University of Windsor
Chapter 9 – Family Care
Chapter 16 – Multicultural Clients, Migrant Workers, and Newcomers

Margaret England, RN, PhD, CNS
Associate Professor, Faculty of Nursing, University of Windsor
Chapter 17 – Clients in the Community Mental Health System

Adeline R. Falk-Rafael, RN, PhD
Associate Professor, School of Nursing, York University, Toronto
Chapter 2 – Financing, Policy, and Politics of Health Care Delivery

Elizabeth Battle Haugh, RN, BA, MScN
Director of Health Promotion, Windsor-Essex County Health Unit
Adjunct Assistant Professor, Faculty of Nursing, University of Windsor
Chapter 4 – Practice Settings, Roles, and Functions

Janet B. Hettler, RN, BScN, MN
Independent Consultant, Airdrie, Alberta
Chapter 21 – Sexually Transmitted Infections and Blood Borne Pathogens

Joan Wharf Higgins, PhD
Associate Professor, School of Physical Education, University of Victoria
Chapter 5 – Concepts of Health

Bonnie Kearns, RN, BScN
Victoria Order of Nurses, Sarnia
Consultant, College of Nurses of Ontario
Chapter 26 – Expanding Community Health Nursing Practice

Elizabeth Kinnaird-Iler, RN, BScN, MSc
Manager, Healthy Babies, Healthy Children Program, Windsor-Essex County Health Unit
Chapter 16 – Multicultural Clients, Migrant Workers, and Newcomers

Sue LeBeau, RN, BScN, MScN, PHC Practitioner
Laurentian University and University of Ottawa
Chapter 26 – Expanding Community Health Nursing Practice

Ann Malinowski, RN, BScN, MSc, MD
McMaster University
Chapter 23 - Adolescent Pregnancy

Patricia Malloy, RN, MScN
The Hospital for Sick Children
Cross-appointed to University of Toronto, Faculty of Nursing
Chapter 12 – Communicable Diseases
Chapter 20 – Poverty and Homelessness

Margaret M. Malone, RN, C-PHN, BA, BAAN, MA, PhD
Associate Professor, School of Nursing, Ryerson University
Chapter 19 - Family Violence

Marion McKay, RN, PhD(c)
Faculty of Nursing, University of Manitoba
Chapter 1 – Community Health Nursing in Canada

Barbara L. Mildon, RN, MN, CHE
Community Health Nurses Association of Canada
Chapter 4 – Practice Settings, Roles, and Functions

Bonnie Myslik, RN(EC), BA, BScN, MScN, ACNP
Primary Health Care Nurse Practitioner
Canadian Mental Health Association, Windsor, Ontario
Chapter 24 - Suicide

Joanne K. Olson, RN, PhD
Professor and Assistant Dean, Graduate Services, Faculty of Nursing, University of Alberta
Chapter 26 – Expanding Community Health Nursing Practice

Linda J. Patrick, RN, MSc, MA, PhD(c)
Assistant Professor, Faculty of Nursing, University of Windsor
Chapter 9 – Family Care
Chapter 26 – Expanding Community Health Nursing Practice

Elizabeth Peter, RN, PhD
Assistant Professor, Faculty of Nursing, University of Toronto
Chapter 3 – Ethical and Legal Considerations

Joanne Shaw, RN, BN
Senior Nursing Consultant, Ministry of Community Safety and Corrections Services, Government of Ontario
Chapter 18 – Clients in the Correctional Setting

Dawn Smith, RN, BScN, MN, PhD(c)
Population Health PhD Program, University of Ottawa
Chapter 6 - Primary Health Care

Lynnette Leeseberg Stamler, RN, PhD
Associate Professor and Director, Nipissing University/ Canadore College Collaborative BScN Program
Chapter 7 – Epidemiology
Chapter 20 – Poverty and Homelessness
Chapter 27 – Challenges and Future Directions

Eric Staples, RN, BAAN, MSN, ACNP, ND(c)
Assistant Professor, Faculty of Nursing, McMaster University; Regional Coordinator, Western Region, Ontario Primary Health Care Nurse Practitioner Program
Chapter 26 – Expanding Community Health Nursing Practice

Louise R. Sweatman, RN, BScN, LLB, MSc
Director of Regulatory Policy, Canadian Nurses Association
Chapter 3 – Ethical and Legal Considerations

Helen Thomas, RN, MSc
Associate Professor, School of Nursing, McMaster University; and Clinical Consultant, Hamilton Public Health and Community Services, Public Health Research, Education and Development Program (PHRED)
Chapter 14 – Research

Christine Thrasher, RN(EC), BScN, MScN, PhD(c)
Assistant Professor and Program Coordinator PHC Nurse Practitioner Program, Faculty of Nursing, University of Windsor
Chapter 26 – Expanding Community Health Nursing Practice

Janet L. Wayne, RN, BScN, MN
Independent Consultant, Calgary, AB
Chapter 21 – Sexually Transmitted Infections and Blood Borne Pathogens

Hélène Philbin Wilkinson, RN, BScN, MN(c)
Senior Health Planner, Northern Shores District Health Council, North Bay, ON
Chapter 22 – Substance Abuse

Lynne E. Young, RN, PhD
Associate Professor, School of Nursing, University of Victoria
Chapter 5 – Concepts of Health

Lucia Yiu, RN, BSc, BA, BScN, MSN
Associate Professor, Faculty of Nursing, University of Windsor; Educational and Training Consultant, Yiu Health Consulting
Chapter 10 – Community Care
Chapter 12 – Communicable Diseases
Chapter 26 – Expanding Community Health Nursing Practice
Chapter 27 – Challenges and Future Directions

Part One

PERSPECTIVES ON COMMUNITY HEALTH NURSING IN CANADA

CHAPTER 1

Community Health Nursing in Canada

Marion McKay

OBJECTIVES

AFTER STUDYING THIS CHAPTER, YOU SHOULD BE ABLE TO:

1. Identify the social conditions and beliefs which were the impetus for the development of community health nursing in Canada.
2. Discuss the theoretical and practical distinctions between the practices of visiting nurses and public health nurses.
3. Describe how the emergence of the welfare state shaped the evolution of public health and visiting nursing programs.
4. Discuss the role that women played in the development of public health and visiting nursing programs.
5. Compare and contrast the work of community health nurses in urban, rural, and remote areas of Canada.

INTRODUCTION

The purpose of this chapter is to explore the history of community health nursing programs delivered by professionally educated nurses. From their origins in the late nineteenth century, community health nursing programs have been profoundly influenced by a variety of social, political, and economic forces. The **public health movement**, well established in Canada by the beginning of the twentieth century, put the health of Canadians on the public agenda. **Maternal feminists**, who believed that the unique nurturing capacity of women made them particularly suited to the development of programs to assist women and children (Ladd-Taylor, 1994), also played a major role in the creation of the Canadian welfare state. Their searching critiques of the prevailing social order sparked many of the social reform programs established in early twentieth-century Canada, including the child welfare movement, services for childbearing women, and the establishment of mothers' allowances and other programs to assist families in need (Christie & Gauvreau, 1996). In addition, social beliefs about gender and appropriate roles for women shaped the social system in which community health nurses (CHNs) lived and practised. Finally, the tensions between professional medicine and nursing created both opportunities for and barriers to the development of nursing practice in the community.

It is impossible, in the space of a single chapter, to describe and analyze the development of community health nursing in each Canadian province and territory. Instead, this chapter will trace trends in the development of community health nursing using specific examples drawn from published sources and from research in progress. It will trace the evolution of community health nursing from its dual origins in philanthropic health care organizations and publicly funded municipal health departments, examining the role that the evolving concepts of charity and citizenship played in shaping current models of community health nursing. It will also examine the challenges that confronted nurses as they carved out a role in the community. In the final analysis, community health nursing was always both a response to and a product of its particular time and place.

THE ORIGINS OF COMMUNITY HEALTH NURSING IN CANADA

Community health nursing evolved in two streams. The earliest form was **district nursing** or **visiting nursing**, which evolved in late nineteenth-century Britain, the United States, and Canada. Charitable agencies, often organized and operated by maternal feminists, employed visiting nurses (VNs) to provide care to poor and destitute families. Working-class and lower-middle-class families also were recipients of visiting nursing services. These families could not afford to hire full-time private-duty nurses, and their homes were not large enough to provide accommodation for a nurse during the term of her employment. In Canada, visiting nursing services were organized at both the national and the local level. The best known of these, the Victorian Order of Nurses for Canada (VON), was founded in 1897 "to supply nurses, thoroughly trained in Hospital and District Nursing, and subject to one Central Authority, for the nursing of the sick who are otherwise unable to obtain trained nursing in their own homes, both in town and country districts" (Lady Aberdeen, cited in Gibbon, 1947, p. 8).

The public health nurse (PHN) was a civil servant employed by the local, provincial, or federal government. **Public health nursing** emerged in Canada in the early twentieth century when civic departments of health established health education and preventive programs to combat communicable disease, infant mortality, and morbidity in school-age children. Nurses were perceived as the ideal professionals to deliver these programs because of their medical knowledge and their ability to interact with women and children in private homes and in the public school setting (Sears, 1995).

Although these definitions are theoretically distinct, in practice there was considerable blurring of the boundaries between the practices of VNs and PHNs. For example, in some Canadian cities, the VON provided programs on behalf of the local health department. In other communities, the VON provided public health programs to supplement those provided by the local government. PHNs in rural and remote areas of the country, however, often provided bedside nursing care and obstetrical care because no VNs were available to undertake this work.

In her analysis of twentieth-century Canadian nursing, McPherson (1996) divides the profession into three sectors: hospital nurses, private-duty nurses, and public health (including visiting) nurses. During the late nineteenth and early twentieth centuries, when community health nursing emerged as a distinct specialty, the majority of all nurses were self-employed as private-duty nurses. Public health and visiting nurses were counted amongst the profession's elite. Employment in this speciality practice required additional clinical skills such as midwifery training and, particularly after World War I, post-diploma training at a university (Baldwin, 1997; Green, 1974; McPherson, 1996; Miller, 2000; Penney, 1996). Myra (Grimsley) Bennett, who worked for fifty years as a nurse along Newfoundland's northwestern coast, took two courses in midwifery under the auspices of the Overseas Nursing Association prior to leaving England (Green, 1974). "To my way of thinking... there is still no more important work in all the world than that of helping a mother bring new life into the world" (Green, 1974, p. 24).

As an occupational group, nurses came from a variety of social backgrounds, including middle-class, working-class, and agricultural families. The majority were female, white, and Canadian or British born. Nursing, one of the few respectable careers available to women, offered young women seeking autonomy from their family the prospect for both financial independence and social status (McPherson, 1996). Many women married and left the profession soon after completing their hospital training programs. Others, usually those who remained single or those whose marriages had ended, forged life-long careers in nursing.

Public health and visiting nurses were different from nurses employed in other sectors of the health care system in several ways. They tended to remain in their community practices longer than those employed in hospitals and private-duty nursing. They also enjoyed greater financial stability and higher salaries (McPherson, 1996). Published biographical material also indicates that these nurses actively sought opportunities that combined challenging work with travel and adventure. "I had always wanted to travel," wrote Margaret Giovannini, another Newfoundland outpost nurse, "... and when the opportunity arose to work as well as travel I liked it" (Giovannini, 1988, p. 1). Other pioneer CHNs wrote of their eagerness to find a place where they could fulfill their desire to use their hard won knowledge and skills in a meaningful way (Colley, 1970; Miller, 2000). "When I first arrived at my little northern hospital in Granite Springs," wrote Mary E. Hope, "I felt that my search for the end of the rainbow was over.... With my shining new public health nursing diploma under my arm, I was a consecrated scientist about to enlighten this benighted wilderness village.... This was my kingdom" (Hope, 1955, p. 5–6). Still others sought a practice free (or at least more distant) from the hierarchy and constraints of supervisors and large institutions (Green, 1974). Bessie J. Banfill, who worked in rural Saskatchewan, found that her work amongst that province's settlers, many of whom were immigrants from Eastern Europe, fulfilled a deep personal need. "[I]mpulsive by nature, and restless and dissatisfied with hospital routine and nursing patients surrounded by luxury, I longed for more challenging adventure and freedom" (Banfill, 1967, p. 9). Many genuinely enjoyed interaction with people and embraced opportunities to learn about other cultures (Baldwin, 1997). Banfill (1967) wrote that her "Scottish blood boiled" in response to comments that foreigners were not welcome in Canada. Their sense of adventure, independence, courage, and humanitarianism led pioneering Canadian CHNs to offer their services in Canada's poorest urban districts and most isolated rural communities. These qualities also placed them at the forefront of efforts to place health care within reach of all Canadians.

HEALTH, THE INDIVIDUAL, AND THE STATE

The idea that health care was a right of citizenship, rather than a privilege based upon social rank and income, developed slowly during Canada's first century. The British North America Act (1867) made only limited provisions for the establishment and maintenance of a health care system. The Act specified that the federal government was responsible for quarantine and for the establishment of Marine Hospitals. All other responsibilities for the organization of health care, including public health services, devolved to the provinces. These responsibilities were not specified within the Act, nor did the provinces, in the early years after Confederation, make much effort to undertake them. Such organized health care as did exist was provided at the local (municipal) level through public welfare or, more frequently, charitable organizations. Many provinces passed enabling legislation in the late nineteenth century, which allowed for the establishment of local and provincial departments of health. However, even at the local level, there was considerable reluctance to provide public health services on an ongoing basis. Most early health departments were organized in response to specific local emergencies. When the emergency was over, they were dissolved (Bilson, 1980; Bliss, 1991). Similarly, Medical Officers of Health (MOHs) were appointed on a part-time basis until the 1880s. Toronto, for example, appointed its first full-time MOH in 1883 (MacDougall, 1990). Nurses were an even later addition to the staff of local health departments.

These arrangements were consistent with the social attitudes of the time. The state neither undertook nor was expected to undertake any responsibility for the health care of individuals and families. Those who could afford to pay for their own health care did so. Those who did not have the financial means to make these arrangements either went without care or, if sufficiently desperate or destitute, turned to local governments or charitable organizations for assistance. The poverty, poor health, and social unrest created by industrial capitalism, immigration, and urbanization demonstrated the inadequacy of nineteenth-century assumptions about individual and collective responsibility for the provision of health care. They also shaped the organization and financing of the public health system and the nature of community health nursing.

The Emergence of the Public Health Nurse

The Rise of Urban Health Departments The establishment of urban health departments was fraught with controversy. In an era when individuals were expected to provide for their own health care and governments were not permitted to intrude into the personal lives of individual citizens, health departments threatened to blur the boundaries between the private and public domains. Further, they did so at considerable expense to the public purse. A.J. Douglas, Winnipeg's first full-time MOH, summed up the challenges of his office as follows:

> [W]hen I first took office, the health officer, in my community at least, was looked upon by most people as a rather unnecessary appendage to the municipal pay-roll—not only unnecessary, but very often pernicious, for sometimes he had the temerity to interfere with citizens, particularly the so-called best citizens' inalienable right to do as they please.... It was considered that his proper sphere was to supervise the collection of city wastes, to keep the streets clean, to juggle with statistics (always with a view to emphasizing the salubrity of his own locality), and to occasionally show some activity during outbreaks of the more serious communicable diseases.... He was always to use discretion as to whose toes he trod upon; he was not to point out glaring sanitary defects in his community as this spoiled business and kept visitors away (Douglas, 1912, p. 85).

At the end of the nineteenth century, Canada's major urban centres faced a health crisis which matched in substance, if not quite in magnitude, that of cities in the United States and Great Britain. Major Canadian cities such as Montreal, Toronto, and Winnipeg possessed inadequate or non-existent sanitary infrastructures at the time of their most rapid expansion (Artibise, 1975; Bliss, 1991). The problems were most acute in areas populated by new immigrants and the working poor. The unsanitary living conditions, overcrowding, and inadequate nutrition created by urban poverty were a recipe for disaster. Infant and maternal mortality rates climbed steadily. Periodic outbreaks of communicable diseases such as smallpox, cholera, typhoid, and influenza killed thousands of Canadians. Tuberculosis (TB) emerged as the leading cause of death for urban dwellers who had survived early infancy (Humphreys, 1999).

The first cohort of Canadian public health officials focused their efforts on creating adequate systems of waste disposal and a safe water supply. In addition, drawing on the new science of bacteriology, efforts were directed toward establishing a safe food supply. Particular attention was focused on the health hazards created by unpasteurized milk. Many Canadian cities enacted by-laws, which required the inspection of meat, milk, and bread sold within the city limits, and hired inspectors to enforce these regulations.

In the early twentieth century, public health officials identified health education as another strategy to combat unnecessary disease and death. It was at this point that nurses were first employed as civil servants in local health departments. Although the exact chronology varies from one city to another, the first PHNs were responsible for TB control, child hygiene programs, or school inspection programs. Two important trends can be identified from these pioneering initiatives. First, the employment of nurses by civic authorities was often undertaken with considerable reluctance and only after voluntary programs had foundered in the face of overwhelming need and inadequate financial resources. Second, early PHNs were appointed to single, specific programs rather than to a generalist practice.

From Voluntary to Civic Public Health Programs In 1907 in Toronto, the first civic nurse was employed to provide health education and nursing care in the home to TB patients. However, this nurse and her predecessors had previously been employed by the Toronto General Hospital through a special fund donated by a concerned Toronto citizen. When this arrangement ended, Toronto's city council agreed to include the salary of the TB nurse in the Health Department's budget. Her work went on virtually unchanged, except that she was now required to report to the MOH twice a week (Royce, 1983). That same year in Montréal, the Tuberculosis League hired a nurse from the VON to provide instruction to those suffering from TB (Gibbon, 1947). In Winnipeg, TB nursing was established in 1909 by the Anti-Tuberculosis Society, a voluntary association of physicians and interested citizens (City of Winnipeg Health Department, 1910). The health visiting and health education provided by the Society's TB nurse was carefully coordinated with the city's sanitation and health inspection programs. The Winnipeg Health Department took over the TB nursing program in 1914. A major reason for the change from voluntary to civic funding was to enable the TB nurses to "have the power to make people carry out our regulations where at present persuasion and argument are about the only weapons she can personally use" (City of Winnipeg Health Department, 1915, p. 7).

In other cities, the first PHNs participated in initiatives to preserve and promote the health of school-age children. As working-class children were removed from economic production and placed in the public school system, the significant health problems from which they suffered became fully visible (Peikoff & Brickey, 1991). In the opinion of public officials and social reformers, this situation was intolerable. Ill health detracted from the child's educational attainment, and, worse still, the sickly child of the present was destined to become the poverty-stricken and dependent citizen of the future. Programs for the medical inspection of school children were established in major cities across Canada. School-based inspections were often augmented by home visits to educate the parents and to ensure that all recommendations were followed (Sutherland, 1981). In many cities, such as Montréal, Toronto, Winnipeg, and Vancouver, school health programs were initially established by the Board of Education. They were subsequently taken over by the Health Department as part of the process of consolidating all public health programs under one jurisdiction (MacDougall, 1990; City of Winnipeg Health Department, 1910).

Finally, many early PHNs were employed in programs to reduce infant mortality. Despite all efforts to improve urban sanitation and to regulate food and milk supplies, infant mortality rates in Canadian cities continued to climb until well into the second decade of the twentieth century. What made this state of affairs a national crisis rather than a family tragedy was a shift in beliefs about the role that children played in industrial society and in the process of nation building. Every child, even the Canadian-born child of an Eastern European immigrant, became a precious element in the patriotic process of nation-building (Peikoff & Brickey, 1991). An equally powerful concern, which particularly preoccupied Canadian-born, Anglo-Celtic members of the elite and middle classes, was the fear that they would soon be overwhelmed as a social and political force by the waves of immigrants arriving from Southern and Eastern Europe (McLaren & McLaren, 1997). As the failure of sanitarian and bacteriological strategies to reduce infant mortality became evident, MOHs across North America and Western Europe re-examined their assumptions

Canadian Research Box 1.1

Gleason, M. (2002). Race, class, and health: School medical inspection and "healthy" children in British Columbia, 1890–1930. *Canadian Bulletin of Medical History/Bulletin Canadien d'histoire de la médecine, 19*(1), 95–112.

This historical analysis examines the efforts of social reformers and public health professionals to impose urban, Anglo-Celtic, middle-class values about health on school-age children and their parents. Interventions in the school setting included daily personal hygiene inspection of the children by teachers, a regular program of medical inspections, health education, communicable disease control, and home visits by school/public health nurses to ensure that families both understood and complied with health professionals' recommendations to improve identified medical and health problems. Rural families and those of Aboriginal, Asian, Eastern European, and East Indian origin were the primary targets of these programs since their health practices and beliefs were more likely to deviate from the standards set by the white urban middle class. The author concludes: 1) that the standards for school health programs and medical inspection of school children could not be attained in rural and working-class school districts, 2) that these programs stigmatized children whose families were unwilling or unable to conform to white middle-class models of health, 3) that reform programs that targeted non-Anglo-Celtic families were powerful instruments to strengthen and legitimize the existing social and political system, and 4) that public health professionals contributed to this process, both deliberately and inadvertently, through their paternalistic and sometimes judgmental interactions with both children and parents.

Discussion Questions:

1. How do these findings compare with other descriptions you have read about the impact of public health programs on school-age children and their families?
2. If you were asked to plan a school health program, how would you use the findings of this study?

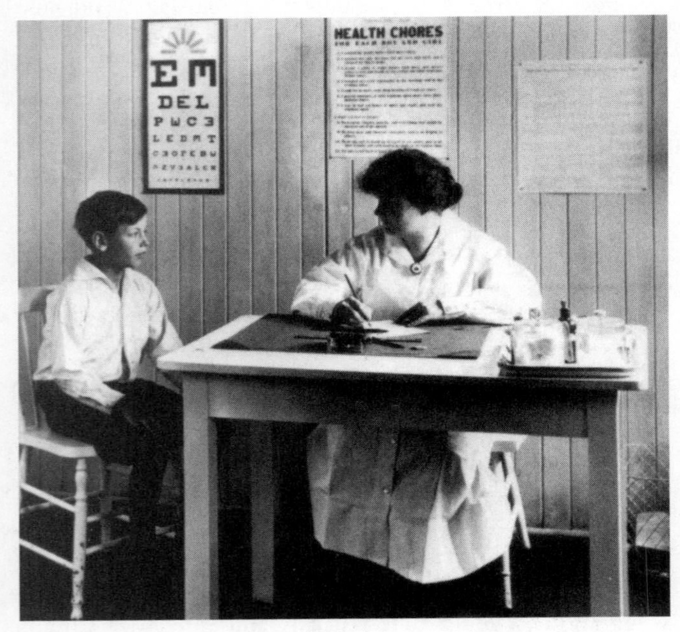

PHOTO 1.1

In Winnipeg, the first public health nurses were hired by the School Board to carry out medical inspections of school-age children. This 1923 photograph shows a provincial public health nurse conducting a health inspection of a school boy in Brooklands, a working-class suburb of Winnipeg.

Credit: Provincial Archives of Manitoba: Public Health Collection 63 (N13039)

FIGURE 1.1 Infant Mortality Rates (per 1000 Live Births) in Selected Canadian Cities, 1908–1918

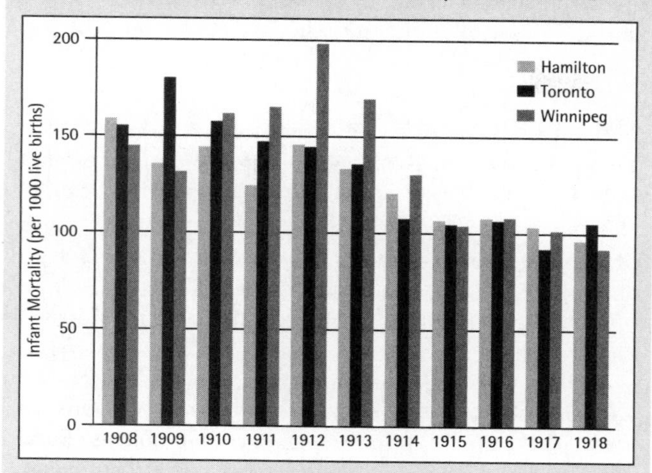

Sources: City of Winnipeg Health Department, 1919; Piva, 1979; Roberts, 1928

Note: Infant mortality statistics were not regularly reported for many other Canadian cities until the early 1920s.

about its etiology and the role that public health might legitimately play in its reduction. Their experiences with poor and immigrant populations convinced them that other factors, particularly those embedded in family and cultural practices, also influenced infant mortality (Meigs, 1916).

Canadian efforts to reduce infant mortality were initiated by elite and middle-class women. Their desire to alleviate the suffering of women and children was inspired by both the **social gospel movement** and maternal feminism. The social gospel movement, which placed priority on the quality of human life on earth, united clergy, politicians, and ordinary citizens in efforts to reform Canadian society (Merkley, 1987). The movement found important allies amongst maternal feminists, who were also advocating sweeping social reform, particularly to protect the interests of women, children, and families (Christie & Gauvreau, 1996).

Public health officials and maternal feminists also turned their attention to the care that infants received from their mothers (Meigs, 1916). They concluded that many parents, particularly the mothers, were "ignorant" and barely capable of providing a safe and healthy environment for the nation's future citizens. Because removing children from their parents was no longer a viable option, educating mothers about infant feeding and hygiene became the intervention of choice (Peikoff & Brickey, 1991). Infant/child welfare/hygiene programs were carried out at milk depots, well baby clinics, and in private homes (Locke, 1918; MacNutt, 1913). VNs staffed the clinics and visited the homes of newborn infants in the early postpartum period. They assessed the health of both the infant and mother, the family's childcare practices, and hygienic conditions in the home. A major focus was to promote the breastfeeding of newborn infants.

In Toronto, a variety of women's groups, settlement houses, and church missions established milk depots and well baby clinics for the city's poorest citizens (MacDougall, 1990; Royce, 1983). Twenty "gouttes de lait" (clinics where mothers unable to breastfeed learned how to properly use cow's milk) were established in Montréal by the Fédération nationale Saint-Jean-Baptiste between 1910 and 1912 (Baillargeon, 2002). In 1915, the VON undertook responsibility for Child Welfare work in Edmonton, and, in 1922, a similar program was established in Ottawa (Gibbon, 1947). In Winnipeg, a child hygiene program was founded in 1910 by the Margaret Scott Nursing Mission (MSNM) with funding from the city's Health Department.

Although voluntary programs confirmed the overwhelming need for both milk depots and child hygiene programs, they could not be sustained. In Winnipeg, for example, the MSNM encountered such severe financial problems that the Health Department took over the program in 1914. A similar pattern of municipal take-over of voluntary programs occurred in other Canadian cities, with PHNs taking the place of VNs in the delivery of child hygiene and milk depot services.

From Specialist to Generalist Practice In the second decade of the twentieth century, urban PHNs began to deliver general rather than specialized services in the community. This change was pioneered in Toronto, where the community

PHOTO 1.2

Child hygiene programs offered public health officials an opportunity to both monitor the health of young children and encourage their mothers to adopt Canadian child-rearing practices. This group, which includes 34 infants and children, gathered on the steps of All People's Mission, Winnipeg, MB in 1921 after having attended a child health clinic staffed by Dr. Ellen Douglas and several nurses.

Credit: Provincial Archives of Manitoba: L.B. Foote Collections 1452 (N2377)

health system had gradually evolved into a confusing mix of programs under the auspices of a variety of private and civic organizations. School health nurses were employed by the Board of Education. VNs were employed by philanthropic organizations to staff milk depots and child hygiene programs. PHNs employed by the Health Department were assigned to several programs, including TB control, measles control, and child welfare. In 1914, Toronto's Child Hygiene and the Communicable Disease programs were amalgamated at the service delivery level and each PHN provided direct care in the home for both programs. The rationale for this reorganization was that the family, rather than the individual, was the basic unit of intervention in public health nursing. "We decided to specialize in homes rather than diseases," stated Eunice Dyke, superintendent of Toronto's PHNs, "and to safeguard the interests of the medical specialist by office organization rather than multiplication of health visitors" (cited in Royce, 1983, p. 49). In 1917, the Board of Education nurses were transferred to the City of Toronto Health Department and their responsibilities were integrated into the role of the generalist PHN (Royce, 1983). Visiting nursing services continued to be provided by the VON and the St. Elizabeth Visiting Nursing Association. These were coordinated with the preventive and health education programs provided by the PHNs (MacDougall, 1990).

The Establishment of Rural Public Health Nursing Public health services in rural and small-town Canada were relatively unorganized until after World War I. A severe shortage of nurses occurred during and after the war (Riddell, 1991), and the majority of available nurses were unprepared for work in public health nursing. Post-diploma programs to prepare nurses for public health work were unavailable in Canada. The VON had established Training Centres in several Canadian cities, including Ottawa, Toronto, and Winnipeg, to prepare registered nurses interested in joining the Order (Gibbon, 1947). However, the impact of the Training Centres was constrained by the Order's limited financial resources.

Fiscal constraints were another factor that delayed the development of rural public health services. Urban centres with a reasonably large tax base found it difficult enough to fund Health Departments. The challenge of raising sufficient funds in small towns and unorganized rural districts was nearly insurmountable. As well, power over the allocation of scarce financial resources rested with far fewer individuals in non-urban settings. Both Stuart (1987) and Riddell (1991) contain first-person accounts by early rural PHNs about the impact that "penny pinching" local officials had on the development of local public health programs.

Popular conceptions about the relative healthiness of urban and rural settings also delayed the development of rural public health programs. Prior to the war, cities had been perceived as more unhealthy environments (Stuart, 1987). The visibility of urban squalor and the relative invisibility of its rural equivalent lulled many social reformers into believing that the pastoral nature of rural life was a healthy antidote to the evils of the city.

After World War I, the development of public health nursing was facilitated by a change in the mandate of the International Red Cross. To support more general efforts at rebuilding social structures in the post-war era, the

Canadian Research Box 1.2

Richardson, S. (1998). Political women, professional nurses, and the creation of Alberta's District Nursing Service, 1919–1925. *Nursing History Review, 6*, 25–50.

This article analyzes the political and professional forces that influenced the establishment of the Alberta District Nursing Service in 1919. Under this program, District Nurses provided obstetrical care (including midwifery), emergency medical care, and public health services to rural and remote districts in the province. Financial responsibility for the program was shared between local districts and the provincial government. Those who could not afford the nursing fees received care free of charge. Enabling legislation under the Public Health Nurses Act allowed nurses who had taken a course in obstetrics to deliver babies in regions of the province where medical care was not available.

The author examines the roles played by the National Council of Women (NCW), the United Farm Women of Alberta (UFWA), the Women's Institutes (WI), and the Alberta Association of Graduate Nurses (AAGN) in the establishment of the District Nursing Service. She concludes that the UFWA was the major force behind the successful establishment of the District Nursing Service. Its members were farm women who had a vested interest in improving services to rural families, particularly women and children. In addition, because the UFWA was an overtly political organization, its members had the political power to lobby the provincial government, then dominated by the United Farmers of Alberta (UFA), to provide the necessary legislation and funding.

The author also concludes that the AAGN's opposition to the District Nursing Program, in particular its midwifery component, was based on its focus on professionalization and the acceptance of professional nurses by the medical profession. The inward-looking focus of both the local and national nursing associations resulted in their gradual withdrawal from and lack of cooperation with social and health reform programs endorsed by other national and local women's groups. In the author's words, "Professionalization took precedence over influencing public policy affecting health care" (p. 42).

Discussion Questions:

1. How do you think professional associations should balance their responsibility to protect the professional status of their members with their responsibility to advocate for health and social reform?
2. What forums would you use to lobby for reform of current community-based health care programs and/or the establishment of new programs?

International Red Cross priorized the development of public health nursing (Hutchinson, 1996). The Canadian Red Cross possessed a substantial fund which had originally been earmarked to support the war effort (VON Minutes, Feb 1920). In the immediate post-war period, it used these funds to establish cottage hospitals and public health nursing services in rural and isolated communities (Miller, 2000; Riddell, 1991; Stuart, 1987), to support visiting nursing services in urban centres (MSNM Minutes, Feb 1920; VON Minutes, Feb 1920), and to provide funding for post-diploma programs in public health nursing at several Canadian universities (Riddell, 1991; Stuart, 1987). In British Columbia, for example, successive classes of nurses graduating from the University of British Columbia's post-diploma and baccalaureate nursing programs accelerated the pace at which rural public health programs could be established (Green, 1984; Riddell, 1991; Zilm & Warbinek, 1995).

The poor health of many military personnel recruited from rural Canada and the horrific loss of life during World War I also redirected political and public attention to the establishment of rural public health programs (Stuart, 1987). The agrarian protest movement in Ontario and the Prairie Provinces also accelerated the development of rural public health services in the post-war era. In Ontario, for example, the election of an agrarian/labour coalition government in 1919 was rapidly followed by the implementation of rural public health programs (Stuart, 1987).

At the local level, rural women's groups such as the Women's Institute and the United Farm Women made community development and the development of health care services a priority. These women lobbied local officials, served tea at Child Welfare Clinics, sewed layettes for destitute families, provided transportation, made referrals, raised funds, and in untold other ways, tried to enable the PHNs to fulfill their professional obligations to the fullest extent possible (Miller, 2000; Riddell, 1991; Stuart, 1987).

Unlike their counterparts in urban settings, the first rural PHNs were generalists. Blurring the boundaries between visiting nursing and public health nursing, these nurses delivered programs in health education, school health, maternal/child health, communicable disease control, social welfare, dental health, and medical/surgical nursing (Riddell, 1991; Stuart, 1987). In addition, they delivered babies and provided emergency medical, dental, and even veterinary assistance on the frequent occasions when these professionals were not available (Giovannini, 1988; Miller, 2000; Riddell, 1991; Stuart, 1987).

To accomplish this work, rural PHNs faced formidable challenges created by distance and climate. Although their urban counterparts, particularly in the early years, often walked many miles to visit homes at considerable distances from street car routes, urban nursing districts were measured in mere city blocks. Rural districts were enormous. As Olive Matthews reported in *The Canadian Nurse* in 1920: "I have a car for my school inspection, given voluntarily by Argyle and Clear Lake districts. It is the only way of covering 925 miles twice a year and paying home visits" (p. 16). The first-hand accounts of early rural PHNs contain vivid descriptions of the various modes of transportation used in the course of their work, and the dangerous road and weather conditions in which they travelled (Colley, 1970; Giovannini, 1988; Miller, 2000; Nevitt, 1978).

In the interwar years, the development of public health services was uneven and often unsuccessful. The time available to follow up on individuals and families needing health education or preventive services was limited, and the nurses' ability to provide long-term follow-up in complex situations was significantly constrained. The need for primary care in rural and isolated areas also limited the successful establishment of public health nursing programs. Many communities wanted VNs who provided bedside nursing care, rather than PHNs who focused on health education and prevention of illness (Matthews, 1920; Stuart, 1987).

On the other hand, local physicians sometimes did not support public health programs because they feared that the PHNs would provide primary care and thus compete with them for both patients and income. It took considerable effort

PHOTO 1.3

Immunization of school-age children was an important part of a rural PHN's work. Small schools and long distances made this a challenging task. In 1932, public health nurse Ina Grenville and an unidentified physician were photographed immunizing a group of school children at Algoma School in Northern Ontario.

Credit: Archives of Ontario. Reference code: RG 10-30-2 (I0005225) Immunizing Children, Algoma, Ontario, 1932

TABLE 1.1
Evolution of Community Health Nursing Programs in Canada

Year	Event	Location
	1891–1900: Laying the Groundwork for Community Health Nursing	
1897	Victorian Order of Nurses for Canada founded	Ottawa
1897	District nurse employed by general hospital outpatient department	Winnipeg
1898	First VON local branch established	Ottawa
	1901–1910: Emergence of Specialized Community Health Nursing Programs	
1901–10	Milk depots and child hygiene programs established by voluntary agencies	Toronto, Montréal, Winnipeg
1901	National anti-tuberculosis society founded	Ottawa
1904	Margaret Scott Nursing Mission founded	Winnipeg
1905	TB nurse employed by general hospital outpatient department	Toronto
1906	TB nurse employed by City Health Department	Ottawa
1907	Medical inspection of school children inaugurated by school board	Montréal
1909	Nurses employed by school board for school inspection program	Winnipeg
1909	Lethbridge Nursing Mission founded	Lethbridge, AB
1910	Civic funding provided to support child hygiene program and milk depot	Winnipeg
	1911–1930: Elaboration and Consolidation of Community Health Nursing Programs	
1914	Child Hygiene program transferred to City Health Department	Toronto, Winnipeg
1914	School Board nurses transferred to City Health Department	Toronto
1914	Public Health Nursing reorganized as a generalist program	Toronto
1916	First provincial public health nurses employed	Manitoba
1918–20	VD control programs established under federal-provincial program	Canada
1919	Provincial District Nursing Service established	Alberta
1919	Red Cross funding supports establishment of public health nursing programs at five Canadian universities	Canada
1920	Provincial school health program established with Red Cross funding	Prince Edward Island
1920	County nursing program established with Red Cross funding	Nova Scotia
1920	Provincial public health nurses employed to work in Northern Ontario	Ontario
1920	First full-time provincial health unit in Canada established	Saanich, BC
1921	Provincial child hygiene program established with Red Cross funding	New Brunswick
	1931–1980: Community Health Nursing in the Evolving Welfare State	
1941–42	Buck Commission recommends major reorganization of public health and visiting nursing programs	Manitoba
1943	Margaret Scott Nursing Mission closes	Winnipeg
1943	VON transfers prenatal, postnatal, and child health programs to provincial health department	Manitoba
1968–70	VON establishes home care demonstration projects	Ontario
1973	*Pickering Report* recommends VON be mandated to deliver home care programs in Canada	Canada
1974	VON included in first publicly funded provincial home care program	Manitoba

Note: Events identified are those found in current literature, and may not, in all instances, be the first such program established in Canada.

on the part of the nurses to assuage these concerns. Stuart (1987), in her analysis of rural public health nursing in northern Ontario, found that PHNs often avoided giving advice to families about the prevention of communicable diseases even when they knew more about immunization programs than did the local physicians. One of the strategies employed to mute the protests of local physicians was to refer all individuals found to have "abnormal" conditions to the attending physician for further follow-up, even in cases where the nurses could have provided this care themselves (Riddell, 1991).

However, tensions surrounding which level of government should finance the public health system likely had the most negative impact on the development of PHN services in rural areas in the interwar years. For example, the nurses sent out to establish a public health system in northern Ontario were not permanently stationed in a community. Instead, they were expected to provide a short-term "demonstration" of the benefits of public health programs, then move on to another location. Should the local authorities agree that these services were necessary, the financing to continue them was to be allocated at the local level. Local authorities were often very happy to accept the services of PHNs financed by the provincial government, but reluctant to employ them out of local funds (Stuart, 1987).

Visiting Nursing in Canada

As is evident from the preceding discussion, previously private health concerns, such as TB and infant hygiene, were redefined as public health concerns in the early part of the twentieth century. In some communities, public health programs replaced services pioneered by visiting nursing organizations. In others, visiting nursing organizations either entered into contractual arrangements with local health departments to provide these services or continued to provide them on their own initiative in the absence of government action. In addition to their occasional involvement in public health programs, visiting nursing organizations also continued to fulfill their original mandate to provide bedside nursing care in the home. This section will examine the experiences and challenges of Canadian visiting nursing organizations between 1897 and 1945.

Established in 1897, the VON is Canada's only national community health nursing organization. Its capacity to respond to local needs and opportunities stemmed from its organizational structure. Local branches were established in communities that had enough volunteers to sustain the organization. They reported to the Central Board, located in Ottawa, which set out guiding principles for the operation of local branches. It also encouraged local branches to seize opportunities to extend their work and to demonstrate the VON's capacity to deliver the whole range of community health nursing services. Visiting nursing services were the backbone of the local branches. In most communities, bedside nursing care was provided to a full range of destitute, working-class, and middle-class families who could not afford to hire private-duty nurses. Families paid what they could for these services. The difference between the actual cost of the service and what was paid in fees was underwritten by charitable donations, fundraising, and, in some cases, grants from city or provincial governments. In this way, the local branches fulfilled a dual mandate: charitable work amongst the poor and the provision of affordable nursing care to the working and middle classes. The history of the VON has been documented in two monographs, one written on the occasion of its 50th anniversary (Gibbon, 1947) and one to celebrate its 100th year of service in Canada (Penney, 1996). The experience of the Winnipeg Branch of the VON will be used as a case study to illustrate how the unique characteristics of specific communities shaped the services offered by the local branches.

In Winnipeg, charitable visiting nursing was pioneered by the Margaret Scott Nursing Mission, founded in 1904 to support the charitable work that Margaret Scott had been carrying out in the immigrant districts of Winnipeg since the 1890s (MSNM Minutes, May 1904). Scott was not a nurse, but in the course of her visits she encountered many people requiring medical and nursing assistance. The Mission performed an important role in preventing the admission of indigent patients to the charity wards of the Winnipeg General Hospital, thus reducing the cost of their care for local taxpayers. In keeping with the goals of the social gospel movement and maternal feminism, the majority of the Mission's patients in the early years were children and pregnant women. After

PHOTO 1.4

The Margaret Scott Nursing Mission provided charitable visiting nursing services to Winnipeg's poor and immigrant citizens from 1904–1943. It was located at 99 George St. on the south edge of Winnipeg's famous North End. This photograph, circa 1914, was taken just prior to the takeover of their child hygiene program by the City Health Department. Margaret Scott is front row centre.

Credit: Allan D. McKay (private collection)

hospital-based obstetrical care became the norm even for poor women, the majority of individuals receiving services from the MSNM were elderly or chronically ill.

The incursion of the Winnipeg branch of the VON into visiting nursing in 1905 forced the two organizations to coordinate their work so that they would not duplicate services. Ultimately, they agreed that the VON would provide services to those who "... did not wish to be classed as charity patients & who were willing to pay moderately for the services of a nurse," while the MSNM would continue to focus its attention on Winnipeg's poor and destitute populations (MSNM Minutes, May 1910). For the first few years, the Winnipeg Branch struggled to establish a non-charitable visiting nursing program in the city and the growth of the organization was relatively slow.

However, new life was injected into the Winnipeg Branch after WWI. In 1919, a new Superintendent of Nurses brought fresh ideas gleaned from her extensive experience in other communities. In 1920, the local Red Cross Society provided the funds to put some of these ideas into action. Between 1919 and 1925, the Winnipeg Branch expanded its visiting nursing services into several suburbs adjacent to Winnipeg. It also established child welfare clinics, mothercraft classes, special clinics for immigrant women, and prenatal visiting in urban and suburban Winnipeg. It pioneered the use of Mothers' Helpers to assist mothers whose primary need was respite rather than nursing care. In addition, the Winnipeg Branch entered into agreements with two major Winnipeg employers to provide industrial (occupational health) nursing services to their employees and opened a Dental Clinic to provide dental care to working-class and indigent families. In 1923, they inaugurated an hourly nursing service for middle-class families who could afford to pay nurses on an hourly basis but not full-time (VON Minutes, May 1923). The enlarged scope of their programs was coordinated with other agencies such as the city and provincial PHNs, the outpatient departments of the Winnipeg General and Children's Hospitals, and the MSNM.

One very important function distinguished VNs employed by charitable organizations from publicly employed PHNs. This was the VNs' responsibility to ensure that the nursing care they provided did not **pauperize** their clients by diminishing their personal initiative and rendering them permanently dependent on the state. Because the provision of charitable health and welfare services was a responsibility of local governments and the wealthy elite (Taylor, 1987), the possibility that charitable assistance might be given indiscriminately was a significant concern for its providers. Charity relieved the suffering of the poor, but it might also pauperize them. Because PHNs were paid out of public funds, they were, at least in theory, required to assist all who requested their services. Visiting nursing services, however, were at least partially funded by charitable donations. Part of their responsibility, therefore, was **investigation work**, which involved the financial assessment of the family and the determination of what portion of the cost of the nursing visit the family could afford. Paying at least part of the cost mitigated the humiliation of accepting charity and enabled families to avoid being classified as paupers. Thus, the VON's major role in their Winnipeg dental clinic was to visit the homes of the clinic patients and determine their ability to pay. In the same vein, the nurses of the Lethbridge Nursing Mission (LNM) could provide charitable assistance to destitute families in addition to providing bedside nursing care, because they had the necessary mandate and experience (Richardson, 1997). Even the MSNM encouraged its clients to pay anything, even a penny, for the services of its nurses.

Summary By the beginning of World War II, the essential elements of community health nursing services had been put in place across the country. Provincial Health Departments had been organized and local Health Departments operated in the majority of Canadian cities. The scope of work in health education and prevention of illness had enlarged to include programs such as mental health, venereal disease control, preschool health, and prenatal education. The VON continued to flourish by using its success in the provision of bedside nursing care in the home as a springboard to also provide public health programs in communities where local attitudes and gaps in services made this possible. The only irony was that, although it had been envisioned by its founders as a nursing service for those living in rural and isolated "country districts," the VON had attained its greatest success and stability in Canada's urban centres.

PHOTO 1.5

Annah L. Prichard, District Superintendent, with the nursing staff of the Winnipeg Branch VON. Prichard served in this capacity between 1919 and 1925 during an era of rapid expansion of the Winnipeg Branch.

Credit: Victorian Order of Nurses, Manitoba Branch Photographic Collection

The Emergence of the Welfare State: Community Health Nursing after World War II

The Political and Economic Context Even prior to WWII, Canadian attitudes toward the provision of health care and financial assistance to the poor had undergone significant change. Canadians were less willing to accept health care as a charitable enterprise. Most had come to believe that health care was a right of citizenship and, therefore, an appropriate responsibility of the government. Poverty had been reconceptualized as an outcome of uncontrollable circumstances such as sickness, death, abandonment, and economic downturns rather than as the result of defects of individual character. All three levels of government had accepted, albeit at times reluctantly, responsibility for the provision of many services which had previously been the responsibility of the individual or family. This acceptance of responsibility by the various levels of government is known as the **welfare state.**The transition from the laissez-faire government of the nineteenth century to the welfare state of the mid-twentieth century gained momentum during the 1930s. The Great Depression dramatically demonstrated the limited capacity of local and provincial governments to provide health care and social welfare for its citizens during times of greatest need. Several western Canadian provinces and many local governments teetered on the verge of bankruptcy under the financial burden of dealing with the social consequences of widespread industrial and agrarian economic failure. However, attempts by the federal government to take greater responsibility for health and social welfare programs had been declared ultra vires (beyond the power of law) by the Judicial Committee of the Supreme Court. The Royal Commission on Dominion-Provincial Relations, which had been appointed in 1937 to examine how federal-provincial relations might be modified to improve the social welfare of all Canadians, brought down its recommendations in 1940. Acknowledging that the provinces had insufficient resources to deal with public welfare, it recommended that the federal government assume responsibility for unemployment insurance and old-age pensions (Owram, 1986). However, it also recommended that the provincial governments retain responsibility for public health programs and hospital care.

In the first decade after WWII, concerns persisted about how the government could protect citizens from the economic disaster that frequently accompanied prolonged illnesses. Several private and provincial medical and hospital insurance programs evolved, but, from the federal government's perspective, inequitable access to programs based on an ability to pay did not meet the needs of all Canadians. In 1948, the federal government provided health grants for a variety of programs (Shillington, 1972). Provincial spending for designated programs was matched dollar for dollar by the federal government. The inclusion of hospital construction costs in this program created a flurry of hospital building projects and hospital admission became the norm for most Canadians requiring obstetrical, medical, or surgical care. In 1957, the institutionalization of medical, surgical, and obstetrical care was further solidified when the Hospital Insurance and Diagnostic Services Act was passed by the federal government. In 1968, the Medical Care Insurance Act made publicly funded medical care available to all Canadians.

Provincial and federal spending on health care increased dramatically between 1948 and the 1970s. In 1977, concerned about uncontrolled health care spending, the federal government replaced its 50/50 cost-sharing arrangement with block funding. Health care costs, however, continued to increase. The economic downturn of the 1990s and the return of a more business-oriented, neo-conservative political climate redirected political and public attention to the reduction of government debt through the curtailment of government programs. In 1993, the federal government capped its contributions to provincial health budgets and announced a gradual reduction of federal transfer payments to support provincial health care programs (Kerr & MacPhail, 1996).

New Roles for Visiting Nurses: The Emergence of Home Care Programs National and local visiting nursing associations were dramatically affected by the emergence of the welfare state. Publicly funded health care programs created a level of social justice that ensured that hospital and medical care was based on need, not on ability to pay or willingness to submit to charity. However, these programs also significantly altered the mandates of visiting nursing associations, whose programs had bridged the gap between need and ability to pay for nearly six decades. Philanthropic support of organizations such as the MSNM and the LNM waned significantly. Unable to sustain either its funding or the quality of the nursing care it provided, the MSNM closed in 1943 and its cases were turned over to the Winnipeg Branch of the VON (MSNM Minutes, 1943). The LNM was succeeded by the VON in 1954 (Richardson, 1997).

Although the VON continued to grow during the postwar years, it faced significant challenges as the face of health care in Canada changed. Expanded local and provincial departments of health took over public health programs, which had been previously provided by the VON (Penney, 1996). The emergence of hospital-based obstetrical care shifted the VON visiting nursing caseloads to the care of convalescent and chronically ill individuals. Further, the erosion of charitable donations, which had at least partially offset the cost of caring for the poor in the past, meant that VNs were most likely caring for those who could afford to pay for these services either directly or through third-party insurance arrangements.

By the early 1970s, rising hospital costs had created both an opportunity and a crisis for the VON. Patients were discharged from hospital earlier but were often unable to obtain bedside nursing care in their homes during their convalescence. No publicly insured programs for home care services existed until 1974, when the first such program was established in Manitoba (Shapiro, 1997). The VON, aware that participation in publicly insured home care programs was an opportunity to both consolidate and strengthen their organization, lobbied provincial and local governments to make them the provider of these services. In "*A case for the VON in home care,"* also known as the *Pickering Report,* Pickering argued that government funding of home care programs did not necessarily require government delivery of the services (Pickering, 1976). It recommended that the VON, Canada's oldest and most experienced visiting nursing organization, be given the mandate to deliver publicly insured home care programs. However, individual provincial governments made a variety of decisions about the organization and funding of home care programs, and these did not always include the participation of the VON (Penney, 1996). Today, as it did in the past, the VON continues to function by offering a mix of services shaped by local circumstances, with a particular focus on creating programs to respond to unmet needs amongst specific segments of the population (Penney, 1996).

New Mandates for Public Health Nurses Increased government responsibility for the health care of Canadians also had a significant impact on public health nursing. Between 1940 and 1970, health departments focused on the elaboration of existing programs. However, this process also included a general shift of emphasis from traditional programs such as child health, immunization, and communicable disease control to programs focusing on the reduction of morbidity and mortality from chronic illnesses and injuries. Early postpartum discharge programs, a modification of the traditional postpartum home visit, placed significant demands on the time and resources of PHNs. In some instances, staffing patterns in health units and community health centres were modified to provide seven-day-a-week early postpartum services to mothers and neonates. PHNs also enlarged the scope of their practices to include health promotion and community development work in collaboration with other agencies and citizen groups with similar interests and mandates.

The reduction in government spending during the 1980s and 1990s affected PHNs both directly and indirectly. Static or reduced nursing staffs decreased levels of service for many programs. Infrastructures for communicable disease control were particularly hard hit. The loss of capacity to monitor, identify, and follow up on communicable diseases has been identified as one of the major reasons for the resurgence of TB and the recent emergence of new diseases such as AIDS and SARS (Garrett, 1994, 2000).

Summary At the end of the twentieth century, many aspects of community health nursing have come full circle. Publicly funded home care programs have created a tremendous growth in the number of nurses working in community settings. However, the role of home care nurses, who provide bedside nursing care and health education to the sick and convalescent, is similar to that fulfilled by the VNs of the late nineteenth and early twentieth century. The number of PHNs, on the other hand, has remained relatively stable. Their mandate has continued to emphasize communicable disease control, healthy child development, prevention of chronic illness, health promotion, and the identification of other factors that create morbidity and mortality in the population. What has changed is their visibility. Although PHNs have worked in the community for nearly a century, their small numbers and the presence of many other community-based service providers have rendered them less visible and more likely to be overlooked by both the funders and the users of the health care system. The challenge for the community health nurses of the future is to regain the visibility of their predecessors and continue to demonstrate the capacity of nurses to provide leadership in the community-based health care systems of tomorrow.

SUMMARY

This chapter traces the development of public health nursing and visiting nursing in Canada from the late nineteenth to the late twentieth century. It describes the emergence of community health nursing in the early twentieth century as part of a more general social-reform movement inspired by advances in scientific knowledge, the social gospel movement, and maternal feminism. The role that lay women played in the development of public health programs is discussed, with particular attention to the part that they played in putting the welfare of women and children on the public agenda. The chapter describes the challenges and barriers that community health nurses encountered in their day-to-day practices. Finally, the impact of the Canadian welfare state on community health nursing in the post-WWII era is examined.

KEY TERMS

public health movement
maternal feminist
district nursing
visiting nursing
public health nursing
social gospel movement
pauperize
investigation work
welfare state

STUDY QUESTIONS

1. Describe the two forms of community health nursing that evolved in Canada in the early twentieth century.
2. What social movements supported the emergence of community health nursing?
3. Which segments of the population were the focus of early community nursing programs?
4. Briefly describe the three earliest public health programs in which nurses were involved and the reasons for their implementation.
5. How did the British North America Act (1867) and nineteenth-century beliefs about the role of government influence the development of community-based health care services?
6. Describe the emergence of the Canadian welfare state.

7. Describe the role that non-governmental organizations, such as the VON, the Red Cross, and local philanthropic agencies, played in the development of community-based nursing programs.

INDIVIDUAL CRITICAL THINKING EXERCISES

The sources listed at the end of each question are cited in full in either the References or the Additional Resources section of this chapter. Each source will provide additional insights into the controversies and debates surrounding the history of public health and visiting nursing.

1. Meryn Stuart (1989), in her analysis of the development of rural public health nursing in northern Ontario, states that "The Board's focus on health education, however delivered by the nurses, would not erase the effects of poverty.... Health education was a facile solution to the serious problem of the lack of permanent human and material resources" (p. 111). Analyze the apparent lack of congruency between the needs of the populations that public health programs served and the typical services that these programs offered. (Sources: Piva, 1979; Stuart, 1989.)
2. Physicians and nurses assumed different roles in early community health organizations. What role did gender play in the assignment of these roles? (Sources: McPherson, 1996, Chapter 1; Stuart, 1992.)
3. Community health nursing has frequently been described as more autonomous than nursing practice in institutional settings. However, Eunice Dyke, Toronto's first supervisor of public health nursing, once stated that "... public health nursing has in the medical profession its greatest friend and not infrequently its greatest stumbling block." How autonomous was the practice of early community health nurses? (Sources: Comacchio, 1993, Chapter 7; Stuart, 1992.)
4. What role did middle-class ideas about class, ethnicity, and gender play in the development of public health programs to protect the health of infants and children? (Sources: Gleason, 2002; Comacchio, 1993, Chapter 3.)
5. Reflect on the constraints/limits on the scope of practice of PHNs in the 1920s and 30s. Do you see any parallels in the practice of PHNs today? Are there recurring patterns, and, if so, what are they? (Sources: Stuart, 1989; 1992.)
6. The major target groups of early public health and visiting nursing organizations were the poor, the working class, and recently arrived immigrants. However, there is little published analysis of how these groups responded to the interventions of middle-class social reformers and public health officials. What do you think some of their responses might have been?

GROUP CRITICAL THINKING EXERCISES

1. Social historians such as Alan Hunt (1999) argue that charity, philanthropy, and welfare programs are essentially efforts by the elite and middle classes to impose their behaviour, values, and culture upon others. Hunt describes these programs of moral or social regulation as being inspired by "... the passionate conviction that there is something inherently wrong or immoral about the conduct of others" (p. ix). Locate an issue of an early public health or nursing journal such as *The Public Health Journal* (now the *Canadian Journal of Public Health*) or *The Canadian Nurse* (particularly the section on public health). Conduct a brief content analysis of the issue, paying close attention to how the recipients of public health interventions are described. What conclusions can be drawn about the attitudes of health care professionals? What anxieties seem to underlie the interventions they describe and recommend to other health care practitioners?
2. Nurses were the intermediaries between the clients they served and the social and political elite who employed them to work in the community. However, their perspective on the objectives and effectiveness of community-based health care programs is often absent from published histories of public health. To fill this gap in the historic record, do one of the following: 1) locate a biographical account written by an early visiting or public health nurse, 2) locate an oral history of an early visiting or public health nurse in an archive, or 3) interview a retired visiting or public health nurse. How does their account resemble and differ from the history of community-based nursing presented in this chapter? How would you account for any differences you identify?
3. Based on what you have learned about the history of community health nursing in Canada, what do you believe are the greatest challenges facing nurses in this practice setting today and in the future?

PRIMARY SOURCES

Margaret Scott Nursing Mission, Board of Management. (n.d.). *Minutes 1904–1943.* (Provincial Archives of Manitoba. MG10 B9 Box IV).

Victorian Order of Nurses for Canada, Winnipeg Branch. (n.d.). *Minutes of Board Meetings 1901–1927.*

REFERENCES

Artibise, A. F. (1975). *Winnipeg: A social history of urban growth, 1874–1914.* Montreal, QC: McGill-Queens University Press.

Baillargeon, D. (2002). Entre la "Revanche" et la "Veillée" des berceaux: Les médecins québécois francophones, la mortalité infantile et la question nationale, 1910–40. *Canadian Bulletin of Medical History/Bulletin Canadien d'histoire de la médecine, 19*(1), 113–137.

Baldwin, D. O. (1997). *She answered every call: The life of public health nurse Mona Gordon Wilson (1894–1981).* Charlottetown, PE: Indigo Press.

Banfill, B. J. (1967). *Pioneer nurse.* Toronto, ON: Ryerson Press.

Bilson, G. (1980). *A darkened house: Cholera in nineteenth-century Canada.* Toronto, ON: University of Toronto Press.

Bliss, M. (1991). *Plague: A story of smallpox in Montreal.* Toronto, ON: HarperCollins.

Christie, N., & Gauvreau, M. (1996). *A full-orbed Christianity: The Protestant churches and social welfare in Canada.* Toronto, ON: University of Toronto Press.

City of Winnipeg Health Department. (1910). *Annual report for the year ending December 1909.* Winnipeg, MB: City of Winnipeg.

City of Winnipeg Health Department. (1915). *Annual report for the year ending December 1914.* Winnipeg, MB: City of Winnipeg.

City of Winnipeg Health Department. (1919). *Annual report for the year ending December 1918.* Winnipeg, MB: City of Winnipeg.

Colley, K. B. (1970). *While rivers flow: Stories of early Alberta.* Saskatoon, SK: Prairie Books.

Douglas, A. J. (1912). Chairman's address, Section of Municipal Health Officers, American Public Health Association. *American Journal of Public Health, 2*(2), 85–86.

Garrett, L. (1994). *The coming plague: Newly emerging diseases in a world out of balance.* New York: Penguin Books.

Garrett, L. (2000). *Betrayal of trust: The collapse of global public health.* New York: Hyperion Press.

Gibbon, J. M. (1947). *The Victorian Order of Nurses for Canada: 50th anniversary, 1897–1947.* Montreal, QC: Southam Press.

Giovannini, M. (1988). *Outport nurse.* St. John's, NL: Memorial University, Faculty of Medicine.

Green, H. G. (1974). *Don't have your baby in the dory!: A biography of Myra Bennett.* Montreal, QC: Harvest House.

Green, M. (1984). *Through the years with public health nursing: A history of public health nursing in the provincial government jurisdiction British Columbia.* Ottawa, ON: Canadian Public Health Association.

Hope, M. E. (1955). *Lamp on the snow.* London, UK: Angus & Robertson.

Humphreys, M. (1999). Tuberculosis: The "consumption" and civilization. In K.F. Kiple (Ed.), *Plague, pox & pestilence: Disease in history* (pp. 136–141). London, UK: Phoenix Illustrated.

Hutchinson, J. F. (1996). *Champions of charity: War and the rise of the Red Cross.* Boulder, CO: Westview Press.

Kerr, J., & MacPhail, J. (1996). *An introduction to issues in community health nursing in Canada.* Toronto, ON: Mosby.

Ladd-Taylor, M. (1994). *Mother-work, women, child welfare and the state, 1890–1930.* Urbana, IL: University of Illinois Press.

Locke, H. L. F. (1918). The problem of our infant population with special reference to the opportunity of the welfare nurse. *American Journal of Nursing, 18*(7), 523–526.

MacDougall, H. (1990). *Activists & advocates: Toronto's Health Department, 1883–1983.* Toronto, ON: Dundurn Press.

MacNutt, J. S. (1913). The Board of Health nurse: What she can do for the public welfare in a small city. *American Journal of Public Health, 3*(4), 1913.

Matthews, O. (1920). Child welfare. *The Canadian Nurse, 16*(1), 15–16.

McLaren, A., & McLaren, A. T. (1997). *The bedroom and the state: The changing practices and politics of contraception and abortion in Canada, 1880–1997* (2nd ed.). Oxford, UK: Oxford University Press.

McPherson, K. (1996). *Bedside matters: The transformation of Canadian nursing, 1900–1990.* Toronto, ON: Oxford University Press.

Meigs, G. L. (1916, August). Other factors in infant mortality than the milk supply and their control. *American Journal of Public Health, 6,* 847–853.

Merkley, P. (1987). The vision of the good society in the social gospel: What, where and when is the kingdom of God? *Historical Papers: Canadian Historical Association,* pp. 138–145.

Miller, G. L. (2000). *Mustard plasters and handcars: Through the eyes of a Red Cross outpost nurse.* Toronto, ON: Natural Heritage/Natural History.

Nevitt, J. (1978). *White caps and black bands: Nursing in Newfoundland to 1934.* St. John's, NL: Jefferson Press.

Owram, D. (1986). *The government generation: Canadian intellectuals and the state, 1900–1945.* Toronto, ON: University of Toronto Press.

Peikoff, T., & Brickey, S. (1991). Creating precious children and glorified mothers: A theoretical assessment of the transformation of childhood. In R. Smandych, G. Dodds, & A. Esau (Eds.), *Dimensions of childhood: Essays on the history of children and youth in Canada* (pp. 29–61). Winnipeg, MB: Legal Research Institute of the University of Manitoba.

Penney, S. (1996). *A century of caring: The history of the Victorian Order of Nurses for Canada.* Ottawa, ON: Victorian Order of Nurses for Canada.

Pickering, E. A. (1976). *A case for the VON in home care.* Ottawa, ON: Victorian Order of Nurses for Canada.

Piva, M. J. (1979). *The condition of the working class in Toronto, 1900–1921.* Ottawa, ON: University of Ottawa Press.

Richardson, S. (1997). Women's enterprise: Establishing the Lethbridge Nursing Mission, 1909–1919. *Nursing History Review, 5,* 105–30.

Roberts, J. (1928). Twenty-three years of public health. *The Public Health Journal, 19,* 554.

Riddell, S. E. (1991). *Curing society's ills: Public health nurses and public health nursing in rural British Columbia, 1916–1946.* Unpublished master's thesis, Simon Fraser University, Vancouver, BC.

Royce, M. (1983). *Eunice Dyke: Health care pioneer: From pioneer public health nurse to advocate for the aged.* Toronto, ON: Dundurn Press.

Sears, A. (1995). Before the welfare state: Public health and social policy. *Canadian Review of Sociology and Anthropology/Revue canadienne de sociologie et d'anthropologie, 32*(2), 169–188.

Shapiro, E. (1997). *The cost of privatization: A case study of home care in Manitoba.* Ottawa, ON: Canadian Centre for Policy Alternatives.

Shillington, C. H. (1972). *The road to medicare in Canada.* Toronto, ON: Del Graphics.

Stuart, M.E. (1987). *"Let not the people perish for lack of knowledge": Public health nursing and the Ontario rural child welfare project, 1916–1930.* Unpublished doctoral dissertation, University of Pennsylvania, Philadelphia, PA.

Sutherland, N. (1981). "To create a strong and healthy race": School children in the public health movement, 1880–1914. In S. E. D. Shortt (Ed.), *Medicine in Canadian society: Historical perspectives* (pp. 361–393). Montreal, QC: McGill-Queens University Press.

Taylor, M. G. (1987). *Health insurance and Canadian public policy.* Montreal, QC: McGill-Queens University Press.

Zilm, G., & Warbinek, E. (1995). Early tuberculosis nursing in British Columbia. *The Canadian Journal of Nursing Research, 27*(3), 65–81.

ADDITIONAL RESOURCES

MONOGRAPHS AND ARTICLES

Buhler-Wilkerson, K. (1989). *False dawn: The rise and decline of public health nursing, 1900–1930.* New York: Garland.

Buhler-Wilkerson, K. (2001). *No place like home: A history of nursing and home care in the United States.* Baltimore, MD: Johns Hopkins University Press.

Comacchio, C. (1993). *Nations are built of babies: Saving Ontario's mothers and children 1900–1940.* Montreal, QC: McGill-Queens University Press.

Copp, T. (1981). Public health in Montreal, 1870–1930. In S. E. D. Shortt (Ed.), *Medicine in Canadian society: Historical perspectives.* Montreal, QC: McGill-Queens University Press.

Gleason, M. (2002). Race, class and health: School medical inspection and "healthy" children in British Columbia, 1890–1930. *Canadian Bulletin of Medical History/Bulletin Canadien d'histoire de la médecine, 19*(1), 95–112.

Hunt, A. (1999). *Governing morals: A social history of moral regulation.* Cambridge, UK: Cambridge University Press.

Stuart, M. (1989). Ideology and experience: Public health nursing and the Ontario Rural Child Welfare Project, 1920–25. *Canadian Bulletin of Medical History/Bulletin Canadien d'histoire de la médecine, 6,* 111–131.

Stuart, M. (1992). "Half a loaf is better than no bread": Public health nurses and physicians in Ontario, 1920–1925. *Nursing Research, 41*(1), 21–27.

WEBSITES

Alberta Association of Registered Nurses:
www.nurses.ab.ca/history.html

American Association for the History of Nursing:
www.aahn.org/

Association of Registered Nurses of Newfoundland and Labrador:
www.anla.nf.ca/regnurse.htm

B.C. History of Nursing Group:
www.bcnursinghistory.ca/bchn.html

Canadian Association for the History of Nursing:
www.ualberta.ca/~jhibberd/CAHN_ACHN/

Margaret M. Allemang Centre for the History of Nursing:
www.allemang.on.ca/

Nurses Association of New Brunswick:
www.nanb.nb.ca/

United Kingdom Centre for the History of Nursing:
www.qmuc.ac.uk/hn/history/

About the Author

Marion McKay, RN, PhD(c) holds a bachelor's and master's degree in nursing from the University of Manitoba, and an MA (History) from the University of Manitoba/ University of Winnipeg. She is currently a PhD student in the History Department at the University of Manitoba. She has held an SSHRC Doctoral Fellowship in support of her research on the early years of public health in Winnipeg. Prior to joining the Faculty of Nursing at the University of Manitoba, she worked for several years as a public health nurse.

The author acknowledges with deep gratitude the assistance and advice of several valued colleagues and friends, including Dr. Meryn Stuart, Dr. Nicole Rousseau, Dr. Janet Beaton, Benita Cohen, and Sandra Gessler. A special thanks to Ulysses Lahaie, who translated several articles written in French and got hooked on nursing history in the process. Thank you also to the four anonymous peer reviewers whose comments did much to improve the initial draft of the chapter. A Doctoral Fellowship from Social Sciences and Humanities Research Council of Canada supported the research necessary for the preparation of this manuscript and is acknowledged with thanks.

CHAPTER 2

Financing, Policy, and Politics of Health Care Delivery

Adeline Falk-Rafael and Sue Coffey

OBJECTIVES

AFTER STUDYING THIS CHAPTER, YOU SHOULD BE ABLE TO:

1. Summarize milestones in the development of the Canadian health care system.
2. Identify federal, provincial, municipal, and regional responsibilities for the delivery of health care in Canada.
3. Examine delivery models and funding mechanisms for health care in Canada, specifically those that apply to community health care.
4. Critique current health care reform initiatives and their implications for community health nursing practice.

INTRODUCTION

> To many Canadians, the Canada Health Act provides for a health care system that helps to define this country. The Act symbolizes the values that represent Canada; it articulates a social contract that defines health care as a basic right and it describes the features of the health care system (Auditor General of Canada, 2002, Chapter 29, p. 13).

The Canadian health care system, **Medicare**, is a feature of Canadian culture that expresses its unique value system. Evolving from the traditions of the religious orders that first provided health care in Canada, Medicare reflects values of social justice, equity, and community. The fundamental principle that all members of our society, including the most vulnerable, are entitled to receive the health care they need contrasts sharply with the American system, which is grounded in the value of individuality and the belief that health care is a commodity to be sold to those who can afford it.

Yet there are increasing pressures to "Americanize" the Canadian health care system. Almost every day, reports in the media suggest that health care in Canada is in a crisis state, that spending is spinning out of control, and that drastic changes are needed to ensure its sustainability. Numerous polls conducted over the last decade show that Canadians are concerned that their health care system will not be there when they need it (Sullivan & Baranek, 2002; Pollara Research, 2002). It is important for community health nurses (CHNs) to understand how our health care system evolved; how the funding, allocation, and delivery of community health services differ from medical and hospital care; and what factors are driving health care reform in this country.

BIRTH OF CANADIAN MEDICARE

Although the 1867 Constitution Act (also known as the British North America Act) did not explicitly assign responsibility for health policy to either the federal or provincial governments, historically both levels of government have been involved in ensuring the availability of health services and funding those services. Deber (2000) notes that because the Constitution assigned responsibility for hospitals exclusively to provinces, health care in Canada has been erroneously interpreted to fall under provincial jurisdiction. With only a few exceptions, such as the direct health services provided by the federal government to Aboriginal populations, veterans, and military personnel, provincial governments have assumed responsibility for the delivery of health care. However, funding for health care is another matter. The Canadian Constitution contains an equalization clause requiring provinces to provide "reasonably comparable levels of public service for reasonably comparable levels of taxation" (Sullivan & Baranek, 2002, p. 21). Because provincial and territorial wealth varies considerably, the federal government's involvement has been necessary to equalize services across provinces. Since 1957, the federal government has done that in two ways: first by contributing money (in effect, transferring money from wealthier to poorer provinces), and second, by stipulating specific conditions the provinces must meet in order to receive that money. Before further discussing the Canadian health care system as it currently exists, a review of key points in the evolution of the system is warranted.

In 1919, access to medical care was of sufficient concern that Mackenzie King, then leader of the Liberal party, convinced his party to include national health insurance as part of its platform (Rachlis & Kushner, 1994). Rachlis and Kushner note, however, that partly because of provincial objections to federal involvement in health care, attempts to implement national insurance for both hospital and physicians' services were initially unsuccessful. North America's first universal health insurance program was actually implemented at a provincial level. In Saskatchewan in 1947, Tommy Douglas and the Cooperative Commonwealth Federation (CCF) party introduced legislation to institute Medicare. For his role in bringing about this historic change, Tommy Douglas is still sometimes referred to as the father of Medicare. It was not until 1957 that similar legislation, the Hospital Insurance and Diagnostic Services Act (HIDS), was passed by the federal government (Rachlis & Kushner).

The HIDS provided financial incentives for the provinces to establish hospital insurance plans. It assured that if provincial plans included five key principles, the federal government would pay half the costs. Those principles, still the legal cornerstone of Medicare, are comprehensiveness, accessibility, universality of coverage, public administration, and portability of benefits. The incentive provided powerful motivation for the provinces' participation and resulted in both the rapid expansion of cost-shared institutional care and the neglect of programs that focused on home care support and health promotion.

Once again, in 1962, Saskatchewan led the country with legislation providing universal, publicly funded medical insurance. In 1966, the federal government followed suit with the passage of the National Medical Care Insurance Act (Medicare). This act, enshrining the right of Canadians to physicians' services, stipulated that the same five principles as required by the HIDS were necessary to ensure the federal government's payment of 50% of provincial health care costs. The act was implemented in 1968, and by 1971 all provinces were fully participating (Rachlis & Kuschner, 1994).

The blanket 50/50 cost-sharing quickly placed a great strain on the federal budget and made fiscal planning increasingly difficult (Rafael, 1997). As a result, in 1977, the federal government passed the Established Programs Financing Act (EPF), which changed the federal share of health costs from a 50/50 split to per capita block grants. These grants were tied to economic performance through being linked to the Gross National Product (GNP) and consisted of both cash and tax points, which allowed the provincial governments a greater share of collected taxes (Rachlis & Kushner, 1994). This new cost-sharing arrangement was adjusted several times over the next 20 years, with each adjustment decreasing the federal contribution (Begin, 1987). Both the Liberal and Conservative parties slashed cash contributions during their terms in power, clearly benefiting federal coffers. However, the changes might also have represented deliberate attempts to decrease federal involvement in health care. Former Minister of Health and Welfare, the Honourable Monique Begin, reflected on the difficulties that the EPF created:

> The EPF legislation had not repealed the two pillars of Medicare: HIDS and the Medical Care Act. So their conditions and regulations... still applied, with one major drawback: the feds could no longer refuse to reimburse their half of the costs when it was felt there was a problem, for we [now had a transfer process]... with no enforcement mechanism (Begin, 2002, p. 2).

The Canada Health Act

Soon after the passage of the EPF, Begin was appointed federal Minister of Health and Welfare (Begin, 2002). She quickly became aware that extra-billing by physicians and user fees by provincial institutions were rising dramatically. Her analysis revealed a number of factors: (a) the popularity of neo-conservative economics, which generally promoted a reduced role for governments and a larger role for the private sector, (b) partisan politics with a liberal government at the federal level and conservative governments in 8 of 10 provinces, and (c) wage-and-price controls, which had included physicians' incomes. Begin believed the extra-billing and user-fee trends posed a serious threat to Medicare and so on December 12, 1983, introduced to parliament Bill C-3, the Canada Health Act.

Passage of the **Canada Health Act** (CHA) in April 1984 was a proud moment in Canadian nursing history. Begin faced tough opposition to the Act from lobby groups, opposition parties, and even from members of the Liberal cabinet (Begin, 2002). Intense lobbying and support by the Canadian Nurses Association (CNA) was instrumental in the bill's passage. In the words of Mme Begin: "Nursing became a big player during the Canada Health Act. They made the difference; it's as simple as that" (Rafael, 1997). Not only were nurses instrumental in passing the CHA into law, they were successful in amending it. As it was introduced into Parliament in 1983, Bill C-3 identified only physicians as providers of insurable services. The CNA amendment changed the language to include other health care workers as potential providers of insurable services (Mussallem, 1992). To date, no provincial legislation has been enacted to allow nurses to bill provincial health insurance plans directly.

The purpose of the CHA was to ban extra-billing and user fees by providing the federal government with the legal authority to penalize provinces that permitted such practices (Canada, House of Commons, 1984). Under the CHA, federal funding for essential medical services would continue so long as the provinces' health insurance plans met the criteria of being **publicly administered** (administered by a public authority accountable to the provincial government), **comprehensive** (must cover necessary in-hospital, medical, and surgical-dental services), **universal** (100% of residents must be covered), **portable** (available after a maximum of three months of residency and no extra charge for care out of province), and **accessible** (no user fees and health care providers must be reimbursed adequately). These five principles of Medicare will be discussed more fully later in the chapter. The CHA represented a significant accomplishment in ensuring that Canadians' access to health care continued regardless of ability to pay or province of residence. It also perpetuated, however, the dominance of a biomedical approach to health care by identifying only essential medical and hospital services as those qualifying for federal cost-sharing.

The EPF continued to be the mechanism for transferring money from federal to provincial governments for health care until 1996. At that time, the EPF and the existing payment plan for welfare, the Canada Assistance Plan (CAP), were replaced by the Canada Health and Social Transfer (CHST) block fund, which included federal transfer payments for health, post-secondary education, and welfare (Sullivan & Baranek, 2002). Allocations to provinces continued in the same proportion as the previous combined EPF and CAP entitlements (Canada, Department of Finance, 2002). However, the EPF funding formula had been severely cut by Prime Minister Mulroney's Conservative government between 1986 and 1991, reducing its growth to 3% less than the GNP growth (Rachlis & Kushner, 1994). As a result, the actual amount of the federal transfer in combined tax points and cash declined steadily until it reached a new low of $25.8 billion in 1997–98. As well, the cash–tax points proportion of the transfer had been changing steadily with less and less of the transfer involving cash payment (Department of Finance, 2002). In 1997–98 and 1998–99, the federal government's cash contribution was $12.5 billion, less than 50% of the CHST. However, recent revisions to CHST funding have begun to reverse this problematic trend. The funding arrangement for the years 1998–2003 includes an increase to CHST growth to the GNP –1% (up from –3%), a revision of the funding formula to account for provincial population growth rates, and adjustments to narrow funding disparities (Department of Finance). As a result, in the 2001–02 fiscal year, the cash portion of the transfer increased to over 50% for the first time since 1996–97, and the total CHST increased to $31.9 billion.

Assessment of the Canada Health Act In assessing the degree to which the CHA was successful in ensuring that all Canadians have access to the health care they need, we need to look first at the express purpose of the Act. Secondly, it is important to examine the extent to which other aspects of health care, explicitly and implicitly addressed by the Act, have been implemented. Finally, the performance of the Canadian health care system should be compared to health care in other countries.

Express Purpose of the CHA Has the Canada Health Act accomplished what it set out to do, that is, "establish criteria and conditions in respect of insured health services and extended health care services provided under provincial law that must be met before a full cash contribution may be made" (Canada, House of Commons, 1984, Introduction)? Within the first three years of the CHA's passage (1984–1987), penalties amounting to $245 million had been levied against 7 of 10 provinces (Auditor General of Canada, 2002). When each of the penalized provinces abolished extra-billing and user fees, all penalties were reimbursed, as provided for in the Act. Thus, with respect to these issues, the CHA fulfilled its purpose. However, the issue of provincial/territorial non-compliance with the five criteria of the Act remains to be adequately addressed. The 1999 Auditor General's report noted that the federal government had "never imposed discretionary financial penalties on provinces and territories for non-compliance with the Canada Health Act" (p.15), choosing instead a non-intrusive approach. Although some cases of non-compliance had been resolved in this way, others had not, including the violation of the portability criterion by five provinces and suspected cases involving the criteria of comprehensiveness and accessibility. Furthermore, the Auditor General chastised the government for not even collecting sufficient information to ensure compliance, noting that, "parliament cannot readily determine the extent to which each province and territory has satisfied the criteria and conditions of the Canada Health Act" (Auditor General of Canada, p. 17).

The intent of the CHA was to relate federal cash contributions not only to insured health services but also to extended health care services. The CHA defines the latter as "nursing home intermediate service, adult residential care service, home care services, and ambulatory health care services" (Canada, House of Commons, 1984, Section 2). However, funding for extended health care was not linked to compliance with the five principles of Medicare. As a result, provinces can decide what they want to spend. Sullivan and Baranek (2002) report a "threefold variation in public spending support across the provinces in extended health services like home care and pharmaceuticals" (p. 23). Thus, one would have to conclude that the CHA has not been effective with respect to the growing fields of home care and pharmaceuticals. Recognition of this limitation was evident in the final report of the National Forum on Health (1997), which urged both the extension of public funding to home care and pharmacare and the reform of primary care.

A Broader Focus on Health In addition to its stated purpose, the Act also implicitly and explicitly suggests a broader purpose. For example, Section 3 of the Act strongly endorses health promotion, stating that the "primary objective of Canadian health care policy" is twofold: to facilitate reasonable access to health services and "to protect, promote and restore the physical and mental well-being of residents of Canada" (House of Commons, 1984, Section 3). Despite this, the Act limited its focus to medically necessary hospital and physicians' services (and dental services in hospitals). Protective, promotive, and preventive services were not required to meet the five criteria of Medicare and were not subject to the conditions of the Act. Thus these services, which were provided largely by provincial public health systems and which added a critical balance to the treatment-focused insured services addressed by the CHA, were left unprotected by federal legislation. As a result, the extent to which these services are offered may vary considerably from one province/territory to another, in violation of the very intent of the Act.

International Comparison The two aspects of the Canadian health care system that can be compared with other countries are the level of health Canadians enjoy and the relative cost of their health care system. The Organization for Economic Cooperation and Development (OECD) provides data that are helpful in making such international comparisons. Table 2.1 reports selected health outcomes by country for 1970 and 1999. Canada's life expectancies for both women and men rank among the highest in the world. Although Canadian infant mortality rates have dropped significantly since 1970, the 1999 rate of 5.3 deaths per 1000 live births is still higher than a number of other developed countries.

TABLE 2.1
Comparisons of Health Outcomes by Country

	Infant Mortality Rate/1000		Life Expectancy at Birth: Females		Life Expectancy at Birth: Males	
	1970	1999	1970	1999	1970	1999
Australia	17.9	5.7	74.2	81.8	67.4	76.2
Canada	18.8	5.3	76.4	81.7	69.3	76.3
Germany	22.5	4.5	73.6	80.7	67.2	74.7
Japan	13.1	3.4	74.7	84.0	69.3	77.1
New Zealand	16.7	5.4*	74.6	80.8	68.3	75.7
Sweden	11.0	3.4	77.1	81.9	72.2	77.0
United Kingdom	18.5	5.6	75.0	79.8	68.7	75.0
United States	20.0	7.1	74.7	79.4	67.1	73.9

**1998 figure; 1999 data not available*
Source: Organization for Economic Cooperation and Development, 2002

When comparing health outcomes to expenditures, one message is very clear: increased spending on health care does not result in better health. In 2000, the United States spent more per capita on health care than any of the other 29 countries compared by the OECD. Health expenditures in the U.S. also represented the highest percentage of gross domestic product (GDP). Yet American health outcomes compare poorly with those of other countries. Japan, for example, spent less than half as much per capita on health than the U.S. yet ranks first on all three measures of health. Canada's per capita spending in 2000 was about 55% that of the U.S., and health care spending amounted to 9.1% of the GDP, compared with 13% in the U.S. However, on all three health outcomes, Canada fared substantially better than the United States. Perhaps this is related to the fact that the American health care industry relies to a larger extent on private funding than in any of the other 29 countries compared (see Table 2.2, last columns).

These and more comprehensive data analyses suggest that Canada's universal health coverage is less costly and more effective than the privatized health system of our U.S. neighbour (Deber, 2000; Rachlis & Kushner, 1994; Rachlis, Evans, Lewis, & Barer, 2001; Sullivan & Baranek, 2002; Alberta Association of Registered Nurses, Canadian Nurses Association, Ontario Nurses Association, Registered Nurses Association of Ontario, & United Nurses of Alberta, 2000; Registered Nurses Association of Ontario, 1999). There is still room for improvement, however, as noted by the Commissioner on the Future of Health Care:

> First and foremost, I am convinced that the Medicare house needs remodelling but not demolishing. Medicare was, and continues to be, the right choice. But the mix of publicly available health services currently covered under Medicare needs to be adapted to today's medical realities and delivery systems.

TABLE 2.2
Comparisons of Health Expenditure by Country

	Total per capita Expenditures in US$		Total Expenditures as Percentage of GDP		Public Expenditure as a Percentage of Total Health Expenditure	
	1970	2000	1970	2000	1970	2000
Australia	175	2211	4.9	8.3	57.2	72.4
Canada	260	2535	7.0	9.1	69.9	72.0
Germany	223	2748	6.3	10.6	72.8	75.1
Japan	130	2012	4.5	7.8	69.8	76.7
New Zealand	174	1623	5.1	8.0	80.3	78.0
Sweden	270	1748*	6.9	7.9*	86.0	83.8*
United Kingdom	144	1763	4.5	7.3	87.0	81.0
United States	349	4631	6.9	13.0	36.4	44.3

**1998 figure; 2000 data not available*
Source: Organization for Economic Cooperation and Development, 2002

When we first started debating Medicare 40 years ago, "medically necessary" health care could be summed up in two words: hospitals and doctors. Today, hospital and physician services account for less than half of the total cost of the system. More money is spent on drugs than on physicians. There are more specialists and more care is delivered in homes, in communities, and through a wide array of health care providers. In short, the practice of health care has evolved. And despite efforts to keep pace, Medicare has not (Romanow, 2002, p. 2).

The Federal Role in Health Promotion

As Mr. Romanow observed, when the legislative pillars of Canadian Medicare were enacted in 1957, 1966, and 1984, the biomedical model dominated public and political thinking about health. The clinical definition of health was the absence of disease and the term "health promotion" was often used interchangeably with "disease prevention." Labelling the illness-centred, treatment-focused physicians' and hospital services that were insured under the Acts as "health care" attests and contributes to this confusion. As challenges to the idea that health was related exclusively to a country's health care emerged, the federal government provided some leadership in the development of health promotion policies and resources.

The first federal acknowledgement of the limitations of the primacy of the funded medical/treatment system in Canada was *The Lalonde Report* of 1974 (Lalonde, 1974). It explicitly presented a vision for health promotion services as a critical component of this country's health care system. The Report was influenced significantly by McKeown's 1958 British research (McKeown, 1979). McKeown asserted that improvements in sanitation, nutrition, and the ability to space pregnancies were much stronger determinants of health than health care alone. The influence of his thinking is evident in the health framework proposed in the Lalonde Report, which identified four **determinants of health**: environment, lifestyle, human biology, and the health care system.

Despite its identification of environment as a determinant of health, the Lalonde Report is often linked primarily to an emphasis on lifestyle. Some have suggested that the Report was less a critique of the dominance of a biomedical approach to health than an attempt to undermine Medicare.

Canadian Research Box 2.1

Romanow, R. J. (2002). Building on values: The future of health care in Canada. Final report of the Commission on the Future of Health Care in Canada.

The long-awaited report of the Commission on the Future of Health Care in Canada was tabled in the House of Commons on November 28, 2002. The recommendations of the report resulted from extensive consultations with the Canadian public and with expert, professional, and stakeholder groups and were grounded in a rigorous review of related evidence. The full report is available on-line (see Additional Resources at the end of this chapter).

The report contained 47 costed recommendations that provide a plan for health care reform over the next 20 years. Five high-priority areas, requiring an immediate infusion of money from the federal government, were identified and include: funds for rural and remote access, diagnostic services, primary health care, home care (post-acute hospitalization, mental health, and palliative care), and catastrophic drug coverage. In addition, the report specifically addresses human health resource planning and management; globalization, including the threat of international trade agreements to the Canadian health care system; and Aboriginal health. Stable, sustained funding and accountability are key features of the recommendations. Although it strongly supports primary health care, including an emphasis on disease prevention and health promotion, a disappointment in the report is that its focus in that regard is limited to a behavioural approach to health promotion. It is silent on a national public health plan and, despite encouraging statements by the Commissioner at the Canadian Nurses Association Annual General Meeting in June 2002, refers only minimally to broad determinants of health and population health.

Discussion Questions

1. What would be the advantages to making changes to health care legislation through companion legislation, rather than re-opening the Canada Health Act?
2. How would a legislated requirement for accountability improve health care?
3. What gaps in home care can you envision if the recommendations on home care are implemented? How would/should they be funded?

PHOTO 2.1

CNA Executive Director Lucille Auffrey with Commissioner Roy Romanow at the CNA Annual General Meeting, June 2002.

Credit: Mone Photography, Ottawa. Used with permission of the Canadian Nurses Association.

However, the Lalonde report was revolutionary in its time, leading a global reconceptualization of health promotion.

Four years later, Canada and other countries around the world met at The International Conference on Primary Health Care in Alma Ata, USSR. They urged governments to take action to "protect and promote the health" of the people of the world by issuing the *Declaration of Alma Ata* (World Health Organization, 1978), to which Canada was a signatory.

In the years following Alma Ata, federal leadership in health promotion policy continued. In 1986, the federal Minister of Health at the time, the Honourable Jake Epp, published the document, *Achieving Health for All: A Framework for Health Promotion* (Epp, 1986). The Epp Framework expanded Lalonde's definition of health promotion; incorporated some of the tenets of primary health care; and emphasized the role of broad social, environmental, and political determinants of health. The document concluded with a denouncement of strategies that focus on individual responsibility for health, or "blaming the victim," while ignoring the social and economic conditions that contribute to disease and disability.

The Epp Framework formed the basis for the Ottawa Charter for Health Promotion that emerged from the First International Conference on Health Promotion, hosted by the federal government in November, 1986 (World Health Organization, Canadian Public Health Association, & Health and Welfare, 1986). The Charter, authored jointly by Health Canada, the Canadian Public Health Association (CPHA), and the World Health Organization (WHO), identified prerequisites for health, strategies for promoting health, and outcomes of those strategies. The Charter acknowledged that caring for one's self and others is conducive to health and identified caring, holism, and ecology as essential concepts in health promotion.

The federal government has continued to support health promotion through policy and development of resources. It created a Health Promotion and Programs Branch, which has evolved into the Population and Public Health Branch. Many of the resources that have been developed, such as the *Population Health Template* (Health Canada, 2001) and the *Population Health Promotion Model* (Hamilton & Bhatti, 1996), have proven useful to CHNs. Strong and consistent support for health promotion services as an integral part of Canada's health care system was evident in the final report of the National Forum on Health and was reiterated by at least one federal Minister of Health in June 1998, when the Honourable Allan Rock vowed to make "health promotion and the prevention of illness true national priorities" (Rock, 1998).

CANADIAN HEALTH CARE: FUNDING, ALLOCATION, AND DELIVERY

Health care services in Canada, including community services, are provided through an array of programs with vastly different philosophies, funding mechanisms, and goals. Hospital and physicians' services are largely publicly financed. Public sector revenue (taxes collected by federal, provincial, and municipal governments) accounts for approximately 70% of the money spent on health care with out-of-pocket expenses or private health-insurance claims accounting for the remainder (see Table 2.3). The proportion of services paid for through public funding has shifted substantially since the inception of Medicare. In 1960, prior to Medicare, less than half the health services were publicly funded. Public funding for health services reached its peak in the mid-1970s and stayed stable at just over 75% for the next decade. Since the mid-1980s, the portion of publicly funded services has steadily declined.

TABLE 2.3
Percentage of Canadian Health Care Costs Publicly and Privately Funded since Inception of Medicare

Year	% Publicly Funded	% Privately Funded
1960	42.6	57.4
1970	69.9	30.1
1980	75.6	24.4
1995	71.4	28.6
1997	70.2	29.8
1999	70.8	29.2

Source: Organization for Economic Cooperation and Development, 2002

The actual distribution of funds is also an important consideration. Table 2.4 reflects the emphasis on funding essential medical and hospital services stipulated in the CHA. Table 2.4 shows that although hospital and institutional funding have decreased somewhat, comparable increases in home care funding, for example, are not evident. Although they have quadrupled since 1992 (Sullivan & Baranek, 2002), home care expenditures remain somewhat invisible in the Canadian Institute for Health Information (CIHI) statistics. Public health expenditures, contrary to the emphasis on health promotion in federal policy statements, have remained a relatively stable and minute portion of total health spending.

In order to understand and evaluate the effectiveness of the various means of providing community health services, it is critical to use an appropriately broad framework. Deber (2000) proposes three key elements—financing, delivery, and allocation—for such a framework. For the purposes of this chapter, these three central components are defined in the following way:

- **Financing** refers to the methods by which money is collected by governments, insurers, and providers (e.g., taxes, premiums) as well as to the decisions about the extent of coverage (e.g., what kinds of services are covered and who receives that coverage).
- **Delivery** refers to the way in which health care services are organized and the mechanisms by which they are provided.
- **Allocation** refers to the links created between financing and delivery. Decisions about how providers are reimbursed and the incentives inherent in the way

TABLE 2.4
Selected Health Expenditures by Use of Funds Over Time (% Distribution)

	Hospitals and Other Institutions	Other*	Physicians	Other Professionals**	Drugs	Public Health & Admin
1975	53.9	2.1	15.1	9.0	8.8	4.2
1980	53.2	2.4	14.7	10.1	8.4	4.3
1985	51.1	2.9	15.2	10.4	9.5	4.5
1990	48.4	4.0	15.1	10.6	11.3	4.3
1995	44.2	4.8	14.3	11.6	13.5	5.4
1997	42.6	4.8	14.2	12.3	14.4	5.5
1999	41.6	5.1	13.6	12.1	14.9	6.1

**Home care, medical transportation services, occupational health, and others*
***Dental care, vision care, and others*
Source: Canadian Institute for Health Information, 2001

providers are paid are considered when one examines allocation of services.

Application of this model to the case of acute care hospitals sheds light on these interrelated components. *Financing* is derived largely from public funds (Deber, 2000). Provincial/territorial governments then determine funding formulae to *allocate* this money to boards of directors of the hospitals. In some jurisdictions in which regionalization has occurred, monies flow to regional governments to be allocated to hospital boards.

Deber (2000) points out that hospital care is primarily privately *delivered* in Canada. Although Canadian hospitals are frequently referred to as "public hospitals," they are run by private boards and their employees are not government workers. To be consistent with the meaning of "public funding," the term public hospital should be reserved for those institutions that are administered and staffed by employees of various levels of government, such as many psychiatric hospitals. Such is the case in countries in which the health system is socialized, for example, the U.K. and Scandinavia, in which health care providers are government employees (Deber). Clarity about these three aspects of health care is important in understanding current health-care-reform initiatives. The changes made by Premier Klein in Alberta, for example, are often referred to as "privatization" when they are, in effect, a shift from not-for-profit private delivery to for-profit private delivery (Deber). The distinction will become more fully apparent as Deber's framework is used to analyze public health, primary care, and home care services in Canada.

Health Care in the Community

This section will examine the financing, allocation, and delivery of three community health services: primary care/primary health care, public health, and home care or home health nursing. Since each of these service areas is continuing to evolve, a number of models used in different areas of the country will be highlighted.

Primary Care/Primary Health Care The terms primary care and primary health care are often erroneously used interchangeably. The definition of **primary health care** in the *Declaration of Alma Ata* can be summarized as accessible, acceptable, affordable health care (World Health Organization, 1978). Other specific tenets of primary health care identified in the charter include its basis in research; its breadth, encompassing the full spectrum of services from promotive to rehabilitative; the identification of health education, proper nutrition, disease prevention and control, and maternal and child health care as minimum services; the recognition that intersectoral and interdisciplinary approaches are necessary for success; and an emphasis on community participation and empowerment.

Primary care, on the other hand, refers simply to the services that a person commonly accesses at the first point of contact with the health care system. In many "developed" countries, primary care services have been dominated by medicine and thus have focused mainly on acute care and treatment of disease. While the largest group of primary care providers in Canada continues to be physicians, other providers include nurse practitioners, dentists, chiropractors, pharmacists, dieticians, midwives, optometrists, and, to some extent, public health nurses. The medicalized focus of primary care is reflected in our current funding mechanisms that overtly favour physicians as privileged health care providers. As a result, most Canadians access primary care in the community in physicians' office, commonly through a family or general practitioner (GP), who is reimbursed on a fee-for-service basis. A small portion of the Canadian population receives primary care services through community health centres, walk-in clinics, or emergency rooms (Shah, 1998).

Legislation As noted previously, the effect of legislation has been to limit the influence of the federal government, define services in terms of physician and hospital care, and maintain physicians at the centre of the decision-making system (Hutchinson, Abelson, & Lavis, 2001; Tuohey, 2002).

Financing Both the funding and focus of primary care services are directly related to the provisions of the CHA. Because essential medical services are the only primary care services identified as eligible for federal/provincial cost-sharing, physicians have enjoyed a monopoly in the provision of such services, severely disadvantaging other primary care providers and the public.

Delivery Like hospitals, primary care services in Canada are largely publicly funded and privately delivered. It is widely recognized that the most cost-effective and comprehensive models of primary care delivery involve the provision of services by salaried, multidisciplinary teams (Rachlis & Kushner, 1994). However, currently fewer than 10% of primary care physicians are involved in this type of model (Hutchison et al., 2001).

Allocation Allocation of funds and resources (the decisions that tie funding to delivery) is based on many factors, which may include availability of resources (e.g., ratio of health care professionals to the population), characteristics of the community which affect the need for service (e.g., age distribution), personal factors that affect the need for service (e.g., education, income), and characteristics of the health care system (e.g., points of entry, accessibility of resources, cost, and barriers to care) (Shah, 1998). At the present time, allocation decisions are generally provincial responsibilities and, with the exception of Ontario, are carried out by regional authorities (Sullivan & Baranek, 2002). Funds are transferred either directly to providers (Ontario), or first transferred to the regional authority and then forwarded to providers.

Physicians' fees account for 13.6% of total health care costs (see Table 2.4). The most expensive form of remuneration for physicians' services is fee-for-service (FFS), yet the overwhelming majority of physicians earn almost all of their income in this way. Hutchinson, Abelson, and Lavis (2001) noted that "for the 89% of Canadian family physicians/GPs who receive some FFS income, FFS payments account for an average of 88% of their total income" (p. 117). Increasing criticism for this traditional and costly model of primary care has led to significant innovations over the past quarter century.

Primary Care Reform: Community Health Centres

In the early 1970s, primary care reform surfaced at the national level. Community Health Centres (CHCs) were recognized for controlling health care costs while also more "fully reflecting the objectives, priorities, and relationships which society wishes to establish for health care in the future" (Canadian Council on Social Development, Research and Development Branch, 1972, p. ii). An inquiry was commissioned to examine the possibility of using CHCs as part of a plan aimed at restructuring health care delivery and funding mechanisms. However, in failing to take into account the opposition of powerful hospital and physician organizations, the Commission significantly hampered this type of reform (Chrichton, Gordon, Robertson, & Farrant, 1997). By the early 1980s it was apparent that CHCs had failed to evolve outside of Ontario and Quebec. Eschauzier (1983) identified the following reasons:

- lack of political commitment and uncertain/inappropriate funding methods,
- professional resistance,
- inter-professional conflict,
- unclear role for community participants,
- resistance from other established organizations,
- lack of models and practical guidelines for operators, and
- lack of evidence documenting worth.

As the twenty-first century begins, primary care restructuring is no longer only a matter of fiscal concern but also a required response to the reality of critical provider shortages. Hence, a brief description of the CHC models currently in place in Quebec and Ontario is instructive.

Quebec's Solution In 1972, Quebec introduced one of the first primary care reforms in the form of a model based on Centres Locaux de Service Communautaires (CLSCs). These centres arose out of a growing desire to bring about reform to health and social services. Philosophically, they are based on the ideal of a global, integrated system of care, delivering a broader, less costly range of services (Hutchison et al., 2001). In addition to providing primary care treatment, these local community service centres also emphasize health promotion, disease prevention, and the provision of expanded services (Shah, 1998). There are currently 146 CLSCs in Quebec, which employ approximately 1500 salaried physicians and more than 5000 full-time-equivalent nurses. All CLSCs are required to provide services during extended evening and weekend hours as well as during regular business hours. Despite the growth of CLSCs, they have been largely underused in an environment in which private physician practice still dominates.

Ontario's Solution Currently, there are 56 CHCs in Ontario providing primary care to approximately 2% of the provincial population (Hutchison et al., 2001). They employ 139 salaried physicians and 90 nurse practitioners. CHC primary care teams also include nurses, social workers, health promoters, community health workers, and often chiropodists, nutritionists, or dieticians. Each centre is incorporated as a non-profit agency with a volunteer, community-elected Board of Directors (Ontario Ministry of Health and Long Term Care, 2002).

Ontario also has Health Service Organizations (HSOs), which are essentially group medical practices providing mainly medical care to individuals enrolled as clients. A review of program costs in the early 1990s suggested that newly recruited physicians were actually being paid more to practise in essentially the same way (Gillett, Hutchison, & Birch, 2001). As a result, a moratorium on further expansion of the programs exists. Currently, 200 physicians work in 60 HSOs in Ontario, most of them in or around Toronto.

The most recent primary care reform initiative of the Ontario government has been to establish Family Health Networks (FHNs), groups of family practice physicians voluntarily organized into multidisciplinary teams. The emphasis is on prevention and providing more comprehensive care while increasing accessibility of services for enrolled patients. Between

1998 and 2002, 14 pilot FHNs were created in seven communities, involving more than 170 family physicians and serving approximately 277 000 enrolled patients (Ontario Family Health Network, 2002). There appears to be slow progress in recruiting physicians to this collaborative model of practice.

Primary Care Reform: Nurse Practitioner as Primary Care Provider

Nurse practitioners have the potential to significantly contribute to primary health care reform. The Canada Health Act (1984) allows provinces to establish reimbursement mechanisms for health care professionals other than physicians and dentists. Although a number of provincial governments have enacted legislation which defines an extended scope of practice for nurse practitioners, no province has established associated funding mechanisms for their reimbursement. This failure to act has resulted in the slow growth and severe underutilization of nurse practitioners.

Primary Care Expansion: Telehealth Nurses as First Contact

Telehealth, a fairly new field of nursing in Canada, uses technology to facilitate patients receiving health care. While applications include video-conferencing, health information lines, Internet Nurses, and tele-home care (home visits over distance), the rapidly expanding area of telephone triage is now most commonly associated with telehealth.

Telephone triage has existed in Canada for the last six years. This health service, in operation in New Brunswick and most recently Ontario, is financed through contracts awarded by the provincial governments to private companies. Initially begun in Moncton, New Brunswick in 1995, telephone triage employs registered nurses to essentially act as a "strainer" between patients and health care services (Lightstone, 2002). The aim of telephone triage is "patient education with the subsequent goal of self-care" (p. 80). Nurses use evidence-based protocols and software to provide standardized advice based on information provided by callers. A comprehensive analysis of this type of service has yet to be completed.

Public Health

Whereas hospital and physicians' services have been governed by federal legislation for at least the last half of the twentieth century, public health was decentralized at the outset so that sole responsibility for public health rested with the provinces (Ostry, 1995). Yet the same principles of comprehensiveness, universality, portability, public administration, and accessibility have been hallmarks of Canadian public health services. **Public health** augmented Medicare by ensuring that health promotion and protection services were among the affordable, acceptable, essential health services that were "universally accessible to individuals and families in the community" (World Health Organization, 1978). Together, Canada's public health services and national health care system provided health services that were consistent with the tenets of primary health care.

Over the last decade, however, the public health infrastructure in Canada has been severely eroded. In 1996, the Canadian Public Health Association (CPHA) warned of the erosion by noting that in some jurisdictions "Public Health units and specific categories of workers (e.g., Public Health nurses) are disappearing"(CPHA, 1996, p. 1–12). Further warnings were issued by Justice Horace Kreever's report in 1997 and the Auditor General's report in 1999 (Canadian Medical Association (CMA), 2002). However, all admonitions seemed to fall on deaf ears and the deepening crisis recently prompted editors of the *Canadian Medical Association Journal* to devote an entire issue to exposing a Canadian public health system "on the ropes" (CMA, 2002). Sullivan (2002) reported the key findings of a report of the Federal, Provincial, and Territorial Advisory Committee on Population Health that identifies severe problems in public health in Canada, such as disparities among provinces and regions, severely inadequate and decreasing funding, critical human resource problems, and the development of public health policies without consideration of relevant data. There was a consensus that the water contamination in Walkerton, Ontario in 2000 was a "wake-up call" for Canadian public health, occurring because "institutions vital to the infrastructure of public health were neglected" (Schabas, 2002, p. 1282). Less than a year after the issue was printed, a new public health crisis in the form of the SARS outbreak in Toronto, Ontario again pointed to the inadequacy of Canada's public health infrastructure to protect the public's health.

Legislation No specific and comprehensive federal legislation defines core public health services across the country. According to a survey conducted by the CPHA (1997), public health is the responsibility of the provincial health ministry in all provinces and territories except British Columbia. In that province, public health is shared between a number of ministries such as Health, Ministry Responsible for Seniors, and Ministry for Children and Families.

Each province/territory has one primary piece of legislation that governs public health functions such as health protection, health promotion, disease prevention, communicable disease management and control, and environmental health protection (CPHA, 1997). However, often other provincial/territorial acts may include aspects of public health function (e.g., environmental or occupational health).

Financing Public health in Canada is funded by a combination of provincial and/or municipal tax dollars, although federal grants may be available for specific initiatives. It accounts for between 2 and 4% of all health care expenditures (CPHA, 2000). The CPHA survey in 1997 identified significant differences in funding among provinces and territories. Without a national public health program, however, provinces are free to make changes in funding mechanisms that can further destabilize the system and deepen disparities among and within provinces. Ontario is a prime example of the consequences of such funding changes.

In 1998 in Ontario, legislation came into effect that downloaded the full responsibility for public health funding to the municipal level, where it competed with other municipal responsibilities such as roads and garbage disposal. The decision was made in direct opposition to the government's own Health Services Restructuring Commission, which had warned that downloading would dis-integrate the province's health services. The province's decision was made for financial reasons, as public health became a bargaining chip in the negotiations to balance the transfer of costs between the provincial and municipal tax collectors. In 1999, just prior to a provincial election, the Ontario government agreed to upload 50% of public health costs retroactively to January 1, 1998. The net result of these changes in funding was approximately a 25% reduction to the provincial responsibility for public health funding that had existed prior to 1998 and significant destabilization of the province's public health infrastructure. It is within that destabilized environment that the Walkerton water contamination crisis occurred, resulting in extensive illness and a number of deaths.

Delivery Not surprisingly, the delivery of public health services also varies considerably across the country (CPHA, 1997). According the CPHA survey, regional health boards in most provinces govern public health as part of regional health services. Approximately 50% of respondents indicated that public health services were delivered through one of the region's departments or divisions. Whereas some had more than one department, 13% indicated that no public health structure was identifiable within their regional organization. Ontario and New Brunswick are the exceptions in that they continue to maintain separate public health organizations. Public health in Canada is delivered largely by municipal, regional, or provincial employees. However, in the tumult of reorganization, some services have been contracted out to private companies (e.g., water testing), while the elimination of others has created a market for private delivery of services that once were publicly available and thus more widely accessible (e.g., school nursing services).

Allocation Allocation of funds for public health services depends in large part on provincial governance and delivery structures. Funds may be generated by provincial taxes and distributed to regions and municipalities through funding formulas designed to share some or all of the funding responsibilities for specific public health programs. In such shared funding arrangements, there may be dual approval mechanisms at the provincial and regional/municipal level for allocation of funds. On the other hand, regional governments may have the complete authority to allocate funding. In those cases, public heath services often compete for funds with other health services such as acute care.

Home Care/Home Health Nursing

Home care aims to support individuals to remain at home by providing professional services (e.g., nursing, physiotherapy), homemaking or personal support services, and/or social services (Sullivan & Baranek, 2002). The use of home care services has been steadily growing in Canada over the past 25 years. In fact, in that time frame, home care expenditures have increased at the staggering average annual rate of 17.4%, compared with 8.5% for general health expenditures. The increase in use and funding has been attributed to several factors, most significantly the belief that services that are provided in the home are both a less costly and a more desirable means of receiving necessary care. These claims, however, have yet to be proven.

In 1997–98, almost 1 million Canadians or approximately 3% of the population received home care services from territorial or provincial programs. While all of the provinces offer a package of basic services, there are significant interprovincial variations in the degree to which services are publicly funded versus privately financed (Health Canada, 2002b). Even after adjusting for provincial population differences, there exists significant inequity in accessing publicly funded home care across different regions of the country. Although the actual figure is difficult to verify, Coyte and McKeever (2001) calculate that private payment (a combination of out-of-pocket and private insurance coverage) for home care services approximated almost 20% of total home care expenditures in 1997. Thus savings associated with the provision of services in the home versus in an acute care setting may not so much reflect an actual decrease in cost but rather a transfer of costs to patients and their families (Shah, 1998).

Legislation Currently, six provinces have legislation that addresses the financing and provision of home care services at provincial and regional levels (Health Canada, 2002a). However, in the glaring absence of common national standards, legitimate concerns exist in relation to equal access to type, amount, and quality of home care services (Sullivan & Baranek, 2002).

Financing Home care is the fastest growing area of health spending in Canada, currently expanding at a rate four times greater than other health services. However, home care expenditures represent <5% of total health spending (Coyte & McKeever, 2001). In all 13 provinces and territories, the ministries or departments of health and/or social/community services maintain control over home care budgets and funding levels. However, home care has retained a significant private sector component, often requiring user fees or co-payments.

Delivery Most provinces have delegated responsibility for service delivery decisions to regional or local health authorities, while still maintaining control over policy guidelines, standards for regional service delivery, reporting requirements, and monitoring outcomes. For example, in British Columbia, Alberta, Saskatchewan, Manitoba, Prince Edward Island, Newfoundland and Labrador, Nunavut, and the Northwest Territories, the delivery of home care services has been completely devolved to local or regional authorities. Ontario employs a model that delivers home care services through 43 Community Care Access Centres (CCACs). In Quebec, the 146 Centre Local de Services Communautaires (CLSCs) deliver home care services. In New Brunswick, two programs under the department of health and community services administer home care whereas in Nova Scotia, regional offices of the department of health administer and make delivery decisions about home care. Finally, in the Yukon, the social services branch of the department of health and social services administers home care.

Across the provinces, services are delivered using four basic frameworks (Health Canada, 2002b). The models, summarized below, all provide some element of streamlining (intake, assessment, referral, case management), but vary in their approach to delivery of care, most significantly in the degree to which contracting out services to private agencies (both for-profit and not-for-profit) occurs.

- Public-provider model: Professional and home support services are delivered mainly by publicly funded employees (Saskatchewan, Quebec, Prince Edward Island, Yukon, Northwest Territories, Nunavut).
- Public-professional and private home support model: All professional services are delivered by public employees. Home support services are contracted out to for-profit and/or not-for-profit agencies (New Brunswick, Newfoundland and Labrador, British Columbia, Alberta).
- Mixed public-private model: Streamlining functions are provided by public employees. Professional services are provided by a mix of public employees or through contracting out to private agencies. Home support services are contracted out to for-profit and/or not-for-profit agencies (Nova Scotia, Manitoba).
- Contractual model: Streamlining functions are provided by publicly funded employees. Professional services and home support services are contracted out by a public authority to private agencies (for-profit and not-for-profit), which provide care to clients (Ontario).

Allocation Once funding has been designated for home care, it is typically allocated across a province. The recent trend for provinces to allocate funds using a population needs–based funding model is viewed as a step forward in the equitable allocation of home care funds.

Within their home care budget, each region must then decide how much is allocated to home care versus acute care services, how much is set aside for support services, and which programs receive support. Public funding for home care is allocated to home care organizations which then coordinate and/or deliver home care services. While major budgetary decisions are made at the regional level, case managers are then required to make decisions at the individual level.

Not All Change Is Progress: Home Care in Ontario through Managed Competition In Ontario, the Long Term Care Branch of the Ministry of Health funds home care services. Historically, the funding process favoured not-for-profit providers of in-home services. However, when reforms were undertaken in 1996, a contractual model for the delivery of home care services was adopted. This new process has favoured any provider willing to enter the lowest bid for the service contract.

Forty-three regionally based Community Care Access Centres (CCACs) were established to determine eligibility and service needs of home care clients, select and remunerate service providers, and monitor performance. Service providers, a mix of for-profit agencies and not-for-profit agencies, are required to compete for contracts to provide the required in-home services by submitting requests for proposals. This process allows private, for-profit agencies to profit from public funding earmarked for the delivery of health services. This new situation, sometimes referred to as passive privatization, requires serious consideration (Sullivan & Baranek, 2002).

It is critical to understand that competition necessarily takes place along two divergent dimensions: price and quality of care (Anderson & Parent, 2000). In the six years since the adoption of this model of "managed competition," there have been no studies demonstrating valid or reliable quality of care indicators for in-home services. The obvious conclusion is that the single critical dimension considered in this model is cost. Given that home care services are labour intensive, the necessary fall-out is significantly lower wages and benefits for nurses and other personnel providing this type of care (Coyte & McKeever, 2001). Currently, nurses providing home care services earn as much as 25% less than their counterparts in traditional health care settings, leading to consequences in terms of recruitment, morale, retention, and quality of care.

In 2000, Price WaterhouseCoopers (PWC) was commissioned by the provincial government to conduct a program review to determine the extent to which this method of "managed competition" was meeting the stated goals of health reform in the province (Mildon, 2002). Recommendations for improvement included the following:

- more resources, including human resources,
- more consistent policies and practices,
- improved waiting-list management,
- outcome-based performance measures, and
- improved financial management.

As a result, Bill 130, the Community Care Access Corporations Act, was passed by the legislature late in 2001. While the PWC report indicates areas of improvement related to function, the new legislation instead focuses on governance, actually initiating a process whereby CCACs may, in future, be even less able or willing to express concern over inadequacy of funding or systemic issues (Mildon, 2002).

HEALTH CARE REFORM IN CANADA

Canada's health care system, while widely cherished and considered a hallmark of Canadian culture, clearly has some problems. Issues such as the skewed distribution of funding toward acute care and curative services, the dominance of a biomedical approach in insured services, and increasing inequities in uninsured services warrant substantial changes to create the equitable, accessible, integrated health care system that was envisioned when Medicare was initially conceived. Health care practices have changed: for example, patients are discharged "sicker and quicker" to their homes. Concerns that an aging population will place increasing demands on the health care system give rise to concerns that it will be inadequate.

Shortages of health care personnel, economic recessions, and the election of governments with an agenda to slash taxes and government involvement in health and social services have all contributed to the reduced availability of services. Media reports of waiting lists and relocation practices that transport Canadians in need of medical interventions away from their homes to the Unites States alarm Canadians and lead them to consider whether alternative models could provide a better, sustainable health care system.

Before examining some of the arguments in the private versus public health care system, it is important to understand that not all pressure for health care reform is simply a desire for a better system. The Canadian health care system's values of social justice, equity, and community are incompatible with others such as individualism and market economics. Privatization of Canadian health care offers a substantial opportunity to for-profit providers. In one analysis, if the private portion of health care rose only 20%, an additional $16 billion dollars per year would be available to health care businesses (Registered Nurses Association of Ontario, 1999). Such a potentially lucrative market is attractive to the large for-profit health care corporations that monopolize the American health care industry. As globalization trends continue, threats that international trade agreements may be able to compromise Canadian sovereignty in determining the structure and scope of its own health care system need to be taken seriously (Barlow, 2002).

The value conflict between those who favour a sustainable, universally accessible health care system and those who favour privatization and a market-driven health care system are summed up in the words of an American cardiologist. Speaking of the decline of American health care, he describes a situation that seems eerily familiar to the current Canadian health care debate:

> Like most social transformations, there were ample warnings of an impending crisis. It was not precipitated by an invasion of barbarians scaling down the ramparts of an ethical profession. Rather, it began when doctors were seduced by financial incentives, with unquestioning third-party payers providing an open till.... For-profit health care is an oxymoron. The moment care

Canadian Research Box 2.2

Standing Senate Committee on Social Affairs. (2002). The health of Canadians – the federal role: Final report on the state of the health care system in Canada. [also known as the Kirby Report]

The final report and recommendations of the Senate Committee for reform, chaired by the Honourable Michael J. Kirby, were released in late October 2002. The cited work, Volume 6 of the committee's report, recommended reforms to the health care system. The full report is available online (see Additional Resources at the end of this chapter).

Many critiques and responses to the report by various stakeholder groups can be found online and were reported by the media. Those of professional nursing groups included a news release by the Alberta Association of Registered Nurses (2002), which highlighted the report's recommendations to use interdisciplinary teams of health care workers, expand publicly funded services to home care, and emphasize a primary health care model. A comprehensive analysis was provided by the Registered Nurses Association of Ontario (RNAO) (2002). The RNAO response provided a brief summary of the Report's recommendations and highlighted both encouraging and problematic aspects from its perspective. It also brought to light what it sees as a conflict of interest on the part of the Committee's chair, Senator Kirby, because of his involvement on the boards of both a for-profit health care agency and a pharmaceutical company.

Briefly, RNAO (2002) identifies as "good news" the report's affirmation that Canadian Medicare is affordable and sustainable, its rejection of user fees and two-tier medicine, its recommendations for increasing public spending on health care, and its proposals to increase accountability. While the recommended expansion of Medicare into home care and pharmaceuticals is welcome, RNAO believes it does not go far enough.

The concerns identified by RNAO (2002) include the report's endorsement of for-profit delivery systems in the face of research evidence that suggests it is costlier and provides poorer clinical outcomes; its proposal of health care insurance premiums as a revenue-raising mechanism; the introduction of service-based hospital funding, which would create a competition among hospitals; and its silence on the vulnerability of Canadian health care and social programs to international trade agreements.

Although the author found no other comprehensive analysis of the Kirby report, other stakeholder groups voiced concerns similar to RNAO's through media releases and advisories. One called the report a "disgraceful sham" (National Union of Public and General Employees, 2002) while another labelled it a recipe for "commercialization and privatization" (Canadian Health Coalition, 2002). A few groups, such as the Ontario Medical Association, welcomed the report's findings (Ontario Medical Association, 2002) or endorsed specific aspects of the report (Ontario Pharmacists Association, 2002).

Discussion Questions

1. To what extent do you believe that Senator Kirby's membership on boards of for-profit agencies compromised his ability to chair the Senate Committee examining health care?
2. How is funding health care through levying a special health care premium different from simply raising general taxes by the same amount and using the increases to pay for health care?

is rendered for profit, it is emptied of genuine caring. This moral contradiction is beyond repair. It entails abandoning values acquired over centuries of professionalizing health care into a humanitarian service (Lown, 1999).

Volumes have been written about health care reform in Canada and all but a brief overview is beyond the scope of this chapter. The Romanow Report represents extensive consultations with the public and stakeholder groups and a comprehensive review of evidence related to health care costs and clinical outcomes associated with various models. During the consultations, Canadians overwhelmingly support a publicly funded health care system, delivered by not-for-profit organizations. However, although fewer in number, others argued strongly for privatization. The most common arguments advanced by proponents of each side of the argument are discussed briefly below.

Common Arguments against Continuance of a Publicly Funded, Not-for-Profit Delivered Health System

A common argument for change in health care is the increased demand expected because of changing demographics, the greying of Canadians. This argument does not stand up in the face of empirical Canadian and international research that demonstrates that aging, per se, has accounted for little increase in health care expenditures in the past (Barer, Evans, Hertzman, & Johri, 1998). Barer et al. suggest that the myth that an aging population will escalate spending makes intuitive sense but changing medical practices with relation to elders has more bearing on health care costs than aging. They are supported by recent research conducted in Manitoba that suggests it is healthy seniors, rather than sick ones, who are responsible for significant increases in health care use (Canadian Health Services Research Foundation [CHSRF], 2001a).

Another frequently advanced argument is that user fees will make the health care system more efficient by eliminating abuse of the system. However, most health care spending is beyond patients' control and requires the order of a physician (CHSRF, 2001b). In analyzing the results of the Rand Health Insurance Study in the U.S., the CHSRF reported that medical services declined for everyone but more so among poor people. They noted that "sick people were more likely to die when user charges were installed." The CHSRF pamphlet also reports Saskatchewan's experience with user fees between 1968 and 1975 in which similar barriers to care occurred, and furthermore, the province's overall health care costs did not decrease! Barer et al. (1998) point out that unlike taxation, which draws contributions most heavily from people with the highest income, user fees take a larger share from those with the lowest incomes.

The third commonly advanced argument is for a parallel health system in which those who could afford to pay would have the "choice" to pay out-of-pocket and jump waiting lists. Such a parallel system, the argument goes, would relieve pressure on the public health care system. Like most arguments, this one has an intuitive appeal. Every Canadian has heard reports of waiting lists. CHSRF counters this argument by noting that the measurement of waiting lists is inaccurate and their management is poor (CHSRF, 2002b). Moreover, after examining parallel systems already in place, the researchers conclude that rather than shortening waiting lists, a secondary system actually increases waiting times because when practitioners are working in the private system, they are not available in the public one. They conclude that increased "choice" in a private system is a luxury for those with higher income levels.

Another myth to advance the argument for privatization is that it would lead to more efficiency. Again, experiences in the U.S. and in Alberta suggest otherwise. According to an CHSRF analysis, cataract surgeries in Calgary, which are now all purchased from private companies, are more expensive and create longer waiting lines that those in neighbouring cities (CHSRF, 2002a). Studies of for-profit and not-for-profit institutions in the U.S. suggest that the quality of care is better when the profit motive is not at cross-purposes with care.

The debate about privatization is not about private delivery, since most of health care in Canada is already privately

PHOTO 2.2

RNAO executive director Doris Grinspun (centre) joins Canadian celebrities in giving health care a helping hand. From left, Fiona Reid, Shirley Douglas, Dan Lett, Doris Grinspun, Sonja Smits, and Rick Mercer. The actors took to the virtual stage at a Toronto Internet cafe on January 10, 2003, joining tens of thousands of other Canadians who have signed an on-line petition urging the federal and provincial governments to quickly implement the full Romanow Report.

Credit: Registered Nurses Association of Ontario

CASE STUDY: Establishing a Nursing Centre

Primary health care, despite being a central ideal in many governmental policy documents, has been slow to be realized in Canada. It has not been possible to realize the principles of primary health care because of the continuing dominance of a biomedical approach to health care. At the same time, nurses have been underutilized and their potential for contributing to health and healing undervalued. The Comox Valley Nursing Centre is an example of an innovative approach to health care that has successfully met a community's needs.

In the early 1990s, the Registered Nurses Association of British Columbia secured funding from the provincial government to establish the Comox Valley Nursing Centre as a 16-month primary health care project that would demonstrate the "breadth of nursing practice when constraints were removed" (Attridge et al., 1997, p. 34).

The next step was to establish a steering committee, consisting of nurses and a community representative. Planning was centred on achieving the following goals (Attridge et al., 1997):

- increasing coordination and integration of health services,
- providing essential health care,
- increasing client self-reliance and participation in health care,
- addressing social determinants of health, and
- providing health care that gave good fiscal and clinical outcomes.

A few months later, a Community Advisory Committee (CAC) was established to represent more voices from the community, and the steering committee was replaced by a Nursing Practice Council (NPC). The Centre opened approximately eight months after receipt of the funding.

One full-time coordinator and four part-time nurses, along with 31 volunteers, provided a range of health promotion services to the community (Attridge et al., 1997). Over the 16-month demonstration project period, 437 individuals visited the centre with a wide range of health issues, including acute or chronic physical complaints; psychological, spiritual, or social concerns; and/or a need for health counselling, health assessment, or health networking. Support groups, advocacy groups, and therapeutic groups, such as a group of compulsive over-eaters, were formed (Attridge et al., 1997). In addition, the nursing staff were involved with over 30 community outreach projects, such as foot-health groups for seniors, health promotion sessions at shopping malls, and asthma information sessions.

The impact of the nursing centre was evaluated by researchers at the University of Victoria. Written questionnaires indicated that the clients' average satisfaction rating was 33.9 in a possible range of 9–36. Interviews likewise revealed very positive client experiences. Clients valued being respected, not rushed, and obtaining better information than they had in previous encounters with the health system. Eighty-nine percent reported positive physical health changes that could be attributed to visiting the nursing centre; none reported any negative physical changes (Attridge et al., 1997). Cost-effectiveness was difficult to demonstrate because of the lack of comparable services and Attridge et al. suggest further research is needed in this area.

Clarke and Mass (1998) analyzed the project's evaluation reports and examined how collaboration and empowerment, two tenets of primary health care, manifested themselves in the nurses' practice. Various antecedents and outcomes of collaboration were identified. Empowering nursing practice was based in a client-nurse relationship and ranged from personal empowerment, small-group development, community organization, and coalition advocacy to political action. The authors concluded that clients were empowered in large part because of the empowerment nurses felt in being able to practise to the full scope of nursing. They reflect on a reality that many nurses experience:

> When professionals are not granted professional status, they have great difficulty in establishing an empowering contract with their clients because they lack enough voice in the situation to be able to do so. The Comox Valley Nursing Centre Demonstration Project provided the context for nurses to practice autonomously, to be independent, self-directing, and self-governing, and to be accountable for their own decisions and actions within a project that was responsible to expressed community needs (Clarke & Mass, 1998, p. 222).

The Comox Valley Nursing Centre received funding to extend its services for an additional 16 months. It ended in December 1996 (Attridge et al., 1997). According to the evaluations, the Nursing Centre was highly successful and had the potential to make an important contribution in the provision of health care.

Discussion Questions

1. The Comox Valley Nursing Centre was established because the Registered Nurses Association of British Columbia capitalized on an opportunity: the provincial government's reform initiatives. What opportunities exist at the present time to establish a nursing centre in your area?
2. If you wanted to establish a nursing centre in your area, how would you go about developing a proposal? Who would you involve? Identify one or two goals that the project might have.
3. Discuss Clarke and Mass' conclusion that an empowering nursing practice was possible because the nature and structure of the nursing centre empowered the nurses who practised there. To what extent do you agree that nurses' ability to facilitate the empowerment of clients is dependent on their own empowerment?

provided (Alberta Association of Registered Nurses et al., 2000; Deber, 2000). However, as Evans, Barer, Lewis, Rachlis, and Stoddart (2000) observe, the concern is about for-profit delivery. Most hospitals are run by private boards, despite being publicly funded. Most physicians, dentists, and other health care entrepreneurs are, in fact, private businesses. And some long-standing home nursing associations, such as the Victorian Order of Nurses and St. Elizabeth Health Care, are private, not-for-profit agencies. The concerns are that, when responsibilities to shareholders for profit margins supersede those to patients for high-quality care, clinical decisions move away from the provider-patient partnership and rest instead with business administrators. It is in the context of protecting profit margins that cherry-picking (that is, restricting eligibility for insurance to those who are at lowest risk) becomes problematic. Expensive redundancies enter the equation when services are increased to the extent that there are no waiting lines. And increased competition adds duplication and increased administrative expenses to overall costs.

What, Then, Needs to Be Changed?

Much of the discussion thus far has established that changes to Medicare are needed both to sustain its principles and to expand the services to which they apply. Organizations such as the CPHA have urged the Romanow Commission to broaden its focus to health promotion and disease prevention services (Canadian Public Health Association, 2001). The decimation of the public health infrastructure has elicited a call for a firm funding base for public health, disentanglement of public health professionals from political demands, and the creation of an arm's-length federal agency to provide leadership in issues related to disease control and surveillance (Schabas, 2002).

Other groups have also advocated for expansion of the services protected by the five principles of the CHA. For example, the Canadian Nurses Association, along with several provincial nursing associations and a nursing union, have suggested that primary care needs to be reconceptualized to primary health care, effecting a move away from biomedical dominance (Alberta Association of Registered Nurses et al., 2000). This coalition of nursing organizations also advocates for expanding principles of Medicare to home care, long-term care, pharmaceuticals, and rehabilitation services. The Registered Nurses Association of Ontario has proposed a Community Care Act in its submission to the Romanow Commission (RNAO, 2002). Such an Act would extend the principles of the CHA to other community health services through parallel legislation without opening up the CHA. The recommendation reflects a common fear that the pressures to dismantle Medicare are so intense, that opening up the CHA to amend it would result in the destruction of the Canadian health care system that Canadians love and have come to expect over the last 30 years.

SUMMARY

To varying degrees, federal, provincial, regional, and municipal levels of government are involved in Canadian health care. A universally accessible, publicly funded, not-for-profit-delivered health care system is steeped in Canadian values and embraced by the Canadian public. Efforts to enshrine those values in federal legislation began as early as 1919. The present legislation, the Canada Health Act, is limited in that its principles of public administration, portability, accessibility, universality, and public administration apply only to essential medical and hospital services. Nevertheless, the publicly funded and largely privately delivered health care system has served Canadians well with respect to both health outcomes and cost-effectiveness.

Pressures to reform Canadian Medicare have come not only because of its narrow focus but also from individuals and groups who favour augmenting the public system with services provided by the for-profit sector. Numerous reports at provincial and federal levels over the last five years have recommended reforms to the health care system. The most comprehensive of those, the Romanow Commission Report, made 47 recommendations for both the immediate future and next 20 years.

The federal government has played a leadership role, not only in Canada, but also in the world, in health promotion policy. However, a coordinated approach to implementing health promotion policy at the community and population levels has been hampered by the lack of a national public health plan. Serious erosions to public health in Canada have led to withdrawal and reductions of many public health nursing services.

Likewise, incorporation of primary health care has been slow in Canada despite this country's endorsement of its principles 25 years ago. Some provincial initiatives with relation to primary care reform (those that focus only on first point of contact with the health care system) can be seen across Canada. More and more provinces are enacting legislation to provide a legal framework for the practice of nurse practitioners. Interdisciplinary primary care models exist in several provinces. Evolving technology has provided access to health care through telephone information and triage services generally staffed by nurses.

Home care services and expenditures have increased disproportionately over the last quarter century because of early discharge practices, hospital bed closures, and technological advances that make care in the home possible. Great variability exists across the country with respect to the degree to which such services are publicly insured.

The arguments advanced for an increased role of the private, for-profit sector in health care have not been supported by evidence of decreased cost or greater effectiveness. Rather, evidence suggests that for-profit delivery of health care, even if publicly funded, produces poorer clinical outcomes (Devereaux et al., 2002). The weight of such studies and overwhelming public support for a publicly funded, universally accessible health care system underpinned the Romanow Report tabled in late 2002. What happens to the report and its 47 recommendations is now in the hands of federal and provincial governments and the public that elects them.

KEY TERMS

Medicare
Canada Health Act
publicly administered
comprehensiveness
universal
portable
accessible
determinants of health
financing
delivery
allocation
primary health care
public health
home care

STUDY QUESTIONS

1. Identify the origins of Medicare in Canada and summarize the essential provincial and federal laws that created the present Canadian health care system.
2. Discuss the events that led up to and necessitated passage of the Canada Health Act.
3. What role did organized nursing play in the passage of the Canada Health Act?
4. Discuss the federal and provincial responsibilities for health according to the Canadian Constitution Act.
5. Contrast the funding mechanisms for public health and home health nursing services.
6. Describe how the Canada Health Act was or was not successful in achieving the intended goals.

INDIVIDUAL CRITICAL THINKING EXERCISES

1. How would your life be different if health care in this country were provided based on ability to pay, rather than need?
2. How can you as a nursing student influence the extent of implementation of the recommendations of the Romanow report?
3. How is health care in Canada both different and the same now than it was for your parents? For your grandparents?
4. How do your own values fit with the societal values that are reflected in the five funding criteria described in the Canada Health Act (1984)?
5. This chapter has shown that health policy decisions may leave a legacy for generations. Describe briefly one policy revision you would make in the areas of primary care/primary health care, public health, and home care.
6. In an ideal world, create a health care system designed to provide the best care, to the most people, in the most cost-effective manner. Describe mechanisms for financing, allocation, and delivery. Compare and contrast this system with the current Canadian system.

GROUP CRITICAL THINKING EXERCISES

1. Who stands to gain from health care privatization? How? Who stands to lose?
2. Discuss the advantages and disadvantages of opening up the Canada Health Act to introduce changes to Medicare.
3. What would be the advantages and disadvantages of a national Canadian Public Health Act?

REFERENCES

Alberta Association of Registered Nurses, Canadian Nurses Association, Ontario Nurses Association, Registered Nurses Association of Ontario, & United Nurses of Alberta. (2000). *Towards a sustainable, universally accessible health-care system.* A discussion paper prepared for the National Nursing Forum.

Alberta Association of Registered Nurses. (2002). *Kirby's committee recommendations identify key steps for effective health care reform.* Retrieved December 24, 2002 from **www.nurses.ab.ca/newsrel/Kirby%202.html**

Anderson, M., & Parent, K. (2000). *Care in the home: Public responsibility—private roles?* (University of Toronto: Dialogue on Health Reform). Retrieved October 27, 2002 from **www.utoronto.ca/hpme/dhr/pdf/Anderson_Parent.pdf**

Attridge, C., Budgen, C., Hilton, A., McDavid, J. C., Molzahn, A., & Purkis, M. E. (1997). The Comox Valley Nursing Centre. *Canadian Nurse,* February, 34–38.

Auditor General of Canada. (2002). *1999 Report of the Auditor General of Canada to the House of Commons* (chapter 29). Retrieved September 3, 2002 from **www.oag-bvg.gc.ca/domino/reports.nsf/html/9929ce.html/$file/9929ce.pdf**

Barer, M. L., Evans, R. G., Hertzman, C., & Johri, M. (1998). *Lies, damned lies, and health care zombies: Discredited ideas that will not die* (HPI Discussion Paper #10). Houston, TX: University of Texas, Health Policy Institute.

Barlow, M. (2002). *Profit is not the cure: A call to citizens' action to save medicare.* Council of Canadians. Retrieved September 17, 2002 from **www.canadians.org/documents/profit_not_cure.pdf**

Begin, M. (1987). *Medicare: Canada's right to health.* Montreal, QC: Optimum.

Begin, M. (2002). *Revisiting the Canada Health Act (1984): What are the impediments to change?* Address to the Institute for Research on Public Policy, 30th Anniversary Conference, Ottawa, ON.

Canada, Department of Finance. (2002). *A brief history of the Canada Health and Social Transfer (CHST).* Retrieved September 2, 2002 from **www.fin.gc.ca/FEDPROV/hise.html**

Canada, House of Commons. (1984). An Act Relating to Cash Contributions by Canada in Respect of Insured Health Services Provided Under Provincial Health Care Insurance Plans and Amounts Payable by Canada in Respect of Extended Health Care Services and to Amend and Repeal Certain Acts in Consequence Thereof. (The Canada Health Act). Ottawa, ON: Government of Canada.

Canadian Council on Social Development, Research and Development Branch. (1972). *Case studies in social planning: Planning under voluntary councils and public auspices.* Ottawa, ON: Author.

Canadian Health Coalition. (2002). *A recipe for commercialization and privatization.* Retrieved December 24, 2002, from **www.healthcoalition.ca/kirby-release.html**

Canadian Health Services Research Foundation. (2001a). *Myth: The aging population will overwhelm the healthcare system.* Ottawa, ON: Author.

Canadian Health Services Research Foundation. (2001b). *Myth: User fees would stop waste and ensure better use of the healthcare system.* Ottawa, ON: Author.

Canadian Health Services Research Foundation. (2002a). *Myth: For-profit ownership of facilities would lead to a more efficient healthcare system.* Ottawa, ON: Author.

Canadian Health Services Research Foundation. (2002b). *Myth: A parallel private system would reduce waiting times in the public system.* Ottawa, ON: Author.

Canadian Institute for Health Information. (2001). *National health expenditure database: National health expenditure trends, 1975–2001.* Ottawa, ON: Author.

Canadian Medical Association. (2002). Public health on the ropes. (Editorial). *Canadian Medical Association Journal, 166*(10), 1245.

Canadian Public Health Association. (1996). *Focus on health: Public health in health services restructuring.* Ottawa, ON: Author.

Canadian Public Health Association. (1997). *Public health infrastructure in Canada: Summary document.* Ottawa, ON: Author.

Canadian Public Health Association. (2000). *An ounce of prevention: Strengthening the balance in health care reform.* Ottawa, ON: Author.

Canadian Public Health Association. (2001). *Creating conditions for health: Recommendations to the Commission.* Ottawa, ON: Author.

Chrichton, A., Gordon, C., Robertson, A., & Farrant, W. (1997). *Health care: A community concern? Developments in the organization of Canadian health services.* Calgary, AB: University of Calgary Press.

Clarke, H. F., & Mass, H. (1998). Comox Valley Nursing Centre: From collaboration to empowerment. *Public Health Nursing, 15*(3), 216–224.

Coyte, P., & McKeever, P. (2001). Home care in Canada: Passing the buck. *Canadian Journal of Nursing Research, 33*(2), 11–25.

Deber, R. B. (2000). Getting what we pay for: Myths and realities about financing Canada's health care system. *Health Law in Canada, 21*(2), 9–56.

Devereaux, P. J., Choi, P. T. L., Laccjetto, C., Weaver, B., Schunemann, H. J., Haines, T. et al. (2002). A systematic review and meta-analysis of studies comparing mortality rates of private for-profit and private not-for-profit hospitals. *Canadian Medical Association Journal, 166*(11), 1399–1406.

Eschauzier, J. (1983). *Community health centres.* Ottawa, ON: Canadian Council on Social Development.

Epp, J. (1986). *Achieving health for all: A framework for health promotion.* Ottawa, ON: Health and Welfare Canada.

Evans, R. G., Barer, M. L., Lewis, S., Rachlis, M., & Stoddart, G. (2000). *Private highway, one-way street: The deklein and fall of Canadian medicare?* University of British Columbia, Centre for Health Services and Policy Research. Retrieved September 17, 2002 from **www.chspr.ubc.ca/hpru/pdf/2000-3d.PDF**

Gillett, J., Hutchison, B., & Birch, S. (2001). Capitation and primary care in Canada: Financial incentives and the evolution of health service organizations. *International Journal of Health Services, 31*(3), 583–603.

Hamilton, N., & Bhatti, T. (1996). *Population health promotion.* Ottawa, ON: Health Canada, Health Promotion and Development Division.

Health Canada. (2001). *The population health template: Key elements and actions that define a population health approach.* Retrieved July 6, 2002 from **www.hc-sc.gc.ca/hppb/phdd/pdf/discussion_paper.pdf**

Health Canada. (2002a). *Health is everyone's business.* Retrieved July 9, 2002 from **www.hc-sc.gc.ca/hppb/phdd/collab/index.html**

Health Canada. (2002b). *Provincial and territorial home care programs: A synthesis for Canada.* Retrieved June 11, 2002 from **www.hc-sc.gc.ca/homecare/english/syn_2.html**

Hutchison, B., Abelson, J., & Lavis, J. (2001). Primary care in Canada: So much innovation, so little change. *Health Affairs, 20*(3), 116–131.

Lalonde, M. (1974). *A new perspective on the health of Canadians: A working paper.* Ottawa, ON: Health and Welfare Canada.

Lightstone, S. (2002). Health-care-by-phone services spreading across country. *Canadian Medical Association Journal, 166*(1), 80.

Lown, B. (1999, August 1). For-profit care's morbid results. *Boston Sunday Globe,* pp. E1, E5.

McKeown, T. (1979). *The role of medicine: Dream, mirage or nemesis?* Princeton, NJ: Princeton University Press.

Mildon, B. (2002). Bill 130: Of issues and imperatives. Community Health Nurses Initiatives Group. Retrieved November 24, 2003 from **action.web.ca/home/chnig/alerts.shtml?sh_itm=59e734c63a12db563d4e4fbfd02bd703**

Mussallem, H. K. (1992). Professional nurses' associations. In A. J. Baumgart & J. Larsen (Eds.), *Canadian nursing faces the future* (2nd ed., pp. 495–518). Toronto, ON: Mosby.

National Forum on Health. (1997). *Canada Health Action: Building on the legacy.* Retrieved September 2, 2002 from **www.hc-sc.gc.ca/english/care/health_forum/forum_e.htm**

National Union of Public and General Employees. (2002). *Kirby report on health care is a disgraceful sham.* Retrieved December 24, 2002 from **www.nupge.ca/news_oc02/n25oc02b.htm**

Ontario Family Health Network. (2002). *About the Ontario Family Health Network.* Retrieved October 27, 2002 from **www.ontariofamilyhealthnetwork.gov.on.ca/english/about.html**

Ontario Medical Association. (2002). *OMA welcomes Kirby commission report continues calling for national debate.* Retrieved December 24, 2002 from **www.oma.org/pcomm/kirby.htm#1**

Ontario Ministry of Health and Long Term Care. (2002). *Your community health services: Community health centres.* Retrieved October 27, 2002 from **www.health.gov.on.ca/english/public/contact/chc/chc_mn.html**

Ontario Pharmacists Association. (2002). *OPA's response to Kirby report: Ontario pharmacists applaud Kirby Report's greater role for health care professionals.* Retrieved December 24, 2002 from **www.opatoday.com/public/opanews.asp**

Organization for Economic Co-operation & Development. (2002). *OECD health data 2002.* Retrieved September 03, 2002 from **www.gdsourcing.ca/works/OECD.htm**

Ostry, A. (1995). The history of public health in Canada: Differences in the history of public health in nineteenth century Canada and Britain. *Canadian Journal of Public Health, 86*(1), 5–6.

Pollara Research. (2002). *Health care in Canada survey 2002.* Presented at the National Nursing Forum, Toronto, ON.

Rachlis, M., Evans, R. G., Lewis, P., & Barer, M. L. (2001). *Revitalizing medicare: Shared problems, public solutions.* Tommy Douglas Research Institute. Retrieved September 01, 2002 from **www.tommydouglas.ca/reports/revitalizingmedicare.pdf**

Rachlis, M., & Kushner, C. (1994). *Strong medicine: How to save Canada's health care system.* Toronto, ON: Harper Perennial.

Rafael, A. R. F. (1997). *Every day has different music: An oral history of public health nursing in Southern Ontario, 1980–1996.* Unpublished doctoral dissertation, University of Colorado, Denver, CO.

Registered Nurses Association of Ontario. (1999). *The Canada Health Act: To preserve and protect.* Toronto, ON: Author.

Registered Nurses Association of Ontario. (2002). RNAO response to the recommendations of the Kirby Commission (Volume Six). Retrieved January 26, 2004 from **http://www.rnao.org/html/PDF/RNAO_Kirby_Response_Nov02.pdf**

Rock, A. (1998). Address to the Canadian Nurses Association Annual General Meeting, Ottawa, ON.

Romanow, R. (2002). *Shape the future of health care: Interim report.* Retrieved September 2, 2002 from **www.hc-sc.gc.ca/english/care/romanow/index1.html**

Schabas, R. (2002). Public health: What is to be done? *Canadian Medical Association Journal, 166*(10), 1282–1283.

Shah, C. P. (1998). *Public health and preventive medicine in Canada* (4th ed.). Toronto, ON: University of Toronto Press.

Sullivan, P. (2002). Canada's public health system beset by problems: Report. *Canadian Medical Association Journal, 166*(10), 1319.

Sullivan, T., & Baranek, P. (2002). *First do no harm: Making sense of Canadian health reform.* Toronto, ON: Malcolm Lester & Associates.

Tuohey, C. H. (2002). The costs of constraint and prospects for health care reform in Canada. *Health Affairs, 21*(3), 32–46.

World Health Organization. (1978). *Declaration of Alma Ata.* Retrieved September 4, 2002 from **www.who.dk/AboutWHO/Policy/20010827_1**

World Health Organization, Canadian Public Health Association, & Health and Welfare Canada. (1986). *Ottawa charter for health promotion.* Ottawa, ON: Health and Welfare Canada.

ADDITIONAL RESOURCES

Fooks, C., & Lewis, S. (2002). Romanow and beyond: A primer on health reform issues in Canada. Canadian Policy Research Network. **www.usask.ca/lists/hplink/2002/msg00338.html**

Canadian Health Services Research Foundation. Mythbuster Series: A series of essays giving the research evidence behind Canadian health care debates. **www.chsrf.ca/docs/resource/index_e.shtml**

Evans, R. G., Barer, M. L., Lewis, S., Rachlis, M., & Stoddart, G. (2000). Private highway, one-way street: The deklein and fall of Canadian medicare? **www.chspr.ubc.ca//hpru/pdf/20003D.PDF**

About the Authors

Adeline R. Falk-Rafael, RN, PhD, is an Associate Professor in the School of Nursing at York University, Toronto, Ontario, where she currently teaches community health nursing. Her program of research has focused on power and empowerment in public health nursing, and her findings have been reported in journals such as *Advances in Nursing Science, Public Health Nursing,* and the *Journal of Professional Nursing.* She is currently the president of the Registered Nurses Association of Ontario.

Sue Coffey, RN, DNSc, is an Assistant Professor in the School of Nursing at York University, Toronto, Ontario. In addition to extensive experience working in acute care settings, Ms. Coffey has a master's degree in community health nursing. She has worked with aggregates experiencing acute and chronic health conditions as well as with those focusing on health promotion.

Adeline Falk-Rafael and Sue Coffey prepared this chapter except for the Appendix.

APPENDIX 2A

Funding for Health Services for First Nations and Inuit in Canada

First Nations and Inuit Health Branch, Health Canada

The First Nations and Inuit Health Branch (FNIHB) is a branch within Health Canada (HC) that is responsible for the delivery of health services in Aboriginal communities. Services are federally funded and regionally managed. FNIHB is divided into seven regions (Atlantic, Quebec, Ontario, Manitoba, Saskatchewan, Alberta, and British Columbia) that roughly correspond to the provincial boundaries. Atlantic Region includes all four Atlantic provinces. The Yukon, Northwest Territories, and Nunavut are overseen by the Northern Secretariat.

FNIHB regions are separate, parallel structures to the HC regional offices that exist in each region. Regional authority is decentralized and each region has its own unique organizational structure and relationship to its First Nations (FN) constituents. Most of the First Nations and Inuit (FN/I) communities in Atlantic, Quebec, and British Columbia regions manage their own health care services in whole or in part. In the remainder, community-based health services are managed by the regional office.

First Nations people are Canadian citizens and as such, have access to provincially and territorially funded health services that fall under the Canada Health Act, 1984. Aboriginal people are included in the per capita allocations of federal funding that are transferred to the provinces for "medically necessary" health services. First Nations communities (formerly termed "reserves") below the 60th parallel are, however, considered to be federal or crown land. For this reason, the federal government has historically funded public health and primary health care services on reserves. "North of 60" Aboriginal people comprise most of the population of the Canadian territories; reserves are largely absent; and health services for Aboriginal people are completely integrated into the health and social services systems.

Indian Health Policy, 1979

The Federal Indian Health policy is one of the cornerstones of current policy regarding First Nations people and the Canadian Government. The Indian Health Policy of 1979 stated that it was based on the special relationship of the Indian people to the federal government and to the Crown. This relationship is committed to addressing access issues and health disparities that exist for Aboriginal people.

Policy for federal programs for Indian people (of which the health policy is an aspect), flows from constitutional and statutory provisions, treaties, and customary practice. It also flows from the commitment of Indian people to preserve and enhance their culture and traditions. It recognizes the intolerable conditions of poverty and community decline, which affect many Indians, and seeks a framework in which Indian communities can remedy these conditions. The federal government recognizes its legal and traditional responsibilities to Indians, and seeks to promote the ability of Indian communities to pursue their aspirations within the framework of Canadian institutions (Health Canada-FNIHB, 2001a).

Many Aboriginal communities exhibit conditions that are comparable to the level of poverty and community decline present in many rural and remote parts of Canada. Combined with this economic disadvantage are cultural isolation and the effects of a colonial past. For this reason, addressing the determinants of health is a key feature of federal policy for FN communities. Thus the Indian Health Policy of 1979 noted that improving the level of health in First Nations communities is founded on three policy fundamentals:

- community development (socioeconomic, cultural, and spiritual) to remove the conditions of poverty and powerlessness which prevent the members of the community from achieving a state of physical, mental, and social well-being;
- the traditional relationship of the First Nations people to the federal government, in which the federal government promotes the capacity of First Nations communities to manage their own local health services; and
- the Canadian health system consisting of specialized and interrelated services funded by federal, provincial, or municipal governments, Indian bands, or the private sector.

The federal role lies in public health activities on reserves, health promotion, and the detection and mitigation of hazards to health in the environment. The most significant provincial and private roles are in the diagnosis and treatment of acute and chronic disease and in the rehabilitation of the sick (Health Canada-FNIHB, 2001a).

Ten years later, the "Treasury Board approved authorities and resources to support the transfer of Indian health services from Medical Services, Health and Welfare Canada (now Health Canada) to First Nations and Inuit wishing to assume responsibility" (Health Canada-FNIHB, 2001b). This "transfer process" (also called the "transfer initiative"):

- permits health program control to be assumed at a pace determined by the community, that is, the community can assume control gradually over a number of years through a phased transfer;
- enables communities to design health programs to meet their needs;
- requires that certain mandatory public health and treatment programs be provided; and

- strengthens the accountability of Chiefs and Councils to community members.

Further, the transfer process:

- gives communities the financial flexibility to allocate funds according to community health priorities and to retain unspent balances,
- gives communities the responsibility for eliminating deficits and for annual financial audits and evaluations at specific intervals,
- permits multi-year (three to five year) agreements,
- does not prejudice treaty or Aboriginal rights,
- operates within current legislation,
- is optional and open to all First Nations communities south of the 60th parallel (Health Canada-FNIHB, 2001b).

Financial Highlights

FNIHB is responsible for funding the delivery of community-based health services to 638 Aboriginal communities and about 700 000 persons, most south of the 60th parallel. FNIHB directly manages health services in about half those communities and administers integrated agreements and transfer agreements for the rest, who manage their own health services in whole or in part following the process outlined above.

FNIHB also funds an extended health benefit program, the Non-Insured Health Benefits program (NIHB). The NIHB is a payer of last resort for health services that are not covered under the Canada Health Act for all status Indians in Canada, both on and off reserve. This includes, for example, medical transportation, dental care, eyeglasses, other assistive devices, and drugs. The total budget for FNIHB in 2002–3 was $1.4 billion dollars, of which approximately 50%, or $700 million, was allocated to the NIHB program.

The total amount of funding in First Nations and Inuit control as of March 31, 1999 was $491 million. Other contributions include NIHB contributions and NIHB pilots. Some FN/I communities have undertaken pilot projects as a step towards the transfer of NIHB.

Recently, FNIHB implemented a home care program that receives about $90 million annually in federal funding. Home care services are community based and band managed. As First Nations and Inuit assume greater control of health services through mechanisms such as integrated agreements and transfer agreements, the involvement of FNIHB in direct service delivery has steadily declined.

Demographic Highlights: South of the 60th Parallel

Across Canada there are 638 FN/I communities. The transfer initiative only applies, however, to those 599 communities south of the 60th parallel. Ten years after the transfer process was initiated, 244 communities of the 599 eligible (41%) had signed Health Services Transfer Agreements. Of those 244 communities, 43% were individual community transfers and 57% were part of a multi-community transfer.

The total population of all 599 eligible communities is 388 712, of which 193 060, or 46%, are living in transferred communities (communities that have completed all or part of the transfer process and are autonomous for those areas of health care). Communities of 1001–3000 represent 21% of the eligible communities, and 54% of those communities have signed transfer agreements.

Delivery of health services is administered in First Nations and Inuit communities in various ways. Those communities interested in having more control of their health services can decide from a menu of approaches: health services transfer, integrated community-based health services, and self-government, based on their eligibility, interests, needs, and capacity.

Community Types

In order to better allocate resources, communities have been classified according to their degree of access to provincial or territorial health services. For example, a remote-isolated community may require professional nursing services 24/7. However, funding for these services also depends on community size.

- Type 1: Remote-Isolated: No scheduled flights, minimal telephone or radio services, and no road access.
- Type 2: Isolated: Scheduled flights, good telephone services, and no year-round road access.
- Type 3: Semi-Isolated: Road access greater than 90 km to physician services.
- Type 4: Non-Isolated: Road access less than 90 km to physician services.

Remote, isolated communities of fewer than 200 people may have only a lay community health representative (CHR) on site, who consults with a community health nurse in a neighbouring community nursing station. Alternatively, a nurse may visit for one or more days a month. Larger centres may have a nursing station with two or more nurses. Nurses in these settings function in an expanded role and provide essential public health, primary care, and physician and pharmacist replacement services on a 24-hour-a-day, seven-day-per-week basis.

FNIHB has more than 600 FTE-registered nurse employees. The transferred bands employ a roughly equivalent number.

Larger, less isolated communities have community health centres that provide more typical public health and primary care services during standard business hours. A physician may visit on a regular basis and/or clients are referred out for doctor visits. Rarely, a community health centre may provide expanded role nursing services after hours.

In both cases, FNIHB's NIHB program provides funding for medical transportation for the community member to visit a doctor or a hospital when required.

Other Federally Funded Programs

Health Canada currently funds 53 National Native Alcohol and Drug Abuse Program (NNADAP) Treatment Centres and seven

National Youth Solvent Abuse Treatment Programs (NYSATP) through FNIHB. To date, eight NNADAP treatment centres and one NYSATP have been transferred to FN/I control.

As of March 31, 1999, FNIHB still operated four hospitals. Sioux Lookout Zone Hospital in Sioux Lookout, Ontario was transferred to provincial control in 2002 as part of an amalgamation with the local community hospital. Manitoba Region has two hospitals: Norway House Hospital in Norway House, and Percy E. Moore Hospital in Hodgson, Manitoba. Alberta Region has The Blood Indian Hospital in Cardston, Alberta. Originally established to serve First Nations peoples, these hospitals are available to anyone in need and are linked to provincial health care systems. Transfer of hospital services must be considered in the light of the individual circumstances of each hospital and the communities in which they are located.

Health Canada also provides funding for early childhood development and targeted programs for fetal alcohol syndrome/fetal alcohol effects, Aboriginal Head Start, Brighter Futures, tobacco reduction, food safety, HIV/AIDS, diabetes, tuberculosis elimination, and the Canada Prenatal Nutrition Program. Many of these programs are allocated to the communities on a per capita basis, which can result in very small sums for tiny communities. FNIHB also provides funds for scholarships for FN/I who are pursuing careers in the health field. These funds are administered by the National Aboriginal Achievement Foundation (NAAF), a non-governmental organization.

Other government departments and branches provide funding to FN/I communities that contributes to addressing determinants of health. FNIHB and Indian and Northern Affairs Canada (INAC) jointly resource on-reserve water quality: FNIHB is accountable for monitoring and testing and INAC for infrastructure. INAC is responsible for housing and community-based education. The Solicitor General funds community policing or support from the Royal Canadian Mounted Police. Human Resources Development Canada has an Aboriginal division that works with FN/I communities on strategies to improve access to trades.

In these ways, the federal government attempts to address determinants of health while FNIHB ensures access to community-based health services and supports community development.

REFERENCES

Health Canada-FNIHB. (2001a). Indian health policy 1979. Accessed November 24, 2003 from **www.hc-sc.gc.ca/fnihb-dgspni/fnihb/bpm/hfa/transfer_publications/indian_health_policy.htm**

Health Canada-FNIHB. (2001b). Ten years of health transfer First Nations and Inuit control. Accessed November 24, 2003 from **www.hc-sc.gc.ca/fnihb-dgspni/fnihb/bpm/hfa/ten_years_health_transfer/index.htm**

Health Canada-FNIHB. (2002). First Nations and Inuit Control – Annual Report, 2000–2001. Accessed November 24, 2003 from **www.hc-sc.gc.ca/fnihb-dgspni/fnihb/bpm/hfa/fnic_annual_report_2000_2001.htm**

CHAPTER 3

Ethical and Legal Considerations

Elizabeth Peter, Louise Sweatman, and Kathleen Carlin

OBJECTIVES

AFTER STUDYING THIS CHAPTER, YOU SHOULD BE ABLE TO:

1. Describe the central values of Canadian nursing and how they relate to community health nursing.
2. Understand the relevance of feminist bioethics for community health nursing.
3. Articulate and reflect upon the central ethical and legal issues in community health nursing.
4. Understand the political nature of ethical problems in the community.

INTRODUCTION

Community health nurses (CHNs) encounter ethical issues in all facets of their everyday nursing lives. Ethical nursing practice requires CHNs to be able to reflect critically upon their practices, make sound ethical decisions, and to take appropriate actions. These capacities must reflect the central values of Canadian nursing: safe, competent, and ethical care; health and well-being; choice; dignity; confidentiality; justice; accountability; and quality practice environments (Canadian Nurses Association, 2002).

The term ethics has been defined and used in numerous ways. For the purposes of this chapter, **ethics** refers to those values, norms, moral principles, virtues, and traditions that guide human conduct. Ideas that reflect what is right and good and what we ought, and ought not, to do are often associated with ethics. Ethics is also a specialized area of philosophy. Moral philosophers, who study and reflect upon ethics, have developed formal ethical theories. These theories can be helpful in identifying, articulating, and analyzing ethical issues. The term **bioethics**, also defined as health care ethics, refers to the study of ethical issues that are related to health and health care. Bioethics has made use of a range of ethical theories and approaches, including deontology, utilitarianism, casuistry, principlism, virtue ethics, and feminist ethics. It is beyond the scope of this chapter to describe all of these in a meaningful and comprehensive fashion. Instead, one approach, feminist bioethics, will be used to frame the chapter along with the CNA Code of Ethics for Registered Nurses (2002) and the Community Health Nurses Association of Canada's (CHNAC) Canadian Community Health Nursing Standards of Practice (2003).

Canadian Nurses Association Definitions of Nursing Values

- **Safe, competent, and ethical care:** Nurses value the ability to engage in nursing care that allows them to fulfill their moral obligations to the people they serve.
- **Health and well-being:** Nurses value health promotion and well-being and assist persons to achieve their optimum level of health in situations of normal health, illness, injury, disability, or at the end of life.
- **Choice:** Nurses respect and promote the autonomy of persons and help them to express their health needs and values and obtain appropriate information and services.
- **Dignity:** Nurses respect the inherent worth of each person and advocate for respectful treatment of all persons.
- **Confidentiality:** Nurses safeguard information learned in the context of a professional relationship and ensure it is shared outside the health care team only with the person's permission or as legally required.
- **Justice:** Nurses uphold principles of equity and fairness to assist persons in receiving a share of health services and resources proportionate to their needs and in the promotion of social justice.
- **Accountability:** Nurses are accountable for their practice, and they act in a manner consistent with their professional responsibilities and standards of practice.
- **Quality practice environments:** Nurses value and advocate for practice environments that have the organizational and human resources necessary to ensure safety and support for all persons in the work setting.

Source: Canadian Nurses Association. (2002). Code of Ethics for Registered Nurses. Ottawa, ON: Author.

The focus of the chapter is to identify and discuss the everyday ethical problems and concerns that frequently arise in the work of CHNs, as opposed to focusing exclusively upon ethical dilemmas. It will help nurses and nursing students gain the capacity to reflect critically upon the multiplicity of ethical and legal dimensions inherent in community health nursing. The purpose is to raise an awareness of both the ethical problems and possibilities in this area of nursing.

FEMINIST BIOETHICS

Feminist bioethics brings feminist perspectives and methods to bear on ethical issues that arise in health and health care (Sherwin, 1998). It is important to note that although feminism began as a response to the oppression of women, many feminist perspectives, such as feminist bioethics, address not only gender oppression, but also other abuses of power, such as forms of oppression that are associated with race, class, ethnicity, age, disability, sexuality, and professional status within the health care hierarchy. As such, feminist bioethics is not a perspective only for or about women, nor is it anti-male. It addresses inequities that both women and men experience and it seeks to make visible and valuable caring practices, such as those of nursing (Liaschenko & Peter, 2003).

Feminist bioethics can be characterized by several generally common features:

- the ethical use of power,
- the inclusion of ethics of care and justice,
- the view of persons as interdependent and situated socio-politically, and
- a focus on everyday ethical issues.

First, feminist bioethics is concerned with the ethical use of power in health care. It examines the broad political and structural dimensions of problems in health care as well as the day-to-day use of power by health professionals. Power, in itself, is ethically neutral. How power is used, however, is of ethical significance. Worthley (1997) defines professional **power** as "the influence stemming from the professional position we hold. It is the ability to have an impact on the state of being of a person—physically, mentally, emotionally, psychologically, spiritually—in the context of the professional role" (p. 62). Nurses and other health professionals can use their professional influence to improve the health and well-being of individuals, but they can also use this professional power to deny individuals the right to make choices regarding their health.

Second, feminist bioethics tends to suggest that the ethic of care is a necessary perspective for bioethics, but it is not sufficient. The ethic of justice must also play a role. Gilligan (1982) identified these contrasting ethics in her research that compared the moral reasoning of men and women. She describes an **ethic of care** as reflecting the moral reasoning of women. It embraces the following moral considerations: the care and nurturing of self and others, the alleviation of hurt and suffering, the maintenance of relationships, and the emphasis upon contextual details of concrete situations. In contrast, the **ethic of justice**, which has been associated with the moral reasoning of men, is characterized by the following moral considerations: abstract rules and principles, fairness and reciprocity, and duties and obligations for self and society.

One factor to use when comparing the two ethics is the type of human relationship each tends to promote. The ethic of care tends to focus on close, personal relationships with others while the ethic of justice tends to focus on impersonal relationships or abstract issues involving groups or society as a whole. It is important to note that although women tend to use care-focused moral reasoning more frequently than men do, both men and women generally use both justice and care considerations in their moral reasoning. Jaffee and Hyde (2000) conducted a meta-analysis to review quantitatively the work on gender differences in moral orientation. They concluded that the care and justice orientations are more strongly related to the context and content of the moral dilemma than to gender, emphasizing that both orientations are needed to fully represent moral life.

Third, feminist bioethics tends to view persons as unique, connected to others, and interdependent, in other words, vulnerable and unequal in power (Sherwin, 1998). It focuses on how persons are situated or positioned in society, that is, the entire context of their lives, including culture, history, politics, and socioeconomic status. This relational definition of persons is appropriate for community health nursing because CHNs often work with vulnerable individuals and groups who are socially disadvantaged. CHNs also emphasize the importance of their relationships with the clients they serve as a means of caring and empowering.

Fourth, feminist bioethics tends to be concerned not primarily with crisis issues, like euthanasia, but with issues of everyday life (Warren, 1989). Not all ethical issues or problems are ethical/moral dilemmas. **Ethical dilemmas** are "situations and issues that arise where equally compelling ethical reasons both for and against a particular course of action are recognized and a decision must be made, for example, caring for a young teenager who is refusing treatment" (CNA, 2002, p. 5). In this situation, a nurse would be compelled not only to honour the choice of the teenager, but also to protect their health and well-being. **Everyday ethics** in nursing is "the way nurses approach their practice and reflect on their ethical commitment to the people they serve. It involves the nurses' attention to the minor ethical events of the day such as protecting the person's physical privacy" (CNA, 2002, p. 5). These everyday ethical concerns can also include those related to advocating for clients, working with limited resources, assessing the competence of fellow caregivers, and relieving human suffering. Feminist bioethics expands the agenda of bioethics by examining broad health care issues that impact on everyday practice, such as the need to examine the implications of the dominance of the medical model within the health care system and the broader Canadian society. It also recognizes that some perspectives, such as those of clients and nurses, have not been adequately brought into the dialogue and debate on ethical issues nor have they been drawn upon fully in the development of bioethical theory.

Feminist Bioethics in Community Health Nursing

Feminist bioethics is a suitable ethical framework for community health nursing because some of its specific features can address common ethical concerns and ideals found in the community. These specific features, derived from the general features of feminist bioethics, include:

- emphasis on social justice,
- acknowledgement of difference (e.g., gender and race),
- sensitivity to context and place, and
- critique of medicalization.

Leipert (2001) suggests that community health nursing could benefit from a feminist perspective because it facilitates critical thinking about power, gender, and socioeconomic structures, all of which impact significantly upon health. Fundamental to community health nursing is an understanding of the socio-environmental context of health that recognizes that basic resources and prerequisite conditions are necessary to achieve health (CHNAC, 2003). Gebbie (2001) has also discussed how feminism promotes collaboration with oppressed groups to create social change in a way that is consistent with health promotion strategies. Underlying these strategies is a view of health that goes beyond the narrow individual and disease orientation of the medical model.

Feminist bioethics also has the capacity to focus not only on individuals, but also on entire groups because it goes beyond traditional individual-focused caring to include considerations of social justice. Traditionally, bioethics has focused upon ethical issues that individuals face in the context of receiving care in a hospital setting. In contrast, public health requires a framework that expresses its values in broader societal terms, that is, social justice. Drevdahl (2002) states, "**Social justice** postulates that important social factors (e.g., gender, age, or income) disadvantage some and limit the fair distribution of goods and hardships. Collective action (particularly by the government) is therefore required to reduce the effects of these factors. Underlying the public health's mission of social justice is the implicit valuing of collectivism over individualism" (p. 163).

With respect to home care nursing, feminist bioethics is also a highly relevant perspective because it emphasizes the ethical significance of difference, such as gender and race, and makes visible the societal value of caregiving. The provision of home care services is largely a gendered activity. Home care's paid labour force in Canada is composed mainly of women who are frequently drawn from immigrant and visible minority populations (Aronson & Neysmith, 1996). The work is poorly paid and of low status. Similarly, informal care is generally provided by women—wives, daughters, and daughters-in-law (Neysmith, 2000). Moreover, approximately two thirds of Canadian home care recipients are women, largely because women have a greater life expectancy, often have chronic conditions, and can rely on less spousal assistance (Wilkins & Park, 1998).

Feminist bioethics is also highly sensitive to context. It can capture the importance of place or setting in health care delivery (Peter, 2002). The notion of **place** has several related meanings. "A place may be thought of as a location... Other conceptualizations of place include the ideas of locale; a specific setting in which social relations are constituted" or of having "a sense of place," which refers to "the meaning, intention, felt value, and significance that individuals or groups give to particular places" (Curtis & Jones, 1998, p. 645–6). In other words, a place is "an operational 'living' construct which 'matters' as opposed to being a passive 'container' in which things are simply recorded" (Kearns & Moon, 2002, p. 609).

Understanding the meaning and impact of various places or settings is central to community health nursing because CHNs deliver nursing services where clients live, work, learn, worship, and play (CHNAC, 2003), not in hospitals. MacPhail (1996), whose research explored the ethical concerns of Canadian CHNs, concluded that, "The most obvious and significant factor influencing ethical issues in community-based practice is the setting, the location or environment in which the nurses practice" (p. 50). This conclusion is not surprising because different places/settings accomplish different kinds of work; have different values, operational codes, and philosophies; and are influenced and structured by different kinds of knowledge and power. These factors combine to influence a person's agency within a particular place or environment (Liaschenko, 1994; 2001). Thus, the experience of receiving and providing health care services cannot be overtly detached from the place in which it is received or provided (Andrews, 2002; Kearns, 1993). Bioethics has generally assumed that the hospital, not the community, is the setting of health care delivery. This has resulted in the neglect of many issues facing CHNs that are strongly shaped by the uniqueness of the settings/places in which they arise.

ETHICAL AND LEGAL ISSUES ARISING IN COMMUNITY HEALTH NURSING PRACTICE

A number of specific ethical and legal issues can arise in community health nursing practice. The following five interrelated standards of practice (CHNAC, 2003) that form the foundation of CHN practice will be used to structure the discussion:

1. promoting health,
2. building individual/community capacity,
3. building relationships,
4. facilitating access and equity, and
5. demonstrating professional responsibility and accountability.

Standards of practice are broad descriptions of desired and achievable levels of performance. They are expressions of the minimum knowledge, skills, judgments, and attitudes expected of nurses. As such, they are considered authoritative statements that set out the ethical, legal, and professional basis of nursing practice (College of Nurses of Ontario (CNO), 2002). Failure to maintain these standards can lead to findings of professional misconduct and incompetence, termination of employment, and exposure to civil and criminal liability.

Standard 1: Promoting Health

CHNs promote health through a) health promotion; b) illness and injury prevention and health protection; and c) health maintenance, health restoration, and palliation (CHNAC, 2002). These strategies can each raise specific ethical and legal concerns that require awareness on behalf of CHNs.

Health Promotion CHNs focus on the health promotion of individuals and communities in a variety of ways. The CHNAC's (2002) Standards state, "Health promotion is a mediating strategy between people and their environments—a positive, dynamic, empowering, and unifying concept that is based in the socio-environmental approach to health... Community health nurses consider socio-political issues that may be underlying individual/community problems" (p. 10). Interventions can include facilitating community action, assisting in the development of skills, and increasing client knowledge and control over the determinants of health (CHNAC, 2003).

Liaschenko (2002) comments that much of the health promotion work that nurses have engaged in has not focused upon the material and socio-political conditions necessary for health. Instead there has been an overemphasis upon individual behaviour patterns. She explains that this may be the result of nurses working within a biomedical system that primarily values repairing diseased or injured bodies and not the social fabric in which those bodies live. CHNs are also not always in a position to directly influence those socio-political factors, such as poverty, that they have identified as moral concerns in their work. There is a collective moral responsibility that goes beyond individual CHNs to bring about broad social and political change.

Nevertheless, there are potential moral harms in health-promoting activities that need to be discussed. First, because health is a value-laden concept, CHNs can influence individuals to conform to social norms through health promotion strategies (Liaschenko, 2002). In other words, CHNs can unwittingly become agents of social control and medicalization. **Social control** is "usually conceptualized as the means by which society secures adherence to social norms; specifically, how it minimizes, eliminates, or normalizes deviant behaviour" (Conrad & Schneider, 1985, p. 7). The concept of **medicalization**, introduced by Zola (1972), refers to the social process whereby more and more aspects of daily life are understood in terms of health and illness. Many activities, such as madness, child abuse, and alcoholism, were once considered immoral or criminal, but later were frequently redefined in medical terms. As a consequence, these behaviours now fall into the realm of medical treatment and control (Verweij, 1999).

Second, a possible moral harm of health promotion is its potential to create adversarial relationships between those who actively strive to improve their health and those who do not (Liaschenko, 2002). A danger exists that the former group may view the latter group as morally weak and inferior because they are not always trying to improve their health through such things as diet, exercise, meditation, and so on. If this type of adversarial relationship existed between CHNs and their clients, nurses' respect for the dignity of those they serve could be compromised. That they respect the inherent worth of the persons they serve is a fundamental ethical responsibility of Canadian nurses (CNA, 2002).

Ultimately, health promotion activities are powerful tools that must be used with careful reflection as to their consequences for the health and well-being of individuals and communities. CHNs must be mindful of the social and professional power they possess as respected health professionals. Because they are often trusted by society to be promoting or providing what is good and healthy, they have an ethical responsibility to reflect upon whose good and whose conception of health is being promoted and why.

Illness and Injury Prevention and Health Protection CHNs engage in a variety of strategies that minimize the occurrence of diseases and injuries and their consequences. These activities are often prescribed and regulated by mandated programs and laws and can include education and services regarding such things as birth control and breastfeeding, disease surveillance, immunization, risk reduction, outbreak management, and education of communicable diseases. Social marketing techniques such as media releases and radio interviews may be used to deliver key information to the public (CHNAC, 2003).

While preventive and health-protective measures can greatly improve the well-being of populations, they are not without their potential moral harms. Some of these harms are similar to those associated with health promotion in that they can further medicalization. First, prevention and health protection information can weaken people's confidence and security in their health. Constant surveillance of one's body can be anxiety-provoking and could possibly lead to an excess of diagnostic testing. These iatrogenic risks are of ethical concern because they can erode a person's sense of well-being (Verweij, 1999). CHNs must strive to find a balance between providing information to protect their clients without unduly alarming them.

Second, it is important to recognize that efforts to prevent disease and injury restrict the liberty of individuals, thereby limiting their choice and autonomy. For example, seatbelt laws and speed limits restrict the liberty of individuals but can protect their health. Other strategies such as communicable disease surveillance and reporting not only can restrict liberty, but can also go against the ideals of confidentiality and privacy. Sound ethical reasons must exist to impose these liberty-limiting strategies upon clients. In some instance, interventions are targeted at one group of people to protect another group's health, such as mandatory reporting of some communicable diseases. These interventions can be ethically justified if they distribute benefits and burdens and limit burdens as fairly as possible. The greater the burdens posed, in terms of constraints on liberty and confidentiality, financial cost, or the targeting of already vulnerable groups, the stronger the evidence must be that a program will be effective (Kass, 2001). In other words, on balance, the potential well-being of a population must exceed the burden placed on individuals. This type of ethical reasoning brings to the fore the CHN's valuing of collectivism over individualism (CHNAC, 2003).

Third, how the prevalence of disease is understood and explained by CHNs also has ethical implications. Krieger and Zierler (1996) describe two distinct theories that explain the interplay between social and biological factors that shape disease susceptibility and the public's health—the lifestyle and social production of disease frameworks. The lifestyle theory suggests that individuals choose ways of living that have health consequences. For example, promiscuity, prostitution, and injection drug use have been posited as lifestyle factors that explain the distribution of HIV/AIDS in a population. In contrast, a framework of social production of disease conceptualizes disease determinants to be economic, social, and political. The relative social and economic positioning of people shapes their behaviours and their exposure to disease. With respect to HIV/AIDS, groups that are economically deprived and experience racial discrimination are at increased risk for infection. Gender-based economic inequalities, for example, influence a woman's ability to determine the sexual use of her body. Prostitution may provide a woman a strategy for economic survival for herself, and possibly also her children, as opposed to being a lifestyle choice per se.

Without a conscious awareness of these differing perspectives, it is possible that CHNs could too easily judge persons who do not heed health information and acquire a disease. Alternatively, CHNs could view these persons as powerless victims of their socio-political and economic positioning, thereby absolving them from any responsibility for their health and absolving CHNs from any responsibility to provide information or other support to assist them in making health choices. Either extreme would not respect the dignity of these persons.

A more helpful perspective would put together these explanatory frameworks in a way that does not eliminate the possibility of choice, but situates it. Sherwin's (1998) notion of relational autonomy is helpful here. She describes how individuals are inherently social and relational beings who are significantly shaped by interpersonal and political relationships. Individuals exercise autonomy and choice within this web of interconnected and sometimes conflicting relationships. Options available to individuals are constrained by circumstances and the availability of resources. Pressure from significant others and social forces can also greatly influence decision-making. For example, a woman with limited financial means may engage in unprotected sexual intercourse with her male partner who refuses to wear a condom. She may understand the risk of unprotected sex, but "chooses" to have unprotected intercourse with him because she is financially dependent upon him and finds it difficult to say no to his requests for sex. While she makes a choice, this choice is limited by her economic dependency and perhaps also by societal expectations upon women to sexually satisfy their male partners. Nevertheless, it is possible that future partners will be more receptive to her request for protection and/or her economic situation may improve. Having health information regarding disease prevention in the latter instance could assist her in making choices that protect her health.

Health Maintenance, Health Restoration, and Palliation

CHNs also provide clinical nursing, palliative care, health teaching, and counselling to individuals and families as they experience illness and life crises such as the birth or death of a family member. In doing so, CHNs engage in a process of mutual participation with their clients in planning, implementing, and evaluating nursing care while maximizing the capacity of individuals and families to take responsibility for and manage their own care. Nursing interventions are wide ranging and can involve health promotion, disease prevention, and direct clinical-care strategies. The variability in settings for this care delivery can lead to challenges in providing care (CHNAC, 2003).

This section of the chapter will address the ethical dimensions of several aspects of this multi-faceted CHN role, including community settings as sites of care, informed consent, family caregiving, and palliative care.

Community Settings as Sites of Care Providing care in the community can be challenging because, unlike hospitals, many community settings were not designed primarily for the purposes of caregiving. Because of the variety of settings, CHNs must often adapt their approaches and procedures and may travel significant distances to reach their clients. For example, CHNs working for the AIDS Prevention Street Nurse Program in Vancouver go where their clients are to provide care. Not only do these nurses have established sites such as jails, detoxification centres, clinics, and drop-in centres, they also go door-to-door in single-room-occupancy hotels and make contacts on the street either by foot or by mobile van (Hilton, Thompson, & Moore-Dempsey, 2000). As a result, CHNs and other community health workers often face a number of potential threats to their health and safety, including violence from clients and others, tobacco smoke, pets, ergonomic issues (e.g., lifting patients), and physical conditions (e.g., poor lighting, temperature, broken stairs, and snow and ice on walkways). Travelling from place to place also poses risks (Health Care Health & Safety Association of Ontario & Workplace Safety & Insurance Board, 2000). Here again, nurses have an ethical responsibility, one that is expressed in the CNA (2002) Code of Ethics. It requires nurses to value and advocate for quality practice environments that have the organizational structures and resources necessary to ensure safety, support, and respect for all persons in the work setting.

When care is provided in the home, special ethical considerations arise because the home is a highly significant place that is imbued with multiple meanings, including personal identity, security, and privacy (Williams, 2002). As nursing services are increasingly offered in homes as opposed to hospitals, it is necessary for nurses to become mindful of the social and ethical implications of this change. McKeever (2001) aptly states: "The devolution of health care to the home setting is changing the meanings, material conditions, spatio-temporal orderings, and social relations of both domestic life and health care work. Unlike institutional settings such as hospitals, homes are idiosyncratic places with aesthetic, physical, and moral dimensions that reflect their occupants' gendered, socioeconomic, and ethnic characteristics. Little is known about the suitability of contemporary homes for providing and receiving extraordinary care, or about the effects of superimposing one major institutional order (health care) over another (the family) in light of the changes in structure and function that both have undergone in recent decades" (p. 4).

The potential lack of suitability of homes for the provision and receipt of care raises ethical concerns. Anderson (2001) suggests that assumptions have been made in health policy, for example, that we all have homes with family and friends readily available to provide care, as well as the necessary resources for care such as bedding and laundry facilities. The privileged middle class may possess these things, but many others do not. Poverty and homelessness are increasing in Canada, thereby limiting the access to needed health services for large segments of our population. This potential barrier to the receipt of health services is of serious ethical concern. Nurses have a moral responsibility to promote social justice to ensure that all persons receive their share of health services and resources in proportion to their needs (CNA, 2002).

Canadian Research Box 3.1

Committee to Advance Ethical Decision-Making in Community Health. (2001). *Final Report. March 2001–December 2001.* Toronto, ON.

The Community Care Access Centres (CCACs) and Community Health Centres (CHCs) of Toronto, recognizing the value of using ethics as a foundation for human resource planning, conducted a qualitative research study to identify ethical issues in practice that may affect the recruitment and retention of qualified workers. Fourteen focus groups were conducted with personal-support workers, nurses, therapists, care coordinators, and consumer representatives to explore the perspectives of frontline workers and care recipients. Fifty-two in-depth interviews with representatives of 39 organizations in the Toronto area were also conducted to obtain a management perspective. Four major themes were identified:

1. Resource allocation: Participants expressed concern that the current allocation of funds for health services favours facility-based care at the expense of the community sector. Workers have inadequate time to care for those with complex clinical conditions.
2. Situational variables: These include the gaps and discontinuities of current legislation, time allocation, content of work, impact of technology, multiple delivery agents, and employer policy.
3. Safety issues: The increased complexity of conditions treated outside of hospitals without the support of on-site resources was identified. Conditions of homes may be less than ideal for delivering care, and workers can be exposed to illegal activity, unsafe family situations, domestic violence, and various forms of abuse.
4. Issues related to consent: The capacity of clients to make informed choices was found to fluctuate. Differences in language and culture, time constraints, and knowledge and interpretation of legislation resulted in barriers to effective decision-making.

Discussion Questions

1. How are ethics and the recruitment and retention of workers related?
2. How does the complexity of the community setting affect the types of ethical issues identified by the participants in this research?

Informed Consent As in all areas of nursing practice, CHNs must support and respect the informed choices of their clients (CHNAC, 2003). In order for CHNs to assist clients in making informed choices, at least two elements must be considered: the exchange of information between the client and CHN and respect for the client's autonomy. These two elements are often subsumed in the concept of **informed consent.** Consent is a basic principle underlying the provision of care such that, without it, a case for negligence and professional misconduct can be made against the nurse. The process of consent includes CHNs disclosing, unasked, whatever the average prudent person in the client's particular position would want to know. CHNs must provide information about the nature of the treatment/procedures they are providing, including benefits and risks, alternative treatments, and consequences if the treatment is not given. The presentation of this information must consider the client's education, language, age, values, culture, disease state, and mental capacity. When clients provide their consent it must be done voluntarily (i.e., without being coerced), and they must have the capacity (i.e., mental competence) to do so. The only times when consent is not required for treatment are in emergency situations and as required by law.

Family Caregiving The family's role in caregiving, or informal care, has greatly expanded as responsibility for the provision of health care services has progressively shifted from the state to the family or individual (Anderson, 2001). As it is for formal caregiving in the home, women also provide most of the informal care in the home (Neysmith, 2000). The level of care provision can be extraordinary, encompassing both personal and high-tech care. It can include assistance with activities of daily living, for example, bathing, eating, cooking, laundry, cleaning, and transportation, as well as the provision and management of medications, injections, IVs, catheterizations, dialysis, tube feeding, and respiratory care. These informal caregivers are often responsible for 24-hour care with little available public support and often with inadequate training for the responsibilities they have been expected to assume (Arras, 1995; CARP, 1999; Collopy, Dubler, & Zuckerman, 1990). It has been reported that they have an increased rate of morbidity and mortality (Shultz & Beach, 1999).

The transfer of caregiving responsibilities to family members raises a number of ethical concerns. CHNs have a responsibility to promote and preserve the health and well-being of their clients. Because persons are relational in nature, nurses also have a similar responsibility to a client's family. At times, it may be somewhat difficult to determine who is or should be the focus of care. The evidence cited above illustrates that the health and well-being of clients may be threatened when their informal caregivers are stressed and inadequately educated for their role. Moreover, CHNs, when delegating responsibilities to family caregivers, may be compromising safe, competent, and ethical care in situations where these caregivers do not have adequate support or resources. Choice is also limited because clients may have no other options than to provide and receive care at home.

Ultimately, however, the source of these ethical problems lies outside the nurse-client relationship. It is important to recognize that the situations of both CHNs and their clients are the result of broader political forces and agendas that have limited the availability of resources in order to reduce costs. The CNA Code of Ethics (2002) addresses the importance of nurses upholding principles of justice and equity to ensure that persons gain access to a fair share of health services and resources that is of their choosing. Advocacy for clients is one way for CHNs to promote justice. Advocating change for clients would also improve the health and well-being of CHNs because it would lessen the frequency of nurses practising in a way that compromises their ethical ideals.

Palliative Care A very special and increasingly frequent part of a CHN's practice is palliative care. Although most deaths occur in institutions, many people are now spending the last days of their lives at home. In fact, both the Kirby Report (Standing Senate Committee on Social Affairs, Science and Technology, 2002) and the Romanow Report (Commission on the Future of Health Care in Canada, 2002) have identified palliative home care as a priority area. The Hospice Palliative Care Nursing Standards of Practice (Canadian Hospice Palliative Care Association (CHPCA), 2002) guides nurses working in palliative care and complements the CHNAC (2003) standards and the CNA (2002) code. The CHPCA standards emphasize "respect for the worth of all humans" and respecting "individual(s) based on recognition of their characteristics and abilities" (p. 11). Here again, the feminist emphasis on context can help to illuminate the different moral stances and decisions of clients, family members, and formal and informal caregivers.

While performing palliative care is extremely rewarding, it can also be stressful for the CHN, the client, and the family. This intimate area of practice is one in which respecting a client's dignity and right to choice may be difficult for some CHNs. The philosophy of palliative care is holistic and client-centred. Each CHN may hold their own values regarding end-of-life care practices such as artificial nutrition and hydration, pain control, withholding cardiopulmonary resuscitation (DNR) and other treatments, and assisted suicide or euthanasia (both illegal in Canada). When these conflict with the choices made by clients or their families, ethical dilemmas may arise. Clients often have cultural and religious practices or rituals that are important to them around the time of death. For example, a Catholic client may ask for a priest to administer the Sacrament of the Sick, and some religions have restrictions on who may care for the body after death. Respecting and facilitating these customs are part of the CHN's care.

One of the most important aspects of palliative care is relief of pain. Promoting the client's health and well-being includes the imperative to provide for the client's comfort. Some CHNs may have moral reservations about advocating for or administering adequate amounts of pain medication.

Canadian Research Box 3.2

Ward-Griffin, C., & McKeever, P. (2000). Relationships between nurses and family caregivers: Partners in care? *Advances in Nursing Science*, *22*(3), 89–103.

This Canadian study examined the relationships between community nurses and family members caring for frail elders. It used a critical ethnographic method guided by a socialist-feminist framework of caring. Twenty-three family caregiver–nurse dyads (pairs) were interviewed privately and asked to talk about their experiences of working together.

Four types of nurse-family caregiver relationships were identified: 1) nurse-helper, 2) worker-worker, 3) manager-worker, and 4) nurse-patient. The latter two were most frequent. In the nurse-helper relationship, the least common found, nurses provided and coordinated most of the care while family caregivers assumed a supportive role. Because of the cost of providing this type of care, nurses quickly moved to the second form of relationship—the worker-worker relationship. Care work was transferred to family caregivers with nurses teaching them technical skills. These caregivers learned to assume much responsibility with little authority. Some family caregivers reported feeling afraid and unqualified to assume this level of responsibility. In time, these relationships moved to the manager-worker type when family caregivers had taken on virtually all of the care. At this stage, nurses no longer provided actual caregiving, but focused on the monitoring of family caregivers' coping skills and competence. Many family caregivers resisted this type of support, wanting assistance with actual caregiving instead. The final type of relationship, the nurse-patient relationship, occurred as frequently as the previous one. With this type of relationship, many caregivers, because of pre-existing health problems and the heavy demands of caregiving, became the nurse's patient too.

The authors concluded that these family caregiver–nurse relationships were not partnerships, but were exploitative in character. The work of caring was transferred to family caregivers who were left socially isolated and without adequate resources to provide care.

Discussion Questions

1. What ethical concerns are raised by the findings of this research?
2. How could advocacy play a role in supporting family caregivers and nurses?

They may worry that they are causing the client's death. Yet, ethically, providing comfort at the end of life is part of effective, dignity-preserving care. The Canadian Senate Subcommittee in its report *Quality End-of-Life Care: The Right of Every Canadian* (2000) recognizes that providing pain control may also shorten life and recommends the clarification of the Criminal Code so that both the public and health professionals can learn that this is an acceptable and legal practice. The Senate also recommends increased training for health care professionals in pain control. It is up to CHNs working in this area of practice to keep up-to-date. Adequate pain control means having not only an appropriate dosage of medication, but also a plan in place so that clients get the medication when it is needed, that is, they do not have to wait for a doctor's order or pharmacy delivery at the last minute.

While clients have the right to make informed choices about their care, as their illnesses progress, they often become unable to make decisions (incapable). When clients cannot understand and appreciate the consequences of their choices, a substitute decision maker, usually the next of kin, steps in to make decisions for the person. CHNs need to be aware of the laws in their province regarding the process for substitute decision makers. When clients and their families or substitute decision maker have discussed the client's preferences for treatment or withholding treatment, the substitute decision maker is able to make decisions based on the client's wishes. One way in which clients can communicate their wishes for future health care is by writing an advance directive (living will). Advance directives are not only for people who are terminally ill. Anyone may stipulate what medical treatments they will accept or reject in certain situations. It is used only if the person becomes incapable of making choices. The advantage of an advance directive is that it gives people, while they are still capable, the opportunity to express wishes about treatments such as cardiopulmonary resuscitation (CPR), artificial feeding, and pain control. Advance directives, however, cannot substitute for communication between patients, their families, and their caregivers.

An advance directive contains two sections. The instructional directive sets out wishes for treatment. For example, it may state that if the person becomes terminally ill, antibiotics should not be used for an infection. Another person may stipulate not to be transferred to a hospital in a crisis. The second section, the proxy directive, is a power of attorney for personal care. This means that a person may designate one or more substitute decision makers for health care. This could be a family member or a friend but should be someone who knows the person well and is comfortable carrying out their wishes. Each section of an advance directive may exist separately: wishes concerning treatment may be set down without naming a proxy, or a proxy may be named without making any stipulations about treatment.

Standard 2: Building Individual/Community Capacity

CHNs work collaboratively with individuals/communities to build individual and community capacity. CHNs begin where the individuals and communities are, helping them to identify relevant health issues and to assess their strengths and resources. CHNs use strategies that involve advocacy and empowerment (CHNAC, 2003). The CHNAC (2003) has described **empowerment** as follows: "Community health nurses recognize that empowerment is an active, involved process where people, groups, and communities move toward increased individual and community control, political efficacy, improved quality of community life, and social justice" (p. 6).

Schroeder and Gadow (1996) propose an **advocacy** approach to ethics and community health that embraces the character of the CHNAC's (2003) perspective on empowerment. Their ethic of advocacy calls for the development of partnerships between CHNs, other professionals, and community members to enhance community self-determination. In these relationships, CHNs can help a community to discern its values, needs, and strengths in the form of a unique and encompassing health narrative. The goal of the relationship is "improved community health as defined by the members of the community rather than as defined by the professional" (p. 79). Communities are experts regarding their own health. They are not deviants in need of the normalizing efforts of professionals. Advocacy also requires that all persons within a community are heard and represented, not just those with power or authority (Schroeder & Gadow, 1996).

Actions based on empowerment and advocacy foster the everyday ethical practice of CHNs. Empowerment and advocacy enhance the choices and the health and well-being of communities because they draw on a community's fundamental strengths and needs without the values of others being imposed upon them. CHNs can exercise their professional power ethically, that is, in a manner that promotes, rather than restricts, the expression of community choices.

For example, CHNs designed the Elderly In Need (EIN) Project, an action-research project conducted in a predominantly French-speaking urban community in the Ottawa region. Over a three-year period, CHNs linked with community groups and agencies to make contact with frail and isolated older persons living at home. At an individual level, the CHNs and the older persons developed contractual relationships through which self-care was promoted and supportive ties were fostered. At a community level, the CHNs worked with community groups, such as churches, social committees, clubs, and home support agencies, to strengthen outreach to these older persons and to create initiatives that would strengthen community support for older persons more generally. Together, these interventions reduced the social isolation and dependency of the older persons and built community capacity (Moyer, Coristine, MacLean, & Meyer, 1999).

Standard 3: Building Relationships

The CHNAC's standards describe how CHNs establish and nurture caring relationships with individuals and communities that promote maximum participation and self-determination. They state, "Caring involves the development of empowering relationships, which preserve, protect, and enhance human dignity. CHNs build caring relationships based on mutual respect" (CHNAC, 2003, p. 14). CHNs must build a network of relationships with many others, including clients, groups, communities, and organizations.

In building relationships, CHNs must recognize the uniqueness of their own attitudes, beliefs, and values regarding health, as well as of those of their clients. They must also maintain professional boundaries while involving and trusting clients as full partners in the caring relationship. Maintaining professional boundaries can become particularly challenging in the home environment, where nurses and clients often spend sustained periods of time together in relative isolation (CHNAC, 2002). A **professional boundary** in the nurse-client relationship has been defined as "the point at which the relationship changes from professional and therapeutic to non-professional and personal. Crossing the boundaries means the care provider either misuses the power in the relationship to meet his/her own personal needs rather than the needs of the client, or behaves in an unprofessional manner with the client" (CNO, 1999, p. 4). In other words, the CHN must be cautious that the focus of the relationship remains on meeting the needs of the client and not on the CHN's own needs. As such, the relationship is therapeutic rather than social in nature.

PHOTO 3.1

Street nurses who work on AIDS prevention in Vancouver.

Credit: Photo by Chuck Russell. Photo used with permission from Gold, F. Supervised Injection Facilities, *Canadian Nurse 99*(2), 2003, 14–18.

The connecting and caring aspects of the CHN's work reflect some of the fundamental elements of nursing ethics. In recent years, much emphasis has been placed on the caring nurse-client relationship as foundational to nursing ethics. A caring approach has merit in that it emphasizes the moral importance of reducing human suffering and the relational aspect of nursing practice. Nevertheless, an approach based solely on caring has limitations, since without moral obligation, justice, and attention to political structures, caring relationships can be exploitative or unfairly partial (Peter & Morgan, 2001). In other words, CHNs require other elements in their moral repertoire beyond caring, such as social justice, that can assist them in focusing not only upon the health needs of those immediately connected to them, but also of those who are more distant.

The AIDS Prevention Street Nurse Program in Vancouver exemplifies the importance of building relationships in the work of CHNs. These street nurses work with diverse populations, including hard-to-reach and high-risk street-involved adults and youth, to prevent HIV and STD within a broader mandate of harm reduction and health promotion. At the core of their work is their capacity to reach marginalized populations and form trusting relationships with them. These connections are fostered through the nurses' accessibility; consistency; flexibility; and non-threatening, non-judgemental approach. These nurses' roles involve a wide range of activities, from the provision of condoms, bleach, and clean needles to counselling, crisis intervention, and wound care. Through these relationships, these CHNs also help clients gain access to mainstream services and STD and HIV testing (Hilton, Thompson, & Moore-Dempsey, 2000).

Standard 4: Facilitating Access and Equity

CHNs collaboratively identify and facilitate universal and equitable access to available health care services and the socioeconomic, social, and physical environmental determinants of health. They employ a number of strategies, including advocating for appropriate resource allocation; ensuring access for vulnerable populations (such as the poor, elderly, isolated, and illiterate) through strategies such as home visits and outreach; case finding; advocating for healthy public policy by participating in legislative and policymaking activities; and taking action on identified service gaps and accessibility problems (CHNAC, 2003).

It is through the activities of facilitating access and equity that CHNs strive for social justice. CHNs must take into consideration that social factors such as age, sexual orientation, and socioeconomic status restrict the equitable access and distribution of health services and determinants of health. These activities can be at the local or international level and can entail promoting awareness and action regarding human rights, homelessness, poverty, unemployment, stigma, and so on.

Achieving social justice is extremely difficult. Bayer (2000) describes how the ultimate causes of human suffering and premature death are poverty, inequality, and disregard for fundamental human rights. Therefore, he argues, improvements in health status can often only come with radical social change. Bayer also states, however, that because "public health officials rarely wield the requisite instruments of power, they can only fulfill their mission as advocates for social transformation" (p. 1838). Bayer has termed this perspective "public health nihilism" because public health officials can do so little to alter existing patterns of morbidity and mortality in the absence of social change.

Bayer's (2000) perspective illustrates well the link between ethics and power. It is important to recognize that small changes are nevertheless important in working toward social justice. Two examples of community health professionals facilitating access and equity are described below to illustrate this possibility.

Lisa Brown, a mental health nurse, is the founder and artistic director of the Workman Theatre Project (WTP) at the Centre for Addiction and Mental Health in Toronto. She was inspired and challenged by the talents of her clients and began to promote their creative expression through theatre. The WTP employs both professional actors and people who receive mental health services. The mission statement of WTP states, "Workman Theatre will promote individuals' well being, expand public awareness of mental health issues and enhance the quality of life in Ontario by providing to people who receive mental health services, to artists and to others, opportunities for creative expression and other arts activities" (WTP, 2002). The activities of the WTP promote social justice because they promote access to some of the determinants of health for people with mental illnesses, an often highly vulnerable and disenfranchised group. The WTP not only provides employment and income, it also promotes community participation and awareness.

The Public Health Alliance (PHA) for Lesbian, Gay, Bisexual, Transsexual (LGBT) Equity, a subcommittee of the Ontario Public Health Association (OPHA), is another example of CHNs promoting social justice. The oppression of gay men, lesbians, and bisexual, transsexual, and transgendered persons can lead to significant health impacts such as depression, suicide, homelessness, substance abuse, the transmission of life-threatening infections, and violence. Many public health professionals offer care; however, they are often inexperienced, uninformed, or uncomfortable with the diverse experiences and situations of these individuals. In addition, the lack of acknowledgement of the holistic nature of LGBT issues across the lifespan limits the possibility of consistently providing accessible and appropriate services. The goals of the PHA include the elimination of heterosexism and homophobia in Ontario health units and community agencies, the formation of accessible and inclusive health services, and the development of communities and organizations that will support and celebrate sexual orientations and diversity. Specific activities include creating opportunities for social support and providing education, research, and programing. In doing so, the PHA recognizes that oppression related to sexual identity is a determinant of health and strives to promote access and equity (Duncan, et al., 2000).

Standard 5: Demonstrating Professional Responsibility and Accountability

CHNs work with a high degree of independence, and, like all nurses, they are accountable for the quality of their own practices. At times they are also accountable for the care and services others provide. In demonstrating accountability, CHNs must adhere to federal and provincial professional standards, laws, and codes of ethics and must use resources effectively and efficiently. They have a responsibility to be knowledgeable, competent, and current, and must also help others around them, such as colleagues and students, to develop and maintain competence (CNA, 2002; CHNAC, 2003).

Professional Competence When CHNs do not practise competently, allegations of negligence may be made against them, situations that are very stressful for nurses. It is important to know what comprises negligence in Canadian law. There are four key elements that must be proven to make a finding of negligence:

- that there was a relationship between the person bringing the claim (the plaintiff, e.g., client, family) and the person being sued (the defendant, e.g., nurse),
- that the defendant breached the standard of care,
- that the plaintiff suffered a harm, and
- that the harm suffered was caused by the defendant's breach of the standard of care.

A nurse-client relationship is usually established from the instant the nurse offers assistance and the client accepts it (Grant & Ashman, 1997). A duty of care is established when a nurse owes a duty to another—the nature and extent will depend on the circumstances. The standard of care has been legally defined as bringing a reasonable degree of skill and knowledge and exercising a degree of care that could reasonably be expected of a normal prudent practitioner of the same experience and standing (*Crits v. Sylvester*, 1956). The determination of the standard of care is often based on professional standards, such as those set by regulatory bodies and professional associations, for example, CHNAC. Breaches of the standard of care often stem from an action the nurse should have done (i.e., omission) or an action that the nurse did negligently (i.e., commission). The mere breach of the standard of care, however, is insufficient to support a negligence claim. There must be harm suffered that was reasonably foreseeable from the breach, and there must be a causal connection between the harm suffered and the nurse's conduct.

CHNs, either individually or in partnership with others, also have the responsibility to take preventive and/or corrective action to protect clients from unsafe or unethical practices or circumstances. This action may entail reporting to appropriate authorities instances of unsafe or unethical care provided by family or others to children or vulnerable adults (CNA,

Canadian Research Box 3.3

Oberle, K., & Tenove, S. (2000). Ethical issues in public health nursing. *Nursing Ethics, 7*(5), 425–438.

The purpose of this study was to identify ethical issues experienced by Canadian CHNs. This study incorporated an exploratory descriptive design involving 22 CHNs, 11 in rural and 11 in urban settings. Nurses were asked to describe a frequently recurring ethical problem. Additional questions were focused on determining what support nurses received when they encountered ethical problems and how they resolved those problems. Five major themes were identified:

1. Relationships with health care professionals: Both intraprofessionally and interprofessionally, CHNs struggled with providing the best information and optimal practice when colleagues were providing sub-optimal practices or poor information to clients. In short, it was difficult for these nurses to balance the responsibility to maintain standards and to preserve important working relationships.
2. System issues: CHNs expressed moral concerns related to their ability to optimize client welfare in a system that both supported and constrained them. Specific concerns included diminishing resources and policies and laws that were occasionally restrictive.
3. The character of relationships with clients: CHNs described challenges in being guests in their clients' homes, establishing trust, maintaining confidentiality, and preserving relationships. They also described concerns with boundaries and fostering too much dependency in clients.
4. Respect for persons: Respecting autonomy through advocacy and informed choice was central to these CHNs who expressed their mandate as a responsibility to support clients in making decisions for themselves concerning their needs.
5. Putting themselves at risk: This included both physical danger and value conflicts.

The authors concluded that the ethical issues that CHNs face are contextual and relational in nature, where seldom a clear right or wrong existed, suggesting that CHNs require an exquisite sense of balance and sensitivity to define what is good and to determine whose good should be promoted.

Discussion Questions

1. How are the ethical concerns of CHNs related to accountability?
2. Why do the authors conclude that the ethical concerns of CHNs are relational or contextual in nature?
3. What political changes would diminish the ethical concerns of CHNs?

2002; CHNAC, 2003). Every Canadian jurisdiction has statutory laws that require nurses to report instances of physical or sexual abuse of persons, situations where a child's welfare is at risk, and information related to communicable and sexually transmitted diseases. These circumstances are supported by a legislated duty to report because the protection of the individual and community takes priority over the confidentiality of the client.

Other instances also require disclosure, including court order or *subpoena* and common law duties to warn. The latter are situations that are less clearly defined because they are not outlined in statute. However, they entail the principle of warning, that in some circumstances it is necessary to avoid possible and probable harm to others or to the client. These situations illustrate that the duty of confidentiality is not absolute as the prevention of harm outweighs the protection of confidentiality.

In a well-known California case, a psychologist did not warn a client's girlfriend that the client repeatedly threatened to kill her. The court held that the psychologist ought to have warned the girlfriend because he had reasonable grounds to believe that she would be harmed (*Tarasoff v. Regents of the University of California*, 1976). In a Canadian case, Mr. Trikha (*Wendan v. Trikha*, 1992), a voluntarily admitted psychiatric patient, escaped from hospital. He drove a car at high speed through a red light, crashing into Ms. Wenden who suffered severe injuries. In this case, however, the psychiatrist was under no obligation to warn because there was no way to foresee that Mr. Trikha would pose a threat to himself or others. The general principle is that when nurses are aware that a client represents serious and probable danger to the well-being of another, then they owe a duty of care to take reasonable steps to protect such persons, that is, to warn the third party. This principle is supported by the CNA Code of Ethics (2002) that indicates that nurses may disclose information if there is substantial risk of serious harm to the person or to other persons.

As part of demonstrating professional responsibility and accountability, CHNs must document "in a timely and thorough manner..." (CHNAC, 2003, p. 17). Proper documentation supports professional and legal requirements. Documentation is a primary tool of communication in the interest of providing efficient, safe, and competent care. Invariably, nursing standards of practice, legal requirements, and institutional/agency policies require that health care professionals document. Nurses' notes can be used as evidence (*Ares v. Venner*, 1970). In one Canadian case, nurses had not written notes contemporaneously, a practice that the Supreme Court found to be unacceptable: "the absence of entries permits the inference that nothing was charted because nothing was done" (*Kolesar v. Jeffries*, 1974).

SUMMARY

In this chapter, common ethical and legal considerations in community health nursing were discussed. Feminist bioethics along with the CNA (2002) Code of Ethics and the CHNAC (2003) standards were introduced as relevant ethical perspectives and standards to articulate and address these

CASE STUDY

Jane was recently hired by a visiting nurses agency. She is providing overnight nursing care for five-year-old Anthony who is ventilator-dependent. Anthony lives with his mother, Susan, and two siblings, ages six months and three years. Susan asks Jane if she could care for all three children while she goes to buy groceries at a 24-hour grocery store. Although the children are all sleeping, Jane is reluctant to assume care for Anthony's siblings. She explains to Susan that she cannot. Susan then becomes upset, stating that she cannot afford to pay for a babysitter and that the other nurses have no problem looking after all of the children for short periods of time. Jane does not know what to do.

1. What ethical and legal issues are raised by this situation?
2. What sociopolitical factors situate these issues?
3. How could Jane help Susan in ways that do not violate professional and ethical standards?

considerations. The unique responsibilities of CHNs and the variable settings in which they work raise particular ethical concerns that must be understood sociopolitically. While health promotion and protection activities can enhance the well-being of clients, they can also be means of social control that can compromise client choice and confidentiality. Legislation can often provide guidance to CHNs in these instances, for example, legislative requirements regarding the reporting of some communicable diseases. In many instances, CHNs are in a position to advocate for social justice such that the health and well-being of their clients can be protected. Although Canada is a developed nation, many Canadians do not have access to the determinants of health.

The health and well-being of CHNs and clients may be threatened when community settings are not suitable for the provision of care and when informal caregivers do not have the necessary resources to assume responsibility for caregiving. CHNs providing palliative care to clients in their homes must possess an excellent knowledge of the ethical and legal considerations regarding end-of-life care, such as advanced directives, pain control, and DNR. Like nurses in all settings, CHNs are ethically required to develop caring relationships with their clients that remain within the limits of professional boundaries. They must also be accountable for their work and often for the work of others and must adhere to provincial and national ethical, legal, and professional standards.

KEY TERMS

ethics
bioethics
safe, competent, and ethical care
health and well-being
choice
dignity
confidentiality
justice
accountability
quality practice environments
power
ethic of care
ethic of justice
ethical dilemmas
everyday ethics
social justice
place
social control
medicalization
informed consent
empowerment
advocacy
professional boundary

STUDY QUESTIONS

1. Identify and define the eight central ethical values of Canadian nurses.
2. Identify and describe the four common features of feminist bioethics.
3. How is feminist bioethics suitable for community health nursing?
4. What are CHNAC's five standards of practice?
5. What does the process of informed consent involve? What information must the CHN provide and what factors must be taken into consideration?
6. What are the four key elements that must be proven to make a finding of negligence?

INDIVIDUAL CRITICAL THINKING EXERCISES

1. How are power and ethics related in community health nursing?
2. What aspects of community health nursing bring about social control? Can these be ethically justified? How?
3. How are nurse-client relationships in the community different from those in hospitals?
4. What are the ethical implications of these differences?
5. Why are the working conditions of many CHNs of ethical concern?
6. How can the CHN promote the health and well-being of family caregivers?

GROUP CRITICAL THINKING EXERCISES

1. Divide the group into two. Have one group argue for the merits and relevance of the ethic of care in CHN practice

and have the other do the same for the ethic of justice. How can these ethics work together? Are there any potential conflicts between the two perspectives?

2. After all group members write their definitions of health, share these with the group. How are these definitions similar and different? How do they reflect different values?
3. Identify a nursing leader in your community and explain how he or she is promoting social justice.

REFERENCES

Anderson, J. M. (2001). The politics of home care: Where is "home"? *Canadian Journal of Nursing Research, 33*(2), 5–10.

Andrews, G. J. (2002). Towards a more place-sensitive nursing research: An invitation to medical and health geography. *Nursing Inquiry, 9*(4), 221–238.

Ares v. Venner. (1970). SCR 608; (1970), 14 DLR (3d) 4; 73 WWR 347; 12 CRNS 349.

Aronson, J., & Neysmith, S. M. (1996). "You're not just in there to do the work": Depersonalizing policies and the exploitation of home care workers' labor. *Gender and Society, 10*(1), 59–77.

Arras, J. D. (Ed.). (1995). *Bringing the hospital home: Ethical and social implications of high-tech home care.* Baltimore, MD: The Johns Hopkins University Press.

Bayer, R. (2000). Editor's note: Public health nihilism revisited. *American Journal of Public Health, 90*(12), 1838.

Canada, Senate, Standing Committee on Social Affairs, Science and Technology. (2002). *The health of Canadians – the federal role.* Ottawa, ON: Author.

Canada, Senate, Subcommittee to Update *Of Life and Death* (2000). *Quality of end-of-life care: The right of every Canadian.* Retrieved March 13, 2002 from **www.parl.gc.ca/36/2/parlbus/commbus/senate/com-e/upda-e/rep-e/repfinjun00-e.htm**

Canadian Association of Retired Persons (CARP). (1999). *Putting a face on home care.* Kingston, ON: Queen's University, Health Policy Research Unit.

Canadian Hospice Palliative Care Association (CHPCA). (2002). *Hospice palliative care nursing standards of practice.* Retrieved July 16, 2002 from **www.chpca.net/sigs/Hospice_palliative_care_nursing_standards_of_practice.pdf**

Canadian Nurses Association. (2002). *Code of ethics for registered nurses.* Ottawa, ON: Author.

College of Nurses of Ontario (CNO). (1999). *Standard for the therapeutic nurse-client relationship.* Toronto, ON: Author.

College of Nurses of Ontario (CNO). (2002). *Professional standards (revised 2002) for registered nurses and registered practical nurses in Ontario.* Toronto, ON: Author.

Collopy, B., Dubler, N., & Zuckerman, C. (1990). The ethics of home care: Autonomy and accommodation. *Hastings Centre Report, 20*(2), 1–16.

Commission on the Future of Health Care in Canada. (2002). *Building on values: The future of health care in Canada.* Saskatoon, SK: Author.

Committee to Advance Ethical Decision-Making in Community Health. (2001). *Final Report.* Toronto, ON: Author.

Community Health Nurses Association of Canada (CHNAC). (2003). *Canadian community health nursing standards of practice.*

Conrad, P., & Schneider, J. W. (1985). *Deviance and medicalization: From badness to sickness.* Columbus, OH: Merrill.

Crits v. Sylvester et al. (1956). 1 DLR. (2d) 502 (Ont.C.A.) (Court 1956), *aff'd* (1956) SCR. 991, (1956) 5 DLR. (2d) 601 (SCC).

Curtis, S., & Jones, I. R. (1998). Is there a place for geography in the analysis of health inequality? *Sociology of Health & Illness, 20*(5), 645–672.

Drevdahl, D. (2002). Social justice or market justice? The paradoxes of public health partnerships with managed care. *Public Health Nursing, 19*(3), 161–169.

Duncan, K., Clipsham, J., Hampson, E., Krieger, C., MacDonnell, J., Roedding, D. et al. (2000). *Improving the access to and quality of public health services for lesbians and gay men.* Toronto, ON: Ontario Public Health Association.

Gebbie, K. M. (2001). Response to "Feminism in public health nursing: Partners for health." *Scholarly Inquiry for Nursing Practice: An International Journal, 15*(1), 63–66.

Gilligan, C. (1982). *In a different voice: Psychological theory and women's development.* Cambridge, MA: Harvard University Press.

Grant, A., & Ashman, A. (1997). *A nurse's practical guide to the law.* Aurora, ON: Canada Law Book.

Health Care Health & Safety Association of Ontario (HCHSA), & Workplace Safety & Insurance Board (WSIB). (2000). *Health and safety in the home care environment.* Retrieved June 16, 2002 from **www.hchsa.on.ca/products/resrcdoc/lap_301.pdf**

Hilton, B. A., Thompson, R., & Moore-Dempsey, L. (2000). Evaluation of the AIDS Prevention Street Nurse Program: One step at a time. *Canadian Journal of Nursing Research, 32*(1), 17–38.

Jaffee, S., & Hyde, J. S. (2000). Gender differences in moral orientation: A meta- analysis. *Psychological Bulletin, 126*(5), 703–726.

Kass, N. (2001). An ethics framework for public health. *American Journal of Public Health, 91*(11), 1776–1782.

Kearns, R. A. (1993). Place and health: Towards a reformed medical geography. *Professional Geographer, 46,* 67–72.

Kearns, R. A., & Moon, G. (2002). From medical to health geography: Novelty, place and theory after a decade of change. *Health and Place, 26*(5), 605–625.

Kolesar v. Jeffries. (1974). 59 DLR (3d) 367, 9 OR (2d) 41 (HCJ) (Court 1974), *aff'd* 68 DLR (3d) 198, 12 OR (2d) 142 (CA), *aff'd* (1978) 1 SCR 491, 77 DLR (3d) 161, 2 CCLT 170, 15 NR 302, sub nom. Joseph Brant Memorial Hospital v. Koziol.

Krieger, N., & Zierler, S. (1996). What explains the public's health? – A call for epidemiological theory. *Epidemiology, 7,* 107–109.

Leipert, B. D. (2001). Feminism and public health nursing: Partners for health. *Scholarly Inquiry for Nursing Practice: An International Journal, 15*(1), 49–61.

Liaschenko, J. (1994). The moral geography of home care. *Advances in Nursing Science, 17*(2), 16–26.

Liaschenko, J. (2001). Nursing work, housekeeping ethics, and the moral geography of home care. In. D. N. Weisstub, D. C. Thomasma, S. Gauthier, & G. F. Tomossy (Eds.), *International library of ethics, law and the new medicine: Aging* (pp. 123–136). Boston, MA: Kluwer Academic Press.

Liaschenko, J. (2002). Health promotion, moral harm, and the moral aims of nursing. In L. E. Young & V. E. Hayes (Eds.), *Transforming health promotion practice: Concepts, issues and applications* (pp. 136–147). Philadelphia, PA: F.A. Davis.

Liaschenko, J., & Peter, E. (2003). Feminist ethics. In V. Tschudin (Ed.), *Approaches to ethics: Nursing beyond boundaries* (pp. 33–43). Oxford, UK: Butterworth, Heinemann.

MacPhail, S. A. (1996). *Ethical issues in community nursing.* Unpublished master's thesis, University of Alberta, Edmonton, AB.

McKeever, P. (2001). Home care in Canada: Housing matters. *Canadian Journal of Nursing Research, 33*(2), 3–5.

Moyer, A., Coristine, M., MacLean, L., & Meyer, M. (1999). A model for building collective capacity in community-based programs: The Elderly in Need Project. *Public Health Nursing, 16*(3), 205–214.

Neysmith, S. M. (2000). *Restructuring caring labour: Discourse, state practice, and everyday life.* New York: Oxford University Press.

Peter, E. (2002). The history of nursing in the home: Revealing the significance of place in the expression of moral agency. *Nursing Inquiry, 9*(2), 65–72.

Peter, E., & Morgan, K. (2001). Explorations of a trust approach for nursing ethics. *Nursing Inquiry, 8*, 3–10.

Schulz, R., & Beach, S. R. (1999). Caregiving as a risk factor for mortality: The caregiver health effects study. *Journal of the American Medical Association, 282*(23), 2215–2219.

Schroeder, C., & Gadow, S. (1996). An advocacy approach to ethics and community health. In E. T. Anderson & J. McFarlane (Eds.), *Community as partner: Theory and practice in nursing* (pp. 78–91). Philadelphia, PA: Lippincott.

Sherwin, S. (1998). A relational approach to autonomy in health care. In S. Sherwin (Ed.), *The politics of women's health: Exploring agency and autonomy* (pp. 19–47). Philadelphia, PA: Temple University Press.

Tarasoff v. Regents of the University of California, 17 California Reports, 3rd Series, 425 (California Supreme Court, July 1, 1976).

Verweij, M. (1999). Medicalization as a moral problem for preventative medicine. *Bioethics, 13*(2), 89–113.

Warren, V. (1989). Feminist directions in medical ethics. *Hypatia, 4*(2), 73–87.

Wendan v. Trikha. (1993). 124 AR 1 (QB) (Court 1992) *aff'd* (1993), 135 AR 382 (CA), leave to appeal denied (1993), 149 AR 160n, (1993) SCCA 126.

Wilkins, K., & Park, E. (1998). Home care in Canada. *Health Reports, 10*(1). (Available from Statistics Canada, Ottawa, ON.)

Williams, A. (2002). Changing geographies of care: Employing the concept of therapeutic landscapes as a framework in examining home space. *Social Science & Medicine, 55*, 141–154.

Workman Theatre Project (WTP). (2002). *Mission statement.* Retrieved June 28, 2002 from **www.workmantheatre.com/**

Worthley, J. A. (Ed.). (1997). *The ethics of the ordinary in health care: Concepts and cases.* Chicago, IL: Health Administration Press.

Zola, I. K. (1972). Medicine as an institution of social control. *Sociological Review, 20*, 487–504.

ADDITIONAL RESOURCES

WEBSITES

Canadian Bioethics Society:
www.bioethics.ca/

Canadian Nurses Association:
www.cna-aiic.ca

Community Health Nurses Association (CHNAC):
www.communityhealthnursescanada.org

Dalhousie University, Department of Bioethics:
http://bioethics.dal.ca/

McGill University, Biomedical Ethics Unit:
www.mcgill.ca/bioethics/

NursingEthics.ca:
www.nursingethics.ca/

Programmes de Bioethique, University of Montreal:
www.fes.umontreal.ca/bioethique/cadres.htm

University of Alberta, John Dossetor Health Ethics Centre:
www.ualberta.ca/BIOETHICS/

University of British Columbia, Centre for Applied Ethics:
www.ethics.ubc.ca:80/

University of Toronto, Joint Centre for Bioethics:
www.utoronto.ca/jcb/

About the Authors

Elizabeth Peter, RN, PhD is an Assistant Professor in the Faculty of Nursing, University of Toronto. She is also Member, Joint Centre for Bioethics; Collaborator, Home Care Evaluation and Research Centre; and Coinvestigator, Nursing Effectiveness, Utilization and Outcomes Research Unit. Her academic preparation is in nursing, philosophy, and bioethics. Her research focuses upon theory and method development in nursing ethics and the identification and analysis of ethical issues in home and community care.

She is the principal investigator of a study funded by the Social Sciences & Humanities Research Council entitled "Home Care Ethics: Identification & Analysis of Issues" and a study funded by The Hospital for Sick Children Foundation entitled "Ethical Dimensions of Home Care Policies for Children and Youth."

Louise R. Sweatman, BScN, RN, LLB, MSc, is a nurse lawyer. She received her bachelor of nursing and master of science—with a focus on ethics—from the Faculty of Nursing, University of Toronto. She worked as a psychiatric nurse and then went back to school for a law degree from Osgoode Hall Law School, York University in Toronto. She has worked in various provincial, national, and international organizations such as the Ontario Nurses Association, Canadian Medical Association, and International Council of Nurses. She currently is the Director of Regulatory Policy at the Canadian Nurses Association where she oversees the Code of Ethics, Certification Program, Canadian Registered Nurse Examination, and the development of regulatory frameworks such as for Nurse Practitioners.

Kathleen Carlin, RN, PhD, is a Registered Nurse who now specializes in health care ethics. She received her master of science and PhD degrees at the University of Toronto, specializing in bioethics.

In 1997, with Louise Sweatman, she cofounded the annual community health ethics workshop day at Victoria College at the University of Toronto. She currently teaches health care ethics at Ryerson University. She is also the consultant to the Ethics Committee, St. Joseph's Health Care Centre for Mountain Services (formerly Hamilton Psychiatric Hospital) in Hamilton, Ontario, and to community and long-term care agencies.

She was the lead author of the chapter on ethics in "A Guide to End-of-Life Care for Seniors." In addition to numerous presentations on ethics, she writes a continuing "Ethics Corner" for a palliative care newsletter.

This work was supported through the funding of the Social Sciences and Humanities Research Council of Canada.

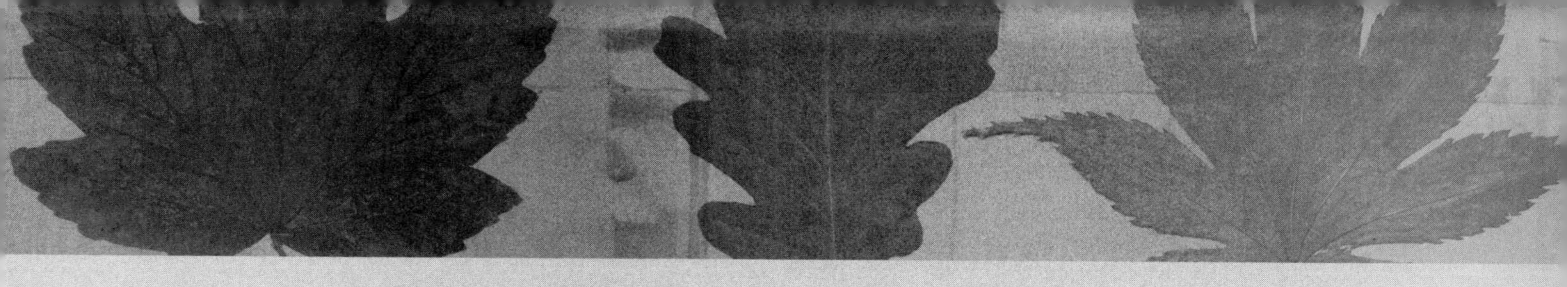

CHAPTER 4

Practice Settings, Roles, and Functions

Elizabeth Battle Haugh
and Barbara L. Mildon

OBJECTIVES

AFTER STUDYING THIS CHAPTER, YOU SHOULD BE ABLE TO:

1. Recognize the diversity of roles and practice settings within community health nursing.
2. Differentiate between the roles of the public health nurse and the home health nurse when caring for individuals, families, groups, and communities.
3. Identify key macro health promotion strategies used in community health nursing.
4. Discuss attributes of quality community health nursing practice.
5. Discuss the role of professional associations in supporting community health nursing.
6. Identify current issues and societal trends for community health nurses.

INTRODUCTION

The goal of promoting health is based on the assumption that the community environment plays a large role in supporting the health of the individuals in the community. The socioeconomic and physical environments of a community are strong predictors of the community's health status (Health Canada, 1999). Community health nursing interventions must take this into consideration when attempting to achieve the goal of healthier communities. This obvious long-term goal is achieved through a comprehensive variety of health promotion strategies. "The interplay of individual, group, community, and population level interventions in health promotion is complex.... Community health nurses (CHNs) may therefore undertake many roles and implement a range of interventions within the goal of promoting health. Each role calls upon different elements of nursing expertise" (Hayward et al., 1993, p. 8).

This chapter describes the goals and practice competencies of CHNs across the range of community nursing roles and settings, with an emphasis on home health and public health practice settings. Strategies that contribute to quality practice settings and healthy workplaces for CHNs are identified and the current trends and issues in CHN practice are described. Lastly, the role of professional associations in supporting CHNs and their practice is explained.

AN OVERVIEW OF COMMUNITY HEALTH NURSING ROLES

With characteristic work excitement and autonomy, CHNs embrace their specialty nursing practice within a breathtaking diversity of roles, functions, and practice settings (Baldwin & Price, 1994). Combining their foundational nursing education with specialized knowledge of community nursing concepts and competencies, they use a multiplicity of frameworks and theories in their practice, which span the complete continuum of **primary prevention** (reducing risks for a potential problem), **secondary prevention** (providing screening and early treatment), and **tertiary prevention** (maintaining health) (see Chapter 7). Key characteristics of their practice include a high level of independence/autonomy, resourcefulness, collaboration with the client/family, strong health assessment skills, critical thinking and problem solving, and an understanding of the overall health care system (Benefield, 1998; Bramadat, Chalmers, & Andrusyszyn, 1996; Clarke & Cody, 1994; Coffman, 1997; Kaiser & Rudolph, 1996). CHNs work within an array of legislation and policy, but the concepts of health promotion and primary health care are the foundation of their practice.

"Community nursing is associated with providing continuity of care and a continuum of care from health promotion and prevention to clinical treatment, rehabilitation and palliative care" (Canadian Nurses Association, 2003, p. 1). **Health promotion** is most commonly defined in global terms by the World Health Organization (1984) as "the process of enabling people to increase control over and to improve their health." It is a broad definition and includes the spectrum of health enhancement, health protection, disease prevention, health restoration/recovery, and care and support. **Primary health care** (PHC) was defined at the 1978 Alma Ata conference as health care made universally accessible to individuals and families, through their full participation and at a cost the community and country can afford. CHNs have a mandate to integrate the principles of PHC into their care of individuals, groups, communities, and populations.

Because a key role of all CHNs is to assist clients to link to the range of community resources, knowledge of other community nursing roles is vital. Tables 4.1 and 4.2 provide a summary of the various roles enacted by community health nurses. CHNs with different levels of preparation may function in each role, for example, primary care nurse practitioners bring their expanded scope of practice to any of the roles. While Table 4.2 identifies several categories of CHN, this chapter focuses on the two most commonly recognized community roles—public health nursing and home health nursing. Table 4.1 highlights some of global differences and shared areas in each type of practice.

"From womb to tomb" is an old cliché used to describe the scope of public health nursing practice. It reflects the diversity of the clientele and describes how public health nursing touches everyone's life throughout the life span. From prenatal classes, newborn home visiting, routine immunization, school health, infectious disease control, healthy lifestyle promotion, and injury prevention, including preventing falls in the elderly, public health is entwined through everyone's life. Public health fits comfortably within a community model of primary health care, which is holistic and multi-levelled (Canadian Nurses Association, 1996). Table 4.2 outlines the practice settings for CHNs.

PHOTO 4.1

Telephone counselling is an important intervention for individuals.

Credit: Aneta Garlinski

ROLES OF COMMUNITY HEALTH NURSE AND CARE OF CLIENTS

Individual as Client: Public Health Nursing

The most common practice settings for individuals as recipients of public health nursing services are clinics and homes. However, telephone counselling, which reaches clients wherever they may be, is one strategy that is used uniquely for providing individualized client health teaching. Most public health agencies have **telephone help lines** that provide callers with information, referral, and consultation services on such topics as newborn and childcare, healthy lifestyle advice, sexual health issues, smoking cessation, and communicable diseases.

Clinic services in public health are diverse, including communicable disease control and follow-up, birth control, travel health, immunization, and well baby and child health. In these latter clinics, developmental screening and anticipatory counselling is provided. The majority of nursing interventions within the clinic setting involve client assessment and counselling. Home visits are rarely provided to individuals because as soon as the nurse visits individual clients in their home, a family focus is assumed, be it a neighbour, friend, or family member. In contrast to home care nursing, most individual client contact in public health is short term with very specific objectives for the individual's need for education and possible referral to community agencies for further support or follow-up.

Control of infectious diseases has become a high profile role of public health departments (see Chapter 12). With the emergence of newer diseases such as Severe Acute Respiratory Syndrome (SARS) and West Nile Virus, public health professionals have had to readjust priorities to collate and track

TABLE 4.1
Roles and Functions of Home Health Nurses (HHN) and Public Health Nurses (PHN)

	Health Promotion (e.g., health education)	Health Protection (e.g., prophylaxis for prevention of communicable disease)	Active Treatment (e.g., dialysis, IV meds, palliative care)	Health Maintenance (e.g., support/sustain through chronic disease process)
Individual	PHN & HHN	PHN & HHN	HHN	HHN
Family	PHN & HHN	PHN & HHN	HHN	HHN
Group	PHN & HHN	PHN	HHN	HHN
Community	PHN	PHN	–	–

TABLE 4.2
Practice Settings for Community Health Nurses

Characteristic	Public Health Nurse	Home Health Nurse	Community Health Centre/Outreach Nurse	Outpost or Rural Nurse	Parish Nurse	Occupational Health Nurse
Defining goals	"A community health nurse who synthesizes knowledge from public health science, nursing science and the social sciences, in order to promote, protect and preserve the health of populations."[(a)] The goal of public health, and therefore of public health nursing, is to increase the health of the community (i.e., reduce mortality and morbidity rates) by preventing disease and promoting healthy behaviours.	Home health nursing is a specialized area of nursing practice in which the nurse provides care in the client's home, school, or workplace. Clients and their designated caregivers are the focus of home health nursing practice. The goal of care is to initiate, manage, and evaluate the resources needed to promote the client's optimal level of well-being and functioning. Nursing activities necessary to achieve this goal may warrant preventive, maintenance, and restorative emphases to prevent potential problems from developing.[(b)]	A nurse who works in a non-profit organization that provides primary health and health promotion programs for individuals, families, and communities. Community Health Centres work with individuals, families, and communities to strengthen their capacity to take more responsibility for their health and well-being. CHNs work together with others on health promotion initiatives within schools, in housing developments, and in the workplace. They link families with support and self-help groups that offer peer education or support in coping, or are working to address conditions that affect health. As such, the CHC program contributes to the development of healthy communities.[(c)]	A CHN or PHN who works exclusively in a rural or outpost setting, generally in isolation from traditional health-care-team support. They provide primary health care and make referrals for more in-depth assessments.	A parish nurse is a registered nurse with specialized knowledge who is called to the ministry and affirmed by a faith community to promote health, healing, and wholeness. Parish nurses are concerned with the entire person—body, mind, and spirit. They believe there is a strong relationship between faith and health.[(d)]	"An occupational health nurse is a registered nurse practicing in the specialty of Occupational Health & Safety to deliver integrated occupational health and safety services to individual workers and worker populations. Occupational health nursing encompasses the promotion, maintenance, and restoration of health and the prevention of illness and injury."[(e)]
Place of work	Official public health agency (i.e., Health Unit or Health Department within municipal or provincial government). Unlimited range from client's homes, schools, workplaces, community centres, and clinics to coalitions in partnership with other community agencies.	Client's private home, school classroom, clinic, or street (i.e., for homeless population).	Community health centre building, community location, or the street.	Outpost clinic, client's home, or other community locations.	Place of worship, client's home.	Workplace

TABLE 4.2
Continued

Characteristic	Public Health Nurse	Home Health Nurse	Community Health Centre/Outreach Nurse	Outpost or Rural Nurse	Parish Nurse	Occupational Health Nurse
Work team/ colleagues	May include RNs, LPNs/RPNs, public health inspectors, epidemiologists, health promotion specialists, dietitians, dental professionals, family support personnel, and physicians.	Other nurses (RNs and LPNs/RPNs), physicians, supportive care staff, and allied professionals (physio, OT, etc.).	Multi-disciplinary	Limited to visits from travelling physicians and dental teams, etc. Relies on technology; phone, e-mail, faxes and telehealth technology for communication.	Clergy, parish volunteers.	Human resource personnel, physician on consult.
Role focus	Public health is mandated in legislation to promote and protect the health of populations. Focus is on health enhancement, health protection, and disease prevention.	Client as individual or family; provides direct clinical care, and case management.	Client as individual, family, group, or population; provides direct clinical care.	Client as individual, community, group, or population; provides primary care including primary, secondary, and tertiary preventive services.	Client as individual or group; focuses on education, counselling, and referrals.	Client as individual or group; provides direct care including primary, secondary, and tertiary preventive services.
Minimum qualifications	Usually defined in provincial legislation; generally baccalaureate level preparation.	RN, RPN/LPN	RN	RN	RN	RN with certification in occupational health.
Unique characteristics of nursing practice	Primarily work with a healthy population; minimal contact with unwell people; may have entire community as client.	Work alone; practice highly autonomous and independent; adaptable to client-controlled environment.	Flexibility to follow client/ family from clinic to home.	Long travel distances; adaptable to range of dwellings; manages broad spectrum of health needs; works in isolated communities.	Integrates faith-based approach to care. U.S.-based credential available.	Addresses health, safety, and well-being of employees. May earn specialty credential from CNA COHN (C).
Funding	Combination of provincial and local revenues.[f]	Provincial government: may be contractual model (e.g., ON) or global funding (e.g., Regional Health Authority).	Fixed budget from province.	Provincially or federally funded.	Independently funded.	Funded by the employer.

TABLE 4.2
Continued

Characteristic	Public Health Nurse	Home Health Nurse	Community Health Centre/Outreach Nurse	Outpost or Rural Nurse	Parish Nurse	Occupational Health Nurse
Scope and standards of practice	Generally provide government-mandated core programs and services. Standards of Practice outlined in 1990 CPHA booklet and 2003 standards from CHNAC. Less requirement for clinical/technical skills.	1987 standards of practice now updated via the CHNAC (2003) standards. High requirement for technical/clinical skills. Movement toward standardized care pathways and measurement of client care outcomes.	Community Health Centre or region specific.	In development through Health Canada.	Working on standards of practice.	Standards of practice in place for credentialing purposes.
Relevant professional associations (Canada)	Community Health Nurses Association of Canada (CHNAC); Canadian Public Health Association (CPHA).	CHNAC, Community Health Nurse Interest Groups in various provinces (e.g., NS, BC, ON).	Province specific (e.g., Association of Community Health Centres in ON); Canadian Alliance of Community Health Centre Associations.	CHNAC	Canadian Association for Parish Nursing Ministry	Canadian Association of Occupational Health Nurses

(a) Community Health Nurses Association of Canada (CHNAC), 2003, p. 7.
(b) American Nurses Association (ANA), 1999.
(c) Ontario Ministry of Health and Long-term Care, 2002.
(d) RNAO, 2001.
(e) Canadian Occupational Health Nurses Association, 2000. p. iii.
(f) Baumgart, 1988.

PRACTICE EXEMPLAR: Public Health Nursing, Individual as Client

A PHN, who worked in the Communicable Disease Control Department of a large urban Health Unit, explained, "I am responsible for community follow-up and contact tracing for all reportable communicable diseases. Sometimes we have to be part private investigator to locate people while preserving their confidentiality. Once we do contact them, we have to counsel them about their diagnosis, refer them to places they can get treatment and support, and try to locate anyone else they may have been in contact with so that, if necessary, screening can begin. The focus is always on the community and preventing the spread of the disease."

cases. Any kind of outbreak of a communicable disease in a community must be dealt with expeditiously. Therefore, contact tracing and individual case management (which may include daily surveillance) of reportable diseases is an important PHN function. Containment of infectious diseases like SARS is achieved through the excellent assessment skills of PHNs who help determine who should be in quarantine based on previous possible exposures and personal histories.

Individual as Client: Home Health Nursing

The separation of home health nursing from what is now recognized as public health has occurred over the years as an outcome of health system development and funding structures. Accordingly, while the focus of home health nursing today is the client, the family, and/or the caregivers, care is provided within the context of the principles of primary health care with an emphasis on health promotion. The majority of care is delivered in the practice settings of client's home, school, or community clinic. The practice standards and competencies of home health nurses (HHNs) are demonstrated throughout the home care length-of-stay. The HHN's relationship with the client is based on the understanding that the nurse is a "guest in the house" and therefore adapts all care according to the client's environment and direction. Holistic health assessment skills are critical (Bramadat, Chalmers, & Andrusyszyn, 1996) in order to determine not only the physical and psychosocial needs of the client, but as importantly, the role played by the family/caregivers and home environment in supporting or challenging the client's achievement of health goals. A collaborative approach, based on a nurse-client partnership model, is a hallmark of the HHN's work with clients to identify the client's desired health goals, develop the care plan, and obtain consent for the care.

Clinical expertise in a wide range of tasks and interventions is another requisite for the HHN. With the high rates of day surgery and the short lengths of hospital stay that characterize today's health care system, HHNs manage the full spectrum of acute treatment regimens such as intravenous drug therapies (including chemotherapy) via a host of venous access devices and infusion pumps, complex wounds, chest drainage systems, new tracheotomy care regimes, and post cerebrovascular and cardiac event monitoring and treatment programs. HHNs also possess considerable competency in the nursing care of chronic conditions, including peritoneal dialysis, respiratory disease (including ventilator-dependent clients), long-term mental health and psychogeriatric conditions, acquired brain injuries, and infants and children with complex and life-long care needs. These clinical aspects of home health care demand highly effective critical thinking and problem-solving skills (Bramadat, Chalmers, & Andrusyszyn, 1996; Meyer, 1997).

Although the role of the HHN is commonly categorized as generalist in nature (ANA, 1999; Kaiser & Rudolph, 1996), the trend to well-informed consumers who increasingly expect care from nurses specializing in the relevant clinical area has given rise to numerous specialty roles for HHNs. These roles include Wound Ostomy Resource Nurse, Psychogeriatric Nurse, Continence Advisor, Diabetes Nurse Educator, Palliative Care Nurse Consultant, Respiratory Nurse Specialist, and many others. These specialty home health care nurses ideally do not take over client care, but rather provide expert client assessment and care-plan guidance that contributes to client care excellence while augmenting the generalist nurse's knowledge base and competencies. Thus the specialty nursing roles promote client satisfaction while also positively influencing career satisfaction for both the specialty nurse (by offering career diversity) as well as the generalist nurse (by contributing to practice confidence and competence).

Additional competencies required by the HHN include (a) detailed knowledge of community resources in order to link the client to appropriate ongoing resources to support their health goals both during the home care length-of-stay and upon discharge, (b) understanding and utilizing culture care principles, (c) knowledge of health policy and the overall health system, and (d) client teaching strategies (Bramadat, Chalmers, & Andrusyszyn, 1996; Clarke & Cody, 1994; Kaiser & Rudolph, 1996).

PRACTICE EXEMPLAR: Home Health Nursing, Individual as Client

"My patient was an 82-year-old woman who had suffered a devastating CVA, leaving her with expressive aphasia," described an HHN. "Added to that was a long-standing dependence on peritoneal dialysis, requiring four exchanges per day. Despite her inability to verbalize comprehensible words, her fierce determination to be independent resulted in her discharge from hospital to her beloved home of many years, with 24-hour homemaking. The visiting nurses arrived four times a day to perform the dialysis, soon realizing the depth of the communication difficulty. 'Alma' was unable to read or nod yes or no reliably and couldn't dial numbers correctly. Intense speech therapy was unable to improve her verbalization ability.

"Alma was able to say 'bacon,' usually repeated three times in sequence. I soon learned that Alma's tone of voice with 'bacon, bacon, bacon' varied according to her needs. For example, after many weeks of four visits per day, Alma began saying 'bacon, bacon, bacon' with great intensity when the dialysis was performed. I eventually asked Alma if she wanted to do the tasks herself. My reward was a much gentler 'bacon, bacon, bacon,' and over time Alma learned to perform the dialysis exchange procedure herself. She then made it clear that she did not want the nurse to visit four times a day. As you can imagine, we were quite concerned about leaving her on her own. How could she get help if needed? We set up a speed-dial mechanism connected to the nurse's office, and after many hours of repeated teaching, Alma was able to use the speed-dial correctly. We then set up a system whereby we would phone Alma just after she would have performed the exchange. We were able to tell from the tone of her voice if she needed us to visit.

"One day the anxiety in her words 'bacon, bacon, bacon' was so evident when I phoned that I almost flew to the house to find that she couldn't do the dialysis exchange because one of the clamps had broken. Alma also made it clear she found 24-hour homemaking intrusive and over time the homemaking hours were decreased. She also indicated that she wished as few nursing visits as possible, but she was agreeable to one visit per day so that we could monitor her vital signs and weight and choose her dialysis bags appropriately. We would help her phone her relatives to ease the loneliness she seemed to convey.

"We cared for Alma that way for two years—years in which she was in her familiar surroundings and had as much independence as possible. Years in which she avoided the institutionalization she dreaded. One day she was not found by the nurse to be in her accustomed place. She was in bed, having passed away peacefully. I will always feel grateful for knowing Alma and for being able to help her be as independent as possible in spite of such profound physical challenges."

Source: Reproduced by permission from Registered Nurses Association of Ontario, Community Health Nurses Initiatives Group. (2000). Understanding the practice of home health nursing: A discussion paper. Retrieved November 29, 2003 from http://www.chnig.org

Family as Client: Public Health Nursing

There are many ways to define a family. It includes significant others for any given person, whether they are living together or related by blood or marriage (Roberts, 1983). Family-centred nursing is a substantive part of a PHN's practice in the multitude of practice settings in which a PHN may work. Family members are most visibly involved in the home setting and the nurse's interventions can include all family members in the reinforcement of health teaching and as part of the entire assessment (see Chapter 9).

Home visiting is one strategy that makes public health nursing services completely accessible to families. There is no need for the family to be concerned about transportation or the physical stress of leaving the home. Visiting in the client's home provides the nurse with an opportunity for a very holistic assessment. Socioeconomic, cultural, and psychological issues are more obvious in the home setting, and, therefore,

PRACTICE EXEMPLAR: Public Health Nursing, Family as Client

"Since all new moms and babies are screened for certain risk factors before they leave the hospital," explained a PHN, "I usually have a fairly good idea how to prioritize her postpartum follow-up telephone screening calls. Some risk factors are not noted and my colleagues and I often walk into situations that are unexpected. One example was the case of 'Sherri,' who was 20 years old and doing well in hospital breastfeeding her second child. 'Justin,' the dad, and the two-year-old, 'Trevor,' had been up to visit, and it appeared that Sherri was going home to a stable, supportive home environment. This was confirmed when I called the day after discharge and made an appointment to visit in two weeks.

"I arrived to find an exhausted-looking mom holding a screaming infant with an agitated two-year-old pulling at mom and begging to be picked up. Mom clearly had no patience for the two-year-old. The small, one-bedroom apartment was very cluttered. An odour of stale air and unwrapped garbage permeated the room. A crib was set up in the corner of the bedroom and a bassinette for the baby was beside the bed.

"My immediate concern was for the welfare of the children. I needed to assess the safety issues and mom's capacity to manage the toddler and the newborn. After a gentle probing, it was discovered that the baby's father was trying to work at two full-time jobs. He was gone 16 hours a day and had been staying at a buddy's house because the baby had been crying and preventing him from getting any sleep. Sherri thought she could manage on her own. The possibility of having to call Children's Aid Society was in the forefront of my mind as I asked all my questions and discreetly assessed the physical environment.

"I had to confront Sherri with my concerns. She acknowledged she felt overwhelmed and quite depressed. I asked permission to call her husband and discuss the situation with him. Justin said there was little he could do because he had to work so much so they could afford bigger living accommodations. I encouraged him to talk to his wife about her needs right now and expressed my concerns about Sherri's mental health and the children's well-being.

"Both Justin and Sherri were present for the next visit. They had agreed they could do with one paycheque until things settled down with the new baby. Justin had been able to take care of the children and do some housework so Sherri could get a bit more rest. I arranged for a lay home visitor to come twice a week and reinforce some of the parenting strategies we had discussed in dealing with the two-year-old. Later, Sherri was able to get out and attend a six-week-parenting group session for moms and babies."

the nursing intervention can be more individualized to meet the specific needs of each unique family.

The birth of a new baby is always a stressful time for families. Intergenerational family patterns and roles change and family members try to adapt to new roles as parents, grandparents, and siblings (Sherwin, Scoloveno, & Weingarten, 1999). PHNs have a long tradition of being pivotal in supporting families as they adapt to the complexities of these role changes and caring for a new infant.

A PHN may also be involved with visiting a family for follow-up for infectious disease control and have several members of the family as the primary clients. The nurse addresses the needs of the individuals within the family, but much of the education and support is provided in the context of the family unit as a whole. As well, such families often access PHN services within a clinical or community centre setting.

The composite of the family's value system and family dynamics are a major part of the PHN's holistic assessment (Neuman, 1983). While establishing a relationship with the family, the nurse is able to assess priorities for the family and capitalize on the strengths of some family members to support and empower others. Often family health nursing requires the recognition of cultural sensitivities, which may be different among other generational family members.

Family as Client: Home Health Nursing

Home health nursing views the family as inseparable from the client as focus of care (Benefield, 1998; Coffman, 1997; Meyer, 1997). Assessing the strengths and needs of the family is fundamental to maximizing the self-care abilities of the client/family. Accordingly, an understanding of family theory is a prerequisite for HHNs. HHNs mobilize and/or augment the ability of family members to assist the client in meeting the health goals. Where the health support needs of the client are short-term, HHNs may teach family members about the particular health alteration and implications (e.g., care considerations for diabetes), specific skills (e.g., wound care), reportable signs and symptoms, and appropriate community supports. Situations where the HHN has a long-term relationship with the family (e.g., when providing care to a chronically ill child over months or years) require an in-depth understanding of alterations in the family dynamics arising from the nurse's presence. These care situations may be stressful for both nurse and family because the nurse may be seen not only as supportive and helpful, but also as a "stranger in the family" (Coffman, 1997). In addition, the closeness and longevity of the relationship may lead to a blurring of the nurse-client boundaries, requiring the nurse to be vigilant in avoiding boundary violations.

The complexity of HHNs' family-centred care is further illustrated by the need for the nurse to be knowledgeable and responsive to any indications of child, elder, or spousal abuse.

Numerous success indicators provide evidence of the effectiveness of HHNs in caring for clients and families in home and school environments. These indicators include observable improvements in caregivers' confidence and knowledge in providing care, reductions in the stress levels of clients and caregivers, remediation of abusive situations, and the appreciation of clients/caregivers as expressed by verbal and written thanks, often to employers, newspapers, or regulatory colleges.

PRACTICE EXEMPLAR: Family as Client, Home Health Nurse

An HHN described a situation she had experienced. "I admitted a 57-year-old male to our home care program. His diagnosis was metastatic liver cancer, and he was in the terminal stage of the illness. A loving family of his wife and two sons cared for him. Before I was escorted to the client's room, the family took me aside and explained that the client had not been told he had cancer and did not know the seriousness of his diagnosis. I was asked not to reveal this information during my care. Knowing that this situation needed to be addressed over time, I proceeded with my visit and provided the care indicated.

"Over the first few subsequent visits, I established relationships with both the family and the client. As the client became weaker, he questioned me increasingly about the nature and expected outcome of his illness. At the same time, the family exhibited greater signs of emotional distress. I explored the family's feelings, offering them a different perspective on their desire to protect the client from what was happening to him. As the family's anticipatory grief became more evident and the client's questions more insistent, I asked the family to consider that both they and the client may benefit greatly from having the chance to share emotions, memories, and messages at this time. I explored their spiritual beliefs, encouraging them to seek additional counsel from their spiritual advisor. Eventually, the family decided to tell the client his diagnosis and condition. They requested that the family doctor and myself be present at the initial discussion. We facilitated the discussion and then left the room, waiting nearby as the client and family began the process of openly sharing their love and impending loss."

Group as Client: Public Health Nursing

Many public health nursing services are provided in the small group setting. Much like traditional classroom teaching, the PHN applies adult learning theory to engage the group in the health promotion issue. More recent trends in adult education identify the adult learner as having unique needs (Selman & Dampier, 1991). Adult teaching strategies are routinely incorporated into the PHN practice, but in the group setting they assist the nurse to meet the common learning needs of a group of individuals who are potentially very diverse demographically. Prenatal classes, smoking cessation workshops, and sessions on general healthy lifestyle education issues are prime examples of education about health issues that are relevant only to a small subset of the population. The group may have very different cultural and socioeconomic status but the learning objectives are similar. The PHN is required to be flexible to ensure inclusiveness of all group members.

Canadian Research Box 4.1

O'Brien-Pallas, L., Doran, D. I., Murray, M., Cockerill, R., Sidani, S., Laurie-Shaw, B., and Lochhaas-Gerlach, J. (2001). Evaluation of a client care delivery model. Part 1: Variability in nursing utilization in community home nursing. *Nursing Economics, 19,* 267–276.

O'Brien-Pallas, L., Doran, D. I., Murray, M., Cockerill, R., Sidani, S., Laurie-Shaw, B., and Lochhaas-Gerlach, J. (2001). Evaluation of a client care delivery model. Part 2: Variability in client outcomes in community home nursing. *Nursing Economics, 20,* 13–21, 36.

The context for the above studies was an environment of increased complexity and challenge for home health nursing in light of health care system restructuring and the movement of health care from the hospital to the community. To promote effective use of health system resources, a new imperative was needed to understand the nature of health care services required by the client recovering at home and the factors associated with variability in the delivery of that care. The researchers posed the following questions: "What factors affect nursing resource utilization in the community, and how can we accurately predict and measure nursing resource utilization? Specifically, how do nurse, client, work environment, and community nursing system influence the number and length of client visits and outcomes?

A total of 96 Registered Nurses (RNs) and Registered Practical Nurses (RPNs) from St. Elizabeth Health Care in the City of Toronto participated in Part 1 of the study. They described the factors that affected their daily workload. Data were captured for each day of the week and both day and evening shifts. In Part 2, 38 RNs and 11 RPNs collected client data, including health care needs and self-reported health status. At the end of each client visit, nursing diagnoses (drawn from the North American Nursing Diagnosis Association's taxonomy) were collected using the client's chart and the nurse's current assessment. The total number of nursing diagnoses reflected the intensity of client needs. The client's medical diagnosis was drawn from the official referring information and the client. The nurses also provided data about themselves, including their years of nursing experience (collective and community specific), educational preparation, and professional designation. Workload data for a total of 751 clients were captured on the Workload Variable Factor Form and reflected the time required to complete the assigned work.

The studies found that while clinical factors were predictive of visit time, provider, organizational, and/or environmental complexity factors also explained variation in visit time and were more predictive of number of visits. Other key findings included:

- Clients with one or more nursing or acute medical diagnoses, or with diagnoses of neoplasm or mental health problems, required significantly longer visits.
- Continuity of care (i.e., the same nurse makes the majority of the visits) reduced the number of visits.
- Longer visit times were associated with fewer visits.
- Visit duration decreased when the nurses' daily nursing caseload was greater.
- Clients visited by baccalaureate-prepared nurses required fewer visits and had greater improvements in knowledge and behaviour scores.
- Baccalaureate-prepared nurses were more satisfied with adequacy of treatment and prevention times.

The study findings suggested that factors associated with environmental complexity are also predictive of nursing workload in the community. Factors such as unanticipated case complexity (e.g., deteriorating client condition, palliative care client) and unanticipated admission (e.g., new admission, or client not known to nurse) were positively associated with greater average visit time. Formal information exchange between nurses and clients decreased the number of visits while use of voice mail by nurses to relay information to clients increased the number of visits.

Overall, the study demonstrated that workload and outcomes of care in home care nursing are associated with several client, nurse, and community system factors. Environmental complexity also significantly affects variability in nursing workload.

Discussion Questions

1. Compare and contrast the influence of hourly compensation versus fee-per-visit compensation on length of visit and number of visits per day/shift.
2. Identify six environmental complexity factors unique to home health nursing (e.g., weather, client-controlled environments, traffic patterns, locating addresses, conditions of the home, communication methods).

The classroom venue provides a good opportunity to deliver specific health education to a segmented target group. The composition of group classes is generally 10 to 20 clients in a classroom format, or a small circle format for groups of fewer than 10 participants. This may occur in a myriad of settings, such as workplaces, schools, or community centres, and through a variety of strategies, such as didactic teaching, small groups, or larger interactive health fairs where two or three people gather around a display at a health booth and the nurse engages them in a game to teach them about a particular health issue.

In terms of hours worked per client numbers, working with groups is a more efficient use of the PHN's time than the one-to-one in the clinic or home setting. The average home visit is logged as comprising 1.5 hours of nursing time (Applied Research Consultants, 2002). An average prenatal class with 30 participants may only take four hours of nursing time, including preparatory and evaluation time. But one must weigh the benefits of direct service, which is individualized to meet personal needs, with the more generalized health education approach. The benefits of the group setting are focused around the communal support and sharing of questions and concerns. Peer support and education are powerful health education allies. Often clients learn as much from each other as from the PHN in regard to the practical application of theories in the group setting. However, if the group format requires clients to go to a centralized location, the more motivated and privileged sector of the population is more likely to be able to access them. Many people in need of education and support either do not have the capacity to access it or feel uncomfortable participating in the formalized group setting (Hayward et al., 1993). Thus, it is important that PHNs be able to identify the clients who are in need of services.

Prenatal classes are traditional techniques to educate parents on the health aspects of pregnancy, labour, delivery, and the postpartum period. Parenting classes on coping with the stages of infant and child development are beneficial in fostering healthy, well-adjusted future generations. Support and intervention during the early years of child development have proven to be critical to maximizing a child's full potential development (Mustard & McCain, 1999).

A train-the-trainer model is an even more efficient model of delivering a health promotion message. Education on content and teaching strategies is provided to a special group, who then feel prepared to present the content in turn to other groups. The multiplier effect assumes that a small number of specially trained individuals will disseminate health information to a large number of other groups. Some very large groups can be termed as "populations" because they share a common characteristic such as a place of work or study. PHNs working within the school setting have opportunities to provide comprehensive health promotion strategies to the school populations on several levels. They may deliver classroom presentations or organize interactive health fairs where students visit booths and play games to raise awareness about lifestyle issues, sexual health, or injury prevention. To be most effective, health education needs to be incorporated into other aspects of the general curriculum and supported with healthy school policy. Knowledge about a particular health issue frequently does not translate into a behaviour change. For example, safe-sex behaviours among youth are rarely the result of direct education; they require social support and skills such as comfort with condom use and an environment that facilitates access to condoms (Rew, Fouladi, & Yockey, 2002). Likewise, teaching children about the benefits of a healthy diet, physical activity, and a smoke-free lifestyle is not effective unless it is reinforced within the school environment through opportunities for physical activity throughout the day, healthy food choices in the cafeteria, and smoke-free school grounds. The PHN can be a key player in policy advocacy within the school setting by working with parent councils and school staff to develop healthy school policies.

PHOTO 4.2

Public health nurse in pamphlet room selecting educational resources.

Credit: Sue Weins

The same process can be used within the workplace setting. **Comprehensive workplace wellness programs** include a combination of education and policy support for a healthy work environment. Often, health screening is incorporated into a workplace model. A health fair that includes education about physical activity, nutrition, and tobacco cessation may also allow employees to have their blood pressure and blood checked to rule out potential cardiovascular problems. Large community health fairs are another means of engaging the general population in health-promoting behaviours (Dillon & Sternas, 1997). Although an education strategy, the target is very broad, with awareness of services as the general outcome.

Group as Client: Home Health Nursing

Although opportunities are limited for HHNs to work with groups as the focus of care, some such roles are now in existence. Actual examples include an HHN who was contracted by a school setting whose student body comprised children with complex and long-term health needs. The role of the nurse was to provide client-specific care interventions such as medication administration and tube feedings, as well as to consider and provide for the overall health needs of all the school children. This latter aspect of the role involved assessing the safety of the school environment, planning activities for the entire school population, and acting as an advisor to the teachers on the intersection of the children's health needs and classroom performance. In another role involving care to a group, an HHN provided clinical care to individual residents of a religious residence, contributing to the overall health care and well-being of all residents as a member of the facility's planning committee. HHNs also provide client care in clinic settings. While attending to the client as an individual, they simultaneously identify the needs or care patterns common to the group of clinic clients. These shared needs may be addressed by a strategy implemented for all clients, for

PRACTICE EXEMPLAR: Public Health Nursing, Group as Client

A public health nurse explained, "There was a set [prenatal] program but certainly you could assess the needs of the group and there was a lot of latitude to allow people to grow, to question, and to prepare.... I saw the benefit was increasing their awareness and knowledge of one, the delivery process; that's important to get out of the way because at least if you have an idea of what is going to happen, you decrease fear and it's going to be a much better experience. But the whole course really helped couples prepare to be parents; it helped them to clarify and crystallize some of their issues. They weren't always resolved in the class for them. I mean, you would hope that they would go home and talk about some of the issues around abuse, for example, or stress or... [finances] or adjustment of even the grandparents. There are just so many life issues that you could discuss.

"Often it would come from the group if you had a... [really] aware group but if they weren't forthcoming then you would really have to try to do that with them.... You just got to love these people because over a seven-week period you have now formed an intimate relationship. People remember; I saw somebody the other day at the grocery store... and we both looked at each other and he said my name and 'We had different instructors in our first class and we still talk about you and we still meet with four other couples from that class and, you know, it made such a difference in our lives'.... I think, if you can't build those kinds of relationships with individuals and even with groups, you just can't be effective in my mind; you are just that stranger, that expert, who comes in and it's certainly not as good an experience."

Source: Reproduced by permission from Rafael, A. R. F. (1999). From rhetoric to reality: The changing face of public health nursing in Southern Ontario. Public Health Nursing, *16(1), 50–59.*

example, the development of a common wound assessment form that becomes part of the clinic admission process for each client.

Community as Client: Public Health Nursing

A **community** is generally viewed as comprising many subgroups or sub-populations (see Chapter 10). It can be as big as an entire city or a municipal region serviced by a Public Health Department. It can be very large in geographical size and small in population, such as a rural outpost region in the far north of Canada. Working with an entire community provides an opportunity for very broad or **macro health promotion** strategies to complement the direct education done with smaller groups or populations. It is acknowledged, however, that education sessions in isolation of other reinforcers are not effective in changing health behaviours (Green & Kreuter, 1991). A comprehensive macro-health-promotion approach entails **social marketing**, which uses mass media, in conjunction with community events and promotional material, to raise community awareness and motivate people to create a social change. Social marketing has been described as a process to influence the acceptability of a social idea or cause (Kotler & Andreasen, 1993). It usually involves targeting a large segment of the community, although the community-at-large may benefit from the message with increased awareness. Promotion of breastfeeding to six months of age is an example of a targeted communication campaign to preconception parents and pregnant and new mothers. Within the public health setting, nurses are usually involved in social marketing projects as content consultants and work on a multi-disciplinary team to plan, execute, and evaluate the project.

Community mobilization is a term that describes a process of activating a community to achieve healthy public policy and/or enhance the capacity of a community to sustain a positive change. PHNs are often involved in community mobilization through coalitions with community partners, a prime example being tobacco policy advocacy. Although the federal government enforces the ban on sales of tobacco products to minors and many provincial governments have some smoking restrictions, each local government is responsible for its own control of environmental tobacco smoke in some public places. PHNs join forces with other local health agencies, such as the Lung Association, Heart and Stroke Association, and Cancer Society, to create awareness in the community. Residents, in turn, get involved and make their voices heard to local politicians and a smoking by-law is created.

Community development is a less concrete strategy that often involves PHNs. This strategy facilitates a community's efforts to establish its goals and take steps to achieve positive change. The nurse cannot assume a strong leadership role in this process because the community members must own the change themselves for sustainability purposes. Reducing youth crime and illegal drug use in an urban housing project are examples of goals of community development. The PHN may assist community members to lobby local politicians, find resources to build a youth activity centre, and recruit volunteers to act as mentors for local youth. But this type of project must be in the total control of the community members themselves; the nurse is only a consultant.

Although broad, the role of the PHN in this type of community involvement is often elusive. Although PHNs are often quite integrated in the community or doing macro health promotion strategies directed at the community as a whole, they and their work may not be as visible and concrete as other community health nurses who provide direct care and hands-on interventions within the curative aspect of health promotion.

All of the most common macro health promotion strategies described here can be effective in reinforcing the need for policy change to create supportive environments for healthy communities. From healthy food policies in schools and family-friendly workplace policies to municipal no-smoking by-laws, healthy public policy is a sustainable means of reinforcing health behaviour. Nurses have an important role in advocating for public policy in general, but PHNs (as well as nurses in

PRACTICE EXEMPLAR: Public Health Nursing, Community as Client

"I currently chair a community-wide coalition to prevent falls in seniors," said a PHN. "We received money about a year ago to look at better ice and snow removal and develop some strategies around that.... Some of [the members of the coalition] are representatives of other organizations for seniors and in some cases they're volunteers, seniors themselves.... I'm [also on a specific local council]. I'm on their board and chair [one of their committees]. Two years ago [our committee] put out telephone inserts—we got a corporation to sponsor it—so the seniors could read this larger print and easier format and [find] the information that they might want for their area. Now we have quarterly newsletters that go out and we're now looking at possibly a directory of some sort."

Source: Reproduced with permission from Falk-Rafael, A. R. (1997). Every day has different music: An oral history of public health nursing in Southern Ontario, 1980–1996. Unpublished doctoral dissertation, University of Colorado. (Available from CNA library, Ottawa).

general) tend to be effective because of their credibility within a community. All of these macro strategies can work in synergy to ensure prerequisites to health exist in all communities.

Evaluation of these larger-scale projects is just as vital to ensure continuous quality improvement in nursing practice as it is at the individual or small group level. Assessment of nursing interventions beyond the individual or family level in public health has often been problematic, mainly because the focus is on prevention. Process and utilization standards are often more available than outcomes (Hilton, Budgen, Molzahn, & Attridge, 2001). Nonetheless, it is important for the PHN to follow the steps in the nursing process and remember to incorporate evaluation strategies into the macro or population-based projects as well.

ATTRIBUTES OF QUALITY COMMUNITY HEALTH NURSING PRACTICE

As demonstrated by the preceding text, CHN practice is complex, diverse, and demanding. As in all nursing sectors, the degree to which community health nurses are able to realize their practice goals and aspirations is significantly influenced by the practice settings they work in, and more specifically the supports provided in the setting. Practice setting attributes are also important factors in nursing recruitment and retention—as much an issue for community health nursing as other nursing sectors. Recent literature has clearly identified attributes of quality practice settings and healthy workplaces that apply to both hospital and community-based settings and that promote nursing recruitment and retention (Baumann et al., 2001; Clarke et al., 2001; College of Nurses of Ontario, 2001; Lowe, 2002). The following discussion of these attributes includes reference to current issues for CHNs.

The degree of influence CHNs exert over their practice environments is a key measure of a quality practice setting. Such influence is to be achieved through several strategies, including designated nursing leadership roles that contribute to senior decision-making. For example, the appointment of a Chief Nursing Officer (CNO) for each public health unit, a goal of Ontario's PHNs and the Provincial Chief Nursing Officer, has been achieved in some of the province's health units. There is little uniformity amongst home health nursing organizations in designating CNO positions, and, if such positions are in place, they often lack visibility or legitimate influence on financial and management decision making.

Control over practice, or autonomy, is another attribute of a quality practice environment. Since PHNs focus on empowerment of clients rather than direct client care, they require an empowered work environment as a prerequisite (Haugh & Laschinger, 1996). Similarly, working in isolation in uncontrolled environments, HHNs also require support for their autonomous practice. These supports include access by CHNs to clinical experts for consultation and/or assistance in managing challenging clinical situations (Baumann et al., 2001; CNO, 2001). Since community practice is usually provided by a nurse working alone in a client-controlled environment, personal safety is an important measure of the practice setting. Some employers provide staff with safety training by community police and/or an environmental safety assessment tool for nurses to use on their first visit (J. Warner, personal communication, May 2000). Driving education for urban, rural, and adverse weather conditions, as well as avoidance of injuries from sharps or client lifting/transfer activities, is pivotal to workplace safety for CHNs. Similarly, control over scheduling has also been associated with satisfying practice settings (Baumann et al., 2001; Clarke et al., 2001).

Most community health employers provide flexible work environments to enable nurses to have control over their practice, adjusting their own hours within the work week to meet the demands for their service. This level of autonomy allows nurses to plan and organize their time effectively. The balance between "effort and reward" (Baumann et al., 2001, p. 4), as measured by remuneration, recognition, and reward, also requires attention by employers. For CHNs, strategies to address the balance between effort and reward include wage parity between nursing sectors, long-term contracts, payment for or provision of communication devices such as cell phones, recognition for specialty knowledge and education, and opportunities for socialization (Baumann et al., 2001), as well as providing benefits such as sick leave and pension and minimizing unpaid work (Canadian Home Care Human Resources Study, 2001). Workload is another key influence on practice settings. Where staff shortages exist, CHNs and their colleagues in other sectors are particularly vulnerable to workloads that contribute to burnout and high turnover (Clarke et al., 2001). It is clear that the establishment of quality practice settings for CHNs is pivotal to ensuring an adequate supply of CHNs to meet the health needs of the public where they live, work, worship, and play.

Canadian Research Box 4.2

Falk-Rafael, A. R. (2001). Empowerment as a process of evolving consciousness: A model of empowered caring. *Advances in Nursing Science, 24,* 1–16.

This study, conducted in three southwestern Ontario public health units from 1998–1999, explored the following questions:

- What is the PHN's understanding of empowerment?
- What are the strategies they use to foster empowerment in the individuals, groups, and communities with which they work?
- What outcomes of empowerment do they identify?
- How do clients experience nursing practice that nurses identify as empowering?

The research was designed as a two-phase process. In Phase One, a separate focus group addressed each of the first three research questions. The same population of nurses attended each of the focus groups, which were held in two rural and one urban/rural health unit. A total of 24 nurses attended, 17 of whom were able to participate in all three focus groups.

In Phase Two of the study, PHNs approached clients with an information letter about the study and invited them to participate. A total of six clients consented to participate and were interviewed by the researcher. Client data was collected as a method to answer the question of "How do clients experience nursing practice that nurses identify as empowering?" Clients spoke about the degree of change they perceived in themselves related to such areas as self-confidence and making healthier choices.

PHNs "conceptualized empowerment as an active, internal process of growth" (p. 4). They identified the client's participation in the process of self-empowerment as essential. Accordingly, they saw themselves as facilitators and not creators of empowerment. Additional factors identified by nurses as critical to the empowering process included awareness of one's own strengths and limitations, the right to have control over personal/family health issues, and the political factors that influence health and health care.

The nurses identified a client-centred approach as central to an empowering approach to care. Clients validated this understanding by stating the importance of the nurse's flexibility in meeting their preferred visit time and place and responding to the needs identified by the client as the priority. Additional concepts linked to empowerment included the development of trusting relationships, advocacy, information sharing, and skill development. The outcomes of client empowerment were categorized as "changes in self, changes in relationships with others, and changes in behaviours" (p. 10).

The model of empowerment that the study illuminated was found to be congruent with the "Freirean concept of conscientizacao"—i.e., that "the process of increasing awareness and concomitant action or praxis is liberating" (p. 13). Additionally, the focus of empowerment was found to be not only on its facilitation but also on the process of becoming empowered. Accordingly, the nurses' client care activities directed toward "increasing awareness, interacting with the client's active participation, and developing knowledge and skills is an evolving helical process of empowerment" (p. 13). This conceptualization of empowerment is consistent with modern definitions of consciousness that underscore "awareness, intention, or free will" (p. 13).

This research is valuable and relevant to nursing practice by providing insight into client empowerment as a process of evolving consciousness. The nursing interventions that support client empowerment are clearly identified and will assist nurses in all settings to address this important aspect of nursing care.

Discussion Questions

1. The questions from the study are replicated here to stimulate reflective practice related to empowerment within the client-nurse therapeutic relationship.
2. What do you do in your practice that you believe is empowering for clients?
3. Identify one client example from your practice in which you perceived an increase in client empowerment.

CASE STUDY

You are a nursing student in your final year of study to obtain your baccalaureate degree in nursing. After writing your registration examination, you will apply for nursing positions in your area. You have enjoyed the community practicums in your nursing education and would like to pursue a career in that area. You are aware of the diversity in practice settings in the community, but the concept of working autonomously, which seems to be a consistent feature in most of them, really appeals to you. You want to make the position a good match for your personality as well as your clinical interests and skills.

Discussion Questions

1. From reading all the practice exemplars in this chapter, assess which one appeals to you the most in terms of the kind of nursing interventions described.
2. What kind of research would you do before submitting an application to a community health nursing agency?
3. How would you prepare for an interview with your employer of choice?

CURRENT ISSUES AND TRENDS IN COMMUNITY HEALTH NURSING

Established and emerging trends in health care and nursing will continue to challenge community nurses to evolve their practice in order to continue to play a central role in the health care system and provide effective and relevant care to their clients. Several such trends are described below from the authors' perspectives as nursing administrators currently working in community health.

Consumerism Increasingly knowledgeable and empowered consumers rely on nurses not only to provide skilled clinical care, but also to work in partnership with them to navigate the health system and provide knowledge that contributes to informed decision-making.

Multiculturalism Changes in Canadian immigration patterns mean nurses are providing services within increasingly multicultural communities and a more diversified clientele (see Chapter 16). Sensitivity to cultural care needs is an essential competency. Communication challenges within a diverse community are prompting innovation in health teaching strategies, such as the use of multilingual health literature and pictograms in health classes or counselling sessions.

An Aging Society Demographic changes and the increase in aging baby boomers will make geriatric care and health promotion for seniors more critical issues for nurses in the community. There is a stronger focus on prevention of chronic diseases as the life span increases.

Technological Advances Technological innovation continues to advance, and nurses need to be ready to embrace the resulting changes. In the community, technology such as voice mail, e-mail, and wireless devices have enhanced connectivity. In some settings, nurses document in the client health record on laptops or palm pilots. Nurses working in the far North or rural outposts now send test results electronically and receive a diagnosis and treatment order without having to transport a client to a remote medical centre. Telehealth applications have also reduced this travel by enabling medical and nursing specialists in major centres to provide assessment, diagnosis, and treatment protocols. Telemonitoring applications are providing new opportunities for remote assessments of wound healing, cardiac and respiratory status, and other health indicators, thus making optimal use of scarce nursing and medical resources. Nurses in many regions of Canada are now identifying and evolving telehealth nursing competencies that continue to support a therapeutic nurse-client relationship.

The Global Nursing Shortage The shortage of nurses will continue to be a factor in health human resources. Nurses' openness to providing services through distance technology will assist in ensuring that clients benefit from the nursing care most relevant to their needs, whether that need is for information, clinical care, or counselling.

Ethics Identifying, analyzing, and resolving ethical dilemmas will continue to characterize nursing and health care, particularly at a time of cost constraints and limited resources. The nature of the community nurse's relationship with the client gives rise to unique ethical issues in areas such as nurse-client boundaries, access to health services, and risk and vulnerability of the infant, child, or isolated elder. Nurses will need to know their employers' policies and procedures related to ethical dilemmas and to mobilize assistance as appropriate.

Changing Educational Requirements for Nurses In many regions of Canada, the educational requirements for both RNs and LPNs are changing. A comprehensive understanding of scope of practice for RNs and LPNs will be increasingly important, as will collaboration that contributes to optimal client outcomes in all practice settings.

Evidence-Based Practice and Outcome Monitoring Because of a growing emphasis on an evidence-based approach to health care, critical pathways and care maps will increasingly provide important foundations from which to individualize nursing care and promote consistency and optimal client health outcomes. The ability to identify, measure, and benchmark the nursing contribution to health outcomes is emerging as an essential competency for all nurses.

Health System Costs It is expected that health system costs will remain a central concern of governments at all levels, as well as of all stakeholders. The advocacy skills of nurses will be pivotal to ensuring that the public has access to the required health care in a universal, publicly funded health care system.

Career Planning and Management A fundamental requirement of a strong nursing profession is the engagement and retention of nurses throughout a long career. The vast scope of nursing roles and settings presents unlimited opportunities for nurses to thrive in roles that offer both challenge and reward. Cultivating the competency of career reflection, planning, and management will contribute to career growth and satisfaction and demonstrate nursing as a profession of choice.

Evolving Roles of Nursing Regulatory and Professional Associations In most provinces and territories in Canada, a single nurses' association or college fulfills the functions of regulatory body and professional association. Regulatory functions include setting standards of nursing practice, identifying and monitoring educational requirements for the profession, assessing eligibility for registration as a nurse, receiving and investigating complaints about nursing care (along with appropriate discipline), and maintaining the register of nurses for that province/territory. Professional association functions include articulating and publicizing the roles and contributions of nurses; advocating, on behalf of the public, access to nursing services and a strong, publicly funded, universal health care system; promoting excellence in nursing practice; and providing services to nurses such as educational courses and conferences, nursing position statements, discussion papers, or other documents, recognition awards, and career counselling. All of the provincial/territorial associations, with the exception of that in Quebec, are members of the Canadian Nurses Association (CNA), and CNA is the voice of nursing at the federal level in Canada.

Every nurse practising in Canada must pay an annual registration fee and belong to their provincial regulatory nursing association. In all jurisdictions except Ontario, the nursing regulatory and professional functions are fulfilled by a single organization. The College of Nurses of Ontario, the regulatory body for all nurses in that province, is completely separate from the professional organizations to ensure the perception of public protection over advancement of the profession.

In addition, both provincially and nationally, nurses also join many nursing associations on a voluntary basis. Nationally, these voluntary nursing associations include all of the groups associated with the Canadian Nurses Association, such as the Community Health Nurses Association of Canada, the Canadian Orthopedic Nurses Association, and many others. These voluntary nursing associations exist to link nurses who are working in the same specialty area (e.g., strengthening the specific practice area through standards development and educational programs or information sharing, and supporting members through benefits such as scholarships, newsletters, and research). Through these activities, voluntary nursing associations influence nursing, governments, and practice-setting decision-makers; create provincial, national, and international connections among nurses working in the same practice area; and provide leadership and professional development opportunities. Choosing membership in a voluntary nursing association is an important way to demonstrate professionalism, contribute to practice excellence, and positively influence the overall health care system.

SUMMARY

This chapter described the practice of community health nurses (CHNs), with an emphasis on home health nurses (HHNs) and public health nurses (PHNs). It discussed the key concepts of community health nursing and provided a table listing several different community practice roles. Both home health nursing and public health nursing interventions were augmented by practice exemplars for individuals, families, groups, and communities. The attributes of quality practice settings for CHNs were outlined and trends in CHN practice identified. It is clear that community health nurses are key players in promoting the health of individuals, groups, communities, and populations across Canada. [T]hey form the concrete link between a policy of empowerment and the participation of individuals" (Hayward et al., 1993, p. 22) and represent "a meaningful presence actively promoting health and quality of life in family and community patterns of daily living" (Clarke & Cody, 1994, p. 43).

KEY TERMS

primary prevention
secondary prevention
tertiary prevention
health promotion
primary health care
telephone help lines
comprehensive workplace wellness programs
community
macro health promotion
social marketing
community mobilization
community development

STUDY QUESTIONS

1. Describe the different practice settings for CHNs.
2. List the variety of roles a CHN may perform.
3. List effective strategies that will encourage healthy lifestyle behaviours?
4. How do home health nurses incorporate primary health care strategies into their practices?
5. What are the key attributes of quality practice settings for CHNs?

INDIVIDUAL CRITICAL THINKING EXERCISES

1. Identify five key roles that are unique to public health nursing as opposed to home health nursing. Explain how each meets the objective of achieving a healthier community.
2. Describe some examples from your own community that show how public health has empowered groups to achieve a healthier community.
3. What personal characteristics might draw nurses toward community nursing as opposed to institutional nursing?
4. Describe some attributes for a quality practice setting in the community and explain why they would ultimately enhance nursing outcomes.
5. Describe how you could apply theories and practices from other disciplines and sectors to any of the areas of community health nursing.

GROUP CRITICAL THINKING EXERCISES

1. Outline a comprehensive plan that a PHN might implement for reducing tobacco use among a school-age population in your community. Include the micro- and macro-strategies your team would employ and describe the collaboration you would have with community partners.

2. Identify strategies to promote an understanding of community health nursing roles amongst nurses in other sectors.
3. Debate the merits of legislation similar to the Canada Health Act that would provide standardized community care services across Canada.
4. What questions would you ask of a community health nursing organization before accepting employment in that setting?

REFERENCES

American Nurses Association. (1999). *Scope and standards of home health nursing practice.* Washington, DC: Author.

Applied Research Consultants. (2002). *Evaluation of the Healthy Babies Program: Project report, Windsor Essex County 2001–2002.* Toronto, ON: Ontario Ministry of Health and Long-Term Care, Child Development Branch, Integrated Services for Children. (NG265)

Baldwin, D. R., & Price, S. A. (1994). Work excitement: The energizer for home healthcare nursing. *JONA: The Journal of Nursing Administration, 24*(9), 37–42.

Baumann, A., O'Brien-Pallas, L., Armstrong-Stassen, M., Blythe, J., Bourbonnais, R., & Cameron, S. (2001). *Commitment and care: The benefits of a healthy workplace for nurses, their patients and the system.* Canadian Health Services Research Foundation. Retrieved November 27, 2003 from **www.chsrf.ca/docs/finalrpts/pscomcare_e.pdf**

Baumgart, A. J. (1988). Evolution of the Canadian health care system. In A. J. Baumgart & J. Larsen (Eds.), *Canadian nursing faces the future* (pp. 19–37). St. Louis: C. V. Mosby.

Benefield, L. E. (1998). Competencies of effective and efficient home care nurses. *Home Care Manager, 2*(3), 25–28.

Bramadat, I. J., Chalmers, K., & Andrusyszyn, M. A. (1996). Knowledge, skills and experiences for community health nursing practice: The perceptions of community nurses, administrators and educators. *Journal of Advanced Nursing, 24*(6), 1224–1233.

Canadian Home Care Human Resources Study. (2001). *Phase 1 Highlights: Setting the stage: What shapes the home care labour market?* Ottawa, ON: Author. **www.homecarestudy.ca/en/news/docs/highlights-final.pdf**

Canadian Nurses Association. (1996). *Commitment required: Making the right changes to improve the health of Canadians.* Ottawa, ON: Author.

Canadian Nurses Association. (2003). *The value of nurses in the community.* Ottawa, ON: Author.

Canadian Occupational Health Nurses. (2000). *Information booklet.* Retrieved November 26, 2003 from **www.cohna-aciist.ca**

Canadian Public Health Association. (1990). *Community health – public health nursing in Canada: Preparation and practice.* Ottawa, ON: Author.

Clarke, H. F., Laschinger, H. S., Giovannetti, P., Shamian, J., Thomson, D., & Tourangeau, A. (2001). Nursing shortages: Workplace environments are essential to the solution. *Hospital Quarterly, 4*(4), 50–56.

Clarke, P. M., & Cody, W. K. (1994). Nursing theory-based practice in the home and community: The crux of professional nursing education. *Advances in Nursing Science, 17* (2), 41–53.

Coffman, S. (1997). Home-care nurses as strangers in the family. *Western Journal of Nursing Research, 19*(1), 81–96.

College of Nurses of Ontario. (1999). *Attributes of a quality practice setting.* Toronto, ON: Author.

Community Health Nurses Association of Canada (CHNAC). (2003). Community health nursing standards of practice. Retrieved November 30, 2003 from **www.communityhealthnursescanada.org/newpage22.htm**

Dillon, D., & Sternas, K. (1997). Designing a successful health fair to promote individual, family, and community health. *Journal of Community Health Nursing, 14*(1), 1–14.

Federal, Provincial, and Territorial Advisory Committee on Population Health. (1999). *Toward a healthy future: Second report on the health of Canadians* (Cat H39–468/1999E). Ottawa, ON: Health Canada.

Green, L. W., & Kreuter, M. W. (1991). *Health promotion planning: An educational and environmental approach* (2nd ed.). Toronto, ON: Mayfield.

Haugh, E. B., & Laschinger, H. S. (1996). Power and opportunity in public health nursing work environments. *Public Health Nursing, 13*(1), 42–49.

Hayward, S., Ciliska, D., Mitchell, A., Thomas, H., Underwood, J., & Rafael, A. (1993). *Public health nursing and health promotion: A background paper for the systemic overviews of the effectiveness of public health nursing interventions* (Paper 93–2). Hamilton, ON: McMaster University, Quality of Nursing Worklife Research Unit.

Hilton, B. A., Budgen, C., Molzahn, A. E., & Attridge, C. B. (2001). Developing and testing instruments to measure client outcomes at the Comox Valley Nursing Centre. *Public Health Nursing, 18*(5), 327–329.

Kaiser, K. L., & Rudolph, E. J. (1996). In search of meaning: Identifying competencies relevant to evaluation of the community health nurse generalist. *Journal of Nursing Education, 35*(4), 157–162.

Kotler, P., & Andreasen, A. (1993). *Strategic marketing for nonprofit organizations.* Englewood Cliffs, NJ: Prentice Hall.

Lowe, G. S. (2002). High-quality healthcare workplaces: A vision and action plan. *Hospital Quarterly, 5*(4), 49–56.

Meyer, K. A. (1997). An educational program to prepare acute care nurses for a transition to home health care nursing. *The Journal of Continuing Education in Nursing, 28*(3), 124–129.

Mustard, J. F., & McCain, M. N. (1999). *Reversing the brain drain: Early years study final report.* Toronto, ON: Ontario Children's Secretariat.

Neuman, B. (1983). Family interventions using the Betty Neumann health care systems model. In I. W. Clements & F. B. Roberts (Eds.), *Family health nursing; A theoretical approach to nursing care* (pp. 239 –254). New York: John Wiley & Sons.

Ontario Ministry of Health and Long Term Care. (2002). *Community Health Centres.* Retrieved November 27, 2003 from **www.health.gov.on.ca/english/public/contact/chc/chc_mn.html**

Registered Nurses Association of Ontario, Community Health Nurses Initiatives Group. (2000). Understanding the practice of home health nursing: A discussion paper. Retrieved November 29, 2003 from **http://www.chnig.org**

Rew, L., Fouladi, R. T., & Yockey, R. D. (2002). Sexual health practices of homeless youth. *Journal of Nursing Scholarship, 34*(2), 139–145.

Roberts, B. (1983). The American family. In I. W. Clements & F. B. Roberts (Eds.), *Family health nursing; A theoretical approach to nursing care* (pp. 239–254). New York: John Wiley & Sons.

Selman, G., & Dampier, P. (1991). *The foundations of adult education in Canada.* Toronto, ON: Thompson.

Sherwen, L. N., Scoloveno, M. A., & Weingarten, T. C. (1999). *Maternity nursing: Care of the childbearing family.* Stamford, CT: Appleton Lange.

World Health Organization. (1984). *Health promotion: A discussion document on the concepts and principles.* Copenhagen: WHO Regional Office for Europe.

ADDITIONAL RESOURCES

WEBSITES

The Community Health Nurses Initiatives: Group of the Registered Nurses Association of Ontario
www.chnig.org

The Canadian Public Health Association:
www.cpha.ca

A typical public health unit website in Ontario:
www.wechealthunit.org

Association for Nurse Directors and Supervisors in Official Health Agencies in Ontario:
www.andsooha.org

The Community Health Nurses Association of Canada (CHNAC): A federation of provincial and territorial community health nurse interest groups:
www.communityhealthnursescanada.org

The Association of Ontario Health Centres:
www.aohc.org

The College of Nurses of Ontario:
www.cno.org

About the Authors

Elizabeth Battle Haugh, RN (St Joseph's Regional School of Nursing, London), DPHN, BA (Psychology), and BScN (Windsor), MScN (Western Ontario), is Director of Health Promotion at the Windsor-Essex County Health Unit in Ontario. She has over three decades of public health nursing experience at the staff nurse, manager, and director level and is currently an adjunct Professor at the University of Windsor. She has had a lengthy involvement with the board of the local Children's Aid Society, Ontario Nurses Association, and more recently with the College of Nurses of Ontario, where she served as President from 2001–03. She is a member of several other organizations such as OPHA (being the 2003 conference chair), CNA, CHNIG, RNAO, Sigma Theta Tau, and the University of Windsor Nursing Honour Society.

Barbara L. Mildon, RN (Seneca College), BScN, MN (Toronto), has acquired her community nursing expertise over a 20-year period in the roles of clinical care, clinical education, and nursing administration in home health care. She also gained experience in nursing regulation while at the College of Nurses of Ontario. Barbara is a past Chair (1997–98) of the Community Health Nurses Initiatives Group of the Registered Nurses Association of Ontario (RNAO) and presently serves as RNAO's Member-at-Large for Nursing Practice. Currently president of the Community Health Nurses Association of Canada (2000–2004), her present studies toward a PhD in Nursing through the University of Alberta have led her to her current role as Research Associate at the Nursing Effectiveness, Utilization and Outcomes Research Unit at the University of Toronto.

Part Two

FOUNDATIONS AND TOOLS FOR COMMUNITY HEALTH NURSING PRACTICE

CHAPTER 5

Concepts of Health

Lynne E. Young and
Joan Wharf Higgins

OBJECTIVES

AFTER STUDYING THIS CHAPTER, YOU SHOULD BE ABLE TO:

1. Understand health as discourse, the systems view of health, social determinants of health, and lay perspectives on health.
2. Examine how these often conflicting yet parallel perspectives on health influence the practice of community health nursing.

INTRODUCTION

> I know people who have such low self-esteem that they have allowed themselves to become infected with HIV, and yet they are people visually who would be seen by society and treated by society as very healthy people. They compensate for such low images that they're in the gym four or five days a week so they see themselves as healthy. I have come to know some of them to be very unhappy or very shy socially, they feel inadequate. So to me they are not healthy. —Glen (pseudonym), a mid-life man (Maxwell, 1997, p. 112).

Health is a ubiquitous but confusing term, as Glen so thoughtfully observed in the above quote. We drink to our health, but some people drink themselves to death. We run for our health, but some people are injured running. Health professionals promote health, but patients/clients may choose to live unhealthfully in spite of these urgings. (In this chapter, "client" is defined as an individual, a family, a community, or a population.) As nurses, we hold to a belief that health is wholeness, but then speak of "heart health" or "breast health." There are Health Acts, Health Care Systems, Health Management Organizations, Health Fairs, and so on. Health is at the heart of the language of daily living, as expressed when we clink glasses with companions as well as front and centre in the policy, program, and practice arenas that affect nursing (Rootman & Raeburn, 1994). Thus, the term "health," often used in everyday life as well as in circumstances that shape our nursing world, is a term for which we generally assume a shared meaning. But can we? Should we?

DEFINING HEALTH

Definitions of health abound, derived from medicine, nursing, psychology, anthropology, sociology, politics, holism, and lay perspectives (Rootman & Raeburn, 1994; Dubos, 1961). Such definitions portray health as objective and subjective, a state and a process, naturalist and normative. A phenomenon such as health that is portrayed dichotomously is understandably confusing when one attempts to "pin it down." Dubos (1959) captures the nature of health by likening perceptions of health to a receding mirage: from a distance the health concept is clear but is slippery and elusive as one approaches its meaning. What is consistent across definitions is that health is desirable because it encompasses positive qualities such as physical strength and emotional stability.

Health emerged as a central concept for nursing in the writings of Florence Nightingale. In spite of its elusive nature, health as a guiding concept is increasingly embraced by the nursing profession (Meleis, 1991). Because nursing activities comprise a large portion of health expenditures in Canada, the health-related actions of nurses need to be designed to achieve the overall health-related goals of the wider society. With the multitude of definitions of health, what is the relationship between definitions of health and nursing actions?

Reflecting on this in light of numerous scholarly writings on health, what is most important and most interesting to us as chapter authors about the concept of health is not how health is defined, but rather what it means to speak of health in a particular way. Thus, exploring health as discourse, or a patterned way of speaking of something for some purpose, has potential to clear up some of the confusions that nurses face when trying to think about the meaning of the term "health" relative to their nursing work.

Defining Discourse

Discourse, the noun, can be defined as formal, orderly, and usually extended expression of thought on a subject. Lupton (1992), a nurse theorist, notes that **discourse** is "a patterned system of texts, messages, talk, dialogue, or conversations which can be identified in these communications and located in social structures" (p. 145). In the philosophical literature (e.g., Habermas, 1973; Foucault, 1972), discourses are commonly understood to play major roles in shaping relations of power—what is valued in society—and subsequently receive attention and resources. Borgman (1992) argues that discourses of prediction and control are characteristic of traditional quantitative science and research, whereas the universal principle of qualitative and naturalistic research in health is to "let everyone speak in the first person, singular and plural" (p. 144). Since traditional science has dominated Western thought from the seventeenth century, with critiques of this approach emerging in the late twentieth century (Borgman), current discourses of health will have elements of both the traditional and naturalistic ways of thinking.

Discourses of Health

Health is desirable, a social good, and therein lies its power to shape action. What is considered healthy and unhealthy is influenced by cultural context (Capra, 1982). In North America, health is currently conceptualized within two major discourses: the medical model and the systems view. In the medical model, health is conceptualized as the absence of disease, whereas in the systems view, health is understood to be constructed through the interrelatedness and interdependence of all phenomena (Capra). In addition, an emerging sub-discourse on health within the systems view, particularly in Canada, is the **social determinants of health**, wherein health is held to be constructed primarily by social conditions. Finally, lay definitions of health are apparent in scholarly and lay literature.

Medical Model of Health

Health, according to the medical model, is the absence of disease. This definition of health has dominated our culture for the past three centuries (Capra, 1982) and is therefore a deeply entrenched perspective on health. As the dominant health discourse in Western societies (Fox, 1999), the medical model of health has the power to influence massive individual and collective activities and expenditures (Green & Kreuter, 1999; Rachlis & Kushner, 1994).

Current perspectives on medicine can be traced to the seminal work of scholars of the Intellectual Revolution, for example, William Harvey (1578–1657) and Vesalius (1514–1564) (Donahue, 1985). By charting anatomy through investigational procedures with animal and human cadavers, Harvey and Vesalius advanced the view of the body as machine (Donahue). From these early beginnings, the goal of medicine emerged as primarily to diagnose malfunctioning of the "human machine" and to "fix" it. This legacy pervades modern medicine. Here, achieving and maintaining health is a mechanistic, technical process in which physicians play the role of experts on body functioning (Capra, 1982; Ehrenreich & English, 1978). Thus, the body is conceptualized as a machine disconnected from mind, soul, and social and environmental contexts or settings. Health is the state of a perfectly functioning, decontextualized mechanical entity. Health professionals, including nurses, who adopt this view of health are technical experts and, by association, guardians of a "social order" that build capacities to predict and control health.

Systems View of Health

A competing discourse to the medical model of health is the systems view of health, a shift in understanding health initiated by the World Health Organization (WHO) in 1948 (WHO, 1948). Here, health is "a state of complete physical, mental, and social well-being, not merely the absence of disease and infirmity" (p. 100). Health then is more than a physical, mechanistic state; rather, health is conceptualized in terms of dynamic interrelatedness and integration. The systems view of health is embraced by diverse stakeholders: public, population, and community health; health psychology; holism (Larson, 1999); health promotion from an ecological perspective (Green & Ottoson, 1999); holistic nursing models; and proponents of primary health care, to name a few.

This discourse on health began to gain currency in Canada in the mid-1970s with the release of the 1974 report, *A New Perspective on the Health of Canadians* (hereafter called the Lalonde Report) (Lalonde, 1974). Signalling the beginning of the current vision for health care in Canada, this report reintroduced lifestyle and environment as key determinants of health, positing that health is tied to overall conditions of living, a long-standing position of the public health tradition (Lalonde; Raeburn, 1992). The central argument of this report is that health is not achievable solely as a result of medical care, but rather from the interplay of determinants from four health field elements: human biology, lifestyles, the environment, and health care systems (Labonte, 1994). The Lalonde Report shifted the focus of a vision for the health of a population from illness care to health care and advanced health promotion as a science. Lalonde called this perspective the health-field concept of health.

The Ottawa Charter of Health Promotion (WHO, 1986), written to expand on the 1948 WHO definition of health, stated that, "Health is... a resource for everyday living, not the objective of living" (p. 426). The Charter also proposed five major strategies for promoting health: building healthy public policy, creating supportive environments, strengthening community action, developing personal skills, and reorienting health services. Advocating, enabling, and mediating were identified as central strategies for health promotion practice. It also articulated prerequisites for health: peace, shelter, education, food, income, a stable ecosystem, sustainable resources, social justice, and equity, thereby entrenching specific determinants of health into this discourse on health in Canada.

In the same year, the Epp Report, *Achieving Health for All* (Epp, 1986), was introduced by the Canadian government. It built on the Lalonde Report by identifying specific challenges to achieving health for all Canadians: reducing inequities, increasing prevention, and enhancing coping. In addition, the Epp Report postulated that these challenges could be addressed by the health promotion mechanisms of self-care, mutual aid, and healthy environments, and that central implementation strategies are fostering public participation, strengthening community health services, and coordinating public policy.

In these documents, family plays second fiddle to community as a unit of concern for health professionals, yet the family unit is of particular importance to the development and maintenance of the health of its members (Young, 2002). An **ecological perspective** on health promotion reflects a systems view and does much to highlight broad contextual factors (such as family) that influence health (Green & Ottoson, 1999; Green, Richard, & Potvin, 1996; Richard, Potvin, Kishchuk, Prlic, & Green, 1996). Ecology is concerned with the relationships between organisms and their environment (Kleffel, 1991), and social ecology is concerned with the nature of the relationships between humans and their social, institutional, and cultural worlds (Stokols, 1992). Health here is the consequence of the interdependence between the individual and the family, community, culture, and the physical and social environments (Green & Kreuter, 1999; Moos, 1979).

The next wave of thinking in this systems view of health was disseminated in the report entitled *Strategies for Population Health: Investing in the Health of Canadians* prepared by the Federal, Provincial, and Territorial Advisory Committee on Population Health (FPTACPH, 1994). This report further clarified key factors that influence health: the social and economic environment, the physical environment, personal health practices and coping skills, biology and genetic endowment, and health services. According to the population health approach, health is the capacity of people to adapt to, respond to, or control life's challenges and changes (Frankish et al., 1996). The population health movement in Canada, in collaboration with Health Canada, set out a template to guide action to achieve population health. Key elements of the Population Health Template are depicted in Figure 5.1.

The Canadian Nurses' Association led an impressive effort to incorporate these new ideas, beginning with the document *Putting Health into Health Care* (Rodger & Gallagher, 1995). Subsequently, provincial nursing associations across Canada produced position statements and discussion documents that captured these ideas (McDonald, 2002). For example, the Registered Nurses' Association of British Columbia (RNABC) incorporated strategies from the Ottawa Charter (WHO, 1986) in their New Directions for Health Care policies and programs. As well, these ideas were incorporated into a document entitled *Determinants of Health: Empowering Strategies for Nursing Practice* that was a socio-environmental framework for health-promoting nursing practice. It directed nurses' attention to concerns of not only individuals, but also families, small groups, communities, and society (McDonald). In keeping with the evolution of thinking within the systems view of health, the RNABC has recently published a position statement on primary health care (RNABC, 2002).

According to the systems view, health is envisioned as a dynamic process embedded in a web of relations within which, and as a result of, capacities for living are constructed. In Canada, the systems view of health has been entrenched in our thinking over the past three decades through a series of government documents, frameworks, and blueprints and their related professional practices. Health professionals, including nurses, who practise from a systems, process-oriented perspective, hold to a view that attends carefully to a multitude

FIGURE 5.1 Population Health Key Elements

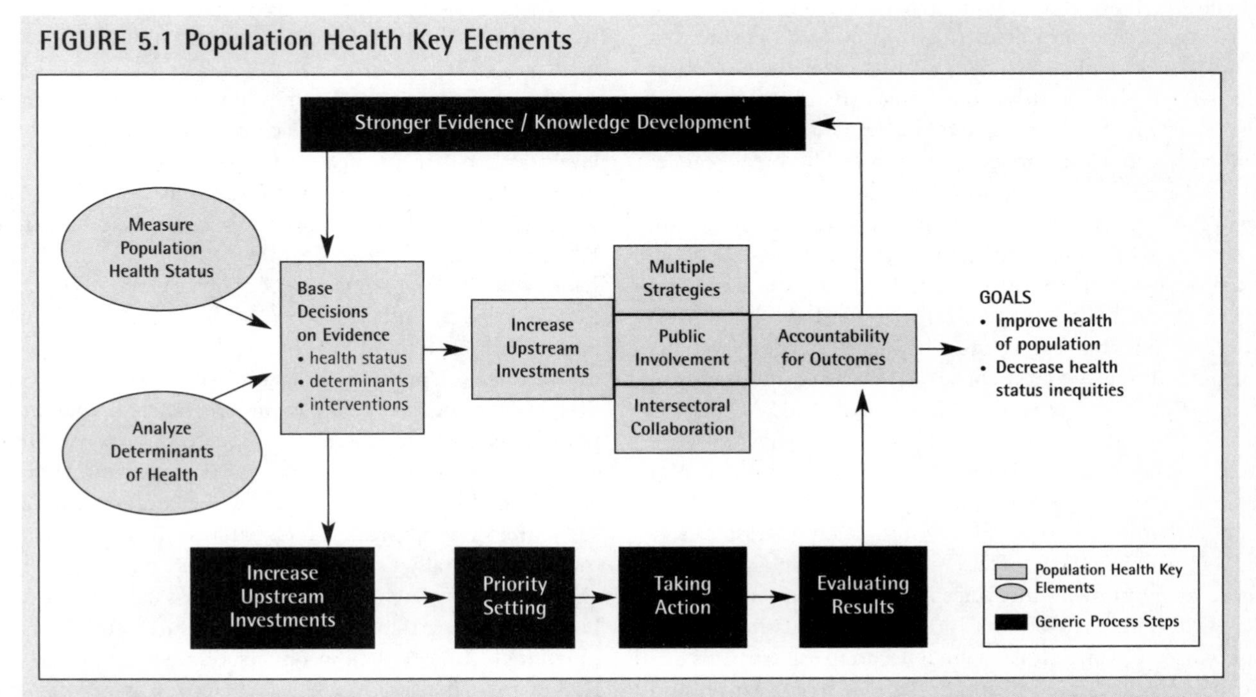

Source: Health Canada. (2001). Population health template: Key elements and actions that define a population health approach. *www.hc-sc.gc.ca/hppb/phdd/pdf/discussion_paper.pdf.* Reproduced with the permission of the Minister of Public Works and Government Services of Canada, 2004.

of capacity-building social and economic relationships, including the relationship between practitioner and client.

Medical Discourse Versus Systems Discourse

Following the Second World War and the discovery of penicillin, the medical model of health irrefutably eclipsed other discourses of health. The near-miraculous discoveries emerging from medical science (e.g., the control of and near-eradication of some communicable diseases, procedures such as heart transplantation, and more recently genetic engineering) have captured our money and imagination. Anyone who has witnessed the recovery of a loved one from a near-death traumatic experience because of innovative surgical procedures, or the prolongation and improved quality of life of an aging parent because of newly developed cardiac medications, stands in awe of medical science and practice. While these successes are real and tangible, they are not the whole story.

Critics of the medical model make strong arguments that such an approach to health does not make for a healthy society (Batt, 1994; Evans & Stoddard, 1990; Illich, 1975; Rachlis & Kushner, 1994; Raphael, 2001). In a seminal work, *Medical Nemesis*, published over 25 years ago, Illich attacked the value of the medical model in producing healthy societies. He opens the book with: "The medical establishment has become a major threat to health" (p. 11) and goes on to argue that a medicalized health care system is a monopoly that serves the interests of medical and paramedical personnel. To this end, he posits that such a health care system obscures the political conditions that render society unhealthy, while seizing the power of individuals to heal themselves.

Heartened by such arguments, consumers have taken steps to regain control over their own health and ensure that medical care and medical science truly serve their interests rather than those of health professionals (Batt, 1994; Porter-O'Grady, 1995). Such consumers understand their health to be embedded in a web of social relations. The breast cancer movement is a consumer movement that exemplifies a challenge to the medical model as a dominant discourse on health. Batt, an award-winning Canadian journalist, charts the journey of breast cancer activism in her book, *Patient No More*. The idea for the book emerged from her need as a breast cancer survivor to better understand why breast cancer treatments were regarded widely as a medical success when thousands of women die each year in spite of those treatments. At first she was hesitant to take on the experts, but her investigative work revealed themes that pointed to the detrimental influence of vested interests and world views on the medical care of women with breast cancer. She writes, "Our [breast cancer survivors'] central task is precisely to develop and advance a perspective of our own. Our voice must be a counterweight to the medical point of view that dominates discussions of the disease" (Batt, p. xiii). Thus, women began to ask why it is difficult to access accurate information about breast cancer and its treatments and moved on to explore how funding decisions are made. Batt writes, "Many now question the premises of past policies, such as the emphasis on treatment rather than prevention, and the strictly biomedical model of cancer" (p. xiv). Batt notes that the activists have inspired breast cancer specialists to examine the world view that guides their research. She writes, "A new order is forming..." (p. xiv).

While the medical view of health as discourse can silence voices and distinguish ideas that do not fit, there are those, such as breast cancer activists, who take issue with the dominance of the medical model and, by their actions, open minds to new ways of thinking about health.

Social Determinants of Health: An Emerging Sub-Discourse

As mentioned earlier, Canadian governments prioritize the funding of health care based on the medical model, but fund interventions aimed at discouraging unhealthy lifestyles to a much lesser extent, a perspective that reflects the health-field concept of health. (This fact exemplifies the power of a dominant discourse to shape social and political action.) However, it is estimated that only five of the 30 years added to life expectancies during the last century can be attributed to clinical medicine (Bunker, Frazier, & Mosteller, 1994). This is in spite of the fact that about 95% of health expenditures in Canada are spent on medical treatment and 5%, at most, are devoted to prevention (Brown, Corea, Luce et al., 1992). Thus, researchers have begun to explore what constellations of factors that determine health status lie "upstream" of medical treatment (McKinlay & Marceau, 2000). An emerging body of research on the social determinants of health provides compelling evidence that challenges the dominance of the medical model as a key perspective. Such research indicates that factors with the greatest impact on the development of life-threatening diseases are usually out of an individual's personal control, factors tied to culture and socio-economic status (Wilkinson & Marmot, 1998).

Indeed, large-scale studies conducted in recent years point to poverty, income, place of residence, and education levels, rather than medical and lifestyle factors, as better predictors of individuals' health (Colhoun, Rubens, Underwood, & Fuller, 2000; Diez Roux et al., 2001; Feldman, Makuc, Kleinman, & Coroni-Huntley, 1989; Lantz, House, Lepkowski, Williams, Mero, & Chen, 1998). For example, Lynch, Kaplan, and Salonen (1997) found that poor adult health behaviours and psychosocial characteristics (sense of hopelessness, depression, or lack of coherence or meaning in life) were more prevalent among men whose parents were poor, regardless of their own socioeconomic standing as adults. The authors suggested that the environmental influences in childhood play themselves out later in adulthood. As such, the "free choice" associated with lifestyle behaviours may not be totally under an individual's control.

Supporting such a thesis, Chernomas (1999) argues that health habits, particularly exercise, smoking, and diet, are less individual choices than products of one's place in society. Rather than focusing on health practices as rational behaviours that one chooses to do at random, the notion of lifestyle is more useful once we understand the determinants of lifestyle choice, that is, what factors and conditions influence our lifestyle habits (Gillies, 1998). In 1998, the World Health Organization defined a healthy lifestyle as a way of living based on identifiable patterns of behaviour that are determined by the interplay between an individual's personal characteristics, social interactions, and socioeconomic and environmental living conditions (WHO, 1998). With this definition in mind, Lyons and Langille (2000) offered the following determinants of lifestyle choice:

1. Personal life skills are those abilities for adaptive and positive behaviours that enable people to deal effectively with the demands of everyday life. Personal life skills include literacy, numeracy, decision making and problem solving, creative and critical thinking, empathy, mutual support, self-help and advocacy, communication, and coping. These are not necessarily linked to specific health practices, but all contribute to helping people increase control over their lives and health.
2. Perceived stress in life influences the choices people make about their lifestyle. To cope with the time pressures they face, Canadians report watching television, eating comfort foods, smoking cigarettes, or consuming alcohol. In fact, "health enhancing" activities such as exercise are perceived as even more stressful when time is limited (Heart and Stroke Foundation of Canada, 1999).
3. The influence of community norms and culture both reflect and limit lifestyle choices.
4. Control over one's life and a sense of coherence about the world enhance one's ability to choose healthy behaviours over unhealthy ones.
5. A sense of belonging is critical to health. To a large extent, connectedness and belonging may overcome the traditional epidemiological risk factors of smoking, physical inactivity, obesity, and poor nutrition (Putnam, 2000); risks that are more prevalent among those with lower incomes (FPTACPH, 1999).
6. Healthy choices in life are not always the most pleasurable, and the benefits of healthy living are not always immediately reaped nor apparent. To make matters worse, persons living with low incomes are more likely to engage in risk behaviours as they provide respite from difficult and painful life situations (Stewart et al., 1996).
7. Personality traits such as learned helplessness or individuals who are "other" directed (believe that luck/fate is responsible for their lot in life) can discourage uptake of healthy behaviours.
8. Overabundance of choice and information about what is the "right" thing to do can confuse and paralyze people rather than galvanize them into action.

Shaping environments in support of healthful living and healthy lifestyles and addressing the social determinants of health require a new way of thinking. The **primary health care** model offers such a way and has gained some currency in the discourse on health care in Canada. Primary health care (PHC) is perceived to be the key to reforming a health care system dominated by the medical model (Green & Ottoson, 1999). PHC was conceived by participants representing 134 nations at the WHO Alma Ata Conference in 1978. They pledged their support for a worldwide effort to shift the emphasis from hospital-based medical treatment to a community-based, participatory model of care (Green & Ottoson, 1999). The catchphrase that emerged from this conference was "Health for All by the Year 2000." Many influential Canadians who believe that the tenets of PHC will indeed improve the health of Canadians have been in a prolonged, difficult, and often embittered battle to expand the vision for health care in Canada beyond the medical model. Such tensions speak to the power of the medical discourse on health to shape political will. Recently, social and health researchers, policy experts, and professionals gathered in Toronto to network and discuss the health of Canadians. On the final day, delegates composed "Strengthening the Social Determinants of Health: The Toronto Charter for a Healthy Canada" (Social Determinants of Health Across the Life-Span Conference, 2002). This document outlines ten social determinants of health, which include early life experiences, education, food security, housing, and income distribution.

In the U.S., the 1990s were a decade of failed health care reform (Oberlander, 2002). Although the Clinton plan for

Canadian Research Box 5.1

Clark, J. P., Feldberg, G. D., & Rochon, P. A. (2002). Representation of women's health in general medical versus women's health specialty journals: a content analysis. *BMC Womens Health, 20(2)*, 5–10.

In this Canadian study, the authors addressed the following question: "How is women's health represented in leading medical journals (GM) versus in women's health specialty journals (WS)?" To answer this question, the authors accessed articles published between January 1 and June 30, 1999 in leading GM journals (n=514) and WS journals (n=82). Using a semi-structured content-analysis instrument to capture key elements of each article—sample characteristics, study design, and health topic—articles were categorized as traditional (reproductive conditions), non-traditional (all other health conditions that afflict women to a greater extent than men), or both. The investigators found that topics were indeed distributed differently between the GM and WS journals with 53.5% of GM articles addressing traditional women's health topics compared with 26% of the WS articles. The WS articles more often combined a traditional view of women's health with non-traditional topics. This analysis identified important gaps in the women's health literature and serves as a baseline for appraising how women's health topics are represented in the literature over time.

Discussion Questions

1. How is women's health represented in your community?
2. Why do you think women's health is represented in this way? Are there tensions in your discussion group around this point? If so, why? If not, why not?

universal insurance failed, it nonetheless spawned the spread of managed care, which, for a time, controlled the costs of health care. Now, however, medical care costs are rising again, and 40 million Americans lack health insurance (Oberlander). In Canada, each day brings new challenges to the universal, single-payer health care system. Reports on the Romanow commission on health care in Canada indicate widespread support for health care policy consistent with a public system, with key aspects of primary health care embedded in its principles. Nonetheless, power and money interests have a foothold in private clinics and ever-more-effective technologies that promise quick and effective diagnoses and cures, a direction consistent with a medical model view.

Social Determinants of Health: Heart Health, a Case Example

Low-income, lone mothers are a particular cohort in which operates a constellation of factors detrimental to health. Such women are more likely to live in poverty, to achieve low levels of education, and to be on social assistance than are partnered mothers (Young, James, & Cunningham, in review; Young, Cunningham, & Buist, 2002). Overall health status is poorer among lone mothers (Perez & Beaudet, 1999), as are health behaviours. In particular, Canadian lone mothers are three to four times more likely to be smokers than partnered mothers of any income (Young, James, & Cunningham). In a U.S. study, women who had experienced a cardiovascular disease event were 3.28 times more likely to be a lone mother than a partnered mother (Young, Cunningham, & Buist). Females across their lifespan, but particularly after age 16, are the least likely to be physically active (FPTACPH, 1999). Heart disease accounts for 38% of all deaths among Canadian women (Heart and Stroke Foundation of Canada, 1999) and 53.5% among American women (American Heart Association, 2002). These facts support the position that female-headed households are associated with a higher risk for heart disease among women (LeClere, Rogers, & Peters, 1998).

The established approach to promote heart health and prevent heart disease has been, and continues to be, individually focused and behaviourally oriented (Raphael, 2003) despite findings that suggest that only a portion of inter-individual variability in CVD incidence can be explained by the major risk factors (Nettleton, 1997; Marmot, 1996). Indeed, Raphael (2001) estimates that 23% of all premature years of life lost prior to age 75 in Canada can be attributed to income differences. Of these premature deaths related to income differences, heart disease and stroke cause the greatest proportion of these years lost: 22%. As such, health policymakers have been encouraged to address issues of poverty, powerlessness, and a lack of social support in addition to the usual care of risk reduction (Marmot & Wilkinson, 1999; Petrasovits, 1992).

Gender is also a critical determinant of heart health. The social determinants of health do not affect women and men in the same way: women are relatively disadvantaged compared to men (Jones & Ste. Croix Rothney, 2001). Marked differences exist between men's and women's ability to access, and gender role expectations of accessing, health-promoting opportunities (e.g., recreation, continued education, satisfying work). Moreover, the gendered effects of reduced funding to health and social services include fewer jobs for women, more unpaid care work, and reduced access to health care (Kaufert, 1996). As a result, low income is especially concentrated among women. In 1998, 56% of Canadian sole support mothers lived below the low income cutoff (Townson, 2000). For lone mothers aged 16 to 24, it jumps to 80% (National Council of Welfare, 1992).

Gender needs to be treated as an important explanatory variable in determining health. As well, more focused efforts are required to ensure that policies and programs take into account existing and new knowledge about women's health. Thus, while the "determinants" model is receiving (deserved) increasing attention for situating lifestyle behaviours and risk factors in their proper social, cultural, and economic contexts, the current health issues facing women have nevertheless been left woefully unchanged by North America's health care model (Jones & Ste. Croix Rothney, 2001). A further challenge to the epidemiological tradition of studying heart disease is its ignorance of the lived experience of women (Raphael, 2001).

Lay Definitions of Health: Giving Voice to Our Clients

Before we move on, let's return to the opening scenario in which Glen points to the tension between what "society" defines as healthy and what he observes in his friends. In pointing to what society says about health, Glen refers to society's dominant discourse on health. Reflect on how health is portrayed by society in Canada as a discourse on health. Now, reflect on the difference between what society says is health and how Glen defines health. Reflect on what this difference means to Glen.

Lay perspectives on health are diverse, ranging from popular Western definitions that reflect the medical perspective—health as the absence of disease—to a perspective evident in many non-Western cultures—health as living in harmony with nature (Calnan, 1987; Spector, 1985). In our view, lay perspectives orient nurses to the views on health of those in their care. In this section, an overview of the findings of a qualitative study (Maxwell, 1997), designed to reveal lay perspectives on health, is presented and then discussed relative to research in the field. Participants in the study were male and female, ranged in age from 7 to 81, and lived in urban and rural settings. The researcher met with families in their own homes for 1–2 research interviews that lasted for 1.5–2 hours.

Health was perceived by most to be fundamental to living a functional, meaningful life. As one middle-aged woman put it, "This sounds very cliché but being healthy is... if you don't have your health, obviously you don't have anything." Another female participant, a financially strained, married mother of three, elaborates:

> You need your health to have energy to raise your family and everyone wants to raise healthy, happy kids, you know, for the future (p. 112).

For several people, having energy was an indicator of health. One man observed:

> Healthy is a mental attitude, physically feeling well, and having an energy level to get through the day, and, it's a lifestyle (p. 111).

Health emerges as an energized state that has physical, mental, and social dimensions, and health is a lifestyle. A health care professional male in his 60s provides a well-thought-through position on his lived experience of health:

> I feel healthy if my back isn't sore or if things don't hurt or my throat is not sore. To me personally, on any given day, whether I feel healthy that day or not is an absence of complaints. But, what does health count as a year? What is a healthy year? Or, what is a healthy decade? Then, we get into that more holistic definition of health. You know the background thing... we're comfortable, we have a nice home, we have adequate money and live with it well, and we're not living in fear and this sort of thing. So that background is okay and so that you can sit around and worry about whether or not you've got a sore throat. If you lived in a war-torn country, you really wouldn't give a damn if you had a sore throat or not.
>
> Researcher: So if you had a healthy year, what would that have been like?
>
> Man: I guess free from relatively, well number one, good physical health, free from sort of major worries, free from family worries, that there weren't a lot of things pressing down and adequate rest so that I am not overtired (p. 113).

This man evaluates his state of health by noting his physical state and the context within which his physical health is experienced, including his family, socioeconomic circumstance, and the political climate of the country. His idea of health counting "as a year" or "decade" is unique.

Not all participants found it easy to speak of health however. One woman, married with three children under age six and employed full time, observed:

> I've never thought of "I feel healthy." It's either you feel tired or you don't feel tired. I've never said, "Oh I feel healthy today." I wouldn't even know where to start with that one (p. 115).

A single mother coping with the aftermath of breast cancer treatment and living meagrely with two early teens views health in the following way:

> Gee, I just can't answer that. Isn't that amazing? I don't know. I'm not grasping what health is, being healthy? [pause] Being fit? Is there more? (p. 115).

While most participants openly discussed their views on health, not all found it an easy term to define. Some participants offered thoughtful definitions of, or personal theories about, health. From these interviews, health emerged as an energized, balanced, dynamic, multidimensional state related to self-perception, interpersonal processes, and socio-economic context, a perspective aligned with a systems view of health but with unique and individualized twists and variations.

A systematic review of 112 qualitative studies that was conducted to develop theory regarding an individual's experience of health and disease was revealing (Jensen & Allen, 1994). These studies involved informants with disease or chronic illness as well as those who considered themselves to be "healthy." Participants ranged in age from early adulthood to very old. The authors identified the following themes to describe the lived experience of health and disease:

- **abiding vitality,** the idea that when one is healthy there is sparkle and animation;
- **transitional harmony,** the idea that, when healthy, one has a sense of harmony and balance, a notion that resonates with the words of participants in the Maxwell (1997) study;
- **rhythmical connectedness,** the idea that, when healthy, one experiences wholeness and an accompanying attachment to the world and that these social connections provide a positive sense of personal contribution or effectiveness as well as positive identity;
- **unfolding fulfillment,** the notion that engaging with life's challenges is meaningful; and
- **active optimism,** the idea that one can cope with life and meet its challenges, that is, one has the attitude and resources to do so.

Two recent qualitative studies revealed meanings of health similar to but also different from those claimed by the above authors. Maddox's (1999) study of older women and the meaning of health reported that the primary themes arising from research interviews were interactions with a being greater than themselves, acceptance of self, humour, flexibility, and being other-centred. Mexican-American women view health as a compilation of good physical health, sound mental health, and a socially and spiritually satisfying life (Mendelson, 2002). Health for these women exceeded more than these component parts, an embodied experience that transcends illness and is grounded in relationships with family and supported by their spirituality.

The lay perspectives on health presented here mirror each other and resonate with both the medical and systems models of health. A study in Alberta found that survey respondents recognized that their health is broadly influenced by social and environmental variables, including issues of social support, supportive environments, and income (Reutter, Dennis, & Wilson, 2001). In an attempt to understand how people arrive at a subjective evaluation of their health, Kaplan and Baron-Epel (2003) surveyed people in three broad age groups (20–40, 41–60, and 61+). When they probed respondents about what factors may have influenced their rating, they found that:

> [H]ealth is a social construction and our beliefs and conceptions of it are rooted in wider socio-cultural contexts. People's perceptions of health are also found to be influenced by biomedicine and by prevailing social and medical ideologies.... People's perceptions and judgements about their own health are at once individual and social (p. 6–7).

As health professionals, our practice is enriched if we listen carefully for our clients' definitions of health and choose this as a starting point.

Canadian Research Box 5.2

Young, L., Turner, L., Bruce, A., & Linden, W. (2001). Evaluation of a mindfulness-based stress reduction intervention. *Canadian Nurse, 97*(6), 23–26.

Select BSN students in a B.C. university participated in an 8-week stress reduction intervention, Mindfulness-Based Stress Reduction (MBSR). The MBSR has been evaluated for its effectiveness in the treatment of anxiety disorders, chronic pain, and cardiac disease. In a pilot study, using a participatory approach, the MBSR was evaluated for its effectiveness by qualitative and quantitative methods. In the qualitative component, 15 students participated in six sessions. Data were analyzed for key themes. Findings indicate that, while at school, juggling multiple demands altered the students' sense of balance, compromising their health and school performance. During the MBSR, students became aware of the effects of stress on their health. They acquired new stress-management skills and learned to "let go" of stress. Quantitative findings are consistent with those of the qualitative component. Students recommended that programs such as the MBSR be included in nursing curricula to ensure greater congruence between what is taught about self-care practices and what is supported by their educational institution.

Discussion Questions

1. What are the effects of school stress on your own health?
2. What discourse on health is central to your school's nursing curriculum?
3. In your nursing program, is the curriculum designed in such a way that your lived experience of health is addressed? If not, in discussion with faculty, explore why not.
4. How do you as students and the nursing faculty honour the idea of the determinants of health in the everyday life of your school? Brainstorm factors that could be addressed in your school community to make your school a healthier place to be. Synthesize your ideas into a summary for presentation to the committee governing your school. In discussion, reflect on the response to your summary from the committee with a view to better understand who gets to say what about health in an institution and why and how this affects policy.

DISCOURSES ON HEALTH AND THE ROLE OF THE COMMUNITY HEALTH NURSE

In the previous sections, we discussed health in terms of medical and systems discourses and lay perspectives on health. These are "lenses" on health that community health nurses can draw on as they perform their roles. Used in this way, "lens" refers to a particular way of understanding a concept, in this case, health. One of the primary challenges nurses face is to sort out how each lens on health can be applied to or incorporated into their practice. However, the first step in addressing this dilemma is to understand how and why a particular lens on health shapes health care practice, be it nursing, medicine, or another health care discipline such as physiotherapy, family therapy, or community health promotion.

For purposes of stimulating thinking, discussion, and debate, we suggest that the medical model of health, with its focus on prediction and control, has the potential to engender nurses who enact their role as experts who can predict the causes of, and intervene to control, the health of those in their care. Nurses who fall within this genre take on the role of the expert in identifying problems and catalyzing solutions. When functioning in this role, nurses may seem like heroines, charging in to instigate a "fix" or solution, or they may act to guard the social order to ensure health: "Xena, the Warrior Princess" nurses. Society needs nurses who can detect health problems and offer effective solutions, for example, when a community experiences the outbreak of a communicable disease.

In contrast, nurses who practise from a systems view, in which health is wholeness, carry out a relational practice in which relationships with clients are paramount to the clients' constructions of health and experiences of wholeness. In such a nursing practice, the nurse builds trusting relationships, collaborates with clients to identify and address their health-related issues, fosters clients' strengths, promotes and protects clients' rights, practises in an intersectoral manner to address the determinants of health, and strives for a respectful, integrated, accessible system of health care delivery. A metaphor for such a nurse might be nurse as dancer, in which the nurse and client strive to connect across life space—a delicate, gentle act, beautiful in its execution but nonetheless precarious.

Community health nurses may find themselves caught between the roles of Xena, the Princess Warrior, and the nurse as dancer, roles that may at times feel untenable. Nurses in British Columbia experienced such tensions and took action to change their practice (Griffiths, 2002). The Public Health Nursing Practice Advisory Committee (PHNPAC) in the South Fraser area of the Fraser Health Authority received a referral from nursing colleagues concerning dissatisfaction with the problem-oriented recording system (POR). The POR was incongruent with the philosophy of nursing that the nurses shared. The PHNPAC initiated a series of consultations to assist them in addressing this concern. A presentation by a nursing professor on "The Power of the Text" raised the nurses' awareness of the incompatibility between the way the documentation system was shaping their practice and their philosophy of nursing. More specifically, the POR documentation system, as a problem-oriented practice, shaped their practices to emphasize detecting problems rather than fostering family strengths. Yet, the act of acknowledging and fostering family strengths was what these nurses held to be fundamental to health promotion practice with families.

Tackling this issue head on, the PHNPAC created its own model for working with high-risk families through a brainstorming process. Key themes that emerged to inform the development of the model included strengths-based practice, collaboration with clients, and taking steps to increase choices and control for families. As one participant noted, "As nurses, we support people to live in ways that are productive for them" (Griffiths, 2002, p. 16). They linked their work to a systems view of health, citing the Ottawa Charter definition of health promotion, "the process of enabling people to increase control over and improve their own health" (WHO, 1986), as a conceptual and philosophical guide for their newly conceived practice standards.

A **population health** model, offered by McKinlay and Marceau (2000), is a useful framework for thinking about where one's nursing practice fits within the discourses of health. This model suggests that there are three streams to promoting population health:

1. **downstream**, an individual-focused orientation to treatment and cure (e.g., pharmacology, surgery, and rehabilitation);
2. **mid-stream**, support at the community and organization level for creating environments conducive to living healthfully (e.g., opportunities for physical activity, prenatal care programs); and
3. **upstream**, in which healthy public policies, programs, and services deal with macro-level issues of employment, education, and reimbursement mechanisms that affect all in a community (e.g., universal health care).

"Downstream" practice falls within a biomedical view of health whereas "mid-stream" and "upstream" practices fit within a systems view of health. Where does your usual practice fit?

SUMMARY

In this chapter, we discussed discourses of health suggesting that there are two primary discourses of health in Canada, the medical model and the systems view on health. Health, a concept of primary importance to community health nurses, is not a concrete entity, but rather a concept that has a range of meanings to various groups of health care professionals. What is important about the concept of health for community health nurses is to clearly grasp who and how health is defined, and for what purposes. Understanding health as a discourse is a first step in grasping who is defining health and for what purposes. Community health nurses can engage in client-centred care when they can link a particular definition of health to whoever is making claims on the definition, and then determine how well a particular definition aligns with clients' definitions of health in addition to clients' health care needs. Community health nurses,

CASE STUDY Community-Based Project in Preventing Type 2 Diabetes

The Saanich Peninsula Diabetes Prevention Project explores how community recreation programs and services can delay the onset or prevent type 2 diabetes in "at-risk" populations. Rather than adhering to a medical model orientation and relying on bio-medical variables, such as glucose intolerance, as identifying risk factors, the definition of "at-risk" used in this project is consistent Health Canada's population health framework and a social determinants view and includes low-income citizens, isolated seniors, persons living with disabilities, and Aboriginal populations. Working with recreation professionals, community nutritionists, diabetes educators, social workers, and public health nurses, project staff work to dismantle the barriers to a diabetes-healthy lifestyle for these at-risk groups, as well as create a supportive community environment. In response to an identified need from these populations, a Diabetes Education and Awareness Fair was held in the fall of 2002. The goal of the Fair was to increase the at-risk groups' education and awareness of type 2 diabetes, as well as provide information about, and access to, the resources and supports available in the community for healthy living. The overall focus was to facilitate a change to a diabetes-healthy life while acknowledging the social, economic, and cultural contexts within which lifestyle behaviours occur. The Fair consisted of brief seminars on risk factors and conditions, healthy eating, meal preparation, physical activity, and stress management. As well, on-site booths provided information concerning community resources and supports for healthy and active living and access to dieticians, community nurses, kinesiologists, and other health professionals. Participants could also visit booths to have their heart rate, blood pressure, body-mass index, and blood glucose levels measured. The Fair was held in the local recreation centre, thought to be a more welcoming and non-threatening environment than a health department or hospital.

Despite an emphasis on the broader social determinants of health to the project, the nursing staff at the Fair found it difficult to communicate the importance of such factors to visitors, whose questions and search of information reflected a medical model understanding of diabetes. Although the design of the Fair and its staff acknowledged and appreciated the population health, systems approach, Fair participants were mired in the medical model and intent on gathering information concerning physiological and behavioural risks and solutions.

Discussion Questions

1. How might you, as a community health nurse, think about why the nursing staff reported difficulty communicating the importance of the social determinants of health to Fair visitors?
2. Is it necessary to emphasize one understanding or discourse of health over the other?
3. How might the Fair be reorganized/restructured to encourage a systems understanding of health over a medical one? What different activities, resources, staff, etc. would be important to include?

because of their location in the community, are well positioned to work in intersectoral relationships to address the social determinants of health, factors that are increasingly held to be the key to health.

KEY TERMS

discourse
social determinants of health
ecological perspective
primary health care
abiding vitality
transitional harmony
rhythmical connectedness
unfolding fulfillment
active optimism
population health
downstream
mid-stream
upstream

STUDY QUESTIONS

1. Define "discourse."
2. What are the principles of primary health care?
3. What is the difference between the medical model and the systems view of health?
4. What is the challenge to nurses working within these two views of health?
5. Why was the Lalonde Report important?
6. Why does the ecological perspective on health fit within a systems view of health?
7. What is a relational nursing practice?
8. Where do the traditional and non-traditional articles presented in Canadian Research Box 5.1 fit into the discourses of health as discussed in this chapter?
9. What has been Canada's role in shaping discourses of health?
10. What are your responses to the metaphors of nursing offered by the authors of this chapter?

INDIVIDUAL CRITICAL THINKING EXERCISES

1. How do you define your own health?
2. Within which view or discourse of health did you frame your response to the previous question?
3. When you assess clients, what questions would you include to help you understand their perspectives on health?
4. Locate the majority of your nursing work on the McKinlay and Marceau (2000) model and identify distinct tasks that fit on the stream continuum.
5. If you were to move your work more "upstream," what would that look like so that you achieved similar outcomes to your present work?

GROUP CRITICAL THINKING EXERCISES

1. What are the sources of stress for you as students? How might you balance study, work, and family to "let go" of stress?
2. Relative to the above discussions about discourses of health, what does it mean to frame school-related stress as a problem that requires an individual-level solution?
3. How do you as students and the nursing faculty honour the idea of the determinants of health in the everyday life of your school? Brainstorm factors that could be addressed in your school community to make your school a healthier place to be.

REFERENCES

American Heart Association. (2002). *Heart and statistical update.* Dallas, TX: Author.

Batt, S. (1994). *Patient no more: The politics of breast cancer.* Charlottetown, PE: Synergy.

Borgman, A. (1992). *Crossing the post-modern divide.* Chicago, IL: University of Chicago Press.

Brown, R., Corea, J., Luce, B., Elixhauser, A., & Sheingold, S. (1992). Effectiveness in disease and injury prevention—estimated national spending on prevention—United States 1988. *MMWR: Morbidity and Mortality Weekly, 41*(29), 529–531.

Bunker, J. P., Frazier, H. S., & Mosteller, F. (1994). Improving health: Measuring effects of medical care. *Millbank Quarterly, 72*, 225–258.

Calnan, M. (1987). *Health and illness: A lay perspective.* London: Tavistock.

Capra, F. (1982). *The turning point: Science, society, and the rising culture.* New York: Simon and Schuster.

Chernomas, R. (1999). *The social and economic causes of disease.* Retrieved November 27, 2003 from **www.policyalternatives.ca**

Colhoun, H. M., Rubens, M. B., Underwood, S. R., & Fuller, J. H. (2000). Cross-sectional study of differences in coronary artery calcification by socioeconomic status. *British Medical Journal, 18*, 1262–1263.

Diez Roux, A. V., Stein Merkin, S., Arnett, D., Chambless, L., Massing, M., Nieto, F. J. et al. (2001). Neighborhood of residence and incidence of coronary heart disease. *New England Journal of Medicine, 345*, 99–106.

Donahue, P. (1985). *Nursing: The finest art.* Toronto, ON: C.V. Mosby.

Dubos, R. (1959). *Mirage of health, utopias, progress, and biological change.* New York: Anchor Books.

Dubos, R. (1961). *Mirage of health.* New York: Doubleday.

Ehrenreich, B., & English, D. (1978). *For her own good.* Toronto, ON: Doubleday.

Epp, J. (1986). *Achieving health for all: A framework for health promotion.* Ottawa, ON: Health and Welfare Canada.

Evans, R. G., & Stoddard, G. L. (1990). Producing health, consuming health care. *Social Science & Medicine, 31*, 1347–1363.

Federal, Provincial, and Territorial Advisory Committee on Population Health. (1994). *Strategies for population health:*

Investing in the health of Canadians. Ottawa, ON: Minister of Supply and Services.

Federal, Provincial, and Territorial Advisory Committee on Population Health. (1999). *Toward a healthy future: The 2nd report on the health of Canadians.* Ottawa, ON: Health Canada.

Feldman, J. J., Makuc, D. M., Kleinman, J. C., & Cornoni-Huntley, J. (1989). National trends in educational differentials in mortality. *American Journal of Epidemiology, 129,* 919–933.

Foucault, M. (1972). *The archaeology of knowledge and the discourse on language.* New York: Pantheon Books.

Fox, N. (1999). *Beyond health: Postmodernism and embodiment.* London: Free Association Books.

Frankish, C. J., Green, L. W., Ratner, P. A., Chomik, T., & Larsen, C. (1996). *Health impact assessment as a tool for population health promotion and public policy.* Vancouver, BC: University of British Columbia, Institute of Health Promotion Research.

Gillies, P. (1998). Effectiveness of alliances and partnerships for health promotion. *Health Promotion International, 13,* 99–120.

Green, L., & Ottoson, J. (1999). *Community health and population health.* Toronto, ON: McGraw-Hill.

Green, L. W., & Kreuter, M. W. (1999). *Health promotion planning: An educational and ecological approach* (3rd ed.). Mountain View, CA: Mayfield.

Green, L. W., Richard, L., & Potvin, L. (1996). Ecological foundations of health promotion. *American Journal of Health Promotion, 10,* 270–281.

Griffiths, H. (2002). Participatory action research. *Nursing BC, 34,* 15–17.

Habermas, J. (1973). *Theory and practice* (J. Viertel, Trans.). Boston, MA: Beacon Press.

Health Canada. (2001). *Population health template: Key elements and actions that define a population health approach.* Retrieved November 27, 2003 from **www.hc-sc.gc.ca/hppb/phdd/pdf/discussion_paper.pdf**

Heart and Stroke Foundation of Canada. (1999). *The changing face of heart disease and stroke in Canada 2000.* Ottawa, ON: Author.

Illich, I. (1975). *Medical nemesis: The expropriation of health.* Toronto, ON: McClelland and Stewart.

Jensen, L., & Allen, M. N. (1994). A synthesis of qualitative research on wellness-illness. *Qualitative Health Research, 4,* 349–369.

Jones, E., & Ste. Croix Rothney, A. (2001). *Women's health and social inequality.* Retrieved November 27, 2003 from **www.policyalternatives.ca**

Kabat-Zinn, J. (1990). *Full catastrophe living: using the wisdom of your body and mind to face stress, pain, and illness.* New York: Delacorte.

Kaplan, G., & Baron-Epel, O. (2003). What lies behind the subjective evaluation of health status? *Social Science and Medicine, 56*(8), 1669–1676.

Kaufert, P. (1996, August). *Gender as a determinant of health.* Paper presented at the Canada-US Forum on Women's Health, Ottawa, ON. Abstract retrieved November 27, 2003 from **www.hc-sc.gc.ca/canusa/papers/canada/english/genderab.htm**

Kleffel, D. (1991). Rethinking the environment as a domain of nursing knowledge. *Advances in Nursing Science, 14,* 40–51.

Labonte, R. (1994). Death of a program, birth of a metaphor. In A. Pederson, M. O'Neill, & I. Rootman (Eds.), *Health promotion in Canada* (pp. 72–90). Toronto, ON: W.B. Saunders.

Lalonde, M. A. (1974). *A new perspective on the health of Canadians.* Ottawa, ON: Health and Welfare Canada.

Lantz, P. M., House, J. S., Lepkowski, J. M., Williams, D. R., Mero, R. P., & Chen, J. J. (1998). Socioeconomic factors, health behaviors, and mortality. *Journal of the American Medical Association, 279,* 1703–1708.

Larson, J. S. (1999). The conceptualization of health. *Medical Care and Review, 56,* 123–136.

LeClere, F. B., Rogers, R. G., & Peters, K. (1998). Neighbourhood social context and racial differences in women's heart disease mortality. *Journal of Health and Social Behavior, 39,* 91–107.

Lupton, D. (1992). Discourse analysis: A new methodology for understanding the ideologies of health and illness. *Australian Journal of Public Health, 16,* 145–150.

Lynch, J. W., Kaplan, G. A., & Salonen, J. T. (1997). Why do poor people behave poorly? Variation in adult health behaviours and psychosocial characteristics by stages of the socioeconomic life course. *Social Science and Medicine, 44,* 809–819.

Lyons, R., & Langille, L. (2000). *Healthy lifestyle: Strengthening the effectiveness of lifestyle approaches to improve health.* Ottawa, ON: Health Canada, Population and Public Health Branch.

Maddox, M. (1999). Older women and the meaning of health. *Journal of Gerontological Nursing, 25,* 26–33.

Marmot, B. G. (1996). Socio-economic factors in cardiovascular disease. *Journal of Hypertension, 14*(5), S201–S205.

Marmot, M., & Wilkinson, R. G. (1999). *Social determinants of health.* Oxford, UK: Oxford University Press.

Maxwell, L. (1997). *Family influences on individual health-related decisions in response to heart-health initiatives.* Unpublished dissertation, University of British Columbia, Vancouver, BC.

McDonald, M. (2002). Health promotion: Historical, philosophical and theoretical perspectives. In L. E. Young & V. E. Hayes (Eds.), *Transforming health promotion practice: Concepts, issues, and applications* (pp. 25–42). Philadelphia, PA: F.A. Davis.

McKinlay, J., & Marceau, L. (2000). US public health and the 21st century: Diabetes mellitus. *The Lancet, 356,* 757–761.

Meleis, A. I. (1991). *Theoretical development in nursing: Development and progress.* New York: J.B. Lippincott.

Mendelson, C. (2002). Health perceptions of Mexican American women. *Journal of Transcultural Nursing, 13,* 210–217.

Moos, R. H. (1979). Social ecological perspectives on health. In G. Stone & F. Cohen (Eds.), *Health psychology: A handbook* (pp. 523–547). San Francisco, CA: Jossey-Bass.

National Council of Welfare. (1992). *Poverty profile: Update from 1991.* Ottawa, ON: Author.

Nettleton, S. (1997). Surveillance, health promotion and the formation of a risk identity. In M. Sidell, L. Jones, J. Katz,

& A. Peberdy (Eds.), *Debates and dilemmas in promoting health* (pp. 314–324). London: Open University Press.

Oberlander, J. (2002). The US health care system: On the road to nowhere? *Canadian Medical Association Journal, 167*, 163–168.

Perez, C., & Beaudet, M. P. (1999). The health of lone mothers. *Health Reports, 11*(2), 21–31.

Petrasovits, A. (1992). *Promoting heart health in Canada: A focus on heart health inequities.* Ottawa, ON: Minister of Supply & Services.

Porter-O'Grady, T. (1995). Consumer ownership of health. *Advances in Practical Nursing Quarterly, 1*, 87–88.

Putnam, R. D. (2000). *Bowling alone, the collapse and revival of American community.* New York: Simon & Schuster.

Rachlis, M., & Kushner, C. (1994). *Strong medicine: How to save Canada's health care system.* Toronto, ON: HarperCollins.

Raeburn, J. (1992). Health promotion with heart: Keeping a people perspective. *Canadian Journal of Health Promotion, 1*, 3–5.

Raphael, D. (2001). *Inequality is bad for our hearts: Why low income and social exclusion are major causes of heart disease in Canada.* Toronto, ON: North York Heart Health Network.

Raphael, D. (2003). Bridging the gap between knowledge and action on the societal determinants of cardiovascular disease: How one Canadian community effort hit - and hurdled - the lifestyle wall. *Health Education, 103*(3), 177–189.

Registered Nurses' Association of British Columbia. (2002). Primary health care. *Nursing BC, 34*(4), 13.

Reutter, L., Dennis, D., & Wilson, D. (2001). Young parents' understanding and actions related to the determinants of health. *Canadian Journal of Public Health, 92*, 335–339.

Richard, L., Potvin, L., Kishchuk, N., Prlic, H., & Green, L. (1996). Assessment of the integration of the ecological approach in health promotion programs. *American Journal of Health Promotion, 10*, 318–328.

Rodger, G., & Gallagher, S. (1995). The move toward primary health care in Canada: Community health nursing 1985–1995. In M. Stewart (Ed.), *Community nursing: Promoting Canadian's health* (pp. 2–36). Toronto, ON: W.B. Saunders.

Rootman, I., & Raeburn, J. (1994). The concept of health. In A. Pederson, M. O'Neill, & I. Rootman (Eds.), *Health promotion in Canada* (pp. 139–151). Toronto, ON: W.B. Saunders.

Social Determinants of Health Across the Life-Span Conference. (2002). Strengthening the social determinants of health: The Toronto charter for a healthy Canada. Retrieved November 21, 2003 from **www.socialjustice.org/subsites/conference/TorontoCharterfinal.pdf**

Spector, R. E. (1985). *Cultural diversity in health and illness.* Norwalk, CT: Appleton-Century-Crofts.

Stewart, M. J., Brosky, G., Gillis, A., Jackson, S., Johnston, G., Kirkland, S. et al. (1996). Disadvantaged women and smoking. *Canadian Journal of Public Health, 87*, 257–260.

Stokols, D. (1992). Establishing and maintaining healthy environments: Toward a social ecology of health promotion. *American Psychologist, 47*, 6–22.

Townson, M. (2000). *A report card on women and poverty.* Canadian Centre for Policy Alternatives. Retrieved November 27, 2003 from **http:www.policyalternatives.ca**

Wilkinson, R., & Marmot, M. (1998). *Social determinants of health: The solid facts.* Geneva, Switzerland: World Health Organization, Centre for Urban Health.

World Health Organization. (1948). *Constitution of the World Health Organization as adopted by the International Health Conference* (Official Records of the World Health Organization, No. 2). Geneva, Switzerland: Author.

World Health Organization, Canadian Public Health Association, & Health and Welfare Canada. (1986). *Ottawa charter for health promotion.* Ottawa, ON: Health and Welfare Canada.

World Health Organization. (1998). *World's largest and longest heart study produces some surprises* [Press release]. Geneva, Switzerland: World Health Organization. Retrieved November 27, 2003 from **www.ktl.fi/monica/public/vienna/press_release.htm**

Young, L. E. (2002). Transforming health promotion practice: Moving toward holistic care. In L. E. Young & V. E. Hayes (Eds.), *Transforming health promotion practice: Concepts, issues, and applications* (pp. 1–25). Philadelphia, PA: F.A. Davis.

Young, L., Cunningham, S., & Buist, D. (2002). Health disparities in women: Parenting status and risk of cardiovascular disease in women. In *WIN Assembly: Vol. 10. Health disparities: Meeting the challenge* (pp. 133). (Published in *Communicating Nursing Research Conference Proceedings, Vol. 35.*)

Young, L., James, A., & Cunningham, S. (in review). Heart health behaviours in lone versus partnered mothers: National Population Health Survey (NPHS 1998–99). *Canadian Journal of Public Health.*

ADDITIONAL RESOURCES

BOOKS

Douglas, P. (Ed.). (2002). *Cardiovascular health and disease in women.* Toronto, ON: W.B. Saunders.

Keating, D., & Hertzman, C. (1999). *Developmental health and the wealth of nation: Social biological and educational dynamics.* New York: Guilford Press.

Pederson, A., O'Neill, M., & Rootman, I. (1994). *Health promotion in Canada: Provincial, national and international perspectives.* Toronto, ON: W.B. Saunders.

Youngkin, E. Q., & Davis, M. S. (Eds.). (2003). *Women's health: A primary care clinical guide* (rev. ed.). Upper Saddle River, NJ: Pearson Prentice Hall.

Kawachi, I., Kennedy, B., & Wilkinson, R. (Eds.). (1999). *The society and population health reader: Income inequality and health.* New York: New York Press.

WEBSITES

BC Centre of Excellence for Women's Health:
www.bccewh.bc.ca/index.htm
Health Canada Publications:
www.hc-sc.gc.ca/pphb-dgspsp/publications_e.html
No easy task – a general health resource website:
www.noeasytask.com/
Social determinants approach to HIV/AIDS:
www.healthplanning.gov.bc.ca/hiv/determinants.html
Women's Breast Cancer Resource Centre:
www.michellesplace.org
World Health Organization publications:
www.who.int/pub/en/

About the Authors

Dr. Lynne Young is an Associate Professor in the School of Nursing, University of Victoria. Her research focuses on health promotion and families in the context of cardiovascular care.

Dr. Joan Wharf Higgins is an Associate Professor in the School of Physical Education, University of Victoria. Her research and teaching interests include the social determinants of health and physical activity and social marketing.

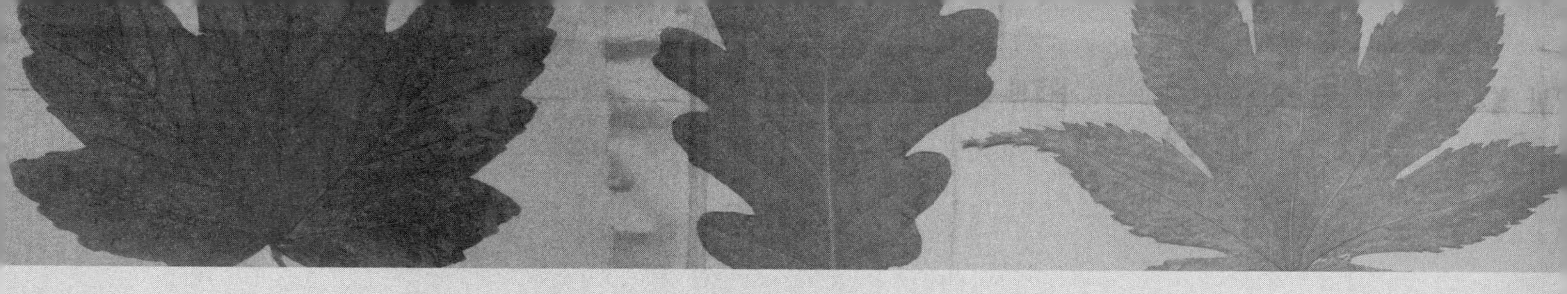

CHAPTER 6

Primary Health Care

Dawn Smith

OBJECTIVES

AFTER STUDYING THIS CHAPTER, YOU SHOULD BE ABLE TO:

1. Describe the concept of primary health care.
2. Define primary health care and describe its values, principles, and elements.
3. Describe differences and similarities between primary health care, primary care, health promotion, and population health.
4. Describe community development and empowerment strategies to implement primary health care, including personal care, small group development, coalition formation, and policy advocacy.
5. Briefly describe primary health care reform and related community health nursing involvement as well as its future directions.

INTRODUCTION

The primary health care approach was first described in the landmark document, *The Declaration of Alma Ata*, produced at the WHO-UNICEF conference in Alma Ata, Kazakstan in the former Soviet Union in 1978. In 1977, the World Health Assembly recognized the unsatisfactory state of health of the world's population and adopted the goal to achieve "Health for All by the Year 2000." The approach required to meet this goal was dubbed "Primary Health Care." **Primary health care** was defined as "essential health care based on practical, scientifically sound and acceptable methods and technology made universally accessible to individuals and families in the community through their full participation and at a cost that the community and country can afford to maintain at every stage of their development in the spirit of self-reliance and self-determination" (World Health Organization [WHO], 1978, p. 2).

More specifically, primary health care can be summarized as:

- evidence based;
- universally accessible;
- the first level of contact, providing for essential health needs;
- providing a full spectrum of needs, including health promotion, prevention, treatment, and rehabilitation;
- addressing the main determinants of health;
- affordable to community and country;
- relevant to the social, cultural, economic, and political context;
- addressing community priorities;
- multi-sectoral and integral to overall social and economic development;
- requiring and promoting individual and community self-reliance and participation;
- sustained by an effective health information system; and
- relying on a diverse team of appropriately trained and responsive health workers.

As a landmark document, the *Declaration of Alma Ata* explicitly outlines the intersectoral and community-driven nature of the approaches to improving health and reducing inequities in health. Primary health care is based on an ecological understanding of health (Smedley & Syme, 2000). However, the *Declaration of Alma Ata*'s explicit attention to the importance of changing structures and policy and enabling socially just values and beliefs to flourish is often missed. Interpretations of primary health care have often been influenced by the social, political, and economic contexts within which they are conceived and have become bounded by the existing approaches to health care.

PRIMARY HEALTH CARE: VALUES, PRINCIPLES, AND ELEMENTS

Primary health care principles describe the nature and scope of action to enact the values. These values shape the "elements," which describe more concrete actions fundamental to achieving health and well-being.

Primary Health Care Values

Achieving "health for all" is a fundamental value of primary health care. Primary health care values are comparable to those of the Canadian Nurses Association's *Code of Ethics for Registered Nurses* (Canadian Nurses Association [CNA], 1997) and the *Standards for Community Health Nursing in Canada* (Community Health Nurses Association of Canada [CHNAC], 2003). Social justice and equity are two distinctive primary health care values.

Social justice refers to the degree of equality of opportunity for health made available by the political, social, and economic structures and values of a society. The extent to which a society provides opportunities for its citizens to develop socially and economically productive roles influences the well-being of individuals as well as the healthfulness of the whole population (Wilkinson, 1996). One example is the inequities that exist in health status where the rich are healthier than the poor. It is important that community health nurses (CHNs) consider how the concept of social justice is enacted in their practice and by the health care organization that employs them.

Equity in health is "the absence of systematic and potentially remediable differences in one or more aspects of health status across socially, demographically, or geographically defined populations or population subgroups" (Macinko & Starfield, 2002, p. 3). Equity is a "political concept, expressing a moral commitment to social justice" (Kawachi, Subramanian, & Almeida-Filho, 2002, p. 647). The distinction of an inequality as inequitable requires a value-based judgment that depends upon one's views of justice and society and the reasoning behind how the inequality was created (Kawachi et al., 2002). Socioeconomic inequality is emerging as perhaps the biggest factor affecting the health of populations (Evans, Barer, & Marmor, 1994; Raphael, 2002; Wolfson et al., 1999). We are beginning to understand how the stresses experienced by those lower down the social and economic ladder in societies with large gaps between the rich and poor (called a steep gradient) have profound direct and indirect influences on the health of individuals and societies. The intermediate steps on the pathway between an unequal society and poor health may include such things as social support, the social organization of work, the psychosocial effects of job insecurity, unemployment, and the divisiveness of material inequality (Wilkinson, 1996). Moreover, relationships also exist between inequality in macro-level social structures, meso-level social processes, and micro-level health effects (Bezruchka, 2002). Usually the term **macro** refers to the "big picture" levels of influence such as policy and **micro** refers to the very smallest levels of influence or impacts such as the individual person or even cells. The **meso** level is the "in between," such as family, group, community, and organization. Planning and implementing interventions that take action on causes of poor health at all levels is fundamental to the primary health care approach.

Principles of Primary Health Care

The CNA (2000) formulated its position on primary health care based on the five principles embodied in the WHO's (1978) original definition, with an emphasis on structural and political reform necessary to reduce inequities in health. These principles include: accessibility, public participation, health promotion, appropriate technology, and intersectoral cooperation.

Canadian Nurses Association's Five Principles of Primary Health Care

Accessibility: The five types of health care (promotive, preventive, curative, rehabilitative, and supportive/palliative) must be universally accessible to all clients regardless of geographic location. In many cases, the principle of accessibility can best be established by having communities define and manage necessary health care services. Distribution of health professionals in rural, remote, and urban communities is key to the principle of accessibility. Accessibility means that clients will receive appropriate care from the appropriate health care professional within an appropriate time frame.

Public participation: Clients are encouraged to participate in making decisions about their own health, identifying the health needs of their community, and considering the merits of alternative approaches to addressing those needs. Adoption of the principle of public participation ensures respect for diversity. It also means that the design and delivery of health care is flexible and responsive. Participation ensures effective and strategic planning for, and evaluation of, health care services in a community.

Health promotion: Health education, nutrition, sanitation, maternal and child health care, immunization, and prevention and control of endemic disease are the goals of health promotion. Achieving these would reduce the demands for curative and rehabilitative care. Through health promotion, individuals and families build an understanding of the determinants of health, thereby developing the skills to improve and maintain their own health and well-being. School-health programs are an important method of promoting health and self-esteem.

Appropriate technology: Modes of care must be adapted appropriately to the community's social, economic, and cultural development. The principle of appropriate technology recognizes the importance of developing and testing innovative models of health care and of disseminating the results of research related to health care. However, it also means considering alternatives to high-cost, high-tech services.

Intersectoral cooperation: Health and well-being are linked to both economic and social policy. Intersectoral cooperation is needed to establish national and local health goals, healthy public policy, and the planning and evaluation of health services. The adoption of the principle of intersectoral cooperation will ensure that providers from different disciplines collaborate and function interdependently to meet the needs of health care consumers and their families and that health professionals will participate in government policy formulation and evaluation, as well as in the design and delivery of health care services. It also suggests that services must be designed and delivered in an integrated and congruent fashion.

Source: Excerpted with permission from the Canadian Nurses Association. (2000). Fact Sheet on Primary Health Care. www.cna-nurses.ca/_frames/policies/policiesmainframe.htm

The Elements of Primary Health Care

The eight essential elements (concrete mechanisms for achieving health for all) articulated in the *Declaration of Alma Ata* (WHO, 1978, p. 2) are:

- education concerning prevailing health problems and the methods of preventing and controlling them;
- promotion of food supply and proper nutrition;
- an adequate supply of safe water and basic sanitation;
- maternal and child health care, including family planning;
- immunization against the major infectious diseases;
- prevention and control of locally endemic diseases;
- appropriate treatment of common diseases and injuries; and
- provision of essential drugs.

These elements have been used extensively to guide health programs and policy development in developing countries. However, it was the emphasis on these elements that initially stamped primary health care as a developing country approach. The strong biomedical and behavioural approach to thinking about health during the 1970s and 1980s in developed nations contributed to the fact that the political, social, and economic messages in the *Declaration of Alma Ata* were

CASE STUDY

In Toronto, over 6000 people are homeless, twice the number in 1996. At that time, the Ontario government drastically cut spending on welfare and low-cost housing. The number of apartments that rent for less than $500 a month has decreased by about 70% since then. Toronto built almost 25 000 public housing units between 1984 and 1996, but fewer than 100 units between 1996 and 2001. Shelters now have 95% occupancy and six times the number of beds.

One result was a tent city, built and lived in by 80 people in downtown Toronto. They lived on five acres of undeveloped, polluted land with portable outhouses, no running water (except one hose), and no electricity.

Discussion Questions

1. Homelessness and poverty in Canada are growing. Access local statistics to identify key data (e.g., vacancy rates, low-income housing units, homelessness demographics). Interview three CHNs about antipoverty initiatives in your home community. During and after your discussion, consider if and how the five principles of primary health care are being enacted.
2. Use Figure 6.2 to describe how you would intervene to promote health in the tent city here or in your own community.
3. Use Figure 6.3 to help you identify how CHNs could increase access to the elements of primary health care in the tent city here or in your own community.

Definitions

Primary health care: "essential health care based on practical, scientifically sound, and acceptable methods and technology made universally accessible to individuals and families in the community through their full participation and at a cost that the community and country can afford to maintain at every stage of their development in the spirit of self-reliance and self-determination" (WHO, 1978, p. 2).

Social justice: equal opportunity for health (e.g., socially and economically productive lives) made available by the political, social, and economic structures and values of a society.

Primary care: the point of first contact with the health care system, generally referring to preventive, curative, and rehabilitative care provided to individuals (Stanhope & Lancaster, 2002).

Primary nursing: a model of nursing care whereby a nurse is primarily responsible for planning and delivering total care for a specific patient. Like primary care, primary nursing is an illness-oriented concept.

Health promotion: "the process of enabling people to increase their control over and improve their health" (WHO, 1986, p. 1).

Population health: "the health of a population as measured by health-status indicators and as influenced by social, economic, and physical environments; personal health practices; individual capacity and coping skills; human biology; early childhood development; and health services. As an approach, population health focuses on the interrelated conditions and factors that influence the health of populations over the life course, identifies systematic variations in their patterns of occurrence, and applies the resulting knowledge to develop and implement policies and actions to improve the health and well-being of those populations" (Federal, Provincial and Territorial Advisory Committee on Population Health, 1999, p. 7).

Determinants of health: factors and conditions that have been shown to influence health over the life course. They include social, economic, and physical environments; early childhood development; personal health practices; individual capacity and coping skills; human biology; and health services (Health Canada, 2002).

Community development: "the planned evolution of all aspects of community well-being (economic, social, environmental, and cultural). It is a process whereby community members come together to take collective action and generate solutions to common problems" (Frank & Smith, 1999, p. 6).

Empowerment: "a social action process in which individuals and groups act to gain mastery over their lives in the context of changing their social and political environment" (Wallerstein & Bernstein, 1994, p. 142).

overlooked. More recently, the growing emphasis on the determinants of health underscores the relevance of these elements across the globe regardless of a nation's level of wealth or development. For example, the increase in homelessness in Canada demonstrates the relevance of these elements (see Case Study).

PRIMARY HEALTH CARE: WHAT IT IS AND WHAT IT IS NOT

Primary health care, primary care, health promotion, and population health: what do these terms mean and how are they related, if at all? There has been considerable confusion, and often fairly heated debate, about the meanings of and relationships among these terms. CHNs can make a significant contribution to primary health care by understanding differing perspectives and developing clear and simple definitions of terms. Table 6.1 compares the focus, the principle actors, and the level and primary emphasis of action commonly associated with each of these terms.

Considerable confusion remains between the terms primary health care and primary care. Although practitioners are encouraged to assess social and environmental impacts on health (primary health care), primary care interventions are often biomedical in focus (Starfield, 1998). Accessibility to primary care is an essential component of primary health care, so primary care is much narrower in scope than primary health care. The Yukon Registered Nurses Association's (2002) Model of Health and Illness shown in Figure 6.1 describes clearly and effectively the relationships between health, illness care, and primary health care.

The distinctions between primary health care, health promotion, and population health are less clear. As Lavis (2002) points out, "the language used to discuss ideas about non-medical determinants of health has changed with each passing decade." Canadian policymakers and researchers talked about "health fields" in the 1970s, "health promotion" in the 1980s, and "population health" in the 1990s. There is a close relationship between health promotion and primary health care in both philosophy and methods. However, primary health care also involves curative, rehabilitative, and palliative care methods as a part of provision of first line contact with the community.

Population health focuses on maintaining and improving the health of entire populations and reducing inequities in health status among population groups. It encompasses "the entire range of factors and conditions (commonly referred to as the determinants of health), and their interactions—that have been shown to influence health over the life course" (Health Canada, 2002, p. 2). Population health is often associated with a "top-down" approach to reducing inequities in health such as developing healthy public policy (Lavis, 2002). This approach to population health is congruent with the original thinking of primary health care outlined in the *Declaration of Alma Ata* (WHO, 1978); it has a strong orientation to evidence-based interventions (Health Canada, 2001).

COMMUNITY DEVELOPMENT AND EMPOWERMENT STRATEGIES

Community development is an approach used by CHNs to put primary health care values and principles into action. Community development is "the planned evolution of all aspects of community well-being (economic, social, environment and cultural). It is a process whereby community members come together to take collective action and generate solutions to common problems" (Frank & Smith, 1999, p. 6).

TABLE 6.1
Comparison of Terms

Term	Focus	Principle Actors	Level and Primary Emphasis for Action
Primary care	Disease	Health professionals	• Micro level • Provision of essential care to individuals with health problems
Primary health care	System-wide (e.g., from provision of care to individuals to action on the determinants of health)	Intersectoral partners, community members	• Micro, meso, and macro levels • Multifaceted: from provision of essential care to individuals to changing social and economic policy
Health promotion	Determinants of health	Community members, health professionals, government and non-governmental organizations	• Micro level (e.g., individuals and small groups); Meso level (e.g., organizations and community coalitions) • Bottom-up development of capacity of individuals and groups to change the things that affect health in the community
Population health	Determinants of health	Government and non-governmental organizations	• Macro level (e.g., government policy and legislative change); Meso level (e.g., organizational change) • Top-down strategies to influence broad social and economic factors

FIGURE 6.1 Yukon Registered Nurses Association Model of Health and Illness

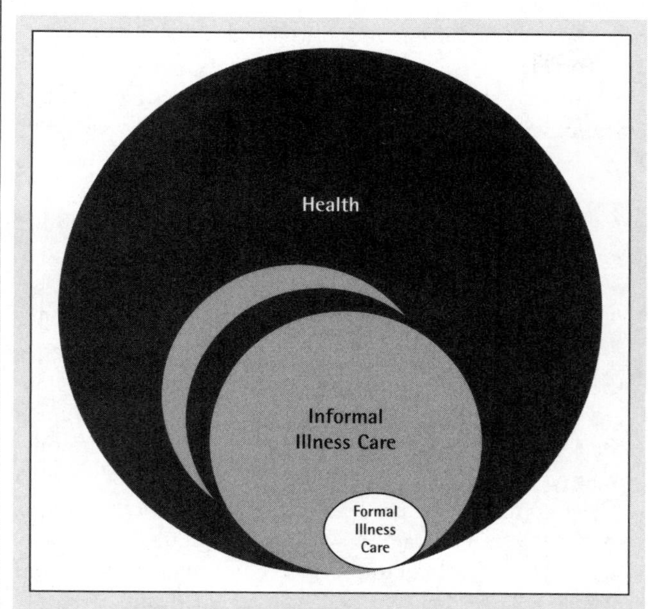

Source: Reproduced by permission from Yukon Registered Nurses Association. (2002). The Preferred Future for the Health and Illness Care of Canadians: Statement to the Commission on the Future of Health Care. Whitehorse, YT: Author.

The largest circle in Figure 6.1 represents health, whether individual, family, community, or society. "Health encompasses all the determinants that support our biological, psychological, social, and spiritual components. Clean air and water; appropriate shelter; adequate food; opportunities for physical activity and social interactions in families, schools, communities and groups; meaningful work; and freedom of worship" (Yukon Registered Nurses Association [YRNA], 2002, p.1) are necessary prerequisites or determinants of health (Health Canada, 2001). Primary health care identifies these as the basic requirements for people to lead "socially and economically productive lives." The importance of these determinants of health has been repeatedly acknowledged (Health Canada, 2001; Health & Welfare Canada, 1986; WHO, 1986; 1997); however, they are only marginally addressed within the current illness-oriented system.

The smaller circle "represents illness and particularly, informal illness care. This circle has a dashed outline to represent that illness is a part of health and that we move in and out of this circle throughout our lives" (YRNA, p. 2). The YRNA model is congruent with primary health care in that it acknowledges that informal illness care handles most of our health needs and illnesses through self-care and with the support of family and friends. A primary health care approach acknowledges the importance of supporting individual and community capacity to manage their health through such preventive, promoting, and healing activities.

The slightly larger rings around informal illness care "represent the formal health promotion and illness prevention work of organizations such as home care, public health, health inspection, hospice, and so on." The smallest circle "represents the formal illness care and includes primarily hospital and physician services" (YRNA, p. 2) and consumes the largest proportion of our health care dollars. This circle includes both frontline and tertiary medical care. The system is dominated by a biomedical orientation and tends to focus on pathology—the diagnosis and treatment of disease. While these illness-care services are important and highly valued by Canadians, they are only a small part of a much more broadly health-oriented, multi-faceted, community-driven approach in a system based on the primary health care model.

As suggested in Figure 6.2, community development requires an understanding and careful handling of community history, resources, and key players.

While the process shown in Figure 6.2 resembles the nursing process of assessment, planning, implementation, and evaluation, there are several key differences. Foremost is the CHN's role as facilitator, rather than as definer or controller of the process. In a community development approach, CHNs engage with citizens to develop a mutual understanding of issues and priorities, resources, and challenges. Their essential ability to actively listen to and understand the experiences of people and organizations in a community enables them to effectively promote dialogue and synthesize similarities and differences among community members. "Through multiple ways of knowing, community health nurses develop the ability to question the status quo and take action for health" (CHNAC, 2003, p. 9). Creating a climate of trust and curiosity, along with exploratory dialogue, also facilitates others to question the status quo, and is an important precursor to a shared envisioning and creation of plans for action (Lindsay & Hartrick, 1996).

Primary health care values and principles are respected in a community-owned and -driven process, from entry right through to intervention and evaluation. This approach builds the skills and capacity of those involved in the process, contributing to sustainability. For professionals accustomed to externally imposed deadlines, hierarchical control, and differential valuing of expert versus lay knowledge, community development requires considerable patience, humility, and learning. Finally, CHNs using this philosophical and practice approach would include themselves as part of the community being "developed," rather than as external controllers of the process. Thus, Figure 6.2 offers a practical guide for a process that is philosophically congruent with primary health care despite outward resemblances to an expert-controlled model.

FIGURE 6.2 Healthy Communities: The Process

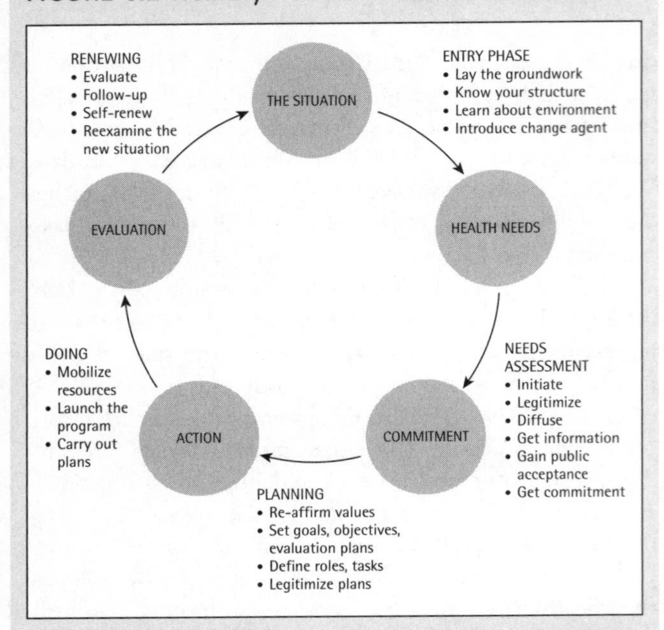

Source: Reproduced by permission from BC Ministry of Health. (1994). Healthy communities: The process. Victoria, BC: Author.

Essential to CHNs' work in community development is the notion of empowerment. Empowerment is a concept closely related to social justice. "Empowerment is an active, involved process where people, groups, and communities move toward increased individual and community control, political efficacy, improved quality of community life, and social justice" (CHNAC, 2003, p. 10). CHNs use empowerment in their work with all levels of clients, whether they be individuals, families, small groups, or whole communities. The variety in the relationships that they have with all levels of clients often enhances their effectiveness.

Labonte's (1993) Empowerment Holosphere (Figure 6.3) shows the overlap in CHNs' work with individual clients (personal care), families or small groups as client, or whole communities as client (community organization, coalition advocacy, and political action). CHNs practise all of these five roles to implement the principles of primary health care. For example, in their individual and family as client work during postnatal visits, a CHN develops an intimate understanding of the joys and challenges unique to each new mother's experiences. As is common in rapidly growing suburbs, some new mothers may be at home alone with their babies and not yet socially integrated into their new community. Individual and family health promotion is a critical part of supporting the woman and her family, helping them develop their capacity to manage the challenges of new parenthood in a new community setting. CHNs also use their understanding of the issue, the relationships they develop through one-on-one interactions with many new mothers during postnatal visits, and their knowledge of community organizations in order to facilitate "women-owned" education, support, and activity groups. This health promotion strategy builds the capacity of the individuals who choose to get involved and develops linkages between the women who have a variety of strengths and challenges but who just happen to be new to the community. Small-group development builds linkages, shares resources, and provides support in a variety of sectors, as well as between women with similar interests and experiences. This kind of community health nursing intervention may go well beyond

Canadian Research Box 6.1

Valaitis, R. (2002). "They don't trust us; we're just kids." Views about community from predominantly female inner city youth. *Health Care for Women International, 23*, 243–266.

The aim of this qualitative research was to "explore youths' perceptions about the meaning of community, their experiences of 'being heard' by adults about community issues, their understanding of their ability to effect community change, and their perceptions of ways to get adults to hear their thoughts about community" (p. 251). The participating inner city school was located near the steel mills in southwestern Ontario. Twenty-three of 35 students approached consented to participate in the study. Eleven students were in Grade 7, and 12 in Grade 8. Seven students were members of visible minorities, 13 were on the school honour roll, and 19 were female. Data were collected via focus groups, sentence-completion exercises, and field notes from facilitators taken during one-hour debriefing sessions after the focus groups. Sentence completion exercises were completed individually by students in the school computer lab.

"The results of this study revealed that youth were able to articulate the meaning of community. [They described community as] physical infrastructure, people, and community functions and relationships" (p. 261). Interestingly, incongruencies between youths' idealized views of community and their negative community experiences were detected. Two other themes included "threats to empowerment" and "empowerment." Threats to empowerment included youths' perception of having little control in decision making ("grown-ups run everything"), being low in the social hierarchy ("we're just kids"), and a strong mistrust between youth and adults in the broader community ("they don't trust us"). Empowerment subthemes related to a perceived sense of support from certain adults; feelings of self-efficacy in smaller, more familiar settings; and a belief in group action and procuring support from adults who know them to overcome their perceived lower social status.

Discussion Questions

1. Identify how CHNs could use the methods in this study to facilitate empowerment of youth through community development.
2. How could CHNs in your community use the results of this study to enhance youth participation in health-related activities?

FIGURE 6.3 The Empowerment Holosphere

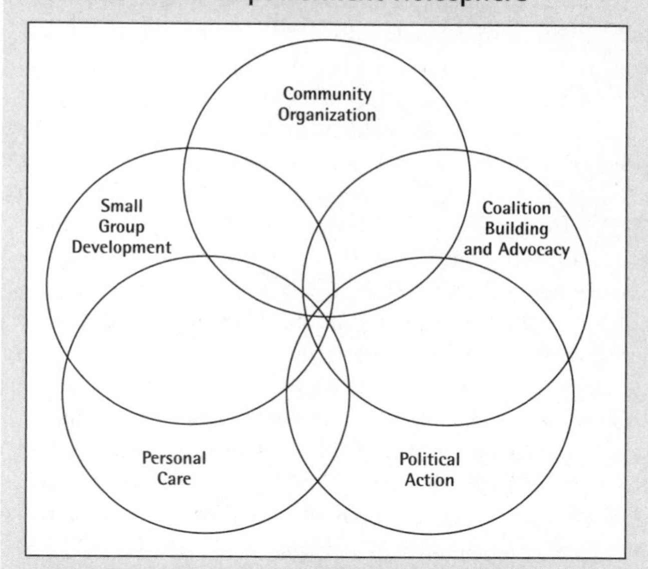

Source: Reproduced with permission from Labonte, R. (1993). A holosphere of healthy and sustainable communities. Australian Journal of Public Health, 17, *4–12.*

the impact that a health professional could provide in a one-to-one client-professional relationship.

CHNs can also use their understanding of individual and community issues to mobilize interested citizens and organizations to take action. For example, CHNs have often facilitated the opening of Planned Parenthood Services in their communities in response to poor access to sensitive and relevant reproductive health services. Development of such initiatives often requires full and sensitive engagement in the community development process. CHNs are also involved in community organization and coalition advocacy for heart health, being key players in the Canadian Heart Health Initiative. This initiative has engaged private and public sector partners to participate in environmental change that supports heart health, injury prevention, and tobacco-use reduction (Canadian Heart Health Initiative, 1998; Kuhn, Doucet, & Edwards, 1999). This work demonstrates the primary health care principle of intersectoral cooperation. For example, the recreation sector has developed walking trails and other environmental factors that support a more active lifestyle. Private sector restaurants are increasingly implementing "heart healthy" menu choices.

The primary health care principles of accessibility, health promotion, and public participation are often used in CHNs' community development work in which the community is the client. For example, political action has been used by CHNs to increase access to adequate housing and change legislation to prevent drunk driving and make bicycle helmets mandatory. A well-known example is the work of Cathy Crowe, a street nurse, educator, and social activist. She co-founded Nurses for Social Responsibility, the Toronto Coalition Against Homelessness, and the Toronto Disaster Relief Committee. The latter organization seeks to have homelessness declared a national disaster (Ward & Piccolo, 2001).

The text box, Canadian Community Health Nursing Practice, illustrates how CHNs used community development to enact the five principles of primary health care (CNA, 2000) in the development of the Brock Youth Centre. Critical thinking exercises related to the Brock Youth Centre are provided at the end of the chapter.

CHNs use their expertise with empowerment and community development to enact the larger primary health care values of equity and social justice in a variety of ways. Though not a linear process, identification of health and socioeconomic inequalities and taking action on their root causes are critical components of practising primary health care. The rapid growth of homelessness in Canada provides a contemporary example of CHNs' practise of primary health care to tackle this worsening social-justice issue. Changes in Canada's social, political, and economic structures are widening the gap between the rich and poor and creating inequalities in opportunity for health. Toronto's shantytown, described in the Case Study, is an example of homelessness that is typical in many communities across Canada. An approach is required that focuses on rectifying those macro-level factors that enable homelessness to flourish. In addition, a stronger emphasis on a primary health care approach will be needed to prevent the further growth of homelessness in Canadian society, while at the same time caring for those who are currently disenfranchised. The part that CHNs have played in tackling this issue demonstrates the key concepts in this chapter (e.g., primary health care, empowerment, community development) and is portrayed in the video, *Street Nurse* (Ward & Piccolo, 2001).

ACHIEVING A PRIMARY HEALTH CARE SYSTEM IN CANADA

The World Health Organization's primary health care approach (WHO, 1978) was predominantly viewed as an approach to address health issues in developing countries. Eight years later, the *Ottawa Charter for Health Promotion* (WHO, 1986) was developed. The *Ottawa Charter* shares many of the key values and principles of primary health care and has been more readily adopted by developed nations. For example, the Canadian government's *Achieving Health for All* framework (Health and Welfare Canada, 1986) reflected the rapid and extensive acceptance of the Ottawa Charter in Canada. Despite these endorsements of the charter's values and principles, Canada has been slow in implementing primary health care. Systemic and attitudinal barriers must be acknowledged and addressed before the country can move forward on the road to primary health care.

Hutchinson, Abelson, and Lavis (2001) describe how systemic and attitudinal barriers become self-reinforcing and increasingly resistant to change through the creation of institutions. In Canada, a change to different systems such as primary health care is stifled by the structural and ideological legacy of three major policies. First, the *BNA Act* of 1867 gave responsibility for health care to the provinces, presenting a significant legislative barrier to *national* health care reform. Second, the limitation of compulsory coverage to hospitals

Canadian Community Health Nursing Practice

The Brock Youth Centre

The Brock Youth Centre is one example of a community development project initiated by CHNs. The project began in 1998 with a series of community needs assessments implemented by local CHNs, the Brock Township municipal council, and youth service organizations with some assistance from non-governmental agencies (e.g., the Addiction Research Foundation). This group found that area youth were at risk due to lack of access to services and few youth-friendly spaces and environments. Youth also reported feeling that they were negatively perceived by area adults. Interventions were needed to create youth-friendly spaces; increase youth knowledge, leadership, and decision-making skills; and contribute to healthy self-esteem and a sense of community belonging.

This initially led to creation of Summer Camp 1999, a capacity-building intervention that sought to change the image of youth within the community from negative to positive. The success of this summer camp led to development of a community-supported, youth-created, and youth-led organization. Now in its fourth year, "Youth for Youth" has evolved into an incorporated, non-profit, grassroots, community organization. The project has its own space and identity in the historical Town Hall in Cannington, Ontario and provides services on a rotating basis to the surrounding areas of Beaverton and Sunderland. Essential to the program's success is leadership from youth and local community members and in-kind and administrative support from key community organizations such as Brock Township. Examples of how the primary health care principles used a community development approach to develop the Brock Youth Centre are described below.

Accessibility

The community needs assessment identified that youth lacked access to health, social, employment, and recreation services. Survey results and community consultation suggested that this lack of access was due to inconsistency of political borders, lack of available health and social services within Brock Township, and a generally negative attitude toward youth in the community. Improvements achieved through community development include greater access to supportive adults and peers, more recreation opportunities at the youth centre, a summer camp program, enhanced crisis intervention, behaviour management, and health education services through linkages with community partners.

Public Participation

The Brock Youth Centre project aims to engage youth and community organizations in genuine rather than token forms of participation (Arnstein, 1969; Wilcox, 2002). Connecting youth and community members with opportunities to use their voice in ways that are meaningful to them was critical to capacity building and the creation of a more socially just local society. Providing support to enable "quieter" voices to be heard at the decision-making table was critical to CHNs' advocacy role. Numerous outcomes of youth participation are evident in the Brock Youth Centre programs. Youth have developed the program logo "Kids Helping Kids Have Fun" and the Youth Centre name and logo, "Brockin-Dropin." However, CHNs provided important support and facilitation. They facilitated youth involvement, creatively identified and accessed resources, and ensured public celebration of achievements and outside recognition. They accessed resources to support the logo development by youth through the Youth Services Canada Project Kick Off Contest. Additional resources to support youth ownership and voice in the project were secured through Youth Participation Study, Youth Services Canada Project (Administered by Brock Township), and connections to Town Youth Participation Strategies (TYPS) Provincial Network. Youth and community participation has been officially recognized by winning the first ever, *Rural Youth in Action Achievement Award* through the Community Foundation for Rural Living.

Health Promotion

Capacity building is key to health promotion and community development (Frank & Smith, 1999). The Brock Youth Centre has maintained a capacity building approach. For example, multi-level mentorship initiatives involve youth at various stages of growth and leadership development, strengthening program effectiveness and sustainability. Flexibility and creativity have enabled many youth to remain involved in spite of moving on to diverse work and study opportunities. After four years of consistent facilitation and follow-through with the principles of community development and primary health care, the project is now focusing on developing the capacity of the community board. For example, 30 adults and 30 youth will be trained to work in genuine partnership to fulfill administrative, program development, and media relations functions of the centre. The Brock Youth Centre demonstrates how balancing small group development, advocacy, community organizing, and political action is essential to achieving sustainability in community development. Community development skills such as grantsmanship, conflict resolution, and advocacy for inclusion of previously marginalized groups were vital throughout this process.

Appropriate Technology

The Brock Youth Centre exemplifies how CHNs used a community development approach to implement and achieve the principles of primary health care. The resulting activities and interventions succeeded at reducing risk-taking behaviours and highlighting youth's positive contributions to their communities. Rather than developing a "high-tech" model of service delivery by health care specialists to manage "troubled youth," the community came up with low-tech, capacity-oriented interventions that matched the youth and community needs with local resources.

Intersectoral Cooperation

Engagement in an extensive network of intersectoral organizations requires consistent and sustained communication, networking, coordination, and reciprocal exchanges of ideas and support. Careful nurturing of partnerships with youth and the support of the local community remains central to the vision and success of the Brock Youth Centre. Intersectoral linkages have been developed and continue to be nurtured at the local, regional, and provincial level. Local partnerships have been developed with agencies such as the Cartwright Youth Activity Centre, the Brock Community Needs Project, local school councils, the North Durham Homeless Initiative, and the Brock Community Employment Resource Centre, as well as with local businesses and service clubs. Regional engagement and resource sharing has occurred through involvement with the North Durham Social Development Council and the newly formed Regional Youth Centre Network. The Brock Youth Centre is involved in several provincial organizations, including the Ontario Healthy Communities Coalition, TeenNet at the University of Toronto, the Town Youth Participation Strategies network (TYPS), and the Youth Services Network.

Note: Many thanks to community health nurses Tracy Prinzen, Kathy McLaughlin, and Pam Frisby and supporting participants of the Brock Youth Centre for sharing their stories.

and physician services was entrenched by the *Hospital and Diagnostic Services Act* of 1957, which has resulted in a lingering belief system that equates technology and curative intervention with health care. Third, public payment for private medical practice was established through the *Medical Care Act* of 1968, further reinforcing the curative focus for the health system. Despite the successful lobbying by the Canadian Nurses Association and other organizations to broaden the scope of providers in the Canada Health Act, the entrenchment of physicians as the point of entry into the health care system remains relatively unchanged.

In order to succeed, a change to a primary health care approach would require a window of opportunity or receptiveness to new values, the willingness of key stakeholders to overcome the barriers to change that have been imposed by existing legislative arrangements, and an additional source of funding. There has been a slow but steady development of conditions to support such a change. In the late 1980s and early 1990s, significant interest in health system change was evident in the numerous commissions on health care across the country (Angus, 1995). The conclusions reached by a majority of the commissions reflected a growing recognition for the need to address inequities in health and supported the approach and philosophy of primary health care (Mhatre & Deber, 1992). These resulted in several concerted efforts on behalf of provincial and territorial governments and institutions to advance the primary health care agenda. For example, in Nova Scotia, the provincial government funded a Task Force on Primary Health Care. From 1994–1999, the Federal Government sponsored the National Forum on Health, a forum of experts and citizens from across the country. They produced several reports and emphasized the need for action on the determinants of health, the importance of using evidence to inform health system intervention and change, and the need to shift to more upstream approaches. As a result, the Health Transition Fund was created to support initiatives that would test and demonstrate effectiveness of alternative approaches. As Hutchinson et al. (2001) suggest, small, incremental, localized changes, through mechanisms such as demonstration projects, are often a more effective approach to broad policy change. Although operationalizing primary health care was not its fundamental aim, the Eskasoni Primary Care Project is an example of a small incremental step (see Canadian Research Box 6.2). Its successes and challenges also demonstrate the magnitude and complexity of health care reform.

Nursing Involvement in Primary Health Care Reform

CHNs have been active in promoting primary health care since its adoption by the World Health Assembly (Maglacas, 1988; Labelle, 1986). The numerous primary health care demonstration projects that have been fought for and initiated by CHNs have made significant contributions to advancing the "health for all" agenda in Canada. CHNs' roles and close relationships with individual and community clients enable them to observe the strengths and gaps in the current health care system. Their expertise with community development has been vital to their success in implementing primary health care demonstration projects. For example, nurses in Newfoundland have gained key insights into health care reform based on the Danish–Newfoundland Primary Health Care Project and other primary health care initiatives (Association of Registered Nurses of Newfoundland & Labrador, 2002). In Nova Scotia, nurses were integral to the development and success of the Cheticamp Primary Health Care Project, which focused on cultural awareness, economic development, education, general community development, organizational development, self-help, and social support (Downe-Wamboldt, Roland, LeBlanc, & Arsenault, 1994). The Registered Nurses Association of Ontario has been closely involved in the formation and ongoing action of the Coalition for Primary Health Care. This organization continues its public education, coalition advocacy, and political action strategies to promote adoption of a primary health care approach (Coalition for Primary Health Care, 2000).

Canadian Research Box 6.2

Hampton, M. J. (2001). *The Eskasoni story: Final report of the Eskasoni Primary Care Project.* Health Transition Fund, Health Canada.

Sims-Jones, N. (2003). The Eskasoni Primary Care Project. *Health Policy Research Bulletin, 5,* 14–15.

"Eskasoni [is] a classic case of a community having many of the right health care resources available, but lacking integration of health information, coordination among programs, collaboration among providers, and a strategy to improve overall health status" (Hampton, 2001, p. 28). In the Eskasoni Primary Care Project, the traditional fee-for-service approach was replaced with a multidisciplinary primary care team employing salaried physicians for an on-reserve First Nations community of 3200 people with a high incidence of chronic disease, addictions, and utilization of the health care system. The high morbidity and mortality were associated with high rates of substance abuse, smoking (60%), diabetes (40%), heart disease, and respiratory illnesses among adults. Complications of diabetes, including vision impairment, kidney disease, and amputations, were not uncommon (Hampton, 2001). Prior to this project, each resident of Eskasoni made an average of 11 medical visits per year. Community health nursing, communicable disease control including immunization, and nutrition education during pregnancy services were provided in this community. However, these preventive services were neither coordinated nor integrated with one another nor with the physician. Gaps in service were common, such as little prenatal care available for pregnant women.

The project resulted in more appropriate utilization of physician services, hospital-based services, prescription drugs, and health promotion programs. Salaried physicians had adequate time to spend on preventive care and encouraged interdisciplinary management of clients with complex medical needs. The number of physician visits per client has dropped to four visits per year and visits to the emergency department declined by 40%. Referral from local family doctors to the team's nutritionist/health educator for diabetic management increased by 850%. Fewer antibiotics, antihistamines, and cough preparations were prescribed, and the overall costs for prescriptions decreased. Prenatal care improved significantly, with 96% of pregnant women in the community receiving appropriate care.

Despite considerable efforts at integration, federally and provincially funded staff continued to work in isolation. Furthermore, procedural difficulties in diverting funding from the fee-for-service system to support alternative primary care models is a significant barrier to adoption of this new approach. While it emphasized a change in delivery of primary care services, the Eskasoni Project demonstrated that health care reform requires readiness and acceptance from the community, willingness and personal commitment from government stakeholders, and partnership with stakeholders from other key sectors (e.g., an educational institution to facilitate recruitment of appropriate personnel). It also shows how significant health care reform in Canada may need to be achieved community by community, as opportunities for progressive incremental change arise.

Discussion Questions

1. Which of the principles of primary health care were operationalized in the change from the old to the new approach to providing primary care services?
2. Discuss how residents of Eskasoni may have received most of the interventions in this project. Were interventions directed primarily at individuals, families, groups, or the community as client?

The Registered Nurses Association of British Columbia (RNABC) was at the forefront of developing models for the application of the primary health care approach in British Columbia. Their New Directions initiative made a significant contribution through the development of a series of background papers, a concerted professional and public education strategy to inform nurses and the public about primary health care, and policy development on nurses' potential to contribute to improved health within a primary health care-based system (RNABC, 1998). The RNABC advocated for and achieved government commitment to launch primary health care demonstration projects and initiated a community-determined process that resulted in establishing a nursing centre in a small rural community on Vancouver Island (Clarke & Mass, 1998). Other provincial nursing associations in Canada have also been active in promoting primary health care.

Future Directions of Primary Health Care Reform in Canada

CHNs have been effective in implementing innovative approaches to primary health care in a number of provinces and settings in Canada. They have been active as care providers, researchers, administrators, and educators in building the capacity needed to implement primary health care in Canadian and international contexts. CHNs have used their organizational base to influence the direction of health policy in Canada and abroad. And they have contributed to the research base needed to inform the design of interventions with special populations and in challenging contexts.

However, CHNs must critically evaluate the consistency and coherence of their own efforts with respect to the values of primary health care. As Labelle (1986) stated more than 25 years ago, CHNs have several sources of power close at hand, including their presence in multiple settings and at all levels in society, direct and continuous contact with the public, access to and control over massive amounts of information, and access to communication channels and linkages between each other through their organizational structures. What Labelle identified then, and what has been validated through research, is that CHNs' fundamental commitment to equity and social justice has made them some of the most trusted members of society (Buresh & Gordon, 2000). While they have demonstrated that they can use these sources of power effectively, they must do so more consistently and strategically.

At a time of growing inequities in health in Canada and waning political commitment to implementing social and economic interventions to narrow that gap (Raphael, 2002), CHNs must continue to work in multiple roles to create the environments and capacity needed to achieve health for all. Primary health care was at the forefront of the movement that recognized and insisted that "health is not simply a repair business after the fact.... Health has a lot to do with individual lifestyle choices, how safe our communities are, how well designed our roads and cars are, and other aspects of public policy" (Decter, 1994, p. 25). Now more than ever, CHNs must expand their participation in community organization, coalition building and advocacy, and political action activities to increase awareness and action on the inequities in health.

On an international scale, "global health inequities" has recently attracted the attention initially called for in the *Declaration of Alma Ata* (Canadian Nurses Association, 2003). Just as they have made significant contributions to the action on gaps in health between groups within Canada, CHNs must add their expertise to the growing imperative to address inequities in health between countries (Labonte & Spiegel, 2001). Thus, at various levels, CHNs can contribute to creation of local to global health care delivery systems that exemplify the values and principles of primary health care. However, similar to the act of recycling to protect the environment, individual CHNs can implement these same values and principles in their practice on a daily basis. One person alone may not make a big impact at a macro level, but if each CHN works toward the same goals, it is more likely to impact the entire system.

SUMMARY

This chapter discussed the concept and definition of primary health care and a description of its overall approach. The importance of understanding primary health care based on its original description in the *Declaration of Alma Ata* was highlighted. Its principles and elements, as well as the philosophy and values at its heart were identified, and its fit with nursing values explored. Primary health care and related terms were defined and compared. The Yukon Registered Nurses Association model of health and illness provided an example of how to articulate differences between primary health care and related terms. Community health nursing's practice of community development and empowerment to implement primary health care values and principles were discussed, using models that depict these two practice strategies.

A case study demonstrated the community health nursing practice of community development and empowerment in a rural area, providing an example of how these approaches are put into practice and emphasizing the intersectoral and community owned nature of primary health care. The example of homelessness in urban Canada demonstrates how political, social, and economic structures contribute to socio-economic inequalities and inequities in health. Provincial and regional examples of primary health care reform efforts, including those initiated by nursing, are described. A description of the Eskasoni Primary Care Project illustrates the difference between primary health care approaches aimed at root causes of poor health and primary care interventions. Factors influencing the shape and extent of primary health care reform in Canada are summarized. Finally, CHNs are challenged to develop and implement strategies that address these macro- and meso-level root causes of inequities in health.

KEY TERMS

primary health care
social justice
equity in health
macro, micro, meso levels
accessibility
public participation
health promotion
appropriate technology
intersectoral cooperation
primary care
primary nursing
health promotion
population health
determinants of health
community development
empowerment

STUDY QUESTIONS

1. Describe the difference between primary health care and primary care.
2. Describe the differences and similarities between primary health care, population health, and health promotion.
3. Describe and illustrate with examples how CHNs in your home community incorporate the principles of primary health care into their practice.
4. Describe and give an example of each of the five roles shown in Figure 6.3.
5. Define the five principles of primary health care developed by the Canadian Nurses Association.
6. Describe various interventions to promote the health for homeless people in Canada.

INDIVIDUAL CRITICAL THINKING EXERCISES

1. Why is it important for CHNs to study and understand the *Declaration of Alma Ata*?
2. Visit the website of your provincial/territorial Ministry of Health. Search for information on primary health care or health care reform (you may have to be creative in your search). What (if any) attempts have been made to implement a primary health care model? Are roles for CHNs and other health care providers described? Do reform efforts address the principles of primary health care?
3. Visit the website of your provincial/territorial nursing association. Search for policy or position statements on primary health care. Look for description of activities that influence or contribute to health care reform. Discuss the initiative with your peers and colleagues. Identify opportunities for CHNs to participate in the initiative, and reflect on how you can become involved.
4. Why is it important for you as a CHN to understand your own values? How does this relate to the role of CHNs as facilitators of primary health care policy and action at local, regional, provincial, or national levels? Practise writing reflectively about your experiences in community health nursing practice.
5. Compare your findings on nursing association policy with that of your provincial ministry.

GROUP CRITICAL THINKING EXERCISES

1. Practise explaining primary health care to your friends and family members. Describe how nursing has and will continue to contribute to reform efforts aimed at the root causes of poor health.
2. Working in small groups, identify how a primary care approach may have differed from the broader primary health care actions taken by the CHNs in the development of the Brock Youth Centre.
3. As community developers in small communities such as Eskasoni, how might community health nurses apply the *Healthy Communities: The Process* model?

REFERENCES

Angus, D. (1995). *Health care reform: Revisiting the review of significant health care commissions and task forces.* Ottawa, ON: Canada Community Health Nurses Association.

Arnstein, S. (1969). Ladder of citizen participation. *American Institute of Planners, 35,* 216–224.

Association of Registered Nurses of Newfoundland & Labrador. (2002). *Sustaining our public health care system.* Submission to the Commission on the Future of Health Care in Canada.

Bezruchka, S. (2002). Forward. In D. Raphael, *Social justice is good for our hearts: Why societal factors—not lifestyles—are major causes of heart disease in Canada and elsewhere.* Toronto, ON: Centre for Social Justice, Foundation for Research and Education. Retrieved July 2002 from **www.socialjustice.org/pdfs/JusticeGoodHearts.pdf**

British Columbia Ministry of Health. (1987). *Healthy communities: The process.* Victoria, BC: Author.

Buresh, B., & Gordon, S. (2000). *From silence to voice: What nurses know and must communicate to the public.* Ottawa, ON: Canadian Nurses Association.

Canadian Heart Health Initiative. (1998). *Canadian Heart Health database centre.* St. John's, NF: Memorial University of Newfoundland. Retrieved January 2003 from **www.med.mun.ca/chhdbc/**

Canadian Nurses Association. (1997). *Code of ethics for registered nurses.* Ottawa, ON: Author.

Canadian Nurses Association. (2000). *Fact sheet: The primary health care approach.* Ottawa, ON: Author.

Canadian Nurses Association. (2003). Global health and equity. Position statement. Retrieved November 30 from **www.cna-nurses.ca/pages/policies/global health and equity_june 2003.pdf**

Clarke, H., & Mass, H. (1998). Comox Valley Nursing Centre: From collaboration to empowerment. *Public Health Nursing, 15*(3), 216–224.

Community Health Nurses Association of Canada (CHNAC). (2003). *Canadian community health nursing standards of practice.* Ottawa, ON: Author.

Coalition for Primary Health Care. (2000). *Primary health care coalition: Backgrounder.* Toronto, ON: Author.

Culyer, A. (1992). *Equity in health care policy. A discussion paper.* Toronto, ON: Premier's Council on Health, Well-Being and Social Justice.

Decter, M. (1994). *Healing medicare: Managing health system change the Canadian way.* Toronto, ON: McGilligan Books.

Downe-Wamboldt, B., Roland, F., LeBlanc,B., & Arsenault, D. (1994). Cheticamp primary health care project. *Nurse to Nurse, 3,* 14–15.

Evans, R., Barer, M., & Marmor, T. (Eds.). (1994). *Why are some people healthy and others not. The determinants of health of populations.* New York: Aldine de Gruyter.

Federal, Provincial, and Territorial Advisory Committee on Population Health. (1999). *Toward a healthy future: Second report on the health of Canadians.* Ottawa, ON: Health Canada.

Frank, F., & Smith, A. (1999). *The community development handbook: A tool to build community capacity.* Ottawa, ON: Human Resources Development Canada.

Hampton, M. J. (2001). *The Eskasoni story. Final report of the Eskasoni primary care project.* Health Transition Fund, Health Canada.

Health Canada. (2001). *The population health template: Key elements and actions that define a population health approach.* Ottawa, ON: Health Canada, Population and Public Health Branch, Strategic Policy Directorate.

Health Canada. (2002). *The population health template working tool.* Ottawa, ON: Health Canada, Population and Public Health Branch, Strategic Policy Directorate. Retrieved November 2003 from **www.hc- sc.gc.ca/hppb/phdd/pdf/template_tool.pdf**

Health and Welfare Canada. (1986). *Achieving health for all: Framework for health promotion.* Ottawa, ON: Author.

Hutchinson, B., Abelson, J., & Lavis, J. (2001). Primary care in Canada: So much innovation, so little change. *Health Affairs, 20,* 116–131.

Kawachi, I., Subramanian, S., & Almeida-Filho, N. (2002). A glossary for health inequalities. *Journal of Epidemiology and Community Health, 56,* 647–652.

Kuhn, M., Doucet, C., & Edwards, N. (1999). *Effectiveness of coalitions in heart health promotion, tobacco use reduction, and injury prevention: A systematic review of the literature 1990–1998.* Toronto, ON: Ontario Ministry of Health, Public Health Branch, Effective Public Health Practice Project.

Labelle, H. (1986). Nurses as a social force. *Journal of Advanced Nursing, 11,* 247–253.

Labonte, R. (1993). A holosphere of healthy and sustainable communities. *Australian Journal of Public Health, 17,* 4–12.

Labonte, R., & Spiegel, G. (2001). *Setting global health priorities for funding Canadian researchers.* Ottawa, ON: Canadian Institutes for Health Research, Institute of Population and Public Health.

Lavis, J. (2002). Ideas at the margin or marginalized ideas? Non-medical determinants of health in Canada. *Health Affairs, 21*(2), 107–112.

Lindsey, E., & Hartrick, G. (1996). Health promoting nursing practice: The demise of the nursing process? *Journal of Advanced Nursing, 23,* 106–112.

Macinko, J., & Starfield, B. (2002). Annotated bibliography on equity and health. *International Journal for Equity and Health, 1*(1), 1–20.

Maglacas, A. (1988). Health for all: Nursing's role. *Nursing Outlook, 36*(2), 666–671.

Mhatre, S., & Deber, R. (1992). From equal access to health care to equitable access to health: A review of Canadian provincial health commissions and reports. *International Journal of Health Services, 22*(4), 645–668.

Raphael, D. (2002). *Social justice is good for our hearts: Why societal factors—not lifestyles—are major causes of heart disease in Canada and elsewhere.* Toronto, ON: Centre for Social Justice, Foundation for Research and Education. Retrieved July 2002 from **www.socialjustice.org/pdfs/JusticeGoodHearts.pdf**

Registered Nurses Association of British Columbia. (1998). *The new health care: A nursing perspective.* Vancouver, BC: Author.

Smedley, B., & Syme, L. (2000). *Promoting health: Intervention strategies from social and behavioral research.* Washington, DC: National Academy Press.

Stanhope, M., & Lancaster, J. (2002). *Foundations of community health nursing: Community oriented practice.* St. Louis, MO: Mosby.

Starfield, B. (1998). *Primary care: Balancing health needs, services and technology.* New York: Oxford University Press.

Wallerstein, N., & Bernstein, E. (1994). Introduction to community empowerment, participatory education, and health. *Health Education Quarterly, 21*(2), 141–148.

Ward, M., & Piccolo, C. (2001, Winter). It's because I am a nurse. *Medhunters,* 1–4. Retrieved January 2003 from **www.medhuntersmagazine.com/PDFstories/winter2001/ItsBecauseIAmANurse.pdf**

Wilcox, D. (2002). *The guide to development trusts and partnerships.* London: Development Trusts Association. Retrieved November 2003 from **www.partnerships.org.uk/pguide/pships.htm**

Wilkinson, R. (1996). *Unhealthy societies: The afflictions of inequality.* New York: Rutledge.

Wolfson, M., Kaplan, G., Lynch, J., Ross, N., Backlund, E., Gravelle, H. et al. (1999). Relation between income inequality and mortality: Empirical demonstration. *British Medical Journal, 319,* 953–957.

World Health Organization. (1978). *The Declaration of Alma Ata.* Geneva, Switzerland: Author. Retrieved November 2003 from **www.who.dk/eprise/main/WHO/AboutWHO/Policy/20010827_1**

World Health Organization. (1986). *Ottawa charter for health promotion.* Geneva, Switzerland: Author.

World Health Organization. (1997). *The Jakarta Declaration.* Geneva, Switzerland: Author.

Yukon Registered Nurses Association. (2002). *Submission to the Romanow Commission on the Future of Health Care.* Whitehorse, YT: Author.

ADDITIONAL RESOURCES

BOOKS

British Columbia Ministry of Health. (1987). *Healthy communities: The process.* Victoria, BC: Author.

Canadian Nurses Association. (2000). *Fact sheet: The primary health care approach.* Ottawa, ON: Author.

Community Health Nurses Association of Canada (CHNAC). (2002). *Canadian community health nursing standards of practice.* Ottawa, ON: Author.

Evans, R., Barer, M., & Marmor, T. (Eds.). (1994). *Why are some people healthy and others not. The determinants of health of populations.* New York: Aldine de Gruyter.

Federal, Provincial, and Territorial Advisory Committee on Population Health. (1999). *Toward a healthy future: Second report on the health of Canadians.* Ottawa, ON: Health Canada.

Frank, F., & Smith, A. (1999). *The community development handbook: A tool to build community capacity.* Ottawa, ON: Human Resources Development Canada.

Labonte, R. (1993). A holosphere of healthy and sustainable communities. *Australian Journal of Public Health, 17,* 4–12.

Registered Nurses Association of British Columbia. (1998). *The new health care: A nursing perspective.* Vancouver, BC: Author.

Wallerstein, N., & Bernstein, E. (1994). Introduction to community empowerment, participatory education, and health. *Health Education Quarterly, 21*(2), 141–148.

WEBSITES

Canadian Nurses Association:
www.cna-nurses.ca

The Canadian Health Network:
www.canadian-health-network.ca/

The Canadian Public Health Association:
www.cpha.ca

The Canadian Institute for Health Information:
www.cihi.ca

Canadian Population Health Initiative:
http://secure.cihi.ca/cihiweb/dispPage.jsp?cw_page=cphi_e

Canadian Health Indicators Project:
http://secure.cihi.ca/cihiweb/dispPage.jsp?cw_page=indicators_online_e

Canada Council on Social Development:
www.ccsd.ca/

Defining and Redefining Poverty:
www.ccsd.ca/pubs/2001/povertypp.htm

Centre for Social Justice:
www.socialjustice.org/

Primary Health Care Transition Fund:
www.hc-sc.gc.ca/phctf-fassp/english/

The Guide to Development Trusts and Partnerships:
www.partnerships.org.uk/pguide/pships.htm

United Kingdom Health Equity Network:
www.ukhen.org.uk/

International Society for Equity and Health:
www.iseqh.org/index.html

World Health Organization:
www.who.int/en/

About the Author

Dawn Smith, BScN (British Columbia), MN (Community) (Dalhousie), is a PhD candidate in Population Health at the University of Ottawa. Her passion for primary health care began during her undergraduate education. The values of primary health care, principles of health promotion, social justice, and caring underpin her work in practice, research, policy, and teaching. Her work in community health nursing often involved community development and population-based health promotion activities. She has also practised primary health care with displaced people on the Thai/Burma border. She continues to be drawn to opportunities for developing the knowledge and skills that will make the principles and values of primary health care more evident in the institutions and processes that influence health and nurses' work.

CHAPTER 7

Epidemiology

Lynnette Leeseberg Stamler

OBJECTIVES

AFTER STUDYING THIS CHAPTER, YOU SHOULD BE ABLE TO:

1. Describe the theoretical underpinnings of the epidemiologic process and its historical and present value to community health nurses.
2. Identify the various measurements used in epidemiologic research and reports, understand how the measurements were calculated, and identify their meaning for community health nurses.
3. Describe the research study designs commonly used in epidemiologic research and link the research question with the appropriate design.
4. Differentiate between association and causality and explain some of the criteria that, when satisfied, suggest a causal relationship.
5. Discuss how epidemiology has expanded to include not only the study of disease, but also the factors that promote health.

INTRODUCTION

Throughout history, humans have ascribed different causes for disease. During the religious era, disease was thought to be a consequence of divine intervention. The environment was the next general cause of disease, which was attributed to miasmas (vaporous atmospheres) or other physical forces. It was not until the 1870s that specific bacteria were recognized as causing disease. During the past century, health professionals have come to understand that there are multiple factors or influences on many diseases and health challenges. In addition to learning the many causes of disease, health researchers are working to discover the factors that promote health.

In this chapter, you will learn the basics of the science of epidemiology, understand the types of data used in community health nursing, and begin to acquire the skills to identify and ask questions, using epidemiologic data to find some of the answers.

WHAT IS EPIDEMIOLOGY?

A simple definition of epidemiology is the scientific collection and analysis of data that assists health professionals to understand factors that promote and impede disease and health. In the original Greek, *epi* (upon), *demos* (people), and *logos* (thought, study) would lead one to define epidemiology as the study of people or populations (Harkness, 1995). Another definition describes epidemiology as "the study of the distribution and determinants of health-related states or events in specified populations and the application of this study to the control of health problems" (Last, 1988). A more recent definition expands epidemiology to embrace not only the goal of controlling health problems, but also of improving the health of the population:

Epidemiology is the study of the health of human populations. Its functions are:

- to discover the agent, host, and environmental factors which affect health in order to provide the scientific basis for the prevention of disease and injury and the promotion of health;
- to determine the relative importance of the causes of illness, disability, and death in order to establish priorities for research and action;
- to identify those sections of the population which have the greatest risk from specific causes of ill health in order that the indicated action may be directed appropriately; and
- to evaluate the effectiveness of health programs and services in improving the health of the population (Terris, 1993, p. 142).

This definition clearly links prevention and promotion, both functions of the community health nurse (CHN). The science of epidemiology assists CHNs to examine and understand the past and to predict the future. From that understanding and those predictions, CHNs can plan, implement, and evaluate appropriate and timely actions.

Historical Background of Epidemiology

While large-scale, focused epidemiologic studies are a relatively new phenomenon, the basis or understanding for such studies has been noted throughout history. Hippocrates is credited with being the first to notice and record a possible relationship between the environment and the health or disease of people.

He suggested that physicians study "the mode in which the inhabitants live and what are their pursuits, whether they are fond of eating and drinking to excess, and given to indolence, or are fond of exercise and labour, and not given to excess in eating and drinking" (Hippocrates, 400 BCE).

While history has recorded the existence and duration of epidemics such as the plague or the Black Death, few large-scale efforts were made to accurately record data that would increase the understanding of these epidemics. By the 1600s, statistics such as numbers of births and deaths were being recorded in London, England, and a haberdasher, John Graunt, was the first to study these statistics. He noted, for instance, gender differences in births (more males than females), seasonal variations in deaths, and high levels of infant deaths.

It was not until 1839 that Dr. William Farr initiated a more complete gathering of statistical data in England. With these data he was able (among other things) to compare death rates between workers in different types of jobs, as well as between prison inmates and the rest of the population. During a cholera epidemic in the mid-1850s, Dr. John Snow noticed an apparent relationship between the number of cholera deaths in various neighbourhoods and the source of the drinking water. He clearly demonstrated that people who lived in areas/homes served by particular water companies had much higher death rates from cholera than those in neighbourhoods served by other water companies.

Florence Nightingale, a contemporary of Snow and Farr, was also convinced of the effect of the environment on disease and death. When she arrived at Scutari during the Crimean War, she discovered horrendous conditions and a lax method of recording deaths and their causes. She increased the recording of these statistics and used them to explain and publicize the reality of the situation. Her polar diagrams, for instance, clearly demonstrated that in January 1855, 2761 soldiers died from contagious diseases, 83 from wounds, and 324 from other causes. It became clear that without ongoing recruitment, the entire army could have been wiped out from disease alone (Cohen, 1984). It was through her influence and her record-keeping that she was able to persuade authorities to allow her to implement sanitation practices that significantly decreased the death rates during and after the war.

In the 1900s, it became evident that while vital statistics of death and illness were important, following populations for a period of time to ascertain the progression of various diseases and their treatments was also important. As well, new research methodologies were developed to gather and compare data appropriately. As medicine discovered and implemented new treatments, the primary causes of death changed over time from predominantly contagious diseases to chronic diseases that were influenced by lifestyle behaviours. For instance, between the 1920s and the 1970s, health challenges such as cardiovascular and renal diseases rose in terms of death rates, while death rates for diseases such as tuberculosis and influenza decreased (see Figure 7.1). In 1949, the first cohort study—the Framingham Heart Study—was begun, followed in 1950 by the publication of the first case-control studies of smoking and lung disease. Four years later, the Salk polio vaccine field trial was conducted. Modern epidemiological studies have all been developed from these pioneering works.

FIGURE 7.1 Comparison of the Most Common Causes of Death of Canadians over Time

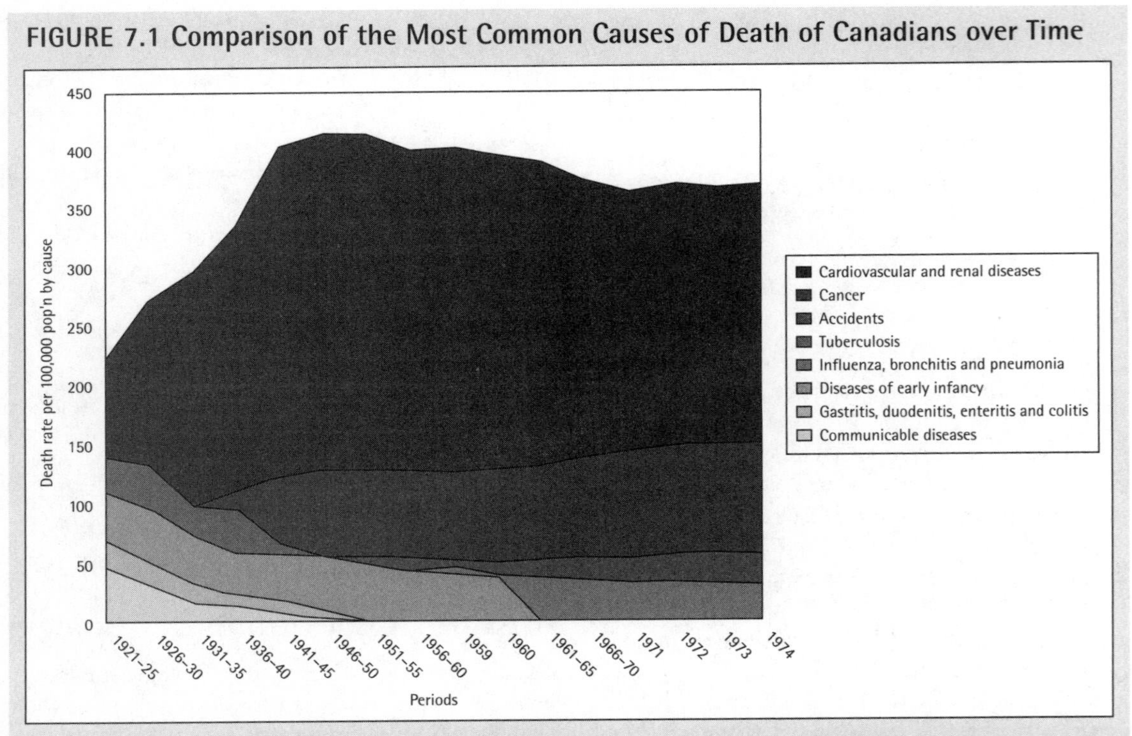

Source: Statistics Canada, www.statcan.ca/english/free[in/11-516-XIE/sectionb/sectionb.htm. *Reproduced with permission.*

Basic Building Blocks in Epidemiology

Several concepts and processes are the basic building blocks to understanding the science of epidemiology. These include the epidemiologic model, the concept of susceptibility, modes of transmission, the natural history/progress of disease, association and causation, and the web of causation. These concepts and processes arose from early epidemiologic observations and analysis and were developed to help scientists understand the hows and whys of disease. Modern CHNs use these same concepts and processes to determine and test appropriate interventions.

Epidemiologic Model While several versions of the epidemiologic model exist, each contains the same elements: host, agent, and environment. The model is frequently presented as a triangle (see Figure 7.2). The **host** is the human being in which the disease occurs. The **agent** is the contagious or noncontagious force that can begin or continue a health problem. Agents include bacteria and viruses, as well as "stimuli" such as the absence of vitamin C or smoking. The **environment** is the context that promotes the **exposure** of the host to the agent. The **epidemiologic model** posits that disease is the result of the interaction among these three elements.

Some authors have included other elements in the epidemiologic model. For example, Gordis (2000) included the vector as an additional concept. He defined **vector** as a factor (such as a deer tick) that moves between the agent and the host, assisting the movement of the disease between the other two elements. Timmreck (1998), on the other hand, added the concept of time to the model. Harkness (1995) noted that using a **Venn diagram** instead of the classic triangle emphasized the interrelatedness within the model. A Venn diagram uses curves and circles to represent relationships (see Figure 7.3).

Susceptibility One might think that if a group of people were all exposed in the same manner to the same disease, all would get the disease to the same degree. However, the combination of characteristics of each individual within that host group, interacting with the factors present or absent in the other elements of the epidemiologic triangle, determines the **risk** (or degree of **susceptibility**) of each person to a particular agent. Susceptibility and risk can also be described as vulnerability, which determines the individual host response.

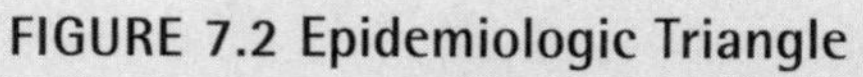

FIGURE 7.2 Epidemiologic Triangle

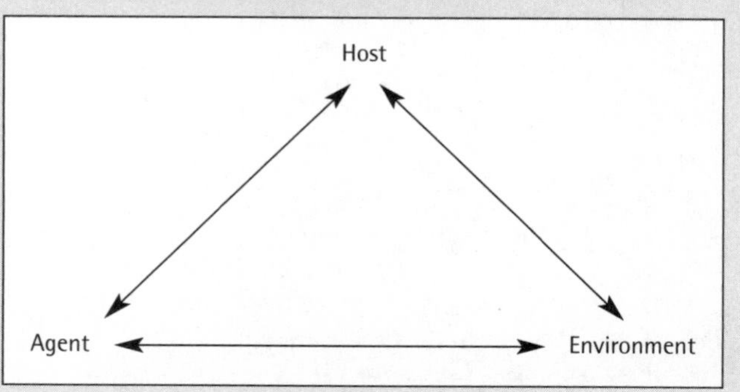

FIGURE 7.3 Epidemiologic Triangle as a Venn Diagram

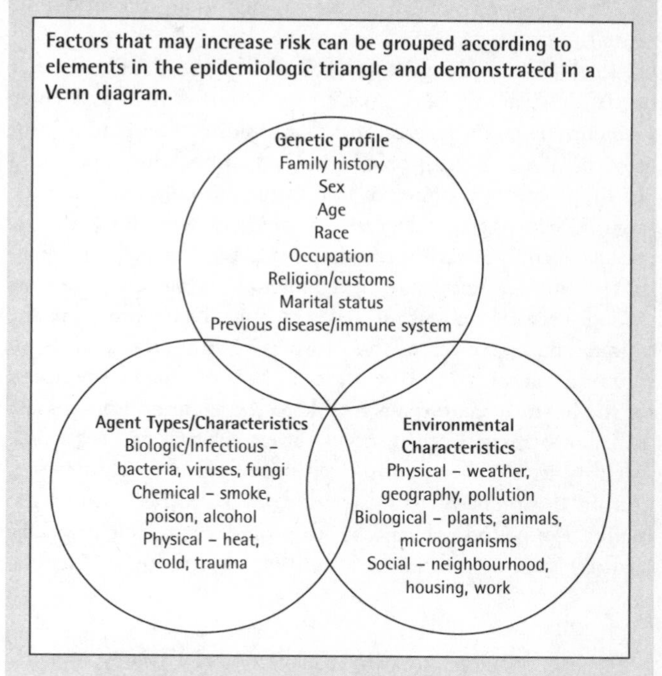

Within each element of the epidemiologic triangle are factors or characteristics that may increase or decrease the risk or susceptibility of the host to the disease. Figure 7.3 identifies some of these factors/characteristics. It is evident that some factors (e.g., lifestyle behaviours) may be changed or modified by the individual while others (e.g., age, gender, genetic makeup) are not under the control of the individual.

Modes of Disease Transmission A **mode of transmission** is one way in which a disease moves to a new host. There are two main modes of transmission: direct and indirect. **Direct transmission** involves contact between the person with the disease and another person. This may be accomplished through touching with contaminated hands, skin-to-skin contact, or sexual intercourse. **Indirect transmission** involves a common vehicle or vector that moves the disease to the new host. An example of a common vehicle is a contaminated water supply or lake. A mosquito can also function as a common vector in disease transmission. Indirect transmission may be airborne (droplets or dust), waterborne, vectorborne, or vehicleborne (contaminated utensils, hygiene articles, or clothing). Different **pathogens** (microorganisms or other substances that cause disease) are viable under different conditions; therefore, one needs to ascertain the potential mode of transmission for each disease.

Because a given disease may have more than one mode of transmission, understanding those modes is central to controlling the disease. For example, when AIDS first became recognized as a threat to public health, the mode of transmission was greatly misunderstood: it was not known whether the disease could be contracted through everyday contact such as by using a toilet seat used by someone with AIDS or by shaking that person's hand. It soon became clear that such minimal contact did not result in disease transmission. However, the fear of AIDS greatly increased the use of universal precautions by health professionals—a positive outcome.

Natural History/Progression of a Disease A disease in a human host should be seen as a process rather than as a single incident. In 1965, Leavell and Clark plotted the natural progression of the disease process and identified prevention and health promotion strategies that could be employed at each stage. As illustrated in Figure 7.4, the first stage in the disease process is the **prepathogenesis** period. During prepathogenesis the human host may be exposed to a variety of agents through several modes of transmission. Depending on the unique characteristics of the prospective host, repeated exposure or a combination of additional stressors may be required for the host to become susceptible to the agent and the disease to begin. **Stressors** are events or situations that cause discomfort to a person, for example, chronic fatigue or a poor diet. During the prepathogenesis period (also has been called the **incubation** period), general health promotion as well as specific health promotion interventions may be employed. General health promotion interventions, such as physical activity and attention to proper diet, optimize health. Specific health promotion activities are directed at particular challenges, such as increased personal hygiene during cold and flu season. Both general and specific health promotion activities are referred to as **primary prevention**.

When the human host begins to react to the agent (or stimulus), the period of **pathogenesis** begins. Depending on the disease, the host may or may not experience symptoms, but microscopic changes take place that indicate the presence of the disease. Pathogenesis ends with recovery, disability, or death. Two categories of health promotion activities are used during the period of pathogenesis. The first category is early diagnosis and treatment, which occurs early in the pathogenesis period. For instance, screening mammography is used for early detection of breast cancer. The second category, disability limitation, occurs later in the pathogenesis period when the disease is active or there are recognizable symptoms. During this period, health promotion activities are aimed at preventing complications, for example, ongoing examination and care of the feet in persons living with dia-

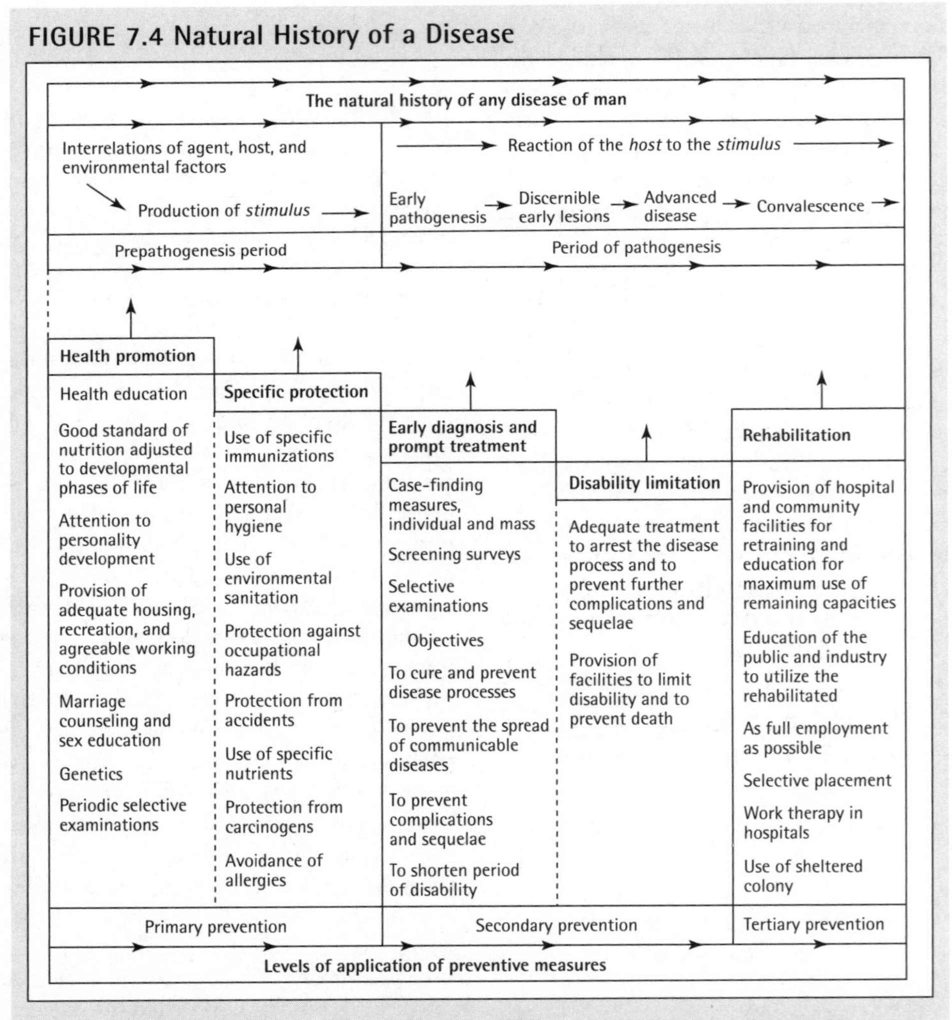

FIGURE 7.4 Natural History of a Disease

Source: Leavell, H. F., Clark, E. G., Preventive Medicine for the Doctor in his Community, *1965, McGraw-Hill, p. 21. Reproduced with permission of the McGraw-Hill Companies.*

betes. Early diagnosis and disability limitation may also be called **secondary prevention**.

Tertiary prevention is the term given to the last health promotion category and occurs during the latter phases of the pathogenesis period. At this stage, health promotion activities might include client/family education to understand the chronicity of the disease, to adapt to sequelae of the disease process, or to maximize the health of the individual through use of aids such as a walker or adapted eating utensils. Figure 7.4 identifies this period as rehabilitation, but it may also be the time when palliative care and assistance for the individual and family to move toward a dignified death would also be appropriate. It is important to recognize that the presence of chronic diseases/health challenges in individuals also increases their vulnerability or susceptibility to additional health challenges. This has become increasingly evident as more and more of our population ages through enhanced medical care and health practices. Disease processes that would have ensured a speedy death only a few decades ago are now managed with little ongoing medical care.

Association and Causation Before planning interventions that prevent or ameliorate diseases or health problems, one first has to clearly understand what is causing the disease or health problem. Two terms are used to describe the relationship between a stressor and a disease: association and causation. An **association** occurs when there is reasonable evidence that a connection exists between a stressor or environmental factor and a disease or health challenge. For example, a CHN might notice that many patients who exhibit a certain condition spent their childhoods in a particular geographic location. Thus, the relationship is first noticed through observation. Based on these observations, the CHN or epidemiologist examines the data to see if the relationship or association is strong or weak—is it all patients or just a few? If the association appears strong from the limited data sample, then a larger, more comprehensive exploration might be conducted. Such investigations often generate data from several sources.

When a relationship or association has been demonstrated statistically, **causation** (or causality) is said to be present. In other words, causality occurs when one can state that there is a definite, statistical, cause-and-effect relationship between a particular stimulus and the occurrence of a specific disease or health challenge, or that the occurrence could not happen by chance alone.

In some ways, causation was simpler when the majority of the diseases were infectious, as they were more likely to have only one cause. For example, streptococcus bacteria produce strep infection. Two important concepts in establishing causality are "necessary" and "sufficient." "Necessary" refers to the notion that a particular stressor *must* be present before a given effect can occur. For example, exposure to *Mycobacterium tuberculosis* is required before a person becomes ill with tuberculosis. "Sufficient" refers to the amount of exposure required to result in the disease. For instance, some people exposed to *Mycobacterium tuberculosis* only once (minimal dose) become ill, and some do not become ill unless exposed several times (larger dose).

In the past 40 years, several authors have identified factors or criteria that researchers and practitioners could use to assess a causal relationship between a stimulus and the occurrence of a disease (Hill, 1965). Timmreck's (1998) criteria of causation

TABLE 7.1
Illustrations of Causation Criteria

Criterion	Example
Consistency	Everyone who eats food contaminated with a certain bacteria gets sick. If other food at a different time and place is contaminated with the same bacteria, the illness recurs.
Strength	Persons who are most exposed to the contaminated food (e.g., ate the most) are the most ill.
Specificity	The cause is linked to a specific problem: *Mycobacterium tuberculosis* does not cause chickenpox.
Time relationship	A person does not get a disease until after exposure to the cause. Similarly, an intervention designed to decrease complications in diabetes is unlikely to be the cause of an immediate decrease since the development of complications is a lengthy process.
Congruence (coherence)	Since the possibility of contamination of raw meat is quite high, it is more logical to assume that eating raw meat is more likely to expose the person to the disease than eating well-cooked meat.
Sensitivity	A test is used to discriminate between persons who get ill from one source and those who get ill from another source—the greater the discrimination, the stronger the sensitivity.
Biological/medical	If children play with a child who has a disease (cold, measles), they will be more likely to get the disease than if they played with children who were not sick.
Plausibility	People used to think that only vigorous, painful exercise was valuable. Research has demonstrated that sustained moderate exercise may be more helpful for maintenance of cardiovascular health.
Experiments and research	Rigorous, scientific comparisons replicated over time add weight to the evidence that an association is present.
Analogy factors (transfer of knowledge)	Since vaccinations have been found to decrease chances of becoming ill with a viral disease, it was reasonable for early researchers to search for a vaccination for the AIDS virus.

were chosen for this text because of their comprehensiveness and clarity. Timmreck's criteria are summarized in Table 7.1.

While strict adherence to these criteria is perhaps the purview of researchers, CHNs can use them as well. When reading research that examines a particular nursing practice or new intervention, it is prudent to examine the presented results/recommendations in light of the ten criteria in Table 7.1. Similarly, when CHNs observe a recurring phenomenon that appears to have a relationship with a human or environmental factor, a close examination of the data in light of the ten criteria may assist them in planning subsequent observations.

Web of Causation Previous chapters have introduced the concept of determinants of health. In contrast to the time when each illness was thought to have a unique and specific cause, it is now recognized the many health problems have multiple causal factors, both direct and indirect. For instance, issues of poverty, education, and environment (e.g., pollution) have been shown to be influential in many health challenges.

A model called a **web of causation** can be helpful to CHNs in visualizing the relationships amongst the many causes or influences of a given health challenge. Within that model, the relationship between the direct and indirect causes can be hypothesized, at which point research studies can be designed to test the hypotheses suggested by the web of causation.

Figure 7.5 illustrates a web of causation for teenage pregnancy. Obviously, the most direct causes of teen pregnancy are sexual activity and lack of use of contraceptives. However,

FIGURE 7.5 Web of Causation for Teen Pregnancy

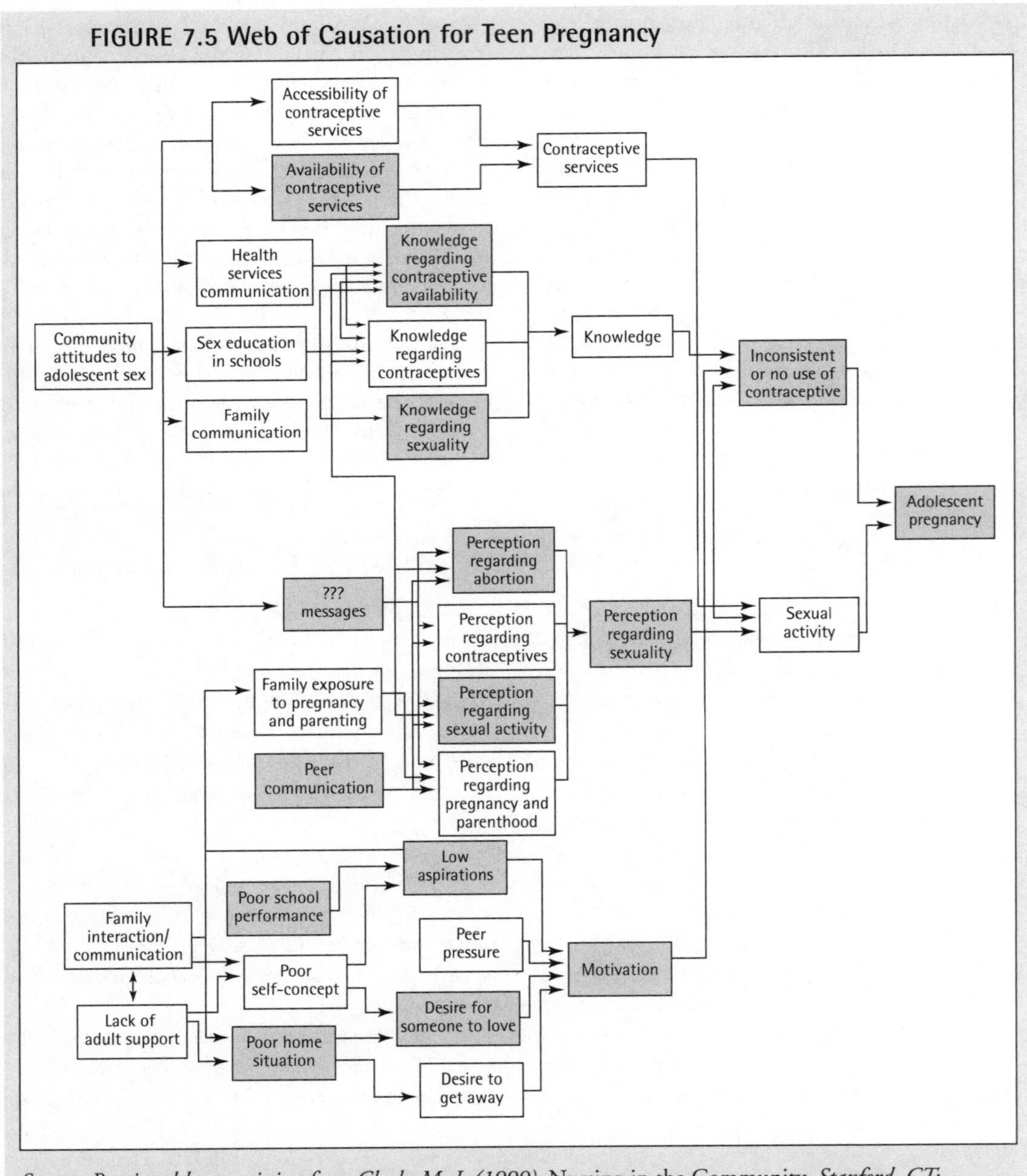

Source: Reprinted by permission from Clark, M. J. (1999). Nursing in the Community. *Stanford, CT: Appleton and Lange.*

behind those primary causes are several other causal factors possessing various levels of influence. For instance, the causal factor of knowledge can be stratified into knowledge of several topics and the sources of the knowledge. Both are influenced by community attitudes.

At any one time, each individual is subjected to multiple agents delivered through many modes of transmission. If one compared webs of causation for several common health challenges, some specific health promotion activities would appear to serve more than one purpose. Conversely, there may be a health promotion activity that is helpful for one challenge, but contributes to susceptibility for another challenge. CHNs must examine all possible benefits and consequences of an intervention.

MEASUREMENT IN EPIDEMIOLOGY

In order to determine the extent of a disease process or health challenge and its final effects on a population, data must be collected and analyzed. However, in order for the resulting measurements to be useful to the CHN, the raw data or crude numbers must be presented in conjunction with other factors such as population, time frame, or human characteristic (e.g., gender, race, age). These numbers, expressed as fractions, are known as **rates**. The numerator of each fraction is generally the crude count of the disease in question, and the denominator is generally the size of the population in question. In each case, the population or subpopulation of the numerator and denominator of the fraction are the same. For example, a rate of teen pregnancies might look like this:

$$\text{Rate} = \frac{\text{number of live births delivered to teen mothers in the population}}{\text{total number of teen women in the population}}$$

This fraction or rate is usually expressed for a set number of the population (e.g., per 100 000 people, per 100 cases, or per 1000 births) so that different-sized populations can be compared. Table 7.2 presents the formulae for commonly used rates, and the following section describes these rates and shows how they are calculated and how they might be used by CHNs.

Mortality Rate (Death Rate)

Physicians are legally required to complete death certificates for all deaths and file them with the government authorities. Thus, death or **mortality rates** are generally complete and easily obtainable. Mortality rates can be crude or specific in nature. **Crude mortality rates** compare the number of deaths from a specific cause with the entire population, while **specific mortality rates** compare the number of deaths from a specific cause in a particular subgroup with that whole subgroup. For example, if one examined all deaths from motor vehicle collisions and compared them with the total population, one would have a crude mortality rate. However, if one examined only teenage male deaths from motor vehicle collisions, one would compare that with the number of male teens driving at that time, a specific mortality rate. Mortality rates from a specific cause are often different when different subgroups (e.g., teenage males, children aged 4–8, elderly persons) are examined. For example, Figure 7.6 illustrates the age-specific suicide rates for Canada for 1997, stratified by gender. Note the line that represents the specific total mortality rate for each age group. If only these data were presented, it would be statistically correct, but would fail to inform the reader that the rate for males is higher than for females in each age group. These data would lead one to conclude that males are more susceptible (or at least more successful) than females to death by suicide.

Proportional mortality rates can be used to stratify (divide) crude mortality rates. The number of deaths from a specific cause in a given population for a particular time period is compared with the total number of deaths in that same population and time period. A common use of proportional

TABLE 7.2
Commonly Used Rates in Epidemiology

Rate	Formula
Crude mortality rate	$\frac{\text{Total deaths from any cause in a given year in a population}}{\text{Average total population for the same year}}$
Specific mortality rate	$\frac{\text{Total deaths from a specific cause in a given year in a population (subgroup)}}{\text{Average number of population (subgroup) for the same year}}$
Infant death rate	$\frac{\text{Total deaths of infants in given year in population}}{\text{Total number of live births in same year in population}}$
Prevalence rate	$\frac{\text{Number of people with given disease in given population at one point in time}}{\text{Total in given population at same point in time}}$
Incidence rate	$\frac{\text{Number of new cases of given disease in population in given time (1 year)}}{\text{Average total population in same time}}$
Relative risk	$\frac{\text{Incidence rate of disease in exposed population}}{\text{Incidence of disease in unexposed population}}$

FIGURE 7.6 Suicide Rates by Age and Gender, Canada, 1997

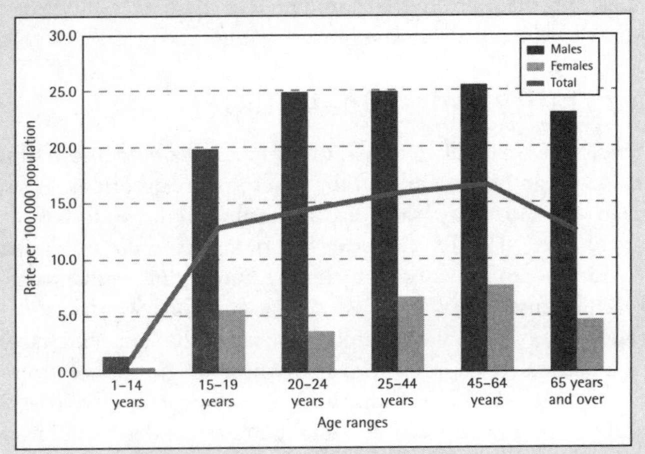

Source: Statistics Canada, www.statcan.ca/english/Pgdb/People/Health/health01.htm

mortality rates is to state that *x*% of the deaths in a given year were due to breast cancer or motor vehicle collisions (see Figure 7.7). Note that two causes of death, cancers and diseases of the heart, account for over half the deaths.

Historically, the health of a population has been exemplified by maternal and infant mortality rates. Families used to have many children, partly because few were expected to live past the first years of life (assuming the mother and child survived the birth and neonatal period). With the advent of better hygiene as well as prenatal and postnatal care, maternal and infant mortality rates decreased. CHNs often compare infant mortality rates across developing and developed countries, the assumption being that the lower the maternal and infant mortality rates, the healthier the population in general. When looking at these statistics, it is particularly important to determine the stage (e.g., perinatal vs. infant) that has been studied so that the comparisons are accurate. The following are definitions used in maternal and infant mortality statistics. In all but the perinatal rate, the denominator is the number of live births in that year in that population.

- Maternal or puerperal death rate: any deaths of the mother resulting from pregnancy-related causes.
- Perinatal death rate: fetal deaths occurring during the last few months of pregnancy and during the first seven days of life. Here the denominator includes both live births and fetal deaths.
- Neonatal death rate: deaths occurring in infants in their first 28 days of life.
- Infant death rate: deaths occurring in the first year of life.

A more recent way of presenting mortality statistics in is terms of potential years of life lost (**PYLL**). This has arisen from the assumption that a person who dies early in life has lost greater potential than has a person who dies much later in life. PYLL statistics give CHNs additional information on which health challenges or diseases contribute the greatest lost potential to the population. While this may raise some ethical issues in terms of where a society or country chooses to place its resources, PYLL statistics are certainly a part of the picture that must be heeded.

Survival (Prognosis) Rates

Survival rates are often used to describe the effect of a given disease (e.g., cancer) and are also referred to as prognosis rates. Survival rates partially answer the common client question, "How bad is it?" Survival rates can also be used to compare the efficacy of various treatments for a specific disease. For diseases such as cancer, and to compare its treatments, the prognosis or survival rate most frequently used is the five-year survival rate. This is determined by calculating the percentage of persons with the disease who are alive five years after diagnosis. While five years is a convenient time period to use for comparing the effect of various treatments, it is easy for clients and health professionals alike to fall into the trap of somehow equating five-year survival with a decreased risk of future mortality from that disease. One of the arguments presented in favour of widespread breast screening is early detection of the disease. While it is hoped that early detection coupled with prompt treatment will increase the survival time, there is still conflicting evidence that these actions in fact contribute to decreased mortality rates from breast cancer.

The **case-fatality rate** is calculated by dividing the number of people who die from a disease by the number of people who have the disease, answering the question, "How likely is it that I will die from this disease?" For instance, while recent advances have greatly increased the length of time between the diagnosis of a person with a positive HIV test and that person's death, the case-fatality rate for HIV/AIDS remains very high, as most people will die from the complications of the disease. The case-fatality rate for a person with arthritis, for instance, is much lower.

FIGURE 7.7 Selected Leading Causes of Death, Canada, 1997

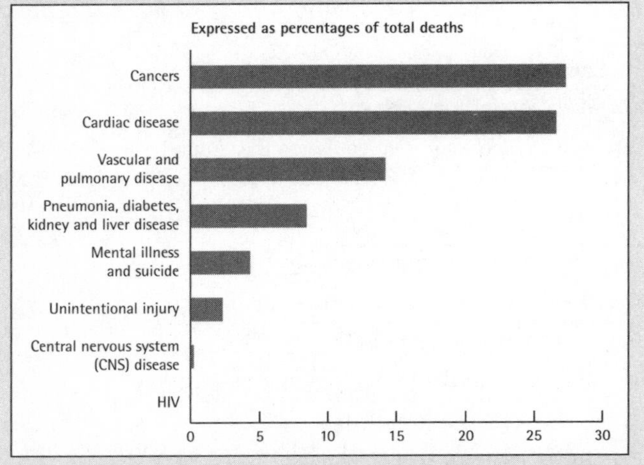

Source: Statistics Canada, www.statcan.ca/english/Pgdb/People/Health/health36.htm

Morbidity (Illness) Rate

Illness or morbidity rates are valuable for the CHN. **Morbidity rates** give a picture of a population and a disease or health challenge over time, suggesting questions about the susceptibility of the population or subpopulation and the effectiveness of either health promotion or treatment strategies. Two types of rate are commonly used to describe morbidity in a population. The first is **prevalence**, which provides a picture of a specific disease process in a population at one given point in time. The second is **incidence**, which describes the identification of new cases of a disease in a population over time. Together with mortality rates and survival rates, they present a fairly complete picture of the population's response to a disease or health challenge.

If the disease is short-lived, such as measles or the flu, the prevalence does not reveal much except in an epidemic situation, when CHNs might use this rate to plan for extra pediatric clinics or teleheath staff to deal with increased inquiries or clinic visits from concerned clients and parents. If the disease is short-lived, resulting in few deaths, the incidence and prevalence rates are very similar. If, on the other hand, the health challenge is chronic in nature, the incidence rate (number of new cases) stays fairly static over time, while the prevalence rate increases as more people live with the disease. If the disease is long-term with complications, such as diabetes or multiple sclerosis, the prevalence rate over time informs CHNs about the need for community and institutional support for the future. This is very important in terms of public and community health planning.

The population in question is usually the population at risk for the disease. For instance, when calculating the incidence of prostate cancer, the number of cases is compared with the population of males, rather than with the whole population. Incidence rates, when calculated within the same population over several years, show whether the population seems more or less susceptible to the disease in question. For example, the number of motor vehicle collisions in a given year involving teenage drivers might change over time in response to changes in the legal drinking age.

When CHNs test for a specific cause of a health challenge, they compare the incidence of that health challenge in a population exposed to the identified cause with the incidence of the same health challenge in a population not exposed to the same cause. If the suspected cause was indeed a factor, one would expect the incidence rates to be quite different. For example, one would expect the incidence of lung cancer to be much greater in smokers than in non-smokers. If the cause being examined is not the *only* cause of the disease (e.g., lung cancer), one might find that the incidence rates are more similar than expected. Such results might lead the CHN to explore other factors (e.g., second-hand smoke) to explain the incidence rates.

One frequently asked question is, "Are some populations more at risk or vulnerable to a specific disease than others?" To find the answer to that question, a statistic known as **relative risk** is used. This measure divides the incidence of a given problem or disease in a population exposed to a given risk factor by the incidence of the same problem in a population not exposed to the same risk. For example, CHNs might compare the incidence of childhood asthma in a population exposed to a certain air pollutant with the incidence in a population not exposed to that pollutant. If the resulting number is 1.0, it means that both groups have the same risk of the health problem, and most likely the risk factor in question makes little or no difference. If the resulting number is >1.0, it indicates that the risk in the exposed group is higher than the risk in the unexposed group, and the risk factor in question is at least one of the significant risk factors for the problem or disease. Should the relative risk ratio be <1.0, the given risk factor is probably not significant for the problem or disease. However, such results may indicate that the factor in question has a protective effect, for example, a population where the physical activity is high may have a low relative risk for diabetes.

Incidence and prevalence rates can be further stratified to increase the descriptiveness of the statistic. Data are frequently obtained through interviewing members of the population, also known as self-reporting. For instance, the question, "Do you currently smoke?" elicits data that could contribute to a **point prevalence** statistic of smokers in the population. This statistic describes the situation only for that particular point in time. The question, "Have you smoked within the last six months?" gives us data that could be useful for **period prevalence** statistics. However, asking, "Have you every smoked?" gives the researcher data that could be used for **cumulative or lifetime incidence** statistics. This demonstrates why it is important for researchers to clearly state their methods and sources of data in journal articles and reports, and why it is equally important for CHNs reading those articles to critically examine the evidence presented.

RESEARCH IN EPIDEMIOLOGY

Sources of Epidemiologic Data

Epidemiological analyses and research are only as good as the data they are based on. Thus, CHNs need to ensure that they use consistent and accurate sources of data. One of the largest sources of epidemiologic data is the government. Canada has several sources of government or government-funded data such as Health Canada, Statistics Canada, and the provincial government health ministries. As birth and death statistics are required by law to be filed with the appropriate government agency, they are generally very accurate. Birth and death statistics can be teamed with the census data reported by Statistics Canada for further detail. Statistics Canada data can be found in their daily newsletter (*The Daily News*) that reports on recent data and analysis and often provides an historical trend analysis for the disease (e.g., breast cancer) or issue (e.g., family structure in Canada). Statistics Canada also has a website where more detailed information such as profiles of individual communities and archived newsletters can be found.

Health Canada produces statistics about various diseases as well as health promotion topics. The Health Canada website contains information on **reportable diseases** (diseases that are required to be reported by law) and links to non-governmental agencies such as the Infectious Diseases Society. Several provinces also maintain websites that provide information for the province in question. Specifically, many of the provincial health ministry websites provide birth and infant mortality statistics.

The Canadian Institute for Health Information (CIHI) is also an excellent source for data. A non-governmental organization, CIHI collects and collates information from many sources to provide analysis that can inform policy. The epidemiological data that it reports includes data from hospital sources and from the various provincial health plans. Thus, this organization may provide information on incidence and prevalence of non-reportable diseases.

In addition to the above agencies, there are various agencies that focus solely on one or more disease issues, for example, the diabetes division of the Population and Public Health Branch of Health Canada. In cooperation with the Canadian Diabetes Association (a non-governmental agency), they present up-to-date information about the epidemiological status of diabetes in Canada. Similarly, the same Population and Public Health Branch website contains information on heart disease and stroke, prepared in cooperation with the Heart and Stroke Foundation of Canada.

For the CHN wanting to compare data between Canada and the United States, the Centers for Disease Control and Prevention website is a valuable resource. For international data, the World Health Organization's website is very helpful. These and other selected websites are listed at the end of this chapter.

In addition to websites, many organizations produce a variety of reports that are frequently found in university and college libraries. If a personal copy of these materials is desired, it could be downloaded from the organization's website or purchased from the organization.

The final source of data is to gather data oneself. While this can result in accurate data that deals with the specific question being asked, the cost of creating a survey instrument that is clear and understood by all respondents, choosing an appropriate sample (especially a national sample), and gathering the data is often beyond the financial reach of most researchers. If this is the case, researchers may be able to add questions to a survey being conducted by a community health care centre or agency.

Types of Epidemiological Research

Research is one method of finding answers to questions. It is critical that CHNs have a clear understanding of research methodologies in order that they can understand, participate in, and conduct research. The reason for this is that the study design is strongly linked to the research question: if an inappropriate study design is chosen, the results will not provide answers. Basic research designs are presented in this section, illustrated by studies completed using the designs.

There are two basic categories of research in epidemiology, observational and experimental. Observational (or descriptive) research, the more traditional form, is designed to answer questions such as "Are mortality rates for cardiac disease higher for men than for women?", "Does age at diagnosis or geographic residency affect survival rates for persons with multiple sclerosis?," and "What are the current incidence rates for HIV in young homosexual males compared with 5, 10, or 20 years ago?" Observational research data are categorized by the variables of interest (e.g., age, sex, time). The epidemiologist does not manipulate the variables, only observes and notes the reality of the situation. Many times, the factors that increase risk (see Figure 7.3) may be used as a variable of interest, for example, gender may be considered to be a risk factor for heart disease.

During experimental research, the epidemiologist assumes greater control over some of the variables. These studies are used to compare a new treatment with one already in existence, provide support for cause-effect relationships, or study a community intervention and compare rates with communities without the intervention.

Types of Observational Studies Observational studies can be cohort, case-control, or cross-sectional. In **cohort studies**, the researcher examines the individual histories of a group of people manifesting a particular disease to find out what common factors they share and what differences can be discerned. In **case-control studies**, the individuals in the cohort with the disease are matched with individuals who are similar in some characteristics (e.g., age, gender, time, geographic residence) but who have not manifested the disease in question. The health histories or characteristics of the individuals in both groups are then obtained. These data are compared and the common factors/differences are identified between the two populations.

A case-control study of children with type 2 diabetes would include children with the disease in one group and children without the disease in the other group. The two groups would be matched for age and geographic location. The epidemiologist might search for common and different factors such as amount of physical activity, obesity, and family history of diabetes. In each case, the researcher would expect to find some similarities and differences between the two groups that could contribute to theories of causality.

The relative risk ratio compares the risk for a particular disease between two populations: one exposed to a stressor and one not exposed to the stressor. Case-control studies also involve two groups: one group composed of individuals who have the disease and one of individuals who do not have the disease. Relative risk cannot be calculated here because neither the incidence nor the prevalence is known. The **odds ratio** provides epidemiologists with an estimate of the relative risk factor. To demonstrate the calculation of this statistic, consider the following example. A hypothetical Community Health Centre practice has 200 male patients between the ages of 45 and 65; 50 of them have lung cancer and 150 do not. Thirty-five of the patients with lung cancer are smokers, while 15 patients without lung cancer are smokers. Table 7.3 illustrates the calculation of the odds ratio for this example.

Canadian Research Box 7.1

Friedenreich, C. M., Courneya, K. S., & Bryant, H. E. (2001). Influence of physical activity in different age and life periods on the risk of breast cancer. *Epidemiology, 12*(6), 604–612.

The researchers in this study wanted to move past the current evidence that physical activity reduces the risk of breast cancer and discover if there were specific periods in a woman's life when physical activity was most beneficial. Using the Alberta Cancer Registry, 1239 women with breast cancer completed an in-person interview. Random-digit dialing was used to identify and match by age and residence (urban/rural) 1241 women who were cancer free. These women were also interviewed. Extensive data was gathered about family history, medical history, dietary practices, and lifetime physical activity. Physical activity was measured two ways, both lifetime totals and physical activity completed during five different age periods and four different life periods. The odds ratios were calculated for all the different variations. The authors concluded that the greatest risk reduction occurred with physical activity after menopause and before the reference year. They further concluded that postmenopausal women who participated in lifetime physical activity had 30% less risk for breast cancer. Additionally, the authors concluded that moderate activity produced the greatest risk reduction, while light or heavy activity produced no further risk reduction.

Discussion Questions

1. How could the CHN use this study to facilitate a group of postmenopausal women to increase their physical activity?
2. What other determinants of health might influence women's choices to be or not to be physically active at different times in their lives?

Cross-sectional studies—snapshots of the present—are also called prevalence studies. These studies are used to suggest relationships between a disease and environmental factors or to provide health professionals with data that assist in planning further interventions. For example, CHNs may be concerned about the age of initiation of smoking behaviours relative to a specific planned health curriculum. The CHNs may work with the community to develop an anonymous survey that asks about smoking behaviours and administer it to students in various grade levels within the school district. The results of the survey may indicate that over one-third of the students in the Grade 6 classes have already tried smoking, suggesting that beginning health education about smoking in Grade 6 is too late. The CHNs and teachers decide to move their initial anti-smoking education to Grades 1 and 2, in which fewer than 3% of the students have tried to smoke. A time series of cross-sectional studies could also be used with a particular group of students to assess the effectiveness of the intervention. After implementing the new curriculum in Grades 1 and 2, Grade 6 classes would be tested in subsequent years. The data would be compared with those from the present Grade 6 students who did not receive the intervention to ascertain if the program made a difference in smoking behaviours of students in the future.

Cohort studies, which follow a specific group, may be retrospective or prospective. **Retrospective studies** are studies that begin in the present and search the past for information to explain the present. **Prospective studies** (or longitudinal studies) begin in the present and follow the subjects into the future or make predictions about the future that can be tested at a later date. These studies focus on individuals exposed to a particular health problem or potential stressor over time. For a prospective study, it is important to measure the incidence of the problem at various times. For instance, a group of people with high exposure to a stressor (e.g., occupational stress) may be matched with a group of people with low exposure to the problem, and both are followed for a period of

TABLE 7.3
Calculation of Odds Ratio

Risk Factor	Persons with lung cancer	Persons without lung cancer	Total
Smokers	35 (a)	15 (b)	55
Non-smokers	15 (c)	135 (d)	145
Total	50	150	200

$$\text{Odds ratio} = \frac{\text{exposed persons with the disease/unexposed persons with the disease}}{\text{exposed persons without the disease/unexposed persons without the disease}}$$

$$OR = \frac{a/c}{b/d} = \frac{ad}{bc} = \frac{(35)(135)}{(15)(15)} = \frac{4725}{225} = 21$$

The odds ratio for these data is 21. As with the relative risk ratio, a number >1.0 means that the persons exposed to the risk factor are more likely to develop the disease than those who are not exposed. In this example, male smokers are 21 times more likely to develop lung cancer than men who do not smoke.

Canadian Research Box 7.2

Siemiatycki, J., & Sharpe, C. R. (2001). Joint effects of smoking and body mass index on prostate cancer risk. *Epidemiology, 12*(5), 546–551.

This study used data obtained from 399 men aged 45–70 who had been diagnosed with prostate cancer. They supplied data about smoking history, alcohol ingestion history, and height and weight when healthy. They were matched to a group of 476 men aged 45–70 with no diagnosis of prostate cancer who volunteered the same data. Calculations were completed that stratified the two samples by smoking history, alcohol history, and body mass index (BMI) (calculated on weight when healthy). For instance, smoking history was stratified by number of pack-years (number of cigarettes smoked daily × number of years smoking), as well as by type of smoking (cigarettes, pipes, or cigars).

Odds ratios (OR) were calculated for the various risks examined. Results indicated that BMI alone demonstrated only a weak trend (OR for BMI >26.66=1.18). All types of smoking were associated with an OR ≥1.0; however, those combinations that included cigar smoking produced the highest OR. When BMI >26.66 was combined with cigarette smoking, the highest OR was found among persons who smoked >57.0 pack-years (OR=3.07). The conclusion reached by the authors was that "cigar and pipe smoking seemed to be associated with the development of prostate cancer. In addition, among men with high BMI, cigarette smoking was associated with an increased risk of prostate cancer" (p. 551).

Discussion Questions

1. How might the CHN explain the authors' conclusion to a group of men?
2. Canada has a strong public policy on health and cigarette smoking, including warnings on packages of cigarettes. How might the CHN use this research in planning an anti-smoking campaign for male teens?

time. The incidence levels of the health problem being studied (e.g., hypertension or myocardial infarction) in the two groups are compared at each measuring time.

Prospective studies have several problems:

- The sample size must be very large at the beginning to allow for attrition as people move, die, or lose interest.
- It is evident that health problems generally increase with increased age. By its very nature, a longitudinal study follows a group of people who are aging. Thus, a method to control for the effects of aging must be applied to any results.
- Outside factors may affect the different groups differently. For instance, researchers may decide to compare hypertension in Canadian and U.S. executives who live in large cities and experience long commutes to work. The cities chosen are Toronto, Montreal, Chicago, and New York. The time frame is 1990–2010. Might the events of September 11, 2001 have an effect on the data and results?

Ethical Concerns Ethical concerns during observational studies are rare but possible because of the nature of those studies. The researcher is not manipulating the variables, but is systematically collecting and analyzing observations to make inferences and predictions. However, CHNs must always remember that most people are interested in participating in any study that they perceive will help someone else with a health problem. If a researcher has no intention of *using* the data (e.g., to plan interventions that are intended to be carried out), it is unethical to collect them. Ethics approval must be sought for any study where data is collected about or from humans. This topic will be expanded in the discussion on experimental studies.

Canadian Research Box 7.3

Dryden, D. M., Francescutti, L. H., Rowe, B. H., Spence, J. C., & Voaklander, D. C. (2000). Epidemiology of women's recreational ice hockey injuries. *Medicine & Science in Sports & Exercise, 32*(8), 1378–1383.

This study arose from the recognition of the rapidly increasing participation by females in organized ice hockey, a contact sport, and the realization that little information was available about injuries suffered by this population during its participation. A prospective cohort study design was used to follow 314 (74.2% of the population) female hockey players from 33 teams in a Canadian city throughout the 1997–98 hockey season. Attendance and injury data were collected through monthly telephone interviews. The population was stratified by age (midget teams composed of players 18 years and younger, and adult players). The total injury rate for the entire sample was 7.8 injuries/1000 player exposures. The upper extremity was the most frequently injured in adult players (29%), while the lower extremity was the most frequently injured in midget players (40.6%). It was noted that 51% of injuries were reported as treated by health professionals, while 36% were treated by the player herself. This suggests that emergency room records should not be the sole source of data since much data would be missed. This study suggests several areas for future research into ice-hockey injuries among females, with possible protective interventions designed based on the future data.

Discussion Questions

1. How could the CHN use this research in a talk to coaches of recreational hockey teams?
2. How could the CHN use these findings to promote self-care of injuries with young female hockey players?
3. What might the CHN consider when working on injury prevention with teenage vs. adult female hockey players?

Types of Experimental Studies In experimental studies, the researcher manipulates some of the variables in order to ascertain the effect of the manipulation. **Manipulation** means to change something that is happening to some or all of the subjects within the study, rather than only observing what is present. In health care, the manipulation usually involves a new treatment or the encouragement of a new behaviour. The researcher believes that the new treatment or behaviour will positively affect the health of the subjects and uses the research to test that belief or hypothesis.

The "gold standard" of experimental study design is the **randomized controlled trial** (RCT). In fact, some scientists consider this the only valid form of experimental design. In an RCT design, individuals are assigned randomly either to a group that receives the new treatment or to a group that does not receive the new treatment. The latter is known as the control group. After a period of time, specific variables are measured in each group and compared. Frequently, neither the researchers nor the subjects are aware of which group they are part of until the end of the study. This is known as a blind RCT.

In community nursing and health promotion, the treatment or intervention studied may be a new health education or social marketing protocol (e.g., new advertisements for breast screening) or a change in policy (e.g., adding fluoride to drinking water for a community). In the example of new marketing for screening, the outcome examined could be the increase or decrease in numbers of persons participating in the screening. In the case of adding fluoride to the drinking water, the outcome measured might be the number of dental cavities found in six-year-olds.

In the examples above, randomized control groups would be almost impossible. One variation of this might be that several communities may be compared, with one or more serving as treatment groups and the others serving as control groups. Another variation may be that the community might serve as its own control group—measuring the outcome of interest (e.g., participation in screening) before and after the treatment (e.g., advertising for breast screening clinics).

Canadian Research Box 7.4

Carabin, H., Gyorkos, T. W., Soto, J. C., Joseph, L., Payment, P., & Collet, J.P. (1999). Effectiveness of a training program in reducing infections in toddlers attending day care centres. *Epidemiology, 10*(3), 219–227.

Prior research has demonstrated that the risk of infection is higher in children attending daycare centres than in children cared for at home. This intervention study tested the effectiveness of a hygiene program in daycare centres in decreasing the incidence of diarrheal and respiratory problems in toddlers enrolled at the centres. Daycare centres were randomly selected and further randomized by geographic area to the intervention or the control group. The intervention was a comprehensive hygiene training session and was delivered once for daycare centre employees in the treatment group. Each treatment group centre also had materials that could be used as reminders during the data collection period. During data collection, the presence of a cold or diarrhea in a child present at the centre or the absence of children from the centre (with causes, if known) were monitored on a daily calendar in both treatment and control group centres. In addition, each centre was visited on three unannounced occasions, and children's and adults' hands were swabbed for fecal coliform bacteria.

The results indicated that the intervention reduced the incidence rates of respiratory problems in the toddlers over the three months following the intervention, but at one year following, there was little reduction. Monitoring alone did not reduce the incidence rate of the respiratory problems but did reduce the incidence rate of the diarrheal problems. This suggests that the act of monitoring (writing on the daily calendar) may be more effective in reminding everyone about hygiene practices than a one-time intervention.

Discussion Questions

1. If you were part of a public health unit, how might you use this information in planning educational sessions for early childhood educators?
2. What future research questions does this study raise?

CASE STUDY

A recent report discusses the epidemiology of hepatitis A in Ontario between 1992 and 2000. The data presented indicate that in only two of the years were the cases reported for males equal to those for females; in all other years, male rates were higher. In the years when male rates were much higher than female rates, a strong source of infection was males having sex with males. The annual number of cases decreased from 601 to 152.

Of the reported cases, 62% had unknown or missing data indicating source of infection. When a source of infection was noted, person-to-person contact accounted for 17%, food for 12%, and water for 4% of the cases. Travel was a risk factor in 21% of the cases and food and water were found to be greater sources of infection in travellers than in non-travellers. Only 28% of the case data included information regarding hospitalization for the disease.

Discussion Questions

1. What specific health strategies might be used to decrease the incidence in the prepathogenesis period?
2. What other data might the local health unit want to collect?
3. Hepatitis A is a reportable disease. How might data collection methods influence the epidemiologic statistics?

Source: Wilson, S. & Middleton, D. (2002). Epidemiology of hepatitis A in Ontario, 1992–2000. Public Health & Epidemiology Report Ontario, 13*(4)*, 41–45.

Ethical Concerns In any experimental study, the competing issues of strong scientific experimental design and ethical considerations must be addressed. The first ethical concern is how the human subjects are approached. Most health care agencies and university research centres have an ethics committee that reviews research proposals to ensure that humans are treated fairly, the information is gathered and used in a confidential manner, and the privacy of the subjects is protected. However, ethical questions also arise about the design of the research. For instance, is it ethical to withhold a treatment that is felt to be beneficial from people who need it because a research design with a control group would be more scientific? Researchers must consider these questions and consult with appropriate sources for advice when designing scientific and ethical research studies.

SUMMARY

In this chapter, the science of epidemiology, its historical influences, and the evolution of its theoretical underpinnings were examined. The theories have been presented with modern examples, illustrating how the historical continues to have influence in the present. The notions of agent, host, and environment have been discussed, as well as modes of transmission and the natural history of disease.

Measurement is an important concept in epidemiology, and mortality, morbidity, and survival rates were each presented. The notion of risk or susceptibility was examined both theoretically and statistically. The importance of accurate sources for epidemiologic data was noted, as well as sources for Canadian data. Observational and experimental research designs were presented, with the caution that it is very important that the research design fits the research question. Causality as a societal belief as well as a statistical conclusion was noted, with causality criteria that the CHN can use to examine observations as well as published research. The notion of web of causation was presented to coincide with the current belief in multiple direct and indirect causes for most health challenges.

The science of epidemiology is an important one for the CHN. Community health professionals are confronted with increasingly complex health challenges that were unheard of just a few short decades ago, such as type 2 diabetes in children. It is becoming increasingly evident that Hippocrates had it right more than two centuries ago: nurses must look at what the person eats, what the person does, and what the person's habits are. Health practitioners face the task of using the results of epidemiologic research to influence citizens to change or enhance their activities of daily living to actively promote maximum health, while recognizing that the individual and group environment may well influence people in other directions.

Modern CHNs, while facing more complex challenges, also have the advantages of access to strong data, government and societal interest in health, and a better-educated populace. The science of epidemiology is but one of their tools.

KEY TERMS

epidemiology
host
agent
environment
exposure
epidemiologic model
vector
Venn diagram
risk
susceptibility
mode of transmission
direct transmission
indirect transmission
pathogens
prepathogenesis
stressors
incubation
primary prevention
pathogenesis
secondary prevention
tertiary prevention
association
causation
web of causation
rates
mortality rates
crude mortality rates
specific mortality rates
proportional mortality rates
PYLL
survival rates
case-fatality rate
morbidity rates
prevalence
incidence
relative risk
point prevalence
period prevalence
cumulative or lifetime incidence
reportable diseases
cohort studies
case-control studies
odds ratio
cross-sectional studies
retrospective studies
prospective studies
manipulation
randomized controlled trial

STUDY QUESTIONS

1. Identify and define five criteria for causality.
2. Differentiate between mortality and morbidity rates. How does each inform the CHN?
3. Name and define three types of observational studies relating to CHN practice. Using different examples from those in the chapter, suggest two research questions that might be answered with each of the types.
4. Identify the three elements of the epidemiologic triangle and define each.
5. Differentiate between incidence and prevalence. What does it mean when the incidence and prevalence rates for a given health problem are very different? What does it mean when they are very similar?
6. Describe prospective and retrospective studies and give two examples of research questions that could be answered with each.

INDIVIDUAL CRITICAL THINKING EXERCISES

1. Select a health problem. Using Figure 7.4 as a guide, suggest five CHN actions for each level of prevention. How might CHNs collaborate with others to implement the actions?
2. Using the ideas identified in question 1, how might the planned CHN actions be influenced by the demographic data for a given community?
3. One of the more recent mortality statistics is PYLL. Suicide is one health problem that is examined in terms of PYLL. Using the data in Figure 7.6, at what age group would you target your prevention interventions? Why? Did PYLL make a difference in your decision?
4. How can CHNs integrate epidemiological findings into their practice? How can CHNs be involved in epidemiological research and/or the collection and analysis of epidemiological data?
5. Why are infant and child morbidity and mortality considered a measure of the health of a population? How can the CHN use this information?

GROUP CRITICAL THINKING EXERCISES

1. Select a condition that you are familiar with (e.g., type 2 diabetes, asthma, heart attack). From two different province's health websites and the Health Canada website, compare the mortality and morbidity rates for that condition. Are they similar or different? What factors might influence the rates in those jurisdictions?
2. As a group, discuss the pros and cons of using an epidemiological approach to planning CHN actions.
3. Using osteoporosis as the health problem, try to identify as many factors as possible that contribute to this problem. Organize the factors into a web of causation similar to that shown in Figure 7.5.

REFERENCES

Cohen, I. B. (1984). Florence Nightingale. *Scientific American, 3*, 128–137.

Gordis, L. (2000). *Epidemiology* (2nd ed.). Philadelphia, PA: W.B. Saunders.

Harkness, G. A. (1995). *Epidemiology in nursing practice.* St. Louis, MO: Mosby.

Hill, A. B. (1965). The environment and disease: Association or causation? *Proceedings of the Royal Society of Medicine, 58*, 295–300.

Hippocrates. (400 BCE). *On airs, waters, and places.* Internet Classics Archive. Retrieved February 23, 2003 from **http://classics.mit.edu/Hippocrates/airwatpl.1.1.html**

Last, J. M. (1988). *A dictionary of epidemiology* (2nd ed.). New York: Oxford University Press.

Leavell, H. F., & Clark, E. G. (1965). *Preventive medicine for the doctor in his community: An epidemiologic approach.* New York: McGraw-Hill.

Terris, M. (1993). The Society for Epidemiologic Research (SER) and the future of epidemiology. *Journal of Public Health Policy, 14*(2), 137–148.

Timmreck, T. C. (1998). *An introduction to epidemiology* (2nd ed.). Sudbury, MA: Jones and Bartlett.

ADDITIONAL RESOURCES

WEBSITES

PROVINCIAL SITES

BC Ministry of Health Services:
www.vs.gov.bc.ca/stats/

BC Ministry of Health Planning:
www.healthplanning.gov.bc.ca/topic.html

Alberta Health Ministry:
www.health.gov.ab.ca

Saskatchewan Ministry of Health:
www.health.gov.sk.ca/ph_br_population_health.html

Saskatchewan Population Health Branch:
www.health.gov.sk.ca/ph_ph_contact.html

Saskatchewan Information Centre:
www.health.gov.sk.ca/info_centre.html,
www.health.gov.sk.ca/Report.pdf

Manitoba Health, Public Health:
www.gov.mb.ca/health/publichealth/epiunit/index.html

New Brunswick, Health and Wellness 2000-2001 Performance Indicators:
www.gnb.ca/0391/pdf/HEALTHPerformanceIndicators2002-e.pdf

Nova Scotia, Department of Health, 1995 Health Survey:
www.gov.ns.ca/health/reports.htm#1995%20Health%20Survey

Prince Edward Island Health and Social Services:
www.gov.pe.ca/hss/index.php3

Newfoundland and Labrador Health Information System:
www.nlchi.nf.ca/dev.php

EPIDEMIOLOGIC SITES

CCDR (Canada Communicable Disease Report): **www.hc-sc.gc.ca/pphb-dgspsp/publicat/ccdr-rmtc/index.html**

Canadian Infectious Disease Society: **www.cidscanada.com**

Canadian Institute of Health Information: **www.cihi.ca**

Health Canada Population and Public Health Branch: **www.hc-sc.gc.ca/pphb-dgspsp/new_e.html**

Health Canada Population and Public Health Branch, Notifiable Diseases Report: **www.hc-sc.gc.ca/pphb-dgspsp/bid-bmi/dsd-dsm/ndmr-rmmdo/index.html**

Statistics Canada: **www.statcan.ca**

Morbidity and Mortality Weekly Report (CDC–U.S.): **www.cdc.gov/mmwr/**

National Center for Health Statistics (U.S.), CDC Wonder Browser system: **wonder.cdc.gov/**

Centers for Disease Control and Prevention (U.S.): **www.cdc.gov/**

World Health Organization Weekly Epidemiological Record: **www.who.int/wer/**

About the Author

Lynnette Leeseberg Stamler, RN, PhD, is an Associate Professor and Director of the Nipissing University/Canadore College Collaborative BScN Program. She completed her BSN at St. Olaf College, Minnesota; her MEd at the University of Manitoba; and her PhD in nursing at the University of Cincinnati. Her research interests include patient/health education, breast health, diabetes education, and nursing education. She was a VON nurse for four years prior to her career in nursing education. She has been active in research and professional nursing organizations as well as Sigma Theta Tau International, the Nursing Honor Society.

CHAPTER 8

Health Promotion

Benita Cohen

OBJECTIVES

AFTER STUDYING THIS CHAPTER, YOU SHOULD BE ABLE TO:

1. Compare and contrast the main characteristics of the three approaches to health promotion that have been dominant since the early twentieth century, the assumptions underlying each of these approaches, and the main factors influencing their development. Give examples of how each approach may be utilized by community health nurses.
2. Identify the milestones in the development of health promotion as a multidisciplinary field of policy and practice since the 1970s.
3. Discuss how the concepts of (a) "empowering" strategies for health promotion and (b) a microscopic ("downstream") versus macroscopic ("upstream") approach to health promotion can be applied to community health nursing practice.
4. Describe the Population Health Promotion Model and apply it to the analysis of a typical community health nursing scenario.
5. Discuss guiding principles for a health-promoting community health nursing practice.

INTRODUCTION

The view that health promotion is a cornerstone of professional nursing practice is not uncommon, especially in the field of community health nursing (Canadian Public Health Association, 1990; Community Health Nurses Association of Canada 2003; Novak, 1988; Smith, 1990). Yet, there is no consensus about what health promotion means. While one might expect differences in the interpretation of the concept of health promotion between nursing and other disciplines, there is considerable diversity *within* nursing as well (Maben & MacLeod Clark, 1995). This phenomenon is reflected in the responses of a group of Canadian nursing students in a third-year course on community health promotion, who were asked what the term "health promotion" meant to them:

- "Health promotion means educating people to make healthy lifestyle choices."
- "Health promotion is a way of being with clients. It's more a philosophy of practice than something specific you do."
- "Health promotion means taking action on the determinants of health—things like poverty, discrimination, marginalization, and so on. It means getting politically active."
- "Everything nurses do is about promoting health. There isn't something specific that is health promotion" (MacDonald, 2002).

Is one of these descriptions of health promotion the "correct" one and the others "incorrect"? Not at all. As we will see, a variety of factors influences how one defines health promotion. This chapter will explore the different ways of thinking about the concept. The goal is *not* to provide a step-by-step guide on how to "do" health promotion, but rather to help the reader think critically about the various conceptual and philosophical approaches to health promotion and their implications for community health nursing practice. We begin by tracing the historical development of health promotion as a multidisciplinary field, including major approaches and key milestones. We then explore the historical role of health promotion in community health nursing and end with a few general principles that may guide community health nurses' (CHNs) health promotion practice.

HISTORICAL DEVELOPMENTS IN THE APPROACH TO HEALTH PROMOTION

Labonte (1993) provides a useful way of organizing the discussion by suggesting that there have been three major approaches to health enhancement since the beginning of the twentieth century: biomedical, behavioural (lifestyle), and socio-environmental. In the following sections, each of these approaches will be discussed, highlighting the key concepts, documents, and strategies associated with them—but, more importantly, highlighting the dominant theories and values that underlie them. Please note that, although these approaches emerged at different points in time, they are all still present to varying degrees in the health field, depending on one's area of practice. Labonte (1993) suggests that all three approaches are useful and that health professionals may find themselves alternating between them at different times and for different purposes. He recommends that the three approaches should be viewed more as *ideal* types; in reality, the boundaries between them are fuzzy. I would also add that, *within* each of these ideal types, in reality, there is a continuum or range of perspectives.

Dominance of the Biomedical Approach

Beginning with the discovery of disease-causing pathogens in the eighteenth and nineteenth centuries, and gaining momentum with the immense expansion of scientific knowledge during the twentieth century, the **biomedical approach** to health enhancement has dominated mainstream thinking in Western society. (Of course, other perspectives on health and disease have always existed, both within certain populations in Western societies and among non-Western societies. However, it is beyond the scope of this chapter to explore those perspectives and the approaches to health enhancement that they have generated.)

The key features of the biomedical perspective are outlined in the first column of Table 8.1. Essentially, think of this approach as synonymous with preventive health care. It is focused on preventing disease or disability in individuals by decreasing their **physiological risk factors** (e.g., hypertension, hypercholesterolemia, lack of immunity). Although the biomedical approach was never the *only* way that people understood the concept of health, overlapping the behavioural approach, this conceptualization of health and health promotion still remains a powerful perspective in our society today. Biomedical strategies, such as immunization and

TABLE 8.1
Summary of Different Approaches to Health Enhancement

	Biomedical	Behavioural	Socio-environmental
Health concept	• absence of disease or disability	• physical-functional ability; physical-emotional well-being	• goes beyond physical-emotional well-being to include social well-being at individual and community levels; may be viewed as a resource for daily living rather than a "state" that one aspires to
Health determinant	• physiological risk factors (e.g., hypertension)	• behavioural risk factors (e.g., smoking); lifestyle	• psychosocial risk factors (e.g., low self-esteem) • socio-environmental risk conditions (e.g., poverty)
Target	• primarily high-risk individuals (due to above risk factors)	• primarily high-risk groups (due to above risk factors)	• high-risk conditions and environments
Principle strategies	• screening for risk factors • patient education and compliance for behaviour change (e.g., dietary counselling) • immunization	• health education • social marketing • regulatory measures and public policies supporting healthy lifestyle choices (e.g., smoking ban)	• *Ottawa Charter* strategies (strengthening community action, creating supportive environments, developing healthy public policy, developing personal skills, reorienting health systems) • empowerment strategies (personal empowerment, small-group development, community organization/ development, advocacy for healthy public policy, political action)
Program development	• professionally managed	• professionally managed, or may be community-based[1]	• community development[2]
Success criteria	• decrease in morbidity and mortality rates • decrease in prevalence of physiological risk factors	• decrease in behavioural risk factors; improved lifestyles • enactment of healthy public policies related to health behaviours	• improved personal perception of health • improved social networks, quality of social support • improved community group actions to create more equitable social distribution of power/resources • enactment of healthy public policies related to social equity and environmental sustainability

1. Community-based programming: the process of health professionals and/or health agencies defining the health problem, developing strategies to remedy the problem, involving local community members and groups to assist in solving the problem, and working to transfer major responsibility for ongoing programs to local community members and groups.

2. Community-development programming: the process of supporting community groups in their identification of important concerns and issues and in their ability to plan and implement strategies to mitigate their concerns and resolve their issues.

Source: Adapted with permission from Labonte, R. (1993). Health promotion and empowerment: Practice frameworks. *Toronto, ON: University of Toronto, Centre for Health Promotion.*

screening tests for early detection and treatment of disease, remain an important part of public health practice.

The Behavioural/Lifestyle Approach

It is generally agreed that the birth of the modern era of health promotion as an organized and distinct multidisciplinary field in health policy and practice occurred in the 1970s. The major turning point in thinking about the concept of health promotion occurred in 1974 with the publication of a discussion paper by the Canadian Department of Health and Welfare entitled *A New Perspective on the Health of Canadians* (Lalonde, 1974). The Lalonde Report (as it is commonly referred to) noted that, in spite of a massive increase in spending on health services during the previous two decades, the health of Canadians was not improving. In fact, morbidity and premature mortality rates for certain chronic or degenerative diseases (e.g., heart disease, cancer, and sexually transmitted infections) and injuries (especially motor vehicle related) were steadily increasing. Instead of pouring more and more money into services for the sick, the Lalonde Report argued for a "new perspective"—one that paid more attention to the promotion of health.

The Lalonde Report was important for several reasons.

- This was the first time that a national government had made such a statement regarding the importance of health promotion as a key strategy for improving the health of a population.
- Although the Report still defined the concept of health in its most basic form as "freedom from disease and disability" (Lalonde, p. 8), the added reference to promoting "a state of well-being sufficient to perform at adequate levels of physical, mental and social activity" (Lalonde, p. 8) allowed for a slightly expanded interpretation of health that included the idea of increased functional "ability" and a sense of "wellness" (Labonte, 1993).
- Perhaps the most important contribution was that it challenged the dominant thinking of the time, which viewed access to health services as the key to population health. Instead, it suggested that the organization and availability of health services was one of four main categories of factors (or "health fields") that influenced the health of Canadians—the others being human biology, the environment, and lifestyle.

While the Lalonde framework appeared to place equal weight on each of the four fields, a central argument was that much of the premature mortality and morbidity occurring at the time was due to individual behaviours or lifestyles that could be modified (e.g., smoking and other addictions, lack of physical activity, risky sexual behaviour). Therefore, it was argued, the focus of health promotion efforts should be on strategies that encourage the adoption of behaviours or lifestyles that promote functional ability and well-being. This perspective on health and health promotion has come to be known as the **behavioural or lifestyle approach**. The key characteristics of this approach are outlined in the second column of Table 8.1. Essentially, the behavioural approach focuses on the prevention of disease and disability (often expressed in terms of promoting "wellness") in people who are at risk because of their lifestyle or behavioural risk factors such as a high-fat diet, unsafe sexual practices, or the use of tobacco, alcohol, or other drugs.

What is the underlying assumption of the behavioural approach to health promotion? The Lalonde Report explicitly defined health promotion as "a strategy aimed at informing, influencing and assisting both individuals and organizations so that they will accept more responsibility and be more active in matters affecting mental and physical health" (Lalonde, 1974, p. 66). The notion of *individual responsibility for health* has its roots in the ideology or world-view that has been dominant in Western societies for the past 400 years. This ideology, which places greatest value on the rights and responsibilities of the individual and assumes that all individuals have "free will" and "equality of choice," is clearly reflected in the assumptions of health promotion approaches that are concerned primarily with changing individual behaviours (Williams, 1989).

Lalonde emphasized **health education** and **social marketing** as key strategies of formal health promotion programs. Other strategies include **health communication**, **behaviour modification**, and the development of **regulatory measures** that influence behaviours or lifestyle. A brief description of these strategies is found in Table 8.2. For a more detailed discussion of these strategies, see Glanz, Lewis, and Rimer (2002) and McKenzie and Smeltzer (1997).

The common thread in each of these strategies is the underlying belief that the main determinant of health is individual behaviour or lifestyle and that information, persuasion, or any other method (including legal coercion) that encourages people to adopt healthier behaviours or lifestyles is the key to health promotion. Not surprisingly, many of these strategies are based on theories and models (e.g., the Health Belief Model [HBM], the Transtheoretical [Stages of Change] Model, and Social Learning/Cognition Theory) that were developed in the field of psychology to explain, predict, and change health behaviours. For a comprehensive discussion of models used in the behavioural approach to health promotion, see Glanz et al. (2002).

The behavioural approach to health promotion continues to be very popular. National and provincial governments frequently rely on health communication campaigns to deliver "healthy lifestyle" messages, health education programs based on various theories of behaviour change are commonly used in schools, and health teaching remains a major part of health care professionals' practice.

The Socio-environmental Approach to Health Promotion

As noted in Table 8.1, the **socio-environmental approach** represented a significant change in thinking about health promotion. Here the focus was on the elements in the environment that contributed to the health or disease of an individual or a group, rather than on their behaviour in isolation. A number of factors contributed to this new way of thinking

TABLE 8.2
Strategies that Focus on Changing Behaviour/Lifestyle

Strategy	Description
Health education	Usually refers to activities associated with formal education, including use of audiovisual materials, printed educational materials, teaching strategies for the classroom (e.g., lecture/discussion, case studies, brainstorming), teaching strategies outside the classroom (e.g., health fair). May also refer to one-on-one teaching.
Health communication	Usually refers to the use of the mass media, direct mail, product labels, pamphlets, and posters to communicate a health message to the public. May also refer to health professional–client interaction.
Social marketing	Refers to "the application of commercial marketing technologies to the analysis, planning, execution and evaluation of programs designed to influence the voluntary behaviour of target audiences in order to improve their personal welfare and that of society" (Andreasen cited in Nutbeam & Harris, 1999, p. 49). Usually involves health communication techniques mentioned above. May include sponsorship, participation events, direct selling, and competitions.
Behaviour modification	Refers to a systematic procedure for changing a specific behaviour by changing the events that precede or result from the behaviour that is to be modified. Most often used to alter smoking, eating, or exercise patterns.
Regulatory measures	Refers to mandated activities (laws, policies, regulations). Examples include laws requiring the use of seatbelts or motorcycle helmets and banning smoking in public places.

about health promotion in the 1980s. One factor relates to ideological responses to the behavioural approach. Labonte (1993) notes that the 1980s were a time when many of the social movements that emerged in North America in the 1960s and 1970s were maturing. Within these social movements, concepts such as **social justice** (the belief that all persons are entitled equally to key ends such as health protection and minimum standards of income) and the **common good** (where the needs of the many have priority over the needs of the individual) were central principles (Beauchamp, 1976). Many of the activists who took part in these social movements later moved into professional jobs, including those in the health and social services fields. Critical of the individualistic behavioural perspective that had come to dominate the field of health promotion in the early 1980s, these former activists articulated what is sometimes referred to as the **structural or systems critique** of health promotion. From this perspective, health and illness are the result of broad factors such as the socioeconomic and physical environment, the level of social support and social cohesion among individuals and communities, the level of education, and working conditions. **Social change** (as opposed to individual behaviour change) is viewed as the most important goal of health promotion, and **social responsibility for health** is paramount. In other words, change must happen across a culture or population, and each member has some accountability for the health of the whole population. Approaches that focus solely on individual behaviour change and individual responsibility for health are viewed as a form of **victim-blaming**, whereby individuals end up being implicitly blamed for being sick because they have "chosen" unhealthy lifestyles or they have unhealthy coping styles when, in fact, their social and economic circumstances have often left them with limited options (Crawford, 1977; Labonte & Penfold, 1981).

At the same time that this ideological critique of the behavioural approach was being articulated, a theoretical perspective called the **ecological approach** to health promotion emerged from the field of social ecology. The central premise of this perspective is that health is a product of the *interdependence* between the individual and subsystems of the ecosystem (family, community, culture, and physical and social environment). To promote health, this ecosystem must offer economic and social conditions conducive to health and healthful lifestyles. While there is agreement with the structuralist view that the environment largely controls or sets limits on the behaviour that occurs in it, the other side of this equation holds that the behaviour of individuals, groups, and organizations also influences their environments (Green, Richard, & Potvin, 1996). From an ecological perspective, both individual behaviour change and environmental or system change are required elements of health promotion initiatives—neither one on its own is sufficient. This perspective had a major influence on the approach to health promotion that emerged in the mid-1980s. For example, one of the most popular frameworks for health promotion program planning in use today—the "PRECEDE–PROCEED" Model (Green & Kreuter, 1999)—is based on the ecological perspective. For further discussion of this and other ecological models, see chapters in Glanz et al. (2002).

In addition to the ideological and theoretical critiques of the behavioural approach to health promotion outlined above, two other factors influenced the development of the socio-environmental perspective. In the 1980s, several high-profile, population-wide, disease-prevention initiatives to reduce the behaviours that were contributing to coronary heart disease (such as smoking, high intake of dietary fat, low levels of physical activity) failed to achieve their intended results (Syme, 1997). Even where disease prevention initiatives *did* result in reductions in high-risk behaviours, it was primarily the better educated, middle-class members of society who benefited. Many of these programs failed to reach individuals from lower socioeconomic groups who suffer from the poorest social and physical health (Labonte, 1993). As a result, it has been suggested that "effective" health promotion programs that focus on lifestyle change can actually contribute to the *increase* of social inequalities in health (Makara, 1997).

The final contributing factor to the socio-environmental approach was epidemiological evidence that could not be ignored. Beginning in the 1970s and escalating in the 1980s and beyond, a substantial body of research suggested that the distribution of disease in a society is *not* the result of individual behaviours, but *is* the result of the economic, political, and social relationship between individuals and groups in that society. In particular, a powerful body of evidence now indicates that social and economic inequality is one of the major determinants—some would argue, *the* major determinant—for disease (Wilkinson, 1996). There is also a robust body of evidence suggesting that social support is a major influence on the well-being of individuals (Heaney & Israel, 2002). At the community level, social stress (as evidenced by economic deprivation, crowding, family instability, and crime) or social cohesion (the flip side of social breakdown) are important determinants of health and disease (Patrick & Wickizer, 1995). Together, this research suggests that health promotion approaches that focus on individual behaviour change are insufficient to address the key determinants of population health.

Milestones in the Development of the Socio-environmental Approach Several pivotal events and policy statements mark the formal development of the socio-environmental approach to health promotion (see Table 8.3).

The seeds of a social definition of health promotion were sown as early as 1977 and 1978 by the WHO (see Table 8.3) (MacDonald, 2002). **Primary health care** (PHC) was anticipated to be the means of achieving the goals outlined in the WHO (1978) document. Several principles of PHC—for example, the importance of community participation and the need for intersectoral collaboration in order to address the broad social and environmental determinants of population health—emerged as key principles in the emerging socio-environmental approach to health promotion.

Several Canadian conferences in the early 1980s had major influences on the shift in thinking about health promotion both in this country and internationally. In 1980, a handful of delegates critiqued health promotion as lifestyle modification, arguing that "to create a dramatic impact on the health of *all* Canadians... requires, in part, addressing the social context in which personal lifestyle choices are made—something which most current health promotion programs fail to do" (Labonte & Penfold, 1981, p. 4). Few of the early health promotion programs in the 1970s addressed such issues as the economic health of the target group, for example, access to transportation or affordable nutritious foods (Minkler, 1989). The delegates argued that a different perspective was needed in which individual responsibility would

TABLE 8.3
Milestones in the Development of the Socio-environmental Approach to Health Promotion

Year	Milestone
1977	• 30th World Health Assembly; Adoption of World Health Organization's *Health for All by the Year 2000* (WHO, 1977)
1978	• Publication of *Declaration of Alma Ata on Primary Health Care* (WHO, 1978)
1980	• "Shifting Medical Paradigm Conference" in Vancouver and the First National Health Promotion Conference in Ottawa (structural critique of behaviour/lifestyle approach articulated)
1984	• Beyond Health Care Conference, Toronto (introduction of the concepts of "healthy public policy" and "healthy cities")
	• Publication of *Health Promotion: A Discussion Document on the Concepts and Principles* (WHO, 1984) (basis for socio-environmental approach first formally articulated at the international level)
1986	• Publication of *Achieving Health for All: A Framework for Health Promotion* (Epp, 1986) (socio-environmental approach first formally articulated in Canada)
	• First International Conference on Health Promotion, Ottawa, Canada. Release of the *Ottawa Charter for Health Promotion* (WHO, 1986) (socio-environmental approach fully articulated); Note: subsequent WHO International Conferences on Health Promotion in 1988, 1992, 1997, and 2000 have all reinforced the original statements made in 1986.
1996	• Publication of *Population Health Promotion: An Integrated Model of Population Health and Health Promotion* (Hamilton & Bhatti, 1996)
	• Publication of *Action Statement on Health Promotion* (Canadian Public Health Association, 1996); Identified three of the *Ottawa Charter* strategies—strengthening community action, building healthy public policy, and reforming the health system—as priorities for health promotion in Canada.

Source: MacDonald, M. (2002). Health promotion: historical, philosophical, and theoretical perspectives. In L. Young & V. Hayes (Eds.), Transforming health promotion practice: Concepts, issues, and applications *(pp. 22–45). Philadelphia, PA: F.A. Davis Company.*

become synonymous with social responsibility and health promotion would include collective actions to alter the health-damaging aspects of our social environment as well as individual action to alter personally damaging habits.

In 1984, another major Canadian contribution to a new approach to health promotion was the concept of "healthy cities" and the need for healthy public policies that focus on environmental determinants of health (such as housing and other factors contributing to the health of cities). This concept challenged the notion of health as an individual characteristic and focused very much on its social and environmental dimensions. In fact, the Beyond Health Care Conference is widely recognized as having given birth to a worldwide movement to establish **healthy communities** (Raeburn & Rootman, 1998).

An important feature of the new health perspective was the link made at this time by Canadian health promoters between the concept of empowerment and the promotion of health (Labonte, 1993). **Empowerment** refers to the process whereby individuals, communities, and populations gain power, knowledge, skills, and/or other resources that allow them to achieve positive change (Rodwell, 1996). It also refers to the outcome of that process. Wallerstein (1992) distinguishes between individual **psychological empowerment**, which involves self-efficacy and motivation to act, and **community empowerment**, which involves increased local action, stronger social networks, resource access/equity, transformed conditions, and community competence. While health care professionals cannot directly empower others, they can help people and communities develop, secure, and/or use the resources and skills that promote a sense of control and self-efficacy (Gibson, 1991).

At the international level as well, 1984 provided a significant milestone: the WHO discussion document on the concept and principles of health promotion (WHO, 1984). Health promotion was defined as "the process of enabling people to increase control over, and improve, their health" (WHO, p. 3). (This original WHO definition is still very popular. However, in recent years it has been expanded as "the process of enabling individuals and communities to increase control over the determinants of health" (Nutbeam cited in Green, Poland, & Rootman, 2000, p. 6).)

Five key principles of health promotion were identified (WHO, 1984).

- Health promotion involves the population as a whole and the context of their everyday life, rather than focusing on people at risk for specific diseases.
- Health promotion is directed toward action on the determinants or causes of health.
- Health promotion combines diverse, but complementary, methods or approaches.
- Health promotion aims particularly at effective and concrete public participation.
- Health professionals, particularly in primary health care, have an important role in nurturing and enabling health promotion.

This perspective was further elaborated in 1986, popularly identified as the birth date of the "new health promotion." Two key events occurred (see Table 8.3). First, the Canadian Minister of National Health and Welfare, Jake Epp, released a document that clearly distanced itself from the behavioural/lifestyle approach to health promotion (Epp, 1986). Acknowledging the growing body of evidence regarding the social and economic determinants of population health, the Epp Report argued that health promotion was as much a societal responsibility as an individual responsibility. It identified three leading health challenges facing Canadians:

- the need to reduce inequities in the health of low- versus high-income groups;
- the need to find new and more effective ways of preventing the occurrence of injuries, illnesses, chronic conditions, and their resulting disabilities; and
- the need to enhance people's ability to manage and cope with chronic conditions, disabilities, and mental health problems.

In order to meet these challenges, three mechanisms for health promotion were identified:

- self-care, referring to the decisions taken and practices adopted by an individual specifically for the preservation of their health;
- mutual aid, referring to people's efforts to deal with their health concerns by working together (either through informal social support networks, voluntary organizations, or self-help groups); and
- the creation of healthy environments at home, school, work, or wherever else Canadians may be.

Finally, three main health promotion strategies were identified as the basis for putting these mechanisms into action:

- fostering public participation, by helping people assert control over the factors that affect their health;
- strengthening community health services, by allocating a greater share of resources to those services that have an orientation to health promotion and disease prevention; and
- coordinating health public policies between sectors (such as income security, employment, education, housing) that make it easier for people to make healthy choices.

It is important to note that the Epp Report clearly stated that a focus on one strategy or mechanism from the framework on its own would be of little significance; it was only by putting the pieces of the framework together that health promotion would be meaningful.

Presented later in 1986 at the first International Health Promotion Conference in Ottawa, the Epp Report influenced the development of the *Ottawa Charter for Health Promotion* (WHO, 1986), a document that was signed by delegates from 38 countries including Canada. The *Ottawa Charter* adopted the WHO's 1984 definitions of health and health promotion and emphasized that achieving equity in health was considered to be the main focus of health promotion. A number of essential prerequisites for health were identified (peace, shelter, education, food, income, a stable ecosystem, sustainable resources, social justice, and equity), and the importance of coordinated intersectoral action to ensure these prerequisites for health was underlined. The *Ottawa Charter* proposed five key strategies for health promotion (WHO).

- **Strengthening community action** by supporting those activities that encourage community members to participate in, and take action on, issues that affect their health and the health of others. Community development or community empowerment is viewed as both the means and the end result of this process. Priority is given to those individuals and communities whose living and working conditions place them at greatest risk for poor health.
- **Building healthy public policy** by advocacy for any health, income, environmental, or social policy that fosters greater equity, creates a setting for health, or increases options/resources for health.
- **Creating supportive environments** by generating living, working, and playing conditions that are safe, stimulating, satisfying, and enjoyable and by ensuring that the protection of the natural environment is addressed in any health promotion strategy.
- **Developing personal skills** by supporting personal and social development through the provision of information—education for health and enhancing life skills—in order to increase the options available to people to exercise more control over their own health and environments and to make choices conducive to health.
- **Reorienting health services** by moving beyond the health sector's responsibility for providing clinical and curative services in a health promotion direction that is sensitive to the needs of the community.

The publication of the *Ottawa Charter* (WHO, 1986) is widely recognized as marking the transition, at least in theory, from an "old" health promotion practice that focused on medical and behavioural health determinants to a "new" health promotion practice that defined health determinants in psychological, social, environmental, and political terms. See column 3 of Table 8.1 for a summary of the key features of this new socio-environmental approach to health promotion. Some of the challenges in implementing the socio-environmental approach to health promotion will be discussed later in the chapter. Canadian Research Box 8.1 describes a community health problem in which each of the three approaches to health promotion that we have discussed might be applicable.

Canadian Research Box 8.1

Hogan, S. E. (2001). Overcoming barriers to breastfeeding: Suggested breastfeeding promotion programs for communities in eastern Nova Scotia. *Canadian Journal of Public Health, 92*(2), 105–108.

This study was motivated by the discovery in the mid-1990s that the rate of initiation of breastfeeding in eastern Nova Scotia, a region of low economic advantage, was only around 40% compared with the provincial and national rates of 63% and 73%, respectively. Participants completed a questionnaire regarding perceived barriers to initiation and duration of breastfeeding and the perceived need for community resources to support breastfeeding. Perceived barriers to initiation and duration of breastfeeding included lack of knowledge about and management skills required for breastfeeding, lack of support for breastfeeding from the family, employers, and both hospital- and community-based health professionals, and difficulty in continuing to breastfeed while returning to work.

Data from the study was used to revise pre- and postnatal hospital and public health programs in the region. For example, home visits by public health nurses were increased to all mothers requesting pre- and postnatal counselling. By 1998, breastfeeding initiation rates in the region had increased to 60.5% and the duration of breastfeeding increased to four months in 90.2% of mothers. However, both of these rates remained below the national average.

Discussion Questions

1. What roles/activities could CHNs engage in as part of a comprehensive health promotion initiative aimed at increasing breastfeeding initiation and duration in this region?
2. Would your answer to Question 1 differ if you applied each of the approaches to health promotion?

Population Health Promotion

A new era may now be emerging in health promotion—the era of **population health** (MacDonald, 2002). In 1994, the Federal/Provincial/Territorial Advisory Committee on Population Health published a document, entitled *Strategies for Population Health: Investing in the Health of Canadians,* that described an approach to public policy that focuses on taking action on the interrelated conditions that influence population health status. These interrelated conditions were identified as income and social status, social support networks, education, employment and working conditions, safe and clean physical environments, biology and genetic makeup, personal health practices and coping skills, early childhood development, and health services. Since that time, the population health perspective has been adopted at the policy level by the federal government, several provincial governments, and some regional health authorities.

A number of characteristics of a population health approach differ from those of the socio-environmental approach to health promotion. For example, the socio-environmental approach focuses on addressing inequities in health experienced by disadvantaged and marginalized groups, defines health in its broadest sense as a resource for daily living, and identifies a wide range of strategies for change that emphasize individual and community empowerment. In contrast, population health is mostly concerned with gradients in health status across all socioeconomic levels, defines "health" in terms of traditional epidemiological "sickness" indicators, and focuses on identifying determinants of disease and death rather than strategies for change.

In an effort to bridge the gap between population health and health promotion, a **Population Health Promotion Model (PHPM)** was developed by Health Canada (Hamilton & Bhatti, 1996). This model attempts to integrate concepts from both perspectives (see Figure 8.1). This three-dimensional model combines the strategies for health promotion outlined in the 1986 *Ottawa Charter* on one side, with the determinants of population health on another side, and with various levels of potential intervention on the third side of the model. This model can be used from different entry points. One can begin with the health determinant that one intends to influence, the action strategy to be used, or the level at which action is to be taken. Figure 8.2 shows examples of how the model can be used to identify possibilities for influencing various determinants of health. The PHPM can also be used to address the health concerns of groups who are at risk for poor health or to address specific health issues. It's important to remember that, from the socio-environmental perspective, we are primarily concerned with social and environmental risk conditions and psychosocial risk factors that are known to affect health status, either directly or indirectly via behaviours. An example of risk conditions would be a deprived neighbourhood where the housing is substandard, there are few recreational facilities, community spirit is weak, and there are feelings of danger and insecurity (Hamilton & Bhatti, 1996).

The positive contribution of the PHPM framework is that it addresses one of the main criticisms of the population health perspective—that it doesn't provide a model for change

FIGURE 8.1 The Population Health Promotion Model (PHPM)

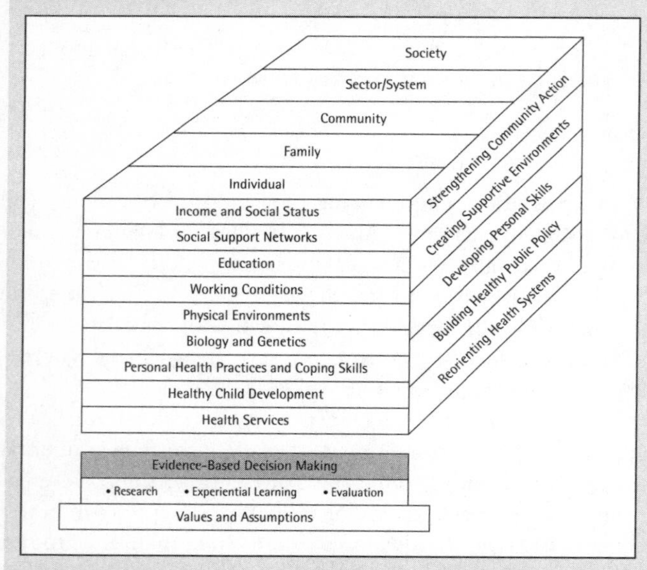

Source: Reprinted with permission from Hamilton, N., & Bhatti, T. (1996). Population health promotion: An integrated model of population health and health promotion. *Ottawa, ON: Health Canada, Health Promotion and Development Division. Reproduced with the permission of the Minister of Public Works and Government Services Canada, 2004.*

FIGURE 8.2 Using the PHPM to Influence Determinants of Health

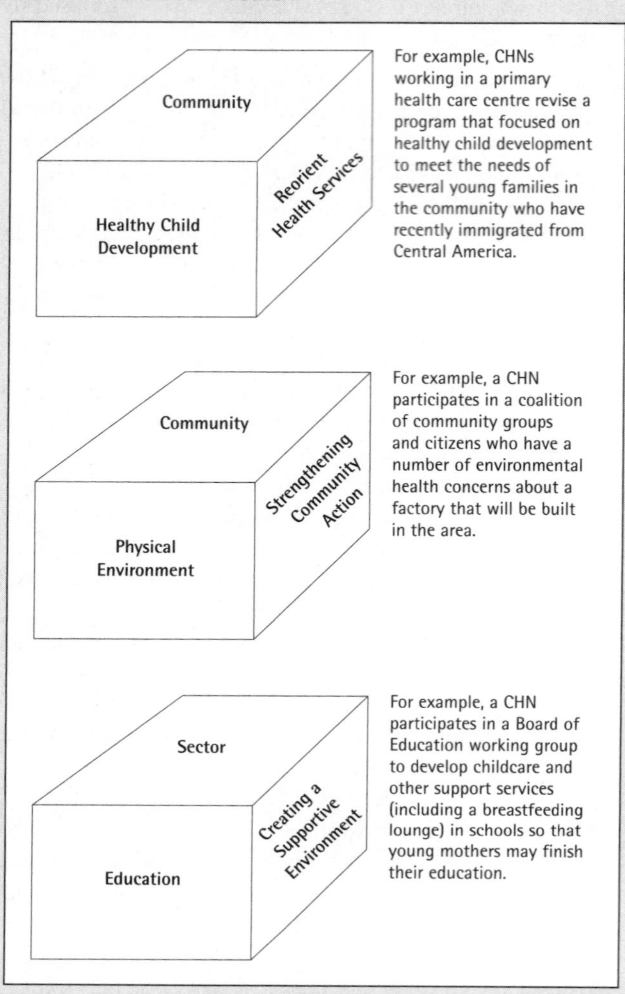

Source: Reprinted with permission from Hamilton, N., & Bhatti, T. (1996). Population health promotion: An integrated model of population health and health promotion. *Ottawa, ON: Health Canada, Health Promotion and Development Division. Adapted and reproduced with the permission of the Minister of Public Works and Government Services Canada, 2004. Health Canada assumes no responsibility for any errors or omissions that may have occurred in the adaptation of its material.*

(Labonte, 1995; Raphael & Bryant, 2000). Rather than simply identifying the broad determinants of health, the PHPM framework proposes strategies for acting on them.

HEALTH PROMOTION IN COMMUNITY HEALTH NURSING

Now that we have explored the major theoretical developments in the multidisciplinary field of health promotion, let's take a look at the role of health promotion in community health nursing. Statements about nurses being at the heart of the practice of health promotion (O'Neill, 1997), in a position to play a strong leadership role in health promotion

(Canadian Nurses Association, 1992; Lowenburg, 1995), and "the most strategically placed health professionals to accomplish health promotion goals with clients" (Innes & Ciliska cited in Dallaire, Hagan, & O'Neill, 2000, p. 320) are not uncommon in the nursing literature. The question is, are all of these authors using the term "health promotion" in the same way? MacDonald (2002) notes that many nursing authors appear to assume that there is a widely shared understanding of the term health promotion, while in reality there is considerable diversity in the interpretation and underlying ideologies of health promotion within the nursing profession. In one review of the nursing practice and health promotion literature, the authors identified six different understandings of health promotion (Maben & MacLeod Clark, 1995):

- as an umbrella term referring to any activity designed to foster health,
- as a synonym for health education,
- as the marketing or selling of health,
- as a strategy concerned with lifestyle behaviour change,
- as health education plus environmental and legislative measures designed to facilitate the achievement of health and prevention of disease, and
- as an approach that encompasses a set of values which includes concepts of empowerment, equity, and collaboration.

Maben and MacLeod Clark (1995) note that the first four understandings are in line with a traditional behavioural approach to health promotion, whereas the latter two are synonymous with the new paradigm approach as outlined in the *Ottawa Charter* (WHO, 1986). Which understanding of health promotion is the most influential among nurses? We will explore this question in the following sections.

The Behavioural Approach in Nursing

In the early 1980s, Brubaker (1983) found that the primary emphasis of health promotion in the nursing literature of the time was on personal responsibility, lifestyle behaviour change, and high-level wellness. In the 1990s, in spite of the emergence of the socio-environmental perspective in the broader health promotion movement and among certain nursing theorists, the behavioural conceptualization of health promotion remained predominant in nursing *practice*, including community health nursing practice (Benson & Latter, 1998; Maben & MacLeod Clark, 1995; O'Brien, 1994).

Why have nurses adopted the lifestyle approach to health promotion? It could be argued that this is simply an extension of what they have been doing for years. Healthy lifestyles and behaviours have long been of concern to nurses, and health education has always been a central focus of nursing practice. This is true in the hospital, where nurses provide health teaching to patients and their families, but it has been even more true for nurses working in the community. In the late nineteenth century, Florence Nightingale, widely considered the founder of modern nursing, wrote about the importance of teaching mothers about proper sanitation methods and childcare under the supervision of district (community) nurses. By the early twentieth century, advising and instructing people on how to avoid illness through personal hygiene and how to promote healthy child development was a primary duty of public health nurses (also referred to as visiting or district nurses, depending on the jurisdiction) (Novak, 1988). Providing information related to healthy child development and health-promoting behaviours remains a central role of CHNs to this day.

Another reason why the behavioural approach appears to be predominant in nursing practice may be because many of the nursing models used in nursing education and practice since the 1970s have been strongly influenced by concepts and theories from the behavioural sciences, in which individual behaviour change is the outcome of interest. For example, Pender's (1996) **Health Promotion Model (HPM)** was the first nursing model to focus *explicitly* on health promotion, and it remains an influential model in community health nursing education and practice (Stewart & Leipert, 2000). Strongly influenced by the Health Belief Model, which was developed to explain why individuals do or do not take action to prevent disease, the HPM suggests that (a) cognitive factors such as perceived benefits and barriers to action and perceived self-efficacy combine with (b) individual biological, psychological, and sociocultural characteristics and experience (e.g., prior related behaviour, age, gender, socioeconomic status) and (c) intrapersonal and situational influences (e.g., family, peers, health care providers, environmental cues) to (d) lead the individual to commit to a plan of action that will (e) result

FIGURE 8.3 Pender's Health Promotion Model (HPM)

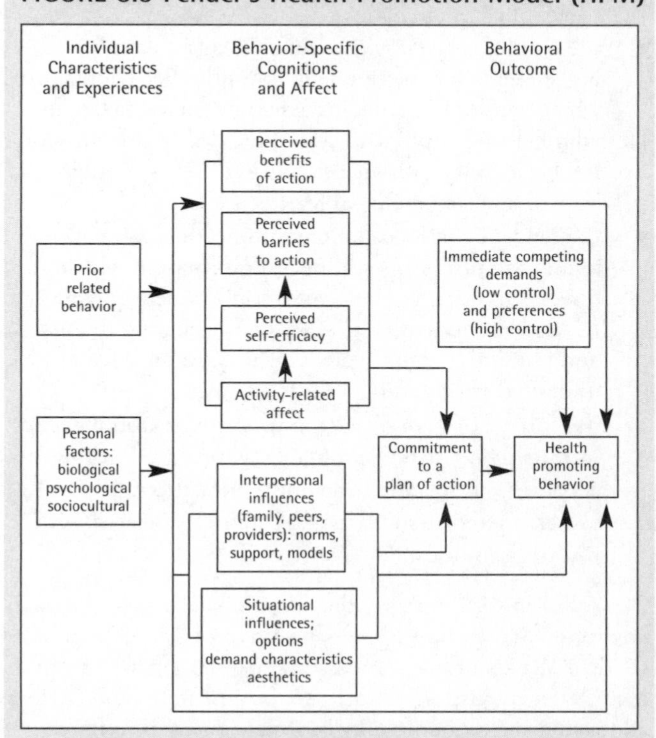

Source: Health Promotion in Nursing Practice (4th ed.). Pender, N.J., Murdough, C.L., & Parsons, M.A. © 2002. Reprinted by permission of Pearson Education, Inc., Upper Saddle River, N.J.

in health-promoting behaviour (see Figure 8.3).

As far as the nurse's role in health promotion is concerned, Pender draws heavily on Orem's (1985) Self-Care Model, which has received wide acceptance in Canada in all areas of nursing (Dallaire et al., 2000). Orem identified three types of professional nursing practice, one of which she called the *educative-developmental* system of nursing, which gives the client primary responsibility for personal health with the nurse functioning in a consultative capacity. According to Pender, this system of educative-developmental nursing is most appropriate for health promotion. The major areas of educative-developmental nursing for self-care identified by Pender include enhancing clients' capacities for exercise and physical fitness, nutrition and weight control, stress management, risk reduction, maintenance of family and other support systems, avoidance of injurious and violent behaviours, and environmental modifications in homes, schools, worksites, and the community to reduce hazards to health. The nurse's role is to assist the client in developing, carrying out, and evaluating a behaviour change plan. Since the individual's *perceptions* regarding the benefits of health-enhancing actions are central to this model, the nurse's role is to change those perceptions and attitudes that are perceived as non-health-enhancing.

Rush (1997) points to several other characteristics of nursing curricula that perpetuate the individualistic, behaviour-focused health promotion ideology among nurses:

- the tendency in undergraduate curricula to gear health promotion to the behaviour of nursing students themselves by requiring them to assess their own lifestyle, identify their personal health goals, and implement a behaviour change plan;
- the emphasis given within nursing curricula to preparing students for role-modelling healthy behaviours, which can lead to students assigning blame to clients who fail to comply with recommended health-promoting behaviours without recognizing the responsibility located at a sociopolitical level;
- the tendency to focus on communication and counselling as nursing roles in health promotion, which directs attention to the coping and problem-solving resources of individuals rather than changing the social and physical environments that may be producing the undesired effect; and
- the format of many health promotion textbooks used in nursing education programs, which section the text according to specific behaviours (nutrition, physical exercise/activity, stress management) associated with health promotion.

All of this is not to say that concepts related to the socio-environmental perspective on health promotion in nursing curricula have not been discussed since the 1980s. The problem is that discussion of socio-environmental issues (such as addressing socioeconomic inequalities in health, intersectoral collaboration, and community participation) tends to occur in one particular course or in one semester that focuses on health promotion, while students are still exposed to the ideas and situations listed above in other parts of their program. In an effort to address this problem, at least one undergraduate nursing program in Canada has completely revised its entire curriculum to reflect a socio-environmental perspective on health promotion throughout (Hills & Lindsey, 1996). Another Canadian undergraduate program has revised its curriculum around the concept of primary health care (Munro et al., 2000).

The Socio-environmental Approach in Nursing

MacDonald (2002) makes several observations worth highlighting about theoretical developments in nursing during the post–*Ottawa Charter* period. First, although a structural critique of the lifestyle/behavioural approach to health promotion by nursing authors emerged in the mid-1980s, it never represented more than a marginal position in nursing until the late 1990s (and, it could be argued, it still doesn't). Second, the critique was articulated in relation to concerns about nursing—in other words, it was a general critique of traditional nursing theory and practice—rather than being discussed within the context of a specific model or framework for health promotion. (This may explain why nursing has not been acknowledged in the broader multidisciplinary health promotion movement as having made any significant contributions to the development of health promotion theory or practice.) Nevertheless, the critique was consistent with the concepts and ideas that were central to the socio-environmental perspective on health promotion. For example, several nursing authors proposed an expansion of the concept of environment in nursing from the traditional focus on the immediate psychosocial environment of individuals to the broader sociopolitical environment of individuals, families, and communities (Kleffel, 1991; Stevens, 1989). Others explored the relevance of concepts inherent in the WHO's statements on PHC and the *Ottawa Charter*—such as empowerment (Rodwell, 1996), community participation (Hudson-Rodd, 1994), community development (Chalmers & Bramadat, 1996), collaboration (Clarke & Mass, 1998), and partnerships (Courtney, Ballard, Fauver, Gariota, & Holland, 1996)—to nursing theory and to practice in particular settings or with particular client groups.

An important point is that a large proportion of the critical analysis of traditional nursing practice and its focus on individual behaviour change emerged from the field of community health nursing. Since CHNs have always functioned within the broader context of the community, the concepts in the "new" health promotion paradigm had particular relevance to them. One of the best-known critiques of traditional nursing practice was articulated by Butterfield (1997), using McKinlay's (1979) famous "upstream-downstream" analogy of people (meaning health care providers) being so caught up with rescuing victims (patients) from a swiftly flowing river (representing illness) that they have no time to look upstream and see who is pushing these people into the water (the root cause of illness). Butterfield suggested that community health nurses needed to adopt a **macroscopic approach** in their practice—more commonly referred to as **thinking**

TABLE 8.4
"Thinking Upstream": Macroscopic vs. Microscopic Approaches in Community Health Nursing

"Downstream" (Microscopic) Approach	"Upstream" (Macroscopic) Approach
• Assessment focuses on individual (and family) responses to health and illness; often emphasizes an individual's behavioural and coping responses to illness or lifestyle patterns	• Assessment focuses on interfamily and intercommunity themes in health and illness • Identifies social, economic, and environmental factors in the community and population that perpetuate the development of illness or foster the development of health
• Nursing interventions are often aimed at modifying an individual's behaviour (including coping behaviours) through changing their perceptions or belief system or providing information	• Nursing interventions may include modifying social or environmental variables (in other words, working to remove barriers to care or improving sanitation or living conditions); this may include social or political action

Adapted, with permission from Elsevier Science, from Butterfield, P. (1997). Thinking upstream: Conceptualizing health from a population perspective. In J. Swanson & M. Nies (Eds.), Community health nursing: Promoting the health of aggregate *(pp. 69–82). Philadelphia, PA: W.B Saunders Company.*

upstream—as opposed to the traditional "downstream" or microscopic approach (see Table 8.4). An important aspect of the macroscopic approach in community health nursing is that it is not usually carried out by one nurse alone, but involves the cooperative efforts of nurses and other service providers from school, occupational, and other community settings (Butterfield, 1997).

The concept of "thinking upstream" is a valuable contribution to community health nursing practice because it encourages CHNs to address the root causes of health issues in individuals, families, and communities. However, two of the central features of the socio-environmental approach to health promotion—the idea of health promotion as a process of empowerment and the belief that reducing social and economic inequalities in health is a central goal—are not immediately apparent in the macroscopic approach outlined by Butterfield. In contrast, other critiques of traditional approaches to nursing—sometimes referred to as **emancipatory nursing** or **critical social nursing**—focus specifically on the nurse's role in addressing inequalities in health and the issue of empowerment. These critiques argue that nursing needs to break away from its preoccupation with helping people to cope with and adapt to oppressive life circumstances; instead, nurses should be assisting people to change their situation (Drevdahl, 1995; Kendall, 1992; Stevens & Hall, 1992). Moccia (1988) challenges nurses to include social activism in their definition of caring. If one accepts the definition of caring as helping people to grow and actualize themselves, she argues, then the responsibilities of the caregiver include activities that create and maintain social conditions that will permit caring to flourish.

Reutter (2000), a Canadian promoter of a critical social approach to community health nursing, notes that this community development approach includes asking critical questions to expose inequities, facilitating community involvement by listening to community needs, and assisting in bringing about changes. Rather than presenting solutions and directing lifestyle changes, the nurse's role is facilitative: assisting individuals and groups to reflect on the social and political factors that influence health, sharing expertise, and providing support. More specifically, Reutter suggests that a critical social approach to reducing inequities in health would include **empowering strategies** at the personal, interpersonal (small group), community, and policy levels (see Figure 6.3 in Chapter 6). At the personal or individual level, Reutter suggests that an empowering nursing strategy would involve not only understanding the psychosocial and socio-environmental context of the individual's concerns and problems and acknowledging these constraints, but also focusing on increasing the capacity of individuals to act upon the roots of their distress and advocating for and with clients to access the resources that they require to change their situation. This level of empowering strategy is similar to the *Ottawa Charter* strategy of "developing personal skills." It may involve the provision of information and advice, but it goes beyond that to building individual capacity for problem-solving, decision-making, and other life skills. At the interpersonal level, Reutter points out that CHNs can be involved in empowering strategies through facilitating the development of small groups that can decrease the social isolation that often accompanies poverty and providing affirmational, informational, and emotional support. Small groups, therefore, can increase personal empowerment and may foster community action. Small-group development also fits with the *Ottawa Charter* strategy of "creating a supportive environment." At the community level, Reutter suggests that CHNs can use a community development strategy to support community groups in identifying important issues related to poverty and in organizing collectively to plan and implement strategies to resolve these issues. This strategy fits nicely with the *Ottawa Charter* strategy of "strengthening community action." At the policy level, Reutter notes that CHNs can play an active role in advocating for structural changes that mitigate the effects of or reduce poverty, and/or they can support community groups in their own advocacy efforts to do the same, an approach that Labonte (1993) referred to as "advocacy with." For example, CHNs can serve on intersectoral boards and committees that influence public policy in areas such as housing, unemployment, income security, childcare, and environmental health, or they may get involved with neighbourhood associations, citizens' groups, and advocacy groups such as anti-poverty organizations. This approach is similar to the *Ottawa Charter* strategy of "advocacy for healthy public policy."

Relatively little has been written about family health promotion compared with individual-level and community-level health promotion (Young, 2002). In the late 1980s, Loveland-Cherry (cited in Bomar, 1990) adapted Pender's HPM for individual health promotion to fit family health promotion. In Canada, several models have been developed that focus on the family as the unit of nursing interactions. The McGill Model of Nursing (Gottlieb & Rowat, 1987) proposed that health promotion within the context of the family is the focus of nursing. The McGill Model emphasizes the nurse's role in engaging family members in a learning process that results in the achievement of health goals. The Calgary Family Assessment Model (Wright & Leahey, 1994) focuses on identifying cognitive, affective, and behavioural aspects of family functioning. The idea is to help families change their perceptions and beliefs about their health problems, to reduce or increase emotions that may be blocking families' problem-solving efforts, and to assist family members to behave differently in relation to one another. Another Canadian model, developed at the University of Victoria School of Nursing, was the first model of family health promotion that was specifically based on the socio-environmental approach to health promotion (Hartrick, Lindsey, & Hills, 1994). This framework suggests that the focus of family assessment is on identifying and resourcing family potential and facilitating the promotion of client autonomy and empowerment as the family itself identifies courses of action for positive change.

The Socio-environmental Approach in Canadian Nursing Practice Between 1987 and 1993 in Canada, there was a major professional mobilization in nursing related to PHC and the "new health promotion" (MacDonald, 2002). Position statements and discussion documents from national and provincial nurses' associations and the community health nursing section of the Canadian Public Health Association identified health promotion, as defined in the *Ottawa Charter* (WHO, 1986) and the Epp Report (Epp, 1986), as the primary goal of nursing practice (Canadian Nurses Association [CNA], 1992; Canadian Public Health Association [CPHA], 1990). For example, the CNA (1992) noted that health promotion "implies a commitment to dealing with the challenges of reducing inequities," while the CPHA's (1990) document, which outlined the philosophy, roles and activities, qualifications, and competencies for community health/public health nurses (C/PHNs), stated that C/PHNs are "leaders in the effort to promote health-enhancing public policy and the empowerment of communities" (p. 4). In 1992, the Registered Nurses Association of British Columbia published a document that provided a socio-environmental framework for health promotion practice (Labonte & Little, 1992). Nurses in that province have been working to put those empowering strategies into practice (Ritchie, Boutell, Buchan, Foster, & St. Aubrey, 1995). Manitoba Health (1998) framed its discussion within the context of the *Ottawa Charter* strategies for health promotion (see Figure 8.4). More recently, the Community Health Nurses Association of Canada (2003) has developed a new set of standards for practice that identifies the socio-environmental approach to health promotion as the basis for CHNs' practice. The role of the CHN, as outlined in

CASE STUDY Application of the PHPM to Community Health Nursing

One of the key roles of the CHN working in a public health setting is to support the family in the first year of the life of a new child. This includes assisting parents in their new role(s), promoting optimal child development, and connecting the family with appropriate community resources.

Imagine that you are a CHN who has been given a postpartum referral from the local hospital. The referral contains the following information: first-time mother, 17 years old; newborn male born at 36 weeks gestation, weighing six pounds; unclear if infant's father is involved; very little contact with the health care system prior to giving birth; receiving social assistance; has no phone. You arrive at the address, which is located in a low-income neighbourhood, and find the mother alone with her infant in a tiny one-bedroom apartment on the third floor of a poorly maintained building without an elevator. You observe that the apartment has very few furnishings, dirty dishes piled in the sink, empty junk food wrappers and containers everywhere, and a strong smell of cigarette smoke. The mother quickly becomes tearful, stating that she doesn't have enough money to pay the rent, and she has no family and few friends in the community.

Using the Population Health Promotion Model (PHPM) as a guide, answer the following.

Discussion Questions

1. What information do you already know and what additional information do you need to obtain about the determinants of health affecting this family?
2. Give specific examples of one or more health promotion strategies that you as the CHN could use at the individual/family or community level to address each of the following determinants of health affecting this family. Consider other health professionals or workers in other disciplines/sectors with whom you might collaborate in these strategies.
   a) Income and social status
   b) Social support networks
   c) Personal health practices/coping
   d) Healthy child development
   e) Access to health services
3. What knowledge/skills/attitudes does the CHN require in order to effectively engage in the strategies identified in question 2?

FIGURE 8.4 Role of the PHN within the Regional Health Authority

Build Healthy Public Policy

Goal

Public policy is developed consistent with improvements in the determinants of health.

Services

- Encourage and support community-based advocacy for healthy public policy at all levels and in all sectors (e.g., justice, education, housing, social services, recreation).
- Direct advocacy for healthy public policy.
- Educate and encourage decision makers in all sectors and at all levels to participate in the development of healthy public policy.
- Foster partnership with community decision makers to evaluate public policy.

An Example of Service

PHNs work with communities to advocate for smoke-free public buildings.

Outcome: Ninety per cent of public buildings are smoke free.

Create Supportive Environments

Goal

Community members live in healthy social, emotional, spiritual, physical and ecological environments.

Services

- Assess and directly act on the factors affecting health in the community's social, emotional, spiritual, physical and ecological environment.
- Encourage and participate in health prompting initiatives with other communities and sectors.
- Increase awareness of the ecological and social environments affecting the health of individuals, families, groups or communities. Encourage and support related action.

An Example of Service

PHNs work with communities to develop strategies to promote safe environments for children.

Outcome: The number of latch-key children under 12 is reduced by 10 per cent.

Reorient Health Services

Goal

Responsibility for the determinants of health is shared among individuals, community groups, health professionals, health service institutions, all levels of government and all sectors, including justice, health, education, business, housing, social services and recreation.

Services

- Primary role in community assessment. Provide consultation with decision makers (e.g., RHA management and board) regarding community strengths and needs as a foundation for health care decisions.
- Promote responsible and effective use of the health care system and community resources.
- Refer individuals, families, groups and communities for appropriate service.
- Engage other sectors in addressing the determinants of health.

An Example of Service

PHNs work with a community to reorient speech and language services from a facility to accessible community locations based on a partnership among health, education and community members.

Outcome: A 5 per cent increase in early identification and intervention for preschool children with speech and language problems.

Strenghten Community Action

Goal

Community members are actively involved in achieving health.

Services

- Mobilize individuals, families, groups and communities to take individual and collective action on the determinants of health in the contexts in which they live, learn, work and play (e.g., schools, workplaces, homes, economic and social environments).
- Develop and support community-based and self-care services in which community members have ownership and an active role.
- Increase awareness of the ecological and social environments affecting the health of individuals, families, groups or communities. Encourage and support related action.

An Example of Service

PHNs work with a community to identify their assets and needs, determine priority issues, develop strategies and take action.

Outcome: An active 'Healthy Community' network is established.

Develop Personal Skills

Goal

Community members will make effective choices to attain an optimal level of physical, emotional, spiritual and social development.

Services

- Mobilize individuals to take individual and collective action on the determinants of health.
- Provide information regarding choices.
- Counsel and facilitate healthy choices.

An Example of Service

PHNs facilitate "Nobody's Perfect" parenting sessions for teen mothers and fathers.

Outcome: All parents involved in the parenting program have identified an improved understanding of early childhood development.

Source: Reprinted with permission of Manitoba Health. Prepared by the public health staff of Manitoba Health and Regional Health Authorities.

these standards, includes seeking to address root causes of illness and disease and facilitating planned change through the application of Hamilton and Bhatti's (1996) PHPM. The Case Study gives an example of applying the PHPM to a community health nursing scenario.

Barriers to Implementing the Socio-environmental Approach in Community Health Nursing The official adoption of the socio-environmental approach at the policy level does not necessarily mean that this approach has filtered down to the frontlines. A number of barriers to putting the socio-environmental approach to health promotion into action have been identified. Some of these barriers originate within nurses themselves and probably relate to the individual behavioural focus of nursing education and practice that we discussed earlier (Chalmers & Bramadat, 1996; Cohen, 2003; Shuster, Ross, Bhagat, & Johnson, 2001). These include:

- a lack of well-developed collaborative and other "upstream" skills,
- anxiety caused by working with uncertainty and a lack of direction,
- a general preference for working directly with individuals or families (probably due to the previous factors), and
- difficulty in giving up control over the agenda and direction of the nurse-client interactions.

In a discussion of community development approaches involving CHNs in various Canadian communities (Shuster et al., 2001), it was noted that nurses have been socialized to be in charge of their professional practice and of the individuals or families in their care. However, community development requires CHNs to share their power with others in the community and to become true partners. One CHN describes how, initially, it seemed easier just to provide services, and she had to constantly resist the temptation to "do for." She eventually learned that her role was to assist community members in finding their own ways to define health and address their own health issues.

A number of barriers to implementing a socio-environmental approach in community health nursing originate from the organizations that CHNs are employed in or from the communities where they work (Benson & Latter, 1998; Chalmers & Bramadat, 1996; Cohen, 2003; Reutter & Ford, 1998; Shuster et al., 2001). These include:

- a lack of recognition, from both their colleagues within the health care system (including other nurses) and the public, that this approach is a legitimate part of CHNs' role;
- a lack of organizational culture/policies that value and support this type of approach in CHNs' practice settings;
- a lack of role models in practice settings with experience in community development work and other "upstream" skills;
- a lack of time for involvement in such strategies due to increasing demands for mandatory disease prevention/health protection services such as immunization, communicable disease follow-up, postpartum referrals, and meeting the immediate needs of individuals or families in crisis—all within the context of cuts to fiscal resources in the community health sector;
- conceptual and practical challenges in defining community participation and empowerment and measuring community change; and
- resistance from sections of the community (based on ethnic, gender, ideological, or social class differences) to community development/empowerment initiatives that they do not see as being in their best interests.

In spite of these challenges, there are some excellent examples of the application of the socio-environmental approach to health promotion in Canadian settings in which CHNs have played an active role. See the text box for a description of a few of these initiatives.

Guidelines for Health-Promoting Community Health Nursing Practice

What conclusions can we draw from the preceding discussion? First, it is clear that there can never be one universally accepted definition of health promotion. How one views health promotion depends on a variety of factors, including one's professional and educational background, the dominant ideology of the time, and one's personal world-view. At the level of nursing practice, health promotion appears to be most widely viewed as a set of specific actions or strategies aimed at changing individual behaviours, with a focus on disease prevention and functional ability. This is in contrast to nursing at the policy and academic levels, where an increasing number of policy and discussion statements and nursing theorists have adopted a broader view of health promotion—one that is based upon specific values and principles such as social justice, equity, and participation—and focused on modifying the social, political, and economic environment that shapes behaviour (either through direct action or by enabling others to do it for themselves). Second, although a certain percentage of the gap between the rhetoric and reality of nurses' health promotion practice may be due to organizational or societal factors over which they have little control, much of this gap can be explained by the way that nurses have been socialized—beginning with their educational experiences and continuing in the workplace. How can CHNs narrow the gap between the rhetoric and reality of health promotion in their practice? The following guidelines are offered as a starting point.

Focus on Health and Build Capacity for Health In spite of the fact that nursing theorists have conceptualized health in positive terms, such as "self-actualization," "positive adaptation," and "optimal functioning" (Novak, 1988), the truth is that CHNs' health promotion practice has often focused on the negative. For example, most individual, family, and community health assessment models used by nurses focus on the identification of needs, deficits, and problems. If CHNs want to truly help to shift the focus of their services to the promotion of *health*, then we need to use a range of assessment tools and empowering strategies that start by

Examples of the Socio-environmental Approach to Health Promotion

Example 1: It was obvious from the heavy utilization of a number of school-based services in a low-income neighbourhood that a larger community service centre would be desirable. CHNs participated in a coalition of agencies to plan for a centre that would meet the needs of the community. Local residents were hired to do a door-to-door survey asking people to list their skills and the strengths of the community and what they would like to see in a neighbourhood centre. A plan was developed that would build upon these strengths and respond to the dreams of the community. A phased-in plan for local staffing and governance was strictly adhered to. This centre has been functioning very well for many years and is well respected by the community. The role of the CHNs in its development is no longer remembered, but the important thing is that people in this neighbourhood have a place where they can meet and join with others in addressing their needs.

Example 2: When working in a program intended to follow individuals with sexually transmitted infections, CHNs noticed that clients who were receiving social assistance payments could not afford to purchase condoms. While many drugs were paid for by social assistance when they were given by prescription, condoms were not. The CHNs successfully worked with their managers to lobby for a change in policy to make condoms available by prescription.

Example 3: Various CHNs have encouraged senior management and the regional health authority to promote breastfeeding as a way to improve population health. This has subsequently become one of the strategic initiatives of the region.

Example 4: A disadvantaged neighbourhood has an annual "Take Pride Week" that is run primarily by residents but is supported in several ways by local community service providers. "Take Pride Week" provides opportunities for area residents (especially people who are new to the area) to meet their neighbours and become involved in ongoing local activities. CHNs support this community-building event in different ways every year, sometimes helping to plan activities and usually being there to staff some events.

Example 5: Based on data gathered in the community on postpartum visits, district CHNs noticed a high level of isolation among young moms, whether it was their first or subsequent child. The CHNs partnered with the local child and family services agency, which was able to secure funding for a one-year pilot of a mom's group, and with the local church, which provided space and other resources. Personal contact was made with all postpartum moms, inviting them to participate in a planning meeting. The moms, not the CHNs, decided that they wanted the group and determined how they wanted it to function and the weekly agenda. The group has been meeting twice weekly for the past two years and now has plans to expand to an evening session to accommodate working parents (they have successfully secured additional funding). The group periodically invites the CHNs to facilitate discussion on topics chosen by the group, but group members now run the group.

Example 6: Cases of head lice in children were not resolving and were spreading to other families. CHNs advocated with the local social assistance office to cover the cost of lice shampoo for families who could not afford this treatment.

Example 7: A CHN is a member of a neighbourhood network that developed in response to several community meetings that identified community needs. The meetings were initiated by a local citizens' group whose original concern was lack of local services and employment opportunities for developmentally delayed students once they became adults. The initial network has expanded to include accessible services related to all areas identified in earlier visioning exercises. The CHN's role is one of consultation, advocacy, and facilitation.

Example 8: The "Baby First" Program is funded by Healthy Child Manitoba and offered through Public Health. Public health nurses work collaboratively with home visitors, who offer regular home visiting during the first three years of life to families who are identified as requiring assistance to ensure healthy early child development—one of the key determinants of health. The focus of the program is on building and enhancing family strengths.

identifying the strengths of individuals, families, and communities, and working with these clients to build their capacity for health. Two useful health assessment tools for community health assessment have been developed by Canadian health promoters: one focuses on assessing community quality of life (Raphael, Renwick, Brown, Steinmetz, Sehdev, & Philips, 2001) and the other, on community capacity (Jackson, Burman, Edwards, Poland, & Robertson, 1999). These models could easily be adapted to the individual and family levels of assessment. A focus on capacity building means that the CHN must strive to form collaborative relationships with clients (whether at the individual, family, or community level) and to maximize their involvement in planning, implementing, and evaluating health promotion actions. Remember—*every* individual, family, or community has some strength that can be capitalized on—your job is to find it and build on it!

Think Upstream It is true that the practices of the majority of CHNs involve a lot of work with individuals and families.

However, these individuals and families live in communities and societies in which the broader ecological, socioeconomic, political, and cultural environment influences their daily lives. "Thinking upstream" means that, in addition to meeting the immediate needs of individual clients or families, CHNs should always be (a) assessing the broader socio-environmental determinants of health, (b) thinking about possible strategies that can influence those determinants in a positive manner, and (c) identifying potential partners with whom they might collaborate for maximum effectiveness (see discussion below). While the majority of CHNs' health-promoting practice may be "downstream" at the level of personal and small-group empowerment, it is essential to identify all possible opportunities for involvement "upstream" in community empowerment and healthy public policy initiatives. Having said that, whether or not one works upstream or downstream may not be as important as *how* one engages in health promotion. It is possible to be involved in "upstream" strategies that are disempowering (e.g., taking the initiative to mobilize community action around an issue that the community has not identified as a priority) and "downstream" strategies that are empowering (e.g., working with a single, teenage mother to identify the specific skills that she feels are important to improve her chances for success in parenting and finding gainful employment).

Look for Partnership Opportunities One of the most challenging aspects of a socio-environmental approach to health promotion for community health practitioners is the recognition that the main determinants of population health, especially social and economic inequalities, lie outside the usual scope of the health system. This has lead many CHNs to feel powerless and has no doubt contributed to a focus in community health nursing practice on helping clients cope with their circumstances, rather than on changing those circumstances. It is imperative that CHNs identify potential partners with whom they might collaborate for maximum impact on individual, family, or community health. The partners may be from other disciplines within the health sector (e.g., community nutritionists or public health physicians) or from other sectors (e.g., social workers, educators, recreation workers). The key is to leave one's sense of ownership of the issue at the door and find ways in which each partner can make a unique but complementary contribution to the ultimate goal. It is even more imperative that the partnerships include members from the community who are directly impacted by the initiative. A partnership made up only of service providers can easily lose track of grassroots concerns and will not result in an empowerment process that benefits those who need it most.

Be Patient Perhaps the most challenging aspect of a socio-environmental approach to health promotion is the fact that it may take a long time to see positive results (unlike many nursing activities). In the case of community development initiatives, this could mean several years. Patience is a virtue in the field of community health nursing. Working with multiple partners, following their lead, and enduring frequent delays can leave nurses impatient with the community development process and make them retreat into "safer" direct service work. Constantly sharing and evaluating one's experiences with colleagues and receiving support and encouragement from one's managers may help to alleviate this problem. Ultimately, keep in mind that the empowerment process—as painfully slow and awkward as it may sometimes be—is the most likely way to achieve long-term positive health outcomes.

SUMMARY

Rather than providing a "how to" guide for health promotion, the goal of this chapter was to help the reader think critically about the various conceptual and philosophical approaches to health promotion and their implications for community health nursing practice. We began by exploring the historical development, underlying assumptions, and key characteristics of the three approaches to health promotion—biomedical, behavioural/lifestyle, and socio-environmental—that have been dominant in the twentieth and early twenty-first centuries. Differences in the conceptualization of health, understanding of main determinants of health, and typical health promotion strategies between the three approaches were outlined. It was noted that, although all three of these approaches may be used by health professionals at different times, the biomedical and behavioural/lifestyle approaches have tended to dominate the health promotion practice of nurses and other health professionals. Several factors appear to have contributed to this phenomenon, including the dominant ideology of individual responsibility for health in Western society and characteristics of typical nursing curricula that perpetuate an individualistic, behaviour-focused health promotion ideology.

One of the salient features of the historical development of approaches to health promotion that was highlighted in the chapter is the significant contribution of Canadian health promoters and policy makers, especially to the socio-environmental perspective. Decreasing social and economic inequalities in health and increasing personal and community empowerment are at the heart of the socio-environmental approach to health promotion. Educating people regarding healthy behaviours is insufficient to achieve health from this perspective and may actually increase inequities in health. The socio-environmental perspective has gained momentum within the field of community health nursing in recent years and, in Canada, has been adopted as the basis for CHNs' practice in several key policy documents. CHNs who would like to practise from a socio-environmental perspective face a number of challenges—some of them related to personal experience, others related to organizational and extra-organizational barriers—and these are discussed here. The chapter ends by providing some realistic guidelines for a health-promoting community health nursing practice that attempts to utilize a socio-environmental perspective, including focusing on health and building capacity for health, "thinking upstream," looking for partnership opportunities, and—perhaps most important of all—being patient.

KEY TERMS

biomedical approach
physiological risk factors
behavioural or lifestyle approach
health education
social marketing
health communication
behaviour modification
regulatory measures
socio-environmental approach
social justice
common good
structural or systems critique
social change
social responsibility for health
victim-blaming
ecological approach
primary health care
healthy communities
empowerment
psychological empowerment
community empowerment
strengthening community action
building healthy public policy
creating supportive environments
developing personal skills
reorienting health services
population health
Population Health Promotion Model (PHPM)
Health Promotion Model (HPM)
macroscopic approach
thinking upstream
emancipatory nursing
critical social nursing
empowering strategies

STUDY QUESTIONS

1. What are the main differences between the three approaches to health promotion in terms of:
   a) type of health determinant most concerned with,
   b) target of the initiative,
   c) program management (including the difference between community-based and community development programs), and
   d) criteria for success?
2. Identify the six different interpretations of the concept of health promotion found in the literature. Which ones reflect the behavioural approach to health promotion? Which ones reflect the socio-environmental approach to health promotion?
3. What were the main strengths and weaknesses of the Lalonde Report?
4. Give a brief description of each of the five key strategies that focus on changing behaviour/lifestyle. Which one of these strategies is also used in a socio-environmental approach to health promotion?
5. What are the four main factors that contributed to the emergence of the socio-environmental approach to health promotion?
6. Why is the year 1986 considered to be the birth of the socio-environmental approach to health promotion?
7. What is the central concept that lies at the heart of the socio-environmental approach to health promotion? How would you define this concept and how does it link with health promotion?
8. What are the five key principles of health promotion from a socio-environmental perspective?
9. Discuss three factors that have contributed to the focus on behaviour change in nursing.
10. There are a number of barriers that a CHN may face when trying to use a socio-environmental approach to health promotion. Identify four barriers that may originate within CHNs themselves, four barriers that may originate from the organizations that CHNs work in, and two barriers that may originate from the communities in which CHNs work.

INDIVIDUAL CRITICAL THINKING EXERCISES

1. Prior to reading this chapter, what did the term "health promotion" mean to you? Has your initial interpretation changed? If so, how?
2. Analyze your personal level of comfort with using the three main approaches to health promotion outlined in this chapter. What factors would increase your comfort in using each one?
3. Think about the community that you live in. What is an important issue affecting your community's well-being or quality of life? Which approach to health promotion would be the most appropriate to deal with this issue (there may be more than one)? What role could a CHN play in a health promotion initiative that addressed this issue?
4. For each of the Examples of the Socio-environmental Approach to Health Promotion (see Text Box), identify which of the *Ottawa Charter* strategies are being implemented (more than one may apply).
5. You are a CHN in a community where there appears to be an increasing number of obese children in the elementary school that you visit. Describe a microscopic ("downstream") versus a macroscopic ("upstream") approach to community health promotion in this situation.

GROUP CRITICAL THINKING EXERCISES

1. Discuss your answers to Individual Critical Thinking Exercise 1 with one or more partners. How do your responses compare? What factors influenced your original understanding of health promotion?

2. With a partner, interview a CHN in your community. Ask what the term "health promotion" means to them. Which approach to health promotion does this interpretation fit with? What are the CHN's perceptions regarding the barriers to utilizing socio-environmental strategies such as community development and advocacy for healthy public policy?
3. With one or more partners, identify examples of each of the behavioural/lifestyle strategies (listed in Table 8.2) that are in use in Canada and/or your region of the country today. Critically assess the strengths and weaknesses of these strategies.

REFERENCES

Beauchamp, D. (1976). Public health as social justice. *Inquiry, 13*, 3–14.

Benson, A., & Latter, S. (1998). Implementing health promoting nursing: The integration of interpersonal skills and health promotion. *Journal of Advanced Nursing, 27*, 100–107.

Bomar, P. (1990). Perspectives on family health promotion. *Family & Community Health, 12*(4), 1–11.

Brubaker, B. (1983, April). Health promotion: A linguistic analysis. *Advances in Nursing Science*, 1–14.

Butterfield, P. (1997). Thinking upstream: Conceptualizing health from a population perspective. In J. Swanson & M. Nies (Eds.), *Community health nursing: Promoting the health of aggregate* (pp. 69–82). Philadelphia, PA: W.B. Saunders Company.

Canadian Nurses Association. (1992). *Policy statement on health promotion.* Ottawa, ON: Author.

Canadian Public Health Association. (1990). *Community health/public health nursing in Canada: Preparation and practice.* Ottawa, ON: Author.

Canadian Public Health Association. (1996). *Action statement on health promotion.* Retrieved December 4, 2003 from **www.cpha.ca/english/policy/pstatem/action/cover.htm**

Chalmers, K., & Bramadat, I. (1996). Community development: Theoretical and practical issues for community health nursing in Canada. *Journal of Advanced Nursing, 24*, 719–726.

Clarke, H., & Mass, H. (1998). Comox Valley Nursing Centre: From collaboration to empowerment. *Public Health Nursing, 15*(3), 216–224.

Cohen, B. (2003). *Building Capacity for Health Promotion in Manitoba's Regional Health Authorities.* PhD. Dissertation., University of Manitoba.

Community Health Nurses Association of Canada. (2003). *Canadian community health nursing standards of practice.* Retrieved December 3, 2003 from **www.communityhealthnursescanada.org/StandardsofPractice.pdf**

Courtney, R., Ballard, E., Fauver, S., Gariota, M., & Holland, L. (1996). The partnership model: Working with individuals, families and communities toward a new vision of health. *Public Health Nursing, 13*(3), 177–186.

Crawford, R. (1977). You are dangerous to your health: The ideology and politics of victim blaming. *International Journal of Health Services, 7*(4), 663–680.

Dallaire, C., Hagan, L., & O'Neill, M. (2000). Linking health promotion and community health nursing. In M. Stewart (Ed.), *Community nursing: Promoting Canadians' health* (pp. 317–332). Toronto, ON: W.B. Saunders Company.

Drevdahl, D. (1995). Coming to voice: The power of emancipatory community interventions. *Advances in Nursing Science, 18*(2), 13–24.

Epp, J. (1986). *Achieving health for all: A framework for health promotion.* Ottawa, ON: Health and Welfare Canada.

Federal, Provincial, Territorial Advisory Committee on Population Health. (1994). *Strategies for population health: Investing in the health of Canadians.* Ottawa, ON: Ministry of Supply and Services.

Gibson, C. (1991). A concept analysis of empowerment. *Journal of Advanced Nursing, 16*, 354–361.

Glanz, K., Lewis, F., & Rimer, B. (2002). *Health behaviour and health education* (3rd ed.). San Francisco, CA: Jossey-Bass.

Gottlieb, L., & Rowat, K. (1987). The McGill model of nursing: A practice-derived model. *Advances in Nursing Science, 9*(4), 51–61.

Green, L., & Kreuter, M. (1999). *Health promotion planning: An educational and environmental approach* (3rd ed.). Mountain View, CA: Mayfield.

Green, L. W., Poland B. D., & Rootman, I. (2000). The settings approach to health promotion. In B. D. Poland, L. W. Green, & I. Rootman (Eds.), *Settings for health promotion: linking theory and practice* (pp. 1–43). Thousand Oaks, CA: Sage Publications.

Green, L., Richard, L., & Potvin, L. (1996). Ecological foundations of health promotion. *American Journal of Health Promotion, 10*(4), 270–281.

Hamilton, N., & Bhatti, T. (1996). *Population health promotion: An integrated model of population health and health promotion.* Ottawa, ON: Health Canada, Health Promotion and Development Division.

Hartrick, G., Lindsey, E., & Hills, M. (1994). Family nursing assessment: Meeting the challenge of health promotion. *Journal of Advanced Nursing, 20*, 85–91.

Heaney, C., & Isreal, B. (2002). Social networks and social support. In K. Glanz, F. Lewis, & B. Rimer (Eds.), *Health behavior and health education: Theory research and practice* (3rd ed., pp. 179–205). San Francisco, CA: Jossey-Bass.

Hills, M., & Lindsey, E. (1996). Health promotion: A viable curriculum framework for nursing education. *Nursing Outlook, 42*(4), 158–162.

Hudson-Rodd, N. (1994). Public health: People participating in the creation of healthy places. *Public Health Nursing, 11*(2), 119–126.

Jackson, S., Burman, D., Edwards, R., Poland, B., & Robertson, A. (1999). *Toward indicators of community capacity: A study conducted with community members of Parkdale, Regent Park, and two sites in Jane-Finch.* Toronto, ON: University of Toronto, Centre for Health Promotion.

Kendall, J. (1992). Fighting back: Promoting emancipatory nursing actions. *Advances in Nursing Science, 15*(2), 1–15.

Kleffel, D. (1991). Rethinking the environment as a domain of nursing knowledge. *Advances in Nursing Science, 14*(1), 40–51.

Labonte, R. (1993). *Health promotion and empowerment: Practice frameworks.* Toronto, ON: University of Toronto, Centre for Health Promotion & ParticipACTION.

Labonte, R. (1995). Population health and health promotion: What do they have to say to each other? *Canadian Journal of Public Health, 86*(3), 165–188.

Labonte, R., & Little, S. (1992). *Determinants of health: Empowering strategies for nursing practice.* Vancouver, BC: Registered Nurses Association of British Columbia.

Labonte, R., & Penfold, S. (1981). Canadian perspectives in health promotion: A critique. *Health Education, 19*(3/4), 4–9.

Lalonde, M. (1974). *A new perspective on the health of Canadians.* Ottawa, ON: Department of National Health and Welfare.

Lowenburg, J. (1995). Health promotion and the 'ideology of choice'. *Public Health Nursing, 12*(5), 319–323.

Maben, J., & MacLeod Clark, J. (1995). Health promotion: A concept analysis. *Journal of Advanced Nursing, 22,* 1158–1165.

MacDonald, M. (2002). Health promotion: historical, philosophical, and theoretical perspectives. In L. Young & V. Hayes (Eds.), *Transforming health promotion practice: Concepts, issues, and applications* (pp. 22–45). Philadelphia, PA: F.A. Davis Company.

Makara, P. (1997). Can we promote equity when we promote health? *Health Promotion International, 12*(2), 97–98.

Manitoba Health. (1998). *The role of the public health nurse within the regional health authority.* Winnipeg, MB: Author.

McKenzie, J., & Smeltzer, J. (1997). Interventions. In J. McKenzie & J. Smeltzer (Eds.), *Planning, implementing, and evaluating health promotion programs: A primer* (pp. 129–156). Boston, MA: Allyn & Bacon.

McKinlay, J. (1979). A case for refocusing upstream: The political economy of illness. In E. Jaco (Ed.), *Patients, physicians, and illnes* (pp. 9–25). New York: The Free Press.

Minkler, M. (1989). Health education, health promotion and the open society: An historical perspective. *Health Education Quarterly, 16*(1), 17–30.

Moccia, P. (1988). At the faultline: Social activism and caring. *Nursing Outlook, 36*(1), 30–33.

Munro, M., Gallant, M., MacKinnon, M., Dell, G., Herbert, R., MacNutt, G. et al. (2000). The Prince Edward Island conceptual model for nursing: A nursing perspective of primary health care. *Canadian Journal of Nursing Research, 32*(1), 39–55.

Novak, J. (1988). The social mandate and historical basis for nursing's role in health promotion. *Journal of Professional Nursing Practice, 4*(2), 80–87.

Nutbeam, D. & Harris, E. (1998). *Theory in a nutshell: A practitioner's guide to commonly used theories and models in health promotion.* National Centre for Health Promotion, Department of Public Health and Community Medicine. University of Sydney, NSW, Australia.

O'Brien, M. (1994). The managed heart revisited: Health and social control. *Sociological Review, 42*(3), 395–413.

O'Neill, M. (1997). Health promotion: Issues for the year 2000. *Canadian Journal of Nursing Research, 29*(1), 71–77.

Orem, D. (1985). *Nursing concepts and practice* (3rd ed.). New York: McGraw-Hill.

Patrick, D., & Wickizer, T. (1995). Community and health. In B. Amick, S. Levine, A. Tarlov, & D. Chapman Walsh (Eds.), *Society & health* (pp. 46–92). New York: Oxford University Press.

Pender, N. (1996). *Health promotion in nursing practice* (3rd ed.). Stamford, CT: Appleton & Lange.

Raeburn, J., & Rootman, I. (1998). *People-centred health promotion.* Chichester, UK: John Wiley & Sons.

Raphael, D., & Bryant, T. (2000). Putting the population into population health. *Canadian Journal of Public Health, 91*(1), 9–12.

Raphael, D., Renwick, R., Brown, I., Steinmetz, B., Sehdev, H., & Philips, S. (2001). Making the links between community structure and individual well-being: Community quality of life in Riverdale, Toronto, Ontario. *Health & Place, 7,* 179–196.

Reutter, L. (2000). Socioeconomic determinants of health. In M. Stewart (Ed.), *Community health nursing: Promoting Canadians' health* (2nd ed., pp. 174–193). Toronto, ON: W.B. Saunders Company.

Reutter, L., & Ford, J. (1998). Perceptions of changes in public health nursing practice: A Canadian perspective. *International Journal of Nursing Studies, 35,* 85–94.

Ritchie, L., Boutell, B., Buchan, C., Foster, P., & St. Aubrey, M. (1995). Practicing what we preach. *Nursing BC,* (November/December), 14–16.

Rodwell, C. (1996). An analysis of the concept of empowerment. *Journal of Advanced Nursing, 23,* 305–313.

Rush, K. (1997). Health promotion ideology and nursing education. *Journal of Advanced Nursing, 25,* 1292–1298.

Shuster, S., Ross, S., Bhagat, R., & Johnson, J. (2001). Using community development approaches. *Canadian Nurse, 97*(6), 18–22.

Smith, M. (1990). Nursing's unique focus on health promotion. *Nursing Science Quarterly, 3*(1), 105–106.

Stevens, P. (1989). A critical social reconceptualization of environment in nursing: Implications for methodology. *Advances in Nursing Science, 11*(4), 56–68.

Stevens, P., & Hall, J. (1992). Applying critical theories to nursing in communities. *Public Health Nursing, 9*(1), 2–9.

Stewart, M., & Leipert, B. (2000). Community health nursing in the future. In M. Stewart (Ed.), *Community nursing: Promoting Canadians' health* (pp. 602–631). Toronto, ON: W.B. Saunders Company.

Syme, S. L. (1997). Individual vs. community interventions in public health practice: Some thoughts about a new approach. *VicHealth, 2,* 2–9.

Wallerstein, N. (1992). Powerlessness, empowerment, and health: Implications for health promotion programs. *American Journal of Health Promotion, 6*(3), 197–205.

Wilkinson, R. (1996). *Unhealthy societies: The afflictions of inequality.* London: Routledge.

Williams, D. (1989). Political theory and individualistic health promotion. *Advances in Nursing Science, 12*(1), 14–25.

World Health Organization. (1977). *Health For All by the Year 2000.* Geneva: Author.

World Health Organization. (1978). *Declaration of Alma Ata.* Retrieved September 4, 2002 from **www.who.int/hpr/archive/docs/almata.html**

World Health Organization. (1984). *Health promotion: A discussion document on the concepts and principles.* Copenhagen: WHO Regional Office for Europe.

World Health Organization. (1986). *Ottawa charter for health promotion.* Ottawa, ON: Canadian Public Health Association and Health and Welfare Canada.

Wright, L., & Leahey, M. (1994). *Nurses and families: A guide to family assessment and intervention* (2nd ed.). Philadelphia, PA: F.A. Davis Company.

Young, L. (2002). Transforming health promotion practice: Moving toward holistic care. In L. Young & V. Hayes (Eds.), *Transforming health promotion practice: Concepts, issues and applications* (pp. 3–21). Philadelphia, PA: F.A. Davis Company.

ADDITIONAL RESOURCES

WEBSITES

The Ontario Health Promotion E-Bulletin, a free weekly electronic news and resources bulletin, includes biweekly feature articles on health promotion issues (e.g., "community capacity building") with relevant print and internet resources: **www.ohpe.ca/ebulletin/intro.html**

A glossary of health promotion terms produced by the World Health Organization: **www.who.int/hpr/NPH/docs/hp_glossary_en.pdf**

PRINT RESOURCES

Stewart, M. (Ed.). (2000). *Community nursing: Promoting Canadians' health* (2nd ed.). Toronto, ON: W.B. Saunders Canada.

Young, L. E. & Hayes, V. (2002). *Transforming health promotion practice: Concepts, issues, and applications.* Philadelphia, PA: F.A. Davis Company.

The following periodicals are good sources of theoretical and practice-based research articles related to community health nursing and health promotion in the community:

Community Health Promotion
Health Education Quarterly
Health Promotion International
Journal of Advanced Nursing
Public Health Nursing

About the Author

Benita Cohen, RN, PhD, is an Assistant Professor in the Faculty of Nursing at the University of Manitoba where she teaches courses in the undergraduate, graduate, and post-RN programs related to prevention of illness and health promotion in the community. She has worked as a Public Health Nurse in the Toronto area, in the Baffin region of the Eastern Arctic as a curriculum development assistant for the community health module of the undergraduate medical education program at the University of Manitoba, and as a community health researcher in several First Nations communities in Manitoba.

The author would like to thank Horst Backe, Bluma Levine, Susan Permut, and Lynda Tjaden—nurses at the Winnipeg Regional Health Authority—for their input into the development of the case study and provision of examples of population health promotion strategies used in their own practice.

CHAPTER 9

Family Care

Linda Patrick and
Kathryn Edmunds

OBJECTIVES

AFTER STUDYING THIS CHAPTER, YOU SHOULD BE ABLE TO:

1. Define family and its basic purposes.
2. Explain the difference between viewing the family as context and the family as client.
3. Describe the theoretical underpinnings of family health nursing.
4. Discuss the components and basic characteristics of family and cultural assessment tools.
5. Describe how family and cultural assessments shape nursing interventions.
6. Discuss the roles for nurses in family-centred community health nursing.

INTRODUCTION

Community health nurses (CHNs) in Canada have a long history of caring for families. According to the Canadian Nurses Association (CNA) (1997), a recent trend has been to describe the meaning of clinical nursing practice with families in more detail. In this chapter, you will study the family as context and the family as client and develop an understanding of cultural and family assessment and relevant theories applied in community nursing settings. You will also examine the skills needed for planning nursing interventions for families, including the case management approach to care.

Why Study Family Nursing?

In Canada, we are seeing an increasing amount of community-based and family-provided health care (Green, 1997). People are spending less time in acute care settings during illness or following surgery. Earlier discharges from hospital settings mean that family caregivers are continuing treatments previously done only in a hospital setting (e.g., medication administration, wound management, and intravenous therapy). This shift also means that nurses who work in community health settings need to develop knowledge and skill in helping families cope with often very complex caregiving situations. Green suggests that, in order to do this, "nurses need an understanding and appreciation of the interactive complexity of family life, and they need to know how to 'think family'" (p. 230).

WHAT IS A FAMILY?

Current definitions of family have evolved from the much narrower traditional definitions of blood, marriage, or legal constrictions that existed before the 1980s (Hanson, 2001). Changing societal family forms have necessitated broader definitions of family. A **family** is described as society's most basic small group (Hitchcock, Schubert, & Thomas, 1999). It consists of "two or more individuals who depend on one another for emotional, physical, and economic support. The members of a family are self-defined" (Hanson, p. 6). The family is also defined as "being unique and whomever the person defines as being family. They can include, but are not limited to, parents, children, siblings, neighbours, and significant people in the community" (Registered Nurses Association of Ontario [RNAO] 2002, p. 18).

Family forms in Canada include nuclear families, extended families, single-parent families, blended families, and homosexual families. For the person who lives alone, a pet may even be considered a family member (Lepage, Essiembre, & Coutu-Wakulczyk, 1996). The CHN who works with families should assess individuals in the context of the family as they define it (RNAO, 2002). Regardless of family form, assessing the family's strengths and resources should take priority over looking for pathology (Harway, 1996).

Family Function

Family function is "the purpose that the family serves in relation to the individual, other social systems, and society" (Hanson, 2001, p. 84). The functions of a Canadian family may include (The Vanier Institute of Family, 2000):

- physical maintenance and care of group members;
- addition of new members through procreation or adoption;
- socialization of children and social control of members;
- production, consumption, and distribution of goods and services; and
- affective nurturance/love.

TABLE 9.1
Varieties of Family Forms

Legally married
- Traditional nuclear
- Binuclear or blended
  - Co-parenting
  - Joint custody
  - One member of the original family remarried
  - Both members of the original family remarried

Dual-career
- Both in same household
- Commuter

Adoptive

Foster

Voluntary childlessness

Unmarried
- Never married
  - Voluntary singlehood, with or without children
  - Involuntary singlehood, with or without children
- Cohabitation with or without children
- Same-sex relationship

Formerly married
- Widowed
- Divorced
  - Custodial parent
  - Joint custody of children
  - Noncustodial parent

Multi-adult household
- Communes and intentional communities
- Multilateral marriage, in which three or more people consider themselves to have a primary relationship with at least two other individuals in the group (Macklin, 1987)

Extramarital sex
- Swinging
- Sexually open marriage
- Co-primary relationships, in which one or both members maintain a primary relationship with at least two partners who may or may not know about the other (Macklin, 1987)
- Home-sharing individuals with or without children

Extended family
- e.g., grandparents, parents, and children; adult children moving home; siblings living together, with or without partners or children

Source: Hitchcock, J. E., Schubert, P. E., & Thomas, S. A. (Eds.). (2003). Community health nursing: Caring in action *(2nd ed.). New York: Thomson Delmar Learning, p. 410. Reprinted with permission of Delmar Learning, a division of Thomson Learning: www.thomsonrights.com. Fax 800-730-2215.*

For nurses who care for families, a "functional" or "healthy" family is one that "provides the protection, nourishment, stimulation for growth, and socialization, among other things, that are necessary for an individual's health" (Whall & Fawcett, 1991, p. 35).

A family experiences dysfunction when unable to meet the definition of a healthy family as stated above. Families experiencing varying degrees of tension may benefit from intervention by CHNs. Interventions may include health teaching or counselling to promote family health and those that specifically target strengthening a family's social support system through referrals to other support services (Hanson, 2001).

Societal Changes Affecting the Canadian Family

The 2001 Census portrays a very different Canadian family as we begin the twenty-first century. The "traditional" Canadian family was once defined as mother, father, and children. The proportion of traditional families is declining, while the number of families with no children living at home is on the increase. To put this into perspective, over a twenty-year period (1981 to 2002), the number of married or common-law couples with children aged 24 and under living at home decreased from 55% to 44%. During the same time period, couples with no children living at home increased from 34% to 41%. The reasons given for this shift include such factors as lower fertility rates and couples who are delaying having children or who are childless. In addition, life expectancy is increasing with one result being that couples have more of their lives to spend alone together after their children have grown up and left the family home (Statistics Canada, 2003). Same-sex couples living together accounted for 0.5% of all couples in Canada in 2001, and of this group, male couples outnumbered female couples. This is the first time that the census has provided data on same-sex partnerships, due to changes in the legal status of same-sex couples.

Other characteristics of Canadian families taken from the most recent census have implications for community health nursing practice. For instance, the proportion of children living with married parents has decreased from 84% to 68% over the past 20 years. In 2001, 13% of children aged 0–14 years lived with parents in a common-law relationship. This is an increase of more than four times the rate of 3.1% in 1981. This suggests that the traditional or historical view—that marriage is a prerequisite for having children—is changing (Statistics Canada, 2003).

The living arrangements of young adults in Canada today are also more flexible. Young adult children stay at home longer or return to the familial home between school, jobs, and marriages or to simply save money. These children are referred to in the literature as "boomerang kids" (The Vanier Institute of the Family, 2000). This trend has continued since the previous census in 1996. The 2001 General Social Survey reports that 33% of men and 28% of women between the ages of 20 and 29 years returned home at least once after initially moving out (Statistics Canada, 2002).

Balancing work and family life can be very stressful for many Canadian families. Having a daily routine that diminishes time with family and friends is a common concern for nearly half of Canadian adults aged 25 to 44 years according to Statistics Canada (2003). One quarter of married men and over one third of married women who are employed full-time with children at home reported time stress as the most significant stressor in their lives. This lack of free time is exemplified in the catch phrase "24/7," which is used to refer to round-the-clock consumer services (24 hours a day, 7 days a week).

The number of Canadian families living below the low-income cutoff is declining (9% in 1998). According to Statistics Canada (2003), just over one million children lived in low-income families, which is a 15% decrease since 1997. Low income was most prevalent (42%) among lone-parent families headed by women. While it is encouraging to report a decrease, the fact that over one million Canadian children live in conditions of economic hardship is very disturbing.

Many Canadians are born into families that have lived in this country for generations, but numerous families have also chosen to immigrate here. The increasing diversity in the structure, form, and ethnicity of families leads to increased awareness of the diversity of family health beliefs, strengths, and adaptability (Friedman, 1997). It is anticipated that Canada will continue to encourage immigration in the future as a means of building its population. This is in part due to an aging society of people who are living longer lives and choosing to have smaller families. It is also due to ten years of decline in the fertility rate in Canada, which reached a record low of 1.49 in 2000. The fertility rate is an estimate of the average number of children each woman aged 15 to 49 will have in her lifetime. Recently, Statistics Canada reported that the fertility rate rose to 1.51 in 2001 with a 28% increase in the number of babies born in 2001 from 2000 (Statistics Canada, 2003). This is encouraging since our economy relies on growth to sustain the way of life that most Canadians expect.

WHAT IS FAMILY HEALTH NURSING?

Family health nursing is an emerging specialty in nursing as well as a new way of thinking about families and nursing (Hanson, 2001). Family health nursing asks how one provides health care to a collection of people, but this does not mean that the nurse must give up providing care to individuals (Allender & Spradley, 2001). Nurses in community settings who have the family as client must take a broader and more comprehensive approach to nursing care. Health promotion of the whole family, as well as of individual members, is a primary goal of family nursing (Bomar, 1996; Hartrick, Lindsey, & Hills, 1994). In order for the care to be most effective, the CHN works within the family's context. Five principles that guide and enhance family nursing practice (Allender & Spradley, 2001, p. 450) are:

- "work with the family collectively,
- start where the family is,
- adapt nursing intervention to the family's stage of development,
- recognize the validity of family structural variations, and
- emphasize family strengths."

Family as Context

Context refers to "the places or settings where community health nursing services are provided" (Hitchcock et al., 1999). The CHN focuses on either the individual within the context of the family or on the family with the individual as context. Viewing the family as context is the traditional focus of nursing, in which the individual is the foreground and the family is in the background (Friedman, Bowden, & Jones, 2003; Hanson, 2001). The nurse who interviews a newly married woman with cancer and her husband concerning the woman's experience with the life-threatening illness is an example of concentrating on the individual within the context of family. The nurse who focuses on the family with the individual as context would interview the adult children of a woman with Alzheimer's disease to discover how the family copes with caring for their mother at home (CNA, 1997).

There are five ways of viewing the family in family nursing (Friedman et al., 2003) (see Figure 9.1).

- The first level is to view the family as context to the client. The CHN focuses nursing care on the individual with the family as a secondary focus.
- In the second level, the family is viewed as a sum of its individual family members or parts. Health care is provided to each individual family member and this is viewed as providing family health care (Friedman et al., 2003). This is not the same as viewing the whole family as the focus of care.
- In the third level of family nursing practice, the focus is on family subsystems. Family dyads, triads, and other family subsystems are the focus of care, for example, a CHN who focuses on the care of the new mother and her baby during a home visit. Other areas of focus could be caregiving issues and bonding attachment issues (Friedman et al., 2003).
- Family as client is the fourth way of viewing the family. The unit of care is the entire family. The nurse does not focus on either the individual or the family, but concentrates on both the individual and the family simultaneously. The interactions that occur among members of the family are emphasized (CNA, 1997). In the family-as-client approach to care, the family is in the foreground and individuals are in the background (Figure 9.1, Level IV). The nurse would assess each person within the family and provide health care for all family members.
- A fifth level of family nursing, identified by Hanson (2001), conceptualizes family as a component of society. The family is seen as one of society's basic institutions.

According to the Canadian Nurses Association (1997), nursing practice that focuses on the family as client is **family systems nursing**. Nurses who practise at this level will have extensive knowledge about family dynamics, family systems theory, and family assessment and intervention. The nurse could choose to be a clinical nurse specialist with a special focus on families. Educational preparation for an advanced practice role would be at a post-graduate level. "The nursing of families and family systems nursing represent different

FIGURE 9.1 Five Levels of Family Nursing Practice

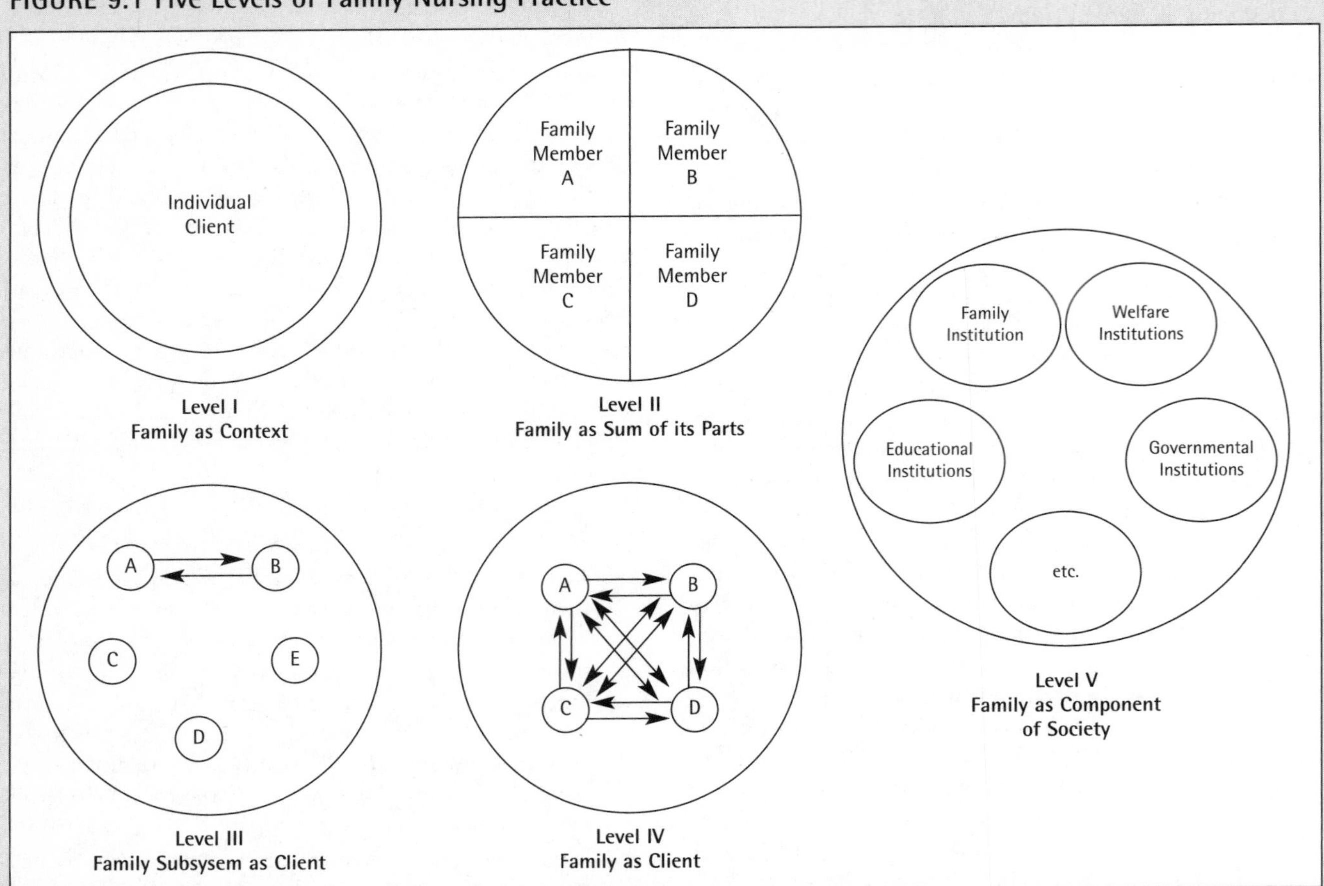

Source: Reproduced with permission from Friedman, M. M., Bowden, V. R., & Jones, E. G. (Eds.). (2003). Family nursing: Research, theory, and practice *(5th ed.). Upper Saddle River, NJ: Prentice Hall, p. 37. © Reprinted by permission of Pearson Education, Inc. Upper Saddle River, NJ.*

types of practice that are distinct in theory. The approach is determined by the situation and by the knowledge and skill of the nurse involved" (CNA, 1997, p. 2).

Health Promotion of the Family Health promotion is "the process of enabling people to increase control over the determinants of health and thereby, improve their health" (World Health Organization, 1986, pp. 1–2), encompassing the family as a whole and each of its members (Bomar, 1996). Health promotion of the family, a primary goal of family nursing, involves promoting family members' health and promoting family system health (Loveland-Cherry, 1996). This means that family health promotion can occur for an individual family member within the context of the family or for the family system as a unit. Areas that a CHN should assess when planning health promotion for the family as a whole include family functioning, family dynamics, communication patterns in the family, relationships between members, and the family's interaction with the community (Friedman et al., 2003).

In health promotion and disease prevention, the role of the nurse is to assist the family to strengthen their capacity to act on their own behalf (Hartrick, 2000). A primary strategy may be to assist families to make informed choices about healthy lifestyle behaviours by increasing their knowledge and skills. Mandle (2002) describes the first step as creating awareness about actual or potential problems. The second step is to recognize families who are at a particular risk and to offer them "the benefits of nursing knowledge about motivating and supporting behavioural change" (p. 195).

Theoretical Underpinnings of Family Health Nursing

Family social science theories, family therapy theories, and nursing models and theories all contribute to the emerging field of family nursing theories (see Figure 9.2). Family therapy theories are relevant to nurses working with families because the theories are oriented to practice (Friedman et al., 2003), for example, Neuman's Health System Model, which is frequently used by CHNs. It is not often that Leininger's theory of Cultural Care Diversity and Universality (Leininger & McFarland, 2002) is mentioned in the discussion of contributions of nursing theory to working with families. The

Canadian Research Box 9.1

Coffman, S. (1997). Home-care nurses as strangers in the family. *Western Journal of Nursing Research, 19*(1), 82–96.

The researcher in this study was interested in gaining a deeper understanding of the meaning of home nursing for nurses in long-term care situations. This study is relevant for CHNs working in Canadian settings even though the study was conducted in the U.S. The method used was phenomenology, as described by van Manen (1990), and the participants were 10 home care nurses employed for more than six months in home care. Each home that the nurses visited required 40 or more hours of nursing care per week for a child dependent on technology. The required special nursing measures included assistance with ventilators, tracheostomy care, enteral feedings, splinting, and positioning. Audiotaped interviews were conducted and transcribed into text.

Following reflection on the data focused on the phenomena, elements that occurred frequently in the text were grouped into themes. The overall theme emerging from the data was "a stranger in the family." Other essential themes included "advocating for the child," "blending with the family," "maintaining family boundaries," "empowering the family," working as a team," and "holding a job" (p. 86). The nurses recognized the vulnerability of the families that they visited and also acknowledged that "walking into the lives" of the families was a complex process that required the nurse to have respect for the family and to be open and flexible. Specifically, attention to the family's well-being was as essential as concern for the child. The child and the family were identified as "inseparable." The author concluded by raising several questions for administrators, educators, and researchers who focus on home care. The discussion questions that follow have been adapted from the questions developed by the author.

Discussion Questions

1. How can nurses in community settings remain open and sensitive to family needs, yet be aware of the boundaries necessary for family autonomy?
2. What content should be required in nursing programs to prepare nurses to deal with the complex family dynamics of the home care environment?

concept of culture is marginalized, yet Leininger's theory contributes to consideration of the whole context and the importance of the family's worldview and perceptions, and to mutually planned and negotiated nursing care.

Although every family is unique, all families share some universal characteristics. Allender and Spradley (2001, p. 428) list five of the most important characteristics for CHNs to consider.

- Every family is a small social system.
- Every family has its own cultural values and rules.
- Every family has structure.
- Every family has certain basic functions.
- Every family moves through stages in its life cycle.

These universal characteristics reflect the importance of culture as well as **systems theory**, **structural-functional theory**, and **theories of family development**, all theories from the social sciences that have been applied to families. Table 9.2 presents an overview of these three theories with examples of nursing assessment questions and interventions.

Family developmental stages and tasks are presented in Table 9.3. This is a life cycle approach, which suggests that families move through typical and shared developmental stages, experiencing growth and development in a similar manner to individuals (Hitchcock et al., 1999).

FIGURE 9.2 Conceptual Sources of Family Nursing Theories

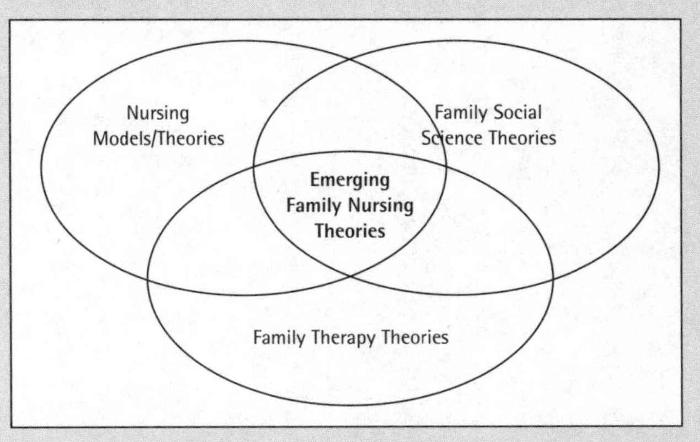

Source: Reproduced with permission from Friedman, M. M., Bowden, V. R., & Jones, E. G. (Eds.). (2003). Family nursing: Research, theory, and practice *(5th ed.). Upper Saddle River, NJ: Prentice Hall, p.63. © Reprinted by permission of Pearson Education, Inc., Upper Saddle River, NJ.*

FAMILY AND CULTURAL ASSESSMENT TOOLS

Regardless of the concepts, models, and tools utilized, a comprehensive **family assessment** uses open-ended questions, is detailed and inclusive, and is similar to a comprehensive cultural assessment. Nursing assessments are ongoing, which means they change, are added to, and develop over time as data are shared with and observed by the nurse. An assessment is not "done to" the family, but is rather a process that the nurse facilitates. This act of facilitation starts to build a relationship between the nurse and the family. The assessment process is part of the nursing process, being the foundation upon which planning, interventions, and evaluation are based. Some aspects of community health nursing can help the nurse and family in the assessment process.

- The interviews often take place in the family's home, where the family is likely to be more comfortable.
- Other family members are more likely to be present, which adds to the family assessment data.

TABLE 9.2
Summary of Family Social Science Theoretical Models

	Structural-Functional Theory	Systems Theory	Family Developmental Theory
Overview	Focuses on family structure and family function and how well family structure performs its functions.	Focuses on interaction between members of the family system and between the family system with other systems. A change in one member of the family system influences the entire system.	Focuses on changes that occur over time in the family system, including changes in interactions and relationships between family members. The roles that family members have within and outside the family that affect family interaction are emphasized.
Concepts	Structural areas include family forms, roles, values, communication patterns, power structure, or support networks. Functional areas include affective, socialization, reproductive, coping, economic, physical care, and health care functions.	Subsystems, boundaries, openness, energy, negentropy (energy which promotes order), entropy (energy promoting chaos), feedback, adaptation, homeostasis, input, output, internal system processes.	Change, roles, developmental tasks, family career or life cycle, family stage marker, family transitions.
Assumptions	Family is a system and a small group that exists to perform certain functions.	Family system is greater than the sum of its parts. Subsystems are related and interact with one another and the whole family system interacts with other systems. Family systems have homeostatic features and strive to maintain a dynamic balance.	Families develop and change over time in similar and consistent ways. Families and their members perform time-specific tasks within the context of their culture and society.
Clinical application	Assess, diagnose, and intervene with the family according to major concepts.	Assess, diagnose, and intervene with the family according to major concepts.	Assess, diagnose, and intervene with the family according to major concepts.
Sample assessment questions	• What impact did _________ have on family structure and function? • What family roles were changed? • What family functions have been affected?	• How are members of the family system relating with one another? • What is the "input" into the family system? • How did change caused by _________ affect all members of the family? • How open is the family system? Does the family system have homeostasis?	• What is the family history? • What is the family's present developmental stage? • How are the family members meeting the developmental tasks of that stage?
Interventions	• Identify typical family coping mechanisms. • Respect and encourage adaptive coping skills used by the family. • Assist the family to modify its organization so that role responsibilities can be redistributed. • Help family members find ways to meet health needs for the family as a whole and for individual members.	• Listen to the family's feelings, concerns, and questions. • Monitor family relationships. • Facilitate open communication among family members. • Collaborate with the family in problem solving. • Provide necessary knowledge that will help the family make decisions.	• Assist the family in describing and articulating their family history. • Provide information about family roles and tasks in the current developmental stage. • Support family members in meeting their developmental tasks. • Provide anticipatory guidance about family roles and tasks during transition and future developmental stages.

Source: Adapted from Artinian, N. T. (1999). Selecting a model to guide family assessment. In G. D. Wegner & R. J. Alexander (Eds.), Readings in family nursing *(2nd ed., pp. 449–450). Philadelphia, PA: Lippincott, and Friedman, M. M., Bowden, V. R., & Jones, E. G. (2003). Reprinted by permission of Lippincott, Williams, and Wilkins.* Family nursing: Research, theory, and practice *(5th ed.). Upper Saddle River, NJ: Prentice Hall. © Reprinted by permission of Pearson Education, Inc., Upper Saddle River, NJ.*

TABLE 9.3
Family Life Cycle Developmental Stages and Tasks

Stage	Task
Forming partnerships and/or marriage	Commitment to and establishing a new family
Childbearing families	Adjustment to parenthood and new family members
Families with • Preschool children • School-age children • Teenagers	Adjusting to changes in the marital relationship Meeting age-appropriate developmental needs of children
Launching Children	Adjustment to needs of young adults leaving and/or re-entering the family
Middle-aged parents	Maintaining supportive relationships with children and across generations
Aging parents	Adjustments to retirement, end of life

- There are often multiple visits, which promote trust and the development of a relationship between the nurse and the family over time.
- The nurse gathers data about the family in their own context.

Much of the care provided by CHNs takes place in client's homes (although care may also be provided in community- or hospital-based settings, for example, hospital liaison for discharge planning). Home visits have many advantages; however, it is a standard of practice for CHNs that a holistic assessment occurs in collaboration with the client (individual, family, or community) wherever the care is provided. It is also an expectation that the nurse can negotiate and provide culturally appropriate care in a variety of settings (Community Health Nurses Association of Canada, 2003).

Leahey and Harper-Jaques (1996) describe five core assumptions relating to the family-nurse relationship.

- The family-nurse relationship is characterized by reciprocity.
- The family-nurse relationship is non-hierarchical.
- Nurses and families each have specialized expertise in maintaining health and in managing health problems.
- Nurses and families each bring strengths and resources to the family-nurse relationship.
- A feedback process can occur simultaneously at several different relationship levels.

Each family member and the nurse bring their own perceptions, values, and beliefs to the interactions. These assumptions "form the basis for the evolution of collaborative relationships between nurses and families" (p. 148).

Family Assessment Tools

Many family assessment tools are available (Allender & Spradley, 2001; Friedman et al., 2003; Hanson, 2001). This section describes the Friedman Family Assessment Model (Friedman et al., 2003), the Calgary Family Assessment Model (Wright & Leahy, 2000), and the McGill Model (Gottlieb & Rowat, 1987). The latter two were developed in Canada. Essential features of these models are presented in Table 9.4.

The Friedman Family Assessment Model has six broad categories (see Table 9.4) (Friedman et al., 2003). Identifying data includes family composition, cultural background, religious identification, social class status, and recreational activities. The developmental stage is assessed along with the family's history and the history of both parent's family of origin. Environmental data includes characteristics of the home, neighbourhood, and community; the family's geographic mobility; associations with the community and use of community resources; and the family's social support system. Family structure looks at communication patterns, power structure, role structure, and family values. Affective, socialization, and health care functions are assessed in the family functions category. The sixth category, family stress and coping, includes assessment of stressors and strengths along with coping strategies (Friedman et al.). Each category has many subcategories. The nurse and the family decide which areas need in-depth exploration based on the focus for nursing intervention.

Wright and Leahey (2000) first developed the Calgary Family Assessment Model (CFAM) in 1983 at the University of Calgary. The CFAM has been conceptualized as a branching diagram (see Figure 9.3) with three major categories: structural, developmental, and functional. As in Friedman's model, it has many subcategories. Each nurse decides which subcategories should be explored and assesses each family accordingly. As derived from Wright and Leahy (1999), some general questions to guide the family-assessment interview are listed in the text box.

Interventions are conceptualized in the Calgary Family Intervention Model (CFIM), which complements the CFAM and provides a framework for family functions in three domains: cognitive, affective, and behavioural. Interventions focus on promoting, improving, and sustaining effective family

TABLE 9.4
Components of Family Assessment Models and Tools

Friedman Family Assessment Model	Calgary Family Assessment Model	McGill Model
• Identifying data • Developmental stage and history of family • Environmental data • Family structure • Family functions • Family coping	• Developmental stage and history of family • Structural • Developmental • Functional	• The family as the subsystem • Health as the focus of work • Learning as the process through which health behaviours are acquired • Family collaborates with the nurse in the learning process

Source: Adapted from Registered Nurses Association of Ontario. (2002). Supporting and strengthening families through expected and unexpected life events. *Toronto, ON: Author (p. 42).*

functioning. The most effective interventions are congruent with the family's beliefs and values, the articulation of which is facilitated during the assessment (Wright & Leahey, 2000).

The McGill Model has been developed and refined over time by faculty and students at McGill University School of Nursing (Gottlieb & Rowat, 1987). This model emphasizes family, health, collaboration, and learning. The family is an active participant with the nurse in their own health care. "One of the goals of nursing, based on the McGill Model, is to help families use the strengths of the individual family members and of the family as unit, as well resources external to the family system, to cope, achieve their goals, and develop" (Feely & Gottlieb, 2000, p. 10). Health consists of processes, which are dynamic and multidimensional, especially the processes of coping and development.

The assessment phase of the McGill Model requires an exploratory approach by the nurse, with the nurse creating a

FIGURE 9.3 Calgary Family Assessment Model

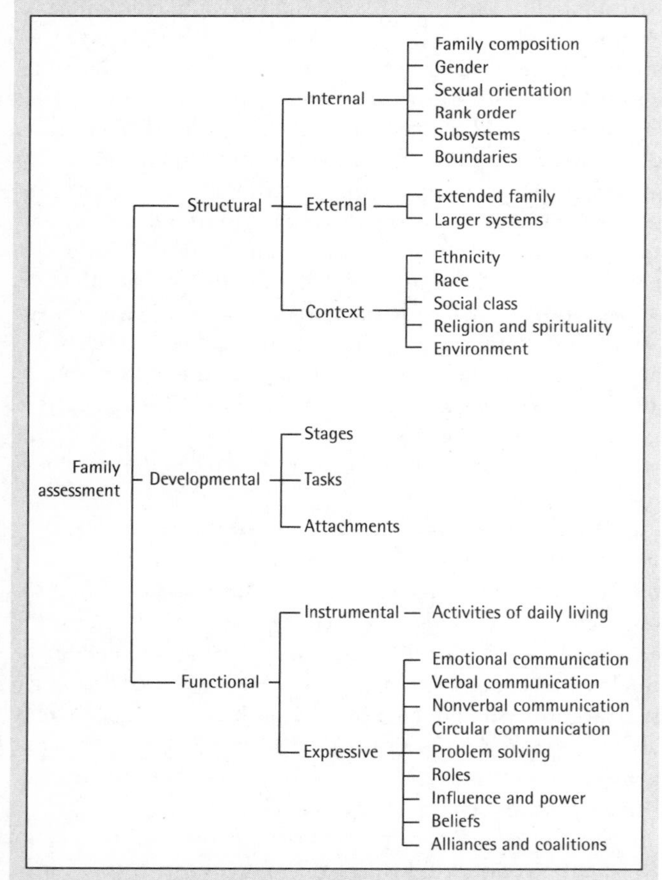

Source: Reproduced with permission from Wright, L. M., & Leahy, M. (2000). Nurses and families: A guide to family assessment and intervention *(3rd ed.). Philadelphia: F. A. Davis, p. 68.*

Examples of Family Assessment and Interview Questions

1. How can I be the most helpful to you and your family at this time? (clarifies expectations and builds partnership between the family and the nurse)
2. What has been the most/least helpful to you and your family in the past? (identifies past difficulties, strengths and achievements)
3. Who of your family and friends would you like to share information with and who not? (identifies alliances, resources, and conflicts)
4. What is the greatest challenge facing your family right now? (identifies actual/potential stress, roles, values and beliefs)
5. What do you need to best prepare you/your family for ______? (identifies appropriate community resources)
6. What strengths does your family have right now? (identifies current positive resources and assists with planning)
7. What is the one question you would like to have answered right now? (identifies the most pressing issue or concern)
8. How have I been the most helpful to you today? How could we improve? (demonstrates willingness to learn from the family and work collaboratively)

FIGURE 9.4 Sample Genogram: The B. Family

Another valuable tool during assessment is the genogram, which is used to build a picture of family structure, relationships, and boundaries. This genogram shows the family of Mr. and Mrs. B., who were married in 1996. Mrs. B. is 27 years old and has just given birth to her third child, a girl. She lives with her 28-year-old husband and their other two children, boys, who are six and two years old. The oldest son has asthma and attends Grade 1 at the local elementary school. Mrs. B.'s father died of cancer in 1998. Her mother and large extended family live close by. Mr. B. provides for the family financially by working as a high-school teacher. The B. family is used for the Case Study later in the chapter.

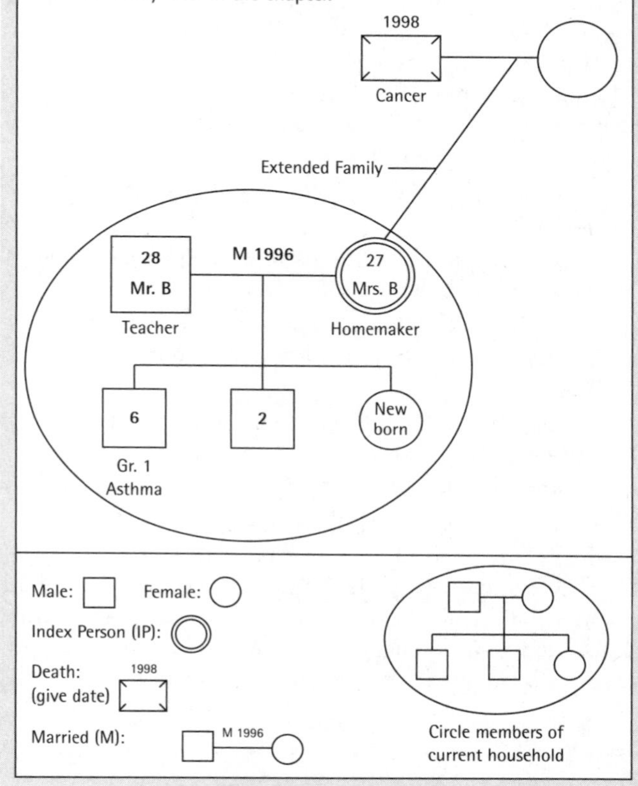

supportive environment so that the family's perceptions and strengths can emerge. Learning needs are identified and the initiative for planning can be with the nurse or the family (Gottlieb & Rowat, 1987). It is during the implementation phase that the family becomes an active learner in collaboration with the nurse.

Cultural Assessment Tools

Cultural assessments can be used with individuals, families, communities, and institutions. As stated by Kulig (1995, p. 254), "The advantages of cultural assessments are that they:

1. provide a systematic strategy to guide practice,
2. show respect for and interest in the client's culture,
3. improve practice by making it potentially more meaningful for the client, and
4. serve as an educational tool for the CHN to understand cultural diversity and learn about various beliefs and practices."

Madeline Leininger (2002) is the founder of transcultural nursing, which evolved from her work in nursing blended with post-graduate studies in anthropology. The purpose of her **theory of Cultural Care Diversity and Universality** is to discover, explain, and predict factors that influence care meanings and practices from both the client's and nurse's perspectives, and to discover care similarities and differences in order to guide nursing practice. For Leininger, care is the central and unifying focus of nursing. Her definition of **culture** is "the learned, shared, and transmitted knowledge of values, beliefs, and lifeways of a particular group that are generally transmitted intergenerationally and influence thinking, decisions, and actions in patterned or in certain ways" (2002, p. 47). Leininger's Sunrise Model (Figure 9.5) depicts her theory of Culture Care Diversity and Universality. Leininger combines cultural assessment with assessments of health and care in diverse settings, which leads to formulating culturally competent nursing actions at three levels.

A variety of cultural assessment guides have been developed (Andrews & Boyle, 2003; Davidhizar & Giger, 1998; Leininger & McFarland, 2002; Spector, 2002; Rosenbaum, 1991, 1995).

FIGURE 9.5 Leininger's Sunrise Model

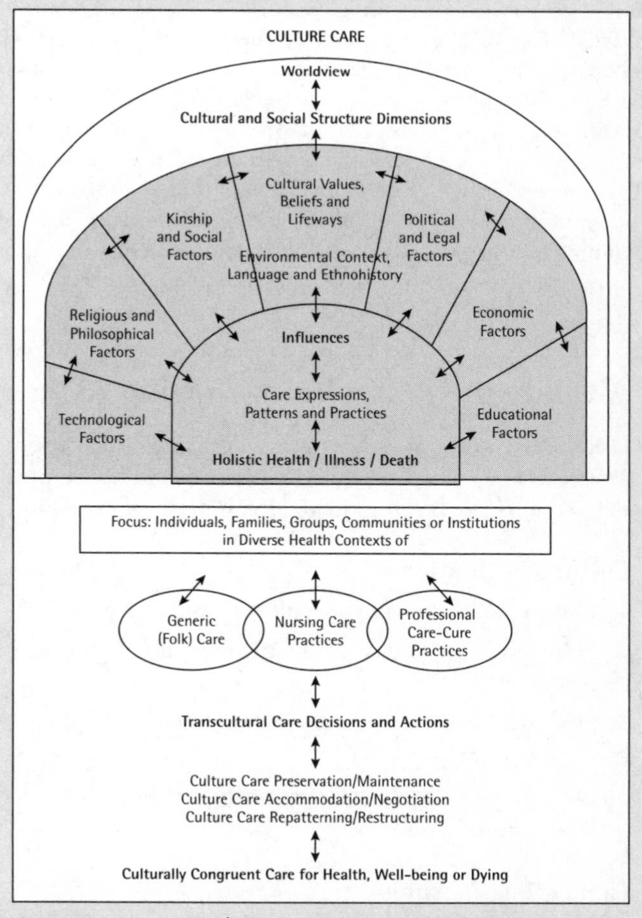

Source: M. Lenninger & M. R. McFarland (Eds.). (2002). Transcultural nursing: concepts, theories, research & practice *(3rd ed.). New York: McGraw-Hill, p. 80. Reproduced with the permission of The McGraw-Hill Companies.*

Useful guides need to provide a format with open-ended questions that facilitate descriptive responses. CHNs using a guide "should be flexible: ask only the appropriate questions, and use a language and conversational level suitable to the client, the nurse, and the setting. The important principle is that in cultural assessment, the client teaches and nurse learns" (Rosenbaum, 1991, p. 33). Yiu and Edmunds (2004) have developed A Guide to Transcultural Assessment (see text box).

When participating in cultural assessments, the CHN must be careful not to focus on how the client differs from the nurse (which we often assume to be the "norm"). Both nurses and clients bring multiple cultures to their interactions. Their own personal ethnicity, the culture of nursing, and the culture of their institution shape nurses. Clients (individuals, families, communities) are shaped by multiple cultures as well. While discovering the clients' values, beliefs, and assumptions, nurses must always be aware of their own.

It is also important to remember that diversity within cultures can be just as strong as diversity between cultures. "Factors such as social class, religion, level of education, and area of origin in the home country (rural or urban) make for major differences within immigrant groups. These factors influence patients' beliefs about health and illness, their help-seeking behaviour, their expectations of health professionals, and their practices regarding health and illness" (Anderson, Waxler-Morrison, Richardson, Herbert, & Murphy, 1990, p. 246). Planning and implementing nursing care is not based on how different (or similar) someone might seem; it is based on bringing the same assessment skills to every interaction so that values, beliefs, and health care practices can be discovered. This process, in which the nurse always tries to work within the cultural context of the client and which leads to mutual planning between the family and the nurse, also takes the nurse on a journey toward cultural competence (see Chapter 16).

Integration of Family and Cultural Assessment

In family assessment models, culture data are considered as a part of the family assessment. In cultural models, family data are considered as part of the culture assessment. The concepts of family and culture are often "taken for granted," that is, assumed and unexamined. This is why open-ended questions are common to both kinds of assessments. The nurse facilitates the family in discovering and articulating the often unexamined assumptions, context, and expectations underlying their perception of reality. As stated before, it is the responsibility of the nurse to examine and be aware of their own perceptions and assumptions about families and cultures, including the culture of nursing and the institution for which the nurse works. The following statements apply to both family and cultural assessments.

- The assessment process takes time, sensitivity, and flexibility.
- The assessment process starts from the perspective of the family and/or the community.
- Assessments take place in an atmosphere of openness, awareness, mutual collaboration, and relationship building.
- Assessments are holistic.
- Assessment tools can be adapted and adjusted to identified needs (identified by the client and the nurse) such as time, area of focus, and/or need for an interpreter.

So how does the CHN decide on an assessment tool that will then guide interventions? It is not a case of "one size fits all" or of designing the "perfect" model. Rather, it is having the openness, knowledge, and skill to evaluate existing theories, models, and guides in light of what would be most appropriate and effective for the client, and adapting as necessary.

A Guide to Transcultural Nursing Assessment

Use the following questions as a guide, and where appropriate, to learn about your client's culture and health practices (client may be an individual, family, or community).

Cultural Affiliation

1. Can you tell me about your cultural group and its heritage?
2. How long have you or your parents/your family been in this country?
3. How did you/your parents/your family decide to come to this country?
4. Do you have close social relationships with people from your cultural group?

Family Relationships

1. How important is family in your culture?
2. Who are your current family members?
3. Can you tell me how your family members communicate with one another? i.e., mother and father, among the siblings, between parents and siblings, and family with extended families (includes verbal and non-verbal communication such as use of silence, personal space, touching, tone of voice, appropriate topics).
4. Who has the authority to make the major and final decisions in your family, and how? Please give examples.
5. What are the roles and responsibilities of mothers, fathers, sons, and daughters in your culture? i.e., what are their duties in the family?
6. Can you tell me about your views of parenting? What do parents expect from their children when they are children and when they are adults?
7. How do families in your culture view marriage? How are single parenthood, divorce, separation, and unemployment viewed?

8. Can you tell me about your views of caregiving? Who takes care of the young children? Who takes care of the aging parents?

Health Beliefs and Practices

1. What does health mean to you?
2. What does being healthy mean to you?
3. What do you do to stay healthy?
4. What are the common health beliefs and practices for the following life events and their significance?
   a. pregnancy
   b. birth
   c. adolescence
   d. marriage
   e. middle years
   f. old age
5. How important is it for you to have regular health care follow-up and why? for example immunization, dental care, regular physical examinations, and screening.
6. Who plays the major role in keeping the family healthy, and how?
7. What does "good nutrition" mean to you and how does food help keep you healthy?
8. What does "care" mean to you? How would you describe someone who is caring/non-caring?

Illness Beliefs and Practices

1. What does being sick or ill mean to you?
2. Can you tell me about your beliefs regarding why people become ill?
3. Can you tell about any illnesses or conditions which are common or of concern for people in your culture?
4. What do you do when you are feeling ill?
5. What are the common health beliefs and practices for the following and their significance?
   a. a major illness or disability
   b. an accident
   c. a chronic illness
   d. a terminal illness
   e. death
   f. other (please describe)
6. Who would usually be involved in caring for the ill family member? Why? What would this person do?
7. In your culture, what traditional healing do you practice, if any? Please describe your experiences with traditional healing practitioners/practices.
8. Please describe your experiences with health professionals. How would you describe a caring/non-caring health professional?
9. How do you determine when to use traditional healers or when to seek care from health professionals?

Religious and Spiritual Practices

1. How would you describe your religious and spiritual beliefs?
2. Are there any special religious and spiritual days in your culture? What are the customs and beliefs for these days?
3. Who in the family usually ensures that these religious and spiritual practices are being followed?
4. Can you tell me your beliefs about life and death?
5. How important are religious and spiritual supports for someone who is healthy/someone who is ill?

World Views

1. Can you describe who you are and how you see your life in relation to the world around you?
2. What is most important in your life?
3. What are your views about education? What level of education do you have?
4. How do you view technology? How does technology influence your life? for example, use of computers, the Internet, health care technology.
5. How important do you view politics, economic, and legal matters in your life?
6. If you are new to the country, have your world views changed since your arrival? Why? How?

Socialization

1. What is the language that you speak and write?
2. What languages are spoken in your home? Why? How do you feel about this?
3. What do you do to socialize with your families and friends?
4. What are the "do's" and "don't's" when teaching children in your family? What do parents encourage their children to do in order to be successful in life?
5. If you are new to this country, what barriers/difficulties did you experience while adapting to the new country? What helped you to adapt to the new country?
6. If you are from an immigrant family, can you tell me how you relate your expectations for your parents and/or children to what you were taught in your own culture?
7. To what extent do you practice or observe the customs and traditions that you learned in your culture? and in the new country?

Yiu, L., & Edmunds, K. (2004). A Guide to Transcultural Nursing Assessment. *Unpublished guide, University of Windsor, Windsor, Ontario.*

Canadian Research Box 9.2

Dicicco-Bloom, B., & Cohen, D. (2003). Home care nurses: A study of the occurrence of culturally competent care. *Journal of Transcultural Nursing, 14*(1), 25–31.

The purpose of this qualitative study was to describe how home care nurses learn about and manage cultural issues that occur during visits to patients. Since understanding culturally competent care requires examining care practices by describing and evaluating nurse-patient interactions, the study methodology included participant observation and interviews. The study sample size was 14 home care nurses from the eastern coastal region of the United States and 14 patients. All the nurses were at least third-generation Americans of European ancestry, and all the patients were first-generation immigrants.

The researchers reported that six of the 14 nurses failed to acknowledge that some of the patient's behaviours might have been culturally prescribed. This means that the nurses did not address the significance of the behaviour and therefore did not adapt their own behaviours toward the patients, nor did they integrate the cultural practices into their care. The article includes rich examples from the data analysis and results. In all the cases analyzed in this study, home care nurses avoided dealing with cross-cultural issues. In some cases, even when the nurses did show an appreciation for the existence of cultural differences, they often attempted to escape from dealing with them by discharging the client or asking to be replaced.

Cultural competence is an important aspect of health care delivery. This study's findings suggest that both the nurses and the agencies that employ them need to develop their skills for providing culturally competent health care.

Discussion Questions

1. Discuss the findings of this and other studies as they relate to nursing behaviour you have observed in practice.
2. What can educational programs do to help student nurses develop their skills in providing culturally competent care when working with families?

PHOTO 9.1

A community health nurse visits a new mother in her home.

Credit: Imagestate/firstlight.ca

CASE STUDY 9.1

Figure 9.4 showed the genogram of the B. family. The family lives in a comfortable three-bedroom home in an established neighbourhood and has developed strong ties with their community and religious organization. You are a CHN required to make follow-up telephone calls to new mothers following discharge from hospital. During your phone conversation, Mrs. B. tells you that she is feeling "very overwhelmed and tearful" after having the new baby. She voices concern and fear that she is not bonding with the baby. She has never experienced anything like this before and has not shared her feelings with her husband or her family.

Discussion Questions

1. How soon should the nurse make the home visit?
2. What should the nurse who made the telephone call do if unable to personally make a home visit within an appropriate length of time?
3. Discuss which assessment tool you will use and describe what beginning information you have about family strengths and community supports.

What Concept Makes Sense for the Situation: "Family" or "Culture"?

Theories arise and are developed and refined within a cultural context. "Family theories are based on assumptions about close relationships. Therefore, when trying to apply a family theory cross-culturally, the researcher should identify the theory's assumptions and then ask, 'How do the assumptions of the theory fit with the assumptions of the culture?'" (Moriarty, Cotroneo, De Feudis, & Natale, 1995, p. 365).

CHNs need to take an inclusive and holistic understanding of family and culture when facilitating assessment, planning, intervention, and evaluation. Culture may seem to be more important for an immigrant family; however, it is just as important for a "mainstream" family in discovering the values and beliefs that have meaning for them. The theories, frameworks, and assessment tools discussed in this chapter have in common that the CHN and the family are engaged in a social process of exploration, negotiation, and mutual goal setting.

CASE MANAGEMENT AND FAMILY-CENTRED CARE

Case management is a systematic and interdisciplinary approach to service delivery (Rheaume, Frisch, Smith, & Kennedy, 1994; Smith, 1998). It is also referred to in the literature as service coordination and service facilitation. Nursing case management is a professional practice model that increases participation by nurses in decisions regarding standards of practice (Zander, 1988). The model was first introduced in 1985 as an outgrowth of primary care nursing and described by Cohen and Cesta (2001) as an opportunity for the nursing profession to define its role in the changing health care industry (p. 3). Traditional nursing care delivery systems are not able to deal with "the many constraints, economic limitations, and continual changes in today's health care settings" (Cohen & Cesta, p. 9). The model also challenges the profession to define nurses' work in terms of its autonomous value to the client.

The goal of case management is to arrive at quality, cost-effective client outcomes. The provision of client care using a case manager is becoming a more recognized strategy. Case management is meant to ensure that patients receive needed care and services and that those services are delivered in an efficient manner (Cohen & Cesta, 2001). Nurses in community settings use the case management approach to identify and assess clients, plan care, provide or delegate care, and follow up with an evaluation of care. For nurses working with families, this would mean the best outcomes for individual clients within families and the family as a whole. Canadian nurses have a lengthy history of providing family-centred care to vulnerable individuals and connecting them to services with the purpose of promoting health and preventing disease (Jack, 2000; Yiu Matuk & Horsburgh, 1989; Rafael, 1999).

In Canada, the restructuring of the 1990s has resulted in two major mechanisms for managed care to save health care dollars. The first is decreasing the length of stay in hospitals (early discharge); the second is decreasing the time spent delivering home care services. The danger of these is that cost containment, not quality of life, becomes the main determining factor (Daiski, 2000). The result has been many complaints about deteriorating home care services and the detrimental impact of the changes on patients and their families. "Inadequate professional follow-up care often forces families to take over these responsibilities" (Daiski, p. 75).

Once embraced as a model to increase nursing's influence in the system, case management has come under criticism for its focus on cost containment. Nurses as case managers are challenged to creatively "integrate financing mechanisms and appropriate utilization management, and ensure high-quality service delivery by prioritizing outcomes (Daiski, p. 75). This is a very challenging situation for nurses who must determine the most appropriate services to meet the needs of the client while providing the most benefit at the least cost. Due to the release of Romanow's Commission on the Future of Health Care in Canada (2002), funding for community-based care may improve dramatically. This will provide nurses with opportunities to reflect on what managed care has become in this country and decide on how to influence changes for the future.

COMMUNITY HEALTH NURSING ROLES

There are many roles for the nurse who works with families in community settings. The Paediatric Consensus Conference, held in Ottawa in 1998, identified major roles/contributions of nurses in meeting the needs of children and families in the next 10–20 years. These roles include provider of direct care, health promoter, partner/collaborator, advocate, teacher, researcher, leader, and administrator/manager. Nurses "help families prevent and manage illness and provide direct care across the continuum—from health promotion to care in the hospital and in the community" (Davies, Ogden Burke, Lynam, Ritchie, & Van Daalen, 1998, p. 4). These authors also recognized that nurses have an additional role responsibility—to themselves and their professional practice. Nurses need to acknowledge that they cannot be all things to all people and need to find a balance. This will enable nurses to maintain their capacity to thrive and to provide quality care by "dealing with stress, recognizing the boundaries of nursing,... and being focused on the provision of care" (Davies et al., p. 11).

SUMMARY

This chapter is an overview of family care in community settings. It is not all encompassing, but rather provides a glimpse into a growing nursing specialty. Changing family composition and increasing cultural diversity of families are discussed, a key message being that it is important for nurses to remain open to the perceptions, values, and beliefs of families and to gather that information as part of a holistic assessment. The nurse does not "conduct" an assessment, but facilitates the process. In community health, this process often occurs in the client's home. Over time, strong relationships between the nurse and the family can develop. Planning, implementation, and evaluating interventions are also collaborative processes between the nurse and the family.

Many assessment tools are available, most based on multidisciplinary theories, but there is no perfect assessment tool or plan of care. The nurse needs to be aware of and use the theories and tools which are consistent with the underlying concepts that will "make sense" of the situation for the nurse and the family. As mutual priorities are set, the tools can be focused and adapted.

KEY TERMS

family
family forms
family function
family health nursing

family systems nursing
systems theory
structural-functional theory
family development theory
family assessment
cultural assessments
theory of Cultural Care Diversity and Universality
culture
case management

STUDY QUESTIONS

1. What are some of the challenges facing families today?
2. What are some of the reasons that young people are moving back home or leaving home at an older age?
3. What are some of the terms that are used to describe nurses' work with families?
4. Describe attributes of a collaborative relationship with a family.
5. What is the definition of a Canadian family?
6. How does a CHN provide effective care while working with the family as client?

INDIVIDUAL CRITICAL THINKING EXERCISES

1. Differentiate between family assessment models and cultural assessment models.
2. Discuss the responsibilities families need to meet for healthy functioning.
3. Describe the shared assumptions for facilitating family and cultural assessments.
4. Discuss the societal changes that have influenced family life in Canada.
5. How does the CHN assist families to strengthen their capacity to act on their own behalf for health promotion?

GROUP CRITICAL THINKING EXERCISES

1. Describe how approaches to family health nursing in the community differ from acute care settings.
2. Case management requires a balance between quality client care and cost-effectiveness. How do family and cultural assessment models help you to meet this goal as a CHN?
3. Explain how the changing demographics of the Canadian family influence community health nursing care.
4. Differentiate between viewing the family as client and the family as context.
5. Elaborate on what it means to "think family."

REFERENCES

Allender, J. A., & Spradley, B. W. (2001). *Community health nursing: Concepts and practice* (5th ed.). Philadelphia, PA: Lippincott.

Anderson, J. M., Waxler-Morrison, N., Richardson, E., Herbert, C., & Murphy, M. (1990). Conclusion: Delivering culturally sensitive health care. In N. Waxler-Morrison, J. Anderson, & E. Richardson (Eds.), *Cross-cultural caring: A handbook for health professionals* (pp. 245–267). Vancouver, BC: University of British Columbia Press.

Andrews, M. M., & Boyle, J. S. (2003). *Transcultural concepts in nursing care* (4th ed.). Philadelphia: Lippincott.

Artinian, N. T. (1999). Selecting a model to guide family assessment. In G. D. Wegner & R. J. Alexander (Eds.), *Readings in family nursing* (2nd ed.) (pp. 447–459). Philadelphia, PA: Lippincott.

Bomar, P. J. (Ed.). (1996). *Nurses and family health promotion* (2nd ed.). Philadelphia, PA: Saunders.

Canadian Nurses Association. (1997). *Nursing now: Issues and trends in Canadian nursing.* Ottawa, ON: Author.

Coffman, S. (1997). Home-care nurses as strangers in the family. *Western Journal of Nursing Research, 19*(1), 82–96.

Cohen, E. L., & Cesta, T. G. (2001). *Nursing case management: From essentials to advanced practice application.* St. Louis, MO: Mosby.

Commission on the Future of Health Care in Canada. (2002). *Building on values: The future of health care in Canada—final report.* Ottawa, ON: Author.

Community Health Nurses Association of Canada (CHNAC). (2003). *Canadian community health nursing standards of practice.* Ottawa, ON: Author.

Davidhizar, R. E., & Giger, J. N. (1998). *Canadian transcultural nursing.* St. Louis: Mosby.

Daiski, I. (2000). The road to professionalism in nursing: Case management or practice based in nursing theory? *Nursing Science Quarterly, 13*(1), 74–79.

Davies, B., Ogden Burke, S., Lynam, J., Ritchie, J., & Van Daalen, C. (1998, October). *A synthesis. Report of the paediatric consensus conference.* Sponsored by The Canadian Nurses Foundation and the Hospital for Sick Children Foundation, Ottawa, Canada.

Dicicco-Bloom, B., & Cohen, D. (2003). Homecare nurses: A study of the occurrence of culturally competent care. *Journal of Transcultural Nursing, 14*(1), 25–31.

Feeley, N., & Gottlieb, L. N. (2000). Nursing approaches for working with family strengths and resources. *Journal of Family Nursing, 6*(1), 9–24.

Friedman, M. (1997). Teaching about and for family diversity in nursing. *Journal of Family Nursing, 3*(3), 280–294.

Friedman, M. M., Bowden, V. R., & Jones, E. G. (Eds.). (2003). *Family nursing: Research, theory, & practice* (5th ed.). Upper Saddle River, NJ: Prentice Hall.

Gottlieb, L., & Rowat, K. (1987). The McGill model of nursing: A practice-derived model. *Advances in Nursing Science, 9*(4), 51–61.

Green, C. P. (1997). Teaching students how to "think family." *Journal of Family Nursing, 3*(3), 230–246.

Hanson, S. M. H. (Ed.). (2001). *Family health care nursing: Theory, practice, and research* (2nd ed.). Philadelphia, PA: F.A. Davis.

Hartrick, G. (2000). Developing health-promoting practices with families. *Journal of Advanced Nursing, 31*(1), 27–34.

Hartrick, G., Lindsey, A. E., & Hills, M. (1994). Family nursing assessment: Meeting the challenge of health promotion. *Journal of Advanced Nursing, 20,* 85–91.

Harway, M. (1996). *Treating the changing family: Handling normative and unusual events.* New York: John Wiley & Sons.

Hitchcock, J. E., Schubert, P. E., & Thomas, S. A. (Eds.). (1999). *Community health nursing: Caring in* action. New York: Thomson, Delmar Learning.

Jack, S. (2000). *Mandating public health nurses to become case managers. Is it necessary?* Unpublished manuscript, McMaster University, Hamilton, Ontario.

Kulig, J. C. (1995). Culturally diverse communities: The impact on the role of community health nurses. In M. J. Stewart (Ed.), *Community nursing: Promoting Canadian's health* (2nd ed.) (pp. 246–265). Toronto, ON: W. B. Saunders.

Leahy, M., & Harper-Jaques, S. (1996). Family-nurse relationships: Core assumptions and clinical implications. *Journal of Family Nursing, 2*(2), 133–151.

Leininger, M., & McFarland, M. R. (Eds.). (2002). *Transcultural nursing: concepts, theories, research & practice* (3rd ed.). New York: McGraw-Hill.

Lepage, M., Essiembre, L. G., & Coutu-Wakulczyk, G. (1996). Variations sur le thème de la famille. *Canadian Nurse, 92*(7), 40–44.

Loveland-Cherry, C. (1996). Family health promotion and health protection. In P. J. Bomar (Ed.), *Nurses and family health promotion* (2nd ed.). (pp. 22–35). Philadelphia, PA: Saunders.

Macklin, E. D. (1987). Nontraditional family forms. In M. B. Sussman & S. K. Stienmetz (Eds.), *Handbook of marriage and the family.* New York: Plenum.

Mandle, C. L. (2002). Health promotion and the family. In C. L. Edelman & C. L. Mandle (Eds.), *Health promotion throughout the lifespan* (5th ed.) (pp. 169–198). Toronto, ON: Mosby.

Moriarty, H. J., Cotroneo, M., De Feudis, R., & Natale, S. (1995). Key issues in cross-cultural family research. *Journal of Family Nursing, 1*(4), 359–381.

Rafael, A. R. F. (1999). From rhetoric to reality: The changing face of public health nursing in Southern Ontario. *Public Health Nursing, 16*(1), 50–59.

Registered Nurses Association of Ontario. (2002). *Supporting and strengthening families through expected and unexpected life events.* Toronto, ON: Author.

Rheaume, A., Frisch, S., Smith, A., & Kennedy, C. (1994). Case management and nursing practice. *Journal of Nursing Administration, 24*(3), 30–36.

Rosenbaum, J. N. (1991). A cultural assessment guide: Learning cultural sensitivity. *Canadian Nurse, 87*(4), 32–33.

Rosenbaum, J. N. (1995). Teaching cultural sensitivity. *Journal of Nursing Education, 34*(4), 188–189.

Smith, J. E. (1998). Case management: A literature review. *Canadian Journal of Nursing Administration, 11*(2), 93–109.

Spector, R. E. (2000). *Cultural diversity in health and illness* (5th ed.). Stamford, CT: Appleton & Lange.

Statistics Canada. (2002). *Census analysis series—Profile of Canadian families and households: Diversification continues.* Retrieved September 29, 2003 from **www.statcan.ca/english/IPS/Data/96F0030XIE2001003.htm**

Statistics Canada. (2003). *The Canada e-book.* Retrieved November 30, 2003 from **www.statcan.ca/start.html**

Vanier Institute of the Family. (2000). *Profiling Canada's families II.* Ottawa, ON: Canadian Nurses Association.

van Manen (1990). *Researching lived experience.* New York: State University of New York Press.

Whall, A. L., & Fawcett, J. (1991). *Family theory development in nursing: State of the science and art.* Philadelphia, PA: F. A. Davis.

World Health Organization, Canadian Public Health Association, & Health and Welfare Canada. (1986). *Ottawa charter for health promotion.* Ottawa, ON: Health and Welfare Canada.

Wright, L. M., & Leahy, M. (1999). Maximizing time, minimizing suffering: The 15-minute (or less) family interview. *Journal of Family Nursing, 5*(3), 259–274.

Wright, L. M., & Leahy, M. (2000). *Nurses and families: A guide to family assessment and intervention* (3rd ed.). Philadelphia, PA: F.A. Davis.

Yiu Matuk, L., & Horsburgh, M. E. C. (1989). Rebuilding public health nursing practice: A Canadian perspective. *Public Health Nursing, 6*(4), 169–173.

Yiu, L. & Edmunds, K. (2004). *A guide to Transcultural Nursing Assessment.* Unpublished guide, University of Windsor, Windsor, Ontario.

Zander, K. (1988). Nursing case management: Strategic management of cost and quality outcomes. *Journal of Nursing Administration, 18*(5), 23–30.

ADDITIONAL RESOURCES

WEBSITES

Child and Family Canada:
www.cfc-efc.ca

A public education website with fifty Canadian non-profit organizations providing quality resources on children and families.

The Canadian Nurses Association:
www.cna-nurses.ca

The Registered Nurses Association of Ontario:
www.rnao.org/bestpractices/completed_guidelines/bestPractice_firstCycle.asp
The Best Practice Guidelines are available for download in abbreviated or full-length versions.

Statistics Canada:
www.statcan.ca

An excellent resource for information from the latest Canadian census.

Transcultural Nursing Society:
www.tcns.org
The links section is especially useful.

The Vanier Institute of the Family:
www.vifamily.ca
A site devoted to reporting and analyzing the Canadian family based on census information.

About the Authors

Linda Patrick, RN (Victoria Hospital, London), BScN, MSc (Windsor), MEd (Central Michigan), PhD Candidate (McMaster), is an Assistant Professor at the University of Windsor. Her areas of research are in prevention or delay of type 2 diabetes in women with previous gestational diabetes through lifestyle changes and education, and the promotion of vehicle safety for vulnerable populations, specifically interventions to increase the safe and effective use of child safety restraints. She was Region One Representative to the Board of Directors for the Registered Nurses Association of Ontario and is a member of the Certification Maintenance Evaluation Committee of the Canadian Diabetes Educator Certification Board.

Kathryn Edmunds, RN, BN (Manitoba), MSN (Wayne State), is an Assistant Professor in the Faculty of Nursing at the University of Windsor. She joins the university after 15 years as a public health nurse with the Windsor-Essex County Health Unit, working in rural Southwestern Ontario. Her graduate education was in the field of transcultural nursing, which remains an area of clinical and research interest. Other research interests include cultural competence and qualitative evaluation. She is a Visiting Research Fellow at the School of Nursing and Midwifery at the University of Southampton, UK and in 2001 was awarded a Registered Nurses Association of Ontario Advanced Clinical/Practice Fellowship in leadership and research.

The authors wish to acknowledge Darlene McDonald and Liana Dass for their assistance with this chapter.

CHAPTER 10

Community Care

Lucia Yiu

OBJECTIVES

AFTER STUDYING THIS CHAPTER, YOU SHOULD BE ABLE TO:

1. Describe the concept of community, its functions, and its dynamics.
2. Briefly describe the common models and frameworks used in community health nursing practice.
3. Explain the community health nursing process.
4. Discuss the purposes, methods, parameters, and participatory tools used in community assessment and planning.
5. Explain the importance of population health promotion and risk assessment.
6. Explain the role of the nurse in caring for clients in the community.
7. Discuss the relevance and application of community nursing process in caring for community clients.

INTRODUCTION

Community health nurses (CHNs) care for people where they live, learn, play, and work. Their goal is to promote, preserve, and protect the health of individuals, families, aggregates, and populations in an environment that supports health. Their practice includes promoting health, building individual/community capacity, connecting and caring, facilitating access and equity, and demonstrating professional responsibility and accountability (Community Health Nurses Association of Canada, 2003). When entering the practice of community health nursing, novice nurses often ask, "Where and how do I begin?" Unlike having clients in hospitals or tertiary care settings, who actively seek episodic care for their presenting problems, community health nurses must determine who and where their clients are and when, why, what, and how best to promote their health in the community. They must understand the relationship of environment and health and work autonomously to build community partnerships that are based on a philosophy of primary health care, caring, and empowerment. This chapter provides an overview of how to care for clients in community settings, with an emphasis on community assessment and population health promotion. The concept of a community, as well as frameworks, models, and participatory tools used in community health nursing practice, will be presented.

COMMUNITY DEFINED

Developing an understanding of a community, its functions and dynamics, and the relationship between these and the health of the people is fundamental to providing community care. A **community** may be defined as a group of people who live, learn, work, and play in an environment at a given time. They share common characteristics and interests and function in a social system that meets their needs within a larger social system such as an organization, a county, a region, a province, or a nation. A community may be also defined by its geographic and political boundaries, which are often used to set the locations of health services delivery (Anderson & McFarlane, 2000). For example, mothers may meet in a local drop-in community centre for parenting support, or seniors may gather in a seniors' centre for socialization or health counselling. Figure 10.1 shows a schematic view of the relationship of the individual and family to their surrounding geographic communities.

Communities, while unique, carry out various functions to sustain the day-to-day livelihood of their residents. These **community functions** include (Higgs & Gustafson, 1985):

- utilization of space for adequate housing, recreation, and accessibility to various health and social services;

Figure 10.1 Schematic Relationships of Community Components

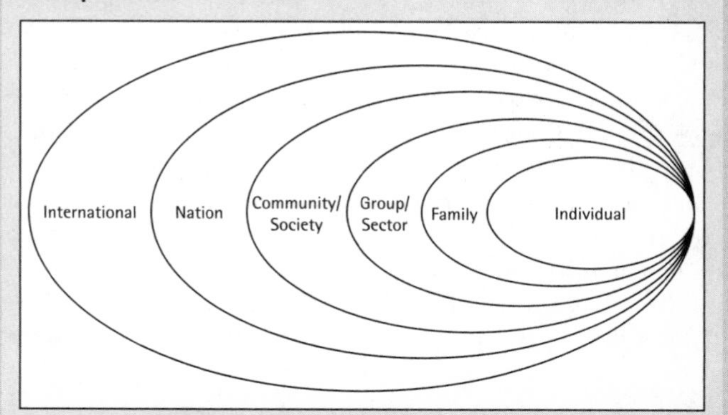

- means of livelihoods that provide secure employment and income;
- productivity and distribution through consumption of goods, trading, and economic growth;
- security, protection, and law enforcement to protect the public from crime;
- education that provides socialization for all community members;
- participation that allows community members to socialize and obtain social support; and
- linkages with other systems for opportunities for growth and capacity building.

Community functions are supported by three interactive **community dynamics**: effective communication, leadership, and decision making (Clemen-Stone, Eigsti, & McGuire, 2002).

Communication

Competent communities possess strong and cohesive vertical, horizontal, and diagonal patterns of communication between the key partners of the community. Vertical communication enables communities to link to larger communities or to those with higher decision-making power. Horizontal communication allows the community to connect to and work collaboratively with its own members, environment, and other service systems. Diagonal communication reinforces the cohesiveness and communication of all system components, both horizontally and vertically, and helps alleviate the silo effects when communication is only done vertically and horizontally.

Leadership

Formal and informal leaders lead their members by influencing the decision-making process using their status and position in the community. Formal leaders are elected official politicians such as the mayors, members of parliament, or the prime minister. Informal leaders are those with prominent positions in the community, such as religious leaders, executives or representatives of community organizations or professionals, elders of community groups, or local heroes.

Decision Making

Formal leaders use government policies to guide their decision making for the community, while informal leaders use their status to influence community groups and to effect change. Based on community needs, these leaders collaborate and negotiate with community groups to advocate for optimal change.

Competent community dynamics lead to public participation, mutual support, and community action that eventually lead to positive change and community growth. Community health nurses are in a unique position to assess community functions and dynamics. They work with people in various community settings, exploring the community's needs and analyzing its strengths and any gaps in relation to the health care system. An understanding of the community goals and needs forms the basis for planning the health services which will promote the health and well-being of the people.

MODELS AND FRAMEWORKS OF COMMUNITY HEALTH NURSING PRACTICE

Models and frameworks are useful in guiding nurses to systematically collect data and to analyze the relationships of various data components. When selecting a model or framework for practice, CHNs must ensure that it is easy to use and that it reflects their agency's as well as their own practice philosophy. This section briefly describes frameworks commonly used in community nursing practice.

Community-as-Partner Model

Community and nursing process are the two main features in Anderson and McFarlane's (2000) Community-as-Partner Model (Figure 10.2). They proposed a **community assessment wheel**, which shows that a community comprises eight subsystems or components: physical environment education, safety and transportation, politics and government, health

FIGURE 10.2 Community-as-Partner Model

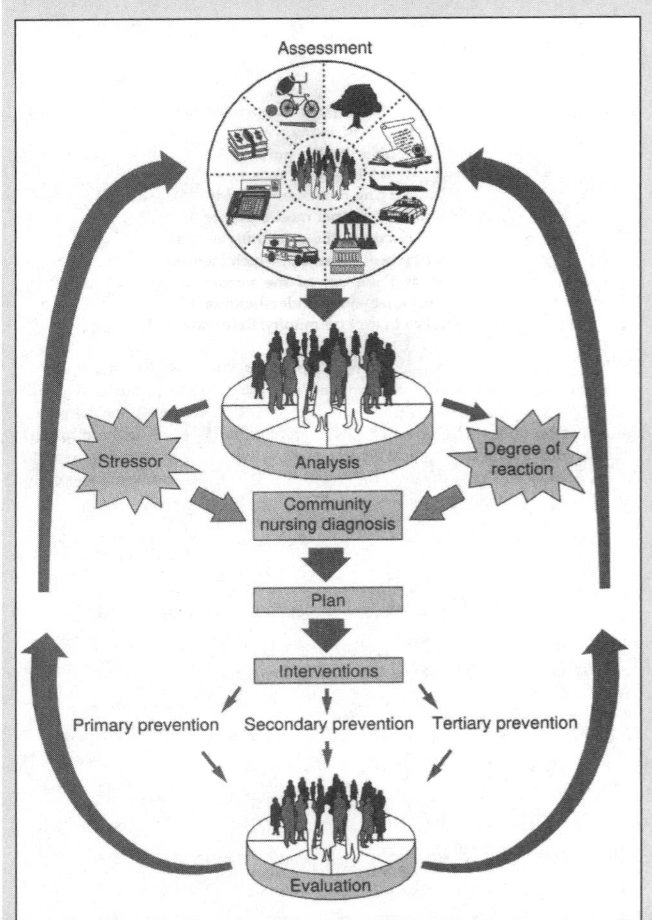

Source: Anderson, E. T., & McFarlane, J. (2000). Community as partner: Theory and practice in nursing (3rd ed.). *Philadelphia, PA: Lippincott. Copyright © 2000 by Lippincott Williams & Williams & Wilkins, p. 158. Used with permission.*

and social services, communication, economy, and recreation. At the core of this community assessment wheel are the community residents who have their unique history, demographics, values, and beliefs. The health of the community is affected by these eight interacting subsystems.

Within the community are the lines of resistance or strengths that protect the community from harm or threats. Surrounding the community are the normal lines of defence that reflect the normal state of health attained by the community. Flexible lines of defence form the outer layer around the community. They serve as a buffer zone, which represents the community's temporary health response to stressors. These stressors produce tension-producing stimuli and may, in turn, penetrate the various lines of defence surrounding the community, affecting the system equilibrium. CHNs work in partnership with members of the community to assess and analyze the degree of reaction to the stressors experienced by the community, to formulate community nursing diagnoses, and to use primary health care principles to plan and deliver primary, secondary, and tertiary preventive care.

Helvie's Energy Theory

As a systems theory, the Helvie Energy Theory (Helvie, 1998) conceptualizes energy as the activity and capacity of communities and individuals to do work. The community includes health, education, and economics as energy subsystems. The community population is in constant energy exchange with its internal environment (e.g., food, air, water, or services) and external environment (e.g., province or nation). CHNs assess the balance and deficit of energies in the community. They target interventions that focus on maintaining, increasing, or decreasing the energies, with a goal to regain balanced energies in the community system.

Community Capacity Approach

The emphasis of McKnight and Kretzmann's (1997) **community capacity** approach is on building community strengths rather than focusing on community deficits. Based on the data collected, a "community assets map" is created that outlines the assets and capacity of the community. Strengths and potential resources are identified for interventions such as community building, resource mobilization, and policy formulation.

There are three categories of data collection for creating the community assets map.

1. Primary building blocks: capacity and assets such as skills and experiences of individuals and organizations located inside the neighbourhood.
2. Secondary building blocks: assets located within the community but controlled by outsiders. These include private and non-profit organizations, physical resources, and public institutions and services.
3. Potential building blocks: resources originating outside the neighbourhood and controlled by outsiders. These include welfare expenditures, public capital improvement expenditures, and public information.

Epidemiologic Frameworks

When studying the distribution of diseases and injuries in populations, CHNs may use the "Epidemiologic Triangle" to collect data and study how man or the host interacts with the agent in his environment. They may also use the "Web of Causation" to study the chains of causation and their effects on a health problem (see Chapter 7).

Primary Health Care

The World Health Organization (1978) endorsed primary health care as an essential health care and a means to achieve health for all (see Chapter 6). In their community assessment and program planning, CHNs may collect data using the eight essential elements of primary health care:

- promotion of food supply and proper nutrition,
- an adequate supply of safe water and basic sanitation,
- maternal and childcare, including family planning,
- immunization against the major infectious diseases,
- prevention and control of locally endemic diseases,
- education about prevailing health problems and methods for preventing and controlling them,
- appropriate treatment for common diseases and injuries, and
- provision of essential drugs.

COMMUNITY HEALTH NURSING PROCESS

While CHNs may select various approaches to work with their community for specific reasons, the process, being continuous and cyclical in nature, remains essentially the same. The first step is to identify the purpose or goal of the nursing care, followed by analyzing the problem or issue, making inferences of the implications and consequences of the problem or issue, formulating nursing diagnoses, planning and implementing the interventions, and evaluating the outcomes. Because of the complexity of the practice setting, CHNs must be independent and self-directed critical thinkers. They use the same basic nursing assessment skills as those in individual and family nursing processes. However, they must expand and broaden their assessment skills when examining the multiple variables that affect the overall functioning of the community.

Community Assessment

The community health nursing process begins with sound community assessment. This assessment is only useful if it is accurate, complete, and realistic. CHNs begin the community data collection process by first asking: "What information about the community should I know and why? How will I use this information?" Specific questions for consideration include:

- What is the purpose of the assessment?
- Who is the target population?

- What are the boundaries of the community and the size of the population?
- What approaches or techniques should be used in the assessment?
- Does the political environment within the community support the assessment?
- What is the time frame to complete the assessment?
- What resources and expertise are available to complete the assessment?
- What are the costs and benefits of doing the assessment?

Purpose of Community Assessment The reason for community assessment may be one or a combination of environmental scan, needs identification, problem investigation, and/or resource evaluation (Allender & Spradley, 2001; Higgs & Gustafson, 1985).

Environmental Scan The most preliminary and fundamental assessment of the community is an **environmental scan**, in which one scans the overall environment through a **windshield survey**. CHNs can drive around the neighbourhood or simply take a walking tour. They can see the people, the housing conditions, the geography, and the physical layout of various services in the community (Figure 10.3). During a walking tour, CHNs can listen to what languages people speak to one another and what concerns them during their daily conversations in their neighbourhood cafes or markets. They can sense the air quality or taste the water. By scanning the environment, CHNs can familiarize themselves with their work environment and connect people to the resources and environment in which they live. Windshield surveys are best done at two different times of day and on different days of the week for data comparison purposes.

Needs Identification Appropriate and cost-effective services that meet the health needs of the population should be based on the community's "needs," not on its "wants." To perform a **needs identification**, CHNs must (a) investigate the nature of the needs, (b) determine if the expressed needs represent the opinions of the community, and (c) determine if the community is willing and has the resources to take action (Werner, Thuman, & Maxwell, 1980). **Needs** can be "felt" and "real." Felt needs are what people feel are their biggest problems (e.g., to get rid of diarrhea). Real needs are steps people can take to correct these problems (e.g., to use clean drinking water to prevent diarrhea). **Wants** are desires that go beyond the basic needs (e.g., to use brand name imported bottled water to prevent diarrhea). Besides needs identification, CHNs also identify the community's strengths and hidden resources and explore ways for community capacity building (Helvie, 1998).

Problem Investigation Community assessments can be **problem investigations**, which are done specifically in response to a problem or concern. For example, with an outbreak of *E. coli*, tuberculosis, or sexually transmitted infections in a community, CHNs investigate the occurrence and distribution of the disease, explore the roots or causes of the problems and their effects, and develop plans to respond appropriately.

Resource Evaluation Financial constraints from the government since the early 1990s have led to downsizing and/or restructuring of many health and social services. Service

FIGURE 10.3 Windshield Survey or Walking Tour

Credit: Camillia Matuk

providers are challenged to plan for cost-effective, efficient, and seamless services through resource allocation and re-allocation. **Resource evaluation** involves the assessment and evaluation of existing community resources and services. This includes an examination of the adequacy of human resources, agency partnerships, service gaps, duplications, delivery, utilization, affordability, and accessibility to the target populations (Essex County District Health Council, 1994).

Components in Community Assessment Various community health nursing practice models may view the community differently, but they all study the basic community components or subsystems as follows.

Community History and Perception Understanding the past allows the CHN to build on existing strengths and avoid repeating the same failures. Areas for examination include previous history of the issues of concern and community actions taken in the past. The perceptions of the residents on the community issues; the attitudes of officials and local politicians; the community's attitudes, beliefs, and felt needs for health, education, and health care services should be specifically explored.

Population The very core of any community is people. A **population** is a diverse group of people or aggregates residing within the boundaries of a community. An **aggregate** is a group of people based on their shared common interests, demographics, cultural heritages, and socioeconomic and education levels. People carry out their daily lives to attain their personal life goals and needs. Personal characteristics and health behaviours of the aggregates may have positive or negative impacts on their own health status and that of the community. For example, communities without anti-smoking by-laws have higher rates of chronic respiratory diseases and cancer, and mainstream Canadians are adopting holistic and Eastern health practices, such as herbal medicine and tai chi, for health maintenance.

An understanding of the *composition of the population* by age distribution, sex, marital status, social class, occupation, birth rate, employment, religion, education level, family size, vulnerable groups, and others enables the CHN to assess and plan for appropriate services that are geared to the population's developmental and situational needs. For example, falls prevention and community support services for elderly clients living alone in their homes could be considered for communities with an aging population.

People tend to reside in areas for a variety of reasons: proximity to their employment and extended family, accessibility to education, amenities, recreational facilities, crime rate, political reasons, and climate. The *density of the population* may shift with time and demographic makeup. For example, an influx of refugees or unemployed workers into a community may be driven by economic or political changes. Health service providers need to respond to the location of the population and make themselves accessible to the residents.

Communities are not static. The needs, characteristics, makeup, and health status of the population change over time within its physical and social environments (Finnegan & Ervin, 1989). For example, occupational hazards such as chemical burns would be a concern for industrial workers but not for the elderly or infants. After the 1992 moratorium on the groundfish fishery in Newfoundland, the province experienced a surge in the unemployment rate, resulting in high family stress, a poor economy, and the relocation of many young people to other provinces for work (Lavigne, 1995). Strengthening community and social services for these fishing communities is a health priority. Similarly, promoting healthy lifestyles and community support to combat social isolation and poverty is much needed in the remote northern communities because of their higher rates of smoking, obesity, and heavy drinking compared to the nation's averages (Statistics Canada, 2002a).

Depending on the economic and political climates and the size, composition, and density of the population, information gathered about a population changes over time. Studying the *rate of population growth or decline* allows the CHN to examine the population trends and anticipate needed services. For example, more seniors with more chronic health conditions in a population puts more demands on home care services. *Health status data* of the community, such as trends in mortality rates (especially maternal and infant death rates), morbidity rates (e.g., common infectious diseases and chronic conditions), and life expectancy, give indications regarding the health of the population. CHNs must clearly identify the target population and its size in relation to the scale of the problem experienced by the community as a whole; collect relevant population data; and examine, compare, and estimate the health outcomes and risk factors within the community or at the regional, provincial, and/or national conditions (Hawaleshka, 2002).

Environment The health of the people in a community is affected by various aspects of their immediate environment. For example, air and water pollution may cause respiratory and digestive problems; geographic isolation may lead to poor access to health services and subsequent inequity in health status; and poor economic development may cause job loss, poverty, malnutrition, and increased individual and family stress or poor coping skills as manifested by drug and alcohol use. **Environmental factors** that affect community health include the following:

- Biological and chemical characteristics: vegetation and forestry, animals and insects, bacteria and other microorganisms, food and water supply, chemicals, and toxic substances.
- Physical characteristics: geography, climate, and natural resources such as soil, mountains, valleys, rivers, lakes, oceans, water, air, oil, buildings, housing, and roads.
- Socio-cultural environment: customs and beliefs, family and kinships, religions, recreational facilities, income and employment level, and support groups.
- Economic environment: trading, business establishments, and entrepreneurship.
- Political environment: leadership, advocacy groups, power, and government structure.

Healthy communities do not exist in isolation. They are separated or connected to other communities by physical or artificial boundaries. **Physical boundaries** include geographic boundaries such as mountains, valleys, roads, lakes, rivers, or oceans. **Artificial boundaries** include (a) political boundaries which depict governance of various townships, counties, cities, and provinces; and (b) situational boundaries which are governed by specific circumstances such as zoning for school children, traffic patterns, or smoking areas. Artificial boundaries exist because of special interests expressed or specific services provided by certain groups. Boundaries need to be permeable for the exchange of services between communities.

Understanding the interactions between people and their environment is key to problem identification and planning for appropriate care. Once the purpose and target population for a community assessment are defined, the next step is to determine the boundary of the community within which the target population lives, works, plays, and learns. CHNs may also examine the geography; percentage of urban versus rural areas; layout of various housing, educational, and recreational facilities; health and social services; transportation system; water and sanitation; safety; available farmland; and population trends in relation to the impact on the health and quality of life of the target population.

Socioeconomic Conditions Income level or wealth is highly associated with level of education achieved and where people reside (Smith & Graham, 1995); wealth is the strongest indicator for good health and quality of life (Premier's Council on Health Strategy, 1991). People with low education levels tend to have low income and many reside in geared-to-income housing. Well-educated professionals with career advancements achieve the income level for living in middle- to upper-class locales. However, upward or downward mobility can be seen in various social classes during economic turmoil. High employment rates, new housing, and business developments are common signs for communities with a healthy economy and/or industrial capacity.

Education Education provides community members the needed life skills for their day-to-day living and technical skills for their career advancement. Educational institutions are a natural socialization setting for children to adopt societal norms and health behaviours in the early years. When assessing a community, policy and practice in primary education and trends in literacy rates of the community and how they relate to infant mortality and industrial accidents, for example, may be examined.

Cultural Characteristics One in every five Canadians belongs to a visible minority group (Statistics Canada, 2002a). Various cultural groups in many Canadian communities work to preserve their heritages through their own social networks, community events, and educational programs. Despite effort from the government to promote multiculturalism, many ethnic groups tend to live and work in their own ethnic communities and are now more isolated than ever. CHNs must examine the diversity of the community population and how the various cultural practices may affect its health beliefs and practices. They must provide culturally competent health services that will meet the clients' needs appropriate to their level of cultural adaptation or integration (Yiu Matuk, 1995) (see Chapter 16).

Religion Religion offers a form of spiritual support for many people, especially when they are in crisis (Mueller, Plevak, & Rummans, 2002). Depending on the religion, it can also affect the health care practices and routines of various members of the population. For example, Jehovah's Witnesses refuse blood transfusions, and Muslims and Jews require adjustment of family, school, and work routines during their religious celebrations and prayers.

Recreation Recreation provides a form of socialization and a means for healthy physical and mental activity for people outside their family, school, and work life. CHNs can assess where and how people spend their time together after school or work, if local recreational facilities/activities are appropriate to people of all ages, and if these activities are accessible and affordable to the public.

Health and Social Services Most communities have an organized network or **service system** of interacting institutions or organizations that deliver essential, quality, and accessible services to meet the health and social needs of their residents. A service system usually includes industry/businesses, a health care system, communication, transportation, churches, schools, fire and police services, and government. Most people, whether sick or healthy, seek health services at some time in their lives. Health services include primary, secondary, and tertiary care, ranging from promotion and protection of health to hospital, rehabilitative, and palliative care services. An infrastructure of a wide range of health and social services can help people emerge from their crises. Welfare, employment, mothers' allowance, and disability pensions are examples of assistance for those who are single parents, unemployed, or have physical and/or mental disabilities. The availability of various community health and social services alone will not improve the health status of the community; people must be aware of how and when to access services that are available to them and use them appropriately.

Transportation Even though all structural components can be in place within a single community, an established and reliable transportation system is essential to ensure that community members have access to all the services they need. CHNs must consider the implications of a lack of public transportation for rural clients, the poor, the frail elderly, and those with physical limitations. They can mobilize local resources (volunteers, family, or neighbours) to meet the clients' transportation needs.

Community Dynamics Effective and efficient communication is crucial for the delivery of quality care to community members. In addition to conveying clear messages, the methods, location, and timing of communication are also pivotal in the communication process. The common modes of communication for community members are usually the local newspapers, newsletters, notice boards, radio, and television.

Governments play a key leadership role to ensure that all essential community services are in place to meet the basic needs of their community members. They set policies and provide funding to support those who are eligible for community services. Territorialism and unwillingness to share information or resources among community agencies, for fear of losing funding to support their own programs, often result in fragmentation and/or duplication of services. A strong, coordinated partnership promotes a seamless health care system and strengthens community capacity. CHNs must be aware of the existing government policies, work with both formal and informal leaders, and be involved in the decision-making process. They can also assess evidence of community development, relationships between the community and other agencies, the degree of cooperation or conflict between agencies and decision-making bodies, and the effectiveness of the decisions made.

SOURCES OF COMMUNITY DATA

Because communities have multi-system components, data concerning them can be abundant and complex. Therefore, the data collected for community assessment must be realistic, and credible sources and appropriate data collection techniques must be used to ensure the validity of the assessment (Ervin, 2002). Two main types of data describe a community:

- quantitative data, or numerical data, such as facts, figures, and lists (e.g., of community resources) that are commonly found in population statistics, and
- qualitative data such as statements or opinions gathered from windshield surveys, focus groups, open forums, key informants, public meetings, or population surveys.

The use of both types of data can identify what may influence the health of the community (Stoner, Magilvy, & Schultz, 1992).

Generally, existing data should be examined first before gathering new data. New data can be gathered from surveys and meetings with community residents and leaders. With today's sophisticated computerized information-management systems, much of the existing data is now easily accessible on the internet and at a low cost. Table 10.1 illustrates the different types of data available from different data sources that can be used to establish a community health profile. Those sources are listed below (Health & Welfare Canada, 1991).

- Statistics Canada provides census data and vital statistics on various communities.
- Local, provincial, and federal health departments and the Canadian Institute for Health Information prepare reports with vital statistics related to determinants of health and diseases.
- Municipal planning departments provide information on housing and business and industrial developments.
- Environmental Canada provides weather reports, including environmental indices.
- Police departments provide crime statistics and trends.
- Local organizations, such as hospitals, school boards, and agencies, provide information related to service utilization by the populations they serve.
- Municipal traffic departments and provincial transportation departments keep track of traffic accidents and resulting injuries and deaths.
- The Worker's Compensation Board provides records of work-related injuries and deaths.

Methods for Community Data Collection

Once the needed data are identified for the purpose of community assessment, CHNs decide how best to obtain the data within the resources available and the time constraints. They may also consult epidemiologists, community stakeholders, and/or residents to help them gather and analyze the data. There are several methods of data collection for community assessments.

TABLE 10.1
Types of Data Sources for Community Health Profiles

Selected Community Data Components	Census	Vital Statistics	Registries	Agency Reports	Treatment Data	Windshield Survey	Key Informants	Forum Discussions	Focus Groups	Surveys
Population	X			X		X			X	X
Education	X	X		X		X	X			X
Economics	X			X		X	X			
Physical environment	X		X	X		X	X	X	X	
Social services			X	X		X	X	X	X	X
Health		X	X	X	X	X	X	X	X	X
Community dynamics						X	X	X	X	
Social support networks	X	X		X		X	X	X	X	X
Industrial capacity	X					X	X	X	X	X

Epidemiologic Data Analysis CHNs use an **epidemiologic data analysis** approach to examine the frequency and distribution of a disease or health condition in the population being studied. They determine *what* the community is, *who* is affected (host), *where* and *when* the condition occurred (environment), and *why* and *how* (agent) it occurred (Allender & Spradley, 2001; Finnegan & Ervin, 1989) (see Chapter 7).

Community Surveys Community surveys contain a series of questions addressing the issue(s) or population(s) being studied. They can produce a broad range of data from a representative sample population in a short period of time. They can be conducted via regular mail, e-mail, telephone, or face-to-face interviews. The data collected provide a snapshot of the population being studied and may be generalized to describe the larger population. Major community surveys (e.g., National Population Health Survey and the Canadian Community Health Survey) are usually repeated every five years to examine changes in the behaviours over time.

Community Forums Community forums are public meetings in which community members discuss issues of concern with their community leaders or decision makers. They provide a two-way dialogue through which members can share their experiences and opinions. They are usually held in neighbourhood community centres, schools, or service clubs. This approach is inexpensive as data can be collected at the end of the meeting. The people who attend these meetings are either directly involved in or affected by the topic being discussed. Community forum topics may include the impact of a school closure or hospital restructuring in a community or the need for safety precautions in a neighbourhood due to increased crime rates.

Often, one person or a few people dominate the meeting discussion and the opinions heard may not represent the majority's view. The following strategies may be used to elicit maximum public response in community forums (Kretzmann & McKnight, 1993).

- Clearly state the purpose and questions for the forum.
- Choose an effective facilitator to lead the forum discussions.
- Plan for small discussion groups after the issue is presented.
- Use a speaker list and allow each person equal "air" time.
- Record the main points discussed by each speaker and encourage the addition of new ideas.
- Gather written comments from participants before they leave the meeting.

Focus Groups Focus groups are small group interviews with 5–15 people who are affected by an issue (Polit & Hungler, 1999). The interviews usually last 1 to 2 hours. There may be a series of focus groups on the same topic across the community, region, province, or nation. Though similar in format and low cost to the community forums, focus groups are smaller in scale, and the participants are more homogeneous in their characteristics or experience related to the topic being discussed. These participants may be aggregates such as women, school children, elderly, or caregivers, or community leaders such as key informants, politicians, or health care providers. Focus groups provide opportunities for **community dialogue** by allowing people to exchange experiences and express opinions. When given a chance to work out issues, community members are far more open to change than most politicians and health care providers imagine (Laughi, 2002).

No single source or method can provide all the assessment data on a community. CHNs may need to use multiple strategies to collect the needed data. Epidemiological and research skills are particularly important for analyzing and interpreting vital statistics and figures (see Chapters 7 and 14). For example, although mortality rates (infant and maternal mortality, life expectancy, and age-specific and disease-specific death rates) and morbidity rates (disability days and prevalence of chronic conditions) have historically been the primary data sources determining the health state of communities, they do not indicate the health status of the population until the members experience the disease or until they die.

Community data collection can be an overwhelming experience but it need not be a time-consuming process. The key is to focus on the purpose of the assessment and to know what the health indictors are and where and how to collect the needed

Canadian Research Box 10.1

McCallum, M. (1999). *Exploring the development of a comprehensive women's midlife health program.* Halifax, NS: Izaak Walton Killam–Grace Health Centre, Women's Health Program.

In 1999, the IWK Health Centre in Halifax invited 40 participants from a local community to explore possible hindering and facilitating factors and actions required for the development of a comprehensive women's midlife health program. These participants represented women in midlife, stakeholders from the community and health care agencies, government, and academic sectors. The group recommended a program that was holistic, multifaceted, coordinated, multidisciplinary, women-centred, based on women's needs, and accessible to all women regardless of income, culture, language, and social class. Primary health care services would be provided to ensure that women would receive the needed education/information to make informed choices. Following this workshop, a consortium was established to define a framework for action for local community groups to use when delivering their women's midlife health services in Nova Scotia.

Discussion Questions

1. Critique the approach used to identify community needs in this study.
2. Explore additional methods that you would use to identify the health needs of women in midlife.
3. Propose how you would mobilize your community to implement the action plan at various community and policy levels in your community.

data. To do so, CHNs must understand what determines health, then identify the health issues and priorities, collect the evidence, measure the health outcomes, and evaluate the effectiveness of different interventions (Erikson, Wilson, & Shannon, 1995). Table 10.2 provides sample population **health indicators** and data sources (Statistics Canada, 2002b).

POPULATION HEALTH

Whether the purpose of the community assessment is needs identification, problem investigation, resource evaluation, or to familiarize the nurse with the community, CHNs must ask key questions related to what makes people healthy and what data indicates the health status of the population. This wellness approach was fundamental to the Healthy Cities/Healthy Communities movement two decades ago in Canada (Manson-Singer, 1994). The concept of **population health** reflects the definition of health and builds on the traditional practice of health promotion and public health in which the focus is on preventive activities and disease management. The health of a population is "measured by health status indicators and is influenced by social, economic, and physical environments; personal health practices; individual capacity and coping skills; human biology; early childhood development; and health service." The overall goal of population health is "to maintain and improve the health status of the entire population and to reduce inequities in health status between population groups," and its approach is to "address the entire range of individual and collective factors that determine health" (Statistics Canada, 2001, p. 2).

CASE STUDY What Does Health Mean to People in a Slum Area?

Study the community scene illustrated in Figure 10.4. List and rank what you think the people in this community would say was needed to improve their health. In a group of 4–6 students, compare the individual rankings and discuss the following questions.

1. By priority, rank the areas that you feel would improve the health of this community and relate them to the determinants of health.
2. If you were a resident of this community, how would you feel to have someone making judgments about your living situation? Why? What do you see as the priority area to improve the health of your community?
3. Who are the experts in identifying the local needs of a community? Why?

Healthy populations contribute to the overall productivity and improved quality of life in the community, and a sustainable and equitable health care system with community participation is key to maintaining a healthy population. Based on this belief, Health Canada (2001a) proposed a **Population Health Template** with eight key elements and corresponding action steps for health practitioners, educators, and researchers (see Appendix 10A at the end of this chapter). The key elements encourage health workers to (a) focus on the health of populations, (b) address the determinants of health and their

FIGURE 10.4
A Slum Area

Credit: Camillia Matuk

TABLE 10.2
Sample Population Health Indicators and Data Sources

Health Indicator	Category	Data Source for Specific Health Indicators: Statistics Canada	Data Source for Specific Health Indicators: Canadian Institution of Health Information
Health status	Well-being	• Self-rated health • Self-esteem	
	Health conditions	• Body mass index (BMI) • Chronic conditions • Low birth weight • Cancer incidence • Injuries	• Injuries • Food- and waterborne diseases
	Human function	• Disabilities/limitations • Disability-free life expectancy	
	Deaths	• Infant/perinatal mortality • Life expectancy • Mortality by selected causes • Potential years of life lost	
Non-medical determinants of health	Health behaviour	• Smoking • Drinking • Physical activity • Breastfeeding practices • Dietary practices	
	Living and working conditions	• Education • Labour force • Income • Housing • Decision latitude at work • Crime	
	Personal resources	• School readiness • Social support • Life stress	
	Environmental factors	• Exposure to second-hand smoke	
Health system performance	Accessibility	• Disease prevention and detection	• Disease prevention and detection
	Appropriateness		• Vaginal birth after caesarean section • Caesarean section
	Effectiveness	• Death due to medically treatable diseases	• Communicable diseases • Pneumonia and influenza hospitalization • Ambulatory care • 30-day in-hospital mortality • Re-admissions
	Efficiency		• May not require hospitalization • Expected compared to actual stay
	Safety		• Hip fracture hospitalization
Community and health system characteristics	Community	• Population attributes • Geographic attributes	
	Health system	• Contact with alternative health care providers • Contact with health professionals	• Inflow/outflow ratios • Utilization rates
	Resources		• Health expenditures • Health professionals

Source: Adapted with permission from Statistics Canada website, www.statcan.ca/english/freepub/82-221-XIE/00502/tables.html, accessed May 9, 2002.

interactions, (c) base decisions on evidence, (d) increase upstream investments, (e) apply multiple strategies, (f) collaborate across sectors and levels, (g) employ mechanisms forming public involvement, and (h) demonstrate accountability for health outcomes.

Implementing a population approach involves the process of analyzing the health issue, setting priorities, taking action, evaluating results, and gaining stronger evidence/developing knowledge. These actions can be collaborated on with agencies such as those seen in the promotion of heart health, physical activity, and cancer prevention across Canada. Delivery of health services alone will not promote population health. Public policy that promotes health is also key, evidenced, for example, by the increase in tobacco taxes to reduce tobacco use. Although the recent emphasis on "population health" may give an impression that this is a new concept, promoting the health of individuals, families, groups, and communities has always been the heart of community health nursing. What is more apparent today is the need for CHNs to provide evidence-based practice by articulating any positive gains in promoting the health of populations.

Risk Assessment

Although CHNs care for clients in community settings, they do not necessarily work with every member in the community. Rather, they assess the conditions of risks and benefits that apply to the entire population or to its significant aggregates and deliver health services to those who are at risk. **Risk** refers to the probability or likelihood that healthy persons exposed to a specific factor will acquire a specific disease. These specific factors, called **risk factors**, can be external (e.g., sources of exposure, cultural practices, patterns of behaviours, local concerns, direct impact from the service delivery system) or intrinsic to the individual (e.g., age, sex, or genetic makeup) (Swanson & Albrecht, 1997). When doing **risk assessment**, CHNs identify and target clients who are most likely to contract the disease or develop unhealthy behaviours and examine attributable factors that affect or potentially affect the health of the population (Omenn, 1996). For example, teens have a higher risk than adults of contracting STDs or getting pregnant as they tend to experiment more with their sexuality; likewise, older adults are more likely to fall than younger adults.

Community Analysis and Nursing Diagnoses

The purpose of data analysis is to identify actual and potential community strengths and needs that are relevant to the improvement of existing health services. This **community analysis** involves *categorization*, *summarization/comparison*, and *inference elaboration* of data, which lead to a community nursing diagnosis formulation (Anderson & McFarlane, 2000) (see Table 10.3). A clear conceptual or philosophical understanding of health, community dynamics, and community health nursing is necessary to guide systematic categorizations of community data. These data, then, should be summarized for conciseness and compared with other relative community systems for significance. Finally, inferences are made to formulate **community nursing diagnoses**, statements that explain the etiology of the community issues with supporting characteristics. Such diagnoses should be based on sound clinical judgments and set directions for nursing intervention. In these aspects, community nursing diagnoses and nursing diagnoses are similar. They differ in that community nursing diagnoses are more general, addressing a community or aggregate, whereas nursing diagnoses address individuals or families living in the community (Ervin, 2002).

All communities have assets as well as problems. Community health nursing diagnoses should include both problem and wellness diagnoses. Depending on the philosophical approach, community nursing diagnoses may be formulated for aggregates and groups in a statement consisting of three parts (Neufeld & Harrison, 1990):

- Who is the specific aggregate or target group?
- What is the actual or potential unhealthy response/situation that a nurse can change?
- What are the related factors to the host or the environment?

Canadian Research Box 10.2

Wong, J., & Wong, S. (2003). Cardiovascular health of immigrant women: Implications for evidence-based practice. *Clinical Governance*, *8*(2), 112–122.

The authors analyzed the data from the National Population Health Survey in Canada between 1996 and 1997 to describe the modifiable cardiovascular disease (CVD) risk factors among Canadian immigrant women. Results showed statistically significant differences in modifiable CVD risk factors with respect to birthplace, language spoken, and the length of time in Canada. While the smoking rate was highest in low- and middle-income groups, the prevalence of obesity, hypertension, and smoking were higher among white immigrant women than their non-white counterparts. Regardless of race and country of birth, immigrant women were more likely to have CVD risk factors than non-immigrant women. Immigrant women are at risk for poor health. They face not only cultural and language barriers, but socioeconomic diversity. Nurses must provide culturally competent care to meet the health promotion needs of these women.

Discussion Questions

1. Discuss possible data sources and community assessment approaches that you would use to identify the health needs or status of various special aggregates in your community.
2. Based on the findings in this study, propose community interventions that will meet the needs of immigrant women.

TABLE 10.3
Community Analysis of Data

Categories of Health Indicators	Summary/Comparison	Inferences
Health behaviour: physical activity	• Integration and implementation of physical activities in the school curriculum exceeding Ministry of Education's minimum requirements • 99% of students selected physical education as a credit course	• Students are interested in healthy lifestyles • Support for promotion of physical activity from school personnel
Non-medical determinants of health: labour force	• High unemployment (25%) among the newcomers because they do not have the needed work and educational requirements • No retraining programs for newcomers • Parents have low self-esteem, lack of sleep, poor appetite, arguments in the home	• High unemployment rate and family stress level among the newcomers • Newcomers not receiving social programs, or there is a lack of services to meet their needs

Table 10.4 illustrates how nursing diagnoses may be formulated using the various approaches described earlier in this chapter. While the 11 health functioning patterns of the commonly known NANDA have been used to formulate community nursing diagnoses (Kriegler & Harton, 1992) (see Table 10.4), the translation to community-oriented diagnoses is still in its infancy. CHNs need to continue to develop their own community diagnoses and cluster themes that are oriented to the health needs of the community. Their community analysis will help develop and organize nursing knowledge and further the continued development of nursing diagnoses.

TABLE 10.4
Approaches to Community Health Nursing Diagnosis

Approach	Target Group/ Host	Potential or Actual Community Response, Situation, Concern, Problem, or Conclusion	Etiology/Agent	Characteristics/Environment
Epidemiological approach	Students in XXX high school	Have potential for healthy lifestyles	Desire to learn about nutrition and physical activities	Supported by integrated school curriculum with an emphasis on healthy lifestyles
NANDA	Community XX	Potential dysfunction in value-belief pattern: ethical conflicts between the public and government	Introducing user fees to the health care system	Debates and public demonstrations over the need for a two-tiered health care system
Community-as-partner approach	West end of community	Optimal waste disposal	Effective management of the community recycling system	98% utilization of the recycling programs and 25% reduction of rodents in the city area
Energy theory	Newcomers	Aggregate energy deficit (inadequate income and resources and high family stress level)	Inadequate language and skill training programs to prepare newcomers to be employable	High unemployment rate (25%), unable to find work because of lack of language skills and Canadian work experience/ requirements, high anxiety and stress expressed by family

Planning, Implementation, and Evaluation

The next part of the community health nursing process is to prioritize the community needs and devise nursing interventions to resolve those needs. Based on the community nursing diagnoses, CHNs must formulate goals and objectives for nursing intervention. Subjective and objective data collected during the community assessment help form the needed indicators for evaluation of any evidence of success (see Chapter 13).

Successful community planning and interventions depend on the following:

1. if the community need or issue is widely and strongly *felt* by the whole community/group,
2. if the community need or issue is *acceptable* to the community/group,
3. if there is *commitment* to work on this community need or issue from the group,
4. if the actions to resolve the community need or issue are *simple, dependable, and feasible* in terms of the local resources and conditions, and
5. if the results *can be achieved* quickly with evidence to support the success.

Above all, CHNs must provide services that meet the key principles of primary health care: accessibility, promotion and prevention, intersectoral cooperation, appropriate technology, and public participation (World Health Organization, 1978). In order to meet the basic health care needs of the community, CHNs must identify the populations who are at risk. These often would be the marginalized or vulnerable aggregates, such as the frail elderly, the poor, the visible minorities, newcomers, teenage mothers, Aboriginals, and persons with physical and mental limitations.

Community Participatory Tools for Community Planning

A **community participatory approach** is key to community planning. The community decides what makes a need into a priority; who is to take the action; what the action will be; when and how it is to be done; and who, when, and how to do what. Community participatory tools assist community dialogue among the residents, community leaders, government officials, and service providers to help quantify and qualify the health issues, needs, or concerns that they identify (Yiu, 2001). All participants share and validate their views and experiences with others. Active participation and learning during the planning process can empower people to take responsibility and ownership in health and to effect change.

To stimulate this type of planning discussion, CHNs initially use a **community needs matrix tool**. The CHN asks participants to discuss, name, rate, and explain what they perceive to be the most important health problems in their community (or the most feasible interventions). As the participants talk, the CHN tallies the degree of concern about each issue on a blank chart similar to that in Table 10.5. The results of the discussion shown in Table 10.5 indicate that this community is more concerned about accidents than about pneumonia.

Canadian Research Box 10.3

O'Connor, R. (2002). *Report of the Walkerton Inquiry: The events of May 2000 and related issues.* Retrieved July 14, 2002 from www.walkertoninquiry.com/report1/index.html#summary

On May 18, 2000, 20 students in Walkerton, Ontario were absent from a school and two children were admitted to the hospital with bloody diarrhea. During the following few days, there was an enteric outbreak among residents of a retirement home, and people began seeking care from the hospitals and doctors' offices, complaining of bloody diarrhea, stomach pain, and nausea. On May 21, a boil-water advisory was issued by the local health unit, announcing that the community water system had been contaminated with the deadly bacteria, *Escherichia coli* O157:H7. Seven people died and more than 2300 were ill. The losses were devastating and the community felt angry and insecure.

Discussion Questions

1. What approaches could you use to learn and understand the experiences of the community?
2. How would you apply your community health nursing process in Walkerton during this crisis? Formulate your nursing diagnoses and devise a plan to care for this community.

This exercise goes beyond asking the community members to fill in the blanks. With good listening and facilitation skills, CHNs can understand what the community has to say and learn from their experiences. They can also validate the data diagnoses, educate the community, and increase their awareness of their choices of action. Mutual planning is pivotal to effective community planning (see Figure 10.5).

During the planning process, the nurse could also ask the community members to look at their accessibility and the resources in their living environment as part of the intervention plan. The participants could use **community mapping** to express their perceptions and experiences: drawing a schematic map of their community indicating the distribution and occurrence of illness, disease, and health; major resources; environmental conditions; and accessibility and barriers to various services. Figure 10.6 is a community map that illustrates the case distribution of spina bifida in the community.

TABLE 10.5
Results of a Community Needs Matrix Tool

Identified Health Need	Not a Concern	Somewhat Concerned	A Concern	Very Concerned
Accidents	X	XXX	XXX	XXXX
Nutrition	X	XX	XX	XXXX
Pneumonia	X	XX	XXX	X
STDs	X	XXX	XXX	X

FIGURE 10.5
Is This Mutual Community Planning?

Credit: Vesna Kratanovich

A **present-future drawing** is a tool that may be used to help the community reflect upon the present situation, and what resources and constraints contributed to it, and to visualize how the future might appear. The present-future drawing (Figure 10.7) allows the nurse to see where the community wants to go and, hence, to formulate mutual intervention goals and objectives.

Implementation of the intervention goals and objectives requires a clear outline of the methods of delivery, a time frame for interventions, and a person who will make the initiatives. Community participation and support are vital for sustained interventions. The community knows what has worked well for them in the past and what will be suitable for them now. CHNs must invite and respect their suggestions, helping them take ownership of the intervention. Plans should be translated into action. However, planning that is not based on a sound assessment of the data results in an intervention that is also not sound. Time and resources must be allowed for monitoring and evaluating the progress, guidance, and supervision of the intervention in order to attain the targeted goals. These can lead to necessary modifications of the plan.

Community interventions must be evaluated to measure whether the expected results were achieved and where the successes and problems lie. The steps involved in **community evaluation** (van Marris & King, 2002) are:

1. getting ready to evaluate,
2. engaging stakeholders,
3. assessing resources for the evaluation,
4. designing the evaluation,
5. determining appropriate methods of measurement and procedures,
6. developing work plan, budget, and timeline for evaluation,
7. collecting data using agreed-upon methods and procedures,
8. processing and analyzing the data,
9. interpreting and disseminating the results, and
10. taking action.

Successes should be shared with the community so that the work can be sustained within the community and become a model to benefit other communities. Lessons learned from challenges or barriers can teach others to avoid making the same mistakes. Plans should be made for any future changes needed in the community. Interventions should be evaluated and documented to support evidence-based practice. The text box provides a summary guide that nurses may use to assess the health of a community, explore the implications and impact of the identified health needs or issues on the overall health of the community, and develop a community intervention plan.

FIGURE 10.6
Community Map Showing Distribution of Spina Bifida

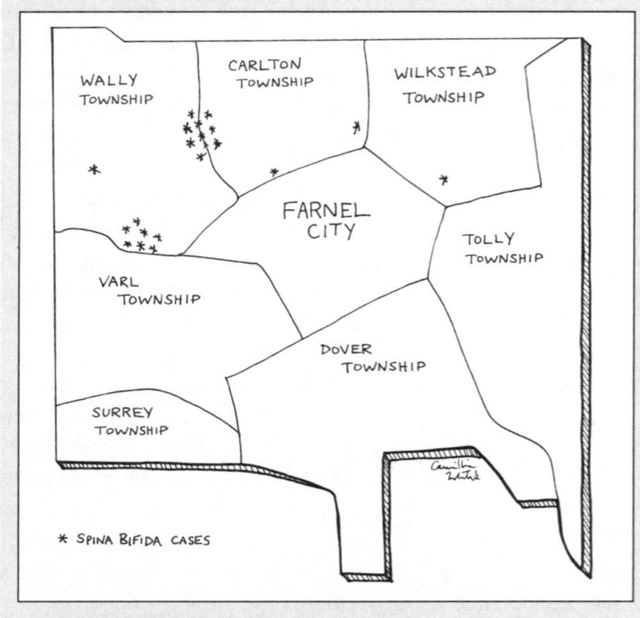

Credit: Camillia Matuk

FIGURE 10.7
Present-Future Drawing

Credit: Camillia Matuk

Guide to Community Assessment and Intervention

A. ASSESSMENT

1. Purpose of Community Assessment
2. Target Group
3. Community History and Perception
   - 3.1 Previous history of community actions by local groups or government
   - 3.2 Perceptions of the residents on the community issues, attitudes, beliefs, felt needs
4. Population
   - 4.1 Total population in the community
   - 4.2 Composition (number and percentages): age group distribution, gender, marital status, birth rate, family size
   - 4.3 Density
   - 4.4 Rate of population growth (increased or decreased?)
   - 4.5 Health status
     - Mortality rates, overall, age-specific, and cause-specific
     - Morbidity rate for specific diseases, their incidence and prevalence
     - How do mortality and morbidity rates compare with previous years? With regional, provincial, and national rates?
     - Life expectancy (trends for males and females)
     - Health status (indicators and influencing factors related to the purpose of the assessment, e.g., nutrition, immunization, lifestyles, stress, sexually transmitted infections, unplanned pregnancy, prenatal care, emergency care, primary, secondary, and tertiary care)
5. Physical Environment
   - 5.1 Location (boundaries, geography, climate, plants and animals posing threats to health, percentage of urban or rural area)
   - 5.2 Housing (type, condition, slum areas, sanitation, adequacy, crowding)
   - 5.3 Safety
   - 5.4 Water supply
   - 5.5 Sanitation (sewage and waste disposal)
6. Socioeconomic Condition
   - 6.1 Social class and mobility (percentages for each social class, patterns and impact of mobility on health needs and health service planning)

- 6.3 Employment (rate, primary occupations, major industries, occupational hazards)
- 6.4 Shopping facilities

7. Education (levels, attitudes, facilities, literacy rates, relationships to health problems)
8. Culture Characteristics (ethnic and racial groups, languages spoken, positive and negative influences on health practices, subcultures, new immigrants' adaptation, perceptions of health)
9. Religion (affiliations, influence on health practices)
10. Recreation (facilities, appropriate, accessibility)
11. Health and Social Services
    - 11.1 Services and community organizations (locations, ratios of health workers to rural and urban populations, number of beds available, type, utilization, spending, culturally sensitive care)
    - 11.2 Health budgets (priority, amount per capita, spending on preventive and tertiary care)
12. Transportation (type, availability, accessible, affordable and usage)
13. Community Dynamic
    - 13.1 Communications (newspapers, radio and television, efficient and effective)
    - 13.2 Leadership (formal and informal leaders, politics, power structure)
    - 13.3 Decision making (policy and planning, human resources, evidence of community development, relationships with other organizations, degree of conflict and collaboration, process and effectiveness of decision making)

B. ANALYSIS
1. Wellness Nursing Diagnoses (potential and actual community strengths)
2. Problem Nursing Diagnoses (potential and actual community needs and gaps)

C. PLANNED INTERVENTIONS
1. Expected Outcomes
2. Responsible Party (Parties) for Implementation
3. Completion Date

D. EVALUATION
1. Progress and Evidence of Success Based on Outcomes Objectives
2. Lessons Learned

SUMMARY

When promoting the health of communities, CHNs use a population approach to work with individuals, families, aggregates, and the community. An understanding of the community makeup and dynamics will guide the implementation of the community nursing process. Sound community assessment requires that the CHNs know the purpose of the assessment, the techniques to use, the data to collect, and where to collect them. The use of a population health approach to community health promotion allows the nurse to look beyond the traditional delivery of health services and to examine various determinants of health, including how social and political environments impact community health. Community analysis requires CHNs to work with the community to analyze the data and devise a mutual plan for community action and evaluation. Throughout this community health nursing process, CHNs may use various community participatory tools to interact with various community stakeholders, interdisciplinary teams, and population groups to address the community's health needs. They must possess critical thinking, leadership, and community development skills to advocate this change. If CHNs are to improve the health of the community and achieve social justice and health for all, they must lead the way.

KEY TERMS

community
community functions
community dynamics
community assessment wheel
community capacity
environmental scan
windshield survey
needs identification
needs
wants
problem investigations
resource evaluation
population
aggregate
environmental factors
physical boundaries
artificial boundaries
service system
epidemiologic data analysis
community surveys
community forums

focus groups
community dialogue
health indicators
population health
Population Health Template
risk
risk factors
risk assessment
community analysis
community nursing diagnoses
community participatory approach
community needs matrix tool
community mapping
present-future drawing
community evaluation

STUDY QUESTIONS

1. Name four community settings where CHNs work. Describe their role and functions.
2. What are the characteristics of a healthy community?
3. What nursing process skills will you use to promote the health of the community?
4. What assessment components are used when assessing community health?
5. What are the next steps following the collection of community data?
6. What is population health?

INDIVIDUAL CRITICAL THINKING EXERCISES

1. Why is it important for the nurse to provide care to the community?
2. How does the community health nursing process differ from the individual nursing process?
3. How would you work with your community to identify their health needs and share their community experiences?
4. Who are the experts in assessing and determining what the community health needs are?
5. In developing a health profile for a community, what assessment questions would you ask for each category of the community components? Where would you collect the needed data?
6. Why is it important to use participatory tools for community planning?

GROUP CRITICAL THINKING EXERCISES

1. Discuss the following based on the Community Needs Matrix Tool (Table 10.5):
   (a) What are some of the questions you would ask the community about their ratings?
   (b) List other information you would want to know from this community.
   (c) What would your next step be?
2. In the community map illustrated in Figure 10.8, compare the accessibility to health services among the communities in the maps, formulate your nursing diagnoses, and propose intervention plans.

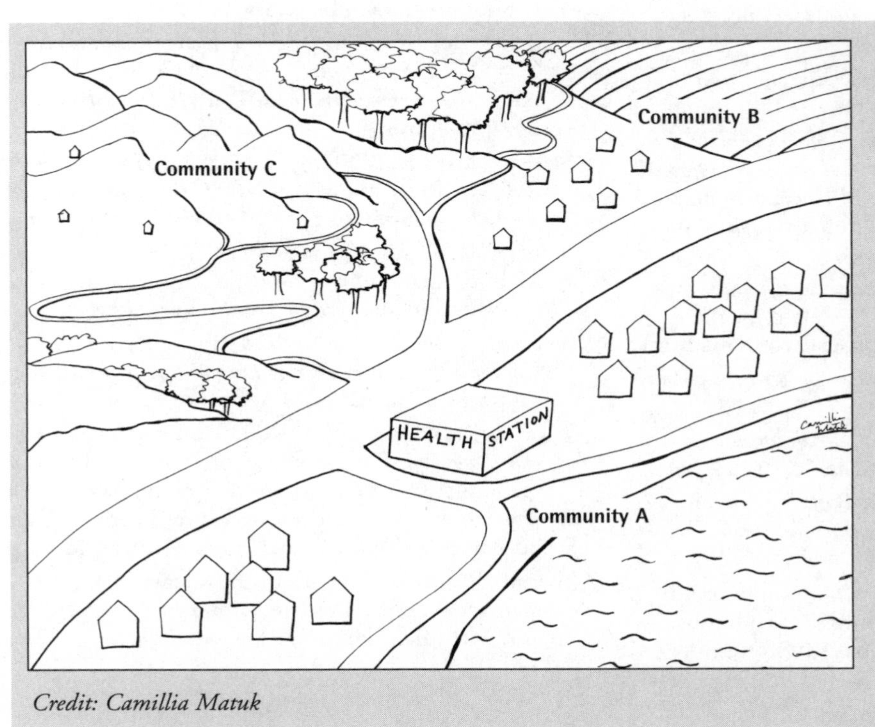

Credit: Camillia Matuk

FIGURE 10.8 Community Map Showing Accessibility to Health Services

3. In a group of 2–4, spend about an hour visiting and talking to people in your local neighbourhood. Describe your community visit and explain your impression about the felt needs, real needs, and wants of the community. Formulate your nursing diagnoses and propose your actions.

REFERENCES

Allender, J. A., & Spradley, B. (2001). *Community health nursing: Concepts and practice.* Philadelphia, PA: Lippincott.

Anderson, E., & McFarlane, J. (2000). *Community as partner: Theory and practice in nursing* (3rd ed.). Philadelphia, PA: Lippincott.

Community Health Nurses Association of Canada (CHNAC). (2003). *Community health nursing standards of practice.* Retrieved November 30, 2003 from **www.communityhealthnursescanada.org/newpage22.htm**

Clemen-Stone, S., Eigsti, D., & McGuire, S. (2002). *Comprehensive community health nursing* (6th ed.). Toronto, ON: Mosby.

Erikson, R., Wilson, R., & Shannon, I. (1995). *Years of healthy life: Healthy people 2000* (Statistical Notes No. 7). Hyattsville, MD: National Center for Health Statistics.

Essex County District Health Council. (1994). *The Essex County "Win/Win" model: An evolving plan for total health system reconfiguration.* Windsor, ON: Author.

Ervin, N. E. (2002). *Advanced community health nursing practice: Population-focused care.* Upper Saddle River, NJ: Prentice Hall.

Finnegan, L., & Ervin, N. (1989). An epidemiological approach to community assessment. *Public Health Nursing, 6*(3), 147–151.

Hawaleshka, D. (2002, June 17). The health report: Measuring health care, the fourth annual ranking. *MacLean's, 24*(115), 23–31.

Health and Welfare Canada. (1991). Assessing community needs. In *Community action pack.* Ottawa, ON: Author.

Health Canada. (2001a). *The population health template: Key elements and actions that define a population health approach.* Updated November 26, 2001. Retrieved November 30, 2003 from **www.hc-sc.gc.ca/hppb/phdd/pdf/discussion_paper.pdf**

Health Canada. (2001b). *Population health in Canada: A working paper.* Retrieved November 30, 2003 from **www.hc-sc.gc.ca/hppb/phdd/docs/social/contents.html**

Helvie, C. O. (1998). *Advanced practice nursing in the community.* Thousand Oaks, CA: Sage.

Higgs, Z. R., & Gustafson, D. D. (1985). *Community as a client: Assessment and diagnosis.* Philadelphia, PA: F.A. Davis.

Kretzmann, J., & McKnight, J. (1993). *Building communities from the inside out: A path toward finding and mobilizing a community's assets.* New York: ACTA.

Kriegler, N., & Harton, M. K. (1992). Community health assessment tool: A patterns approach to data collection and diagnosis. *Journal of Community Health Nursing, 9*(4), 229–234.

Laughi, B. (2002, June 26). Romanow health care commission: Medicare shape up supported, study says. *The Globe and Mail,* A7.

Lavigne, D. (1995). *Seals and fisheries, science and politics.* Retrieved August 3, 2003 from **www.imma.org/orlando1.html**

Manson-Singer, S. (1994). The Canadian health communities project: Creating a social movement. In A. Pederson, M. O'Neill, & I. Rootman (Eds.), *Health promotion in Canada: Provincial national & international perspectives* (pp. 107–122). Toronto, ON: W.B. Saunders Canada.

McKnight, J. K., & Kretzmann, J. P. (1997). Mapping community capacity. In M. Minkler (Ed.), *Community organizing and community building for health* (pp. 157–172). New Brunswick, NJ: Rutgers University Press.

Mueller, S., Plevak, D., & Rummans, T. (2002). Religion and health. *Mayo Clinic Proceedings, 77*(6), 600–601.

Neufeld, A., & Harrison, M. (1990). The development of nursing diagnoses for aggregates and groups. *Public Health Nursing, 7*(4), 251–255.

Omenn, G. S. (1996). Putting environmental risks in a public health context. *Public Health Report, 111*(6), 514–516.

Polit, D. F., & Hungler, B. P. (1999). *Nursing research: Principles and methods* (6th ed.). Philadelphia, PA: Lippincott Williams & Wilkins.

Premiers' Council on Health Strategy. (1991). *Nurturing health: A framework on the determinants of health.* (also known as the Gerstein Report). Ottawa, ON: Author.

Smith, T. E., & Graham, P. B. (1995). Socioeconomic stratification in family research. *Journal of Marriage and the Family, 57,* 930–940.

Statistics Canada. (2001). *Population health approach: Key determinants of health.* Updated 2001-11-26. Retrieved July 5, 2002 from **www.hc-sc.gc.ca/hppb/phdd/docs/common/e_appendix_c.html**

Statistics Canada. (2002a). *The health of Canada's communities* (82-003-SIE), *2000/01*(1). *The Daily.* Retrieved July 5, 2002 from **www.statcan.ca/Daily/English/020704/d020704b.htm**

Statistics Canada. (2002b). Data tables. *Health Indicators, 2002*(1). Retrieved May 9, 2002 from **www.statcan.ca/english/freepub/82-221-XIE/00502/tables.htm**

Stoner, M., Magilvy, J., & Schultz, P. (1992). Community analysis in community health nursing practice: The GENESIS model. *Public Health Nursing, 9*(4), 223–227.

Swanson, J. M., Nies, M. A., & Albrecht, M. (1997). *Community health nursing: Promoting the health of aggregates* (2nd ed.). Philadelphia, PA: Saunders.

van Marris, B., & King, B. (2002). *Evaluating health promotion programs.* The University of Toronto: The Health Communication Unit. Retrieved November 24, 2003 from **www.thcu.ca/infoandresources/publications/EVAL%20Master%20Workbook%20v3.3%2010.21.02.pdf**

Werner, D. (with Thuman, C., & Maxwell, J). (1980). *Where there is no doctor: A village health care handbook.* Palo Alto, CA: McMillan Education. w1–w6.

World Health Organization. (1978). *Primary health care: Report on the International Conference on Primary Health Care, Alma Ata, USSR, 6–12, September 1978.* Geneva, Switzerland: Author.

Yiu, L. (2001). *Monitoring and evaluation: A handbook for maternal and child health workers.* Ottawa, ON: University of Ottawa, Canada-China Yunnan Maternal and Child Health Project & the Yunnan Public Health Bureau.

Yiu Matuk, L. (1995). "Health promotion surveys for newcomers." In M. Stewart (Ed.), *Community nursing: Promoting Canadians' health* (pp. 266–283). Toronto, ON: W.B. Saunders.

ADDITIONAL RESOURCES

WEBSITES

Canadian Public Health Association:
www.cpha.ca

Statistics Canada, *Canadian community health survey (CCHS), 2000/01*:
www.statcan.ca/english/sdds/3226.htm

Canadian Institute for Health Information (CIHI):
http://secure.cihi.ca/cihiweb/dispPage.jsp?cw_page=home_e

Ontario Healthy Communities Coalition:
www.healthycommunities.on.ca/ohcc.htm

READINGS

Federal, Provincial, and Territorial Advisory Committee on Population Health. (1999). *Toward a healthy future: The second report on the health of Canadians* (H39-468/1999E). Ottawa, ON: Health Canada.

Health Canada. (2001). *Population health in Canada: A working paper.* Retrieved May 2, 2002 from **www.hc.gc.ca/hppb/phdd/docs/social/**

O'Connor, R. (2002). *Report of the Walkerton inquiry: The events of May 2000 and related issues.* Retrieved July 14, 2002 from **www.walkertoninquiry.com/report1/index.html# summary**

Romanow, R. (2002). *Analysis of over a decade of public opinion research about health care.* Retrieved July 14, 2003 from **www.healthcarecommission.ca**

About the Author

Lucia Yiu, BScN, BA (Psychology, Windsor), BSc (Physiology, Toronto), MScN (Administration, Western Ontario), is an Associate Professor in the Faculty of Nursing, University of Windsor, and an Educational and Training Consultant in community nursing. She has published on family and public health nursing. Her practice and research interests include multicultural health, international health, experiential learning, community development, and program planning and evaluation. She has worked overseas and served on various community and social services committees involving local and district health planning.

APPENDIX 10A

Summary Table of Population Health Key Elements

The goals of a population health approach are to maintain and improve the health status of the entire population and to reduce the inequities in health status between population groups.

Key Element	Actions
1. Focus on the health of populations	• Determine indicators for measuring health status. • Measure and analyze population health status and health status inequities to identify health issues. • Assess contextual conditions, characteristics, and trends.
2. Address the determinants of health and their interactions	• Determine indicators for measuring the determinants of health. • Measure and analyze the determinants of health and their interactions to link health issues to their determinants.
3. Base decisions on evidence	• Use best evidence available at all stages of policy and program development. • Explain criteria for including or excluding evidence. • Draw on a variety of data. • Generate data through mixed research methods. • Identify and assess effective interventions. • Disseminate research findings and facilitate policy uptake.
4. Increase upstream investments	• Apply criteria to select priorities for investment. • Balance short- and long-term investments. • Influence investments in other sectors.
5. Apply multiple strategies	• Identify scope of action for interventions. • Take action on the determinants of health and their interactions. • Implement strategies to reduce inequities in health status between population groups. • Apply a comprehensive mix of interventions and strategies. • Apply interventions that address health issues in an integrated way. • Apply methods to improve health over the life span. • Act in multiple settings. • Establish a coordinating mechanism to guide interventions.
6. Collaborate across sectors and levels	• Engage partners early on to establish shared values and alignment of purpose. • Establish concrete objectives and focus on visible results. • Identify and support a champion. • Invest in the alliance-building process. • Generate political support and build on positive factors in the policy environment. • Share leadership, accountability, and rewards among partners.
7. Employ mechanisms for public involvement	• Capture the public's interest. • Contribute to health literacy. • Apply public involvement strategies that link to overarching purpose.
8. Demonstrate accountability for health outcomes	• Construct a results-based accountability framework. • Ascertain baseline measures and set targets for health improvement. • Institutionalize effective evaluation systems. • Promote the use of health impact assessment tools. • Publicly report results.

Source: Reproduced by permission from Health Canada. (2001). The population health template: Key elements and actions that define a population health approach. *Retrieved June 8, 2002 from* www.hc-sc.gc.ca/hppb/phdd/pdf/summary_table

CHAPTER 11

Environmental and Occupational Health

Sharon L. Chadwick and Bernice Doyle

OBJECTIVES

AFTER STUDYING THIS CHAPTER, YOU SHOULD BE ABLE TO:

1. Discuss the components of an occupational health and safety program.
2. Identify the legislation and standards that apply to health and safety.
3. Identify the different types of occupational hazards to which workers may be exposed.
4. Describe the occupational health team.
5. Outline the roles and competencies of occupational health nurses.
6. Identify linkages between occupational and community health.
7. Consider occupational health principles when working in the community health setting.
8. Recognize occupational hazards to which community health nurses may be exposed and identify controls.

INTRODUCTION

"Each year, work-related injuries and diseases kill an estimated 1.1 million [people] worldwide. In addition there are 250 million accidents and an estimated 160 million new cases of work-related diseases..." (World Health Organization, 1999). These are significant numbers. Because work affects every part of our lives, injuries and illnesses can significantly affect individuals, families, and communities. Regardless of a nurse's work setting, it is important for all nursing professionals to be aware of the basic principles of occupational health and safety.

The purpose of this chapter is to provide an overview of the specialty nursing practice of occupational health. General principles and the components of occupational health and safety programs are outlined, and include the roles of various members of the occupational health and safety team. Occupational health nursing practice is explained in more detail. The role, competencies, and benefits (to both employees and employers) of occupational health nursing are described and related to the community health setting. Legislation and research are presented in the Canadian context. Health promotion is discussed as an integral part of all components. Community health nurses (CHNs) can only benefit from this brief introduction to the world of occupational health and safety.

GENERAL PRINCIPLES OF OCCUPATIONAL HEALTH AND SAFETY

Health and safety programs support the development of the highest level of worker health by creating a safe and healthy work environment. Basic **occupational health theory** states that it is "aimed at prevention" and includes "health promotion and protection in the context of the work environment" (Doyle, 1997, p. 3-3). In other words, **occupational health and safety programs** prevent ill health from work-related injury or illness and protect workers from existing or potential health and safety hazards at work. This section describes the components of a comprehensive program to meet these objectives.

Workplace programs are often developed because of specific legislated requirements in health and safety. As a minimum, an employer's health and safety program must contain the elements necessary to meet the legislated requirements for the jurisdiction in which a particular work site exists and operates. In addition, numerous standards are related to the field of health and safety at work. The legislation and other standards that may apply in a comprehensive health and safety program are outlined in this section.

Health and safety **hazards** at work are categorized into five basic types: physical, chemical, biological, ergonomic, and psychosocial. This section briefly introduces each category of hazard.

The nurse is just one member of the team that delivers comprehensive occupational health and safety programs. While the next section introduces occupational health nursing, this section discusses all other members of the occupational health and safety team.

COMPONENTS OF AN OCCUPATIONAL HEALTH AND SAFETY PROGRAM

Management Commitment

A number of components make up an occupational health and safety program, and many factors determine the extent to which each component can be developed and implemented at a work site. The first and most important component necessary for an effective program is **management commitment**.

Management is responsible for the overall operation of the workplace, including the development and enforcement of any policies and procedures. Without management commitment to health and safety, an effective program is simply not possible. Evidence of this commitment in any workplace can be seen by policies, procedures, and programs that focus on pertinent issues and are well-known throughout the workforce. In other words, the program must not only address the health and safety hazards, but also be communicated to the workers.

Having appropriate and adequate resources are also evidence of the extent of management commitment to health and safety. Worker commitment, support, and cooperation are more likely to follow when management commitment, focus, and communication are evident. To be effective, policies and procedures must be followed by the workers, and systems must be in place so that supervisors and workers have support in addressing health and safety issues that arise. A workplace culture in which everyone knows the safety rules, takes ownership, and is held accountable at all times for preventing injuries or ill health goes a long way in maintaining worker health and safety at all levels.

PHOTO 11.1

Occupational health and safety nurse on job site with workers.

Credit: Provided by the Canadian Nurses Foundation from the Canadian Nursing History Collection.

Worker Involvement

An effective program promotes health and safety at work in a variety of ways. Training, job analyses, health assessments, and health and safety committees are important components that directly involve workers and impact workplace health and safety.

Training Workers Training begins when workers are hired or transferred into any new job, whether on a permanent, temporary, part-time, or full-time basis. Training is also appropriate if new procedures, new equipment, or different tasks are introduced to existing jobs or processes. Worker training should encompass all aspects of health and safety that apply to the job, including

- hazards;
- company policies;
- legislative responsibilities;
- right to refuse unsafe work;
- safe operating procedures for performing work and using equipment;
- requirements, care, and use of personal protective equipment;
- first aid services, equipment, and supplies;
- emergency procedures for alarms or evacuations; and
- reporting requirements for injuries, illnesses, hazards, incidents, and near misses.

Assessing the Jobs of Workers Ensuring that jobs are analyzed as part of the health and safety program helps to identify potential inherent hazards as well as determine the skills or physical requirements of a job. Often called a **job demands analysis**, this is also known as job task analysis or critical task analysis. Regardless of the name, this component can prevent worker injury. To assess a job's demands, the job is divided into specific tasks and each task is analyzed to determine the physical or mental requirements. In addition, the hazards posed to a worker while performing the work are specified. Information from the analysis is useful in other areas of health and safety. A job demands analysis is essential when conducting a worker health assessment, which determines whether the worker is physically and mentally able to perform a job. This is used for screening workers either on initial hiring or when returning to work after illness or injury. When job accommodation is necessary, the results of a job demands analysis can help identify the necessary job changes that are required so that a worker can perform tasks without risking health and safety.

Formally Involving the Workers The most common mechanism for involving workers in health and safety at work is through a joint health and safety committee. This committee usually consists of both worker and management representatives and is a forum to address workplace health and safety issues. While many jurisdictions in Canada have legislation that requires employers to establish joint health and safety committees, there is no reason for employers to wait for legislation or official orders to establish such a committee. The committee can address health and safety complaints and suggestions, monitor or track work hazards, initiate targeted health and safety projects, investigate work sites, resolve health and safety issues, monitor effectiveness of health and safety programs, and make recommendations for program improvements (Canadian Centre for Occupational Health and Safety [CCOHS], 1999. Committees can go a long way in motivating workers in health and safety and therefore protecting worker health so that injuries and illnesses are prevented.

The Work Environment

An assessment of the work environment, an essential component of a health and safety program, should be done in order to recognize and control hazards. Recognition is the first step in protecting workers from workplace hazards. Hazard identification can be done by trained members of the health and safety committee, other workers who are trained in hazard recognition, or by health and safety specialists who have training in measuring hazards. These people must consider all aspects of the work-site operations, including all processes, all materials used (i.e., from raw materials to end products), and all the actual and potential points of worker contact or exposure. Hazard identification can involve walk-throughs of the work site, either on a regular basis or in response to specific concerns. Review of work-injury statistics can also point to areas on a work site that need to be surveyed and assessed to identify hazards. Another method for identifying hazards is to complete a Job Hazard Analysis. This involves identifying each component of a particular job and then examining it to ascertain any actual or potential hazards. This can be done using a form such as the one found in Figure 11.1. Once the hazards have been identified for each job task, the actual risk must be assessed.

The type of assessment or expertise required depends on the type of hazard. For example, noise is a common hazard in workplaces. Taking a simple noise measurement requires a sound level meter. A more complex measurement of noise exposure involves dosimetry, which requires workers to wear a measuring device throughout a workday. Exposure time and noise levels are then calculated to determine a worker's actual exposure to noise as well as the risk of hearing being affected and occupationally induced hearing loss caused.

Hazard evaluation can help to determine the risk to workers' health from any type of workplace hazard. In addition, hazard evaluation points to those hazards that require controls so that worker exposure and consequent health effects are eliminated or minimized as much as is practicable.

Hazard control can be divided into three general categories: engineering controls, administrative controls, and personal protective equipment. The controls identified or implemented should be entered as part of the Job Hazard Analysis (Figure 11.1).

Engineering controls is the first choice because hazards are removed at the source, preventing exposure and therefore eliminating the risk of harmful health effects. A simple example of an engineering control is a muffler on a car, which reduces the noise of a vehicle. Isolation of either a hazard source (e.g., enclosing noisy machinery) or the workers (e.g., by placing them in a control room) is a common engineering control in many industries.

Administrative controls include strategies such as job rotation to minimize the time a worker is exposed to a hazard in a particular process and instituting safe work procedures. When safe work procedures are followed, they can significantly reduce the risks to health posed by hazards.

The use of **personal protective equipment** is very common in industry to prevent exposure to health hazards. Examples of such equipment include respiratory protective equipment (RPE), gloves, protective eye goggles, hard hats, or fall protection equipment. Personal protective equipment is used as a last resort when a hazard cannot be eliminated or controlled by any other means. Rogers (1994, p. 200–201) gives five things to consider when using personal protective equipment:

- selecting the proper type of equipment,
- ensuring proper fit,
- instructing workers in the proper use of equipment,
- enforcement of standards for using the equipment, whether legislated or workplace based, and
- effective equipment sanitation and maintenance.

It's important to remember that using personal protective equipment does not eliminate a hazard, but it can minimize exposure if it is properly fitted, used, and maintained.

Addressing Injuries, Illnesses, and Incidents

Despite the best intentions and the preventive focus of occupational health and safety programs, injuries and illnesses still occur in the workplace. Because of this, elements such as first

FIGURE 11.1 Sample Job Hazard Analysis Worksheet

Occupation/Job Classification: ____________________

Location/Site: ____________________

Department: ____________________

Specific Job: ____________________

____

Prepared by: ____________________

____

____

Date: ____________________

Job Tasks by Sequence of Events	Potential Hazards	Preventive Actions or Controls

aid, health surveillance for hazard exposures, rehabilitation of workers, incident investigations, and emergency preparedness for major incidents need to be addressed in a program. As a minimum, most jurisdictions require employers to provide first-aid services, the most basic form of worker health assessment as work-related injuries and illnesses must be reported, assessed, treated, and documented by a first-aider. In more comprehensive health and safety programs, more extensive health assessments are done, including health surveillance and rehabilitation. This will be discussed in more detail in the "Occupational Health Nursing" section.

Conducting workplace investigations is another part of a health and safety program. Some investigations are mandated by legislation, such as those done because of a serious injury or a major incident that could cause serious injury or significant property damage. Workplace investigations are done to determine causes and prevent recurrence; they are not intended to find fault. Often, a number of factors or events, not just a single one, leads to injuries, property damage, or near misses. Thorough investigations are necessary so that all factors can be addressed when recommendations are made to prevent future incidents.

Preparing for emergencies is critical for any work site, regardless of the size or type. Being prepared minimizes not only injuries to workers, but also damage to property. "Emergency management is a dynamic process. Planning, though critical, is not the only component. Training, conducting drills, testing equipment, and coordinating activities with the community are other important functions" (Federal Emergency Management Agency, 2003). Although emergency preparedness does not prevent an emergency, it ensures that both human and economic losses are minimized.

Program Administration

Comprehensive records are a necessary component of an effective health and safety program. A variety of records must be kept for the purposes of:

- meeting legislated requirements (e.g., first-aid records or material safety data sheets),
- informing and communicating,
- maintaining baseline measurements (e.g., worker baseline tests),
- determining hazards (e.g., if a number of workers from one department report the same types of health problems, a hazard investigation may be warranted),
- preventing injuries or illnesses (a review of injury or illness records can identify problem areas and preventive steps can be taken to reduce additional problems),
- proving or disproving exposures to hazards (e.g., for insurance or compensation claims),
- program tracking (program objectives should be measurable and tracking helps determine whether objectives are being met), and
- evaluating and planning a program.

Each company will have preferences for different types of records and reports, including policies, procedures, tracking, and evaluation. In addition, members of the health and safety team may have specific professional requirements for record keeping. It is important to constantly assess the records to ensure that they are well maintained and kept up to date.

LEGISLATION AND STANDARDS

Health and Safety

Each province and territory in Canada has legislated standards for health and safety in the workplace. In general, the legislation outlines the rights, responsibilities, and fundamental principles for achieving and maintaining workplace health and safety. Most importantly, health and safety legislation sets standards so that health problems or safety risks at work are minimized. Consequences of not meeting the minimum requirements are also outlined in the legislation.

Both employers and employees have obligations under health and safety legislation. Employers have overall responsibility for ensuring health and safety at their work sites. In turn, workers are responsible for working safely and cooperating with the employer by following health and safety policies and procedures. Standard-setting agencies, such as the government, have legislated duties of inspection and enforcement.

Legislation can set overall general objectives, or it can be very specific and include detailed procedures for preserving safety at work, such as fall protection or confined space entry. First-aid requirements or the need for joint health and safety committees may also be addressed. The laws also deal with specific hazards such as noise, chemicals in the workplace, or biological hazards. Legislation may require that workers have a specific level of competence to perform work safely and can require training in certain areas. Some laws apply to all industries in a given jurisdiction while some are industry specific. Both employers and workers are well advised to find out the legislated requirements for health and safety for their specific workplace.

While provincial or territorial legislation applies to employers and workers within its boundaries, not all work sites fall under provincial or territorial jurisdiction. Industries, such as banks, some communications and transportation businesses, that cross provincial boundaries fall under federal jurisdiction.

The legislation that pertains to hazardous products is slightly different from other health and safety legislation because both federal and provincial/territorial legislation apply. The federal Hazardous Product Act governs all jurisdictions. In addition, each jurisdiction has its own laws in this area, commonly known as the **Workplace Hazardous Material Information System (WHMIS)**. From a practical point of view, there are three major components of WHMIS legislation:

- workers must be informed of the nature of the hazards posed by any hazardous products at work;
- hazardous products must be labelled; and
- hazardous products must have a material safety data sheet that outlines components, physical properties, health hazards, first aid, toxicity, and any other aspects that pertain to health and safety.

Compensation Legislation

Workers' compensation legislation goes hand in hand with occupational health and safety legislation. It was introduced to protect both workers and employers when work-related injuries or illnesses occur. Workers' compensation is a form of no-fault insurance that protects employers from being sued by workers who become injured or ill due to work. In turn, workers receive compensation for work-related injuries or illnesses and do not have to take legal action against an employer to obtain it.

Compensation legislation is in every Canadian jurisdiction. The laws of each dictate reporting requirements, compensation allowances, and procedures for obtaining and providing compensation. Different commissions or boards throughout Canada administer their respective legislation.

Human Rights Legislation

Canada has a Charter of Rights and Freedoms that protects basic human rights. In addition, each jurisdiction has legislation that protects human rights, and this legislation applies at the workplace as well as any other setting. From a health and safety point of view, human rights legislation protects individuals from discrimination at the workplace due to any of the listed protected areas, which include disability, sex, family status, or religion. It requires employers to consider individual differences and outlines a duty to accommodate those differences. For example, if a worker is returning to work after suffering an injury and is unable to perform the job held prior to the injury, the employer must adapt the job so that the worker's new disability is accommodated. An employer who claims that such accommodation is not possible must prove that it would cause undue hardship.

Other Legislation

Many other pieces of legislation can apply at a workplace and affect health and safety programs. While a complete list would be too lengthy, some examples include:

- employment standards;
- cross-jurisdictional legislation (e.g., drug-testing requirements in the transportation industry in the United States);
- public health legislation, including communicable diseases reporting or immunization;
- privacy legislation;
- building standards and codes;
- fire codes;
- disaster services;
- Good Samaritan legislation; and
- legislation pertaining to health and safety professionals.

Other Standards

In addition to the laws of the land, many other standards can apply at a workplace and impact a health and safety program. Manufacturers of equipment and supplies, regardless of the type of industry, often have safety standards that apply to their products. Workers and employers must know and follow these standards to maintain health and safety.

Many industries have what are commonly known as industry-based standards, best practices, or industry safety codes for health and safety at work. An industry association often writes these and recommends that they be used by employers. These types of standards help employers to comply with legislation, and many go further than the minimum legislated standards. Professional associations often develop minimum practice standards for their members. As well, safety associations are a common source for guidelines and recommended practices in health and safety.

Still other standards are set by organizations for equipment, policies, or procedures. The Canadian Standards Association (CSA) is a prominent standards-setting organization. Examples of CSA standards that apply to health and safety programs include those for personal protective equipment such as eye protection, face protection, and respiratory protection. Some, but not all, standards are referenced in legislation and made mandatory. Regardless of whether the standards are a requirement, they are a useful resource for health and safety programs and can provide guidance on a variety of issues. Some standards or guidelines are distributed by governments. While these may not be requirements, they are a valuable resource for anyone developing an effective health and safety program or implementing the requirements of the legislation.

TYPES OF HEALTH AND SAFETY HAZARDS

Safety Hazards

Safety or mechanical hazards are a significant source of injury in the workplace. These types of hazards are generally fairly obvious and include unguarded belts, unprotected gears, shafts without railings, ladders that do not provide proper support, poor housekeeping, or unsecured items that can fall on workers' heads or toes to cause injury. The list is endless.

Physical Hazards

The Canadian Centre for Occupational Health and Safety (CCOHS) defines **physical hazards** as "sources of energy that may cause injury or disease" (CCOHS, n.d., c). Types of physical hazards and some examples include:

- noise: chain saw,
- vibration: jackhammer,
- ionizing radiation: checking welds on pipelines,
- ultraviolet radiation: welding,
- excessive heat: foundry, and
- excessive cold: winter outdoors.

Noise in the workplace is as ubiquitous at work as it is in our homes and other environments. Our ears can tolerate certain levels without long-term effects, but hearing loss can occur after exposure to high noise levels over a period of time. Once the inner ear is damaged from excessive noise, there is no cure. This makes prevention of hearing loss due to exposure to excessive noise extremely important. Vibration sources in the workplace include tools such as jackhammers, sanders, stamping machines, and drills that can cause long-term effects to fingers and hands. Workers who operate excavating equipment can experience effects to their whole body if they sit in a seat that vibrates. "The risk of injury from exposure to either type of vibration depends on the intensity and frequency of the vibration, the duration of exposure (usually measured in years), and the part(s) of the body affected" (Alberta Human Resources and Employment, Workplace Health and Safety [WHS], 2002a, p. 1). Local effects of using vibrating tools can include Raynaud's syndrome, while whole-body vibration can produce a wide range of effects, including back and neck problems.

The uses of ionizing radiation, such as X-rays and radiation for cancer treatment, are well known in the health care industry; however, ionizing radiation is also used in other industries. One example is the use of a radioactive source for checking welds on pipes. The health effects of ionizing radiation can range from mild skin erythema to cancer. Non-ionizing radiation includes various types along the electromagnetic spectrum. The ultraviolet rays of sunlight are probably the best known of the non-ionizing radiation hazards. Ultraviolet radiation, a common hazard in welding, can cause a painful injury known as welder's flash in which the cornea is burned.

A wide variety of industries can expose workers to excessive heat or excessive cold. Factors that determine whether workers suffer heat stress, and the extent of the health effects, include air temperature, humidity, amount of radiant heat, air speed, clothing, physical activity, and individual factors (WHS, 2002b). Health effects can include heat cramps, heat exhaustion, heat stroke, and death. Working outside during a hot summer day in a foundry near molten metal, or in many other work situations, can cause heat stress in workers. Exposure to the other temperature extreme, cold, can occur either outside (e.g., in the construction industry) or inside (e.g., working in refrigeration units, immersing hands in cold water, or using cold equipment or tools). As with heat, a number of factors determine the health effects, which vary from reduced dexterity to hypothermia and death.

Chemical Hazards

Found in almost any work setting, chemicals are a significant hazard in the workplace. **Chemical hazards** can be in liquid, solid, or gaseous form, in mists, vapours, or fumes. Chemicals enter the body in many ways, including ingestion, injection, and skin absorption. Probably the most common route of entry is via inhalation (CCOHS, 1997). The most prudent way to prevent chemical exposures is to become informed about the chemicals used and to minimize exposure as much as possible by using the controls available, including personal protective equipment. Material safety data sheets, required under health and safety legislation, include information about the toxicity of different chemicals, their potential health effects, first-aid measures, and protection from exposure.

Biological Hazards

Biological hazards, such as bacteria, viruses, insects, plants, birds, animals, and even other humans, can cause a variety of health effects, such as skin irritation, allergies, infections, and cancer (CCOHS, n.d., a). Workers who may be exposed to biological hazards include health care workers (to bacterial or viral diseases from their patients), forestry workers (to insects, plants, birds, and animals), and maintenance workers (who may clean an area where there are mouse droppings and therefore may be exposed to hanta virus).

Ergonomic Hazards

Ergonomic hazards are workplace conditions that can cause injury to the musculoskeletal system of the worker (CCOHS, n.d., b). Examples of ergonomic hazards in the workplace include repetitive work, static postures, improper lighting, and poor tool design.

Psychosocial Hazards

Psychosocial hazards can be defined as "factors and situations encountered or associated with one's job or work environment that create or potentiate stress, emotional strain, and/or interpersonal problems" (Rogers, 1994, p. 96). Examples

Canadian Research Box 11.1

Duxbury, L., & Higgins, C. (2003). *Voices of Canadians: Seeking work-life balance.* Retrieved November 30, 2003 from http://labour-travail.hrdc-drhc.gc.ca/worklife/vcswlb-tcrctvp/tm.cfm

Attaining work-life balance is an ongoing issue for many Canadians in today's fast-paced world. Health Canada commissioned a study to address this issue and make recommendations for workers to achieve and maintain a better balance between work and home responsibilities. The authors' report contains a compilation of 10,000 comments regarding the life stresses faced daily by Canadian workers. The study sample included a total of 31,571 workers from 100 of the larger organizations (i.e., >500 employees) across Canada. Workers in companies in both the private and public sectors as well as not-for-profit organizations were surveyed.

Researchers found that the majority of comments addressed challenges faced by workers in balancing home and work life. Those who felt more challenged were more likely to comment.

This survey presents a very real problem that has implications for nursing practice in both occupational health and community health. It can help nurses better understand and address the needs and the concerns of their clients.

Discussion Questions

1. What steps can be taken by (a) employers, (b) workers, and (c) governments at all levels to facilitate a healthier work-life balance in Canadian workers?
2. What strategies could community health nurses include in their practice and services to reduce work-life conflicts and promote a balance for their clients?

of psychosocial hazards include anything that may cause a worker to experience stress, such as high workloads, harassment, inflexible work arrangements, uncertainty, shiftwork, or conflict in the workplace.

THE OCCUPATIONAL HEALTH AND SAFETY TEAM

Occupational health nurses are members of occupational health and safety teams. Their roles on these teams will be discussed in the next section. Other team members include occupational physicians, occupational hygienists, safety professionals, ergonomists, and other specialists who address either work environment issues or workers themselves.

Occupational Health Physicians

Occupational health physicians are medical doctors who have specialized in the field of occupational medicine. They deal specifically with worker health to diagnose and treat injuries, illnesses, and diseases that may stem from workplace exposures. Companies hire these medical specialists on a full-time, part-time, or consultant basis, depending on the needs of the company, its commitment to health and safety, and its economic situation. Occupational health nurses and occupational physicians work closely together to prevent illness and to promote the highest level of health in workers.

Occupational Hygienists

Occupational hygienists focus primarily on recognizing, measuring, evaluating, and controlling health hazards in the workplace. Usually, their educational background emphasizes the sciences, plus special training in the principles and concepts of work environment assessment. They use special equipment to quantitatively measure hazards such as noise or chemicals. Occupational hygienists also understand the health effects of different hazards on the human body.

In Canada, there are two recognized professionals: Registered Occupational Hygienists (ROH) and Registered Occupational Hygiene Technologists (ROHT). To qualify as an ROH, the Canadian Registration Board of Occupational Hygienists (CRBOH) requires a university degree plus experience. An ROHT must have experience in occupational hygiene, the amount of which varies according to the level of education achieved. Professionals must maintain competency in their respective areas to register with the CRBOH.

Ergonomists

An **ergonomist** is a professional who "applies theory, principles, data, and methods to... optimize human well-being and overall system performance" (Association of Canadian Ergonomists, 2003, p. 1). While these professionals have diverse educational backgrounds, all have an interest in and work to improve work situations by addressing the "physical, cognitive, social, organizational, environmental, and other relevant factors" in the workplace (Association of Canadian Ergonomists, p. 1). In other words, ergonomists look at both worker characteristics and work environment characteristics (such as equipment) to prevent injuries and illnesses. For example, ergonomists examine the potential for musculoskeletal problems from repetitive work or inappropriate tools, eyestrain caused by computer screens or improper lighting, or physical or psychological problems caused by shiftwork.

Safety Professionals

Safety professionals, or safety officers, are also integral members of health and safety teams. In Canada, safety professionals can register and receive professional designation as a Canadian Registered Safety Professional (CRSP) from the Board of Canadian Registered Safety Professionals (BCRSP). A **safety professional** promotes workplace health and safety in a variety of ways. General knowledge in the following is helpful in obtaining a CRSP designation (BCRSP, 2003, p. 1):

- accident theory;
- environmental practices;
- ergonomics;
- fire prevention and protection;
- health promotion;
- law and ethics;
- occupational health, safety, and environment systems;
- occupational hygiene;
- risk management; and
- safety techniques and technology.

Others

Other specialists or professionals may be part of the health and safety team at one time or another. These include counsellors, psychologists, physiotherapists, massage therapists, case managers, and rehabilitation specialists. The extent to which these individuals work in health and safety is based on need, economics, and management commitment.

OCCUPATIONAL HEALTH NURSING

Occupational health nursing is a recognized specialty practice under the Canadian Nurses Association (CNA). It is defined by the American Association of Occupational Health Nurses (AAOHN) as "the specialty practice that provides for and delivers health and safety programs and services to workers, worker populations, and community groups. The practice focuses on promotion and restoration of health, prevention of illness and injury, and the protection from work related and environmental hazards" (AAOHN, 2003, p. 1).

Conceptual Framework

An occupational health nursing conceptual framework presents values and beliefs about four aspects: the individual, health, occupational health nursing, and the environment (see text box). The interrelationship of these four components reflects the assumptions and philosophy of occupational

Conceptual Framework of Occupational Health Nursing

The individual is unique in biological, psychological, social, spiritual, and cultural characteristics. The individual has rights to confidentiality of health records, advocacy, and information about health status and potential hazards. The individual also has the right to work in a safe and healthy environment, choose or refuse participation in occupational health programs, and refuse unsafe/unhealthy work. In addition, the individual has responsibilities to maintain his/her own health, know the hazards of the workplace, assume responsibility for the consequences of his/her actions, respect the rights and needs of others, and maintain safe work practices for self and others.

Health is the extent to which an individual or group is able to realize aspirations to satisfy needs and to change or cope with the environment. Health is, therefore, seen as a resource for everyday life, not the objective of living. Health is a positive concept emphasizing social and personal resources as well as physical capacities.

Occupational health nursing is that specialty area of nursing practice that focuses on the worker group by promoting health, preventing illness/injury, protecting workers from risks associated with exposure to occupational health hazards, recommending placement of workers in jobs suited to their physiological and psychological health status, and restoring workers' health in a safe and healthy work environment.

Environment consists of dynamic forces that interact with each other and the individual. The environment can be social, economic, political, physical, and cultural as well as the internal psychological status of the individual. A major focus of occupational health nursing is the work environment because of its unique health hazards.

Source: Canadian Occupational Health Nurses Association. (2002). Occupational health nursing practice guidelines. *Retrieved December 10, 2003, from* www.cohna-aciist.ca. *Reproduced with permission.*

health nursing practice (Canadian Occupational Health Nurses Association [COHNA], 2002).

Role of the Occupational Health Nurse

Nurses have been working in occupational health since the late 1800s when they were employed by industries to care for ailing workers and their families (Levy & Wegman, 1995; Rogers, 1994). Since then, the role of the occupational health nurse (OHN) has expanded to include the areas of epidemiology, industrial hygiene, environmental health, toxicology, safety, management, health education, early disease detection, disease prevention, health promotion, and health and environmental surveillance (Levy & Wegman).

Rogers (1994) identifies five major roles in occupational health nursing practice: clinician/practitioner, administrator, educator, researcher, and consultant. Many OHNs function in several or all of these roles. The **clinician/practitioner** applies the nursing process to direct care for occupational, and often non-occupational, injuries and illnesses at the workplace. The OHN also collaborates with other members of the occupational health team to maintain a safe and healthy work environment.

An **administrator** serves an important function in the operation of the occupational health service by providing the structure and direction for the development, implementation, and evaluation of the program. The administrator is also responsible for communicating and interpreting the occupational health program to management and other members of the occupational health team.

The OHN **educator** teaches and prepares nursing students in the occupational health nursing specialty. The educator must have the appropriate education to teach, as well as experience and knowledge in the concepts of occupational health. The educator must be able to integrate theory with actual practice in the workplace.

The role of the OHN as a **researcher** is growing, and there is increasing focus on this area. The researcher develops researchable questions, conducts research, and communicates the research findings to other occupational health nurses, other researchers, and the public.

The OHN **consultant** serves as a resource to other occupational health professionals, management, and organizations; assists in the development and evaluation of occupational programs and services; and recommends strategies and options for improvement. The consultant generally does not have direct responsibility for implementing or enforcing the recommendations. Consultants must be aware of the "business" of occupational health, as well as having excellent communication skills (both oral and written). OHN consultants may function either internally or externally to the organization.

Occupational Health Nursing as a Specialty Practice

Occupational health nursing is a specialty in which registered nurses generally work outside the traditional health care system. Most OHNs work independently and may be the only health care professional in the workplace setting. Consequently, OHNs must ensure that they have the appropriate education, training, and expertise to practise competently in order to provide a variety of services such as:

- health promotion and injury/illness prevention;
- health surveillance for those workers who may be exposed to health hazards (e.g., audiometric testing for noise-exposed workers; blood-lead levels for lead-exposed workers);
- health monitoring for workers who have health conditions that may impact on their ability to do their jobs safely, or where workplace exposures may have a detrimental effect on their health;
- pre-placement health assessments to match fitness for work with bona fide occupational requirements such as job demands;

- primary care and case management for ill or injured workers;
- counselling;
- referral to employee assistance programs;
- management and administration;
- research;
- worker education;
- job hazard analysis; and
- ergonomic assessments.

Education In Canada, OHNs are registered nurses who hold a diploma or degree in nursing and have a variety of additional qualifications and experience. OHNs may also have a certificate, diploma, or degree in Occupational Health and Safety from a community college or university. Courses may include such topics as hazard identification and control, toxicology, ergonomics, occupational environments, health surveillance, program development, audiometric testing, spirometry, and disability case management. To ensure their competency, registered nurses who choose to work in this field should take this specific education.

Occupational Health Nursing Competencies

Provision of Occupational Health, Safety, and Environment Services

The OHN providing these services:

- practises in accordance with the professional standards of practice and code of ethics of their professional licensing body.
- maintains confidentiality of employee health records.
- uses and interprets relevant legislation to promote workplace compliance.
- manages the occupational health, safety, and environment program by setting goals and objectives and establishing priorities.
- advises management on appropriate record-keeping requirements for due diligence.

Assessment of the Work Environment, Hazard Control, and Surveillance

One of the key components of the occupational health and safety program is the identification of workplace hazards and control of these hazards. The OHN:

- anticipates and recognizes potential environmental hazards including chemical, biological, physical, ergonomic, and psychosocial hazards.
- assesses the level of risk and severity of hazards.
- applies the principles of hazard control including engineering, administrative, and personal protective equipment.

Employee Health Assessment, Surveillance, and Intervention in the Workplace

A major function of the OHN is the assessment of employee health and the surveillance of those employees who may be exposed to hazards within the workplace. The OHN:

- assesses and monitors the health of employees.
- develops, implements, and reviews programs and procedures for health surveillance.
- collects and analyzes aggregate data for prevention, identification of trends, or statistical or research purposes.

Assessment and Care of Injuries and Illnesses in the Workplace

OHNs may be involved in primary care at the workplace and/or in assessment of previously ill or injured employees returning to the workplace. The OHN:

- implements nursing interventions to minimize effects of illness and injury.
- recognizes the implications for fitness to work for the following types of disorders: respiratory, musculoskeletal, skin, neurological, mental health and behavioural, reproductive, cardiovascular, hematological, hepatic, renal and urinary tract, and gastrointestinal.
- identifies when disorders are work related and recommends preventive workplace modifications.
- provides and coordinates ability/case management. This may include contact with the injured/ill worker, referral to the employee assistance program, conducting or arranging fitness for work examinations, and facilitating return to work.
- counsels employees with respect to prevention and management of both occupational and non-occupational illnesses and injuries.

Health, Safety, and Environment Education/Promotion in the Workplace

The role of the OHN includes health promotion and education of employees. The OHN:

- utilizes principles of adult education when developing and providing formal/informal educational activities (e.g., literacy and target population).
- assesses organizational and individual educational needs.
- provides leadership to empower employees and management to adopt a strategy directed toward both organizational and individual health and wellness (e.g., fitness, job design, flexible work hours, smoking cessation, work-family conflict, stress management, and nutritional counselling).
- coordinates and evaluates program development.

Source: Excerpted by permission from Canadian Nurses Association. (2000). Occupational Health Nursing Certification Exam Prep Guide. *Ottawa, ON: Canadian Nurses Association. Retrieved December 3, 2003 from* www.cna-nurses.ca/_frames/certification/certification_frame.html

Certification OHNs in Canada may obtain national certification in their specialty by writing the Canadian Nurses Association certification exam. The first to develop a specialty certification exam, OHNs did this through their own association, the Canadian Council for Occupational Health Nurses Incorporated (CCOHN) in 1984. This certification earned international recognition, and many specialty nursing groups followed. In 1992, the CCOHN certification process was transferred to the jurisdiction of the Canadian Nurses Association.

OHNs who are certified in occupational health nursing have met specific eligibility requirements and passed a written exam to show that they have met a national standard of competency in Occupational Health Nursing. In Canada, expertise unique to this speciality is recognized with the initials COHN(C), granted by the Canadian Nurses Association. The initials COHN or COHN-S recognize U.S. certification. These are marks of distinction for occupational health nursing excellence.

The five major competencies for occupational health nursing required for the Canadian Nurses Association (CNA) certification exam are headlined in the text box. Each major competency is followed by a list of standards.

Specialty Associations and Networking OHNs from across Canada have been meeting informally since 1980. The formal association was founded in 1984 and incorporated in its current form in 1994. The Canadian Occupational Health Nurses Association/Association Canadienne des Infirmières et Infirmiers en Santé du Travail (COHNA/ACIIST) continues to evolve and is the voice of OHNs in Canada.

COHNA/ACIIST has over 2000 members. Members of the provincial occupational health nursing associations are automatically members of COHNA/ACIIST. The Board of Directors is composed of representatives from each provincial association. Nine provinces are represented. Information on the association is available on the COHNA/ACIIST website.

The objectives of COHNA/ACIIST are:

- to improve health and safety of workers by speaking with a national voice to influence health and safety regulations legislation,
- to enhance the profile of OHNs at provincial, territorial, national, and international levels,
- to advance the profession by providing a national forum for the exchange of ideas and concerns,
- to contribute to the health of the community by providing quality health services to workers,
- to promote national standards for OHNs, and
- to encourage continuing education and ensure the certification process meets COHNA/ACIIST (COHNA, 2000a) standards.

Benefits of Occupational Health Nursing

OHNs are a valuable part of an organization's team. Benefits of having an OHN on staff have been outlined by the Alberta Occupational Health Nurses Association (AOHNA) and by COHNA/ACIIST.

Benefits to Employees Having an OHN at the work site benefits employees (AOHNA [n.d.]) by:

- decreasing the risk of workplace illness and injury;
- educating them on health and safety issues that may affect them both on and off the job;
- increasing job satisfaction and morale;
- placing them in jobs that they can perform safely;
- training them in healthy and safe work practices; and
- facilitating a safe return to work following illness or injury by helping such employees maintain a sense of self worth and connection with the workplace, perform modified work, and minimize loss of income from time away from work.

Benefits to the Employer OHNs in the workplace are a valuable asset to the organization and assist the employer (AOHNA, [n.d.]; COHNA, 2000b) by:

- increasing compliance with federal and provincial occupational health and safety legislation;
- allowing managers to spend less time dealing with unfamiliar health and safety issues;
- reducing costs of premiums and penalties on WCB and other insurance and benefit plans;
- lowering the risk of workplace illness and injury;
- reducing lost time/downtime related to both on-the-job and off-the-job illness and injury;
- improving employee morale and productivity;
- decreasing absenteeism;
- assisting placement of employees in jobs that are suitable to their physical and mental abilities;
- enhancing corporate image; and
- decreasing employee turnover, which reduces costs of recruiting and retraining staff.

Cost-Benefit and Cost-Effectiveness Analyses OHNs must be able to demonstrate their contributions, value, business relevance, and return on investment for employers (Morris & Smith, 2001). In today's corporate climate, this must be done using business principles like cost-benefit and cost-effectiveness analyses. Programs that cannot demonstrate that they are financially beneficial will not be maintained.

Cost-benefit analysis is a technique that represents both costs and benefits of the outcomes of a program in monetary terms, permitting a comparison between unlike elements and yielding a benefit-to-cost ratio (American Association of Occupational Health Nurses [AAOHN], 1996). It asks what is the benefit of the program (e.g., reduced WCB costs, increased productivity) compared to what it costs to run the program.

Cost-effectiveness analysis is used to determine which activities or interventions achieve the program's goals and objectives with the most value or greatest impact on cost (AAOHN, 1996). It involves comparing alternative options for the same services. An example of this would be comparing the costs for in-house versus contracted occupational health services.

AAOHN (1996) outlines the following steps for cost-benefit and cost-effectiveness analyses for OHNs.

1. Determine the program/service for financial analysis.
2. Formulate the objectives and goals of the program/service.
3. List alternative ways objectives and goals can be achieved.
4. Determine costs/benefits for all alternatives. Include appropriate cost categories such as personnel costs, supplies, capital expenditures, facility costs, and lost productive time.
5. Determine monetary value for costs/benefits, or determine outcome measures such as absenteeism rates, health services utilization, claims utilization, risk behaviours (such as smoking, obesity, seat belt use, and alcohol use), workers' compensation claims, lost-time incidents, and productivity rates.
6. Calculate discounting, which reduces future costs to their present worth. It answers the question, "What is the cost of providing this service now compared with what it will cost in the future?"
7. Calculate the cost-benefit ratio or cost-effectiveness of the program/service.

Credit: Reproduced with permission of AAOHN Journal.

ORGANIZATIONAL CULTURE AND OCCUPATIONAL HEALTH

Organizational culture is defined as "the learned values, assumptions, and behaviours that knit a community together. It preserves and unifies the social structure through a system of norms, expectations, and assumptions about the way individuals feel or behave within a group" (Rogers, 1994, p. 177). The impact of organizational culture on employee health behaviours is well documented (Allen, Allen, Kraft & Certner, 1987; Bachmann, 2000; O'Donnell, 2000; Pratt, 2001; Rogers, 1994). The literature indicates that employees are more likely to be guided by the cultural "norms" of the organization than by their own values (Allen et al., 1987; Allen & Leutzinger, 1999). These norms may be positive or negative. An organization that values a "safe and healthy" workplace must have organizational goals that reflect this through the implementation of occupational health and safety programs and through role modelling of organizational behaviours that support, promote, and protect health (Rogers). Successful occupational health and safety programs must focus on the development of initiatives that go beyond the traditional physical component, addressing the areas of physical, emotional, social, intellectual, spiritual, and environmental well-being. The key to the success of all comprehensive occupational health and safety programs is to create a culture that supports safe and healthy activities and behaviours and moves toward both personal and organizational health, safety, and well-being. To be successful, this must involve participation from all levels within the organization.

OCCUPATIONAL HEALTH NURSING: LINKAGES WITH COMMUNITY HEALTH

Occupational health nursing is closely linked to community health nursing in both theory and practice (Rogers, 1994). Both nursing types emphasize prevention and health promotion as strategies for improving health and reducing the risks of illness (Rogers). Community health nurses focus on the public, while OHNs focus on the worker population.

Occupational health nursing functions may be categorized into the three levels of prevention: primary, secondary, and tertiary. Primary prevention by OHNs includes health promotion (such as nutrition, physical activity, coping) and disease prevention (such as incident and injury prevention, health risk appraisals, health education, smoking cessation, weight control, and stress management). Secondary prevention activities may include pre-placement assessments, health surveillance, incident reporting, and injury treatment. Tertiary prevention in occupational health includes return-to-work programs, work hardening, and monitoring employees for chronic health conditions (Rogers).

Occupational Health and Safety in the Community Health Setting

Community health nurses (CHNs), as workers themselves, have a responsibility to maintain the health and safety of their workplace and to protect themselves and their co-workers from work-related illness or injury. Whether working on-site at a health facility, in the client's home, or on the road, the community health nurse must be aware of the occupational health and safety hazards and their appropriate controls, as outlined in the beginning of this chapter. Hazards for CHNs may include such things as workplace violence, working alone, driving, exposure to blood and body fluids, repetitive strain injuries, lifting and transferring of materials and clients, and exposure to chemicals. Identified hazards, near misses, and incidents must be reported promptly and investigated to prevent future incidents resulting in illness or injury. Working in a safe and healthy manner should become the "norm" of the community health workplace and part of everyday work performance.

CANADIAN RESEARCH

How does one measure the extent to which occupational health nursing care helps the clients? This is challenging for the occupational health and safety profession because it is difficult to quantify the promotion and maintenance of physical, mental, emotional, and spiritual health as well as the prevention of ill health. In the field of occupational health nursing, as with all other areas of nursing, quantifying effectiveness is particularly important because significant costs are associated with health care. Determining the effectiveness of our nursing practice is a challenge (Graziani, 1996) and any tools for this purpose are valuable.

Canadian nursing research in occupational health is limited and therefore provides opportunities for nurses in the future. Although only a handful of academic research studies have been done by OHNs, research is being done by industry and by other occupational health professionals. Canadian Research Box 11.2 illustrates one example of Canadian nursing research in occupational health nursing.

Canadian Research Box 11.2

Skillen, D. L., Anderson, M. C., Seglie, J., & Gilbert, J. (2002). Toward a model for effectiveness: What Alberta occupational health nurses think. *AAOHN Journal, 50*(2), 75–82.

Four Alberta nurses conducted a study and proposed a model for determining the effectiveness of occupational health nursing practice. The model (see Figure 11.2) identifies five occupational health nursing goals:

- balance,
- communication,
- leadership,
- continuing competence, and
- trust.

To achieve these five goals, ten occupational health nursing functions as well as ten relationships were suggested and discussed. The model states that the base or foundation for occupational health nursing practice is education and experience as a Registered Nurse as well as baseline competence in occupational health nursing, which includes education and experience in occupational health nursing along with knowledge of a number of related disciplines.

The model brings together a number of elements of occupational health nursing in a comprehensive format and provides a basis for further research, discussion, and development. The researchers acknowledge that further work and discussion is needed so that the effectiveness of occupational health nursing practice can be measured using their model.

FIGURE 11.2 Model for Determining the Effectiveness of Occupational Health Nursing Practice

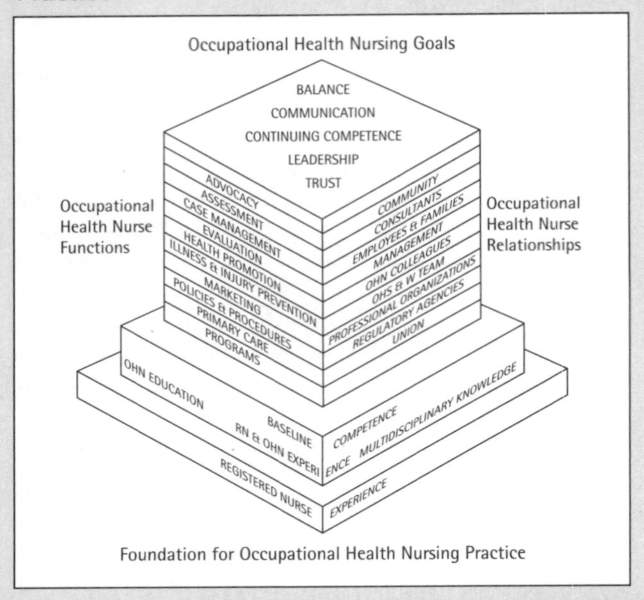

Source: Skillen et al. (2002). (See above.) Reproduced with permission of AAOHN Journal.

Discussion Questions

1. Of what practical use is a model such as this for the practice of nursing?
2. How would you suggest the model be used when effectiveness measures are developed?

SUMMARY

Occupational health nursing is a specialized area of nursing requiring specific education and competence. As well, occupational health and safety issues affect *all* nurses in their everyday work experience. It is important that registered nurses in the community health setting be aware of occupational health and safety issues, which may impact the health of their clients as well as themselves.

This chapter has looked at the components of an occupational health and safety program. Management commitment, worker involvement, legislation and standards, and program administration have all been discussed. The different categories of health and safety hazards were introduced. Occupational health nursing was portrayed both as an integral part of the occupational health and safety team and as a specialty of nursing. A conceptual framework for occupational health nursing and the roles and competencies of OHNs were presented. Finally, the necessity of considering occupational health and safety in all aspects of nursing, particularly community health, was considered.

As you continue your studies and your work in nursing, think about how a patient's work setting can affect health, what nursing care may be required, and what referrals may be indicated. If your patient is young and hasn't yet been introduced to the work world, think about how a family member's work could be a factor in the presenting problem or the family's health. If you're working with a senior, think about how previous work exposures may be a factor in cur-

CASE STUDY

Marie is a 47-year-old community health nurse who has worked in a rural community health setting in northern Saskatchewan for 15 years. Marie works primarily at the local community health centre and frequently travels to visit new mothers and babies in the surrounding area.

Discussion Questions

1. What hazards might Marie encounter when she visits her clients?
2. How might these hazards differ from those of a community health nurse working in an urban setting?
3. What controls should be in place?
4. Identify the responsibilities of the employer for ensuring Marie's health and safety.

rent health issues that senior may be facing. Finally, and most importantly, think about your own health and safety as you work and the steps you can take to protect yourself as a worker and to promote your own health and safety.

KEY TERMS

occupational health theory
occupational health and safety programs
hazards
management commitment
job demands analysis
engineering controls
administrative controls
personal protective equipment
Workplace Hazardous Material Information System (WHMIS)
safety or mechanical hazards
physical hazards
chemical hazards
biological hazards
ergonomic hazards
psychosocial hazards
occupational health physicians
occupational hygienists
ergonomist
safety professional
occupational health nursing
clinician/practitioner
administrator
educator
researcher
consultant
cost-benefit analysis
cost-effectiveness analysis
organizational culture

STUDY QUESTIONS

1. List the components of an effective occupational health and safety program.
2. Who are the members of the occupational health and safety team?
3. Outline the roles of the occupational health physician, occupational hygienist, and the safety professional.
4. Name the categories into which hazards are divided and give one example of each type of hazard.
5. What are the roles identified by Rogers for OHNs?
6. List the major competencies required by the CNA for OHNs.
7. Pick any one member of the occupational health and safety team and describe the similarities and differences between the focus of that member's role and an OHN's role.
8. What are the benefits of having an occupational nurse at the workplace for employees? for employers?
9. How are occupational health and community health similar?
10. Name five hazards to which CHNs may be exposed in their work setting. In addition, state the category of hazard for each.

INDIVIDUAL CRITICAL THINKING EXERCISES

1. What is your role and responsibility as a CHN for occupational health and safety at work?
2. Who is responsible for identifying hazards in the workplace?
3. As a CHN, how can you provide input into a joint health and safety committee?
4. Consider the linkages, similarities, and differences between community health nursing and occupational health nursing.

GROUP CRITICAL THINKING EXERCISES

1. How would you set up a joint health and safety committee in the community health unit? Why would you want to?
2. Identify the legislation pertinent to health and safety in your jurisdiction.
3. Using the Job Hazard Analysis form (Figure 11.1), identify five hazards in a community health nursing workplace. Specify the controls that could be used to eliminate or minimize exposure to these hazards.

REFERENCES

Alberta Human Resources and Employment, Workplace Health and Safety. (2002a). *All shook up—Understanding vibration.* Edmonton, AB: Author. Retrieved December 1, 2003 from **www3.gov.ab.ca/hre/whs/publications/pdf/erg026.pdf**

Alberta Human Resources and Employment, Workplace Health and Safety. (2002b). *Working in the heat.* Edmonton, AB: Author. Retrieved December 1, 2003 from **www3.gov.ab.ca/hre/whs/publications/pdf/mg022.pdf**

Alberta Occupational Health Nurses Association [n.d.]

Allen, R., Allen, J., Kraft, C., & Certner, B. (1987). *The organizational unconscious: How to create the corporate culture that you want and need.* Morristown, NJ: Human Resources Institute.

Allen, J., & Leutzinger, J. (1999). The role of culture change in health promotion. *The Art of Health Promotion, 3*(1).

American Association of Occupational Health Nurses. (1996). *Advisory: Cost benefit and cost effectiveness analysis.* Retrieved September 29, 2003 from **www.aaohn.org**

American Association of Occupational Health Nurses. (2003). *Occupational and Environmental Health Nursing Profession Fact Sheet.* Retrieved December 10, 2003 from **www.aaohn.org/press_room/fact_sheets/profession.cfm**

Association of Canadian Ergonomists. (2003). *Home page.* Retrieved March 16, 2003 from **www.ace.ergonomist.ca/**

Bachmann, K. (2000). *More than just hard hats and safety boots: Creating healthier work environments.* Ottawa, ON: Conference Board of Canada.

Board of Canadian Registered Safety Professionals. (2003). *Home page.* Retrieved March 16, 2003 from **www.bcrsp.ca/Designation/designation.html**

Canadian Centre for Occupational Health and Safety. (1997). *How workplace chemicals enter the body.* Retrieved March 16, 2003 from **www.ccohs.ca/oshanswers/chemicals/how_chem.html**

Canadian Centre for Occupational Health and Safety. (1999). *What is a joint health and safety committee?* Retrieved March 16, 2003 from **www.ccohs.ca/oshanswers/hsprograms/hscommittees/whatisa.html**

Canadian Centre for Occupational Health and Safety. (n.d., a). *Biological hazards.* Retrieved March 16, 2003 from **www.ccohs.ca/oshanswers/biol_hazards/**

Canadian Centre for Occupational Health and Safety. (n.d., b). *Ergonomics.* Retrieved March 16, 2003 from **www.ccohs.ca/oshanswers/ergonomics**

Canadian Centre for Occupational Health and Safety. (n.d., c). *Physical agents.* Retrieved March 16, 2003 from **www.ccohs.ca/oshanswers/phys_agents/**

Canadian Nurses Association. (2000). *Occupational Health Nursing Certification Exam Prep Guide.* Ottawa, ON: Canadian Nurses Association. Retrieved December 3, 2003 from **www.cna-nurses.ca/_frames/certification/certification_frame.html**

Canadian Occupational Health Nurses Association (COHNA-ACIIST). (2000a). *About us.* Retrieved December 10, 2003 from **www.cohna-aciist.ca**

Canadian Occupational Health Nurses Association (COHNA-ACIIST). (2000b). *Canadian occupational health nurses information booklet.* Author.

Canadian Occupational Health Nurses Association (COHNA-ACIIST). (2002). *Occupational health nursing practice guidelines.* Retrieved December 10, 2003 from **www.cohna-aciist.ca**

Doyle, B. (1997). *Introduction to occupational health nursing.* Edmonton, AB: Grant MacEwan College.

Federal Emergency Management Agency. (2003). *Emergency management guide for business & industry.* Retrieved March 12, 2003 from **www.fema.gov/librarybiz1.shtm**

Graziani, C. (1996). Defining "effectiveness" in health development. *Synergy: Canadian Initiatives for International Health, 8*(3), 1, 5.

Levy, B., & Wegman, D. (1995). *Occupational health: Recognizing and preventing work-related disease* (3rd ed.). Toronto, ON: Little, Brown.

Morris, J., & Smith, P. (2001). Demonstrating the cost effectiveness of an expert occupational and environmental nurse. *AAOHN Journal, 49*(12), 547–556.

O'Donnell, M. P. (2000). *How to design workplace health promotion programs* (5th ed.). West Bloomfield, MI: American Journal of Health Promotion.

Pratt, D. (2001). *The healthy scorecard: Delivering breakthrough results that employees and investors will love.* Victoria, BC: Trafford.

Rogers, B. (1994). *Occupational health nursing: Concepts and practice.* Toronto, ON: W.B. Saunders.

World Health Organization. (1999). *Occupational health: Ethically correct, economically sound.* Fact Sheet, 84. Retrieved March 12, 2003 from **www.who.int/oeh/OCHweb/OCHweb/OSHpages/OSHDocuments/Factsheets/Occupational%20Health.htm**

ADDITIONAL RESOURCES

WEBSITES

Canadian Nurses Association:
www.cna-aiic.ca/

Canadian Occupational Health Nurses Association:
www.cohna-aciist.ca

About the Authors

Sharon L. Chadwick, RN, BScN, MSc, COHN(C), COHN-S, has been working in the field of Occupational Health and Safety for over 14 years. Her varied experience in this specialty includes consulting, transportation, healthcare, and government. Sharon has also taught in the Occupational Health Nursing Certificate Program at Grant MacEwan College for over 10 years and has experience writing and developing courses for distance delivery. Currently, Sharon is Best Practices Specialist in the area of Workplace Health and Safety, Legislation, Policy and Technical Services for the Alberta Government. Sharon is also the current President of the Canadian Occupational Health Nurses Association/Association Canadienne des Infirmières et Infirmiers en Santé du Travail (COHNA/ACIIST) and is a member of the Canadian Nurses Association Certification Advisory Committee.

Bernice Doyle, RN, COHN(C), has been working in the Occupational Health Nursing specialty for over 20 years. Her experience includes working in a variety of industries including government. She also has experience writing and developing occupational health nursing courses for distance delivery and teaching occupational health nursing students. Currently, Ms. Doyle is a manager in the Workplace Health and Safety Policy and Standards Branch for the Alberta Government as well as a part-time instructor in the Occupational Health Nursing Program at Grant MacEwan College, Edmonton, Alberta.

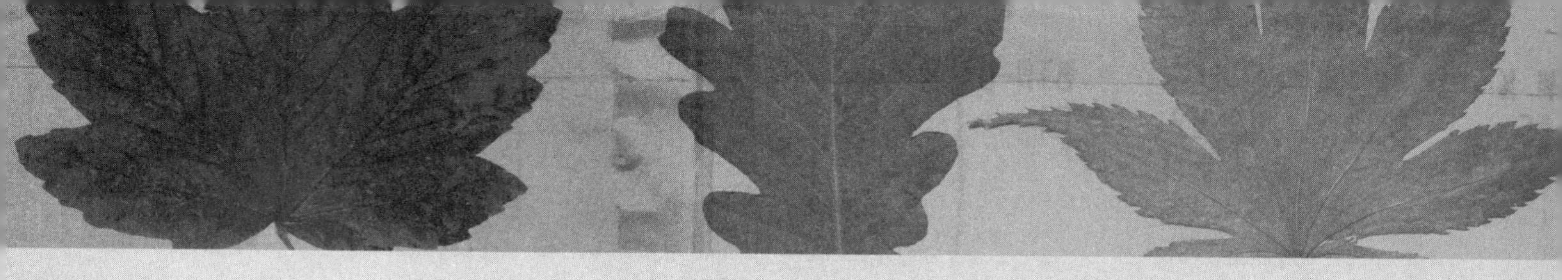

CHAPTER 12

Communicable Diseases

Patricia Malloy and Lucia Yiu

OBJECTIVES

AFTER STUDYING THIS CHAPTER, YOU SHOULD BE ABLE TO:

1. Discuss the changing perspectives of communicable diseases.
2. Explain the different modes of transmission of diseases through an epidemiological approach.
3. Identify natural history and patterns of disease in a community.
4. Describe contact tracing and surveillance in the control and management of communicable diseases.
5. Describe the role of the community health nurse in the control and management of communicable diseases.
6. Discuss the WHO priorities in communicable disease management.

INTRODUCTION

As long as humans have inhabited the earth, communicable diseases have been a part of their lives. Communicable diseases occur in every society, from rural areas to urban cities, from country to country, and without discrimination between the rich and poor. With advances in technology and modern medicine, the severity of the illnesses associated with many of these diseases has been reduced. However, with increasing population mobility due to efficient transportation systems, and with lifestyle and environment changes, communicable diseases from far away countries now threaten Canadians. Community health nurses (CHNs) must have a sound knowledge base of communicable diseases in order to prevent the transmission of these diseases and protect the health of the public. This chapter will describe the general concepts of communicable diseases and discuss the role of CHNs in communicable disease control and management in relation to the legislative mandate within our Canadian health care system.

CHANGING PERSPECTIVES ON COMMUNICABLE DISEASES

For many centuries, communicable diseases such as syphilis, tuberculosis, smallpox, leprosy, cholera, scarlet fever, typhoid, diphtheria, and poliomyelitis have caused many casualties and threatened the health of mankind. The first recorded worldwide threat from a communicable disease was bubonic plague, which killed about 1/3 of the population in Europe in the thirteenth century. More recently, the influenza epidemic in 1918 was a major global threat, resulting in 20 million deaths worldwide (Chin, 2000).

Many communicable diseases were brought to Canada with the arrival and migration of early settlers in the sixteenth century. The Aboriginals at that time had little or no resistance to these diseases. Living with poor hygiene practices and crowded conditions, the Aboriginal peoples were decimated by the infectious and parasitic diseases carried by the settlers.

Since the mid-1800s, advances in scientific and medical knowledge and public health measures have contributed to the declining mortality and morbidity among Canadians from communicable diseases. The development of microscopes, germ theories, and vaccines and the improvement of nutrition, sanitation, and living conditions were instrumental in this decline (Allemang, 2000; Allender & Spradley, 2001). Additionally, the 1974 World Health Organization's (WHO) Expanded Program on Immunization initiative led to the immunization of 85% of the children around the world against measles, mumps, rubella, tetanus, pertussis, diphtheria, and poliomyelitis by 1985. It also successfully eradicated smallpox in 1977 (WHO, 1998). Despite these successes, the WHO continues its efforts to combat infectious diseases that cause life-long disabilities and socioeconomic consequences, such as malaria, tuberculosis, and parasitic and infectious diseases in developing countries (WHO, 2003a).

Over the years, Canada has seen similar trends in its mortality patterns. What were once the top two leading causes of death for Canada, influenza and tuberculosis, are gradually being replaced by chronic illnesses such as cancer and heart diseases (see Table 12.1).

Emerging new infectious diseases are now challenging the public health system in many nations. The most recent infectious diseases in Canada are AIDS, West Nile virus, bovine spongiform encephalopathy (BSE or mad cow disease), and severe acute respiratory syndrome (SARS). The first case of AIDS in Canada was diagnosed in 1979. Between 1979 and 2002, there were 19 123 AIDS cases and 12 674 deaths in Canada. Mortality from AIDS peaked in 1995 with 1481 deaths. With modern medicine and increasing public

TABLE 12.1
Leading Causes of Death in Canada

1900[1]	1925[2]	2000[3]
Influenza	Cardiovascular/renal diseases	Cancer
Tuberculosis	Influenza/bronchitis/ pneumonia	Heart diseases
Diarrhea	Disease of early infancy	Cardiovascular
Heart diseases	Tuberculosis	Bronchitis
Stroke	Cancer	Accidents

1. *Nagnur, D., & Nagrodski, M. (1990). Epidemiologic transition in the context of demographic change: the evolution of Canadian mortality patterns.* Canadian Studies in Population, *17(1). Office of Population Research, Princeton University. Edmonton: Canada.*

2. *Fraser, R. D. (1999, July 29.) B35-50. Average annual number of deaths and death rates for leading causes of death, Canada, for five-year periods, 1921 to 1974. In F. H. Leacy (Ed.), Historical statistics Canada. SOURCE: for 1921 to 1974, Statistics Canada,* Vital Statistics, *vol. III,* Deaths, *(Catalogue 84-206). Retrieved on Dec 20, 2003 from http://www.statcan.ca/english/freepub/11-516-XIE/sectionb/sectionb.htm#health*

3. *Statistics Canada. (2003).* 2003 Canada at a glance. *A publication of Communications Divisions, Catalogue no. 12-581-XPE. Retrieved December 20, 2003 from http://www.statcan.ca/english/freepub/12-581-XIE/12-581-XIE03001.pdf*

awareness, only 61 AIDS deaths were reported in 2002 (Health Canada, 2003b).

Ironically, when treatment protocols to cure tuberculosis were developed in 1948, people hoped the disease would be eradicated by 2000. This old disease has now re-emerged as a new public health threat because of the multi-drug-resistant strains and non-compliant clients to chemotherapy. It affects vulnerable populations such as women, children, and elderly and those who are homeless, poor, or with immune deficiencies. Today's global travel and trade, climate changes, poverty, weakened health systems following political changes, ineffective vector control programs, overuse of antibiotics (WHO, 2000), efficient transportation systems, and changing lifestyle practices have led to transmission of infectious diseases within a very short time.

AN EPIDEMIOLOGICAL PERSPECTIVE IN DISEASE TRANSMISSION

Communicable diseases are illnesses caused by a "specific infectious agent or its toxic products that arises through transmission of that agent or its products from an infected person, animal, or reservoir to a susceptible host, either directly or indirectly through an intermediate plant or animal host, vector, or the inanimate environment" (Health Canada, 2003c). There are four main categories of **infectious agents** that can cause diseases: bacteria, fungi, parasites, and viruses (Stanhope & Lancaster, 2004). Susceptible **hosts** are people and animals who can get the particular disease. **Infected hosts** carry the infectious agent, playing an important role in its successful transmission in the right environment, with the end result being infection. The biological characteristics of a host play an important role in determining susceptibility. These characteristics include age, gender, general health status, genetic make-up, and specific immunity. The general health status of the host includes stage of development, stress, nutritional status, and presence of other diseases or illnesses.

Once the infectious agent has invaded, the infected host becomes the vessel or shelter for the agent to multiply and spread throughout the body. Infection can only occur if the degree of exposure is sufficient and/or the host possesses biological factors that affect its ability to defend itself against the infectious agent. An organism's ability to invade a susceptible host lies in the organism's **infectivity** (ability to invade and multiply in a host), **pathogenicity** (ability to induce disease), **virulence** (a measure of the severity of the disease), and **immunogenicity** (ability to induce specific immunity). These will be further discussed later.

The host's immune response can protect it from contracting infections. **Natural immunity** is innate; the host naturally possesses resistance against certain infections. Hosts may also possess **acquired immunity** through passive or active immunization that protects them against infections. In **active immunization**, the host is exposed to a live pathogen (such as a vaccine or infectious agent) and antibodies develop as a result of the primary immune response. For example, a person is exposed to chickenpox, gets the disease, and then has immunity to chickenpox. A **vaccine**, a substance that contains the antigen, can artificially induce acquired active immunity by stimulating a primary response against the anti-

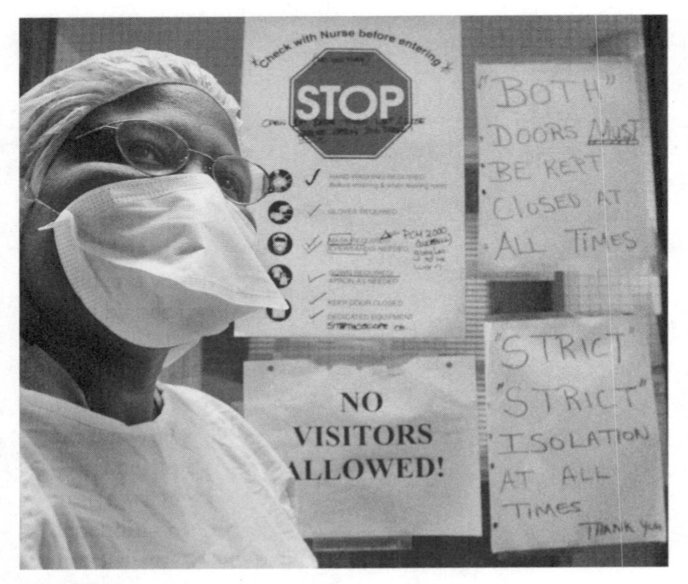

PHOTO 12.1

A Toronto nurse wearing a mask during SARS outbreak.

Credit: CP (Kevin Frayer)

gen without causing symptoms of the disease. **Passive immunization** is gained through maternal transmission of antibodies to infants, for example, through breastfeeding, or through administration of immune globulin. Injecting antibodies that are not produced by the recipient's cells gives short-term, artificially acquired passive immunity. Immune globulin (containing the antibodies to a particular disease) is administered after a person has been exposed to certain communicable diseases. Naturally acquired passive immunity occurs during pregnancy in which certain antibodies are passed from the mother into the fetal bloodstream. **Herd immunity** refers to the resistance of a population group against the spread of an infection. For example, if enough people in the community are immunized against hepatitis B, it is more difficult for the infectious agent to spread to those not immunized.

The **environment**, where the host lives, also affects the transmission of the agent and the susceptibility of the host to the agent. Environmental factors include socio-cultural, employment, biological, and physical variables external to the host. For example, if a person resides in an area where mosquitoes are prevalent, their risk of exposure to West Nile virus is higher than that of a person who resides in an area with fewer mosquitoes. Employment, for example, was an issue during the SARS outbreak in Toronto in the spring of 2003. During this period, health care workers were at greater risk for acquiring SARS than the general public was, since transmission over time became limited to the health care setting. Country of origin can also play a part in the treatment of a communicable disease or in the infecting organism. For example, a person who emigrates from a developing country, such as China or India, to Canada has a greater likelihood of having drug-resistant tuberculosis (TB) when compared with a person born in Canada. This is related to different treatment regimens utilized in the developing countries that predispose those people receiving TB therapy to resistant strains of the infectious agent. Living arrangements can affect the degree of exposure. Living in crowded spaces, such as a shelter, rooming house, or dormitory, can increase people's degree of exposure to communicable diseases.

Mode of Transmission

Prevention through control and management of communicable diseases is achieved through breaking links in the chain of infection. The **chain of infection process** includes the causative or infectious agent, the reservoir, the portal of exit of the agent from the reservoir, the mode of transmission of the agent, the portal of entry into the susceptible host, and the infected host (see Figure 12.1). A sequential order is necessary for the chain to be complete. If the order is disturbed or the links are broken, then the infectious disease process is incomplete and the chain of infection is broken. Each step in the chain of infection and the role of the CHN will be discussed in this chapter.

Some communicable diseases are passed on by direct or indirect contact with infected hosts or with their excretions. Most diseases are spread through contact or close proximity because the causative bacteria or viruses are airborne. This spread is referred to as transmission. **Transmission** is the manner in which the agent communicates from one vertebrate host to another. This can occur through direct contact, droplet, airborne, and indirect contact (common vehicle and vectorborne).

For **direct transmission** to occur, physical contact is necessary between the infected individual and the susceptible host. Examples include skin-to-skin contact such as shaking hands and kissing and exchange of body fluids such as through sexual intercourse, which may spread syphilis, HIV, and other sexually transmitted diseases. In **droplet transmission**, the agent is shed by respiratory secretions and the droplets are greater than five microns in diameter. For transmission to occur, the infected host and the susceptible host need to be less than one metre apart so that the droplets can be inhaled or have direct contact with other mucous membranes such as eyes. Diseases that are transmitted via this route include *Haemophilus influenzae* type B and *Neisseria meningitidis.*

Indirect transmission uses an intermediate object as the vehicle of transmission, such as unwashed hands between patients, contaminated instruments, or other inanimate objects like toys. Examples of diseases transmitted via indirect contact include rotavirus, other gastrointestinal diseases, and those in which the agent is shed via feces.

Common vehicle transmission refers to the transmission of a single contaminated source from an infected host to a susceptible host or hosts via food, water, contaminated medication or intravenous fluids. Transmission by this route can result in widespread outbreaks. Many people in Walkerton, Ontario experienced the transmission of *E. coli* O157:H7 in their contaminated water supply. Seven people died and more than 2300 became ill in May 2000 after drinking contaminated water (O'Connor, 2002). Other diseases transmitted in this manner include typhoid, diphtheria, and salmonella.

Horizontal transmission is defined as the person-to-person transmission of an organism via direct contact, indirect contact, airborne, vectorborne, or common vehicles. Sexually transmitted diseases and common colds are examples of horizontal transmission. **Vertical transmission** is defined

FIGURE 12.1 Chain of Infection

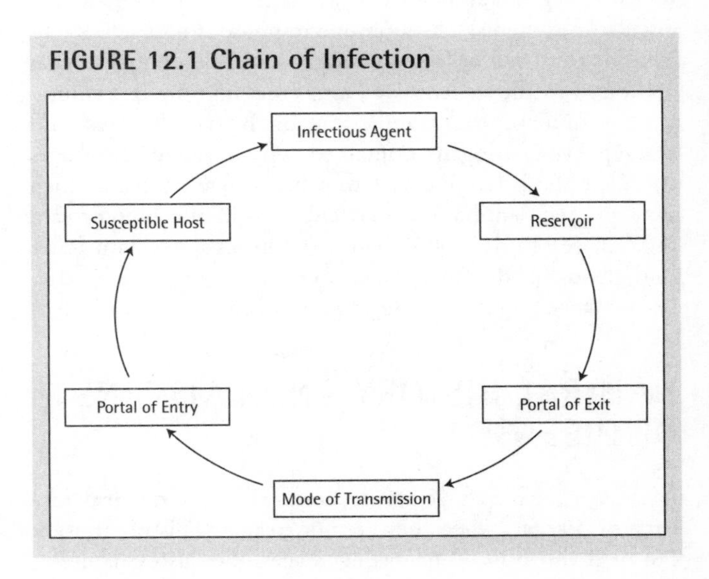

as transmission of an infection from mother to infant via placenta, breast milk, or contact in the vaginal canal at birth (Stanhope & Lancaster, 2004). HIV and rubella are viruses that are transmitted from mothers to infants.

Vectorborne transmission refers to diseases transmitted by insects. The insects can serve as either the vehicle or they themselves may actually be infected with the organism. Houseflies can transport organisms from feces to food. West Nile virus and malaria are both transmitted by mosquitoes from an infected host to a susceptible host.

Airborne transmission involves aerosolization of the organism into the air. The droplets are less than five microns in diameter and the distance between the infected host and susceptible host does not affect transmission of the organism. Tuberculosis, measles, varicella, and smallpox are examples of diseases that are transmitted in this manner.

Infectious Agents

Organisms are characterized by how they enter the host, how well they survive during transmission, how fast they multiply after entering (virulence), and how effective the body is in battling the organism. Infectivity refers to the ability of the organism to enter the host, multiply within the host, and then cause tissue damage. Entry into the host is related to the mode of transmission of the organism, the susceptibility of the host to receiving the organism, and the environment needed to multiply. All factors need to be in place before the organism can "infect" the host.

The pathogenicity of an organism is related to its survival in the environment during transmission between hosts and its ability to attach or adhere to receptor surfaces, to proliferate locally, to damage local tissues, to invade and disseminate, and to alter the cell membrane of the host cell. Virulence is the degree to which the organism multiplies when invasion is successful as well as the organism's ability to survive between hosts. Virulence is closely related to pathogenicity.

Immunogenicity is the host's ability to respond to the infectious agent (antigen) when it enters the lymphatic and circulatory systems. This immune response is induced, mediated, or regulated by T lymphocytes and B lymphocytes that are found in the spleen, liver, and bone marrow. T lymphocytes stimulate the production of B lymphocytes and macrophages. Antigens contained within the macrophages stimulate the B lymphocytes to produce plasma cells, which then produce antibodies, that circulate in the bloodstream (Craven & Hirnle, 2003). Thus, the **immune system** refers to the body's ability to make antibodies to destroy or neutralize the bacterial or viral infective organism.

NATURAL HISTORY AND PATTERNS OF DISEASE

Diseases have a natural progression, called the **natural history of disease**, when they are not treated. This progression can be divided into four distinct stages. (See also Chapter 7, Figure 7.4.)

- The **stage of susceptibility** occurs before the onset of symptoms when the host has contact with the infectious agent. Prevention depends on the host's ability to fight the infection. If the host does not have the capacity to do this, the disease and host then move into the next stage.
- The **incubation period**, during which the organism replicates, is the time interval between exposure to the infection and the onset of the symptoms of the disease.
- During the **stage of presymptomatic disease, or prodromal stage**, the person still does not display signs or complain of symptoms associated with the disease. Transmission may occur during this stage if there is sufficient replication of the organism and a way for the organism to reach the next host. When this occurs, the host is called a **carrier**, a person who transmits an organism without displaying symptoms of the disease.
- Next, the **stage of clinical disease** occurs when the signs and symptoms are visible and vary in degree of severity. Diagnosis and treatment is usually possible at this stage.
- During the **stage of diminished capacity**, the body either begins to convalesce or bears residual disability after the symptoms have disappeared. **Residual disability** is temporary or permanent complications from the disease. For example, poliomyelitis can leave a person with the permanent complication of having difficulty with weight bearing.
- The **convalescent period** occurs when the person has not returned to their former level of health, yet the clinical symptoms have gone.

Patterns of disease are related to geography and population density and affected by global variation, variations within nations, and local patterns of disease. Temporal patterns of disease also occur as infective organisms arise during certain seasons or temperatures, accounting for seasonal variation (Dowell, 2001). An **outbreak** occurs when the new cases of a disease exceed the normal occurrence during a given period of time. For example, measles outbreaks are common in the spring in school-age children who have not been immunized (Dowell, 2001). **Endemic** refers to the steady presence of a disease in a defined geographic area or population group. An example is the presence of tuberculosis among the foreign-born Canadians (Gushulak & MacPherson, 2000). Spatial (geographic location), temporal (time of day or season), and demographic patterns are the where, when, and who of people who have the potential to be infected with a disease. Occasionally, the occurrence of a disease (e.g., flu) is higher than what would be expected normally; this is called an **epidemic**. More rarely, a disease spreads and affects a large number of populations worldwide, such as the Spanish flu, SARS, and AIDS. This is referred to as a **pandemic**.

Preventing the transmission of communicable diseases is key to controlling the number people infected with the organism and breaking that link in the chain of infection. Understanding the infectious agent's characteristics can help health care personnel diagnose, control, and manage the communicable disease. Table 12.2 summarizes several of the common communicable diseases in Canada.

TABLE 12.2
Selected Communicable Diseases in Canada

Disease	Infectious Agent	Mode of Transmission	Incubation	Clinical Presentation	Period of Communicability	Control Measures
Acquired immuno-deficiency syndrome (AIDS)	Human immuno-deficiency virus (HIV), types 1 and 2 (retrovirus)	Unprotected intercourse with an infected person; inoculation with or exposure to infected blood, other body fluids, needle stick injuries/sharing; from infected woman to the fetus during pregnancy or breastfeeding	3 weeks to 20yrs+ (average 10 years)	Initially, mononucleosis-like illness for a week or two; may then be free of clinical signs or symptoms for months or years before developing Pneumocystis carinii pneumonia, opportunistic infections and cancers	From onset of infection and persists for life.	• Contact tracing and HIV testing • Public education • Zidovudine (AZT), dideoxycytidine, (DDC) and dideoxyinosine (DDI) treatment including prophylaxis for the opportunistic infectious diseases that result from HIV infection • Recommendations for HIV postexposure prophylaxias include a basic four-week regimen of two drugs (zidovudine plus lamivudine, stavudine plus lamivudine, or stavudine plus didanosine) for most HIV exposures and an expanded regimen that includes the addition of a third antiretoviral drug for HIV exposures that pose an increased risk of transmission
Chickenpox (varicella)	Varicella zoster	Airborne through respiratory secretions or direct or indirect contact from vesicle fluid of person with varicella-zoster	10–21 days	Low grade fever, maculopapular rash in trunk, face, scalp, mucous membrane of mouth then changed to vesicular for 3–4 days	2–5 days before onset of rash and until skin lesions have crusted	• Exclude from childcare, school or work at least 7 days after eruption first appears • Avoid contact with immunosuppressed persons
Diphtheria	*Corynebacterium diphtheriae*	Droplet spread through direct contact with a patient or carrier or indirect contact with articles soiled with nasopharyngeal secretions	2–5 days	Greyish spots on tonsils; sore throat, enlarged and tender cervical lymph nodes; marked swelling and oedema of the neck in severe cases	If untreated, 2 weeks to several months	• Offer needed immunization to contacts, surveillance for 7 days • Throat culture • Erythromycin treatment for infected persons • Isolate until two cultures taken more than 24–48 hours apart are negative after the cessation of antibiotics; or isolate for l4 days if no culture available • Disinfect contact articles
Hemophilus influenza type B	*H. influenza* type B (Hib)	Droplet infection and discharges from nasopharyngeal discharges	Unknown, probably short, 2–4 days	Upper respiratory obstruction, fever, bulging fontanelle in infants, stiff back and neck in older children, epiglottitis, meningitis, bacteremia, septic arthritis, cellulitis	Most infectious in the week prior to onset of illness and during the illness until treated	• Early surveillance on children under six to prompt early medical treatment as needed • Provide needed immunization and antibiotic prophylaxis

continued

TABLE 12.2 *Continued*

Disease	Infectious Agent	Mode of Transmission	Incubation	Clinical Presentation	Period of Communicability	Control Measures
Hepatitis A	Hepatitis A virus (HAV)	Direct or indirect contact through fecal–oral route transmission, through contaminated water, or non-cooked food contaminated by infectious food handlers.	15–50 days, range is 28–30 days	Non-jaundiced in infants, acute febrile nausea, anorexia, diarrhea, lethargy, abdominal discomfort, jaundice	2 weeks before to 1 week after onset of symptoms	• Exclude from school or work for 1 week following onset of illness • Health education, immunoglobulin treatment, contact tracing
Hepatitis B	Hepatitis B virus (HBV)	Sexual, perinatal and percutaneous exposure through blood, serum and vaginal fluids	60–90 days, range is 45–180 days	Insidious onset of symptoms, nausea, vomiting, anorexia, lethargy, abdominal discomfort, jaundice	Many weeks before onset of symptoms, may persist for life	• Pre-exposure vaccination to at-risk populations; vaccination to susceptible sexual contacts • Exclusion from work and school until diagnosis confirmed • Give HBIG treatment to contacts as needed.
Measles	Measles virus (morbillivirus)	Airborne by droplet spread or by direct contact with infected nasal or throat secretions	8–14 days	Fever ≥38°C, cough, runny nose, conjunctivitis, Koplik's spots on buccal muscosa, red blotching rash appearing on 3rd to 7th day, beginning on face then generalizing to body	1-2 days before onset of symptoms to 4 days after appearance of rash	• Exclude from childcare or school at least 5 days after first appearance of rash • Check immunization of all close contacts and offer vaccination within 72 h of contact for non-immune persons
Meningo-coccal infections	*Neisseria meningitidis*	Direct contact including airborne droplets from nose and throat of infected persons	2–10 days	Acute onset of meningitis and septicaemia with fever, intense headache, nausea, vomiting, stiff neck, purpuric rash on trunk and limbs and body, joint pain	Until 24 hours of effective therapy has been received	• Prompt treatment Parenteral penicillin followed by 24-h respiratory isolation • Close surveillance of all close contacts and exclusion from school or work until at least 2 days after chemotherapy
Mono-nucleosis	Epstein-Barr virus (EBV)	Person-to-person spread by oropharyngeal route via saliva; indirect contact with infected saliva on toys or hands	30–50 days	Asymptomatic in young children; in young adults: fever, exudative pharyngitis, lymphadenopathy, hepatosplenomegaly	A year or more after infection; healthy adults may be long-term oropharyngeal carriers	• Isolation or surveillance not necessary • Disinfect articles soiled with nose and throat discharge
Mumps	Mumps virus (paramyxovirus)	Droplet spread and direct contact with saliva of an infected person	12–25 days	Swelling of salivary glands, orchitis, fever	2 days before to 9 days after onset	• Exclude from childcare, school, or workplace • Isolation not necessary
Pertussis	*Bordetella pertussis*	Direct contact via airborne or droplet spread from respiratory discharges of infected persons	6–20 days, usually 7–10 days	Whooping cough, little fever, non-specific respiratory tract infection in infants	To three weeks after onset of paroxysms if not treated	• Exclude from childcare or school until at least 5 days after a minimum of the 14-day erythromycin treatment • Immunize non-immune infants and children

continued

TABLE 12.2 *Continued*

Disease	Infectious Agent	Mode of Transmission	Incubation	Clinical Presentation	Period of Communicability	Control Measures
Poliomyelitis	Poliovirus, types 1, 2 and 3 (enterovirus)	Direct contact via fecal-oral route where sanitation is poor; pharyngeal spread more common during epidemics and when sanitation is good	3–21 days	Fever, malaise, headache, nausea and vomiting, muscle pain, stiffness of the neck and back with or without flaccid paralysis	Greatest for 7–10 days after onset of symptoms, and up to six weeks or longer	• Isolate • Exclude from school for at least 14 days after onset of illness • Disinfect throat discharges and fecal soiled articles • Vaccinate all non-immunized close contacts
Rubella	Rubella virus	Droplet or direct spread with infected persons through pharyngeal secretions	7–18 days	Fever (≤38.3°C), diffuse, punctate maculopapular skin rash. Malaise, headache, coryza, and conjunctivitis more common in adults	7 days before to 4 days after onset of rash	• Contact should avoid pregnant women • Exclude from school at least 5 days after onset of rash • Routine MMR immunization as preventive measure
Severe Acute Respiratory Sydrome (SARS)	Corona virus	Direct or indirect transmission of respiratory secretions via droplet or air-borne through close contact with a symptomatic person	2–10 days	Sudden onset of high fever (≥40°C), malaise, headache, cough, shortness of breath, sore throat, diarrhea	Early symptoms up to 10 days after fever subsides	• Wear mask; isolation; hand washing • Active daily surveillance for 10 days • Quarantine of close contacts for 10 days • Public education and traveller advisory and screening
Tetanus	*Clostridium tetani*	Bacterial spores may be introduced through contaminated puncture wounds, lacerations, burns, trivial wounds or injected contaminated street drugs	2 days–2 months	Painful muscular contractions generalized from site of injury to back muscles; lockjaw; respiration and laryngeal spasm	Not transmitted from person to person. Spores enter and devitalize tissues in infected wound	• Use IV tetanus immune globulin (TIG) and penicillin in large doses for 14 days • Adequate wound debridement
Tuberculosis	*Mycobacterium tuberculosis* (rarely *Mycobacterium bovis)*	Droplet spread from person with pulmonary TB through respiratory secretion; infection through muscous membranes or damaged skin, ingestion of unpasteurized milk, or contact with infectious urine from persons with renal TB	2 weeks–24 months, highly variable	Fever, night sweats, chronic cough with haemoptysis, weight loss, or no symptoms	As long as organisms are still in sputum	• Screening with tuiberculin testing/x-rays amongst the at-risk populations • Contact tracing • Provide adequate anti-TB chemotherapy and prophylactic treatments • Follow-up and encourage compliance to follow prescribed treatments

Sources: Health Canada, Population and Public Health Branch. (1999). Routine practices and additional precautions for preventing the transmission of infection in health care: Revision of isolation and precaution techniques. Canada Communicable Diseases Report, 25S4. *Retrieved December 4, 2003 from http://www.hc-sc.gc.ca/pphb-dgspsp/publicat/ccdr-rmtc/99vol25/25s4/index.html*
Pickering, L. K. (Ed.). (2003). Red book: 2003 report of the Committee on Infectious Diseases *(26th ed.). Elk Grove Village, IL: American Academy of Pediatrics.*
Government of Victoria Australia. (1997). The blue book: Guidelines for the control of communicable diseases. *Retrieved December 14, 2003 from http://www.dhs.vic.gov.au/phb/hprot/inf_dis/bluebook/index.htm*

CONTROL AND MANAGEMENT OF COMMUNICABLE DISEASES

The successful control and management of communicable diseases are intricately tied to using sound principles of epidemiology (see Chapter 7). **Surveillance** of a disease involves ongoing data collection and monitoring and evaluating all aspects of occurrences and infectivity of the disease essential for effective control and management (Chin, 2000). Through data analysis, the investigator may uncover the cause or source of the disease. For example, investigating a case of salmonella infection may uncover a contaminated food item in a restaurant.

While some infectious diseases are common and mild (such as the common cold or pediculosis), others are serious enough to be defined as **notifiable diseases**, which must be reported to the local health officials. Health care personnel are mandated by the provinces and territories to report all notifiable disease, but reporting to the federal level is voluntary. The list of notifiable diseases is reviewed regularly and approved by provincial and federal health authorities (Health Canada, 2003c). Notifiable diseases will be discussed further later in the chapter.

Effective control and management are achieved through multiple resources and partnerships within the community, health system, and civic governments. **Contact tracing** (beginning with interviewing the patient to discover the close "contacts," people who may have been exposed to the disease), surveillance, and **quarantine** (keeping contacts isolated from each other and from the rest of the community) are ways to control and manage the transmission. Administering vaccines to susceptible people for those vaccine-preventable diseases can help control communicable diseases.

CHNs play a major role in the control and management of communicable diseases. They must know the principles of communicable diseases and be proactive and effective in protecting and improving the health of their communities through prevention, diagnosis, control, and surveillance.

Contact Tracing

After a notifiable communicable disease is reported to the local health unit, the infected person is interviewed by a CHN or designate regarding contacts (people who were exposed to

CASE STUDY

As you listen to the news one evening you hear, "Anyone who has been in contact with Mrs. T., please report to the nearest ER for evaluation." You wonder why they would say the person's name on the radio. The next day, the news broadcast states, "Anyone who has been in contact with Mrs. T. in the last ten days and is now experiencing a cough, fever, and headache, do not go to the ER, call your local health authority."

You started working at the local health authority two months ago. Your role is to develop an educational program about vaccine-preventable diseases. When you arrive at work the morning after hearing the news about Mrs. T., a staff meeting is called. The information presented at the meeting pertains to Mrs. T. and an acute respiratory infection called SARS, a disease that was first identified in Southeast Asia. Mrs. T., recently returned from Hong Kong, died six days ago, and her son is in hospital in critical care. Little is known about the transmission of SARS: possibly airborne or contact. Some of the symptoms associated with SARS are known, but it remains unclear about the order of their appearance. At this point, the local health authority is placing staff on alert; they may be moved from their current roles to work with SARS.

The next morning another person has been diagnosed with SARS. The provincial health authority has issued a code orange (all health care providers must be ready to report to work). You are directed to report to the central SARS command area. More information has been received and it is now necessary to put all SARS contacts in quarantine for 10 days. During these 10 days, those in quarantine must have no contact with other household members. If contact is necessary, a special mask (N-95) must be worn. Contacts are instructed to monitor their temperatures twice daily, and if the temperature goes up or other symptoms appear, they are directed to report to a SARS clinic.

Your role is to visit one hospital each day to collect information on admitted patients with suspected or probable SARS. The information collected includes name of contact, location of this contact (hospital, household, or other activity), symptoms (especially the order of appearance of the symptoms), and treatment. Other CHNs are collecting similar information at other locations. Reviewing the collected data reveals that one hospital is the source of the majority of the contacts, the contacts occurred on the same day, and headache is the first symptom. The provincial health authority closes this hospital to visitors and new admissions. All other hospitals begin screening all people who enter their institution. Visitors are restricted, clinical activity is reduced, and more people are placed in quarantine. Scientists have just discovered that SARS is a virus, transmitted by droplet contact.

One week later, another cluster of contacts is identified; this cluster met at a funeral home. A health care provider from the closed hospital, who had not been placed in quarantine, had attended a funeral there.

Discussion Questions

1. Do you think that the public needed to know Mrs. T's name? If so, did this help or hinder the contact tracing?
2. Why was it necessary to reassign CHNs to work on SARS?
3. Could an event like this happen again?

the patient during the incubation period of the disease, as well as contacts who may already be ill with the disease). The CHN must know the mode of transmission, incubation period, and infective period of the particular disease to order to discover all the contacts. The initial case definition must be formulated based on three elements: host with exhibiting signs and symptoms, and place and time of exposure. The list of contacts must be analyzed to identify the **index case** or first case. Then, a list of contacts must be collected from the index case. With this list, the local health authority proceeds with further assessment and investigation and follows up with treatment as deemed necessary. For example, when investigating a case of HIV/AIDS, the CHN must ask about contacts as far back as three months ago, not just recent contacts. When performing a contact tracing for measles, the CHN would include those people who were in contact with the infectious agent seven days prior to the outbreak of the rash. The degree of exposure (the time spent with the infected person) and where it took place are included in the collected data. Not all communicable diseases warrant contact tracing (e.g., pediculosis, chickenpox).

Contact tracing is a response to disease reporting. As such, it is more comprehensive and inclusive of the population when the community comprehends the scope of the issue. The report is only as reliable and accurate as the person relaying the information and the parameters required for reporting. That is, if the doctor or nurse is unsure of the signs and symptoms of a disease, no report is given. If they report vague symptoms that could be a communicable disease, surveillance and contact tracing may be delayed. Also, if the report system is not uniform in collecting the necessary data, contact tracing may be delayed. Education of doctors and nurses helps to ensure detailed disease reporting.

During the SARS outbreak that occurred in Toronto during March through May of 2003, quarantine acts of the federal and Ontario ministries of health allowed the Health and Safety Commissioner, Dr. James Young, and the Public Health Commissioner, Dr. Colin D'Cuhna, to conduct contact tracing in a public forum by naming those with SARS in the public media. Their purpose was to protect the public as well as notify contacts of those first patients and health care facilities to come forward. Although contact tracing might be viewed as an infringement of a person's right to privacy, it is necessary to contain the spread of the organism.

Surveillance

The listing of contacts is assisted by active or passive surveillance. During **active surveillance,** the local health authority department or designate conducts interviews and collects data. Active surveillance may occur in response to the identification of an outbreak or the notification to the local health authority unit of a communicable disease. Active surveillance is best illustrated by the SARS outbreak. When SARS was first reported in November 2002, the World Health Organization globally applied public health measures to control and manage the spread of this new communicable disease. By July 2003, 774 deaths had occurred among the 8098 reported cases worldwide; Canada had 43 deaths among the 251 reported cases in Ontario (World Health Organization, 2003). The surveillance of SARS was conducted by the Ontario Ministry of Health partly through the development of a screening tool (Table 12.3) that used the principles of epidemiology. Sections A and B of this tool collect data on the epidemiologic risk factors. Section C asks about symptoms associated with SARS.

People with symptoms but without an epidemiologic link did not fulfill the criteria for a possible investigation of SARS. This is because the symptoms ascribed to SARS are not unique; they resemble symptoms of many other respiratory infections. A link had to be made between the potential patient and an original SARS case, a SARS-affected health care facility, or a SARS-affected country. Hospital employees informed local health officials and the Ministry of Health and Long Term Care in Ontario of potential SARS patients. Local health authorities conducted interviews with these patients. Once the patients were identified and quarantined, surveillance consisted of twice-daily telephone calls to the quarantined patients.

In Canada, the Quarantine and Migration Health Act and the Department of Health Act provide the necessary legislation to enact active surveillance. Both are federal acts that fall under the jurisdiction of the Federal Minister of Health. The Department of Health Act provides for the protection of the people of Canada against risks to health and the transmission of disease. The Quarantine Act was amended in May 2003 after the SARS outbreak. These amendments include the distribution of education and screening materials on SARS to incoming and outgoing flights. The list of airports with direct international flights was extended and these airports were asked to report to the local health authority before planes could land with cases of illness or death. As well, SARS was added to the Quarantine Act's schedule of infectious and contagious diseases. Currently, the list includes the bubonic plague, cholera, smallpox, and yellow fever (Health Canada, 2003a; 2003d).

Monitoring of diseases, investigation of disease outbreaks, and research into diseases are responsibilities of local health authorities. The Health Canada Act transfers the responsibility of providing health care delivery and services to the provinces through transfer funds. Each province manages or bears the responsibility for the health of their constituents. For example, in Ontario, individual counties operate local health authority units and report to the province. This process is different from that in British Columbia, which operates and dispatches the necessary manpower to manage local health authorities.

Passive surveillance relies on the health care provider to notify the local health authority unit of signs and symptoms associated with communicable diseases. Passive surveillance also relies on laboratory test results if the disease or infectious agent is in the Reportable Disease list. It differs from active surveillance in which the local authority is actively looking for people with signs and symptoms. The completeness of the notification report depends on health care workers' ability to recognize signs and symptoms and their interest in providing a comprehensive report (Doyle, Glynn, & Groseclose, 2002). A report must include all the necessary demographics of the person, the symptoms and date of onset of the presenting

TABLE 12.3
SARS Screening Tool

Severe Acute Respiratory Syndrome (SARS) SCREENING TOOL For Ontario Healthcare Settings

The screening tool must be completed by
all persons entering this facility.

SECTION A:

1. Have you had contact with a person with SARS in the last 10 days while not wearing protection against SARS? **OR** ❐No ❐Yes → Quarantine applies, notify Public Health
2. Within the last 10 days have you been in a health care facility while it was closed due to SARS? **OR**
3. Have you been to a potential SARS exposure site (see www.health.gov.on.ca) during the exposure period? **OR**
4. Are you under quarantine, or have you been contacted by Public Health and put on home-isolation?

SECTION B:

Have you been to [INSERT AFFECTED AREAS (see www.health.gov.on.ca) in the last 10 days?

❐No ❐Yes

SECTION C: Are you experiencing any of the following symptoms?

- Unexplained myalgia (muscle aches) **OR**
- Unexplained malaise (severe tiredness or unwell) **OR**
- Severe headache (worse than usual) **OR**
- Cough (onset within 7 days) **OR**
- Shortness of Breath (worse than what is normal for you) **OR**
- Feeling feverish, had shakes or chills in the last 24 hours

❐No ❐Yes

SECTION D: Record the temperature if answer to C is yes.

Temperature	°C	(Is the temperature above 38°C?) ❐No ❐Yes

❐ **PASS**
-Response is NO to all Sections A through C
-If only Section B is Yes → Provide education materials about SARS

❐ **FAIL**
-If **only A** is **Yes** → Quarantine and notify Public Health
-If **A or B** is **Yes AND C or D** is **Yes** → Emergency Department or SARS Clinic (Call ahead)
-If **A and B** are **No AND C and D** are both **Yes** → Clinical Evaluation (droplet precautions)
-If only **C** is **Yes** → Home for up to 72 hours with self-isolation and twice daily temperature monitoring; Follow up with Family Doctor, Occupational Health or TeleHealth Ontario (1 866 797 0000) **Or** clinical evaluation and clinical discretion

I declare that to the best of my knowledge the information that I have provided for the purpose of completing the SARS Screening Tool is true.

Interviewee: **Signature:** **Date:**

Source: Ontario, Ministry of Health and Long Term Care (2003 June 16). Severe acute respiratory syndrome (SARS) screening tool for Ontario health care settings. Retrieved January 23, 2004 from www.health.gov.on/ca/english/providers/program/pubhealth/sars/docs/docs2/screening_tool_061603.pdf.

illness, social history, sexual history, diagnostic tests done to date, and prescribed treatment. Tuberculosis, AIDS, and sexually transmitted disease reports tend to be the most complete, possibly related to the perceived seriousness and burden of illness of these diseases (Doyle et al.). Surveillance, whether active, passive, or both, does not end with the notification of the disease to the local health authority unit; rather, it initiates the next steps toward the control and management of the disease.

Community Partnerships Effective contact tracing requires a comprehensive assessment of the infected individual and accurate disease reporting. While performing this process, the CHN is also assessing the individual as part of a community. This community is defined by the individual as the place where they work, live, and play and is not limited by geographic boundaries. For example, contact tracing conducted during a recent outbreak of TB in a homeless men's shelter demanded that the local health authority unit become cognizant of the community defined by this unique population. This involved learning about the soup kitchens, drop-in centres, parks, and other areas these men congregated. Local health authority personnel could not achieve this task without the assistance of the index case (who provided information concerning contacts) and the community partners (who work closely with this population). These partners are not limited to health care providers but include all community agencies that provide services to the homeless. The result of the partnership was to develop a more focused and targeted screening to be used in the future.

Community partnerships are strengthened through the dissemination of information at open forums and educational sessions. At the open forums, the exchange of information is bi-directional: local health authority representatives provide the community with the necessary medical information while the community, in turn, provides the local health authority with social information. These forums are a necessary part of the follow-up. The local health authority should continually evaluate common links between cases and their causative epidemiology, while adding the community's input to the descriptive epidemiology. Other components of these open forums include educating the public and the service providers and discussing different strategies to control transmission to this population and environment.

Control and management of a communicable disease can be a daunting task without the assistance of the community. Partnerships, networks, and other alliances assist the CHN to achieve this goal. Infectious disease experts and infection control practitioners quickly become part of the network, providing up-to-date knowledge on current management guidelines. For example, immigration officials can inform the CHN of patterns of immigration that can assist in identifying patterns of disease or changes in the incidence of diseases, and community agencies can provide information on housing patterns, daycare use, and use of other social services. Legal officials can provide information on sex-trade activities or illicit drug activities, important when tracing sexually transmitted diseases or infections transmitted by the sharing of needles.

Notifiable Diseases

A notifiable disease is identified as such by the consensus of experts in infectious diseases. These experts from around the world identify diseases that have the largest impact on the population by reviewing case reports submitted by local health authorities. The collected information is analyzed to look for disease prevalence and associated morbidity and mortality. The disease then becomes notifiable or reportable. Physicians are obligated to report a case of a notifiable disease to the local health authority. In Canada, all local health units are required to report occurrence of communicable diseases to the provincial authorities, who in turn report to the Centre for Infectious Diseases Prevention and Control in Ottawa. The list of notifiable or reportable diseases (Table 12.4) represents the current thinking in infectious diseases medicine.

Anthrax and smallpox are examples of communicable diseases that may be used in bioterrorism activities; their management is directed by Emergency Preparedness as recommended by Health Canada (Health Canada, Centre for Emergency Preparedness and Response, 2003).

Role of the Community Health Nurse

History has shown that communicable diseases are controlled through changes in practice or environment. The sanitation of water is one of the public health triumphs that occurred in the early 1900s. Typhoid and cholera are two communicable diseases that can be transmitted via contaminated water. Improved sanitation and the development of vaccines for typhoid and cholera have virtually eliminated these two diseases from the developed world. They still continue to plague developing countries where water sanitation and vaccination programs are limited or not available (Chin, 2000; Stanhope & Lancaster, 2004).

The evolution of medicine, the advent of antimicrobial therapy, and the introduction of vaccines have assisted in the control, management, and eradication of some communicable diseases. CHNs play a major role in this control. Canada led the way with the founding of the Victorian Order of Nurses (VON) in 1897 in response to the hardships and illnesses of women and children in remote regions of Canada (Victorian Order of Nurses, n.d.). Victims of the Halifax Harbour explosion (1917), the deadly "Spanish flu" influenza epidemic (1918), the Great Depression (1930s), and other events all received the assistance of the VON (Halamandaris, n.d.). The VON nurses initially focused on prenatal education and women's illnesses and worked in the overcrowded communities in the early 1900s. Sanitation or hygiene education was paramount in controlling the spread of communicable diseases (Ross-Kerr, 2003).

Historically, CHNs broke the chain of infection at the mode of transmission link by educating the public on personal hygiene and the importance of clean drinking water. Today, breaking the chain of infection is achieved through various methods, each one targeted at different links. For example, immunization programs (usually for children) modify the susceptible host into a resistant host. Prophylaxis can diminish or reduce the ability of the infectious agent to multiply after

TABLE 12.4
Notifiable Communicable Diseases, 2000

Acute Flaccid Paralysis	Hepatitis A	Plague
AIDS	Hepatitis B	Poliomyelitis
Botulism	Hepatitis C	Rabies
Brucellosis	Hepatitis non-A, non-B	Rubella
Campylobacteriosis	Human Immunodeficiency Virus	Rubella, congenital
Chlamydia, genital	Influenza, laboratory confirmed	Salmonellosis
Chickenpox	Invasive Group A Streptococcal Disease	Shigellosis
Cholera	Invasive Pneumococcal Disease	Sudden Acute Respiratory Sydrome
Creutzfeld-Jacob Disease	Legionellosis	Syphilis, congenital
Cryptosporidiosis	Leprosy	Syphilis, early latent
Cyclosporiasis	Malaria	Syphilis, early symptomatic
Diphtheria	Measles	Syphilis, other
Giardiasis	Meningitis, pneumococcal	Tetanus
Gonococcal Infections	Meningococcal infections	Tuberculosis
Group B Streptococcal Disease of the Newborn	Mumps	Typhoid
Haemophilus influenzae type b	Paratyphoid	Vertoxigenic *E. coli*
Hantavirus Pulmonary Syndrome	Pertussis	Yellow Fever

Note: The previously notifiable diseases amoebiasis, chancroid, gonococcal ophthalmia neomatorium, listeriosis, meningitis (other bacterial), meningitis (viral), and trichinosis have been removed from national surveillance as of January 1, 2000.

Sources: Adapted from Health Canada, Centre for Infectious Disease Prevention and Control. Notifiable diseases on-line. Retrieved November 6, 2003 from http://dsol-smed.hc-sc.gc.ca/dsol-smed/ndis/list_e.html. *Health Canada. (2003, Nov. 6).* Public health management of cases of clusters of severe respiratory illness in the SARS post-outbreak period: Interim guidelines. *Volume 1. Retrieved December 25, 2003 from* http://www.hc-sc.gc.ca/pphb-dgspsp/sars-sras/pdf/phm-of-cases-and-clusters-sars-pop_e.pdf. *Adapted and reproduced with the permission of the Minister of Public Works and Government Services Canada, 2004. Health Canada assumes no responsibility for any errors or omissions that may have occurred in the adaptation of its material.*

entry into the susceptible host. Sterilization of instruments, proper cleaning of food in restaurants, and harm-reduction methods are strategies targeted at the reservoir, thereby altering the ability of the infectious agent to transmit from one host to another.

Immunization campaigns, screening, ensuring that quarantine requirements are met, instituting isolation, providing prophylaxis, and acting as consultants on communicable diseases to community groups are some of CHNs' clinical activities. CHNs are also responsible for monitoring communicable disease occurrence in the community as reported by health care providers, schools, childcare agencies, laboratories, the general public, and other health care institutions.

CHNs use the nursing process to implement primary, secondary, and tertiary prevention activities in controlling communicable diseases. Primary prevention activities attempt to prevent the disease from occurring. Secondary prevention activities detect a disease or condition in a certain population, usually by screening or testing for the disease. Tertiary prevention involves the reduction of the extent and severity of the health problems in order to minimize the disability.

The main **primary prevention** measures for controlling communicable diseases (Stanhope & Lancaster, 2004) include:

- promoting and implementing immunization programs;
- notifying the contacts and making referrals for the needed follow-up diagnosis;
- providing chemoprophylaxis such as antimicrobial medications and antitoxin for prevention of diseases such as malaria, pertussis, or diphtheria;
- working with legislations concerning protective and control measures for communicable diseases; and
- educating the public on safe sex practices, optimal nutrition, healthy buildings and environments for better air quality and sanitation, and use of preventive measures such as universal precautions.

Every minute, six children die from vaccine-preventable diseases around the world (WHO, 1998). The importance of immunization must be noted. Immunization has a dual purpose: to prevent disease and to eradicate it. Smallpox (globally) and poliomyelitis (in developed countries) have been eradicated through successful immunization programs. Measles, mumps, and rubella have been dramatically reduced in some countries. Diphtheria, *Haemophilus influenzae* type b, hepatitis B, influenza, measles, meningococcal disease, mumps, pertussis, *Streptococcus pneumoniae* (pneumococcus), poliomyelitis, rubella, tetanus, and varicella are vaccine-preventable diseases. Most vaccine-preventable diseases have a timed schedule of immunizations, which provides optimum protection throughout life. Depending on resources and the burden of illness in the specific province, this schedule (Table 12.5), developed by Health Canada, can be modified by the individual provinces. Influenza and varicella are not on the cur-

Canadian Research Box 12.1

O'Connor, D. R. (2002). *Report of the Walkerton inquiry: The events of May 2000 and related issues, part one.* Toronto, ON: Ministry of the Attorney General.

In May 2000, the small rural town of Walkerton, Ontario experienced an outbreak of *E. coli* 0157:H7. The contamination entered their drinking water after four days of heavy rains. Seven people died and more than 2300 became ill. The community was devastated. The tragedy triggered alarms about the safety of the drinking water across the province of Ontario. Among other issues, the inquest found that the chlorinating system did not operate properly, and this was not detected due to human error.

Heavy rainfalls, bovine fecal matter, a low water table, fractured bedrock, and human error all played roles in the outbreak in Walkerton. Contaminated water in this rural town demonstrates the impact of climate, geography, and fauna in the investigation of *E. coli* 0157:H7.

Discussion Questions

1. By what mechanism is contamination with *E. coli* 0157:H7 transmitted?
2. As a CHN, what roles and responsibilities could you play during and after this outbreak?

rent routine immunization schedule. Influenza vaccine is routinely given on an annual basis near or at the onset of "flu season," typically in October.

Secondary prevention measures involve the following activities (Stanhope & Lancaster, 2004):

- screening, which includes case finding, referral, and mass screening for early detection;
- early diagnosis, which includes provision and interpretation of diagnostic results;
- treatment, which involves provision of antimicrobial medications for newly diagnosed contacts;
- education for medication and treatment compliance, including provision of supportive care such as diet, rest, and exercises, and comfort measures for side effects of the medications; and
- advocacy for accessible diagnostic and treatment services for the socially disadvantaged groups such as the poor, the homeless, and people with AIDS or with language and cultural barriers.

There are two reasons for testing or screening for a communicable disease. The first is in response to the disease being identified in the community. Epidemiology reports can reveal or identify a population that is at risk for disease. To validate these reports and to identify the at-risk individuals, CHNs screen the population. The persons being tested have not been identified in the contact screening but are part of the population at risk. For example, a student comes down with tuberculosis. All students in the school, not just those with close contact to the index student, are tested for tuberculosis. The second, more general strategy is testing and screening after broad immunization campaigns, done as a standard of practice. This checks the efficacy of the immunization to ensure that all those (a random sample is taken) who received the vaccine now have antibodies to the disease.

Prophylaxis, another secondary preventive measure, is the utilization of antimicrobial agents or other chemoprophylaxis agents to prevent illness by a suspected pathogen or infectious agent. Prophylactic agents are usually prescribed for vulnerable hosts such as people who have an immune disorder, had recent major surgery or transplanted organs, or are very young, very old, or immune suppressed. For example, an outbreak of varicella or measles in the community will do little harm to the population at large. However, if contact tracing reveals that one of the contacts is a child who is undergoing chemotherapy for leukemia and has no history of varicella, this child may not be able to fight the infection and may be a candidate for varicella-zoster immune globulin (VZIG) as a prophylaxis. The VZIG will either protect the child from acquiring varicella or lessen the symptoms if the disease occurs. It is important to remember that in the case of varicella, VZIG extends the incubation period by an extra seven days.

Isonazid (INH) is administered to children younger than six years of age who have a negative response to the tuberculin skin test yet are identified as contacts in a tuberculosis outbreak. These children are given this medication daily for three months. Such young children may not have the ability to fight the TB organism as well as an older child can. The medication provides the child with the ability to fight the organism, reduces the bacterial load, and reduces the possibility of disseminated disease. A tuberculin skin test is repeated after three months, and if the result continues to be negative and no other immune disorder appears to exist, the INH can be discontinued.

Prophylaxis is part of the control of some communicable diseases. It provides protection to the vulnerable hosts in the general population. The role of the CHN is to identify the vulnerable hosts, monitor the therapy if it is long term, and possibly administer a one-time prophylaxis.

Isolation and quarantine are also secondary preventive measures. Treatment or management of some infectious agents includes isolation or quarantine to reduce the transmission and break the chain of infection. Generally, communicable diseases that are transmitted by direct or airborne routes require that the contacts are isolated from other people and possibly placed in quarantine. The length of time spent in quarantine is calculated as the time the disease or organism is able to communicate or transmit. Thus, the length of the quarantine period is specific to each communicable disease. For example, varicella is considered to be most infectious two days before the onset of the rash, remaining infectious until all lesions are dried and crusted. SARS is considered to have an incubation period of 10 days. During the SARS outbreak, it was uncertain when the infected person was most contagious or when the symptoms displayed by the patient equated to communicability. For this reason, contacts were placed in quarantine for a minimum of 10 days. Patients were often quarantined longer, depending on their symptoms.

TABLE 12.5
Routine Immunization Schedule for Infants and Children

Age at Vaccination	DTaP[1]	IPV	HiB[2]	MMR	Td[3] or dTap[10]	Hep B[4] (3 doses)	V	PC	MC
Birth									
2 months	X	X	X					X[8]	X[9]
4 months	X	X	X			Infancy		X	X
6 months	X	(X)[5]	X			or		X	X
12 months				(X)[6] or		preadolescence	X[7]	X	
18 months	X	X	X	(X)[6]		(9–13 years)			or
4–6 years	X	X							
14–16 years					X[10]				X[9]

DTaP	Diphtheria, tetanus, pertussis (acellular) vaccine
IPV	Inactivated poliovirus vaccine
HiB	*Haemophilus influenzae* type B conjugate vaccine
MMR	Measles, mumps, and rubella vaccine
Td	Tetanus and diphtheria toxoid, adult type with reduced diphtheria toxoid
dTap	Tetanus and diphtheria toxoid, acellular pertussis, adolescent/adult type with reduced diphtheria and pertussis components
Hep B	Hepatitis B vaccine
V	Varicella
PC	Pneumococcal conjugate vaccine
MC	Meningococcal C conjugate vaccine

Notes:

1. DTaP (diphtheria, tetanus, acellular or component pertussis) vaccine is the preferred vaccine for all doses in the vaccination series, including completion of the series in children who have received >1 dose of DPT (whole cell) vaccine.

2. HiB schedule shown is for PRP-T or HbOC vaccine. If PRP-OMP is used, give at 2, 4, and 12 months of age.

3. Td (tetanus and diphtheria toxoid), a combined adsorbed "adult type" preparation for use in people >7 years of age, contains less diphtheria toxoid than preparations given to younger children and is less likely to cause reactions in older people.

4. Hepatitis B vaccine can be given routinely to infants or preadolescents depending on the provincial/territorial policy; three doses at 0-, 1-, and 6-month intervals are preferred. The second dose should be administered at least one month after the first dose, and the third dose at least two months after the second dose. A two-dose schedule for adolescents is also possible.

5. This dose is not needed routinely, but can be included for convenience.

6. A second dose of MMR is recommended at least 1 month after the first dose for the purpose of better measles protection. For convenience, options include giving it with the next scheduled vaccination at 18 months of age, with school entry (4–6 years) vaccinations (depending on the provincial/territorial policy), or at any intervening age that is practicable. The need for a second dose of mumps and rubella vaccine is not established but may benefit (given for convenience as MMR). The second dose of MMR should be given at the same visit as DTaP IPV (+ HiB) to ensure high uptake rates.

7. Children aged 12 months to 12 years should receive one dose of varicella vaccine. Individuals >13 years of age should receive two doses at least 28 days apart.

8. Recommended schedule, number of doses, and subsequent use of 23-valent polysaccharide pneumococcal vaccine depend on the age of the child when vaccination is begun.

9. Recommended schedule and number of doses of meningococcal vaccine depend on the age of the child.

10. dTap adult formulation has reduced diphtheria toxoid and pertussis component.

Source: Health Canada, Population and Public Health Branch, Division of Immunization and Respiratory Diseases. (2002). Table 1: Routine immunization schedule for infants and children. Retrieved December 4, 2003 from www.hc-sc.gc.ca/pphb-dgspsp/dird-dimr/is-cv/index.html. *Reproduced with the permission of the Minister of Public Works and Government Services Canada, 2004.*

Tertiary prevention aims to reduce the extent and severity of the health problems in order to minimize the disability (Stanhope & Lancaster, 2004):

- educating and monitoring treatment compliance to prevent complications, and
- monitoring effectiveness of treatment and identifying and referring for adverse effects.

Education of the public at the individual, family, and community levels through the development of community-based programs is a tertiary-level preventive measure. Education is not directed at a single stage in the chain of infection; rather, it targets the whole chain and teaches measures that can be adopted into the individuals' personal health habits. The goal is to help the client and the community return to baseline functioning.

CASE STUDY

An infant is born at 26 weeks gestation in a community hospital. Five hours after birth, the infant is transported to a Level 3, high acuity nursery. The infant is intubated with central venous and arterial lines for nutritional support and to administer antibiotics. The stay in hospital is complicated, involving frequent intubations and switching from conventional ventilation to oscillating ventilation. On the 59th day of life, the infant succumbs. Histology samples from the autopsy reveal *Mycobacterium tuberculosis* that may have contributed to the infant's death. The organism is grown for culture and sensitivity. The organism is fully sensitive to first-line medications (isonazid, rifampin, ethambutol, pyrazinamide, and streptomycin). Contact tracing begins. The local health authority is notified and becomes actively involved.

Discussion Questions

1. How would you know if the infant had received the tuberculosis congenitally?
2. You have collected sputum samples from some of the contacts. One sample comes back resistant to rifampin. What does this tell you about this strain of TB compared with the strain found in the infant?
3. Describe what steps you will take to conduct your contact tracing.

Throughout various levels of prevention activities, CHNs play major roles in education, health promotion, direct care, community development and mobilization, liaison, research, advocacy, program planning and evaluation, and policy formulation. All are essential skills in the epidemiological investigation for successful management and control of communicable diseases.

WORLD HEALTH ORGANIZATION PRIORITIES IN CONTROLLING COMMUNICABLE DISEASES

Like other nations, Canada works in partnership with the WHO to reduce the incidence and impact of communicable disease on its population. The role of the WHO in communicable disease control is to lead global efforts in surveillance, prevention, control, and research. What continues to be a challenge for all nations can be seen in the following priorities set by the WHO (2000):

- to reduce the negative consequences of malaria and tuberculosis;
- to continue to strengthen surveillance, monitoring, and response to communicable diseases;
- to intensify routine prevention and control; and
- to generate new knowledge through research for development of tools and intervention methods.

SUMMARY

This chapter on the control and management of communicable diseases has discussed the transmission of infectious agents, what factors are necessary for infectivity, how to control the transmission, and finally how to prevent the disease. Two case studies and a Canadian Research Box have been chosen to illustrate transmission, quarantine, contact tracing, treatment, and other factors related to communicable diseases.

The topic of communicable diseases is broad. Each day, the world faces a new disease, which may or may not find itself in your community. It is imperative that you know what resources are available to assist you and that you are prepared to respond to the unexpected. The body of knowledge required changes quickly; one day you are an expert and the next, you are a novice. You must possess a strong relationship with your community partners, a solid knowledge base of epidemiology and current information on communicable diseases, a knowledge of your resources, and strong decision-making and research skills. Integration of these skills will help you be successful in your role in protecting and promoting the health of Canadians.

KEY TERMS

communicable diseases
infectious agents
hosts
infected hosts
infectivity
pathogenicity
virulence
immunogenicity
natural immunity
acquired immunity
active immunization
vaccine
passive immunization
herd immunity
environment
chain of infection process
transmission
direct transmission
droplet transmission
indirect transmission
common vehicle transmission
horizontal transmission
vertical transmission
vectorborne transmission
airborne transmission
immune system
natural history of disease
stage of susceptibility
incubation period
stage of presymptomatic disease, or prodromal stage
carrier
stage of clinical disease

stage of diminished capacity
residual disability
convalescent period
patterns of disease
outbreak
endemic
epidemic
pandemic
surveillance
notifiable diseases
contact tracing
quarantine
index case
active surveillance
passive surveillance
primary prevention
secondary prevention
prophylaxis
tertiary prevention

STUDY QUESTIONS

1. What is the link between epidemiology and communicable diseases?
2. What are the modes of transmission of communicable diseases?
3. You have collected a history of a male that includes dependence on alcohol, long-term unemployment, and participation in the sex trade. The disease you are investigating is transmitted by exchange of body fluids. What control measures would you discuss with the client?
4. What biological factors are important to consider when identifying a potential host?
5. A high school student is diagnosed with tuberculosis. Who might be able to help you as you conduct contact tracing?
6. The local health authority department has just hired you to work on hepatitis A management and control. You are uncertain about the rate of the infection and what age group it affects in your region. This information will help you develop teaching packages. Where would you look to find this information?

INDIVIDUAL CRITICAL THINKING EXERCISES

1. The incubation period of an infectious disease can be used to estimate the time during which further cases may occur and to indicate the most effective time for the introduction of control measures (Richardson et al., 2001). What information would you need from the infectious individual and about the disease to conduct an inclusive contact tracing?
2. Laboratory results indicate an increased incidence of gonorrhea. The reports are from the same geographic location, the identifiers are anonymous, and you have no knowledge of the disease being reported. What steps are needed to differentiate an increased incidence as opposed to repeated testing of the same individual? How would you involve the testing site in your investigation?
3. Newspaper headlines state that the increase in TB is due to a failure of monitoring systems. What information would you need to know to respond accurately to this statement?
4. A colleague reveals, in confidence, that his or her own HIV test has come back positive. As a nurse, what, if any, responsibilities do you have related to this information?
5. You are working in a downtown clinic that provides services to marginalized/vulnerable persons. A patient presents to the clinic with non-specific ailments. You are collecting the history. The patient reveals a history of addictions to crack cocaine and other substances. Your recommendation is to have a full work-up for sexually transmitted infections. The patient refuses. What is your impetus to recommend this work-up?

GROUP CRITICAL THINKING EXERCISES

1. "As migrant and foreign-born populations age, the presentation and frequency of chronic infectious sequelae in these groups may be different from that observed in native-born cohorts. Tuberculosis in foreign-born populations is anticipated to be a significant issue as that segment of the population ages. The arrival of large numbers of migrants from regions where the prevalence of tuberculosis is high has resulted in the importation of a large burden of latent infection, which can be expected to generate future active cases in aging migrants" (Gushulak & MacPherson, 2000). Discuss the implications of this statement on health care, especially communicable diseases. Healthy public policy should be included in the discussion as opposed to local health authority policy.
2. "Most investigations of outbreaks look through a relatively narrow time window of a few months and thus will miss chains of transmission involving links of many years" (Vynnycky & Fine, 2000). Discuss the communicable diseases that have many years of linkages. For example, AIDS can manifest after years of HIV-positive status. A HIV-positive test may not occur until three months after the contact. Another example is tuberculosis, in which the skin test can be negative up to 12 weeks post exposure, and the manifestations of the disease may occur sometime in the person's lifetime. Discuss the implications of contact tracing for these two diseases with this information and in relation to the quotation.
3. Emerging diseases, changes in antibiotic resistance, and threats of terrorism with biologic agents have heightened the awareness of surveillance needs worldwide (Bean & Martin, 2001). Since September 11, 2001, the threat of smallpox and anthrax has been in the media. Discuss the information needed to control the spread of smallpox.

REFERENCES

Allemang, M. M. (2000). Development of community health nursing in Canada. In M. Stewart (Ed.), *Community nursing: Promoting Canadians' health* (2nd ed., pp. 4–32). Toronto, ON: W.B. Saunders.

Allender, J., & Spradley, B. (2001). *Community health nursing: Concepts and practice* (5th ed.). Philadelphia, PA: Lippincott.

Bean, N. H., & Martin, S. M. (2001). Implementing a network for electronic surveillance reporting from local health authority reference laboratories: An international perspective. *Emerging Infectious Diseases, 7*(5). Retrieved December 4, 2003 from **www.cdc.gov/ncidod/eid/vol7no5/bean.htm**

Chin, J. (Ed.). (2000). *Control of communicable diseases manual: An official report of the American Public Health Association* (17th ed.). Washington, DC: American Public Health Association.

Craven, R., & Hirnle, C. (2003). *Fundamentals of nursing: Human health and function* (4th ed.). Philadelphia, PA: Lippincott Williams & Wilkins.

Dowell, S. (2001). Seasonal variation in host susceptibility and cycles of certain infectious diseases. *Emerging Infectious Diseases, 7*(3). Retrieved December 4, 2003 from **www.cdc.gov/ncidod/eid/vol7no3/dowell.htm**

Doyle, T., Glynn, K., & Groseclose, S. (2002). Completeness of notifiable infectious disease reporting in the United States: An analytical literature review. *American Journal of Epidemiology, 155*(9), 866–874.

Gushulak, B., & MacPherson, D. (2000). Population mobility and infectious diseases: The diminishing impact of classical infectious diseases and new approaches for the 21st century. *Clinical Infectious Diseases, 31*, 776–780.

Halamandaris, V. J. (n.d.). Lillian Wald 1867–1940. *Profiles in Caring, 104.* Retrieved December 4, 2003 from **www.nahc.org/NAHC/Val/Columns/SC10-4**

Health Canada. (2003a). *Advisory: Update #1, Severe Acute Respiratory Syndrome.* Retrieved December 4, 2003 from **www.hc-sc.gc.ca/english/protection/warnings/sars/fact_sheet.htm**

Health Canada. (2003b). *HIV and AIDS in Canada: Surveillance report to December 31, 2002.* Retrieved December 20, 2003 from **www.hc-sc.gc.ca/pphb-dgspsp/publicat/aids-sida/haic-vsac1202/pdf/haic-vsac1202.pdf**

Health Canada. (2003c). *Notifiable diseases on line: Glossary.* Retrieved December 20, 2003 from **dsol-smed.hc-sc.gc.ca/dsol-smed/ndis/glossa_e.html**

Health Canada. (2003d). *SARS: Severe Acute Respiratory Syndrome.* Retrieved December 4, 2003 from **www.hc-sc.gc.ca/english/protection/warnings/sars/index.html**

Health Canada, Centre for Emergency Preparedness and Response. (2003). *Bioterrorism and emergency preparedness.* Retrieved December 4, 2003 from **www.hc-sc.gc.ca/english/protection/biotech/bioterrorism.htm**

Health Canada, Population and Public Health Branch. (1999). Routine practices and additional precautions for preventing the transmission of infection in health care: Revision of isolation and precaution techniques. *Canada Communicable Diseases Report, 25S4.* Retrieved December 4, 2003 from **www.hc-sc.gc.ca/pphb-dgspsp/publicat/ccdr-rmtc/99vol25/25s4/index.html**

Health Canada, Population and Public Health Branch, Division of Immunization and Respiratory Diseases. (2002). *Table 1: Routine immunization schedule for infants and children.* Retrieved December 4, 2003 from **www.hc-sc.gc.ca/pphb-dgspsp/dird-dimr/is-cv/index.html**

Nagnur, D., & Nagrodski, M. (1990). Epidemiologic transition in the context of demographic change: The evolution of Canadian mortality patterns. *Canadian Studies in Population, 17*(1), 1–24.

O'Connor, D. R. (2002). *Report of the Walkerton inquiry: The events of May 2000 and related issues, part one.* Toronto, ON: Ministry of the Attorney General. Retrieved July 14, 2002 from **www.walkertoninquiry.com/report1/index.html# summary**

Pickering, L. K. (Ed.). (2003). *Red book: 2003 report of the Committee on Infectious Diseases* (26th ed.). Elk Grove Village, IL: American Academy of Pediatrics.

Richardson, M., Elliman, D., Maguire, H., Simpson, J., & Nicoll, A. (2001). Evidence base of incubation periods, periods of infectiousness and exclusion policies for the control of communicable diseases in schools and preschools. *Pediatric Infectious Disease Journal, 20*(4), 380–391.

Ross-Kerr, J. (2003). Nursing in Canada from 1760 to the present: The transition to modern nursing. In J. Ross-Kerr & M. Wood (Eds.), *Canadian nursing: Issues and perspectives* (4th ed., pp. 15–28). Toronto, ON: Mosby.

Stanhope, M., & Lancaster, J. (2004). *Community & public health nursing* (6th ed.). St. Louis, MO: Mosby.

Statistics Canada & Social Science Federation of Canada. (1983). B35-50: Average number of deaths and death rates for leading causes of death, Canada, for five-year periods, 1921–1974. In F. H. Leacy (Ed.), *Historical statistics of Canada* (2nd ed.). Ottawa, ON: Statistics Canada. Retrieved December 20, 2003 from **www.statcan.ca/english/IPS/Data/11-516-XIE.htm**

Statistics Canada. (2003). *Selected leading causes of death by sex.* Retrieved December 20, 2003 from **www.statcan.ca/english/Pgdb/health36.htm**

Victorian Order of Nurses. (n.d.). *A century of caring.* Retrieved December 4, 2003 from **www.von.ca/english/aboutframe.htm**

Victoria, Public Health Division. (1997). Hepatitis B. *The blue book: Guidelines for the control of communicable diseases.* Retrieved December 14, 2003 from **www.dhs.vic.gov.au/phb/hprot/inf_dis/bluebook/hepb.htm**

Vynnycky, E., & Fine, P. (2000). Lifetime risks, incubation period, and serial interval of tuberculosis. *American Journal of Epidemiology, 152*(3), 247–263.

World Health Organization. (1998). Report of the director-general. *1998 world health report: Health in the 21st century: A vision for all.* Geneva, Switzerland: Author.

World Health Organization. (2000). *Communicable diseases 2000: Highlights of activities in 1999 and major challenges for the future.* Retrieved December 21, 2003 from **www.who.int/infectious-disease-news/CDS2000/PDF/cd2000-e.pdf**

World Health Organization. (2003). *Communicable diseases cluster: Highlights of communicable disease activities, major recent achievements.* Retrieved December 21, 2003 from **www.who.int/infectious-disease-news/IDdocs/highlights-2003/CDS-highlights-2003.pdf**

ADDITIONAL RESOURCES

READINGS

Feigin, R. D., Cherry, J. D., & Fletcher, J. (Eds.). (1998). *Textbook of pediatric infectious disease* (4th ed.). Philadelphia, PA: W.B. Saunders.

Gold, R. (2002). *Your child's best shot* (2nd ed.). Ottawa, ON: Canadian Paediatric Society.

McQuillan, K. (1985). Ontario mortality patterns, 1861–1921. *Canadian Studies in Population, 12*(1), 31–48.

Long, R. (Ed.). (2000). *Canadian tuberculosis standards* (5th ed.). Ottawa, ON: Canadian Lung Association and Health Canada.

Walker, T. (Ed.). (2001). *Infectious diseases in children: A clinical guide for nurses.* Melbourne, Australia: Ausmed Publications.

WEBSITES

Calgary Regional Health Authority, School Health. *Communicable Diseases:*
www.crha-health.ab.ca/schoolhealth/diseases.htm

Centers for Disease Control and Prevention (CDC):
www.cdc.gov

Centers for Disease Control and Prevention (CDC). *MMWR: Morbidity and Mortality Weekly Report:*
www.cdc.gov/mmwr/

Centers for Disease Control and Prevention, National Center for Infectious Diseases. *Emerging Infectious Diseases:*
www.cdc.gov/ncidod/EID/index.htm

Community and Hospital Infection Control Association, Canada:
www.chica.org

Health Canada. *The Canadian Strategy on HIV/AIDS:*
www.hc-sc.gc.ca/hppb/hiv_aids/index.html

Health Canada, Centre for Infectious Disease Prevention and Control:
www.hc-sc.gc.ca/pphb-dgspsp/centres_e.html#cidpc

Health Canada, Centre for Infectious Disease Prevention and Control. *Notifiable Diseases On-line:*
http://dsol-smed.hc-sc.gc.ca/dsol-smed/ndis/list_e.html

Health Canada, Centre for Surveillance Coordination:
www.hc-sc.gc.ca/pphb-dgspsp/csc-ccs/faq_e.html#publichealth

Health Canada, Population and Public Health Branch. *Canada Communicable Disease Report:*
www.hc-sc.gc.ca/hpb/lcdc/publicat/ccdr/indrex.html

Health Canada, Population and Public Health Authority Branch. *Disease Surveillance On-line:*
www.hc-sc.gc.ca/pphb-dgspsp/surveillance_e.html

Health Canada, Population and Public Health Branch. (2000). Waterborne outbreak of gastro-enteritis associated with a contaminated municipal water supply, Walkerton, Ontario May-June 2000. *Canada Communicable Disease Report, 26-20:*
www.hc-sc.gc.ca/hpb/lcdc/publicat/ccdr/00vol26/dr2620eb.html

Health Canada, Population and Public Health Branch. *Travel medicine program:*
www.hc-sc.gc.ca/pphb-dgspsp/tmp-pmv/index.html
or
www.TravelHealth.gc.ca

Orton, S. (n.d.). *Infectious disease epidemiology.* Pittsburgh, PA: University of Pittsburgh:
www.pitt.edu/~super1/lecture/lec1191/index.htm

Statistics Canada. (2003). *Canada at a glance 2003.* (Catalogue no. 12-581-XPE):
www.statcan.ca/english/freepub/12-581-XIE/12-581-XIE03001.pdf

World Health Organization. *Communicable Disease Surveillance and Response (CSR).* Includes news of diseases reported to CSR, the Weekly Epidemiological Record, and more:
www.who.int/emc/

About the Authors

Patricia Malloy, BSN (Northeastern), MSN (Northeastern), is a Clinical Nurse Specialist/Nurse Practitioner in the Infectious Diseases division at The Hospital for Sick Children. Ms. Malloy's clinical area focuses on tuberculosis in children and children living in homeless or underhoused situations. Ms. Malloy is currently involved in a research project on the management of homeless/underhoused youth who abuse substances and have mental illness. With other experts, she has developed the Canadian Nurses' Association Handbook on hepatitis C. She has also developed an intake sheet for patients seen in the tuberculosis clinic. Ms. Malloy is cross-appointed to the Faculty of Nursing at the University of Toronto.

Lucia Yiu, BScN, BA (Psychology, Windsor), BSc (Physiology, Toronto), MScN (Administration, Western Ontario), is an Associate Professor in the Faculty of Nursing, University of Windsor, and an Educational and Training Consultant in community nursing. She has published on family and public health nursing. Her practice and research interests include multicultural health, international health, experiential learning, community development, and program planning and evaluation. She has worked overseas and served on various community and social services committees involving local and district health planning.

CHAPTER 13

Planning, Monitoring, and Evaluation

E. Merilyn Allison

OBJECTIVES

AFTER STUDYING THIS CHAPTER, YOU SHOULD BE ABLE TO:

1. Discuss the influence of social pressures on the development of community health programs.
2. Describe the various components involved in the planning-evaluation cycle, including the PRECEDE-PROCEED Framework, Program Logic Model, and Targeting Outcomes of Programs.
3. Explain the types of evaluations and common program models used in evaluation.
4. Explain how commonly used evaluation models are structured to address program accountability.
5. Provide an overview of the importance of program planning, monitoring, and evaluation in the practice of community health nursing.

INTRODUCTION

In recent decades, social and political pressures have led to increased scrutiny of community health nursing services. Policymakers and funding agencies are demanding that health professionals provide evidence of the value of the programs they deliver. More and more often, community health nurses (CHNs) are required to justify the continuation or expansion of existing programs and the implementation of any new programs to stakeholders and the general public (Cramer & Iverson, 1999; Dwyer & Makin, 1997; McLaughlin & Jordan, 1998). CHNs must engage in ongoing program evaluation activities to determine the effectiveness of programs, improve the quality of their services, and achieve maximum cost-effectiveness.

With the community as the client, the process of planning, monitoring, and evaluating health promotion programs becomes more complex as societal and political factors impact decision making and program design. Collaboration with and involvement of representatives of the target community, key community leaders, and persons in authority and funding positions are essential if program planning is to be successful. These individuals, along with the program participants, also play a significant role in monitoring and evaluating the program. If program planning is done thoroughly, with clearly defined goals, evaluation measures, and indicators of success incorporated into the program design, then the likelihood of success is greatly enhanced (McNamara, 1998). Thus, the concepts and processes presented in this chapter are intended to help students to develop a foundation for effectively integrating program planning, monitoring, and evaluation into their practice as CHNs.

SOCIETAL INFLUENCES ON HEALTH PROMOTION PROGRAMS

Community health promotion programs are experiencing greater public scrutiny. Factors contributing to this closer examination include limited resources, an increased demand for accountability, a growing emphasis on individual rights, advocacy groups, and increased access to information via the internet. Community health promotion programs are funded by a variety of government, community, and private sources. These funding bodies want to feel confident that their monies are well spent and the desired outcomes achieved. They expect both a fiscal accounting and a performance report. Requests for cost-benefit analyses and reports on the return on investment are common in the current economic environment. No longer are funds dispersed without regard for value obtained.

In recent decades, public interest has surged with respect to individuals' rights to be informed and involved in planning and decision-making processes related to care, education, and treatment (Clark, 2003). This demand has been addressed to some degree through legislation, such as provincial laws on informed consent and bills of rights for patients, and by the creation of ombudsman positions. This interest in individual rights is also expressed in the growing number of advocacy groups representing the interests of particular groups of persons, for example, seniors' associations referred to under the rubric of "grey power" and groups promoting the rights of vulnerable populations such as the physically challenged. As champions of human rights, advocates have a strong interest in how programs are planned and conducted and want to know the results of program evaluations.

The growing number of people with access to information through the internet adds new dimensions to health promotion program development. Information is rapidly disseminated. Both health professionals and consumers have easier access to articles, recent research on a wide range of topics, and discussion and support groups. CHNs need to know how to access the internet and how to discriminate between reliable, valid information and undependable information on websites. They may also need to assist people in identifying reliable sources of health information and reputable support groups through the internet. The long-term effects of this rapid dissemination of information on health promotion programs have not yet been determined, but it certainly presents challenges as well as opportunities for expanding the level of knowledge to diverse groups of people.

THE PLANNING-EVALUATION CYCLE

Since these societal influences have led to an increased demand for CHNs to develop programs and implement changes in a planned and accountable manner, CHNs must become familiar with all aspects of the planning and evaluation processes. To help the student understand the various components of the planning–evaluation cycle, planning and evaluation will be presented separately with remarks highlighting the linkages between them.

Planning and evaluation are related to each other in a cyclical fashion. The distinctions between them are not always clear as various aspects of each contribute to the development and management of the other. The **planning-evaluation cycle**, depicted in Figure 13.1, involves the following steps:

- situational analysis or community assessment,
- identification of the problem or issue of concern,
- consideration of a variety of possible solutions,
- selection of the best alternative,
- program design (which includes identification of evaluation measures),
- program implementation,
- program evaluation,
- analysis of evaluation findings, and
- utilization of evaluation findings and recommendations to provide feedback for future program planning, decision making, and situational analysis.

FIGURE 13.1 The Planning-Evaluation Cycle

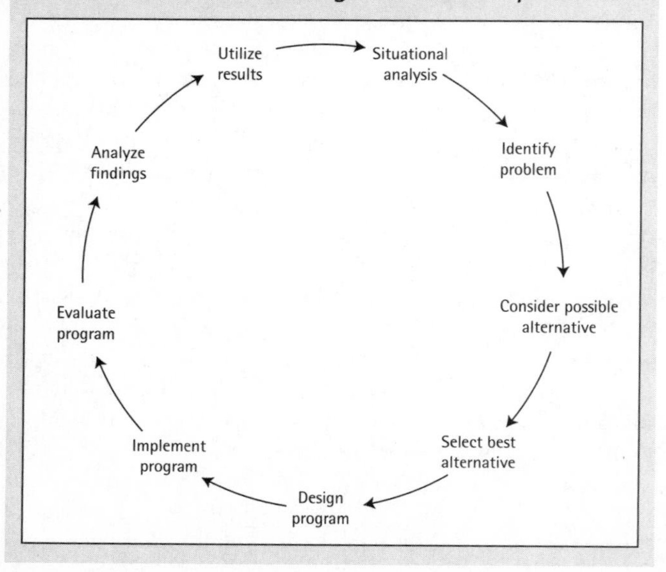

PROGRAM PLANNING

Planners need to know what they want to achieve. To paraphrase the response of the Cheshire Cat in the fantasy story, *Alice's Adventures in Wonderland*, if you don't know where you want to go, it doesn't matter what path you take (Carroll, 1929). After the CHN has completed the community assessment (see Chapter 10) and analyzed the situation to identify the priority needs of the community and the modifiable risk factors prevalent within the community, then the target population for a health promotion program can be determined. This may be in relation to planning a new program or with respect to modifying an existing program. The CHN will then have a purpose for engaging in program planning.

However, before proceeding with the planning process, other factors should be considered as part of the situational analysis (McNamara, 1998).

- Is this the best solution to the problem, or are there other alternatives? The most appropriate organization to develop a program to address the particular concern should be determined.
- Are other agencies already engaged in delivering a related service? If so, the CHN may want to look at a more specific aspect of the general concern or at a more specific population for the program.
- Should a single organization take the lead role in developing the program, or should a partnership be developed among agencies?
- Is there potential opposition to the program? If so, how will this be counteracted?

After considering these factors and deciding to proceed with the planning of a health promotion program, consider using existing tools to assist with the design of the program. A program planning group may consist of people internal to the organization or individuals from a variety of agencies and organizations. Three tools widely used in North America for program development are the PRECEDE-PROCEED framework, the Program Logic Model, and TOP (Targeting Outcomes of Programs). The main features of the PRECEDE-PROCEED framework are briefly outlined below. The other two tools, which integrate program planning, implementation, and evaluation, will be addressed in more detail later in this chapter.

The PRECEDE-PROCEED Framework

The **PRECEDE-PROCEED framework** was developed by Lawrence W. Green in the late 1960s as a planning approach and expanded in the 1980s through collaboration with Marshall Kreuter to include environmental, policy, and organizational factors (Brown, 1999). PRECEDE is an acronym for Predisposing, Reinforcing, and Enabling Causing in Educational Diagnosis and Evaluation. PROCEED is an acronym for Policy Regulation and Organizational Constructs in Educational and Environmental Development. This multidimensional model is founded in the social/behavioural sciences, epidemiology, administration, and education. Two assumptions underlie this model:

- health, health risk, and health behaviours are caused by many factors as individuals are influenced not only by their own behaviours but also by the environment in which they live; and
- a multidimensional and multidisciplinary approach is required to effect changes (Gielen & McDonald, 2002).

In the PRECEDE segment, the program planner begins with the desired outcome and works backward to what causes it or what must precede that outcome. PRECEDE emphasizes that people need to be actively involved in assessing their own needs. It includes five phases which reflect the scientific perspectives on which the model is based: social diagnosis, epidemiological diagnosis, behavioural and environmental diagnosis, educational and organizational diagnosis, and administrative and policy diagnosis. The PRECEDE segment provides for a comprehensive assessment and precedes the development of appropriate interventions.

The PROCEED segment has four phases: implementation, process evaluation, impact evaluation, and outcome evaluation. The components of PROCEED require the planner to incorporate the political, managerial, and economic actions necessary to make the environment more conducive to healthful lifestyles. Interventions targeted at the PRECEDE factors are applied during the implementation phase. In the process evaluation phase, the implementation of the program is evaluated in an ongoing manner. The impact evaluation phase measures the program's effectiveness in terms of its immediate objectives and changes in identified causal factors. In the outcome evaluation phase, changes in terms of overall objectives and in health and social benefits or the quality of life are measured (Brown, 1999).

This framework, which uses a diagnostic approach, has been used extensively in developing health promotion and education programs. Its merits have been confirmed in numerous published studies.

Program Logic Model

The **program logic model** depicts in graphical form the component parts of an overall plan for program development and evaluation. Basic logic model diagrams typically contain inputs, processes (which may also be referred to as throughputs, methods, or outputs), and outcomes (both short-term and long-term). Other elements, such as goals, objectives, assumptions, and environmental factors, may be included to illustrate specific factors associated with a program.

There is no right or wrong way to develop a logic model. They can be built from the bottom up or from the top down, or a mixed approach can be used, but it is preferable to link the model to a sound theoretical base. The bottom-up approach begins by considering the desired outcomes of the program and then designing the activities that will lead to those results. This approach is particularly useful in planning new programs. The top-down approach is more likely to be used to evaluate existing programs since it begins with the activities and then considers how these activities can lead to the desired outcomes (Porteus, Sheldrick, & Stewart, 1997; Rush & Ogborne, 1991).

The development of the logic model for a program is typically a group endeavour. Although logic modelling can be time consuming, the discussions during model development clarify concepts and values about the proposed program and inform the planners about the interventions and resources required to produce the desired results. Logic modelling yields a map or diagram showing what must be done, who needs to participate, and what the expected impact of the program will be. The program logic model makes the implicit theory behind a theory explicit and shows how different facets of a program are linked (Dwyer & Makin, 1997).

When drawing the model, the elements are shown in temporal sequence and relationships are indicated with arrows. Program logic models do not illustrate every aspect of a program; they form the basis for a cascading group of action plans that detail specific components of the program for implementation at the program delivery level. For instance, the program logic model does not contain details about costs, measurement processes, or the rationale behind the boxes and arrows in the diagram.

The program logic model (Figure 13.2) draws on the work of Alter and Murty (1997), McNamara (2000), Porteus et al., and Taylor-Powell (2001). The shared vision is created by the planning group through discussion and negotiation. Underlying assumptions, values, and beliefs about the program's purpose are clarified and a common understanding about the overall goal, objectives, and desired outcomes for the program is attained.

FIGURE 13.2 Program Logic Model

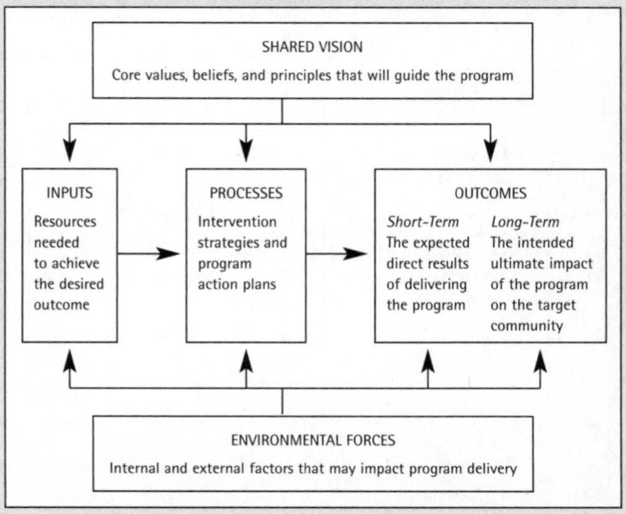

SHARED VISION
Core values, beliefs, and principles that will guide the program

INPUTS
Resources needed to achieve the desired outcome

PROCESSES
Intervention strategies and program action plans

OUTCOMES
Short-Term The expected direct results of delivering the program
Long-Term The intended ultimate impact of the program on the target community

ENVIRONMENTAL FORCES
Internal and external factors that may impact program delivery

Inputs are the resources that must be invested in a program in order to achieve the desired outcomes. Types of inputs include staff, time, partnerships, volunteers, money, equipment, materials, and facilities. In addition, the information obtained from a community assessment is an essential resource for the development of the program.

Processes are the methods for delivering the program. They include the strategies and activities designed to produce desired results. Research-based intervention strategies that are scientifically defensible and appropriate to the community need to be identified when developing the action steps. These strategies may include activities such as recruitment, education, advertising, and social marketing. Collecting statistical data on these activities, for example, the number of participants served, is usually incorporated into the program's action plan, and the results may be referred to as **products** or **outputs** of the activity in some logic models. These quantifiable statistics provide information on services delivered and contribute to the evaluation of the achievement of outcomes. The selection of data collection tools (to gather the appropriate and relevant information in a timely manner) and the resource needs associated with data collection will also have to be determined and built into the action plans.

Outcomes are the changes or benefits from delivering the program. Outcomes include both short-term changes demonstrated by participants in the program and long-term results observed in the target community. Short-term results are often measured in terms of changes in awareness, knowledge, attitudes, skills, opinions, aspirations, and motivations. Long-term outcomes show the ultimate impact of the program on the target community and are causally related to the program goal. Long-term outcomes are directional in nature; that is, the desired outcome is an increase or a decrease in something or some behaviour.

Indicators to measure change both in the short term and the long term should be determined before program implementation in order to build the evaluation of outcomes into the program design from the outset. **Indicators** are observable items of specific information that provide tangible evidence of movement toward or away from goal attainment. A cautionary note is that measuring the consequences of delivering a health promotion program may be frustratingly difficult since the time period over which changes occur can be lengthy and since internal and external environmental forces can influence the outcomes.

Environmental factors such as health policies, safety regulations, economic conditions, culture, political climate, geography, changes in program personnel, employment conditions, changes in funders' requirements, and changes in stakeholder priorities can impact the delivery of the program. As Rovers (1986) states, "The key to a successful evaluation appears to be (1) select those relevant indicators for which it is possible to gather information, and (2) have a contingency plan!" (p. 216).

Program logic models assist program planners to identify all the components required for delivering a program. They help by delineating the linkages and the rationale underlying the program. They assist with the identification of key issues and potentially unintended consequences in program delivery. They integrate planning and evaluation and facilitate program accountability. In addition, as Rush and Ogborne (1991) note, program logic models can function as communication tools to describe the program to the general public, relevant stakeholders, and the media.

To illustrate the use of the program logic model, a hypothetical scenario is described with a sample schematic diagram displayed in Figure 13.3. In this situation, a community assessment identified a higher than provincial average incidence of type 2 diabetes in the community of "Greenacres." The assessment also revealed that elementary school children

FIGURE 13.3 Hypothetical Example of a Program Logic Model

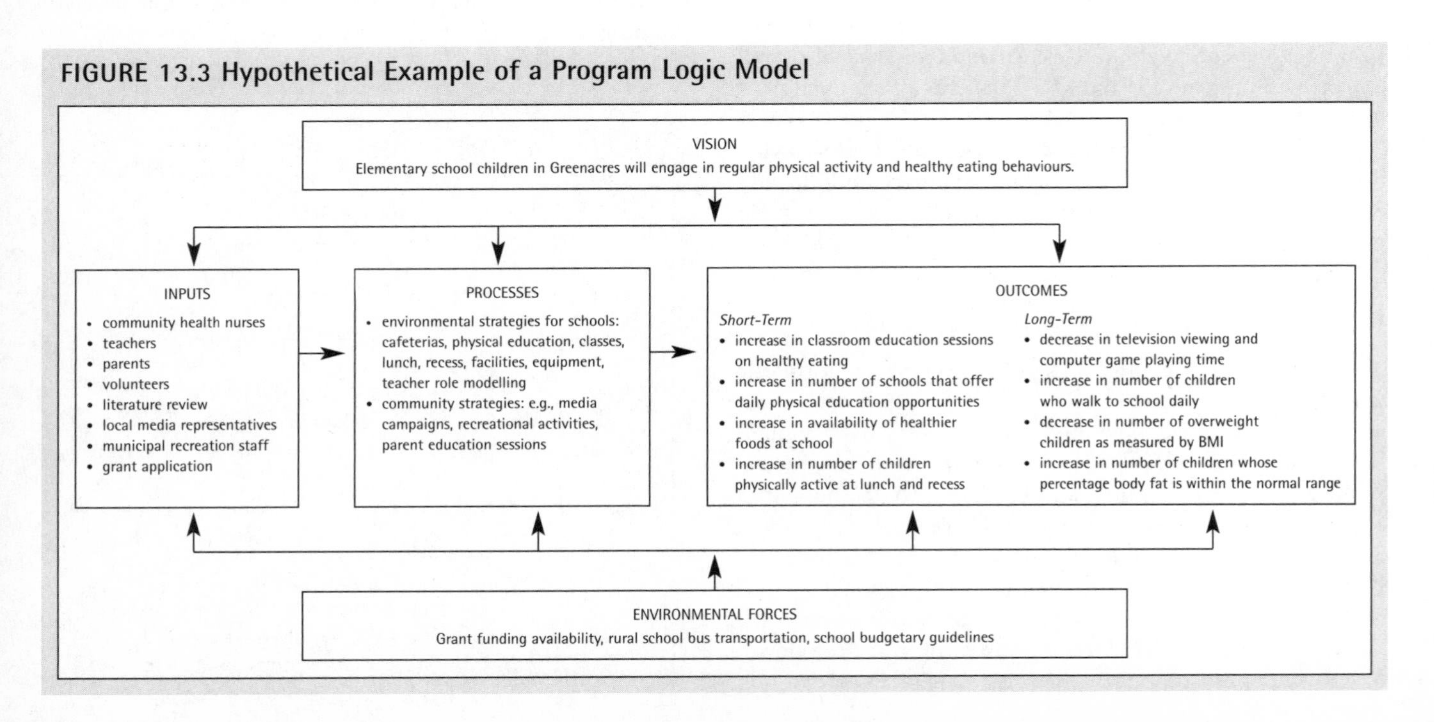

did not engage in daily physical activity at the minimum levels recommended in fitness standards, and archival data indicated that obesity, a modifiable risk factor for developing diabetes, was an increasing problem in the school-age population. There is general concern in the community of Greenacres about their health status, and several newspaper articles have been written about it. The provincial government has announced that grants are available for school-based projects with respect to primary prevention of type 2 diabetes. CHNs in Greenacres have been directed to take a lead role in developing a health promotion program to address this situation. (Note: The examples used throughout this hypothetical scenario are neither exhaustive nor meant to be prescriptive.)

Developing the Program Logic Model

1. Assemble the Planning Group In this sample situation, key stakeholders such as teachers, dieticians and diabetes educators, representatives from the Canadian Diabetes Association, parents, recreation department staff, and community opinion leaders, including media representatives, are contacted. Interested stakeholders meet to form a planning coalition.

2. Establishment of Shared Vision After much discussion and negotiation, a consensus (shared vision) is reached by the planning coalition to promote the adoption of regular physical activity and healthy eating behaviours in elementary school children. The ultimate goal is to increase the likelihood that lifelong healthy eating and physical activity habits will be established, thereby modifying the risk factors for obesity, the main modifiable risk factor for developing type 2 diabetes.

3. Inputs The health department, the municipal recreation department, and the Boards of Education have committed staff and time to the proposed project. Community agency representatives and parents have agreed to volunteer time to conduct activities. The media representatives have offered in-kind donations such as newspaper articles, sponsored ads, and public service announcements. Start-up funds will be requested through the provincial grant application process to cover material items and the hiring of a project coordinator.

4. Identification of Best Practices The CHNs are aware that a review of the literature "to summarize the evidence of the effectiveness of school-based interventions in reducing obesity and promoting physical activity and nutrition in children and adolescents" was conducted for the Ontario Public Health Association (Micucci, Thomas, & Vohra, 2002, p. 9). The results were inconclusive, but practice recommendations contained in the review suggest that programs should be multifaceted, contain a classroom component, include environmental change strategies, be behaviourally focused, and be tailored to address the concerns of different age, sex, and ethnic groups. The report also states, "a dose-response effect was evident in that effective interventions were longer in duration and had frequent booster sessions" (Micucci et al., p. 41). In view of these recommendations, promising strategies will be developed in the program action plans.

To determine which interventions are most appropriate for Greenacres, the coalition members will brainstorm about which theoretical model to use (see Chapter 8) and about each of the proposed strategies. The coalition members intend to consider recruitment, health education, change process, and group process strategies. They also plan to monitor environmental forces in the community such as school budget guidelines and rural school bus transportation issues. Promising interventions may be considered, such as the Walking School Bus program to increase children's physical activity (Greenest City, 1999), walking and bicycling paths in the community, after-school recreational activities, healthy menus for restaurants and fast-food outlets, and media campaigns. The program action plans will be based on the program logic model, expand on each of the selected strategies, and identify the local resources to be used in program implementation.

5. Short-Term Outcomes Changes in awareness, knowledge, attitudes, skills, opinions, aspirations, and motivations are **short-term outcomes** that will be considered. Possible short-term outcomes could be an increase in the number of classroom educational sessions on healthy eating, an increase in the number of students participating in physically active games during lunch and recess periods, an increase in the number of schools that offer daily physical education opportunities, and healthier food choices in school cafeterias, snack shops, and after-school programs.

6. Long-Term Outcomes The main consideration in setting intermediate and long-term objectives is to determine outcomes that measure changes in behaviour. **Long-term outcomes** in relation to physical activity could include reduced time spent on television viewing and playing computer games, increased time spent in regular out-of-school physical activities, increased number of children walking to school daily, an increase in the number of children who meet average fitness standards, a decrease in the number of students who are overweight as indicated by basic metabolic indexes, and a decrease in the number of children who have excessive body fat as shown by skin-fold measures.

Targeting Outcomes of Programs (TOP)

Another framework used in program planning and evaluation is **Targeting Outcomes of Programs (TOP)**, a hierarchy for targeting outcomes and evaluating their achievement, developed by Kay Rockwell and Claude Bennett (2000). Figure 13.4 shows it to be a two-sided, seven-level hierarchical model. It is used in the development of diverse information, training, and educational programs, including school health programs (Cramer & Iverson, 1999). TOP integrates program evaluation within the program development process. It focuses on the degree to which the outcomes of programs are achieved and relies on community input for planning and evaluation. The left side of the TOP framework depicts program development while the right side depicts program performance.

Program development comprises the upper three levels on the left of the diagram: SEE (social, economic, and environmental) conditions, Practices, and KASA (knowledge,

FIGURE 13.4 Framework for Targeting Outcomes of Programs (TOP)

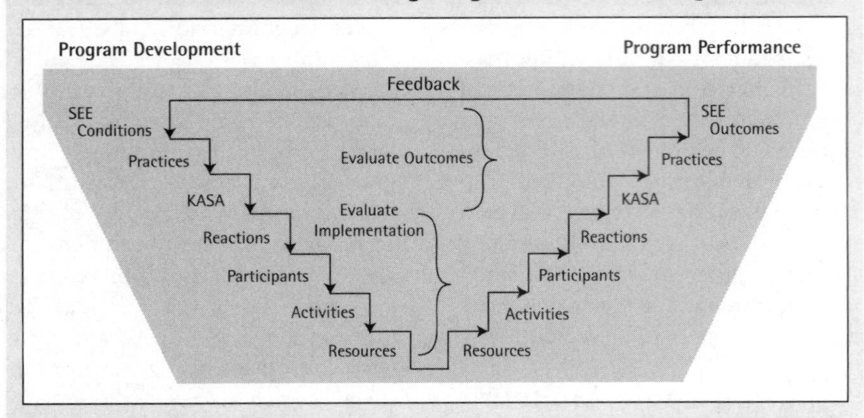

Source: Redrawn with permission from Rockwell, S. K., & Bennett, C. F. (2000). Targeting Outcomes of Programs (TOP): A hierarchy for targeting outcomes and evaluating their achievement. *Lincoln, NE: University of Nebraska, Institute of Agriculture and Natural Resources. Retrieved March 14, 2002 from* http://deal.unl.edu/TOP/

attitudes, skills, and aspirations). These three levels assess the community's needs.

At the **SEE** level, planners investigate and assess the social, economic, and environmental conditions that have an effect on the community of interest. This portion of the assessment examines factors such as mortality rates, household income levels, transportation, water potability, and police and fire services. The assessment incorporates scientific research approaches as well as self-report approaches through participation by members of the community (see Chapter 10). From this information, the planners can identify conditions that need changing and set priority targets for change. The **Practices** level consists of an assessment of the behaviours that exist in the target community, selecting those that could potentially be used to improve the community's social, economic, and environmental conditions, that is, an assessment of the community's capacity to build upon its strengths. The **KASA** level focuses on a determination of the knowledge, attitudes, skills, and aspirations needed by the people in the target group to achieve the desired outcomes. Program activities are aimed at influencing people to adopt the selected practices and technologies that will help them to achieve the targeted outcomes.

Program possibilities are assessed at the lower four levels on the left: Reactions, Participation, Activities, and Resources. When developing the program's activities, the planners must identify the types of reactions needed to change behaviours and acquire the desired KASAs so that sufficient participation in these activities is built into the program plan. They must consider the duration, continuity, frequency, and intensity of program involvement required to provide the participants with an optimal opportunity to acquire the desired behaviours. The participants' reactions, either positive or negative, may be affected by their reactions to the people delivering the program as well as to the subject matter and methods used in delivering the program. Finally, the planners must identify and acquire those resources, such as money, staff, materials, transportation, and facilities, required to implement the program.

The program logic model and the TOP hierarchy framework provide simplified structures for program planning. In actuality, the process can be quite complex and planners will shift between levels or phases of the models as they design and develop the program. These models help planners present to stakeholders, funders, and staff a logical argument to justify the need for a new program or for the continuation or expansion of existing programs.

PROGRAM EVALUATION

While planning is a process for problem solving and a method to initiate change, evaluation is a process to determine what has been achieved and what can be improved. The evaluation portion of the planning-evaluation cycle will now be addressed using the same models that were presented in the planning portion of the chapter to illustrate various aspects of evaluation.

Program evaluation looks at what works and what else needs to be done. During the evaluation process, the program's strengths and weaknesses are reviewed. The raw data collected during the monitoring process are examined and analyzed. The analysis may include an evaluation of the cost-effectiveness of different health promotion strategies (an important consideration for future program delivery), or it can compare the effectiveness of different programs. Based on the results of the evaluation, service delivery can be improved to make it more effective and efficient. The evaluation results may also be fed back into the planning process.

The increased emphasis on evidence-based decision making requires nurses at all levels of an organization to integrate the principles of program evaluation into their practice (Clark, 2003; Porteous, Sheldrick, & Stewart, 1997). These principles include the following beliefs:

- Program evaluation is a structured, systematic process for examining all aspects of programs to obtain data for decision-making and accountability purposes.
- Evaluation activities should be incorporated into all phases of program development and delivery.
- Underlying assumptions, values, and beliefs about the aims of the program must be clearly articulated in order that the questions posed for the evaluation process are relevant.
- The purpose and rationale for any evaluation must be stated explicitly.
- The purposes for conducting an evaluation determine the methodologies selected.
- Confidentiality issues related to the collection of data and the reporting of findings must be dealt with in advance.
- Ethical implications with respect to beneficence and non-maleficence, that is, doing good and not causing harm to staff and clients, must be addressed.
- Evaluation processes should be socially, culturally, and politically sensitive to all persons involved in or impacted by the program.
- Evaluation findings should be made available in a timely manner to all stakeholders.

The importance of conducting evaluations in a responsible and ethical manner is supported by the Canadian Evaluation Society's (1996) Guidelines for Ethical Conduct, which are listed below:

- Evaluators are to be competent in their provision of service.
- Evaluators are to act with integrity in their relationships with all stakeholders.
- Evaluators are to be accountable for their performance and their product.

Types of Evaluation

Knowledge of the various types of program evaluation that may be conducted is essential for community nursing practice. Evaluation methods are broadly grouped into two main categories—formative and summative.

Formative evaluations, also referred to as **process evaluations**, are concerned with improving program operations. They are particularly useful in the early stages of program implementation for identifying operational problems, for example, by having pilot groups provide feedback on the program during a testing phase. On an ongoing basis, formative evaluations are used for monitoring and revising program activities when necessary. This can be accomplished by activities such as collecting continuous feedback from program participants. These evaluations are frequently conducted by internal evaluation groups. Formative evaluations may also provide documented evidence of the historical development of various aspects of a program.

Summative evaluations assess the effectiveness of the program. Because they are performed at the completion of the program activities, the focus is on the outcome. Did the program make a difference? Is the program worth continuing or expanding? Since they examine whether a program has met its stated goals and objectives and whether the outcomes of delivering the program have achieved the intended effect, summative evaluations may also be referred to as **outcome evaluations** (Alter & Murty, 1997; Billings, 2000). Summative evaluations are often mandated by policy or conducted as part of policy reviews and are less likely to address issues of program implementation (Rowe, 1999). Frequently these evaluations are carried out by outside evaluators or by senior managers in an organization. Summative evaluations incorporate impact evaluation and use tools such as population surveys, measures of behavioural change, and tests to show biological changes. These final or summary evaluation findings are particularly valuable when decisions need to be made about the continuation or expansion of a program.

Variations on these two main categories of evaluation also take place. Some organizations are concerned that a summative evaluation does not take into account the process of program delivery and may not provide sufficient information about why a program has succeeded or failed. Therefore, they move to a more comprehensive evaluation, using various approaches to increase the accuracy and depth of their findings. This is referred to as **pluralistic evaluation**, since it combines both formative and summative components. For example, a pluralistic evaluation may involve activities such as periodically observing and interviewing participants in the program (formative component), conducting pre- and post-tests to measure changes in knowledge levels, and collecting other statistical data for use in determining whether the program has been effective or in comparing the program's approach to alternate program delivery models (summative component). Pluralistic evaluations may include documenting aspects of the history of the project and consideration of particularly key decision points and features of implementation processes. Pluralistic evaluation accumulates evidence from a variety of different sources and uses diverse research methods in order to generate conclusions concerning the outcomes of a project (Billings, 2000).

Another variation is called the **participatory, collaborative, or empowerment evaluation** approach. These terms are often used interchangeably, although empowerment evaluation is an outgrowth of and not necessarily synonymous with participatory and collaborative evaluation approaches (Fetterman, 1999), since an evaluation can involve participants but may not be empowering. In discussing empowerment evaluation, Billings (2000) comments, "This approach is described as using evaluation concepts, techniques and findings to facilitate improvement and self-determination and utilizes both qualitative and quantitative methods" (p. 474). The participatory/collaborative approach is formative in nature. It is a constructive process, which uses evaluation concepts, techniques, and findings. The participants in the program, including staff, volunteers, and other stakeholders, exercise control over the entire evaluation process. No external person or individual internal manager is responsible for conducting the evaluation although they may be available to act as facilitators or mentors.

The participants determine whether the program is responsive to their needs and determine future program directions (Billings, 2000; Ellis, Reid, & Barnsley, 1990).

Another evaluation approach is the use of the **balanced scorecard**, which focuses on measuring and improving organizational performance through examining different components of the organization and its programs. This formative approach was developed by Robert Kaplan of Harvard University and David Norton originally for use in business corporations. It has been used by some government and not-for-profit organizations, and, therefore, brief mention is made of it here. The balanced scorecard focuses on four indicators—customer perspective, internal-business processes, learning and growth, and financials—to monitor progress toward an organization's strategic goals. It is based on auditing and accounting principles and is useful for organizations that need to report to funders accustomed to business language reports. It provides feedback around both internal business processes and external outcomes in order to continuously improve strategic performance and results (Arveson & Rohm, 2001; Bozzo & Hall, 1999).

Traditionally, the measures used for evaluation purposes have been categorized as structural, process, and outcome criteria. **Structural criteria** consist of measures of organizational resources, such as staffing ratios, equipment, facilities, and policies, which provide the framework for the work environment. These elements impact efficiency as well as costs for program delivery. Without these resources, provision of service would not be possible. **Process criteria** measure the quality of the interventions used in delivering the program. They assess whether the program is functioning as intended. **Outcome criteria** examine the impact of the program on the target group or community. They assess whether the program is achieving the desired changes. These three types of criteria are incorporated into the evaluation methods described above, with some methods placing greater emphasis on the use of one type over another.

Whether the evaluation is formative or summative in nature, the selection of the evaluation approaches begins with considering the purposes for the evaluation. The evaluators have to establish the intended recipients of the evaluation findings, determine the questions to be answered, ascertain when the results are required, and clarify any planned future uses of the appraisal results. These requirements help determine which evaluation approach should be selected. As noted earlier, these questions should be considered during the assessment and planning phases of program development so that appropriate evaluation methodologies can be selected and integrated into the program's structure. This allows for relevant data collection and for the timely deployment of human and material resources for program monitoring and evaluation. However, if an existing program is being evaluated, the evaluation methodologies may need to be selected and applied at the time the evaluation process is being developed.

Common Program Models Used in Evaluation

Recent years have seen an emphasis on the use of outcome measurement for evaluation in the nonprofit sector. For example, in 1997, the Public Health Branch of the Ontario Ministry of Health issued an educational resource to all

FIGURE 13.5 Program Evaluation Approach

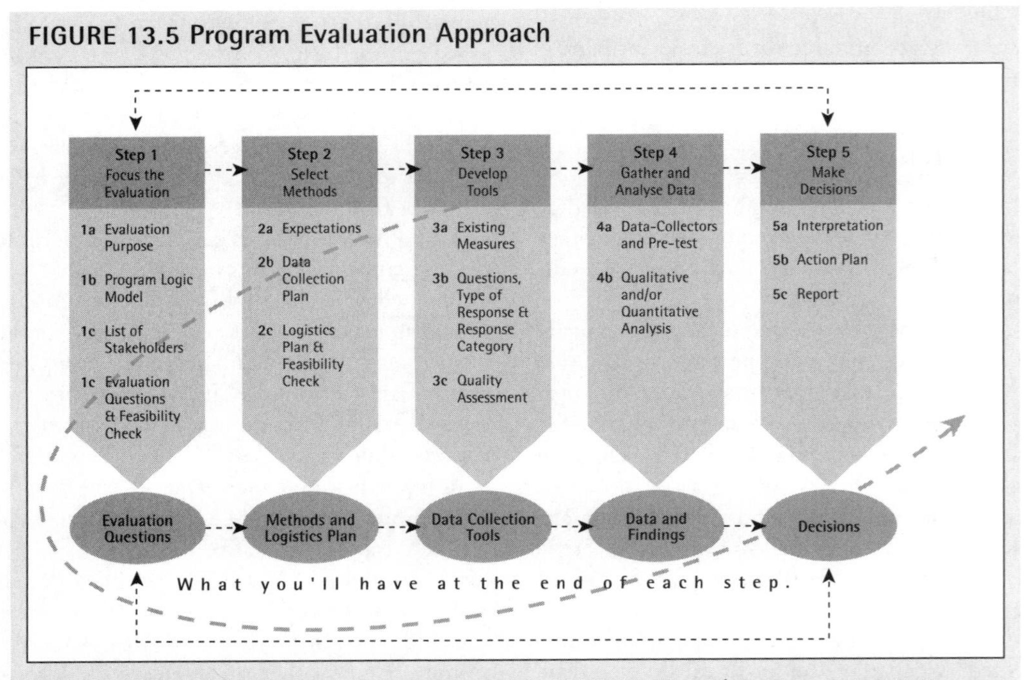

Source: Redrawn with permission from Porteous, N. L., Sheldrick, B. J., & Stewart, P. J. (1997). Program evaluation kit: a blueprint for public health management. *Ottawa, ON: Ottawa-Carleton Health Department.*

FIGURE 13.6 TOP Performance Evaluation

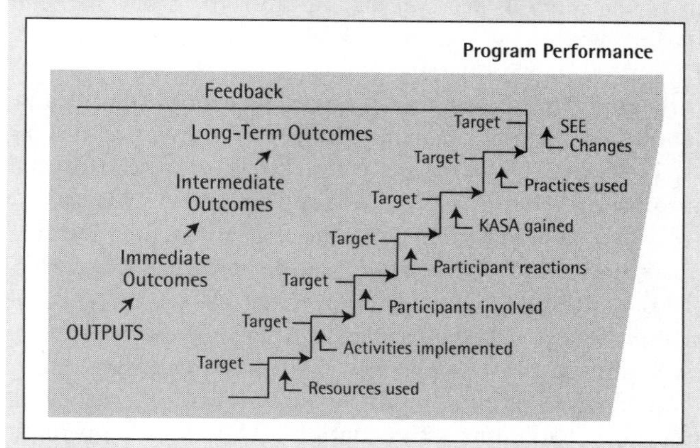

Source: Redrawn with permission from Rockwell, S. K., & Bennett, C. F. (2000). Targeting Outcomes of Programs (TOP): A hierarchy for targeting outcomes and evaluating their achievement. *Lincoln, NE: University of Nebraska, Institute of Agriculture and Natural Resources. Retrieved March 14, 2002 from* http://deal.unl.edu/TOP/

Medical Officers of Health in the province for use in evaluation activities at the local level. The resource, "A Program Evaluation Kit," is based on a program logic model (Porteous, Sheldrick, & Stewart, 1997). Figure 13.5 illustrates the steps this resource uses for evaluation, providing a clear guide to the evaluation process. The dotted lines from Step 5 back to Step 1 show the feedback loop, indicating that as decisions are reached, evaluators should return to the starting step and use the information gained to reshape the program. This framework is consistent with the principles of evaluation listed earlier in this chapter. It depicts a structured, systematic process for developing all aspects of a program.

TOP Framework and Evaluation From an evaluation perspective, the hierarchical levels of the TOP framework are examined in ascending order using the right side of the framework, as shown in Figure 13.6. The four lower levels appraise the effectiveness of program implementation using quantifiable process measures such as cost of resources used, number of program activities delivered, the number of participants involved in the program, and the reactions of the participants as shown by such tools as program satisfaction questionnaires. Feedback from program volunteers and staff also contributes to the evaluation of participant reactions. These findings help to identify whether changes are needed in programming.

The top three levels involve an evaluation of the program's impact on the target outcomes. Ways of measuring changes for KASA evaluation include pre-post differences (differences between before and after the program) in knowledge, attitude surveys using validated measurement scales, pre-post differences in skill scores, self-reports, and focus groups to obtain feedback from participants about changes in their knowledge, attitudes, skills, and aspirations and about their perceptions of the actual or potential benefits of the program. The impact on program participants' practices is evaluated by using specific, scientifically based measures of behavioural change and through self-reports by participants of their adoption of recommended practices. SEE outcomes are evaluated to determine if the program had a public or community impact that went beyond the program participants. Population surveys, morbidity data, cost-benefit analyses, and surveys of stakeholders are possible means for examining SEE outcomes. The evaluation of the program's effectiveness assists in decision making regarding program continuation or modification and its potential for expansion to other areas (Rockwell & Bennett, 2000).

Participatory Monitoring and Evaluation (PME) Over the past few decades there has been mounting pressure from governments and other program funders for greater accountability and transparency, not only in program planning, but also in program monitoring and evaluation. There is also an increasing awareness that the process needs to be more inclusive, that stakeholders and beneficiaries need to be involved in monitoring and evaluation. Program monitoring and evaluation are more likely to be effective when the program has been designed in a participatory manner from the beginning. This focus on participant involvement distinguishes participatory monitoring from conventional monitoring and evaluation. Rather than

TABLE 13.1
Differences between Conventional and Participatory Monitoring and Evaluation

Aspect	Conventional Monitoring and Evaluation Approach	Participatory Monitoring and Evaluation Approach
Process planning and management	Evaluation done by senior managers or outside experts	Done by local people, project staff, managers, and other stakeholders; often helped by a facilitator
Role of primary stakeholders, that is, the intended beneficiaries	Passive role, provide information only	Design and adapt the methodology, collect and analyze data, share findings, and link them to action
Measures of success	Externally defined, mainly quantitative indicators	Internally defined indicators, including more qualitative judgments
Approach	Predetermined; focus is on the final report	Adaptive; more process oriented

having senior managers or outside experts plan and manage the process, the local project staff and stakeholders are involved in the planning and managing with external people acting as information sources and facilitators, rather than as experts with a predetermined approach to the evaluation process (Guijt & Gaventa, 1998). Table 13.1 compares participatory monitoring and evaluation with conventional methods.

The **participatory monitoring and evaluation** approach is widely used in development projects sponsored by governments and non-governmental agencies such as the United Way in Canada and the United Nations and other aid organizations in developing countries. One example is the Yunnan Maternal and Child Health Project, one of largest projects funded by Canadian International Development Agency (CIDA) in China. This six-year project, which began in 1997, has been implemented collaboratively by the University of Ottawa School of Nursing and the Yunnan Provincial Public Health Bureau. A cascading train-the-trainer approach was used to train about 5000 grassroots maternal and child health workers, both in classroom training sessions and community fieldwork practice. Through the participatory process, two Canadian CHNs, Nancy Edwards and Lucia Yiu Matuk, led and worked with local women, health workers, and community leaders in the planning and evaluation process. Participants analyzed their own community situations, exchanged experiences and knowledge, and explored emerging questions and solutions. Community-based processes and participatory tools (see Chapter 10) were used to establish an effective, unique comprehensive referral system for poor, high-risk pregnant women living in ten remote and isolated districts which experienced high rates of maternal mortality and morbidity and infant mortality. By the end of 2002, the Yunnan project had already achieved considerable and impressive reductions in maternal and infant mortality and morbidity rates (Armstrong, 2001).

PME differs from conventional evaluation as well in the way it measures success. In conventional monitoring, success is measured using externally defined indicators that are primarily quantitative in nature. In participatory monitoring, the stakeholders and the beneficiaries decide together how progress should be measured and the results acted upon. The indicators may include more qualitative judgments as the community determines whether the health program is responsive to its needs. The approach is adaptive rather than predetermined. As Guijt and Gaventa (1998) state, "It is a challenging process for all concerned since it encourages people to examine their assumptions about what constitutes progress, and to face up to the contradictions and conflicts that can emerge" (p. 1). PME promotes the development of the community and is particularly attuned to local views and practices rather than the ideas of outside experts.

PME is based on five fundamental principles: participation, negotiation, learning, flexibility, and methodological eclecticism (Clayton, Oakley, & Pratt, 1998; Guijt & Gaventa, 1998). Participation involves the creation of structures and processes that include the persons most directly affected by the program in the design and analysis processes. Strategies to involve these people include clearly identifying and communicating the benefits to potential participants, involving them in decision making from the beginning, and finding ways to give them genuine power (Van Marris & King, 2002). Negotiation requires a commitment to work through differences and reach agreements about what will be monitored and evaluated, the division of responsibilities for data collection, how the evaluation will be conducted, what the data mean, how findings will be shared, and what actions will result. These participatory negotiations lead to learning about what works and what does not, which leads to corrective action and program improvement. Since the circumstances, people, and skills available for the process change over time, flexibility is required. Those involved in and affected by these changes need to modify their strategies so that work toward goal attainment can continue. This requires openness to change and a willingness to try different methods.

Practitioners and beneficiaries can draw on a wide range of methods and tools that have been developed, such as **GANTT charts**, which specify the time frames for tasks and identify the persons to work on each task. An example of a GANTT chart is shown in Figure 13.7. Some new techniques that are relevant to the local situation may also be created. Commonly used methods are displayed in Table 13.2. These methods, which seek to compare the situation before and after a set of events, require the acceptance of less stringent information than is required for conventional research purposes. Thus, they may need to be used in parallel with conventional methods depending on whether or not the program is part of a research study or depending on the specific requirements of funding organizations.

Figure 13.8 shows the cyclical nature of the participatory monitoring and evaluation process. As in the program logic model and TOP, stakeholders and willing partners to the process need to be identified, since there is widespread recognition that to be successful, planning and evaluation require group participation. People in our society are no longer willing to have one person make the decisions about programs that impact their lives; problem solving is based on partnership and cooperation. Values and beliefs need to be clarified, and commitment to the process needs to be obtained from participants at the outset. PME can be an empowering process and must be built on trust and respect.

The program's work needs to be defined and priorities for monitoring and evaluating identified. These priorities must reflect the socioeconomic conditions, political and cultural factors, and other conditions that affect the health of the community and must be selected on the basis of what the participants deem to be important. Participants should select indicators that apply to the local situation and resources and that will also provide the necessary information for evaluation. Methods of data collection, both quantitative and qualitative, are chosen to support the selected indicators. Who will collect the data, and how and when they will be collected, must also be decided. As the program proceeds, data are collected and analyzed. The participants may decide to share the results with others who could benefit from their experience. They may use the information to develop reports for program funders and to modify the program if they agree that the program needs to

FIGURE 13.7 Example of GANTT Chart

This chart specifies an overall project time frame of six months with time frames depicted in two-week allotments and includes a section for identifying the persons working on the different tasks. Note: The time frames shown are suggested task allotment intervals and would need to be determined by the planning group. Actual times taken could vary, requiring adjustments to the times projected on the chart.

Key: △ Begin task ▲ Complete task ——— Duration of task

	Time (in weeks)												
Task	2	4	6	8	10	12	14	16	18	20	22	24	Task group members
Assemble the planning group	△	▲											
Clarify expectations	△	▲											
Establish shared vision		△	▲										
Identify best practices		△	▲										
Identify tasks and group members		△	▲										
Define priorities for monitoring and evaluation			△	▲									
Identify indicators of desired information			△	▲									
Agree on data collection methods			△	▲									
Collect the information				△	—	—	—	—	▲				
Analyze the information									△	—	▲		
Interpret the findings											△	▲	
Determine use of findings											△	▲	
Make recommendations											△	▲	

TABLE 13.2
Common Participatory Monitoring and Evaluation Methods

Maps	To show the location and types of changes in the area being monitored
Venn diagrams	To show direct and indirect impacts of changes and relate them to causes
Flow diagrams	To show direct and indirect impacts of changes and relate them to causes
Diaries	To describe changes in the lives of individuals or groups
Photographs	To depict changes through a sequence of images
Matrix scoring	To compare people's preferences for a set of options or outcomes
Network diagrams	To show changes in the type and degree of contact between people and services

Source: Redrawn with permission from Guijt, I., & Gaventa, J. (1998). Participatory monitoring & evaluation: Learning from change. *IDS Policy Briefing, 12. Brighton, UK: University of Sussex, Institute of Development Studies. Retrieved July 18, 2002 from* www.ids.ac.uk/ids/bookshop/briefs/Brief12.html

FIGURE 13.8 Participatory Monitoring and Evaluation Processes

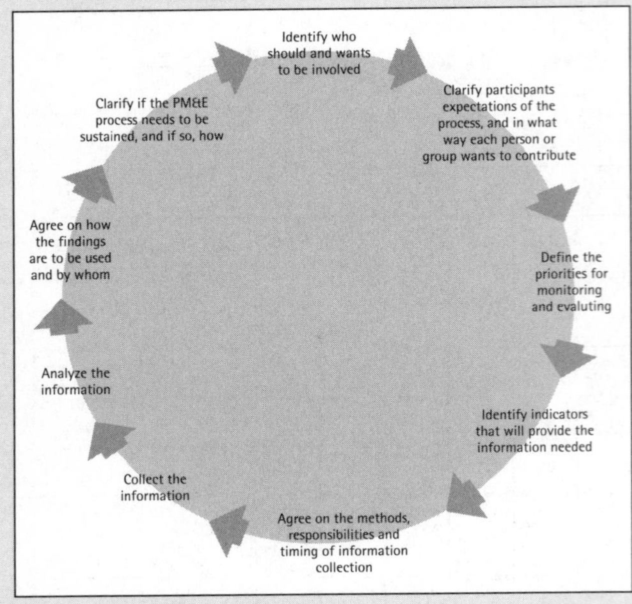

Source: Redrawn with permission from Guijt, I., & Gaventa, J. (1998). Participatory monitoring & evaluation: Learning from change. *IDS Policy Briefing, 12. Brighton, UK: University of Sussex, Institute of Development Studies. Retrieved July 18, 2002 from* www.ids.ac.uk/ids/bookshop/briefs/Brief12.html

continue. In the latter instance, the information would provide feedback for the process to continue in a cyclical manner.

PME recognizes people's capacity to develop solutions to meet their health needs by building on their strengths. This approach is well aligned with Standard 2: Building Individual/Community Capacity in the Canadian Community Health Nursing Standards of Practice (see Appendix A). It requires CHNs to use a collaborative approach in providing leadership that will assist others to reach their goals and gain the skills to become independent problem solvers and decision makers.

Reporting Evaluation Findings

One of the driving forces behind the increasing requirement to conduct evaluations is the growing demand for accountability. **Accountability** has been defined as "a relationship based on the obligation to demonstrate and take responsibility for performance in light of agreed expectations" (Office of the Auditor General of Canada and the Treasury Board Secretariat, 1998, p. 4). The agreement referred to is either explicit or implicit—either explicitly stated by funders through formal agreements or implicitly assumed as an expectation by the general public. When programs are delivered, it is implicitly expected that they are designed to provide a benefit and will be conducted with honesty and integrity.

With their high degree of autonomy and independence, CHNs must conduct themselves responsibly and be answerable for their actions. This means informing and reporting to the public and responding to public requests for information about services and programs. Public pressure is increasing for greater openness or transparency about what organizations and agencies do. Society is less willing to blindly accept assurances that programs are meeting their best interests. This pressure is also reflected in stakeholders' and funders' expectations of reports on the results of services provided.

Evaluations may be conducted for internal and external use. Internal stakeholders who are interested in the evaluation results include the participants, staff, and volunteers who delivered the program; program managers and other organizational administrators; persons or groups who collaborated in designing or delivering the program; and any funders associated with the program. They will want to know the results of their efforts and how they might improve (McNamara, 1998). Other interested parties may include

Canadian Research Box 13.1

Herbert, R., & White, R. (1996). Healthy hearts at work: Prince Edward Island Heart Health Program: CSC worksite pilot project. *Canadian Journal of Cardiovascular Nursing, 7*(2), 12–18.

Based on the principles of community mobilization, this pilot project developed a multi-faceted risk-appraisal tool called Heart Check. The target population comprised 800 civil service employees working in Prince Edward Island. Two hundred and fifty-one persons participated during the six-day Heart Check in June 1992. Evaluation measures to examine process, short-term impact, and long-term outcomes were developed. Process evaluation measures included examination of the planning process, employee participation rates, and partner agency contributions. Outcome evaluation measures were based on a Heart Check intervention model developed by the Ottawa-Carleton Heart Health Program. Components of the Heart Check intervention were body mass index (BMI), blood pressure, total serum cholesterol, smoking, level of physical activity, dietary habits, perceived ability to cope with stress, age, gender, family history of heart disease, and personal history of heart disease. As a result of the program, participants with identified risk behaviours for cardiovascular disease indicated intentions to make necessary behaviour changes to reduce the risk. Participants who were referred to physicians because of elevated blood pressure and cholesterol actually made behaviour changes to reduce their risk. The pilot project concluded that the partnership had a synergistic effect as more programs were delivered than either agency could have done on their own.

Discussion Questions

1. Assuming that the results of the outcome evaluation are positive, what strategies would you develop to implement this project at other work sites?
2. Read three other articles on workplace health promotion programs and compare their evaluation measures with those used in this study.

public officials, community residents, other community providers, the media, and researchers. Because public officials often have to justify to taxpayers what is happening in the community, they frequently have input in funding decisions. Many community residents may be curious about a program's activities and interested in hearing about the evaluation results. Other community providers may want to examine how the program interfaces with their services or may be interested in making or receiving referrals to the program or in contributing to the program in some manner. Community agencies in other areas may be interested in replicating the program. The media provide information to the public and serve a watchdog role. Reports of the evaluation results can promote the program and enhance efforts to be publicly accountable. Researchers exploring programs and strategies for service delivery in other areas or communities may be interested in the findings or in further investigations of some aspects of the program.

When initially identifying the purpose(s) for conducting the evaluation, the potential users of the information should be considered. If the needs of stakeholders are built into the evaluation from the beginning, it is easier to provide a useful report and increase support for the process. Furthermore, when pertinent information is collected, the results will more likely be used for decision making.

Evaluation results can be presented in a variety of ways, such as written reports, oral presentations, report cards, and media releases. Evaluation reports should be prepared in a timely manner, which increases the likelihood that they will be meaningful, and in a manner easily understood by the intended audience. For the latter reason, more than one version of the report may need to be developed, for example, a longer, more detailed report for funders and a briefer version for general audiences.

The format for formal written reports typically includes

- a title page,
- table of contents,
- an executive summary providing a concise overview of the findings and recommendations,
- a background explanation about the program,
- a statement regarding the purpose(s) of the evaluation,
- an explanation of the methods used in conducting the evaluation,
- an account of the findings with interpretations and expressions of limitations about the findings, and
- any conclusions and recommendations arising from the appraisal.

Appendices may also be attached to the report to illustrate or expand on specific aspects of the evaluation such as data collection instruments, tables showing data analyses, references, and related literature (McNamara, 1998).

Brief reports and oral presentations (usually with complementary visual aids) highlighting the evaluation's results can be made to participants, staff, funders, other health practitioners, and community groups. These presentations can emphasize the accomplishments of the program to gain community support for program modifications and continued funding or to advocate for program expansion.

Report cards are being used in the public sector to provide brief synopses of evaluation results. Although they are often presented as comparisons amongst groups of programs, they can present the results of a specific evaluation. They offer an "at-a-glance" view of the evaluation by focusing on the measurement criteria and the evaluation results.

Media releases provide information to the general public and are an important way to meet the demands for public accountability. They generally outline the reasons for the evaluation and the main findings and recommendations arising from the evaluation. They may also provide brief background information about the program. Media releases can help to shape community opinion and gather support for new or continued program funding.

SUMMARY

This chapter presented the effect of societal influences, such as economic constraints, widespread internet usage, a growing emphasis on individual rights, and increased demands for accountability, on program planning and evaluation. In today's society, CHNs at all levels of an organization are expected to play an important role in program planning and evaluation. To meet this role requirement, CHNs need to be educated about the processes involved.

Program planning and evaluation are integrally related and cyclical in nature. The main features of program development and evaluation were presented separately in order to focus on various aspects of the processes. Reminders of the integrated nature of program planning and evaluation were included at various points throughout the chapter, particularly with respect to the importance of building evaluation measures into the planning process and of involving stakeholders at the beginning stages of each of these processes.

The PRECEDE-PROCEED framework, the Program Logic Model, and Targeting Outcomes of Programs (TOP) were briefly outlined and the planning steps for each of these models examined. Formative and summative evaluations were introduced along with common variations in

CASE STUDY

Referring to the Greenacres community example and Figure 13.3, develop a hypothetical scenario for a program logic model using the types of background information provided in this chapter. Apply it to the TOP hierarchical framework in relation to program development.

Discussion Questions

1. What additional background information would you need in order to consider all levels of the framework?
2. What similarities and differences do you see in these two methods?

these approaches, namely, pluralistic, participatory, and the balanced scorecard. Structure, process, and outcome criteria, which are historical ways of classifying measurement criteria, were briefly presented. Use of the Program Logic Model and the TOP framework in evaluation was explored. Finally, the need to report evaluation findings was addressed as there is little value in engaging in the evaluation process if the results are not used to contribute to decision making and future planning.

Program planning and evaluation skills are essential to modern community health nursing practice. The concepts associated with planning, monitoring, and evaluation are reflected in the values and standards for community health nursing practice as set forth in the Canadian Community Health Nursing Standards of Practice. Although beginning practitioners may need a mentor to support them in these activities during the early stages of their career, they can participate with increasing levels of confidence, independence, and expertise as their experience grows.

KEY TERMS

planning-evaluation cycle
PRECEDE-PROCEED framework
program logic model
inputs
processes
products
outputs
outcomes
indicators
short-term outcomes
long-term outcomes
Targeting Outcomes of Programs (TOP)
SEE (social, economic, and environmental)
practices level
KASA (knowledge, attitudes, skills, and aspirations)
program evaluation
formative evaluations
process evaluations
summative evaluations
outcome evaluations
pluralistic evaluation
participatory evaluation
collaborative evaluation
empowerment evaluation
balanced scorecard
structural criteria
process criteria
outcome criteria
participatory monitoring and evaluation
GANTT charts
accountability
report cards

STUDY QUESTIONS

1. Identify and describe five pressures in modern Western society that influence program planning and evaluation.
2. Identify the steps in the planning-evaluation cycle.
3. Identify the steps in a basic program logic model and define the type of information considered at each step.
4. Differentiate between outputs and outcomes in a program logic model and provide examples to illustrate each term.
5. Identify each of the seven levels in the TOP hierarchy and provide examples of the type of information used for planning and evaluation at each level.
6. Differentiate between formative and summative evaluation and give examples of when each type of evaluation might be conducted.
7. Differentiate between conventional and participatory monitoring and evaluation approaches.
8. Identify seven common participatory monitoring and evaluation methods and state the purpose of each.
9. Identify and describe five reasons for reporting evaluation results.

INDIVIDUAL CRITICAL THINKING EXERCISES

1. You are part of a team delivering a program. One of your tasks is to monitor program implementation. How would you plan to do this?
2. You intend to submit an application for project funding. You have been advised that the funder expects an evaluation report. What questions might the funder want addressed in your final report?
3. Describe the kinds of visual aids, with component parts, that you might develop to present the findings of a program evaluation to a non-participant group in the community.
4. The community of Greenacres is developing a grocery store advertising campaign as part of its program to promote healthy eating. What strategies would you propose for use in this campaign? What short-term outcomes would you establish for the program? What types of data would you collect, and how would you measure the short-term outcomes of your proposed strategies?
5. For the past two years, CHNs at the Health Unit in Greenacres (in cooperation with others, such as teachers, psychologist, social worker, student council representatives) have delivered educational programs aimed at preventing teenage pregnancies. What short-term and long-term outcomes might have been determined for the program? What evaluation data might have been collected to measure these outcomes?

GROUP CRITICAL THINKING EXERCISES

1. Select a health problem in your community for which there are modifiable risk factors. Identify key stakeholders in your community who are dealing with the issue already or who might be available to partner with you to address the problem. How can other resources in your community assist with the problem resolution?
2. Discuss ways to involve key stakeholders in a program planning process. What other means of obtaining community input into program development could be used?
3. Explain ways you might deal with opposition to planning a health promotion program.

REFERENCES

Alter, C., & Murty, S. (1997). Logic modeling: A tool for teaching practice evaluation. *Journal of Social Work Education, 33*(1), 103–117.

Armstrong, L. (2001). Experience with participatory monitoring and evaluation in Yunnan, China. *The Participatory Development Forum e-views, 7.* Retrieved July 19, 2002 **from www.pdforum.org**

Arveson, P., & Rohm, H. (2001). *Rolling it all together: A balanced scorecard approach.* Cary, NC: Balanced Scorecard Institute & U.S. Foundation for Performance Measurement. Retrieved July 22, 2002 from **www.balancedscorecard.org**

Billings, J. R. (2000). Community development: A critical review of approaches to evaluation. *Journal of Advanced Nursing, 31*(2), 472–480.

Bozzo, S. L., & Hall, M. H. (1999). *A review of evaluation resources for nonprofit organizations.* Toronto, ON: Canadian Centre for Philanthropy. Retrieved March 5, 2002 from **www.ccp.ca**

Brown, K. M. (1999). *The PRECEDE-PROCEED model.* Tamp Bay, FL: University of South Florida. Retrieved June 8, 2003 from **http://hsc.usf.edu/~kmbrown/PRECEDE_PROCEED_Overview.htm**

Canadian Evaluation Society. (1996). *CES guidelines for ethical conduct.* Ottawa, ON: Author. Retrieved March 5, 2002 from **http://evaluationcanada.ca**

Carroll, L. (1929). *Alice's adventures in wonderland.* Toronto, ON: Alfred A. Knopf.

Clark, M. J. (2003). *Nursing in the community: Caring for populations (3rd ed.).* Upper Saddle River, NJ. Prentice Hall.

Clayton, A., Oakley, P., & Pratt, B. (1998). *Empowering people: A guidebook on participation.* Oxford, UK: United Nations Development Programme, Civil Society Organizations & Participation Programme. Retrieved July 19, 2002 from **www.undp.org/csopp/CSO/NewFiles/docemppeople.html**

Cramer, M. W., & Iverson, C. J. (1999). Developing an evaluation plan for school health programs in Nebraska. *Journal of School Health, 69*(2), 51–57.

Dwyer, J. J. M., & Makin, S. (1997). Using a program logic model that focuses on performance measurement to develop a program. *Canadian Journal of Public Health, 88*(6), 421–425.

Ellis, D., Reid, G., & Barnsley, J. (1990). *Keeping on track: An evaluation guide for community groups.* Vancouver, BC: Women's Research Centre.

Fetterman, D. M. (1999). Reflections on empowerment evaluation: Learning from experience [Special issue]. *The Canadian Journal of Program Evaluation, 14,* 5–37.

Gielen, A. C., & McDonald, E. M. (2002). Using the PRECEEDE-PROCEED planning model to apply health behavior theories. In K. Glanz, B. K. Rimer, & F. M. Lewis (Eds.), *Health behavior and health education: Theory, research, and practice* (pp. 409–436). San Francisco, CA: J. Wiley & Sons.

Greenest City. (1999). *How to organize a walking school bus program.* Draft. Toronto, ON: Author. Retrieved July 23, 2002 from **www.greenestcity.org**

Guijt, I., & Gaventa, J. (1998). *Participatory monitoring & evaluation: Learning from change.* IDS Policy Briefing, 12. Brighton, UK: University of Sussex, Institute of Development Studies. Retrieved July 18, 2002 from **www.ids.ac.uk/ids/bookshop/briefs/Brief12.html**

McLaughlin, J. A., & Jordan, G. B. (1998). *Logic models: A tool for telling your program's performance story.* Retrieved March 5, 2002 from **www.net/education/Logic.htm**

McNamara, C. (1998). *Basic guide to program evaluation.* St. Paul, MN: The Management Assistance Program for Nonprofits, Free Management Library. Retrieved March 14, 2002 from **www.mapnp.org/library/evaluatn/evaluatn.htm**

McNamara, C. (2000). *Guidelines and framework for designing basic logic models.* Retrieved December 12, 2003 from **www.managementhelp.org/fp_progs/np_mod/org_frm.htm**

Micucci, S., Thomas, H., & Vohra, J. (2002). *The effectiveness of school-based strategies for the primary prevention of obesity and for promoting physical activity and/or nutrition, the major modifiable risk factors for type 2 diabetes: A review of reviews.* Toronto, ON: Ontario Public Health Association.

Office of the Auditor General of Canada & Treasury Board Secretariat. (1998). *Modernizing accountability practices in the public sector.* Draft discussion paper. Retrieved July 26, 2002 from **www.tbs-sct.gc/rma/account/OAGTBS_E.html**

Porteous, N. L., Sheldrick, B. J., & Stewart, P. J. (1997). *Program evaluation kit: A blueprint for public health management.* Ottawa, ON: Ottawa-Carleton Health Department.

Rockwell, S. K., & Bennett, C. F. (2000). *Targeting Outcomes of Programs (TOP): A hierarchy for targeting outcomes and evaluating their achievement.* Lincoln, NE: University of Nebraska, Institute of Agriculture and Natural Resources. Retrieved March 5, 2002 from **http://deal.unl.edu/TOP/**

Rovers, R. (1986). The merging of participatory and analytical approaches to evaluation: Implications for nurses in primary health care programs. *International Journal of Nursing Studies, 23*(3), 211–219.

Rowe, A. (1999). Epilogue: Comments on the Special issue [Special issue]. *The Canadian Journal of Program Evaluation, 14,* 193–197.

Rush, B., & Ogborne, A. (1991). Program logic models: Expanding their role and structure for program planning and evaluation. *The Canadian Journal of Program Evaluation, 6*(2), 95–106.

Taylor-Powell, E. (2001). *Logic model.* Madison, WI: University of Wisconsin–Extension, Program Development and Evaluation. Retrieved March 5, 2002 from **www.uwex.edu/ces/pdande/evaluation/evallogicmodel.htm**

Van Marris, B., and King, B. (2002). *Evaluating health promotion programs* (Version 3.3). Toronto, ON: University of Toronto, Centre for Health Promotion, Health Communication Unit. Retrieved August 3, 2003 from **www.thcu.ca/infoandresources/publications/EVAL%20Master%20Workbook%20v3.3%2010.21.02.pdf**

ADDITIONAL RESOURCES

WEBSITES

American Evaluation Association:
www.eval.org

Canadian Centre for Philanthropy:
www.ccp.ca

Canadian Evaluation Society:
www.evaluationcanada.ca

Health Communication Unit, Centre for Health Promotion:
www.thcu.ca

The Management Assistance Program for Nonprofits, Free Management Library:
www.mapnp.org/library/evaluatn/evaluatn.htm

The Participatory Development Forum:
www.pdforum.org

United Nations Development Program, Civil Service Organizations and Participation Program:
www.undp.org/csopp/CSO/NewFiles/docemppeople.html

United Way of America, Outcome Measurement Resource Network:
www.unitedway.org/outcomes

U.S. Bureau of Justice Assistance (BJA) Evaluation Website:
www.bja.evaluationwebsite.org/html/

About the Author

E. Merilyn Allison, BA (Psychology), BScN (Windsor), MScN (Western Ontario), has 28 years of experience in community health nursing, including positions as Director of Public Health Nursing and later as Director of Home Care Programs for the Kent-Chatham Health Unit. She has been an adjunct assistant professor for the Faculty of Nursing at the University of Windsor since 1989. She operated an independent management consulting business for five years, offering services to community health and social service agencies. Currently, she is a sessional professor for St. Clair College of Applied Arts and Technology in the nursing program at the Thames Campus in Chatham, Ontario.

CHAPTER 14

Research

Donna Ciliska and Helen Thomas

OBJECTIVES

AFTER STUDYING THIS CHAPTER, YOU SHOULD BE ABLE TO:

1. Describe evidence-based practice as it relates to community health nursing.
2. Critically appraise research articles reporting on the effectiveness of treatment or prevention or qualitative research to judge whether they should be utilized in practice, management, or policy decisions.
3. Understand the barriers to utilizing research to change practice, management, and policymaking.
4. Define how one might be involved in future community health research.

INTRODUCTION

Community health nurses (CHNs) continuously participate in research and have opportunities, frequently unrecognized, for improving their care by utilizing high-quality research. For example:

- One CHN role is to support breastfeeding, but you are not always sure that you are successful. Are there any interventions that have been shown to increase the duration and exclusivity of breastfeeding? If so, can breastfeeding interventions have any impact on infant eczema and gastrointestinal (GI) tract infections (Kramer, Chalmers, & Hodnett, 2001)?
- The local school board is concerned that there is too little time to teach the required curriculum, so they are considering reducing the time spent in physical activity. At the same time, the region is concerned about the increasing numbers of overweight children. Are school-based physical activity programs effective in improving fitness in children (Dobbins, Lockett, Michel et al., 2001)?
- The rate of delayed development among school-age children is higher in your area than in the rest of the province. Can parenting programs led by CHNs reduce developmental delay in children (Thomas, Camiletti, Cava et al., 1999)?
- As part of the mental health team, you visit families in which one member has a mental illness. How do family members experience the situation, and do they ever reach acceptance (Karp & Tanarugsachock, 2000)?

Every day, questions like these face CHNs. After graduation, how can nurses continue to be educated critical thinkers whose practice is based on high-quality research evidence? How can busy nurses keep current with the research findings? This chapter highlights strategies that CHNs can use to develop and sustain evidence-based nursing practice.

WHAT IS EVIDENCE-BASED NURSING?

The term **evidence-based nursing** (EBN) has evolved from the initial work done in evidence-based medicine and is defined as the conscientious, explicit, and judicious use of current best evidence in making decisions about the care of individual patients. The practice of evidence-based medicine means integrating individual clinical expertise with the best available external clinical evidence from systematic research (Sackett, Rosenberg, Gray, & Haynes, 1996). We have conceptualized "evidence-based nursing" as broader in context than research utilization. The practice of EBN involves the following steps:

- formulation of an answerable question to address a specific patient problem or situation (Flemming, 1998);
- systematic searching for the research evidence that could be used to answer the question (McKibbon & Marks, 1998a; 1998b);
- appraisal of the validity, relevance, and applicability of the research evidence;
- decision making regarding the change in practice;
- implementation of the evidence-based practice decision; and
- evaluation of the outcome of the decision.

In evidence-based practice, research utilization is integrated with other information that might influence the management of health issues and problems, such as clinical expertise, client preference for alternative forms of care, and available resources (DiCenso, Cullum, & Ciliska, 1998). In Figure 14.1, elements in evidence-based decision making are presented. In the figure they all have equal weight; however, this is unlikely in reality. For example, CHNs have the skills to teach and support breastfeeding, know from the research evidence that breastfeeding intervention is effective (Kramer, Chalmers, & Hodnett, 2001), and have employers who encourage them to utilize work time doing the intervention. However, some new mothers may see the home visit as intrusive and be unwilling to allow it to occur. Similarly, you tell your clients with osteoarthritis that glucosamine can be effective (Towheed, Anastassiades, Shea et al., 1999), but some of your patients do not have the money to purchase it. What difference does the use of research make? Heater, Becker, and Olson (1988) conducted a meta-analysis to determine the contribution of research-based practice to client outcomes. They found 84 nurse-conducted studies involving 4146 patients and reported that clients who received research-based nursing care made "sizeable gains" in behavioural knowledge and physiological and psychosocial outcomes compared with those receiving routine nursing care.

So, why don't all nurses base their practice on evidence? Luker and Kenrick (1992) used qualitative techniques in an exploratory study of CHN decision making in the United Kingdom and determined that the nurses had an awareness of research but did not perceive it as informing their practice. Bostrom and Suter (1993) found that only 21% of 1200 practising nurses had implemented a new research finding in the previous six months. Nurses have reported difficulty in accessing and appraising published research, either because they do not have access to journals and libraries or because they have not been taught how to find and appraise research (Blythe & Royle, 1993; Pearcey, 1995).

Estabrooks (1998) surveyed staff nurses about their use of various sources of knowledge. Those most frequently used were found to be experiential, nursing school (even though the average length of time since completing their basic nursing education program was 18 years), workplace sources, physician sources, intuition, and past usual practice. Literature (whether in textbook or journal form) was rated in the bottom five sources of information for frequency of use. The nurses were also asked to identify the one most common source from which they learned about research findings. While 39% identified nursing journals, additional analyses revealed that the primary journals the nurses were reading were not research journals, but rather trade magazines published by nursing professional organizations.

FIGURE 14.1 Evidence-Based Decision Making

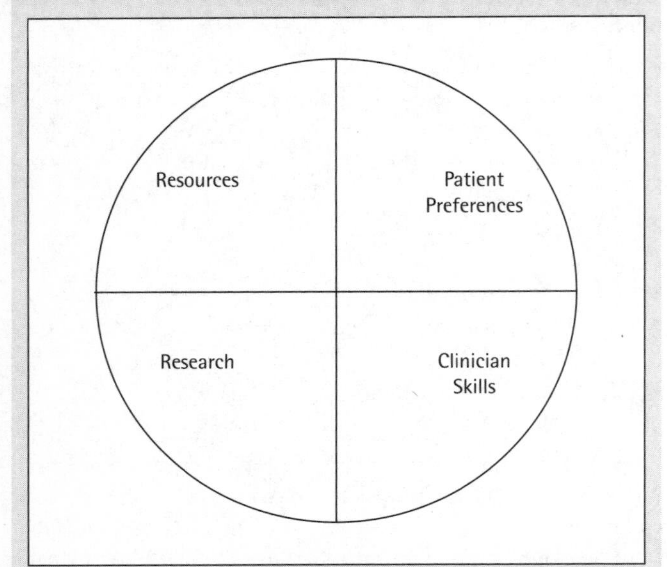

Source: Based on model by DiCenso, A., Cullum, N., and Ciliska D. (1998). Implementing evidence-based nursing: some misconceptions. *Evidence-Based Nursing 1, 38–40, with permission from the BMJ Publishing Group.*

The sheer volume of research is more than any nurse can manage. Nurses working individually cannot hope to find and read even the highest-quality research published each year. This is compounded by the fact that much of the research relevant to community health nursing is published in non-nursing journals.

There is a substantial time lag of eight to fifteen years between the time technical information is generated and the time it is used in actual practice (Lomas, 1991; Utterback, 1974). In addition to barriers faced by individual nurses, multiple political, cultural, economic, and other environmental barriers must be overcome in order to practise in an evidence-based way. However, this chapter will focus more on the abilities and strategies of individual nurses and teams of nurses to implement evidence-based practice.

THE PROCESS OF EVIDENCE-BASED NURSING

Asking Clinical Questions

Nurses need to maintain inquiring minds in order to evaluate interventions and consider options for other interventions. In order to find relevant research, **clinical questions** (also called **structured questions**) need to be structured, usually consisting of the situation, the intervention, and the outcomes (Flemming, 1998). The **situation** is the patient, client, population, or problem being addressed; the **intervention** is the action that is under consideration for some health promotion, disease prevention, or treatment effect; and the **outcome** is the result of interest from the client or clinical perspective. To return to some of the questions in the introduction, the phrasing of the questions might be:

- For new mothers (situation), does a structured breastfeeding support program delivered by a CHN (intervention), affect duration, exclusivity, GI infections, or eczema in the infants (outcomes)?
- Is glucosamine (intervention) effective in reducing pain and increasing functional ability (outcomes) in people with osteoarthritis (situation)?

Conducting an Efficient Search of the Literature

Structuring the question allows one to consider all the possible synonymous search terms for the conduct of an efficient search. The most efficient search is done with the help of a health sciences librarian, taking the original question, the list of synonyms for each component of the question, and any articles already found on the subject. The latter will allow the librarian to see how this type of article is indexed in the relevant databases. It is also important to be clear about the purpose in finding this literature. Is a systematic review needed (which would give direction regarding management or policy and procedure decisions; see section "What is a Systematic Review" below), or are the details of the interventions and their effectiveness needed (in which case the review would give the references for the studies, but one would probably want the individual primary studies as well)?

But what if you don't have access to a librarian? The most time-efficient sources of good data are the websites and journals of pre-appraised research, including *Evidence-Based Nursing, ACP Journal Club, Evidence-Based Medicine, Evidence-Based Cardiovascular Medicine, Evidence-Based Health Policy and Management,* and *Evidence-Based Mental Health.* These journals are similar in format in that they select high-quality research from published journals using explicit quality criteria. Articles that report studies and reviews that warrant immediate attention by nurses attempting to keep pace with important advances are summarized in structured abstracts and commented on by clinical experts. The evidence-based journals are valuable resources that overcome the barriers of time (for example, the time to read all the issues of the over 150 journals that are read for *Evidence-Based Nursing*), search skills, physical access to the original journals, and critical appraisal skills. While each issue of an evidence-based journal may contain only a few articles relevant to community health nursing, searchable on-line databases of abstracts and web-based updates for a specific user profile of clinical interests are available. Generally, *Evidence-Based Health Policy and Management* and *Evidence-Based Nursing* contain the most articles relevant to community health nursing.

Abstracts and commentaries from several abstraction journals (not *Evidence-Based Nursing*) are pooled on the *Best Evidence* CD-ROM (American College of Physicians, 2001). In addition, *Clinical Evidence* (in book format or on-line version; see Additional Resources) is an evidence-based tool organized around common primary care or hospital-based problems. It provides concise accounts of the current state of knowledge, ignorance, and uncertainty about the prevention and treatment of a wide range of clinical conditions based on thorough searches of the literature. *Clinical Evidence* uses information from the Cochrane Library (see below) and the abstraction journals. However, it starts not with the journals, but with the clinical questions such as prevention and treatment of pressure sores or management of acute stroke or acute myocardial infarction.

The Cochrane Collaboration is an international organization that aims to help people make informed decisions about health by preparing, maintaining, and ensuring the accessibility of rigorous, systematic, and up-to-date reviews (including meta-analyses where appropriate) of the benefits and risks of health care interventions (Jadad & Haynes, 1998). Examples of the Cochrane Collaboration's relevance to community health include smoking cessation in the workplace, parent training for improving maternal psychosocial health, and prevention of falls in the elderly. The Cochrane Library is the product of the Collaboration's work and includes reports and protocols from over 1000 systematic reviews produced within the Collaboration; abstracts of over 1800 reviews summarized and critically appraised by the Centre for Reviews and Dissemination at the University of York, UK; and citations for over 200 000 randomized controlled trials. One can search the Cochrane Library, without charge, for abstracts of reviews and, through subscription, for on-line access or the CD-ROM version, which is updated quarterly. Much smaller than Cochrane, the Effective Public Health Practice Project (Hamilton Public Health & Community Services, 2003) is an on-line site for high-quality systematic reviews relevant to public health practice in Canada. Public health practitioners, managers, policy people, and academics from around Ontario are involved in defining important practice and policy questions, setting priorities, conducting systematic reviews, and disseminating and utilizing the information.

If no answer is found to the structured question within the pre-appraised literature, it is necessary to go to other databases. Free on-line access is available for Pub-Med, which can be searched with key words, setting limits for type of publication, year of publication, language, a nursing subset of journals, and so on. Another useful place to search is Cumulative Index of Nursing and Allied Health Literature (CINAHL), but it is not free unless there is access through an academic centre. Similar to Pub-Med, it allows for limits to be set and to search by author or key word.

Critically Appraising Retrieved Articles

Once the articles are found and retrieved, one must decide if their quality is sufficient that one can be confident in using them. Some health care research is too poor in quality to be used in decision making regarding clinical practice. As stated above, this is less critical with some of the pre-appraised sources of research. Several checklists for quality (validity), also known as "Users' Guides," have been developed to help people develop **critical appraisal skills**, that is, the ability to decide if an article is of sufficient methodological quality that it warrants attention for decision making. With a little practice, these skills become easier and quicker to apply.

Outcomes research or evaluative research answers questions about effectiveness or harm and has a quantitative design. As stated in the epidemiology chapter, different research designs are best for answering particular types of questions. For example, questions about effectiveness or harms of certain interventions and prevention are best answered by **randomized controlled trials** in which the investigators have no control over who is placed in the intervention group versus the control group. The most efficient article of this type is a systematic review of randomized trials. However, randomized trials may be unethical, such as randomizing mothers to breastfeed or not to see if breastfeeding is associated with eczema, or randomizing preteens to smoke to see if it causes lung cancer. Also, trials are very expensive. If a trial cannot be done (ethically or financially), the next best design to answer the question is a cohort design, where at least two groups are compared before and after one group receives an intervention. (See Chapter 7 or a basic nursing research text for more information on study designs.)

Questions exploring feelings and experiences are best answered through a qualitative design like phenomenology or grounded theory. Questions and interventions that evolve through partnerships between researchers and participants are best dealt with through participatory action research. **Participatory action research** is action-oriented research in which the researchers and participants are partners in developing the question, intervention, and evaluation. It may be quantitative or qualitative and may involve triangulation of data (Burns & Groves, 2001). One principle when critically appraising articles is to ensure that the appropriate design was used to answer the question.

The Research Boxes in this chapter discuss criteria for critical appraisal of systematic reviews, single intervention studies, and qualitative research and demonstrate the application of the criteria to actual research studies.

Critical Appraisal of Studies of Interventions

The decision to use a study of intervention (usually a treatment or prevention) depends on the findings and the quality of the study design. The quality determines the level of confidence in the findings of the study. The major questions used to evaluate primary studies of interventions or prevention are:

- Are the results valid?
- What are the results?
- Will the results help me in improving the health of clients? (Ciliska, Cullum, & Marks, 2001; Sackett, Strauss, Richardson, Rosenberg, & Haynes, 2000).

The critical appraisal criteria shown in the text box will be explained and applied in relation to the article by Blue et al. (2001a).

Are the Results Valid? This question considers whether the reported results are likely to reflect the true size and direction of the treatment effect. Was the research designed to minimize bias and lead to accurate findings?

Was the assignment of participants to treatment groups randomized, and was the randomization concealed? The purpose of randomization is to remove any control over who is assigned to an intervention or control group. As well, groups should be similar in all respects except for exposure to the intervention. Known and unknown factors (age, sex, socioeconomic status, disease severity) that could influence the outcome of the study are evenly distributed among the groups. Different methods, such as a table of random numbers or computer-generated random numbers, ensure that all participants have an equal chance of being in each of the study groups. The methods section of the article should tell if and how participants were randomized.

The person recruiting the participants into the study should not know to which group each person is allocated. This is called *allocation concealment.* Concealment could happen through a process of a calling a central office to get the allocation of the participant or through the use of numbered, opaque, sealed envelopes. In this way, the recruiter does not know until after the participant is registered to which group they will be assigned, and the participant does not know at all. This prevents the recruiter from exercising bias in recruitment.

Was follow-up sufficiently long and complete? The first of these two criteria has to be judged by the clinician reading the paper. The definition of appropriate length of follow-up varies with different clinical questions. For example, success in weight loss measured at six months after a year-long intervention does not give a true picture of how many people are able to maintain the weight loss. A minimum expectation would be a one-year follow-up. Similarly, with early childhood interventions, follow-up for only two years may mean that some important outcomes that occur later in life for the child or family are missed.

The second part of these criteria relates to completeness of follow-up. Seldom are studies able to retain all participants until the end of the follow-up. If large numbers are lost, it

How to Critically Appraise Studies of Treatment or Prevention

1. Are the results of this study valid?
    a) Was the assignment of participants to treatment groups randomized, and was the randomization concealed?
    b) Was follow-up sufficiently long and complete?
    c) Were participants analyzed in the groups to which they were assigned?
    d) Were participants, clinicians, outcome assessors, and data analysts unaware of (blinded to or masked from) participant allocation?
    e) Were participants in each group treated equally except for the intervention being evaluated?
    f) Were the groups similar at the start of the trial?
2. What were the results?
    a) How large is the effect? Is it clinically important?
    b) How precise is the treatment effect?
3. Will the results help me in caring for my clients?
    a) Are my clients so different from those in the study that the results do not apply?
    b) Is the treatment feasible in our setting?
    c) Were all the clinically important outcomes (harms as well as benefits) considered?
    d) What are my clients' values and preferences for both the outcomes we are trying to prevent and the side effects that may arise?

Sources: Adapted from Cullum, 2000, 2001

reduces the confidence one can have in the results. To continue with the weight-loss example, large dropouts are usual during treatment and follow-up. If the author only reports on those who remained in the study, those participants are more likely to be doing well in terms of their weight loss. Participants who were unsuccessful with the intervention are more likely to drop out, making the intervention look far more effective than it is in reality. A retention rate of 80% is considered good; however, this is somewhat topic dependent, as one would expect the dropout rates of a transient population to be much higher.

Were participants analyzed in groups to which they were assigned? This criterion relates to the fact that participants should be analyzed in the group to which they were randomized, regardless of whether or not they actually received the treatment or completed treatment as assigned. This is called **intention-to-treat analysis**. If the participants who discontinued treatment, for example, due to unpleasant side effects, were omitted from analysis, we would be left only with participants who had better outcomes, making the treatment look more effective than it actually is.

Were participants, clinicians, outcome assessors, and data analysts unaware of (blinded to or masked from) participant allocation? Several of the groups involved in a trial have the potential to bias the outcomes if they know whether a participant is in the intervention or control group. **Bias** means any systematic tendency to produce an outcome that differs from the truth. It includes the tendency to look more carefully for particular outcomes or to probe more deeply for outcomes in one group and not the other, as well as for participants to more likely recall an event or exposure that could have an impact if they have an adverse outcome than if they do not have an adverse outcome (Oxman, Guyatt, Cook, & Montori, 2002). Studies can be labelled single, double, or triple blinded depending on how many of the groups were unaware of the allocation of the participants. Authors should clearly state which groups were blinded or masked. For example, if participants know they are in the intervention group, they may have a sensitivity to the good or bad effects of the treatment. Participant blinding is easier to do in drug trials where placebos can be made to look identical to the active drug. However, it is far more difficult in community nursing to blind participants to a nurse coming to their home, or delivering a physical versus a primarily psychosocial intervention. It is often possible to minimize the potential bias by assuring that the participant does not know the specific outcome. Similarly, clinicians who care for the participants and know the allocation may unconsciously alter the way they give care and may have a heightened awareness of good outcomes or adverse outcomes in a way that biases the evaluation.

The most important group to be blinded is the one who measure the outcomes. Ideally, they are not the clinicians providing care. The measurement of key outcomes can be unconsciously distorted by the clinicians' beliefs about the intervention and its side effects. Objective outcome measures, such as glycated hemoglobin, are less subject to outcome assessor bias. Similarly, data analyses should be done with coded data that does not allow for identification of treatment groups.

Consequently, readers of randomized trials should look for reports of which groups were and were not blinded to the participant allocation. If blinding is not possible, the authors should report on steps taken to minimize possible biases.

Were participants in each group treated equally except for the intervention being evaluated? Randomization should ensure that the only difference between study groups is the treatment being evaluated. An important principle is that additional treatments, or extra care, not be given. Readers of randomized trials should look carefully at the descriptions of interventions received by all groups, especially if the clinicians are not blinded to allocation.

Were the groups similar at the start of the trial? Randomization should ensure that the groups of study participants were similar at the beginning. Usually a table of baseline characteristics is prepared and some analysis is done to check that randomization actually "worked." If the groups show statistically significant differences at the beginning, the impact of the intervention may be altered, which can affect the validity of the result. If imbalances do exist at baseline, adjustment in the analysis can be done with statistical techniques.

What Were the Results? Once one has determined that the results are valid, it important to understand what the results really mean.

How large is the effect? Is it clinically important? How precise is the treatment effect? The effects of treatment are measured using one or more outcome measures. They can be dichotomous (yes/no; alive/dead; pregnant/not pregnant) or continuous (weight, adjustment score, blood pressure, self-esteem). Different statistical tests are used for different types of data. Often statistical test are reported as ***p* values**. The convention is that any *p* value less than 0.05 is considered statistically significant and means that the intervention has an effect on the outcome. More information may be gained about the extent of that difference by the use of other statistical tests such as relative risk reduction (RRR) and absolute risk reduction (ARR).

The **relative risk reduction** is the proportional reduction in rates of poor outcomes (e.g., death or readmission) between the experimental (better outcomes) and control (greater poor outcomes) participants. It is calculated as:

$$\text{Relative risk reduction} = \frac{\text{Event rate in control group} - \text{Event rate in experimental group}}{\text{Event rate in the control group}}$$

For example, an RRR of 50% means that there were 50% fewer deaths in the experimental group compared with the control group.

Relative risk (RR) is the proportion of participants experiencing an outcome in the intervention group divided by the proportion experiencing the outcome in the control group. However, RR does not take into account the number of people in the study who would have died anyway without the intervention.

This is called the **absolute risk reduction** and is calculated as:

$$\text{Absolute risk reduction} = \text{Event rate in control group} - \text{Event rate in experimental group}$$

For example, an ARR of 2% means that there were 2% fewer deaths in the experimental group than the control group.

Yet another approach is to report the **number needed to treat** (NNT). This describes the number of people who must be treated with the intervention in order to prevent one additional negative outcome (e.g., death) or promote one additional positive outcome (e.g., smoking cessation). The NNT is calculated as:

$$\text{NNT} = \frac{1}{\text{Absolute risk reduction}}$$

When researchers report statistical significance, it is imperative to ask if this is clinically important or meaningful. It is quite possible for results to be statistically significant but clinically unimportant. In a hypothetical example studying weight-loss interventions for obese women, the group with a more intensive intervention lost a mean of 5 kg more than the group in the less intensive intervention. While the researchers found this statistically significant ($p = 0.03$), it did not meet the preset goal of a 10% weight loss in order to be a meaningful difference, that is, to be associated with health risk reduction. It also was not personally meaningful to the morbidly obese women.

Precision of the results can never be absolute but is estimated by calculating **confidence intervals** around the RRR or ARR. Confidence intervals (CI) are a range of values with a specified probability (usually 95%) of including the true effect, which can never be known absolutely. Wide confidence intervals indicate less precision in the estimated effect of the intervention. Precision increases with larger sample sizes.

Will the Results Help Me in Caring for My Clients?

- *Are my clients so different from those in the study that the results do not apply?*
- *Is the treatment feasible in our setting?*
- *Were all the clinically important outcomes (harms as well as benefits) considered?*
- *What are my clients' values and preferences for both the outcome we are trying to prevent and the side effects that may arise?*

In order to use the findings of a study, one needs to consider these questions and make judgments in relation to one's own client population. Consider how similar the characteristics of the study participants are to your own clients. Think about reasons why you should *not* apply the study results to your clients, rather than the looking for evidence that the clients are exactly the same as yours. Feasibility in your setting depends on factors such as cost, organizational resources, nursing skills, availability of special equipment, and acceptability to clients. Harms and benefits should be included in the reports by various obvious outcomes such as health but also other outcomes like quality of life and economics. In particular, negative effects or side effects should be included.

Critical Appraisal of Systematic Reviews

What Is a Systematic Review? A **systematic review** is a summary of research evidence that relates to a specific question. It could involve causation, diagnosis, or prognosis, but more frequently involves **effectiveness** of an intervention. Basing a clinical decision on a single study may be a mistake, as the study may have an inadequate sample size to detect clinically important differences between treatments, leading to a false negative conclusion. Discrepant findings across studies of the same question may occur due to chance or subtle differences in study design or participants. Therefore, it is useful to look at a summary of all the research related to a single clinical question.

In a narrative review, authors may selectively pick articles that support their viewpoint and ignore those that do not, so that the conclusion is set before the articles are selected. Systematic reviews differ from an unsystematic narrative review in that they attempt to overcome possible biases by following a rigorous methodology of search, retrieval, relevance and validity (quality) rating, data extraction, synthesis, and report writing. Explicit pre-set criteria are used for relevance and validity. Two people conduct each stage independently, then compare results and discuss discrepancies before moving on to the next stage. Details of the methods used at every stage are recorded. A **meta-analysis** is the quantitative combination of results of several studies to get an overall summary statistic that represents the combined effect of the intervention across different study populations.

The terms "systematic review" and "overview" are often used interchangeably. The reviewers must decide whether the statistical combination (meta-analysis) is appropriate by using both clinical judgment and a statistical test for heterogeneity. The clinical judgment requires the reviewers to examine the methodologies and statistical tests completed in the studies under review and ascertain if it is reasonable to combine them in a meta-analysis. The statistical tests determine the extent to which the differences between results of individual studies are greater than one would expect if all studies were measuring the same underlying effect and the observed differences were only due to chance. The more significant the test of heterogeneity, the less likely that the observed differences are from chance alone and that some other factor, such as design, participants, intervention, or outcome, is responsible for the differences in the treatment effect across studies (Sackett et al., 2000). Readers must use their own expertise to decide if the statistical combination is reasonable in terms of clinical and methodological sense.

Systematic reviews help to answer clinical questions without having to access large numbers of research reports; they overcome the obstacles of lack of time and, sometimes, lack of skills necessary to conduct the critical appraisal. But can one be confident in using all reviews? The search in the scenario of Canadian Research Box 14.2 yielded 195 reviews—are they all of equal value? What does one do if they give conflicting results?

Global Research Box 14.1

Blue, L., Lang, E., McMurray, J. J. V., Davie, A. P., McDonagh, T. A., Murdoch, D. R. et al. (2001a). Randomized controlled trial of specialist nurse intervention in heart failure. *BMJ, 323,* 715–718.

Scenario: You are a CHN nurse on a committee that is studying community care of clients with chronic heart failure (CHF). The hospital readmission rate in this client grouping is higher in your region than the provincial average. You ask if anyone knows if there is any research literature on the topic. Since no one remembers seeing any such literature, they ask you to search and report back at the next meeting. You remember from your evidence-based nursing course that you can search on the Evidence-Based Nursing website (see Additional Resources) to see if there are any pre-appraised topics. You enter "heart failure" and get four hits. One is a citation that appears to be on topic, finding that a specialist nurse intervention reduced hospital readmissions in clients with CHF (Blue et al., 2001b). You decide to use the website to retrieve the full-text journal article (Blue et al., 2001a). Will you present this study to your committee next meeting?

In the article you retrieved by Blue et al., the methods section reports that the participants were randomized to receive either usual care or the specialist nurse intervention. After recruitment, the study personnel phoned a central place to find out the allocation of each participant from a randomization list. Thus, participants were randomized and allocation was concealed to personnel prior to recruitment. The treatment group got a specialist nurse intervention, which consisted of planned home visits of decreasing frequency, supplemented with telephone contact as necessary. The aim was to educate participants about heart failure and its treatment, to monitor electrolytes, to teach self-monitoring and management, to encourage treatment adherence, to liaise with other health care providers, and to provide psychological support. Nurses were trained and followed written protocols on the use of specific drugs. Participants were given pocket booklets that included information on heart failure and treatment, contact information of the nurses, a list of drugs, body weights, blood test results, and details of planned visits. The control group received "usual care" in which participants were managed by the attending physician and then the general practitioner. They did not see the specialist nurse. There is no indication of co-intervention in this study.

Follow-up lasted for one year, probably a reasonable length of time to assess an intervention like this for CHF. Follow-up at one year was 95%. The authors do not state that intention-to-treat analysis was done, but their dropout rate was very low, and a graph of participant distribution shows that there were people in both arms of the trial (intervention and control) who did not receive the intervention as allocated, but stayed within the group anyway. The article does not report on blinding; the abstract reports that the authors provided information that the outcome assessors and the data analysts were blinded (Blue et al., 2001b).

The study does present a table of participant characteristics at baseline, including age, sex, living situation, social services required, other medical problems, disease classification, severity, renal function, and blood pressure at discharge. While a clinician can "eyeball" the results, and they look similar across groups, the article does not tell us if any analysis of baseline characteristics was done.

Rates of death and readmission due to CHF were primary outcomes, with death and readmission due to any other cause as secondary outcomes. One major outcome was worsening heart failure. The researchers found that 32% of those in the usual care group and 14% in the nurse intervention group experienced worsening heart failure in the first year. This was associated with a p value of 0.0044, which is statistically significant, and translates to a relative risk reduction of 57% (95% CI: 21–78); NNT = 6 (CI: 5–16) (Blue et al., 2001b). This means that there was a 57% reduction in the relative risk of hospital readmission for CHF as a result of the intervention. The NNT is interpreted as six people need to be treated with the intervention in order to avoid one additional hospital readmission, but it may be as low as 5 and as high as 16 (as indicated by the confidence intervals).

In summary, the report contains a good description of participants, allowing one to decide if the results could be applicable to one's own client population. It seems that all relevant harms and benefits were considered in the outcome measurement. Considering the opening scenario to this Research Box, you decide that this trial is a strong one with clear positive results that indicate that mortality or readmission for CHF can be significantly reduced. You take this study to your next meeting to discuss its strengths, weaknesses, and the implications for your community. You will also retrieve the other three articles from your initial search to see if they are relevant and if the results are consistent across studies.

Discussion Questions

1. How would you use this research to argue for resources to be reallocated from the current home visiting of CHF clients and directed to the intervention described in this Research Box? Role play that you are the nurse and your classmates are the committee to whom you are reporting.
2. When it is difficult or impossible to randomize people (e.g., when a media or city/community-wide intervention is to be done), what is the next most rigorous design after a randomized controlled trial?

Common misconceptions of systematic reviews are that many readers think that they include *only* randomized trials, that they must adopt a biomedical model, and that they have to have some statistical synthesis (Petticrew, 2001). If these were true, there would be few reviews of interest in community health, as many community health questions have not been or cannot be addressed by randomized trials. Fortunately, review methods are improving to include non-randomized studies such as cohort studies, to use a population health model, and to synthesize without necessarily including meta-analysis. The Cochrane Collaboration Health Promotion/Public Health Field has been a leader in promoting the methods, conduct, and use of systematic reviews and meta-analyses in community health care. Many websites contain high-quality systematic reviews relevant to community health and resources for skill building in critical appraisal of reviews (see Additional Resources).

Appraising Systematic Reviews In this section, we look at how to critically appraise systematic reviews to decide if the methods have sufficient rigour that the results may be applied to client or management decisions. The same major questions used for evaluation of intervention studies can be used to evaluate systematic reviews (see text box).

Are the Results Valid? *Is this a systematic review of randomized trials?* Questions about the effectiveness of treatment or prevention are best answered by randomized controlled trials if it is ethically possible to do so; whereas questions about harm or prognosis are best answered by cohort studies (Roberts & DiCenso, 1999). The reader of systematic reviews should look to see if the authors used randomized trials (if ethically possible) or the next most rigorous design which included a comparison group (quasi-randomized or cohort analytic designs).

Does the systematic review include a description of the strategies used to find all relevant studies? A thorough search for both published and unpublished studies should be done for a systematic review. The publication of research in a journal is more likely to occur in studies that have statistically significant results. Studies in which a new intervention is not found to be effective are frequently not published, a phenomenon known as publication bias (Dickersin, 1990). Systematic reviews that do not include unpublished studies may overestimate the effect of an intervention; that is, it will appear that the intervention is more effective than it really is. Therefore, in addition to searching through relevant databases such as CINAHL, MEDLINE, PsycINFO, ERIC, or Cochrane Library, researchers should hand-search relevant journals, review reference lists from retrieved articles, contact authors and relevant manufacturing companies, and review abstracts presented at relevant scientific meetings. Unless the authors of the reviews tell us what they did to locate relevant studies, it is difficult to know if any were missed.

Every systematic review grows from a focused question, through the development of the search strategies and search terms for each database, to retrieval of studies. Explicit inclusion/exclusion criteria are predetermined and two people independently review each article for inclusion.

Does the systematic review include a description of how the validity of individual studies was assessed? A narrative review often reports on study findings without considering the methodological strengths of the studies. Differences in study quality often explain differences in results across studies, with those of poorer quality tending to overestimate the effectiveness of the interventions (Kunz & Oxman, 1998). Quality ratings are sometimes used in the analysis to compare outcomes across studies by study strength. Or, if there are many studies to consider, the authors may choose to apply a quality rating threshold for inclusion or give greater attention and weight to the stronger studies.

The predefined quality checklist minimizes reviewer bias by helping to ensure that reviewers appraise each study consistently and thoroughly. Having two or more raters helps to reduce mistakes and bias and increases the reader's confidence in the systematic review. The quality rating tools usually include criteria such as those presented for evaluating interventions (see Global Research Box 14.1).

Were the results consistent from study to study? The reader would be most confident using the results of a review if the results were similar in all included studies, that is, showing the same direction of effect, all being positive, all negative, or all showing no effect. But what if the direction of effect differs across studies? Differences may be due to types of clients included; the timing, duration, and intensity of the intervention; the outcomes measured; and/or the ways in which the outcomes were measured.

How to Critically Appraise Review Articles

1. Are the results of this systematic review valid?
   a) Is this a systematic review of randomized trials?
   b) Does the systematic review include a description of the strategies used to find all the relevant trials?
   c) Does the systematic review include a description of how the validity of individual studies was assessed?
   d) Were the results consistent from study to study?
2. What were the results?
   a) How large was the treatment effect?
   b) How precise was the estimate of treatment effect?
3. Will the results help me in caring for my clients?
   a) Are my clients so different from those in the study that the results do not apply?
   b) Is the treatment feasible in our setting?
   c) Were all the clinically important outcomes (harms as well as benefits) considered?
   d) What are my clients' values and preferences for both the outcomes we are trying to prevent and the side effects that may arise?

Source: Adadpted from Ciliska, Cullum & Marks, 2001 and Sackett et al., 2000.

What Were the Results? *How large was the treatment effect? How precise is the estimate of treatment effect?* Comparing a simple count of studies that helped, harmed, or showed no difference in treatments would assume that all studies had equal validity, power of the sample size to detect a difference, and duration and intensity of interventions and follow-up. Meta-analysis, when appropriate, can assign different weight to individual studies so that those with greater precision or higher quality make a greater contribution to the summary statistic. Summary statistics usually used include odds ratio, relative risk (RR, defined earlier), and weighted mean difference. The **odds ratio** (OR) describes the odds of a participant in the experimental group having an event (e.g., pregnancy) divided by the odds of a participant in the control group having the event. In a study such as prevention of pregnancy, one would consider that an RR or OR of <1 represents a beneficial treatment. **Weighted mean difference** is the mean of the difference found between control and intervention groups across studies entered into a meta-analysis. Both OR and RR are used for dichotomous data (dead/alive, pregnant/not pregnant), while weighted mean difference is used for continuous data (blood pressure, blood glucose, stress measurement scale). (For more information on OR and RR, see Chapter 7.)

The precision of the results is estimated by calculating confidence intervals (CI, defined earlier) around the summary statistic. The CI is useful for decision making because we can look at both extremes of the effect. If the lower extreme is 1 or close to it, the effect of the intervention is quite small and probably not worthwhile. A hypothetical display is shown in Figure 14.2 to demonstrate how output tables are read. The summary odds ratio of the three studies in Figure 14.2 is 0.69 (95% CI: 0.51–0.90), which indicates that the treatment was effective in producing the desired outcome.

Will the Results Help Me in Caring for My Clients?

- *Are my clients so different from those in the study that the study results do not apply?*
- *Is the treatment feasible in our setting?*
- *Were all the clinically important outcomes (harms as well as benefits) considered?*
- *What are my clients' values and preferences for both the outcome we are trying to prevent and the side effects that may arise?*

These questions have to be answered by the readers in the context of their own work and client-encounter situations. For example, feasibility in the example in Canadian Research Box 14.2 would relate not only to the skills of the nurses and resources of the health department to do a multi-faceted sexual health program, but also to the ability of the school board to withstand the parental pressures for abstinence programs.

Researchers try to look for all outcomes of interventions, both positive and negative, that might affect the participants and the health care system. Outcomes might include mortality, morbidity, costs, quality of life, and participant satisfaction. Participant and family values must be considered. If, in Canadian Research Box 14.2, families are unwilling to have their children exposed to multi-faceted sexual health education programs, the students must be given an alternative during that school time.

Critical Appraisal of Qualitative Research

Qualitative research is important for the development of nursing knowledge. **Qualitative research** describes, explores, and explains phenomena and is concerned with the process or experience rather than outcomes. Done for the purpose of obtaining rich data, sampling is purposive as opposed to random or the probability sampling in quantitative research. Data collection is done in many ways, but the most common are observation and group or individual interviews. Data analysis is by codes, themes, and patterns, not by statistical techniques, and it produces rich, deep descriptions rather than numbers. Qualitative research does not allow inference to a population as a whole, but allows the researcher to generalize to a theoretical understanding of the phenomena being studied (Ploeg, 1999).

Major types of qualitative research used in nursing include phenomenology, grounded theory, and ethnography. **Phenomenology** seeks to describe the lived experiences of people, such as the experience of people returning home after a stroke. **Grounded theory** generates theories or models of the phenomena being studied, such as the development of a model of coping used by family caregivers of people who have HIV. **Ethnography** describes a culture and answers questions such as what is it like to be a pregnant teen trying to continue with school. Reading qualitative research deepens our understanding of the potential and actual experiences of people we work with and has the potential to enrich our interactions and care.

Once again, the same major questions used to evaluate primary treatment studies or systematic reviews can be used to evaluate qualitative research (see text box).

FIGURE 14.2 Example of Meta-Analysis Display

Each study is shown as a horizontal line with the OR for that study as the point on the line. The ends of the line show the 95% CIs. The numbers of participants are shown to the left of the line, and to the right are the numerical OR and 95% CIs. If a CI touches or crosses the vertical line of 1, that result is not statistically significant. The horizontal line just above the *x*-axis is the summary of the studies (the meta-analysis) that shows the combined impact of the intervention.

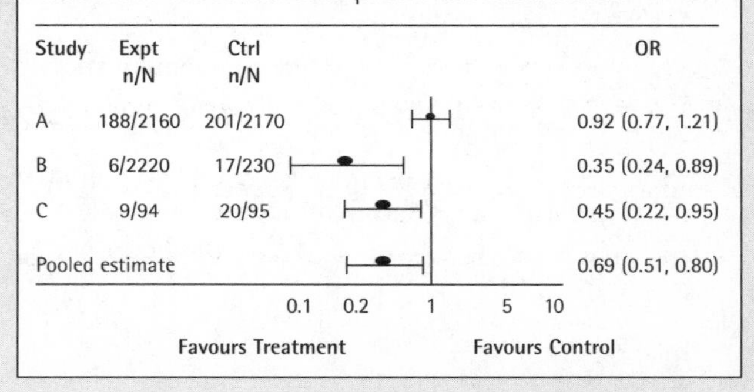

Are the Findings Valid? *Is the research question clear and adequately substantiated?* This question will determine if the qualitative study will be read or not. The article should clearly establish the question and what is already known about the topic.

Is the design appropriate for the research question? On a grand level, it is important to determine that the authors used the appropriate method that fits the purpose of the study (e.g., that phenomenology is used to explore experience and

Canadian Research Box 14.2

DiCenso, A., Guyatt, G., Willan, A., & Griffith, L. (2002). Interventions to reduce unintended pregnancies among adolescents: Systematic review of randomized controlled trials. *BMJ, 324*(7351), 1426–1434.

Scenario: You are the manager of the sexual health program at your health department. A local high school has asked you to offer a sexual health program in their school. They are concerned about the rates of both pregnancy and STDs. You guess that what they really want is an "abstinence" program. You decide to search the literature to find any evidence of effectiveness of sexual health generally, or abstinence programs, specifically. In PubMed, you search "sexual health," limiting the search to "humans," "English," "adolescents," and the publication dates of "January, 1995 to July, 2002." You get 2071 hits. When you try adding "abstinence" you get the same number of hits. When you limit the primary search further by methods terms, the addition of "review" reduces the hits to 195 and with "randomized trials," you still get 69 hits. Over lunch, you explain your discouragement to your colleagues. So many articles! So little time! How can you possibly be reasonably well prepared for the meeting at the school? One colleague suggests you try to further limit your search by choosing "meta-analysis" under publication type. You are elated because there are only four, and you can easily access the review cited above, which is available full-text and on-line. You don't have to retrieve and critically appraise 2071 articles!

The review included only randomized controlled trials, of which there were 22. The review question was narrowed from a starting-point scenario of sexual health. The authors wanted to know if primary prevention programs were effective in "delaying sexual intercourse, improving birth control use, and reducing incidence of pregnancy" in adolescents; this was a clear and focused question. The search strategy was extensive, involving the search of 12 electronic databases back to 1970, a hand search of ten key journals, and contact with experts to discover any unpublished studies. Criteria for study selection included:

- a target population of adolescents 18 years of age or less;
- the intervention being any primary prevention strategy (e.g., sex education classes, school-based clinics, community-based programs);
- the outcome measure being behavioural (e.g., initiation of sexual intercourse, birth control use, pregnancy);
- the study design being a randomized controlled trial; and
- the language being English or any language for which a translator was available.

Studies that were targeted to pregnant teens, high-risk populations, or the outcome of AIDS prevention, or that were conducted in a developing country were excluded. These criteria are quite explicit and help to ensure that the appropriate studies were included.

The appraisal tools used for validity (quality) rating included ratings of the appropriateness of the method of randomization, bias of the data collection, and number of withdrawals and dropouts. In the unplanned adolescent pregnancy review, there is consistency across the studies, with the test for heterogeneity showing no significant heterogeneity ($p = 0.99$).

The review found that interventions did not delay initiation of sexual intercourse for young women (OR: 1.12; 95% CI: 0.96–1.30) or young men (OR: 0.99; 95% CI: 0.84–1.16). Four abstinence programs and one school-based sexual education program were associated with an increase in number of pregnancies among partners of young male participants (OR: 1.54; 95% CI: 1.03–2.29). One study found significantly fewer pregnancies in young women who received a multi-faceted program (OR: 0.41; 95% CI: 0.20–0.83).

These results are directly applicable to the introductory scenario. Potential negative effects of the abstinence programs were documented; costs were not reported. The review was done systematically; focused on a clearly delineated question; did quite an extensive literature search; focused on randomized trials; applied pre-defined inclusion, exclusion, and quality criteria; did a meta-analysis with pooled odds ratios; and considered both positive and negative outcomes. It is a high-quality review that found that primary preventions strategies do not delay initiation of sexual intercourse, improve use of birth control among young men or women, or reduce the number of pregnancies in young women. Four abstinence programs and one school-based sex education program were associated with an increase in number of pregnancies. There were significantly fewer pregnancies in young women who received a multi-faceted program. Returning to the opening scenario, you can certainly present to the high school the evidence to not conduct the abstinence program and to consider a multi-faceted intervention for the students.

Discussion Questions

1. The media attend the meeting at the high school. They ask, "If abstinence does not work, and some of the other interventions do not work, then why should we spend any time or resources on sexual health education for adolescents?" How would you respond?
2. What components would you argue to be included in a multi-faceted sexual health program for adolescents?

meaning for clients following colostomy, rather than using an ethnographic approach). A more sophisticated appraisal considers the fit of the philosophical background of a particular perspective with the purpose of the study.

Was the method of sampling appropriate for the research question? The study should report on how participants were selected. Many different types of sampling are used in qualitative research, including sampling for maximum variation, typical cases, extreme cases, or critical cases.

Were data collected and managed systematically? The study should try to define the breadth (variation, multiple perspectives) and depth (numbers and types of data collected). Also, has each investigator kept track of the process, hunches, data collection, and data collection procedures through the use of journaling and memos?

Were the data analyzed appropriately? The researcher should report on how the data were organized and reduced in order to identify patterns. Often the analysis identifies further areas for data collection and analysis. Usually the researcher uses other team members to assist in the analysis, providing various interpretations of the data. Member checking (taking the results back to the participants or people associated with the issue under study) is sometimes done to gather alternative interpretations of the analysis.

What Are the Findings? *Is the description of findings thorough?* Qualitative research is difficult to write for the word limit of standard journals. It is difficult to fit the rich description and analysis into one publication. It is expected that authors have used direct quotations of the participants to illustrate the descriptions and conceptualizations.

How to Critically Appraise Qualitative Research Reports

1. Are the findings valid?
   a) Is the research question clear and adequately substantiated?
   b) Is the design appropriate for the research question?
   c) Was the method of sampling appropriate for the research question?
   d) Were data collected and managed systematically?
   e) Were the data analyzed appropriately?
2. What are the findings?
   a) Is the description of findings thorough?
3. How can I apply the findings to patient care?
   a) What meaning and relevance does the study have for my practice?
   b) Does the study help me understand the context of my practice?
   c) Does the study enhance my knowledge about my practice?

Source: Russell, C. K., & Gregory, D. M. (2003). Evaluation of qualitative research reports. Evidence-Based Nursing, 6, *36–40. Reproduced with permission of the BMJ Publishing Group.*

How Can I Apply the Findings to Patient Care?

- *What meaning and relevance does the study have for my practice?*
- *Does the study help me understand the context of my practice?*
- *Does the study enhance my knowledge about my practice?*

The authors should establish the need and relevance of the research while both arguing why they conducted the research as well as discussing the results. Readers must use their critique of the study as well as the information presented in the report to decide if any parts of the research findings are potentially transferable to their own practice.

Making the Decision about Implementation

Each Research Box in this chapter shows high-quality evidence around the clinical scenario and clinical question. In community health nursing, many decisions to implement a change in practice are probably beyond the individual; they are decided by a team. In every case, the decision involves all of the four aspects of Figure 14.1: the research evidence, available resources, skills of the practitioners, and the client values and choices. Furthermore, if the decision goes beyond individual clients or small groups, political and organizational elements become involved. This is particularly evident in the final decision of Canadian Research Box 14.2 to implement a comprehensive sexual health program. The students, parents, and high school would all have to be involved in the decision if there is any chance for a school-based intervention for sexual health to be successful.

What does one do if no research evidence is found during the database search? Or if the research that comes up is of consistently poor quality? In those cases, expert opinion or usual practice is the standard for decision making. One may be able to find practice guidelines on the topic. These depend on a thorough literature review, then consensus meetings with expert panels in order to make practice decisions, particularly where research evidence does not exist (Registered Nurses Association of Ontario, 2002; U.S. Department of Health and Human Services, Agency for Healthcare Research and Quality, 2002). Similarly, "best practice" documents describe programs or interventions that seem to be effective, but may not yet have been rigorously evaluated.

Caution must be exercised when implementing interventions for which there is no good evaluation. CHNs must be particularly vigilant in observing for effects, both positive and negative, then charting them. Unfortunately, many effects are not evident until years after the intervention when no one is observing any longer! Areas of clinical interest where evaluation does not exist are prime research questions that should receive priority attention from funding agencies.

Global Research Box 14.3

Sandberg, J., Lundh, U., & Nolan, M. R. (2001a). Placing a spouse in a care home: The importance of keeping. *Journal of Clinical Nursing, 10*, 406–416.

Scenario: You work as a CHN. For several months you have been providing physical and supportive care for an elderly man, who had a stroke some years ago, and his wife, his primary caregiver. Two months ago, the wife suffered a myocardial infarction. She is no longer able to manage her husband's care and has reluctantly moved him to a nursing home. You are very worried about how she will cope with the separation. Once again, you search on the Evidence-Based Nursing website to see if there are any pre-appraised studies. When you search "caregiver," you get nine hits, including an abstract saying that spouses who placed partners in care homes experienced emotional reactions to separation and made efforts to maintain their relationships (Sandberg, Lundh, & Nolan, 2001b). You decide to retrieve the full article (cited above) for critical appraisal.

You use the criteria from Russell & Gregory (2003) to critique the article. You find that the purpose was clear: to explore the experience of placing a spouse in a care home, to better understand the various processes involved, and, ultimately, to produce a theory that might help improve the placement process and subsequent adjustment for caregivers. Therefore, the design of grounded theory was appropriate. A purposive sampling method was used: letters were sent to people who had placed a partner in care within the past 6–12 months. Twelve people participated. Interviews were conducted in the homes of participants, and interviewers kept filed notes of context, settings, and perceptions of the interview process. The data were transcribed and analyzed separately by two authors; constant comparison was used to elaborate the themes. Emerging themes were discussed until agreement was reached.

This method has been recommended as a way to enhance credibility in qualitative research. Results from the first phase of interviewing are briefly presented, regarding "making the decision, making the move, adjusting to the move, and reorientation." This publication, however, focuses on the processes for the spouse, on the "separation and continuity in maintaining the relationship (keeping)." The results are clearly described: a process of separation that includes four elements—"pretending, dawning, putting on a brave face, and seeking solace." Each of these themes is elaborated with quotations from the participants. The core theme of "keeping" explained how the spouses maintained relationships with their partners and the staff. The first themes relate to the partner: "keep it going, keep in touch, keep it special, keep an eye," while the next themes relate to staff: "keep your distance, keep quiet, keep on trying, and keep it close."

The thorough description of results, plus other literature findings (in the introduction and the discussion), provide meaning for nursing home staff as well as for the CHNs, helping both understand the processes involved in having a partner placed in a nursing home. You decide that the methods used in this grounded theory study are more than adequate and that the findings are meaningful for your practice. The study raises several areas for possible assessment and confirmation with your client to see if they are issues and to discuss possible interventions, thus enhancing your knowledge about this area of practice. Qualitative research provides information for the development of interventions that may be tested in a quantitative evaluation.

Discussion Questions

1. Qualitative research, such as grounded theory or phenomenology, does not tell us which interventions are effective, so how can qualitative research enrich our practice?
2. How could you use this research in an anticipatory way?

Planning for Dissemination and Implementation

Once a decision is made to change practice and organizational support is achieved, a comprehensive plan has to address how the others who work within the organization will be informed of the proposed change. Changing the practice of health professionals has been studied extensively with mixed, unclear results. The "Effective Practice and Organization of Care" Review group within the Cochrane Collaboration conducted a systematic review of 44 existing reviews on the topic. They found that **passive dissemination** (as in sending out a report or directive) does not work. A range of interventions work in some circumstances but not consistently; multifaceted interventions targeting different barriers are likely to be more effective than single strategies. A diagnostic analysis should be done to identify factors likely to help and hinder the proposed change (University of York, NHS Centre for Reviews and Dissemination, 1999). For example, opinion leaders have been shown to be effective in some studies with physicians, but not others (University of York, NHS Centre for Reviews and Dissemination), and they were not successful as an intervention with nurses (Hodnett et al., 1996). Thus, evidence of the use of opinion leaders as a strategy of change has been inconclusive.

The diagnostic analysis (environmental scan) must consider barriers and supports in relation to the characteristics of the innovation (the change being introduced), individual clients and practitioners, the organization, and the environment so that barriers can be reduced and supports strengthened. It is important to consider characteristics of the innovation such as the resources it will require (will it cost more or actually be time/resource saving) and how different it is from current practice. Relevant characteristics of individual practitioners include

Canadian Research Box 14.4

Arthur, H. M., Wright, D. M., & Smith, K. M. (2001a). Women and heart disease: The treatment may end but the suffering continues. *Canadian Journal of Nursing Research, 33*, 17–29.

Participatory action research scenario: You are a CHN working as part of a team delivering a cardiac rehabilitation program. You know that heart disease is the leading cause of death for both men and women, yet women have lower attendance and higher dropout rates in your program. The team has discussed this observation, trying to understand what the barriers are for women to attend the program or how the program is not meeting their needs when they do attend. You suggest that some research literature might help address the problem. You are to report back at the next meeting. You again decide to do an initial search in the pre-appraised literature and go to the Evidence-Based Nursing website. You search "women" and "cardiac rehabilitation" and get eight hits. You have a brief look at the abstracts on-line, and one article is about women, their adjustment to heart disease, and their participation in a support group (Arthur, Wright, & Smith, 2001b). You order the full-text article from the librarian (cited above).

The authors establish in the "Background" that women have below-average attendance and higher dropout rates. They suggest, from their literature review, that women's primary need in cardiac rehab is support, particularly from women with the same experience. The purpose of this study was to develop and implement a community-based communication and psycho-educational support group for women with heart disease. Participatory action research, the methodology used, involves bringing representatives from stakeholders (those who will be affected by the intervention) as collaborators in defining the question, the intervention, and the evaluation. This strategy is used more frequently in broad-based community health interventions as it facilitates broad support for the new intervention. When used with disadvantaged groups, participatory action empowers them to have a voice in the program and in how the results will be disseminated (Burns & Groves, 2001). Participatory research strategies were originally developed by Friere, a Brazilian scholar who used these methods to promote social change, and methods of critical social theory to address power imbalances between the target community and the researchers (Friere, 1972). Participatory action involves a large commitment from participants and a variety of skills among the researchers, including group process, qualitative and quantitative design, and data collection and analysis.

Two groups of women met monthly for five months to develop the program. Sessions were facilitated jointly by a nurse clinician and a nurse researcher. Between sessions, participants kept diaries of their experiences. This particular participatory action research study used qualitative data. Sessions were videotaped and transcribed and used along with field notes and the women's diaries for data collection and final evaluation. Analysis revealed that the group helped the women cope with their emotional reactions, offered social support, and helped them manage their health problem. Further iterative analysis revealed that the overall benefit of the group was the acknowledgement and sharing of suffering.

For participatory action studies, use the critical appraisal criteria for qualitative research. To summarize the critical appraisal of this study: it included a clear and focused question, participatory action research was an appropriate method, there was adequate description of context, and data were collected and managed systematically and analyzed appropriately. The report includes a thorough description of results although few actual quotations from the participants are used to substantiate the analysis. The study makes a useful contribution to our knowledge of how women suffer from cardiac disease and how the group offered them social support and helped them manage.

You conclude that the study has been well done, and you will take it to your committee meeting as a possible model to use for program re-development to meet the needs of the women with established heart disease in your community.

Discussion Questions

1. From your community experience, consider other identified problems or issues that you might approach from a participatory action research framework.
2. For each example in question 1, identify all the stakeholders who would need to be involved in order for the participatory action research to succeed.

such issues as level of education, years of experience, and general acceptance or resistance to change. Organizational characteristics include affiliation with an academic setting, size, level of care, funding sources, organizational structure, research participation, research orientation, and usual valuing of research findings. The environment includes factors such as rural/urban, economic status of the community, and health issues valued by the community (Dobbins, Ciliska, Cockerill, Barnsley, & DiCenso, 2002).

Important stakeholders must be identified. They may include the nurses, medical staff, clients, and accounting staff. Each group should attend a different meeting to hear a tailored message about the proposed change, rationale, and timelines. The goal of each meeting is to get support for the practice change from each stakeholder group. A champion may be needed with the enthusiasm and energy to push for this practice change. Identifying opinion leaders and influencing their understanding and attitudes about the proposed practice change is another strategy worth pursuing, despite the inconclusiveness (mentioned above) that this strategy is effective. Interventions to promote dissemination, uptake, and utilization of research results is an area that requires further focused research in order to complete the cycle of evidence-based practice from question identification to implementation and evaluation.

Evaluation

After implementing a practice or policy change, an evaluation period is needed to see if it is working in the organization with the new population and staff. This does not mean replicating the original study that was used as a basis for the practice change. It does, however, mean a period of data collection or chart review to ensure that the desired outcomes are similar to the rates of those in the original study and that the client acceptability and negative outcomes are also similar.

USING RESEARCH FOR MANAGEMENT DECISIONS AND POLICY DEVELOPMENT

While research evidence is useful for individual practitioners working with individual clients, it is also important that management decisions be evidence based. Decisions regarding the implementation of a new intensive intervention in a community, such as the cardiac rehabilitation example, are usually made where there is no additional funding coming to an agency for the new program. Therefore, if the organization wishes to begin such a program, it needs to find the resources within what currently exits. This may mean taking staff away from some other programs or activities. Reviewing the research evidence for both the proposed activity and any existing programs helps managers to make those decisions. For example, following a string of four adolescent suicides, one school requested that the health department offer suicide prevention interventions at the school the following fall. During the summer, the health department conducted a systematic review of the effectiveness of school-based suicide prevention programs for teens. They found that the available research was of poor quality and no evidence supported the decision to implement the suicide prevention programs; furthermore, some studies indicated that there was harm to adolescent males who experienced such a program in that they were more likely to engage in negative coping behaviours and to commit suicide (Ploeg, 1999). The management decided to present this information to the school and to offer instead a comprehensive "healthy school" initiative, which would also be evaluated.

Similarly, people working at institutional or government policy levels are increasingly aware of and value the need for research evidence, yet they face other competing factors (public opinion and pressures, fiscal restraints) when making policy decisions.

The actual conduct (as opposed to the search and discovery) of systematic reviews has contributed to their use by clinicians and policy-level decision makers. Of the many examples, two are chosen from the chapter authors' experiences with the Effective Public Health Practice Project (Hamilton Public Health & Community Services, 2003). Potential review questions are sought from the policy, management, and frontline clinician perspectives. The review groups included the methodological experts along with the community practitioners who were chosen for their content expertise and their understanding of the context and relevance to community health. They assisted in identifying and refining the priority questions, rating articles for relevance to the question, reviewing drafts, and helping to write clinical, management, and policy implications. This process has also been used in Alberta by the Alberta Heritage Foundation for Medical Research.

In a second example, identification, prevention, or treatment of spousal abuse had not been included in minimum policy recommendations (Ontario Ministry of Health, Public Health Branch, 1997). This omission was identified as a weakness by community health clinicians in Ontario. A work group was set up and members carried out a systematic review (Mueller & Thomas, 2001) from which clear guidelines for clinicians, managers, and policymakers were developed. Later, these guidelines were included in new policy recommendations.

Participating in Community Health Research

CHNs are involved in many different types of research, the most common being program evaluation using process outcomes such as numbers of clients, numbers of groups, hours spent, and reasons for home visits. These types of data are important for tracking uses and users of services and how resources are spent within the agency. Client outcome measurement is the next most likely information collected, such as client mortality, morbidity, immunization status or coverage, communicable disease outbreak, goals met, or adolescent pregnancies after a school program. Nurses are usually asked to log these data, at least in formal records. They also may be required to report it in other formats, or the agency may conduct periodic chart reviews or database summaries. These local data often feed into provincial and national databases and registries of statistics. Some of these databases are available to regions within the provinces so that local rates can be followed.

Especially if associated with an academic setting, CHNs are also likely to be involved in effectiveness research, that is, testing an alternate intervention against usual or no intervention. They might deliver interventions such as a falls prevention program for the elderly or a child abuse prevention intervention for families already identified as abusers or at high risk for abuse. CHNs might also collect the data for an effectiveness study, such as assessing functional status in people who have suffered a stroke and who have received the specialist nurse home intervention. Initiation and maintenance of relationships with academic settings is beneficial from the perspective of agencies and the universities. The agency can gain consultation on research utilization and program evaluation, and the nursing faculty can be kept current on clinical issues in the community and priority research needs.

CHNs may also decide that stakeholders need to be consulted about a particular health problem such as inactivity in children, heart disease in women, or mental health needs of immigrant adolescents. In this case, one might do as Arthur and colleagues (2001) did and develop a participatory action research program.

SUMMARY

In this chapter, we reviewed evidence-based practice as it relates to community health nursing. While evidence can be observations made by the nurse, expert "gut hunches," or advice of colleagues, we too often ignore the evidence from research (Estabrooks, 1998). Therefore, this chapter focused on research evidence—finding, critiquing, and using it. Particular detail was presented in relation to critical appraisal of research articles on effectiveness questions (primary studies or systematic reviews) or qualitative research to judge whether they should be utilized in practice, management, or policy decisions.

The process of using quality research evidence does not end with the critical appraisal and individual decisions to implement with clients. In community nursing, it more often involves getting organizational "buy-in" and changing policies and procedures or care maps. Thus, we presented information about understanding the barriers to utilizing research to change practice, management, and policymaking.

Research, in the form of process evaluation, currently takes place daily in every community organization in Canada. Therefore, CHNs can never avoid involvement in research. Further, as the valuing of research evidence increases in community health nursing, the critical attitude to practice will increase so that clinicians will more frequently ask relevant clinical questions. Since there is not a research-based answer for every clinical question within community health, the need to conduct research in community health will continue. CHNs will find they are asked to participate in research by collecting data, providing interventions, or developing research proposals.

KEY TERMS

evidence-based nursing
clinical questions
structured questions
situation
intervention
outcome
critical appraisal skills
randomized controlled trials
participatory action research
intention-to-treat analysis
bias
p values
relative risk reduction
relative risk
absolute risk reduction
number needed to treat
confidence intervals
systematic review
effectiveness
meta-analysis
odds ratio
weighted mean difference
qualitative research
phenomenology
grounded theory
ethnography
passive dissemination

STUDY QUESTIONS

1. Identify four factors to consider for evidence-based decision making.
2. What is the most critical attitude for a nurse in order to practice in an evidence-based way?
3. In what ways might you conduct research as part of your daily role in community health nursing?
4. Why would you seek out systematic reviews to answer clinical questions?
5. Name the four major categories of factors to consider when planning to implement a clinical practice or policy change. Give a few examples under each category.

INDIVIDUAL CRITICAL THINKING QUESTIONS

1. Pick an intervention that has been shown to be effective and discuss how you would plan to implement that practice change in a nursing agency. What factors would you assess? What processes would you use?
2. Answer the following using Figure 14.3.
   a) How many studies were involved in this meta-analysis?
   b) Which of those studies had statistically significant findings?
   c) How would you interpret the result? Is the intervention effective? Is it statistically significant? Is it precise?

FIGURE 14.3 Results of Meta-Analysis

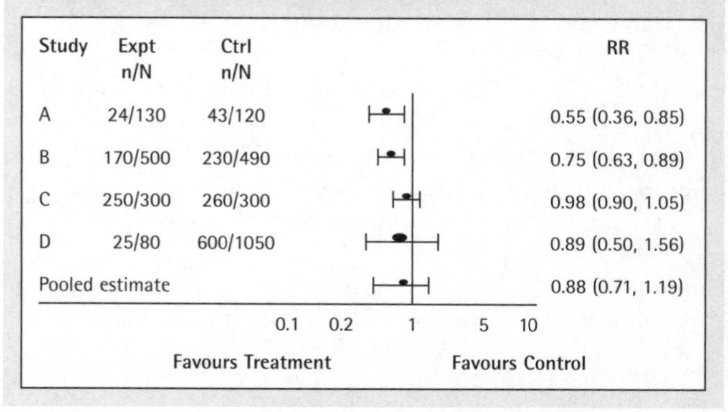

GROUP CRITICAL THINKING QUESTIONS

1. Select an article that evaluates an intervention relevant to community health nursing. Use the criteria in the first text box to critically appraise the article and come to a decision about using the intervention in your own practice.
2. As in question 1, critically appraise a systematic review article using the criteria in the second text box.
3. As in question 1, critically appraise an article on qualitative research using the criteria in the third text box. If it is a valid study, discuss what the study findings contribute to your understanding of the issue that was explored.

REFERENCES

American College of Physicians. (2001). *Best evidence.* (CD-ROM). Philadelphia, PA: Author.

Arthur, H. M., Wright, D. M., & Smith, K. M. (2001a). Women and heart disease: the treatment may end but the suffering continues. *Canadian Journal of Nursing Research, 33,* 17–29.

Arthur, H. M., Wright, D. M., & Smith, K. M. (2001b). Women and heart disease: the treatment may end but the suffering continues. *Canadian Journal of Nursing Research, 33,* 17–29. Abstract obtained from *Evidence-Based Nursing, 2002, 5,* 126. A support group created a caring environment where women with heart disease felt understood, supported, and strengthened by peers and nurse facilitators.

Blue, L., Lang, E., McMurray, J. J. V., Davie, A. P., McDonagh, T. A., Murdoch, D. R. et al. (2001a). Randomised controlled trial of specialist nurse intervention in heart failure. *BMJ, 323,* 715–718.

Blue, L., Lang, E., McMurray, J. J. V., Davie, A. P., McDonagh, T. A., Murdoch, D. R. et al. (2001b). Randomised controlled trial of specialist nurse intervention in heart failure. *BMJ, 323,* 715–718. Abstract obtained from *Evidence-Based Nursing, 2002, 5,* 55. A specialist nurse intervention reduced hospital readmissions in patients with chronic heart failure.

Blythe, J., & Royle, J. A. (1993). Assessing nurses' information needs in the work environment. *Bulletin of the Medical Librarians Association, 81,* 433–435.

Bostrom, J., & Suter, W. N. (1993). Research utilisation: Making the link to practice. *Journal of Nursing Staff Development, 9,* 28–34.

Burns, N., & Groves, S. K. (2001). *The practice of nursing research: Conduct, critique and utilization.* Philadelphia, PA: W.B. Saunders.

Ciliska, D., Cullum, N., & Marks, S. (2001). Evaluation of systematic reviews of treatment or prevention interventions. *Evidence-Based Nursing, 4*(4), 100–104.

Cullum, N. (2000). Evaluation of studies of treatment or prevention interventions. *Evidence-Based Nursing, 3*(4), 100–102.

Cullum, N. (2001). Evaluation of studies of treatment or prevention interventions, part 2: Applying the results of studies to your patients. *Evidence-Based Nursing, 4*(1), 7–8.

DiCenso, A., Cullum, N., & Ciliska, D. (1998). Implementing evidence-based nursing: Some misconceptions. *Evidence-Based Nursing, 1,* 38–40.

Dickersin, K. (1990). The existence of publication bias and risk factors for its occurrence. *JAMA: The Journal of the American Medical Association, 263,* 1385–1389.

Dobbins, M., Ciliska, D., Cockerill, R., Barnsley, J., & DiCenso, A. (2002). A framework for the dissemination and utilization of research for health care policy and practice. *Online Journal of Knowledge Synthesis in Nursing, 9*(7). Retrieved December 3, 2003 from **www.stti.iupui.edu/VirginiaHendersonLibrary/articles/090007.pdf**

Dobbins, M., Lockett, D., Michel, I., Beyers, J., Abate, N., & Feldman, L. (2001). *The effectiveness of school-based interventions in promoting physical activity and fitness among children and youth: A systematic review.* Hamilton, ON: Public Health Research Education and Development Program. Effective Public Health Practice Project.

Estabrooks, C. A. (1998). Will evidence-based nursing practice make practice perfect? *Canadian Journal of Nursing Research, 30,* 15–36.

Flemming, K. (1998). Asking answerable questions. *Evidence-Based Nursing, 1,* 36–37.

Friere, P. (1972). *Pedagogy of the oppressed.* New York: Herder & Herder.

Hamilton Public Health & Community Services. (2003). *Effective public health practice project.* Retrieved June 9, 2003 from **www.hamilton.ca/PHCS/EPHPP/EPHPPResearch.asp**

Heater, B. S., Becker, A. M., & Olson, R. (1988). Nursing interventions and patient outcomes. A meta-analysis of studies. *Nursing Research, 37,* 303–307.

Hodnett, E. D., Kaufman, K., O'Brien-Pallas, L., Chipman, M., Watson-MacDonell, J., & Hunsburger, W. (1996). A strategy to promote research-based nursing care: Effects on childbirth outcomes. *Research in Nursing and Health, 19*(1), 13–20.

Jadad, A. R., & Haynes, R. B. (1998). The Cochrane collaboration: Advances and challenges in improving evidence-based decision making. *Medical Decision Making, 18,* 2–9.

Karp, D. A., & Tanarugsachock, V. (2000). Mental illness, caregiving, and emotion management. *Qualitative Health Research, 10,* 6–25.

Kramer, M. S., Chalmers, B., & Hodnett, E. (for the PROBIT Study Group) (2001). Promotion of breastfeeding intervention trial (PROBIT): A randomized trial in the Republic of Belarus. *JAMA: The Journal of the American Medical Association, 285,* 413–420.

Kunz, R., & Oxman, A. (1998). The unpredictability paradox: Review of empirical comparisons of randomized and non-randomized clinical trials. *BMJ, 317,* 1185–1190.

Lomas, J. (1991). Words without action? The production, dissemination, and impact of consensus recommendations. *Annual Review of Public Health, 12,* 41–65.

Luker, K. A., & Kenrick, M. (1992). An exploratory study of the sources of influence on the clinical decisions of community nurses. *Journal of Advanced Nursing, 17,* 457–466.

McKibbon, A., & Marks, S. (1998a). Searching for the best evidence, part 1: Where to look. *Evidence-Based Nursing, 1*, 68–70.

McKibbon, A., & Marks, S. (1998b). Searching for the best evidence, part 2: Searching CINAHL and Medline. *Evidence-Based Nursing, 1*, 105–107.

Mueller, D., & Thomas, H. (2001). *The effectiveness of public health interventions to reduce or prevent spousal abuse toward women: A systematic review.* Hamilton, ON: Effective Public Health Practice Project. Retrieved November 30, 2003 from **www.health.gov.on.ca/english/providers/pub/phero/pdf/phero_043003.pdf**

Ontario Ministry of Health, Public Health Branch. (1997). *Mandatory health program and services guidelines.* Toronto, ON: Queen's Printer for Ontario.

Oxman, A., Guyatt, G., Cook, D., & Montori, V. (2002). Summarising the evidence. In G. Guyatt & D. Rennie (Eds.), *Users' guides to the medical literature: A manual for evidence-based clinical practice* (pp. 155–173). Chicago, IL: AMA Press.

Pearcey, P. A. (1995). Achieving research-based nursing practice. *Journal of Advanced Nursing, 22*, 33–39.

Petticrew, M. (2001). Systematic reviews from astronomy to zoology: Myths and misconceptions. *BMJ, 322*, 98–101.

Ploeg, J. (1999). Identifying the best research design to fit the questions, part 2: Qualitative designs. *Evidence-Based Nursing, 2*, 36–37.

Registered Nurses Association of Ontario. (2002). *Best practice guidelines.* Retrieved July 30, 2002 from **www.rnao.org/bestpractices/**

Roberts, J., & DiCenso, A. (1999). Identifying the best research design to fit the question, part 1: Quantitative designs. *Evidence-Based Nursing, 2*, 4–6.

Russell, C. K., & Gregory, D. M. (2003). Evaluation of qualitative research reports. *Evidence-Based Nursing, 6*, 36–40.

Sackett, D. L., Rosenberg, W., Gray, J. A. M., & Haynes, R. B. (1996). Evidence-based medicine: What it is and what it isn't. *BMJ, 312*, 71–72.

Sackett, D. L., Strauss, S. E., Richardson, W. S., Rosenberg, W., & Haynes, R. B. (2000). *Evidence based medicine: How to practice and teach EBM.* London: Churchill Livingstone.

Sandberg, J., Lundh, U., & Nolan, M. R. (2001a). Placing a spouse in a care home: the importance of keeping. *Journal of Clinical Nursing, 10*, 406–416.

Sandberg, J., Lundh, U., & Nolan, M. R. (2001b). Randomised controlled trial of specialist nurse intervention in heart failure. Placing a spouse in a care home: the importance of keeping. *Journal of Clinical Nursing, 10*, 406–416. Abstract obtained from *Evidence-Based Nursing, 2002, 5*, 32. Spouses who placed partners in care homes experienced emotional reactions to separation and made efforts to maintain relationship.

Thomas, H., Camiletti, Y., Cava, M., Feldman, L., Underwood, J., & Wade, K. (1999). *The effectiveness of parenting groups with professional involvement in improving parent and child health outcomes.* Hamilton, ON: Public Health Research Education and Development Program. Effective Public Health Practice Project.

Towheed, T. E., Anastassiades, T. P., Shea, B., Houpt, J., Welch, V., & Hochberg, M. C. (1999). Glucosamine therapy for treating osteoarthritis. *Cochrane Database of Systematic Reviews.* (Available to subscribers from The Cochrane Library, Chichester, UK, **www.cochrane.org**)

U.S. Department of Health and Human Services, Agency for Healthcare Research and Quality. (2002). *National guideline clearinghouse.* Retrieved July 30, 2002 from **www.guideline.gov**

Utterback, J. M. (1974). Innovation in industry and the diffusion of technology. *Science, 183*, 620–626.

University of York, NHS Centre for Reviews and Dissemination. (1999). Getting evidence into practice. *Effective Health Care, 5*(1). Retrieved December 3, 2003 from **www.york.ac.uk/inst/crd/ehc51.pdf**

ADDITIONAL RESOURCES

JOURNALS OF PRE-APPRAISED RESEARCH

Evidence-Based Nursing:
www.ebn.bmjjournals.com

Evidence-Based Mental Health:
www.ebmh.bmjjournals.com

Evidence-Based Medicine:
www.ebm.bmjjournals.com

Evidence-Based Healthcare:
www.harcourt-international.com/journals/ebhc

WEBSITES

BMJ theme issues and series:
www.bmjjournals.com/misc/fcissues.shtml

Clinical Evidence. London: BMJ Publishing Group:
www.clinicalevidence.org

The Cochrane Library:
www.update-software.com/cochrane/

The Cochrane Collaboration Health Promotion/Public Health Field:
www.vichealth.vic.gov.au/cochrane

Evidence-Based Nursing:
www.evidencebasednursing.com

Hamilton, Public Health and Comunity Services, Effective Public Health Practice Project:
www.hamilton.ca/PHCS/EPHPP/EPHPPResearch.asp

Teaching/Learning Evidence-Based Practice:
www.mdx.ac.uk/www.rctsh/ebp.htm

U.K. National Health Service, Health Development Agency (formerly the Health Education Authority):
www.hda.nhs.uk/

Users' Guides Interactive:
www.usersguides.org

BOOKS

McKibbon, A. (with Eady, A., & Marks, S.). (1999). *PDQ: Evidence-based principles and practice.* Hamilton, ON: B. C. Decker.

Sackett, D. L., Strauss, S. E., Richardson, W. S., Rosenberg, W., & Haynes, R. B. (2000). *Evidence based medicine: How to practice and teach EBM.* London: Churchill Livingstone.

ARTICLES

Greenhalgh, T. (1997). How to read a paper: Papers that summarise other papers (systematic reviews and meta-analyses). *BMJ, 315,* 672–675. Retrieved December 10, 2003 from **www.bmj.com/cgi/content/full/315/7109/672**

Havelock, P. (1998). Teaching and learning evidence-based practice. In L. Ridsdale (Ed.), *Evidence-based practice in primary care* (pp. 173–190). New York: Churchill Livingstone.

U.S. Department of Health and Human Services, Agency for Healthcare Research and Quality (AHRQ). (2003). *National guideline clearinghouse.* Retrieved December 10, 2003 from **www.guideline.gov**

About the Authors

Donna Ciliska, RN, PhD, is a Professor at the School of Nursing, McMaster University, and has an appointment as Nursing Consultant with Hamilton Public Health and Community Services. Dr. Ciliska is an editor of the journal *Evidence-Based Nursing.* Her research interests include community health, obesity, eating disorders, and research dissemination and utilization.

Helen Thomas, RN, MSc, is an Associate Professor in the School of Nursing at McMaster University and a Clinical Consultant with Hamilton Public Health and Social Services, Public Health Research Education and Development (PHRED) program. She is also the Director of the Effective Public Health Practice Project. Helen's research interests include adolescent health, homelessness, child abuse, and research dissemination, uptake, and utilization.

Part Three

COMMUNITY CLIENTS WITH SPECIAL HEALTH NEEDS

CHAPTER 15

Aboriginal Canadians

Rhonda J. King Blood

OBJECTIVES

AFTER STUDYING THIS CHAPTER, YOU SHOULD BE ABLE TO:

1. Describe First Nations' health care delivery.
2. Identify culturally appropriate nursing practice for First Nations communities.
3. Identify health care issues that are important in First Nations communities.
4. Describe how policy and culture can impact on the health of First Nations communities.

INTRODUCTION

This chapter is a broad overview of community health nursing in Canadian Aboriginal communities. The term **Aboriginal** is used to refer to all peoples of Indian, Inuit, and Metis heritage, including non-status Indians (Waldram, Herring, & Young, 1995). These communities may also be called **First Nations** communities. First Nations peoples have been made **vulnerable populations**, who are more likely to have adverse health outcomes than other populations (Flaskerud & Winslow, 1998). This has occurred not only through colonization, but also by the culture of poverty superimposed on their societies. Community health nurses (CHNs) need to adapt knowledge and skills to provide meaningful community health nursing care to Aboriginal communities. Nurses who choose to practise in First Nations communities must come prepared to deal with complex issues in health and nursing.

In this chapter, the history of Aboriginal people is outlined from **pre-European contact** (prior to exploration and settlement by Europeans) to contemporary populations. The historical context is important in order to provide culturally appropriate community health care to Aboriginal populations. Deagle (1999) contends that Canada's health care system is a three-tier system, with the Aboriginal populations on the last tier. Here, the third tier is described in order to enhance the CHN's understanding that health care is delivered to the First Nations and Inuit by a distinctly different system. Finally, cultural, policy, and health issues important to the Aboriginal people of Canada in the modern context are discussed. The CHN can influence changes to improve the health of the descendants of Canada's First Peoples.

FIRST NATIONS HISTORY

Pre-European Contact

North America's Aboriginal peoples have maintained that they were the original inhabitants of the Americas. That fact has been proven; however, the date and path of the arrival of humans to this continent are still being debated (Dickason, 2002a). Most tribes have a version of a creation story of being the original inhabitants of North America. Unearthed artifacts prove that humans arrived and resided in the Americas during the later Ice Ages. The first inhabitants of the Americas arrived with the necessary skills to survive in harsh environments (Riccuiti, 1990). Despite the hardships, cultures developed and adapted to the locale (Ballantine & Ballantine, 1993). However, the lives of Aboriginal people were profoundly altered by colonization.

Before the arrival of the newcomers to this continent, an estimated 18 million inhabitants and some 2000 languages flourished. First Nations peoples of Canada had an oral history (Dickason, 2002a). Aboriginal languages evolved into dialects spoken in different areas of a region (Waldram et al., 1995). The Aboriginal people comprised distinct cultures: Arctic, Western Subarctic, Eastern Subarctic, Northeastern Woodlands, Plains, Plateau, and Northwest Coast. These cultures were based on the resources of the area that the people inhabited. For example, the Plains people were hunter-gatherers who provisioned the **bands** or **tribes** by hunting and harvesting the flora of the prairies (Schultz, 1962). Thus cultural and historical diversity of Aboriginal people of Canada clearly existed before the arrival of the new immigrants.

Childcare and education were the responsibility of the extended family (Sherman, 1996). The adults provisioned for themselves and the community. Some communities settled into villages and grew crops to sustain themselves. Methods of food preservation were devised to store food for less plentiful seasons. Housing materials included the animal hides or the trees of the woodlands. Any less fortunate members of the band were provided sustenance by the whole group. Sharing of resources among the group was expected; for example, the potlatch was a method of redistributing resources. Transgression by anyone was dealt with according to custom law. The culture of the group included the spirituality that was a characteristic of most Aboriginal people. Life, if not ideal, was valued and individuals knew their roles and purpose (Fleet, 1997).

Aboriginal communities had traditional beliefs about health. Shamans and herbalists held the knowledge of curing illness. Mothers or grandmothers practised folk medicine to care for their families. The Medicine Wheel philosophy that encompassed all nature was extensively used by numerous tribes, with regional variability.

European Contact

Initial contact with Europeans was on Canada's east coast and extended over a significant period of time. Explorers and fur traders from France began to explore and bring settlers to harvest the plentiful animals for the fur trade. Missionaries made their way westward to bring Christian doctrine. The newcomers brought diseases such as smallpox, tuberculosis, and measles, which decimated the population by the thousands. The resources that had supplied Aboriginal livelihoods became scarce. Malnutrition, starvation, and alcohol consumption added to the misery. At the time of European contact, Canada was estimated to have fifty to sixty languages. Many of those languages became extinct, and the rest continued to dwindle over time (Waldram et al., 1995), further contributing to the decimation of Aboriginal culture (Chrisjohn, Young, & Maraun, 1994).

Post-European Contact

Even though there were about 500 distinct tribes in the early 1600s, the land was legally considered empty and therefore claimable (Fleet, 1997). Britain developed the **treaty** method with the Indians to claim land that the Aboriginal people occupied. The British North America Act of 1867 gave Canada its birth as a country, but The Royal Proclamation specified that only the British government could buy Indian lands or negotiate treaties. Private individuals or other nations (including Canada) could not go into Indian communities to buy land directly (Dickason, 2002b). The **Indian Act** of 1876 was passed to ensure that the terms of the treaties were observed.

As a result of the treaties, First Nations were relegated to living on **reserves**. Aboriginal people who came from agrarian cultures had lived their entire lives in villages. However, hunter-gatherers travelled within their territories for their sustenance. Now their territories were reduced to small plots of land, some as small as a few acres. The reserves were governed by the federal government under the Indian Act (Venne, 2002). The **Department of Indian Affairs and Northern Development** was the government department responsible for managing the reserves and the treaty Indians. Individuals called **Indian agents** were assigned to carry out the terms of the treaty. Once accustomed to having freedom, Indians found that they now required written permission from the Indian Agent to leave the reserve. Indians became dependant on the Indian agent for all aspects of their livelihood (Canada, Department of Indian & Northern Affairs, 1997). Churches assumed responsibility for the education of Aboriginal children, often in residential schools. Children were separated from families for extended periods of time and at varying distances, which disrupted family life (Chrisjohn et al., 1994; Fox, 2001).

Treaty Status

An understanding of how Aboriginal status is acquired and defined is indispensable to understanding the health care of Aboriginal people. The status of being a First Nations person in Canada is not only acquired by birth but also legislated by the Indian Act. To be considered a **treaty Indian**, one must be born to parents who are both treaty (registered) members of a recognized band and be registered with the parent under a treaty number. A **registered Indian** is recognized under the Indian Act and has a unique registration number called a treaty number. A **status Indian** is an Indian recognized by the federal government to be "Indian" under the Indian Act, but who does not have a registration number. **Non-status Indians** are culturally Indians, but because their tribe did not sign a treaty, they cannot be recognized as status Indians. A treaty Indian is always considered to be a status or registered Indian. However, a status or registered Indian is not always a treaty Indian. Prior to 1985, if an Aboriginal woman married a non-Aboriginal, she was deleted from the treaty list. The woman and her children were then considered non-status.

The **Inuit** are in a separate category but are treated in the same manner as registered Indians by the federal government (Waldram et al., 1995). The **Metis**, who were the mixed-blood children born of marriages between Aboriginal and non-Aboriginal parents, are legally considered the same as non-status Indians.

In response to complaints that the Indian Act was discriminatory to women, **Bill C-31** was passed in 1985. Women who had married non-Aboriginal men could apply for status and be registered in Ottawa. Bands or tribes could admit the women and their children into the tribe depending on the band membership code. Waldram et al. (1995) state that "Aboriginals are defined in the Canadian Constitution under Section 35, which recognizes the Indian, Inuit, and Metis peoples and their existing Aboriginal and treaty rights recognized and affirmed with a special status within Canada" (p. 6).

CONTEMPORARY ABORIGINALS

The White Paper was written in 1969 (Health Canada, 2001) for the purpose of abolishing the treaties and the Indian Act and disassembling the government departments responsible for reserves and treaty Indians. Generally, a White Paper is a government report on an investigation into a given topic. Often, a White Paper offers recommendations that become policy or law. However, this White Paper never became policy or legislation (Canada, Department of Indian & Northern Affairs, 1997). While the White Paper did not succeed in terminating the First Nations and Inuit relationship with the federal government, its very attempt appears to have created a resurgence in the culture of Canada's Aboriginal people (Schouls, 2002). Today, there is increasing interest in speaking the languages of the remaining 11 language families: Algonquian, Athapaskan, Eskimo-Aleut, Haida, Tlingit, Siouan, Tsimshian, Wakashan, Salishan, Kutenai, and Iroquoian.

Canada's Aboriginal peoples' rights were given recognition in the Canadian Constitution. Several attempts have been made to define the treaty rights. The federal government is currently presenting the First Nations Governance Act (FNGA) to national, regional, and local groups. The FNGA should allow effective self-governance for Aboriginal people (Canada, Department of Indian & Northern Affairs, 2002). However, it was not passed by parliament into law.

Aboriginals on Reserves

Aboriginal reserves are located in all of Canada's provinces, but not in the territories. Some reserves are adjacent to or located within urban centres. The reserves located in the south are easily accessible. Farther north, most reserves are remote and isolated unless they are located near an urban centre. The Inuit live in settlements throughout the Far North. Most reserves are governed by an elected Chief and Council.

The existence of reserves continues to exclude First Nations people from participating in and enjoying a place in Canadian society. The lack of opportunity on reserves is evident. Some residents seek opportunities in urban centres, but because family and social support networks are absent, the result is similar to living on the reserve. Modern housing, taken for granted by other Canadians, is only a dream for too many Aboriginal people. Lack of childcare, low educational achievement, high unemployment, and lack of food security for children in particular, are serious concerns for Aboriginal communities. Health and social indicators of Aboriginals highlight the grim statistics relative to health, justice system, education, and the social and child welfare system. But the resilience of individuals can result in their being educated and participating as members of mainstream Canadian society (Mercredi & Turpel, 1993).

Urban Aboriginals

Some First Nations individuals sought enfranchisement, essentially giving up their treaty rights. These individuals live in mostly urban areas, blending with mainstream Canadian society. Or, in the case of tribes that did not sign a treaty with the British Crown, the people are considered non-status and do not reside on reserves. Metis did not have reserves set aside for them except in Alberta where Metis settlements can be found.

The same problems that plague First Nations reserve communities can also be apparent for urban Aboriginals. Those problems present themselves as unemployment; inadequate housing; social exclusion; lack of childcare, food insecurity, and lack of transportation; and intermittent access to health care. Depending on the resilience of the individuals, poverty may be temporary until they obtain education or job training.

The picture is not all bleak. Aboriginal people are adapting to modern culture and are represented in all occupations. There are doctors, lawyers, and yes, chiefs who govern their communities because they have the education and knowledge. Aboriginal educators administrate schools and teach Aboriginal students. The National Aboriginal Achievement Awards showcase the talent in the Canadian Aboriginal community. It is important to become aware of the positive aspects of being Aboriginal. It counteracts the negative stereotyping of Aboriginal people.

The national profile of First Nations communities and their health status highlights the dire need for change. The relatively new health determinants have emphasized the health needs of the Canadian Aboriginal people. The change has to be made to the social determinants of health, such as income, to overcome the poverty and third-world conditions that are present in too many First Nations communities.

First Nations Health Care

A component of working with First Nations communities is knowing the larger health care system that enacts policy to establish the practice and standards for First Nations health care systems. Health care for First Nations and Inuit is considered a treaty right. Government policy states that health care provided to First Nations is benevolence by the federal government. The federal government, through its Health Minister and department and the **First Nations and Inuit Health Branch** (FNIHB) (formerly Medical Services Branch of Health Canada) provide the health services and support for First Nations, Inuit, and Bill-C31 members. First Nations are increasingly assuming local control for health services through the transfer of health services (see Appendix 2A). Metis are the responsibility of the provinces.

The territories assume responsibility for their Aboriginal populations through their agreements with Ottawa. The FNIHB is based in Ottawa, where policy is planned. The First Nations and Inuit health policy is administered by the Regional Branches in each province, headed by a Regional Director.

Why do CHNs need to know about government and its functions? The answer is that it affects how health care is delivered to First Nations on a daily basis. It is advantageous to know and understand policies, thereby increasing the effectiveness of health care practitioners.

Much has changed in the health care field since Marc Lalonde, Minister of National Health and Welfare, produced the document, *A New Perspective on the Health of Canadians: A Working Document* (1974). In it, he spoke about environmental and behavioural threats to health. He stated that the economy affects the health status of Canadians. Little has changed since the Lalonde Report in the socio-economic status of Aboriginal Canadians to produce improvement in the health and social indicators. The majority of reserve residents are dependant on social services for their subsistence. Considerable economic development must be made to improve the economy of First Nations.

For acute care services, First Nations health care systems interface with the greater Canadian health care system. The degree of interfacing required with the surrounding communities depends on the type and scope of health services that exist on the reserves.

The process for community-based health services is different. The governance for health services is derived from Chief and Council, the governing authority for First Nations. Once the band council resolution is signed, a health committee or health board can be formed to begin the process of exploring community-based health services for its membership. First Nations health authorities were established to prepare for the transfer of control of health services to First Nations. Various types of funding arrangements are available to First Nations groups seeking to administrate their own health programs (see Appendix 2A).

First Nations' health care systems are varied in scope and practice. The nurse may practise in a large health care system that utilizes nursing skills in a limited scope. In contrast, the nurse may arrive in a remote northern community where the expectation is that all of the nursing roles will be met by one individual (Cradduck, 1995). Giger and Davidhizar's (1998) conceptual framework states that there are six key cultural phenomena in all cultures: communication, space, time, social organization, environmental control, and biological variations. The Giger and Davidhizar Transcultural Assessment Model is one tool that can be utilized in assessing Aboriginal populations to develop culturally appropriate community health nursing care. In too many cases, health facilities and health personnel are lacking in First Nations communities.

Cultural Issues in Community Health Nursing in Aboriginal Communities Development of competent, culturally appropriate nursing care (Andrews & Boyle, 1999) for Aboriginal clients requires the CHN to keep in mind the historical, cultural, and changing clinical and health care delivery system. As noted earlier, the traditional lifestyles of Canada's Aboriginals profoundly changed because of colonization. Reserves effectively excluded First Nations from participation in mainstream Canadian society (McMurray, 1999).

Aboriginal populations continue to remain a distinct cultural segment of Canadian society. Traditional holistic health beliefs, traditional medicine, and herbal medicine are acceptable health care. First Nations communities are societies in themselves. Based on a culture continuum, the society may have different members who are traditionalists, traditionalists/modernists, and modernists. Each group's strengths and challenges present for interesting nurse practice. The CHN must learn protocol for communicating with the traditionalists who may still possess cultural manners, diet, and health beliefs that may be contrary to nursing knowledge and skills (Holland & Hogg, 2001). For example, some individuals believe that bear grease is the best treatment for abrasions and wounds. The CHN must respect the client's health beliefs, yet attempt to maintain sterile wound care. The outcome is establishing sufficient trust with the client so that the wound heals without infection and the client continues to seek the required health care.

Rumbold (1999) states that ethics provides a framework for dealing with issues, problems, and dilemmas. An understanding of ethical or moral theories helps a person decide on an appropriate line of action although it may not necessarily provide them with the answer. Nurses need to study ethics since they often have to deal with moral or ethical problems. Nurses need to examine their own beliefs and values. Rumbold makes the case that nurses who move from one culture to another need to be informed of the values and norms of the society to which they are moving. It does not mean that they should abandon their own ethical values (Rumbold, 1999). Aboriginal communities can present CHNs with dilemmas in which it is crucial that they make wise choices. Dilemmas may be related to childcare, family violence, or geriatric abuse (Dumont-Smith, 2001). Aboriginal nurses working with First Nations communities may find different challenges, such as a personal tension between cultural practices and their knowledge of health science. Clients may assume a belief system (e.g., traditional medicine) that is not included in the nurses' practice. The Aboriginal Nurses Association of Canada (ANAC) was formed in 1975. This organization provides support to all Aboriginal and non-Aboriginal nurses practising in First Nations communities.

Nurses contemplating employment with FNIHB or a First Nations health authority should come prepared by doing prior research on the tribe's culture, language, geographic location, education, economy, and health care system. CHNs will require excellent skills for assessment, planning, implementing, and evaluating community health programs (Chapters 10, 13). Knowing your client, whether it is the individual, family, or community, facilitates evidence-based decision making. The nurses should be genuinely interested in the health of the Aboriginal clients requiring community health nursing. Required skill sets include the ability to remain objective and to resist stereotyping the community and its residents. Often nurses arrive in an Aboriginal community having already drawn conclusions from media and other sources.

Health personnel must continually be recruited, and nurses must often relocate to remote or isolated First Nations communities (Tarlier, Johnson, & Whyte, 2003). Retention of health personnel for only short lengths of time can result in some communities becoming distrustful of new nurses. This can provide another challenge to the nurses' communication skills (Sundeen, Stuart, Rankin, & Cohen, 1998).

Formal and informal leadership in First Nations communities can be difficult to grasp. CHNs will require the skills to assess the community and outline the health priorities and health issues of the population. They will have to decide on the course of action in consultation with the community. Historically, First Nations people made decisions on a consensus basis; some communities continue to make decisions in this way (Cookfair, 1991). CHNs will have to find roles that can be filled by a non-member health professional, perhaps as a consultant who provides the information that the community can use to make its best decision. Alternatively, the nurse may be seen as the individual who makes the decisions. The nurse must rely on community development knowledge and allow the community to make its own deci-

Recollections of Nursing—Jennie Nielsen, Aboriginal Registered Nurse

"I remember my mother interpreted for the doctor on his rounds on the Blood Reserve. My first contact with nursing was with two nurses at St. Paul's Anglican Residential School. I completed my high school in Sault Ste. Marie, Ontario. One day, while walking by the hospital, I decided to become a nurse. The director of nurses encouraged me to apply. It was three years of hard, rewarding work. I first worked, near home, at the Cardston General Hospital. Next, I left for Bermuda with an adventurous friend to experience nursing in another country. Later, I was a community health nurse for 17 1/2 years on the Blood Reserve. We tried to meet the immense health needs of our community. Today, community health nursing is provided by Aboriginal nurses with baccalaureate degrees. There have been enormous changes to nursing since I graduated in 1949."

Source: J. Nielsen, personal communication, 2003.

sions over time. It is easy to assume control of the decision-making if you are seen as the individual with the best health knowledge. However, it is important to consult with leaders, whether they are the elected leaders or the administrators of the health care system (McMurray, 1999).

Policy Issues Affecting Community Health Nursing in Aboriginal Communities Unlike public health nursing in urban communities, First Nations and Inuit health care systems vary in size and services offered. Nurses who seek employment in an Aboriginal community need to establish a network of colleagues who can assist with information when required. Health professionals establish liaisons with other service agencies or professional organizations such as the ANAC to promote the population health approach.

CHNs must also be aware of competing policies. For instance, the federal government is responsible for the health care of Aboriginal people; thus, nursing services are provided for home care clients by FNIHB. However, the Department of Indian Affairs is responsible for funding personal care and home support services. The nurse must be innovative in coordinating the home care services for clients from two service agencies.

Health Issues in Community Health Nursing with Aboriginal People Superimposed on the cultural disorganization caused by colonization is the culture of poverty (Bartlett, 2003). Because reserves effectively excluded Aboriginal people from mainstream Canadian society, poverty became permanent (Allender & Spradley, 2001). A people made powerless have no hope. Risk factors accumulated over generations, affecting health. This is demonstrated in the high rates of mortality and morbidity from injury and trauma, chronic illness, depression, and family violence (Sebastian, 2000). The effects of the residential school on individuals, family, and community have only begun to be addressed by the state and the churches. Illnesses such as tuberculosis remain a health threat, while preventable conditions such as fetal alcohol spectrum disorders and HIV/AIDS are on the increase.

Trauma and injury, whether accidental or intentional, are high on the list of health issues besetting First Nations communities. The communities that practise a hunting and gathering culture may be prone to injuries from firearms or other hunting equipment. Burns caused by fires are another area of concern. Housing in these communities may be substandard by Canadian standards, and smoke alarms are not mandatory in such homes. Utilities that are considered essential in urban homes, such as electricity, heating, and indoor plumbing, are not always available to all First Nations community homes. Health determinants cite environment as one of the factors that determine the health of individuals in a community. The nurse must be an advocate for clients and community to improve housing standards and safety for the First Nations community.

Vehicle safety is another area of health education that the nurse must contend with frequently. Perhaps the community is

Canadian Research Box 15.1

Daniel, M., & Messer, L. C. (2002). Perception of disease severity and barriers to self-care predict glycemic control in Aboriginal persons with type 2 diabetes mellitus. *Chronic Diseases in Canada, 23*(4), 130–137.

The purpose of the research was to evaluate the Health Belief Model in secondary prevention of type 2 diabetes mellitus in an Aboriginal population in British Columbia. Health beliefs, knowledge of diabetes, venous blood samples for glycated hemoglobin, two-hour post-load glucose, and behaviour were measured in 34 out of 37 persons diagnosed with diabetes in the initial phase of the study. Eighteen months later, glycemic markers and behaviour were measured for all participants. Data analysis included:

- determining the treatment compliance of the Aboriginal people living with diabetes,
- identifying more effective interventions for treatment compliance,
- understanding how health beliefs affected compliance to treatment, and
- determining how to surmount barriers to healthy behaviour.

This longitudinal study concluded that Aboriginal diabetics' health beliefs can be altered through health education. The primary recommendation was for culturally sensitive education of Aboriginal people emphasizing the severity of diabetes complications and the beliefs about overcoming perceived barriers to diabetes.

Discussion Question

How might a new CHN gather information to provide culturally sensitive diabetes education?

a fly-in community with different modes of transportation such as all-terrain vehicles, which have their own set of safety issues.

Diabetes has reached epidemic proportions in Aboriginal communities. Mortality rates from diabetes for Aboriginal women living in First Nations communities are five times higher than the national average. Diabetes is being diagnosed at a younger age. Amputation, sight impairment, and kidney failure—the dreaded results of diabetes—are common. Nurses must understand the health promotion and health education needed to change the lifestyle of those affected by diabetes (McMurray, 1999). The research box gives an example of research with Aboriginal people living with diabetes.

Grace (2003) cites the grim health outlook for Aboriginal women, particularly Ontario Aboriginal women, who are more prone to heart disease, diabetes, suicide, depression, substance use, and family violence compared with their non-Aboriginal counterparts. While cervical cancer rates are higher in Ontario Aboriginal women, rates for other types of cancer are lower. The types of cancer studied include colon, breast, uterine, and lymphoma.

Health education and promotion are part of the everyday contact with communities and groups. Some communities gravitate to group education sessions, while others need continual encouragement to attend classes.

Part of the community health nursing practice in Aboriginal communities is the evaluation component of health programs. Nurses should recognize that nursing standards of practice can be maintained through continuous quality improvement. First Nations health systems are becoming members of the Canadian Council on Health Services Accreditation.

SUMMARY

The chapter outlined the complexities of working with Aboriginal populations. Aboriginal status must be under-

CASE STUDY

A First Nations community has a total population of 1600. Twelve hundred members live on the reserve and 400 members live off-reserve. The community is located near a mid-size city. The unemployment level is consistently at 70%. Most families rely on Social Services for their subsistence. Sixty percent of the population is 18 years of age or less. The education level is at the junior- to high-school range. The community is governed by an elected Chief and four Councillors.

Most homes are 25 to 35 years old and have indoor plumbing, central heating, and electricity. However, potable water is delivered by water trucks. Sewage disposal is in a community sewage system, but rural homes have a septic tank sewage disposal system. The climate is temperate, with cold winters and dry summers.

The community-controlled school system goes from Kindergarten to Grade 6, and six of the ten teachers are Aboriginal. The community no longer practises their Aboriginal beliefs, and fewer than 5% of the school children speak their language. High school students are bussed for an hour each way to attend school in the nearby city. Most families end up being single-parent households.

The economy is based on school transportation, employment with the band administration, the band-controlled school, and two privately owned gas stations/convenience stores. The school principal has initiated a good recreation program for the students, and Aboriginal teacher assistants keep the students interested in being physically active. The parents participate in the school activities. However, once the students are bussed to attend school in the city, parents do not display much interest in school activities. Most of the adults attended the residential school at the neighbouring First Nations community, and most of them completed middle school.

The Health Centre is readily accessed by the population for all the community health programs. The Chief and Council transferred control of the health programs five years ago to a health administrator hired from another First Nations community. Immunization levels are at 85% for all ages. Chronic disease rates for diabetes, arthritis, and circulatory diseases have not been assessed since prior to the health program transfer. The First Nations and Inuit Health Branch continue to provide support for the CHN.

On weekends, parents leave the community to shop in the nearby city. They frequent the bars to drink alcohol and gamble on the video lottery terminals. Children are often left in the care of elderly grandparents or alone at home to fend for themselves until their parents return.

There have been disturbing developments in the community in the last five years. Family violence, child neglect, and an increased number of motor vehicle accidents and house fires are causing concern for the various community agencies. The frequency of fetal alcohol spectrum disorder is not known. In the last five months, five teenagers have attempted suicide.

You are the new nurse. When you arrive, a lone community health representative is there to welcome you to the Health Centre. She seems to know the community very well as people greet her warmly on the way to the Health Centre. The people that you meet appear very glad that you have arrived at the community. They greet you heartily and make you feel welcome.

Discussion Questions

1. How would you, as the CHN, use the nursing process to begin planning to improve the population health?
2. Who would you ask to help you familiarize yourself with the community?
3. List the resiliency factors of the community.
4. What factors make this First Nations community a vulnerable community?

stood by nurses working in First Nations communities because it affects their provision of nursing services for Aboriginal clients. The employers of nurses working in First Nations communities can be the federal, provincial, or local health authorities, each with their own organizational complexities.

Aboriginal populations have immense health challenges that nurses must assess in order to plan health services. Nurses may be responsible for the implementation of health services and programs and should have the skills to evaluate the efficacy of the health programs for Aboriginal communities. In addition, nurses must have communication skills to allow effective interaction with First Nations leadership and other service agency personnel. Advance preparation for working with First Nations should be a priority for nurses contemplating employment in First Nations communities to lessen the possible effects of culture shock. Nurses working with Canadian Aboriginals face complex challenges in a rewarding practice setting.

KEY TERMS

Aboriginal
First Nations
vulnerable populations
pre-European contact
bands
tribes
treaty
Indian Act
reserves
Department of Indian Affairs and Northern Development
Indian agents
treaty Indian
registered Indian
status Indian
non-status Indian
Inuit
Metis
Bill C-31
First Nations and Inuit Health Branch (FNIHB)

INDIVIDUAL CRITICAL THINKING EXERCISE

The Chief of the First Nations community that employs you has just asked to see the chart of one of the clients in your care. How would you handle the situation?

GROUP CRITICAL THINKING EXERCISE

The routine water sample of the First Nations community indicates contamination. How would you deal with this threat to public health since you are the nurse manager? Whom would you contact?

REFERENCES

Allender, J. A., & Spradley, B. W. (2001). *Community health nursing: Concepts and practice.* (5th ed.). Toronto, ON: Lippincott.

Andrews, M. M., & Boyle, J. S. (1999). *Transcultural concepts in nursing* (3rd ed.). Philadelphia, PA: Lippincott.

Ballantine, B., & Ballantine, I. (Eds.). (1993). *Native Americans: An illustrated history.* Atlanta, GA: Time.

Bartlett, J. G. (2003). Involuntary cultural change, stress phenomenon and Aboriginal health status. *Canadian Journal of Public Health, 94,* 165–167.

Canada, Department of Indian & Northern Affairs. (1997). *First Nations in Canada.* Ottawa, ON: Author.

Canada, Department of Indian & Northern Affairs. (2002). *A summary of the First Nations Governance Act.* Ottawa, ON: Author.

Chrisjohn, R. D., Young, S. L., & Maraun, M. (1994). *The circle game: Shadows and substance in the residential school experience in Canada: A report to the Royal Commission on Aboriginal Peoples.* Published 1997. Penticton, BC: Theytus.

Cookfair, J. M. (1991). *Nursing process and practice in the community.* Toronto, ON: Mosby.

Cradduck, G. R. (1995). Primary health care practice. In M. J. Stewart (Ed.), *Community nursing: Promoting Canadians' health* (pp. 454–471). Toronto, ON: Saunders.

Deagle, G. (1999). The three-tier system. [Editorial]. *Canadian Family Physician, 45,* 247–249.

Dickason, O. P. (2002a). Reclaiming stolen land. In J. Bird, L. Land, & M. Macadam (Eds.), *Nation to nation: Aboriginal sovereignty and the future of Canada* (pp. 34–42). Toronto, ON: Irwin.

Dickason, O. P. (2002b). *Canada's First Nations: A history of founding peoples from earliest times* (3rd ed.). Don Mills, ON: Oxford.

Dumont-Smith, C. (2001). *Exposure to violence in the home: Effects on Aboriginal children.* Ottawa, ON: Aboriginal Nurses Association of Canada.

Flaskerud, J. H., & Winslow, B. J. (1998). Conceptualizing vulnerable populations health-related research. *Nursing Research, 51*(2), 69–78.

Fleet, C. (1997). Introduction. In C. Fleet (Ed.), *First Nations firsthand: A history of five hundred years of encounter, war, and peace inspired by the eyewitnesses* (pp. 7–9). Edison, NJ: Chartwell.

Fox, L. (2001). *Kipaitapiiwahsinnooni: Alcohol and drug abuse education program.* Edmonton, AB: Duval House.

Giger, J. N., & Davidhizar, R. E. (1998). *Canadian transcultural nursing assessment and intervention.* Toronto, ON: Mosby.

Grace, L. S. (2003). Hepatitis A among residents of First Nations reserves in British Columbia, 1991–1996. *Canadian Journal of Public Health, 94,* 173–175.

Health Canada, First Nations and Inuit Branch (2001). Ten Years of Health Transfer First Nation and Inuit Control. Retrieved December 16, 2003 from **www.hc-sc.gc.ca/fnihb/bpm/hfa/ten_years_health_transfer/index.htm**

Holland, K., & Hogg, C. (2001). *Cultural awareness in nursing and health care: An introductory text.* New York: Oxford University Press.

Lalonde, M. (1974). *A new perspective on the health of Canadians: A working document.* Ottawa, ON: Canada, National Health and Welfare.

McMurray, A. (1999). *Community health and wellness: A sociological approach.* Toronto, ON: Mosby.

Mercredi, O., & Turpel, M. E. (1993). *In the rapids: Navigating the future of First Nations.* New York: Penguin.

Ricciuti, E. (1990). *The natural history of North America.* New York: Gallery.

Rumbold, G. (1999). *Ethics in nursing practice* (3rd ed.). Toronto, ON: Bailliere Tindall.

Schouls, T. (2002). The basic dilemma: Sovereignty or assimilation. In J. Bird, L. Land, & M. Macadam (Eds.), *Nation to nation: Aboriginal sovereignty and the future of Canada* (pp. 34–42). Toronto, ON: Irwin.

Schultz, J. W. (1962). *Blackfeet and buffalo: Memories of life among the Indians.* Norman, OK: University of Oklahoma Press.

Sherman, J. (1996). *Indian tribes of North America.* New York: Todri Productions.

Sebastian, J. G. (2000). Vulnerability and vulnerable populations: An overview. In M. Stanhope, & J. Lancaster (Eds.), *Community & public health nursing* (5th ed.) (pp. 638–661). Toronto, ON: Mosby.

Sundeen, S. J., Stuart, G. W., Rankin, A. D., & Cohen, S. A. (1998). *Nurse-client interaction: Implementing the nursing process* (6th ed.). Toronto, ON: Mosby.

Tarlier, D. S., Johnson, J. L., & Whyte, N. B. (2003). Voices from the wilderness: An interpretive study describing the role and practice of outpost nurses. *Canadian Journal of Public Health, 94,* 180–184.

Venne, S. (2002). Treaty-making with the Crown. In J. Bird, L. Land, & M. Macadam (Eds.), *Nation to nation: Aboriginal sovereignty and the future of Canada* (pp. 45–52). Toronto, ON: Irwin.

Waldram, J. B., Herring, D. A., & Young, T. K. (1995). *Aboriginal health in Canada: Historical, cultural and epidemiological perspectives.* Toronto, ON: University of Toronto Press.

ADDITIONAL RESOURCES

WEBSITES

National Aboriginal Health Organization (NAHO):
www.naho.ca

Aboriginal Nurses Association of Canada (ANAC):
www.anac.on.ca/

Aboriginal AIDS Network:
www. caan.ca

First Nations and Inuit Health Branch:
www.hc-sc.gc.ca/fnihb-dgspni/

Population Health Approach:
www.hc-sc.gc.ca/hppb/phdd/approach/linked.html

About the Author

Rhonda J. King Blood, daughter of the late Raymond and Isabella King of the Blood Tribe, is married and the mother to three children and a proud grandmother to Cherilynn. Educated at Blood Reserve, Magrath and Lethbridge schools, Rhonda decided to become a nurse. She obtained a registered nurse diploma in 1970 and subsequently a Bachelor of Nursing in 1982 and a Master of Arts (Honours) from Gonzaga University, Spokane, Washington in 1997. Primarily employed by Health Canada, she was a community health nurse in Alberta's First Nations for more than twenty years. Rhonda was also employed at the Canadian Council on Health Services Accreditation in Ottawa.

Rhonda is a past Vice President and Board Member for the Aboriginal Nurses Association of Canada and a member of the Alberta Association of Registered Nurses. Rhonda now works with Chinook Health Region in Lethbridge, Alberta as a Health Promotions Specialist with the Urban Aboriginal Mental Health Program, Population Health.

CHAPTER 16

Multicultural Clients, Migrant Workers, and Newcomers

Kathryn Edmunds and Elizabeth Kinnaird-Iler

OBJECTIVES

AFTER STUDYING THIS CHAPTER, YOU SHOULD BE ABLE TO:

1. Define and explain culture and multiculturalism.
2. Discuss the relationship of culture and health.
3. Discuss the common experiences of newcomers and migrant workers and the implications for community health nurses.
4. Describe how cultural values shape clients and nurses and their interactions.
5. Apply transcultural nursing principles to community health nursing practice and describe the knowledge, attitudes, sensitivity, and skills that are needed to provide culturally competent care.

INTRODUCTION

Canadian nurses have a long history of providing care to all people and communities, where and when it was required, while adapting to local contexts, resources, and circumstances. The Canadian Nurses Association (CNA) recognizes that nurses are caring for an increasingly diverse population and are expected to learn about cultural diversity in preparation for the Registered Nurse Examination. Expected competencies include "demonstrating consideration for client diversity; providing culturally sensitive care (e.g., openness, sensitivity, and recognizing culturally based practices and values); and incorporating cultural practices into health promotion activities" (CNA, 2000, p. 1). Valuing multiple ways of knowing, engaging in reflective practice, facilitating access and equity, empowering clients through negotiation, and providing culturally appropriate care in multiple settings are all expectations in the standards of practice of the Community Health Nurses Association of Canada (CHNAC) (2003). The College of Nurses of Ontario (CNO) (1999) has also developed standards of practice for providing culturally sensitive care.

In this chapter, we will build on the discussion of culture, cultural assessment, and how cultural values shape nurse-client interactions, which was started in Chapter 9. Some of the issues associated with Canadian multiculturalism will be discussed, as will some of the common experiences of newcomers and migrant workers. Implications for community health nursing practice and the development of cultural competence will be described.

CULTURE

A brief introduction to the field of transcultural nursing was provided in Chapter 9. Madeline Leininger, the founder of the field and the Sunrise Model (see Figure 9.5), defines **culture** as "the learned, shared, and transmitted knowledge of values, beliefs, and lifeways of a particular group that are transmitted intergenerationally and influence thinking, decisions, and actions in patterned or in certain ways" (Leininger & McFarland, 2002, p. 47). Culture is learned, shared, and transmitted over time. It also encompasses all aspects of our lives. What we have learned to value underlies our assumptions about how to perceive, think, and behave in acceptable, appropriate, and meaningful ways.

The underlying assumptions to the provision of culturally sensitive and appropriate care that is centred on the unique and individual culture of each client (person, family, community, or institution) (College of Nurses of Ontario [CNO], 1999, p. 3) are as follows.

- *Everyone* has a culture.
- Culture is individual. Individual assessments are necessary to identify relevant cultural factors within the context of each situation for each client.
- An individual's culture is influenced by many factors such as race, gender, religion, ethnicity, socio-economic status, sexual orientation, and life experience. The extent to which particular factors influence a person may vary.
- Culture is dynamic. It changes and evolves over time as individuals change over time.
- Reactions to cultural differences are automatic and often subconscious and influence the dynamics of the relationship.

- A nurse's culture is influenced by personal beliefs as well as nursing's professional values. The values of the nursing profession are upheld by all nurses.
- The nurse is responsible for assessing the client's cultural expectations and needs.

Five characteristics are shared by all cultures (Spradley & Allender, 2001).

- Culture is learned. Cultural norms, behaviours, and values are acquired through socialization within the family and community. However, socialization is interpreted and shaped individually. Behaviours that the nurse may assume are universal can differ across *and within* cultures.
- Culture is integrated. In this characteristic, culture is viewed as an integrated system. Beliefs and health care practices are usually consistent with the overall paradigms that are used to make sense out of the world. For example, an individual or a community may seek treatment from traditional healers whose care is based on that culture's holistic or spiritual worldview, rather than a biomedical model of disease and illness.
- Culture is shared. Beliefs that have meanings (either positive or negative) and are shared by a group are called **cultural values**. These values are transmitted within a group and over time. "Shared values give people a specific culture stability and security; they provide a standard for behaviour. From these values, members know what to believe and how to act" (Spradley & Allender, 2001, p. 61).
- Culture is largely implicit and tacit. This means that it shapes us at an unconscious level. Most of the time we do not stop to consider the assumptions and expectations that ground our behaviours and decisions. Culture becomes the way we do things in our daily living. It is the responsibility of the nurse to recognize that clients may have very different assumptions and tacit knowledge that guide their health care practices and decisions.
- Culture is dynamic. Culture is always adapting and changing. Consider the changes that have occurred since your grandparents were young adults. Minority cultures are certainly influenced by the dominant culture; however, they also influence the dominant culture.

Shared characteristics and patterns can be used to identify cultural groups; however, individual experiences and meanings vary and everyone participates in multiple cultures. Generalizations can be useful in providing background information about meanings of care and health practices, but must be used with caution and sensitivity (Masi, 1993). What prevents a generalization from becoming a stereotype is a cultural assessment with each client. Clients, whether individuals, families, or communities, may or may not share or value the background information known to the nurse.

Culture is a socially constructed reality that is constantly being renewed, affirmed, and adapted. A nurse learning about the lifeways of people and what is meaningful to them should realize that culture is a phenomenon that is created (Allen, 1996) and needs to be described appropriately. Part of that process is distinguishing between etic and emic perspectives. An **etic** perspective is from an outsider's point of view and often uses an outsider's classification system (e.g., a nursing diagnosis that is made for a client). An **emic** perspective is the insider's point of view, the experience of that culture from someone who is of that culture (e.g., a nurse describing nursing). Both perspectives are useful; however, if outsiders impose their views on a culture without critical reflection of their own assumptions and perceptions, it can perpetuate misinterpretations, judging of "the others," and inaccurate conclusions of the culture being explored (Allen, 1996).

Multiculturalism

Cultural diversity has always existed in Canada. However, formal recognition for language rights and different legal systems were restricted to the English and French at the time of Confederation in 1867. Treaty rights, which were negotiated with some First Nations, took place in the context of colonization and were largely motivated by land and resource acquisition. Multiculturalism was based on European, Christian, and colonial perspectives (Joy, 1995) with layers and separations based on class, race, gender, formal education, and ability to speak English (Lee, 1995). People who look different because of their skin colour, ethnicity, or race may always be considered as "visible minorities" in the mainstream society. In 1971, federal multiculturalism policy acknowledged the contribution of all ethnic backgrounds to Canadian culture (Kulig, 2000). More recently, debate about the assumptions, benefits, and barriers of multiculturalism has been articulated.

Multiculturalism can be defined as the notion of cultural diversity as a valuable resource that should be preserved, extended, and strengthened (Locke, 1992). This is seen to benefit the entire population. The Canadian Multiculturalism Act of 1988 states:

> The Constitution of Canada... recognizes the importance of preserving and enhancing the multicultural heritage of Canadians...; [and] the government of Canada recognizes the diversity of Canadians as regards to race, national or ethnic origin, colour and religion as a fundamental characteristic of Canadian society and is committed to a policy of multiculturalism designed to preserve and enhance the multicultural heritage of Canadians while working to achieve the equality of all Canadians in the economic, social, cultural and political life of Canada (as cited in James, 1999, p. 199).

Ethnicity is a way of describing social identity with a group that is based on a shared history and social structure (James, 1999). The dominant culture tends not to define themselves in terms of ethnicity; it is usually minority groups that are viewed as ethnic. **Race** is often thought of as an objective biological distinction (usually based on visible differences such as skin colour). However, historically the concept of race has been socially constructed and used to maintain the dominant social order. This continues to occur today. "Race is significant as long as groups are determined by their physical traits, and attributes are assigned as a result of these traits. It is significant as long as groups and individuals suffer consequences because of race" (James, 1991, p. 41–42).

Acculturation refers to the adaptation that occurs when cultures are in contact. Culture is dynamic with inevitable change and adjustment. Groups who immigrate to Canada and value retaining their ethnic culture also acculturate to living in a new country. The dominant culture also acculturates but may not recognize this. **Assimilation** refers to total integration into the dominant culture. Kymlicka and Norman (2000) state that one needs to distinguish between assimilation and multicultural integration (acculturation). Both involve a new identity and both seek to integrate people from diverse backgrounds into common social and political institutions. However, assimilation has the intent of eliminating cultural differences. In contrast, multiculturalism "accepts that ethnocultural identities matter to citizens, will endure over time, and must be recognized and accommodated within these common institutions" (Kymlicka & Norman, 2000, p. 14). The "Canadian mosaic" conveys symbolically that the pieces (cultures) that form the mosaic are different, can be distinguished, are all needed to create the entire pattern, and that the whole forms a pattern (the culture of Canada) richer that any one of its parts.

It is important to realize that the different minority groups in Canada experience different challenges to participation in society and means of addressing those challenges (Kymlicka & Norman, 2000). For example, national minority groups such as French-Canadians or First Nations often seek autonomy through self-government. Immigrant groups often identify ways to increase their participation in existing institutions, such as reducing barriers. Community health nurses (CHNs) should not assume that all groups have the same values about being a part of the Canadian mosaic or want the same mechanisms in place. There are issues of power inherent in multiculturalism. The meaning of multiculturalism has gone through phases and changes of interpretation (Srivastava & Leininger, 2002) that are reflected in some positive and negative views, as follows.

Positive views: A celebration of personal and group heritage and of the meaning of that heritage today as a full partner in Canadian culture. Recognition of, commitment to, and the practice of diversity, tolerance, equity, and respect for multiple ways of knowing and being.

Negative views: Being marginalized; considered to be "others;" culture is reduced to "diet, dance, and dialect." Only those who are not a part of the dominant culture are considered ethnic or to have a culture. The underlying assumptions of power, who makes decisions, and who fits in are not questioned.

NEWCOMERS IN CANADA

Newcomers may include "refugees, immigrants, legal or illegal aliens, migrants, international adoptees, and others" (Smith, 2001, p. 53). Newcomers may share some similarities (e.g., language barriers, cultural adaptation) but like all groups of people, there are significant differences both within and across cultures. In 2001, Canadian census data (Statistics Canada, 2003) showed that 5.4 million people (18.4% of the total population) were born outside the country, the highest proportion in 70 years. Canada was second only to Australia, which had the highest proportion of foreign-born residents (22%). In the United States, 11% of the residents were born outside the country in 2000 (which was also the highest proportion for that country in 70 years). Since 1901, 13.4 million immigrants have come to Canada. The decade with the highest number of immigrants in the past 100 years was the 1990s when 1.8 million immigrants were welcomed. "Immigration is one of [the] major sources of ethnic diversity in contemporary societies" (Zolberg, 1996, p. 44). Between 1900 and 1961, immigrants

TABLE 16.1
Top 10 Countries of Birth (Other than Canada), 2001

Immigrated before 1961	Number	Percent	Immigrated 1991-2001[1]	Number	Percent
Total immigrants	894 465	100.0	Total immigrants	1 830 680	100.0
United Kingdom	217 175	24.3	China, People's Republic of	197 360	10.8
Italy	147 320	16.5	India	156 120	8.5
Germany	96 770	10.8	Philippines	122 010	6.7
Netherlands	79 170	8.9	Hong Kong, Special Administrative Region	118 385	6.5
Poland	44 340	5.0	Sri Lanka	62 590	3.4
United States	34 810	3.9	Pakistan	57 990	3.2
Hungary	27 425	3.1	Taiwan	53 755	2.9
Ukraine	21 240	2.4	United States	51 440	2.8
Greece	20 755	2.3	Iran	47 080	2.6
China, People's Republic of	15 850	1.8	Poland	43 370	2.4

(1) Includes data up to May, 2001

Source: Statistics Canada. (2003). Canada's ethnocultural portrait: The changing mosaic. *2001 census: Analysis series (p. 39). Ottawa, ON: Author.*

to Canada were primarily from European countries (Table 16.1). However, since then, most immigrants have been from Asia. Factors that caused this shift include changes to federal immigration policies and changes in the international migration of immigrants and refugees. The changing face of immigrants to Canada increases the need for all nurses to be able to provide culturally competent care.

Almost three-quarters (73%) of newcomers arriving in the 1990s settled in Canada's largest cities: Toronto, Vancouver, and Montreal. Newcomers were younger (46% between the ages of 25–44) than the rest of the population (31% between the ages of 25–44), and nearly one in five (17%) school-age children in Toronto and Vancouver in the last decade were immigrants (Statistics Canada, 2003). Four million Canadians (13.4% of the population) now identify themselves as visible minorities, a three-fold increase since 1981. "Visible minorities are defined by the *Employment Equity Act* as 'persons, other than Aboriginal peoples, who are non-Caucasian in race or non-white in colour'" (Statistics Canada, 2003, p. 10).

In 1997, 69% of children under the age of 15 could not speak either English or French at the time of arrival in Canada (Health Canada, 1999). Language is a significant barrier to seeking and gaining access to health care. CHNs must learn how to use both professional and lay interpreters effectively in order to communicate with clients. For convenience, an English-speaking family member may be considered as an interpreter, but this choice has inherent problems. The family member may not understand the health information given and may not know specific medical terminology used by the nurse. The use of a family member may also inhibit frank discussion of sensitive topics. Children are frequently the first to learn English in a family. However, using children as interpreters is not recommended since the child may no longer recognize the parent in the role of family leader when they are seen as dependent on the child for communication (Anderson, Waxler-Morrison, Richardson, Herbert, & Murphy, 1990). Interpreters must be encouraged to translate accurately since they may paraphrase and add personal interpretations of client feelings and beliefs.

Culture shock is a state of anxiety that occurs when it is difficult to behave appropriately in a new context (Spradley & Allender, 2001). With acculturation, previous beliefs and values that are functional are retained; those that are not functional are adapted and changed over a period of years. Surprisingly, newcomers often integrate themselves quickly into the host culture (Health Canada, 1999). Newcomers to Canada bring significant strengths, such as diversity, determination, and resilience (DeSantis & Thomas, 1997), yet their health is often at risk due to barriers that exist at many levels (Yiu-Matuk, 1995). A low standard of living; language barriers; working to fit in with mainstream society; dealing with stress by using alcohol, tobacco, and consuming high-fat foods; and working in unsafe conditions without benefits such as dental care and eyeglasses all contribute to increased health risks of the newcomer. Stress associated with immigration alone can put an individual at risk for poor health outcomes. Refugees, older people, individuals separated from their families, and those with limited or non-existent support in the host country are at particular risk.

MIGRANT WORKERS

According to Clark (2000), it is estimated that there are 200 000 to 300 000 foreign and migrant workers in Canada. Foreign and **migrant workers** without permanent residence who are authorized for employment include people in the Live-in Caregiver Program (someone who provides care to

Canadian Research Box 16.1

Lynam, M. J., Gurm, B., & Dhari, R. (2000). Exploring perinatal health in Indo-Canadian women. *Canadian Nurse, 96*(4), 18–24.

The goals of this study were to document and reflect the perspectives of Indo-Canadian women on issues of perinatal health and to explore and facilitate ways to enable these women to establish partnerships with health care providers in the community. A total of 133 people participated in 15 focus groups.

The authors recognized that traditional perinatal practices among Indo-Canadian women, particularly those from rural areas, continue to be a vital and important source of support. Women who have immigrated to Canada, who may be isolated from extended family and do not speak English, have limited access to both traditional support and formal health care providers.

Social class, formal education, and English language skills were found to vary within the same community. Perceptions of traditions and nurturing activities differed as well. For example, the traditional 40-day rest period for new mothers was seen in both positive and negative ways. The most frequently mentioned risk factor for poor health outcomes was recent immigration for a woman who was also likely to be newly married. It was felt that such women were more likely to be lonely, isolated, unfamiliar with available resources, and unable to speak English. Women as resources for other women and women's resources within the family were largely viewed as positive. Participants utilized the Canadian health care system, especially physicians. They commented on long waiting times for appointments and that visits did not focus on concerns related to child development.

Implications for CHNs include the need to be aware of the stress associated with immigration, particularly among new mothers since they may have neither traditional cultural nor host society supports available to them. Nurses also need to be aware that perceptions, experiences, and values differ within cultures.

Discussion Questions

1. What do the data in this study reflect about the nature of culture and experience of newcomers?
2. A variety of meanings and realities emerged from each area of discussion. If you were a CHN working with this community, how would you apply the data?

children, the elderly, or the disabled in a private household), seasonal farm workers, and some refused refugee claimants. These workers may travel as a family, or in the case of most foreign workers in sponsored programs, are adults who have left families behind in their home countries. Migrant workers can also include Canadian citizens who travel in search of seasonal agricultural work. It is difficult to accurately report the number of migrant farm workers and their country of origin because some are working illegally and are very mobile and difficult to track as they move from one crop to the next between provinces and states (Sandhaus, 2001).

Farming operations have steadily increased in size since World War II, and farmers have found it difficult to recruit local people to plant, spray, and harvest crops. Reasons for this difficulty may be that local people are unwilling to work in low-paying, hazardous jobs lasting only a few weeks a year (Sandhaus, 2001). Migrant farm workers fill this gap and have come to play a vital role in the success of the agricultural industry (Clark, 2000; Sandhaus, 1998). Unfortunately, limited finances, fear of deportation, language barriers, isolation, difficulty in gaining access to health care, and hazardous living and working conditions, partnered with a nomadic lifestyle, result in complex and frequent health problems for migrant farm workers and their families.

Migrant farm workers are a culturally diverse group, travelling to Canada and the United States from places such as Mexico, Central America, the Caribbean, and Latin America. They may be adults residing in seasonal housing in one location or families travelling by themselves or in groups. For example, some Low German-speaking Mennonites from Mexico travel annually as families between their colonies in Mexico and agricultural work in the Prairie provinces and Southwestern Ontario (Edmunds, 1993). They are often Canadian citizens or have the right to apply for citizenship, and many have settled permanently in Canada, building churches and schools and retaining traditional values and practices while adapting to Canadian culture.

Common agriculturally related injuries include strains from heavy lifting, repetitive task injuries such as carpal tunnel syndrome, and physical and emotional fatigue from long hours in the heat, cold, and rain while being required to complete work within a restricted time period. Physical and emotional stress, compounded with a lack of adequate tools and training, increase the likelihood of injury. Environmental hazards, such as exposure to pesticides, are also of concern (Larson, 2001). Migrant farm worker housing is often substandard. Crowded, unsanitary living conditions promote the spread of infectious diseases, affecting all members of the group or family. Infant mortality, parasitic infection, influenza, tuberculosis, and hepatitis occur more frequently in migrant farm worker families. There are also high rates of dental disease and chronic diseases such as hypertension, anemia, and diabetes (Sandhaus, 1998).

The National Advisory Council on Migrant Health reported that less than 20% of the migrant population access health care (Sandhaus, 2001). Reasons for this lack of access are varied. Migrants may be unfamiliar with the health care system, and language barriers make it difficult to explain symptoms and understand treatment plans. Many have limited transportation and childcare and are often unable to attend appointments during daytime hours without loss of wages (Sandhaus, 1998; Zust & Molene, 2003).

CULTURE AND HEALTH

Determinants of health for all individuals, families, and communities include income, education, social support, and access to health care. As culture is individually and collectively defined and expressed, so is health. Many immigrants define health, health care, and health promotion very differently from the definitions of the dominant culture. This can lead to the perception on the part of health care providers that immigrants "don't care" about their health or the health of their families. Newcomers and migrant workers will continue to utilize health care practices from within their culture and may have no reason to trust that the Canadian health care system will be understanding or responsive to them in ways that are meaningful to them (Edmunds, 1993; Waxler-Morrison, Anderson, & Richardson, 1990). As Canadians welcome ever increasing cultural diversity, CHNs must be willing to accept the responsibility of responding to individual and family health care needs with cultural sensitivity and competence.

PHOTO 16.1

The staff of an Old Colony Mennonite private school pose with their school's community health nurse.

Credit: Kathryn Edmunds

Implications for Community Health Nursing Practice

Since the passing of the Canadian Multiculturalism Act of 1988, much emphasis has been placed on cultural awareness and sensitivity. Cultural competence requires more attention. The concept of **cultural competence** integrates the knowledge, attitudes, and skills that the nurse would use to plan effective and appropriate interventions (Andrews & Boyle, 2003). It is a process that "includes a genuine passion to be open and flexible with others, to accept differences and build on similarities, and to be willing to learn from others as cultural informants" (Camphina-Bacote, 2002, p. 183). So how does one become a culturally competent CHN? It requires reflection of oneself, other cultures, nursing models and theories and the opportunity to practise assessment and collaborative skills.

While it is important to acknowledge the culture of others, it is even more important to examine our own assumptions and values. As a CHN, you bring the values and expectations from at least three cultures to every interaction: your personal culture, the culture of nursing, and the culture of your institution. Self-reflection includes being aware of all these influences (see text box).

Self-reflection is also needed to become aware of the client's (or colleague's) culture. CHNs need to recognize their own values and assumptions; to be open to the different values, assumptions, and worldview beliefs held by the client; and to demonstrate the interviewing and assessment skills that allow the clients to express their realities. There is always interplay between making use of background information the nurse may have and checking that information with every client. Background information that is never checked and is assumed to be true for all becomes a **stereotype**. What must also be assessed is how important an intervention is to the client and how the concept of "care" is perceived, expressed, and demonstrated.

Clients bring multiple cultures to their interactions with nurses. They too are shaped by their personal culture, professional values, and unique life experiences. The key to understanding lies in being open to and appreciating the diversity within each individual. Locke (1992) adds some valuable dimensions with his consideration of global influences on the culture of individuals, families, and communities.

Being open to and aware of multiple ways of knowing and experiencing the world leads to the recognition that decisions can take place in different moral contexts (Baker, 1997). Characteristics of culture can lead to **ethnocentrism**, which is the belief that one's own culture is the best or most desirable. Nurses who believe that the culture and practices of nursing are the only or "best" way to interpret what the client is expressing and to achieve improvements in health are being ethnocentric.

Knowledge of every culture is impossible and unnecessary (Waxler-Morrison et al., 1990). CHNs need to have the assessment, interviewing, and collaborative skills in order to be open to the discovery and reflection required for providing effective care. These skills are not only needed with clients but also with interpreters and community agencies. Leininger's transcultural care decisions and actions (Leininger &

Questions for Self-Awareness

Awareness of self is the first step to understanding others. To seek that awareness, one might attempt to answer the following questions.

- What is my cultural heritage? What was the culture of my parents and my grandparents? With what cultural groups do I identify?
- What is the cultural relevance of my name?
- What values, beliefs, opinions, and attitudes do I hold that are consistent with the dominant culture? Which are inconsistent? How did I learn these?
- How did I decide to become a nurse? What cultural standards were involved in that process? What do I understand to be the relationship between culture and nursing? What are the similarities and differences between the values of my culture and the culture of nursing?
- What are the values of my institution? Are those values compatible with or different from the values of my culture and the values of nursing?
- What unique abilities, aspirations, expectations, and limitations do I have that might influence my relationships with people from my culture and other cultures?

Source: Adapted from Locke, D. C. (1992). Increasing multicultural understanding: A comprehensive model *(pp. 2). Newbury Park, CA: Sage.*

CASE STUDY

You have just accepted a position as a CHN in a small town 50 km from the city where you grew up and went to school. You feel you are familiar with the geographic area and the people. You have been asked to speak to a community group about caring for the elderly at home. This is a topic that is "near and dear" to your heart because your grandmother lives with your parents and geriatrics was of special interest to you as a nursing student. People in the audience look like "regular" people, and you give your presentation emphasizing access to resources in the city, the decline of mental status in the elderly, and safety concerns in the home for the elderly when they are left alone. The audience is polite but non-responsive.

Discussion Questions

1. How would you do a community cultural assessment?
2. You as the nurse used caring behaviours from your nursing knowledge and your own ethnicity. What strengths and limitations did this have?
3. How could the nursing care have been more culturally competent?

McFarland, 2002) provide a framework for planning nursing interventions with individuals, families, and communities. These professional decisions and actions are:

- culture care preservation/maintenance,
- culture care accommodation/negotiation, and
- culture care repatterning/restructuring.

These actions help clients preserve or retain relevant health care values and practices, accommodate and adapt for beneficial health outcomes, and greatly modify or change existing health care patterns while respecting the values of both the client and the nurse.

Cultural safety is the effective nursing practice with a client from another culture, determined by that client. "Unsafe cultural practice comprises any action which diminishes, demeans, or disempowers the cultural identity and well being of an individual" (Nursing Council of New Zealand, 2002, p. 7).

SUMMARY

This chapter has introduced the concept of culture, the Canadian experience of multiculturalism, the experiences of newcomers and migrant workers, and the development of a culturally competent community health nursing practice. CHNs need to bring the same set of skills, behaviours, and expertise to every encounter whether the person looks the same or different from them. A culturally competent approach requires commitment to personal reflection and growth, an understanding of the layers of cultural identity that shape us all, and the development of knowledge and skills so that in every interaction the nurse strives to discover the values and meanings of health for the client.

KEY TERMS

culture
cultural values
etic
emic
multiculturalism
ethnicity
race
acculturation
assimilation
culture shock
migrant workers
cultural competence
stereotype
ethnocentrism
cultural safety

INDIVIDUAL CRITICAL THINKING EXERCISES

1. What is the difference between healthy cultural identification and ethnocentrism?
2. How would you assess if the model or theory you are using is helping you deliver culturally competent care?

GROUP CRITICAL THINKING EXERCISES

1. How would you go about gaining and demonstrating the skills and behaviours needed for culturally competent practice?
2. In pairs, do Yiu and Edmonds' (2004) A Guide to Transcultural Assessment (see text box in Chapter 9). What have you learned about your own culture? What have you learned about your partner's culture?
3. Are the members of your nursing class representative of your community's population? Why or why not?

REFERENCES

Allen, D. G. (1996). Knowledge, politics, culture, and gender: A discourse perspective. *Canadian Journal of Nursing Research, 28*(1), 95–102.

Anderson, J. M., Waxler-Morrison, N., Richardson, E., Herbert, C., & Murphy, M. (1990). Conclusion: Delivering culturally sensitive health care. In N. Waxler-Morrison, J. Anderson, & E. Richardson (Eds.), *Cross-cultural caring: A handbook for health professionals* (pp. 245–267). Vancouver, BC: UBC Press.

Andrews, M. M., & Boyle, J. S. (2003). *Transcultural concepts in nursing care* (4th ed.). Philadelphia, PA: Lippincott.

Baker, C. (1997). Cultural relativism and cultural diversity: Implications for nursing practice. *Advances in Nursing Science, 20*(1), 3–11.

Camphina-Bacote, J. (2002). The process of cultural competence in the delivery of healthcare services: A model of care. *Journal of Transcultural Nursing, 13*(3), 181–184.

Canadian Nurses Association. (2000). Cultural diversity—changes and challenges. *Nursing Now: Issues and Trends in Canadian Nursing, 7*, 1–6.

Clark, T. (2000). *Migrant workers in Canada.* Retrieved December 14, 2003 from **www.december18.net/web/docpapers/doc626.pdf**

College of Nurses of Ontario. (1999). *Standards of practice: A guide to nurses for providing culturally sensitive care.* Toronto, ON: Author.

Community Health Nurses Association of Canada. (2003). *Canadian community health nursing standards of practice:* Ottawa, ON: Author.

DeSantis, L., & Thomas, J. (1997). Building healthy communities with immigrants and refugees. *Journal of Transcultural Nursing, 9*(1), 20–31.

Edmunds, K. A. (1993). Transcultural nursing care with Old Colony Mennonites in a school context. In M. E. Parker (Ed.), *Patterns of nursing theories in practice* (pp. 122–141). New York: National League for Nursing Press.

Health Canada. (1999). *Canadian research on immigration and health.* Ottawa, ON: Author.

James, C. E. (1999). *Seeing ourselves: Exploring race, ethnicity and culture* (2nd ed.). Toronto, ON: Thompson Educational.

Joy, M. (1995). Multiculturalism and margins of intolerance. In C. Pizanias & J. S. Friederes (Eds.), *Freedom within the margins: The politics of exclusion* (pp. 3–13). Calgary, AB: Detselig Enterprises.

Kulig, J. C. (2000). Culturally diverse communities: The impact on the role of community health nurses. In M. J. Stewart (Ed.), *Community nursing: Promoting Canadians' health* (2nd ed.) (pp. 194–210). Toronto, ON: W.B. Saunders.

Kymlicka, W., & Norman, W. (2000). Citizenship in culturally diverse societies: Issues, contexts, concepts. In W. Kymlicka & W. Norman (Eds.), *Citizenship in diverse societies* (pp. 1–32). Oxford, UK: Oxford University Press.

Larson, A. (2001). Environmental/occupational safety and health. *Migrant Health Issues: Monograph no. 2.* Buda, TX: National Center for Farmworker Health.

Lee, J. (1995). Community development with immigrant women: Theory and practice. In C. Pizanias & J. S. Friederes (Eds.), *Freedom within the margins: The politics of exclusion* (pp. 87–109). Calgary, AB: Detselig Enterprises.

Leininger, M., & McFarland, M. R. (Eds.). (2002). *Transcultural nursing: Concepts, theories, research & practice* (3rd ed.). New York: McGraw-Hill.

Locke, D. C. (1992). *Increasing multicultural understanding: A comprehensive model.* Newbury Park, CA: Sage.

Masi, R. (1993). Multicultural health: Principles and policies. In R. Masi, L. Mensah, & K. McLeod (Eds.), *Health and cultures: Exploring the relationships: Vol. I. Policies, professional practice and education* (pp. 11–31). Oakville, ON: Mosaic Press.

Nursing Council of New Zealand. (2002). *Guidelines for cultural safety, the Treaty of Waitangi, and Maori health in nursing and midwifery education and practice.* Retrieved April 3, 2003 from **www.nursingcouncil.org.nz/culturalsafety.pdf**

Sandhaus, S. (1998). Migrant health: A harvest of poverty. *American Journal of Nursing, 98*(9), 52, 54.

Sandhaus, S. (2001). Migrant health. In J. A. Allender & B. W. Spradley (Eds.), *Community health nursing: Concepts and practice* (5th ed.) (pp. 658–681). Philadelphia, PA: Lippincott.

Smith, L. S. (2001). Health of America's newcomers. *Journal of Community Health Nursing, 18*(1), 53–68.

Spradley, B. W., & Allender, J. A. (2001). Transcultural nursing in the community. In J. A. Allender & B. W. Spradley (Eds.), *Community health nursing: Concepts and practice* (5th ed.) (pp. 57–79). Philadelphia, PA: Lippincott.

Srivastava, R. H., & Leininger, M. (2002). Canadian transcultural nursing: Trends and issues. In M. Leininger & M. R. McFarland (Eds.), *Transcultural nursing: Concepts, theories, research & practice* (3rd ed.) (pp. 493–502). New York: McGraw-Hill.

Statistics Canada. (2003). *2001 census: Analysis series. Canada's ethnocultural portrait: The changing mosaic.* Ottawa, ON: Author.

Waxler-Morrison, N., Anderson, J., & Richardson, E. (1990). *Cross-cultural caring: A handbook for health professionals.* Vancouver, BC: University of British Columbia Press.

Yiu, L. & Edmunds, K. (2004). A Guide to transcultural nursing assessment. Unpublished guide, University of Windsor, Windsor, Ontario.

Yiu Matuk, L. (1995). Health promotion surveys for multicultural clients. In M. Stewart (Ed.), *Community nursing: Promoting Canadians' health* (2nd ed.) (pp. 267–281). Toronto, ON: W.B. Saunders.

Zolberg, A. R. (1996). Immigration and multiculturalism in the industrial democracies. In R. Bauböck, A. Heller, & A. R. Zolberg (Eds.), *The challenge of diversity: Integration and pluralism in societies of immigration* (pp. 43–65). Aldershot, UK: Avebury.

Zust, B. L., & Moline, K. (2003). Identifying underserved ethnic populations within a community: The first step in eliminating health care disparities among racial and ethnic minorities. *Journal of Transcultural Nursing, 14*(1), 66–74.

ADDITIONAL RESOURCES

READINGS

College of Nurses of Ontario. (1998). *Practice guidelines for registered nurses providing culturally sensitive care.* Toronto, ON: Author.

Greey, M. (2002). *Honouring diversity: A cross-cultural approach to infant development for babies with special needs* (rev. ed.). Toronto, ON: Centennial Infant and Child Centre.

London InterCommunity Health Centre. (1993). *Culture, health and you: Discussion stimulator video workbook.* London, ON: Author.

WEBSITES

Digital Forest:
www.diversityrx.org

Health Canada:
www.hc-sc.gc.ca

Transcultural Nursing Society:
www.tcns.org

About the Authors

Kathryn Edmunds, RN, BN (Manitoba), MSN (Wayne State), is an Assistant Professor in the Faculty of Nursing at the University of Windsor. She joined the university after 15 years as a public health nurse with the Windsor-Essex County Health Unit, working in rural Southwestern Ontario. Her graduate education was in the field of transcultural nursing which remains an area of clinical and research interest. Other research interests include cultural competence and qualitative evaluation. She is a Visiting Research Fellow at the School of Nursing and Midwifery at the University of Southampton, UK and in 2001 was awarded a Registered Nurses Association of Ontario Advanced Clinical/Practice Fellowship in leadership and research.

Elizabeth Kinnaird-Iler, RN, BScN, MSc (Windsor), is a manager in the Healthy Babies, Healthy Children program at the Windsor-Essex County Health Unit. She provides direct supervision to public health nurses and family home visitors who visit new mothers and young families from a variety of cultural backgrounds. Her interests include areas of women's health, program evaluation, health promotion, and transcultural health.

The authors would like to acknowledge Liana Dass for her assistance in preparing this chapter.

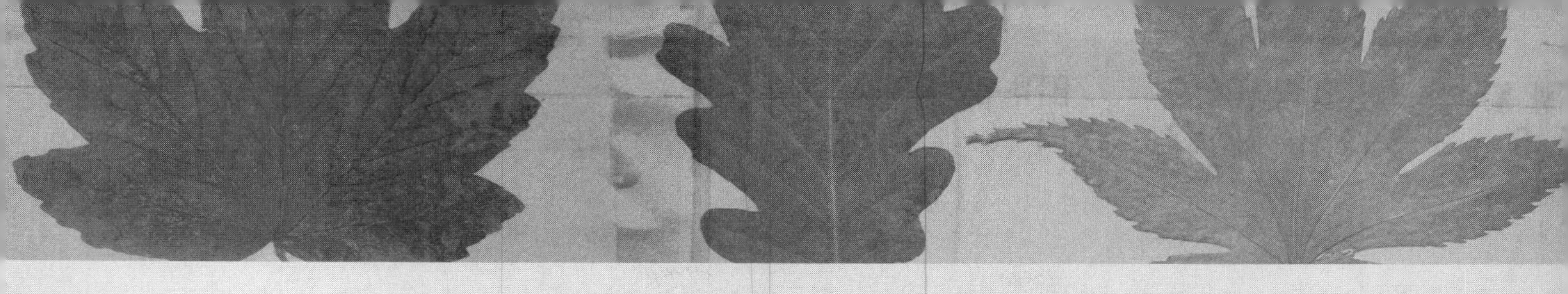

CHAPTER 17

Clients in the Community Mental Health System

Margaret England

OBJECTIVES

AFTER STUDYING THIS CHAPTER, YOU SHOULD BE ABLE TO:

1. Analyze challenges faced by mentally ill persons in your community.
2. Evaluate mental health services and supports in your community.
3. Explain the role of community health nurses in your community using the ACCESS framework.
4. Use the concept of prevention to describe a face-to-face, telephone, and group-based mental health intervention.
5. Plan assessment and intervention services for a person who is to receive assertive community treatment.
6. Cite research that documents outcomes of community mental health services and supports.

INTRODUCTION

Today, psychiatric nurses are taking on roles in the community that focus on mental health promotion, prevention of mental illness, and reduction of deficits linked to mental illness. This trend is occurring largely because of changes in the philosophy and location of psychiatric treatment and mental health care. This chapter provides an overview of challenges facing mentally ill persons in the community and the delivery of community mental health services to these individuals.

HISTORICAL CONTEXT

The history of mental health care in Canada began with the management of mentally ill persons in poor houses. Beginning in the early 1800s, mentally ill persons were gradually shifted to provincial mental hospitals where they were physically isolated from their communities of origin, given custodial care, but provided little in the way of non-custodial treatment. Over of the next 150 years, these facilities became increasingly overcrowded, unhygienic, and inhumane, leading to an erosion of public confidence in their usefulness. Factors that contributed to dissatisfaction with these institutions were the inability of non-medicinal treatments to eradicate mental illness, the discovery of psychotropic medication, and rising concern for individual human rights of the mentally ill (Benjafield & Boudreau, 2000). These factors triggered efforts to depopulate provincial mental hospitals, a process of reform that became known as the **deinstitutionalization** of the mentally ill.

The philosophy of deinstitutionalization shifted mental health care to psychiatric units of general hospitals and the community. The result was a drop in bed capacity in provincial mental hospitals from 47 633 beds in 1960 to 15 011 beds in 1976, and a rise in general hospital psychiatric beds from 844 to 5836 (Wasylenki, Goering, & MacNaughton, 1994). The current trend is to target approximately 35 psychiatric hospital beds per 100 000 adults, with 14 of those beds to be used for long-term mental health care (Goering, Wasylenki, & Durbin, 2000).

Prevention-oriented mental health services evolved at the same time as the deinstitutionalization of the mentally ill because of the shifting of public funds from provincial mental hospitals to local communities. These community-based services targeted not only the needs of mentally ill persons, but also the needs of families and the larger community. Social forces helping to shape this change included advancements in research, improvements in treatment modalities, civil rights legislation, and liberalization of policies for institutional commitment of the mentally ill. The result is that most individuals with mental health problems or mental illness now live and receive mental health services and supports within their own communities.

Despite societal efforts to address mental health and illness in the community, a recent report on mental illnesses in Canada affirms that "stigma and discrimination attached to mental health [as being] the most tragic realities facing people with mental illness in Canada" (Health Canada, 2002, p. 7). **Stigma** is "an unjustified mark of shame or discredit attached to mental illness" (Allender & Spradley, 2001, p. 685). Throughout history, society has viewed persons with mental illness (MI) as being different. Cultural beliefs, superstitions, and poor understanding of MI contribute to fear, stereotyping, and avoidance of persons with MI. This stigmatism is an important reason why so many persons with MI conceal their illness and delay or refuse treatment and follow-up care (Health Canada, 2002).

Canadian Mental Health Association

The provision of community mental health services in Canada is the responsibility of provincial ministries of health. Community mental health programs such as those of the Canadian Mental Health Association, therefore, operate under the general supervision of a provincial mental health division. The **Canadian Mental Health Association (CMHA)** is an umbrella organization founded in 1918 to fight mental illness, prevent mental illness, and promote mental health of residents living in their own communities (see CMHA website listed in Additional Resources). Today, the CMHA is a tri-level enterprise with a national office, provincial divisions, and local community-based branches within each province. Local branches of the CMHA are autonomous, mission-based organizations responsible for the provision of resources, mental health programs, and other human services to individuals, families, and groups within their respective communities. Provision of mental health services is accomplished through self-help, generic community resources and services, and the support and good will of family, friends, and neighbours. These services and supports are tied to factors that determine health and wellness, such as housing, income, education, leisure opportunities, employment, peer and social supports, and self-esteem (Bezzina, 1996).

TABLE 17.1
Estimated One-Year Prevalence of a Mental Illness among Adults in Canada

Mental Disorder	Prevalence
Mood disorders	
Major (unipoloar) depression	4.1–4.5%
Bipolar depression	0.2–0.6%
Dysthymia	0.8–3.1%
Schizophrenia	0.3%
Anxiety disorders	12.2%
Personality disorders	–
Eating disorders:	
Anorexia: Women	0.7%
Men	0.2%
Bulemia: Women	1.5%
Men	0.1%
Deaths from suicide:	12.2/100 000 (1998)
Population of all deaths	2.0%
Aged 15–24 years	24.0%
Aged 25–44 years	16.0%

Source: Health Canada. (2002). A report on mental illnesses in Canada: Chapter 1. *Retrieved October 24, 2003 from* www.hc-sc.gc.ca/pphb-dgspsp/publicat/miic-mmac/chap_1_e.html. *Reproduced with the permission of the Minister of Public Works and Government Services Canada, 2003.*

MENTAL ILLNESS AND ITS EFFECTS

Mental illness (MI) refers to a group of diagnosable diseases or disabilities of the mind (Mental Health Act, 1990, amended 2002). It is described as some combination of altered thinking, mood, behaviour, or will that can be linked with distress or impaired functioning.

Current figures show that approximately one in five Canadian adults will require mental health services or support at some point in their lifetime (Statistics Canada, 2000). Nearly 10% of Canada's adults and 20% of Canada's children and youth require mental health services or supports over the course of a 12-month period. In 1999, 3.8% of all admissions to a general hospital (1.5 million hospital days) were due to mental illness; women were almost twice as likely as men to have been hospitalized for a mental illness (Figure 17.1). Based on estimates from the United States, personality disorders may affect 6% to 9% of the population (Narrow, Rae, Robins, & Regier, 2002).

Serious mental illness (SMI) refers to mental illness that has compromised a person's level of competence and quality of life. **Serious and persistent mental illness (SPMI)** refers to the chronic or enduring nature of a person's mental illness. Presently, 1–3% of Canada's population suffers from SPMI, costing the nation more than 14.4 billion dollars a year to manage (Stephens & Joubert, 2001). However, the societal costs of mental illnesses would be at least three times greater if the illnesses were not treated in a timely manner.

Risk Factors

Many combinations of biological, behavioural, socio-cultural, and environmental variables are linked to the development and progress of mental illness (Tsuang & Tohen, 2002). Biological variables include genetic predisposition, family history of mental illness, father's age at conception, traumatic illness or injury, and age and gender of the MI person. Behavioural variables include psychobiological stress, child neglect or abuse, low self-esteem, and alcohol or other substance misuse or abuse. Socio-cultural variables influencing mental illness include economic stress, poverty, inadequate education or exposure to opportunities for personal development, relocation, family dysfunction and lack of support, violence, social isolation, stigmatization, homelessness, and inadequate health and human resources or services within the community (Pevalin & Goldberg, 2003). Environmental variables include geography, climate conditions, seasonal changes, crowding, noise, pollutants, toxins, and war.

The growing problem of homelessness illustrates how combinations of variables contribute to the burden of MI in a community. Studies estimate that 50 to 75% of homeless adults have at least one diagnosable alcohol-, drug-, or mental illness–related disorder (Kovess, 2002). Moreover, these individuals tend to be socially isolated from family, friends, and other supportive networks. A study of 330 homeless adults in Toronto, for example, found that the study participants became homeless because of poverty, lack of employment, low welfare wages, and lack of affordable housing (Morrel-Bellai,

FIGURE 17.1 Hospitalization for Mental Illness

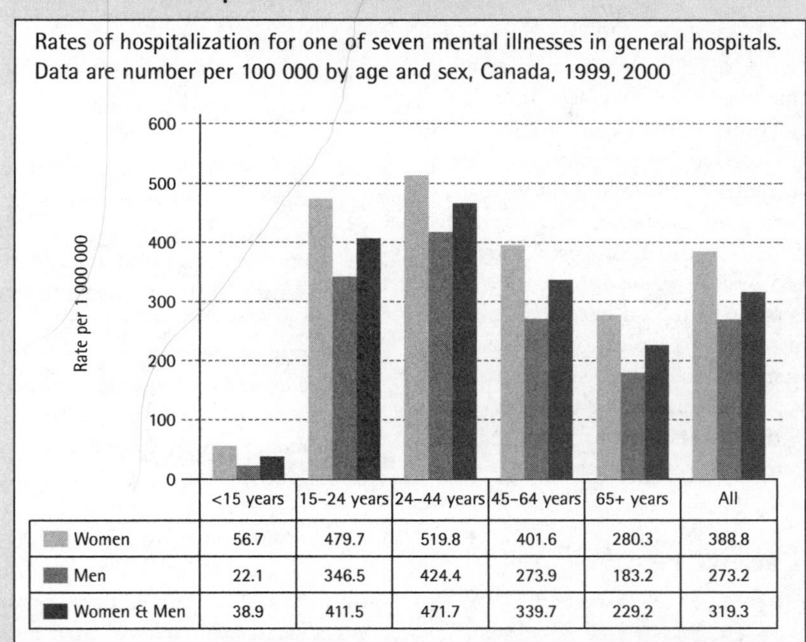

	<15 years	15–24 years	24–44 years	45–64 years	65+ years	All
Women	56.7	479.7	519.8	401.6	280.3	388.8
Men	22.1	346.5	424.4	273.9	183.2	273.2
Women & Men	38.9	411.5	471.7	339.7	229.2	319.3

Source: Reproduced with the permission of the Minister of Public Works and Government Services Canada, 2003, from Health Canada. (2002). A report on mental illnesses in Canada: Chapter 1. *Retrieved October 24, 2003 from* www.hc-sc.gc.ca/pphb-dgpsp/publicat/miic-mmac/chap_1_e.html. *Reproduced with the permission of the Minister of Public Works and Government Services Canada, 2003.*

Goering, & Boydell, 2000). More than 50% of these individuals were diagnosed with a psychotic or mood disorder. Sixty-one percent reported suicidal ideation and 34% had attempted suicide. Factors linked with their risk of suicide were MI, childhood homelessness of at least one week without the presence of a family member, being female, sexual abuse, lack of social opportunities, and periods of homelessness longer than six months (Rahel et al., 2002). The chronically homeless participants in the study often reported experiences of severe childhood trauma and hopelessness and attributed their continued homelessness to substance abuse. These findings suggest that homeless persons need facilitated access to generic community resources and services such as supportive counselling; rehabilitation; income; and safe, affordable, drug-free housing, before they lose hope.

Effects

Major depression, bipolar disorder, schizophrenia, and obsessive-compulsive disorder account for four of the 10 leading causes of disability and approximately 23% of the **burden of disease** on the population of Canada (Murray & Lopez, 1996; World Health Organization, 1999). SMIs are commonly associated with other comorbid conditions, contributing significantly to the degree and duration of disability and the prevalence of premature deaths in the population (Qin, Agerbo, & Mortensen, 2002). Persons diagnosed with schizophrenia, for example, are significantly more likely to acquire diabetes and cardiovascular disease earlier than the population at large. These conditions may be due in part to weight gain and disturbances of glucose and lipid metabolism that are now being linked with new-generation, neuroleptic medication and cardiovascular deaths (Fenton, 2001).

Individuals with MI suffer from exposure to psychological trauma within the family and the larger community. They typically report high levels of anxiety, loneliness, and depression and express negative beliefs about themselves. Those who work have an unstable employment history and may take comfort from nicotine, alcohol, marijuana, or other substances. Their families also suffer from the effects of MI, reporting feelings of fear, grief, shame, or embarrassment. They not only must cope with the dysfunction of their impaired family member, but also with community agencies and institutions that are available to persons with MI. Issues that surface because of a family member's SMI include denial of illness, medication non-adherence, management of medication side effects, lack of energy or will to perform self-care, avoidance of human contact, mood swings, threatening or paranoid behaviour, lack of appropriate reasoning or judgment, inappropriate or incomprehensible communication, persistent risky or dangerous behaviour, and manipulation of others to achieve a simple but desired goal. Persons with SPMI who do not take their medication tend to be hospitalized repeatedly because of disturbing symptoms, stigmatization, or inability to function (Fenton, 2001; Pejlert, 2001).

Needs of the Mentally Ill

According to Benjafield and Boudreau (2000) and Bezzina (1996), clients with MI face a myriad of physical, psychological, social, and spiritual challenges, and they need literal assistance with self-care and symptom management. Common physical challenges include distaste and intolerance of prescribed medication, impairments of vision and motor control (e.g., photosensitivity, dystonia, akathesia, and/or tardive dyskinesia), constipation, sleep disturbances, inadequate nutrition, dental disease, obesity, water intoxication, foot problems, and sunburn. Persons with SMI need to be assessed and treated for symptoms tied to medication, poor eating habits, smoking, and substance abuse. These symptoms often arise as a result of obesity; diabetes; blood dyscrasias; heart, lung, and liver problems; or cancer. Persons with SMI also need to be screened and treated, if necessary, for alcohol or substance abuse and communicable diseases (e.g., tuberculosis, sexually transmitted diseases, and AIDS). With structured support, they can learn to manage basic routines for self-care such as hygiene, dressing, eating, drinking, elimination, sleep, exercise, and medication intake.

Common psychological problems of persons with SMI include fear, anxiety, confusion, depression, frustration and anger, and low self-esteem, as well as impaired memory, concentration, and judgment. These individuals must learn how to manage feelings and thoughts and how to connect with understanding and competent sources of interpersonal support. With structured support, they can improve their overall ability to concentrate, make decisions, feel comfort, and resolve everyday challenges tied to relating with other people.

Common social problems of persons with SMI include low income, unemployment, unstable housing, erratic access or use of community services, and physical isolation from others. These individuals need one-to-one and multidisciplinary supports as well as sufficient funds to construct a physical and social environment in which to live. With supported opportunities and coaching, they can improve on their ability to participate in the lives of their families and the community.

Canadian Research Box 17.1

Pejlert, A. (2001). Being a parent of an adult son or daughter with severe mental illness receiving professional care: Parents' narratives. *Health & Social Care in the Community, 9*(4), 194–204.

The aim of this phenomenological interpretive study was to illuminate the meaning of taking care of a SMI adult son or daughter. In the study, parents talked about past, present, and projected relationships with their MI offspring. According to the narratives, parental care emerged as a lifelong effort that was illuminated in six themes: living with sorrow, anguish, and constant worry; living with guilt and shame; relating with caregivers and care; comfort and hardships; coming to terms with difficulties; and hoping for a better life for their MI child. Parents revealed ongoing grief, sorrow, and losses as chronic sorrow. They disclosed conflicts between the "culture" of the family and the health care system, in which they perceived threat to the parental role as well as comfort and confidence in the care given to their child. Parents interpreted experiences of stigma from how public and mental health professionals labelled MI and how they felt shame. Nevertheless, study participants interpreted a process of coming to terms with difficulties from the ways in which they persisted in giving care to their child, strived to look after themselves, and expressed hopes for the future. Results of the study suggest that nurses and other mental health professionals need to be aware of their own attitudes and treatment of families, improve their cooperation with and support to families, and provide opportunities for family members to interact with one another.

Discussion Questions

1. How would you assess the perceived burden of MI on family caregivers of an adult child with SMI?
2. What communication strategies might you use when interacting with the parent of an adult child with SMI?
3. What community-level resources might you target to support these parents?

COMMUNITY MENTAL HEALTH SERVICE DELIVERY

Communities also face many challenges in the area of MI because persons with MI simply do not have enough personal resources or natural supports to survive on their own with comfort. Illness symptoms prevent many MI persons from seeking help. Failure to appreciate that these people can live meaningful lives in the community may further deter service providers or families from engaging persons with MI in rehabilitation (Bezzina, 1996). Despite these challenges, the 1984 Canada Health Act serves as the stage for establishing health as a daily resource for all Canadians, including those with MI; and embraces the principles of accessibility, universality of coverage, portability from province to province, comprehensiveness, and government administration of services and supports in Canada.

Service Philosophy

ACCESS is a value-based framework for the organization, financing, and delivery of health services and supports within a community (Bezzina, 1996). Used by the National Office of the Ontario CMHA since 1993, ACCESS is an acronym for an accessible, continuous, comprehensive, and seamless system of supports designed to provide high-quality services to vulnerable people (see Figure 17.2). Through this framework, local branches of the CMHA seek to augment mental health services with resources to support determinants of health. Support personnel, including community mental health nurses (CMHNs) and social workers, assure that some level of service is always available to the most vulnerable persons with SPMI.

CMHNs incorporate the ACCESS service philosophy by targeting principles underlying a community's resource base, continuity of service, and seamless delivery of comprehensive

FIGURE 17.2 ACCESS Framework for Nursing

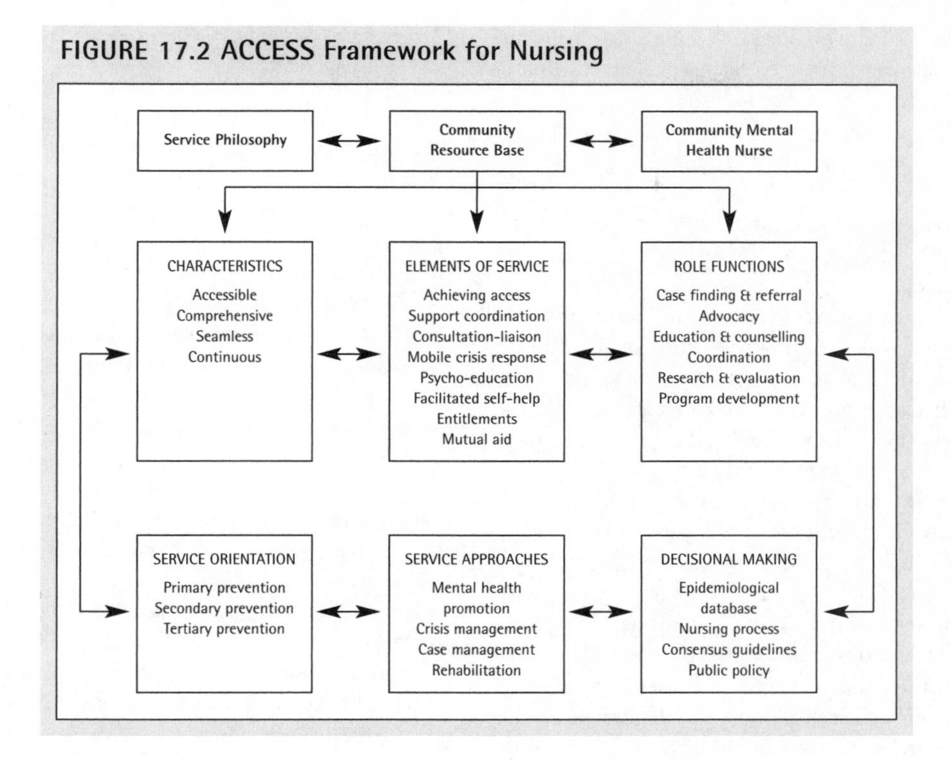

services and supports. The concept of a **community resource base** helps nurses understand the combination of services and opportunities available for the prevention or resolution of MI and its consequences. **Continuity of service** refers to the organized delivery of a balanced combination of specific services for specific individuals in need of specific kinds of help (Bachrach, 1993). These two concepts are based on the idea that vulnerable people, family and friends, and professional support staff work together to achieve health and the quality of life of a community. This collaborative teamwork allows for **seamless delivery of service**, that is, the provision of a "best" balance of services and supports at the best time, in the best place, and at the best level of intensity needed to achieve the best benefits.

Service Orientation

Accessible, comprehensive, seamless, and continuous service delivery within the ACCESS framework is organized around the concepts of primary, secondary, and tertiary prevention. **Primary prevention** involves strategies to promote healthy growth and development, along with resourcefulness of individuals, families, and other stakeholders within a community. It occurs through mental health promotion and case finding of the at-risk individuals. The goal is to reduce the number of new cases or the rate of development of a mental disorder in the community. **Secondary prevention** entails strategies to promote growth and healing of destabilized individuals, families, and other stakeholders in a community. It occurs through crisis intervention and may include the delivery of tangible resources, medication, and other medical or psychological support. The goal is to reduce episodes of acute distress and the prevalence of MI in the community. **Tertiary prevention** entails case management or rehabilitation of stable, functional patterns of behaviour in a community. It occurs through supportive interpersonal technologies, tangible resources, and psycho-education. The goal is to reduce the severity of MI and associated disability in the community.

Elements of Service

A community resource base provides resources in the form of materials, information, personnel, and time. Support personnel deliver resources based on the determinants of health. Elements of service delivery include access to service, support coordination, consultation, mobile crisis response, psycho-education, facilitated self-help, entitlements, and organized mutual aid.

Access to service refers to strategies that help people learn about their service options, including intake and assessment services, information and referral, outreach, consultation, entitlements, and short-term intervention support. Referral services, for example, recommend available resources such as emergency services, psychiatric care, or medical treatment. Outreach consists of case finding, engagement of those in need, crisis management, facilitated self-help, or other intensive support services.

Support coordination is the design, organization, and individualization of service packages for individuals, families, and other community groups in need of help. Its goal is to help vulnerable people develop and maintain interdependent ties to family, friends, and service providers. CMHNs, for example, might use support coordination to help persons with MI recover from acute MI, interact with the wider community, and engage in a widening spectrum of health-promoting activities.

Consultation refers to the diffusion of **consensus guidelines** into community practices. These guidelines are accepted practices designed to treat mental disorders or make the public aware of the challenges facing a community so that it can take appropriate steps to reduce or eliminate such challenges. CMHNs, for example, use consensus guidelines as a basis for how they provide up-to-date knowledge about diagnosis, treatment, and aftercare for a person with a particular MI.

Mobile crisis response is a series of interconnected interventions ranging from least to most intrusive. It can include phone lines, walk-in clinics, mobile crisis teams, freestanding crisis centres, hospital emergency departments with holding beds, and in-patient psychiatric units (Health Canada, 2002). A **mobile crisis team**, available round-the-clock, provides quick-response, intensive service delivery and support to individuals or groups who need immediate help at the scene of a critical life event such as an accident or threat of suicide. Crisis workers stabilize the situation and refer affected individuals to resources for longer term management of injury or trauma.

Psycho-education is designed to enhance a community's ability to cope with stress. Its goals are to enhance awareness, confidence, and mastery of particular situations that place individuals at risk for loss of health. CMHNs typically develop programs of education that focus on attitudes and self-care practices in order to normalize thinking and self-management. This education also helps persons with SMI become more aware of their civil rights under Canada's Mental Health Act.

Education programs are effective to the extent to which they empower individuals to engage in self-care and modify warning signs of relapse. The psycho-education process begins with an assessment of an individual, family, or community's need for learning. The development and implementation of the plan must be evaluated for the learning outcomes; these include the learner's increased understanding of information, competence in an area of living, and satisfaction with the educational experience.

Facilitated self-help is group-based, informal support to individuals who share a common concern or set of problems. Its goals are to develop common understandings of a concern and to share information about resources for coping. CMHNs, social workers, or a designated member of a group typically facilitate these self-help groups, assisting group members to work on particular concerns.

Entitlements involve the delivery of tangible services in a way that empowers people in the direction of health. Entitlements include the procurement of food, income, housing, leisure, education, work, and social support in the community in which people reside. Housing options and supports, for example, can range from short-term residential placement or other communal living arrangement, through transitional apartment living and household management, to assistance with rent or mortgage.

Organized mutual aid refers to formal organizations composed of MI persons, family members, and others who have a stake in the health of the mentally ill. These organizations evolved because of concerns about human rights, including the right of persons with MI to participate fully in the life of the community. They seek to empower the individuals, reduce isolation, and promote effective coping through education and support.

Comprehensive Service Approaches

Many communities have comprehensive service delivery approaches for primary, secondary, and tertiary prevention of MI. Three of these approaches are mental health promotion, crisis management, and case management, including assertive community treatment (Health Canada, 2003). These approaches draw upon elements of service accessible through the community resource base.

Mental health promotion is an educational service designed to strengthen the confidence and biopsychosocial competence of a community. It is intended to enable people to improve and increase control over their overall health through risk reduction and lifestyle modification (World Health Organization, 1986). **Risk reduction** refers to resources and activities that protect individuals from stressors that may lead to MI or disenfranchisement in a community (Institute of Medicine, 1994). **Lifestyle modification** refers to activities, such as good nutrition, rest, exercise, work, and leisure, that sustain and enhance the health of individuals and communities (Allender & Spradley, 2001).

Crisis management addresses initiatives at both the system and individual level for the prevention and resolution of critical life events. On a systems level, 24-hour mobile crisis response teams, partnerships with service providers, and consumer-run alternatives such as a telephone hotlines help individuals resolve urgent problem situations effectively and quickly. Medical services, in-patient hospitalization, and short-term residential placement are used for crisis stabilization, protection, and support when other crisis response strategies have been exhausted. At the individual service level, crisis workers assist persons in acute distress to improve the accuracy of their perception and communication skills and prevent further trauma or crisis (Slaikeu, 1990).

Case management involves the delivery of a complex system of support services by a case manager to small groups of vulnerable persons over time. The goals of case management include improving the health and quality of life of individuals as well as reducing the burden their disability poses for family and other service providers. Case managers access, evaluate, negotiate, plan, and coordinate seamless delivery of services from a variety of community resources. For example, a nurse case manager might target anger management, social skills training, and supported housing services for persons with SPMI so that these individuals can participate more fully in the life of the community.

Assertive community treatment (ACT) is a comprehensive, long-term, intensive case management approach to treating persons who, because of their illness, resist or avoid involvement with more traditional service approaches (Stein & Santos, 1998). It is estimated that 25% of persons with SPMI require this type of case management (Goering et al., 2000). The basic goals of ACT are:

- to attenuate debilitating symptoms of MI in order to minimize recurrent episodes of illness;
- to facilitate the development of functional competence and improve quality of life by providing high-intensity, community supports when needed;

- to broaden the base of support systems available to persons with SPMI to include family members, caregivers, and other significant persons; and
- to facilitate the development and enhancement of vocational and other social roles in the community.

The ACT team is a multidisciplinary team of trained professionals working together to support persons with SPMI. The team typically includes a team coordinator, program psychiatrist, program assistants, psychiatric nurse, licensed social worker, and a vocation specialist or a consulting dual-diagnosis specialist. The team meets regularly to review, target, or plan for the individualized day-to-day needs and status of its caseload. Persons with SPMI, their families, and other key support persons participate in the design, implementation, monitoring, and assessment of services provided. ACT is one of the best-researched, comprehensive service approaches used in community mental health practice to date (Bond, Drake, Mueser, & Latimer, 2001; Dixon, 2000). According to the research, although ACT is costly, it substantially reduces psychiatric hospital use, increases housing stability, and moderately improves symptoms and quality of life.

Role of Community Health Nurses

With their focus on mental health promotion and risk protection and their understanding of the determinants of health, CMHNs create and provide comprehensive systems of service to support the mental health of their clients (Lindeman, 1993). They carry out various roles while performing the following activities.

Epidemiological Base for Decision Making CMHNs must be able to access, contribute to, and use epidemiological data to help them make decisions about how best to respond to the health needs of a community. They retrieve and use information (see Chapter 14) to investigate and link the incidence and prevalence of various mental disorders in a community with known or suspected risk factors in the community. The results of these analyses become the basis for determining the health and service needs of individuals, families, and groups who need support.

Case Finding and Referral Early identification and treatment of mental illness helps reduce its severity and allows for a quicker recovery. Involvement with mental health promotion or risk reduction activities in a community permits nurses to identify individuals who show signs of a mental disorder or who are known to be at risk for development of a mental disorder. CMHNs can then provide oversight or diffuse stressors that threaten the well-being of the community.

Advocacy Advocacy centres on the development of new services, enhancement of existing services, and access of persons to full participation in the life of the community. On the individual level, CMHNs seek to enable a person's access to services, reduce the stigma of MI, and improve public understanding of MI and service delivery. They advocate at the level of the family to help family members acquire informational support about MI and the determinants of health as well as emotional support and respite. At the community level, they serve on committees and community boards where decisions about the health and participation of persons with MI are made. At the provincial level, these nurses can lobby for legislative or policy changes that allocate and distribute resources for housing stock and supported housing services for persons with SPMI.

Education and Counselling CMHNs provide informational support to individuals or families with MI, both individually and in groups. The basic education includes up-to-date information about various mental health conditions, medication and other treatment regimens, community resources, strategies for self-care and coping, and the management of warning signs of distress and relapse. CMHNs also target community groups for informational support and clarification of values. The goals of these exchanges are to increase public awareness and understanding of issues pertaining to the prevention, recognition, and management of the dynamics of MI and stigma expressed within a community (Haghighat, 2001).

CASE STUDY

A confused, combative, hallucinating, dehydrated, and malnourished 70-year-old man with a draining foot ulcer walks unaccompanied into the CMHA Community Mental Health Centre (CMHC) inadequately dressed for the winter. He is carrying a half-empty can of dog food, some candy, and plastic bag full of rags. With much difficulty, you determine that the man's name is Jake. Jake mumbles that he is new in town, having arrived on the freight train. He wants to see his nephew. After several hours you are able to locate Jake's nephew and discover, to your surprise, that Jake was born at a nearby hospital. The CMHC physician assigns Jake a dual diagnosis of chronic undifferentiated schizophrenia and uncontrolled diabetes mellitus.

You are assigned to look after Jake's requirements for self-care and instrumental support. You arrange for Jake's emergency admission to a geri-psychiatric, in-patient setting. Your next decision is to target case management services for Jake following his discharge from the hospital.

Discussion Questions

1. Explain the complexity of Jake's needs for food, clothing, shelter, medicine, nursing care, and a calming environment.
2. Prioritize a system of support services for managing Jake's needs and right to full participation in the life of the community.
3. Identify agencies through which you will arrange a package of support services for Jake.
4. How will you broker a caregiving relationship between Jake and his nephew?

Coordination CMHNs frequently coordinate the care of persons with MI because of their knowledge and experience with interventions that facilitate self-care and role behaviour. They provide screening and assessment, plan for care such as role modelling for life-skills development, arrange for service delivery, monitor and evaluate the progress of clients, and terminate services when they are no longer needed. They collaborate with individuals, families, and human service agencies to assess client needs and plan the delivery of health and other human services.

Nursing Process

Consisting of the phases of assessment, planning, intervention, and evaluation, the nursing process guides CMHNs as they assess and resolve problems concerning mental health and illness. During the assessment phase, the CMHN examines the degree to which signs and symptoms of illness, disability, or injury affect self-care and the ability of clients to manage resources in a community. Next, the nurse examines how the clients react to stressful life circumstances such as poverty, poor housing, inability to communicate, and lack of meaningful activity. Third, the nurse addresses evidence of isolation, loneliness, and loss of meaningful family and social contacts or networks. Fourth, the nurse addresses evidence of stigma, lost opportunities, and abuse that might be affecting the perspective of the person or family being assessed. Finally, the nurse diagnoses the ability of the person or family to cope with a myriad of everyday demands.

When planning care for persons with MI, the CMHN examines barriers that prevent the clients from meeting their needs, stressors they are likely to encounter daily, and the personal resources and informal support network they have. The nurse then determines the type, level, and timing of support services needed and proceeds to engage the clients and their stakeholders in the appropriation of these services.

As intervention strategists and decision makers, CMHNs facilitate engagement, communication, and support service delivery, relying on their knowledge of self-care, signs and symptoms, and human relationships. They develop collaborative alliances and outcome-oriented plans with target individuals, family members, and other service providers in order to establish, monitor, and assess goals of support service delivery.

Evaluation of care entails measurements of type, intensity, duration, costing, and pattern of service delivery; client satisfaction with services received; and the determinants of health targeted by the services and supports. These measures should link logically back to how nursing services interface with the services of other personnel and the overall health care delivery system.

Status and Future Directions in Community Mental Health

Despite ongoing societal interest in enhancing community-based support for persons with MI, community mental health programs remain underfunded, accounting for less than 3% of provincial mental health budgets (Goering et al., 2000). The result is that many persons with MI live impoverished lives in the community, a fact that is eroding public confidence in the philosophy of deinstitutionalization.

The public attributes failure to achieve ideal community-focused mental health care to the insufficient resources for such care and to Canada's overreliance upon hospitals and medical care. It blames the failure of the federal and provincial governments to administer public funds sufficiently to satisfy the principles underlying health promotion as an everyday resource for Canadians. Many of these failings were captured in the recently published Romanow and Kirby Reports. These reports are fuelling incentives to change public health policy, including how community mental health programs are financed and delivered (Romanow, 2002; Kirby & LeBreton, 2001).

Implications for Nursing Leaders of the mental health users' movement emphasize the importance of attitude, hope, self-responsibility, and public policy along with the appropriate use of medication, psycho-education, advocacy, and supported friendship in the amelioration of MI and stigma (Mead & Copeland, 2000). The implication is that CMHNs and other stakeholders in Canada must continue to advocate for comprehensive systems of mental health service delivery that is focused on the determinants of health. CMHNs must also use the best evidence of what works to improve quality of life and include the collective wisdom of individuals and families with MI. Nelson, Lord, and Ochocka (2001), for example, address three decision points concerning the right of all people, including the mentally ill, to participate fully in the life of a community. They are:

- participation and empowerment, that is, "*Nothing about me without me*";
- community support and integration, that is, "*I participate rather than exist in the community where I live*"; and
- social justice and access to valued resources, that is, "*My right to fair and equitable distribution of resources in society.*"

SUMMARY

This chapter provided a description of the characteristics, difficulties, and needs of people with MI for support services in the community as well as a description of concepts underlying the service philosophy of the Canadian Mental Health Association. It described comprehensive seamless service delivery in terms of access and continuity of service, a community resource base, prevention, and service elements. Incorporation of these concepts into comprehensive service approaches to the management of mental health and illness in the community was discussed. Those approaches include mental health promotion, crisis management, and case management, including assertive community treatment. Attention also was given to the role of the CMHN and the reasoning process used to evaluate and resolve challenges associated with mental health promotion, risk reduction, and attenuation of mental illness in the community. The chapter closed with a view to the future of community mental health in Canada, focused on the right of all individuals to participate fully in the life of the community.

KEY TERMS

deinstitutionalization
stigma
Canadian Mental Health Association (CMHA)
mental health
mental illness (MI)
serious mental illness (SMI)
serious and persistent mental illness (SPMI)
burden of disease
ACCESS
community resource base
continuity of service
seamless delivery of service
primary prevention
secondary prevention
tertiary prevention
access to service
support coordination
consultation
consensus guidelines
mobile crisis response
mobile crisis team
psycho-education
facilitated self-help
entitlements
organized mutual aid
risk reduction
lifestyle modification
mental health promotion
crisis management
case management
assertive community treatment (ACT)

INDIVIDUAL CRITICAL THINKING EXERCISES

1. What are the functions of a nurse case manager working with SMI persons?
2. What communication strategies might you use while providing a psycho-educational or counselling service to a MI client residing in the community?

GROUP CRITICAL THINKING EXERCISES

1. What needs and challenges do the mentally ill face in their community?
2. How might you prepare a comprehensive assessment and treatment plan for a SPMI client residing in the community?
3. What is the relationship between evaluation, research, and Canadian mental health policy?

REFERENCES

Allender, J. A., & Spradley, B. W. (2001). *Community health nursing: Concepts and practice* (5th ed.). Philadelphia, PA: Lippincott.

Bachrach, L. L. (1993). Continuity of care: A context for case management. In M. Harris & H. C. Bergman (Eds.), *Case management for mentally ill patients: Theory and practice. Vol. 1* (pp. 183–187). Langhorne, PA: Harwood Academic.

Benjafield, J. G., & Boudreau, F. (2000). Introduction: Canadian community mental health: Our past, our future. *Canadian Journal of Community Mental Health, 19*(2), 5–8.

Bezzina, A. (1996). *ACCESS: A framework for a community based mental health system.* Toronto, ON: Canadian Mental Health Association, Ontario Division.

Bond, G. R., Drake, R. E., Mueser, K. T., & Latimer, E. (2001). Assertive community treatment for people with severe mental illness: Critical ingredients and impact on patients. *Disease Management & Health Outcomes, 9*(3), 141–159.

Dixon, L. (2000). Assertive community treatment: Twenty-five years of gold. *Psychiatric Services, 51*(6), 759–765.

Fenton, W. S. (2001). Co-morbid conditions in schizophrenia. *Current Opinion in Psychiatry, 14*(1), 17–23.

Goering, P., Wasylenki, D., & Durbin, J. (2000). Canada's mental health system. *International Journal of Law and Psychiatry, 23*(3–4), 345–359.

Haghighat, R. (2001). A unitary theory of stigmatization: Pursuit of self-interest and routes to destigmatization. *British Journal of Psychiatry, 178*(2), 207–215.

Health Canada. (2002). *A report on mental illnesses in Canada.* Retrieved October 24, 2003 from **www.hc-sc.gc.ca/pphb-dgpsp/publicat/miic-mmac/index.html**

Health Canada. (2003). *Mental health.* Retrieved December 11, 2003 from **www.hc.sc.gc.ca/hppb/mentalhealth/**

Institute of Medicine. (1994). *Reducing risks for mental disorders.* Washington, DC: National Academy Press.

Kirby, M. J., & LeBreton, M. (2001). *The health of Canadians: The federal role: Final report on the state of health care system in Canada.* Ottawa, ON: Senate, Standing Committee on Social Affairs. Retrieved December 11, 2003 from **www.parl.gc.ca/37/2/parlbus/commbus/senate/Com-e/SOCI-E/rep-e/repoct02vol6-e.htm**

Kovess, V. (2002). The homeless mentally ill. In N. Sartorius, W. Gaebel, J. J. Lopez-Ibor, & M. Maj (Eds.), *Psychiatry in society* (pp. 221–240). New York: Wiley & Sons.

Lindeman, C. (1993). To prepare a preventionist. *Nursing & Health Care, 14*(9), 486.

Mead, S., & Copeland, M. E. (2000). What recovery means to us: Consumers' perspectives. *Community Mental Health Journal, 36*(3), 315–328.

Mental Health Act, RSO 1990 § Chapter M7. (2002). Retrieved December 16, 2003 from **www.e-laws.gov.on.ca/DBLaws/Statutes/English/90m07_e.htm**

Morrell-Bellai, T., Goering, P. N., & Boydell, K. M. (2000). Becoming and remaining homeless: A qualitative investigation. *Issues in Mental Health Nursing, 21*, 581–604.

Murray, C. J. L., & Lopez, A. D. (Eds.). (1996). *Summary: The global burden of disease: A comprehensive assessment of mortality and disability from diseases, injuries, and risk factors in 1990 and projected to 2020.* Cambridge, MA: Harvard University Press.

Narrow, W. E., Rae, D. S., Robins, L. N., & Regier, D. A. (2002). Revised prevalence estimates of mental disorders in the United States. *Archives of General Psychiatry, 59*, 115–123.

Nelson, G., Lord, J., & Ochocka, J. (2001). *Shifting the paradigm in community mental health: Towards empowerment and community.* Toronto, ON: University of Toronto Press.

Pejlert, A. (2001). Being a parent of an adult son or daughter with severe mental illness receiving professional care: Parents' narratives. *Health & Social Care in the Community, 9*(4), 194–204.

Pevalin, D. J., & Goldberg, D. P. (2003). Social precursors to onset and recovery from episodes of common mental illness. *Psychological Medicine, 33*(2), 299–306.

Qin, P., Agerbo, E., & Mortensen, P. B. (2002). Suicide risk in relation to family history of completed suicide and psychiatric disorders: A nested case-control study based on longitudinal registers. *Lancet, 360*(9340), 1126–1130.

Rahel, E., Langley, J., Tolomiczenko, G., Rhodes, A. E., Links, P., Wasylenki, D. et al. (2002). The association between homelessness and suicidal ideation and behaviors: Results of a cross-sectional survey. *Suicide and Life-Threatening Behavior, 37*(4), 418–427.

Romanow, R. J. (2002). *Building on values: The future of health care in Canada.* Saskatoon, SK: Commission on the Future of Health Care in Canada. Retrieved December 11, 2003 from **www.hc-sc.gc.ca/english/pdg/care/romanow_e.pdf**

Slaikeu, K. A. (1990). Crisis intervention: A handbook for practice and research (2nd ed.). Needham Heights, MA: Allyn & Bacon.

Statistics Canada. (2000). *Health.* Retrieved December 11, 2003 from **www.statcan.ca/english/Pgdb/health.htm**

Stein, L. I., & Santos, A. B. (1998). *Assertive community treatment of persons with severe mental illness.* New York: W. W. Norton.

Stephens, T., & Joubert, N. (2001). The economic burden of mental health problems in Canada. *Chronic Diseases in Canada, 22*(1), 18–23.

Tsuang, M. T., & Tohen, M. (Eds.). (2002). *Textbook in psychiatric epidemiology* (2nd ed.). New York: Wiley-Liss.

Wasylenki, D., Goering, P., & MacNaughton, E. (1994). Planning mental health services: Background and key issues. In L. L. Bachrach, P. Goering, & D. Wasylenki (Eds.), *Mental health care in Canada* (pp. 21–30). San Francisco, CA: Jossey-Bass.

World Health Organization, Canadian Public Health Association, & Health and Welfare Canada. (1986). *Ottawa charter for health promotion.* Ottawa, ON: Health and Welfare Canada.

World Health Organization. (1999). *The world health report 1999: Chapter 2.* Geneva, Switzerland: Author. Retrieved December 11, 2003 from **www.who.int/whr2001/2001/archives/1999/en/pdf/chapter2.pdf**

Pyke, J., Morris, L., Rabin, K., & Sabriye, A. A. (2001). Improving accessibility: The experience of a Canadian mental health agency. *Psychiatric Rehabilitation Journal, 25*(2), 180–185.

Roberge, M.-C., & White, D. (2000). L'ailleurs et l'autrement des pratiques communautaires en santé mentale au Québec. *Canadian Journal of Community Mental Health, 19*(2), 31–56.

Stip, E., Caron, J., & Lane, C. J. (2001). Schizophrenia: People's perceptions in Quebec. *Canadian Medical Association Journal, 164*(9), 1299–1300.

Thesen, J. (2001). Being a psychiatric patient in the community—reclassified as the stigmatized "other." *Scandinavian Journal of Public Health, 29*(4), 248–255.

Zygmunt, A., Olfson, M., Boyer, C. A., & Mechanic, D. (2002). Interventions to improve medication adherence in schizophrenia. *American Journal of Psychiatry, 159*(10), 1653–1664.

ADDITIONAL RESOURCES

READINGS

Goldman, H. H., Morrissey, J. P., Rosenheck, R. A., Cocozza, J., Blasinsky, M., & Randolph, F. (2002). Lessons from the evaluation of the ACCESS program. *Psychiatric Services, 53*(8), 967–969.

Leenaas, A. A. (2000). Suicide prevention in Canada: A history of a community approach. *Canadian Journal of Community Mental Health, 19*(2), 57–73.

WEBSITES

Canadian Association for the Mentally Ill:
www.cami.org

Canadian Mental Health Association:
www.cmha.ca

Canadian Psychiatric Association:
www.cpa-apc.org

Canadian Psychiatric Research Foundation:
www.cprf.ca

Health Canada, Mental Health:
www.hc-sc-gc.ca/hppb/mentalhealth/mhp/index.html
and
www.hc-sc-gc.ca/english/lifestyles/mental_health.html

National Network for Mental Health:
www.nnmh.ca

Registered Psychiatric Nurses of Alberta:
www.rpnaa.ab.ca

Schizophrenia Society of Canada:
www.schizophrenia.ca

About the Author

Margaret England, RN, PhD (Case Western Reserve University), completed a postdoctoral fellowship in gerontological nursing at the University of Iowa. She is now an associate professor in the Faculty of Nursing at the University of Windsor. During the past 20 years, Dr. England has been engaged in research on caregiver strain and decision making of adult children who look after the welfare of cognitively impaired parents. In 1998, she initiated a second program of research on voice hearing and has conducted several projects to date. She currently works with voice hearers at a community mental health centre of the Canadian Mental Health Association, Windsor-Essex branch. She also supervises nursing students at IRIS House, a not-for-profit supported residence in Windsor, Ontario for persons who have been diagnosed with severe and persistent mental illness.

CHAPTER 18

Clients in the Correctional Setting

Joanne Shaw

OBJECTIVES

AFTER STUDYING THIS CHAPTER, YOU SHOULD BE ABLE TO:

1. Identify challenges of and opportunities for nursing interventions in the correctional setting.
2. Identify nurses' professional and ethical responsibilities for inmate health care.
3. Identify the most common inmate health care conditions.
4. Identify areas in which health promotion and patient advocacy are needed.

INTRODUCTION

Nurses working in a correctional setting provide ambulatory care to a large diverse population. They use advanced clinical assessment and triage skills to provide early case finding, disease prevention, infection control, treatment and medication administration, health teaching, and health promotion. Clients housed in correctional facilities are entitled to the same level of health care as they would be if they were in the external community. Provision of health care to inmates is important so that their health care conditions can be identified early and treated, managed, or controlled for both the individual and the health and safety of other inmates and facility staff.

The populations housed in correctional facilities consist of many legal subsets. First, some inmates are on a remand while awaiting their trial. Other inmates were found guilty and sentenced to various periods of time in custody. Inmates receiving a sentence of two years less a day are housed in **provincial correctional centres**, while those with a sentence of two years or greater are housed in **federal correctional facilities** (operated by **Correctional Service Canada [CSC]**). Males, females, and youths make up the inmate population. On an average day, approximately 7900 adults and 670 youth are in custody in Ontario's correctional and detention centres, jails, and youth centres (Ferris, personal communication, 2003). The average age of the adult inmates is approximately 33 years; the average age of youth is approximately 17 years (Davis, personal communication, 2003). In Ontario, women accounted for 6% of adult inmates and 10.6% of youth inmates in January 2003 (Ferris, personal communication, 2003). The oldest inmate in Ontario facilities in January 2003 was 83 years old (Davis). In the federal penitentiaries, there were 12 418 male offenders and 337 female offenders in 2001 (CSC, 2003). (See Tables 18.1 and 18.2.)

PRACTICE SETTING

The practice setting in correctional facilities is unique and poses many challenges to providing health care. Security and protection of the public are the main concerns of the correctional system. Health care has to be provided while considering security precautions. For example, a correctional officer accompanies the nurse for every inmate contact, and this officer must maintain visual contact with the inmate at all times. The nurse respects the officer's job responsibility but must provide health care and maintain the confidentiality of health care information being elicited from the client. Often the nurse must wait while the officer completes security-related tasks. On the day and evening shifts, there is generally one RN for 200 inmates. This large caseload means that nurses in correctional facilities must set priorities based on assessment of individual client needs.

The protection of confidential health care information is but one method the nurse uses to build trust with the client. Other ways to build trust include only making commitments that can be met and telling the inmate straight up why some requests cannot be met. Most inmates respect and appreciate health care staff because they provide much needed health care and are not usually involved in inmate discipline.

Most inmates are housed in units with two-person cells and a common day area. Inmates are allowed out of their cells 12 hours per day, and the majority of health care must be provided during these 12 hours. Emergency care may be delivered at any time. Health care may be delivered in the inmate's living area or in a centralized health care unit. Care is generally delivered to individual clients; however, treatment facilities often provide the opportunity for group work.

Correctional nurses must be alert in order to prevent introduction of health care equipment that could be used as a weapon. When providing health education material, they must ensure that it will not pose a security risk. For example,

TABLE 18.1
Crime Statistics in Canada, 2001/02*

Item	Numbers
Cases processed	452 450 cases
Charges processed	992 567 charges
Found guilty	60% (271 470 cases)
Sentenced to incarceration	44% (range 59% in PEI** to 23% in Saskatchewan) (119 447 cases)

*Representing 90% of national adult criminal caseload (statistics missing from Manitoba, Northwest Territories, and Nunavut)
**One reason for the high incarceration rate in PEI is that first offenders convicted of impaired driving are frequently sent to prison. This is an excellent example of a public policy outside the health care policy affecting the health status of individuals. The offender is rehabilitated and the risk of accidents as a result of an impaired driver is decreased.

Source: Robinson, P. (2003). Juristat. *Ottawa, ON: Canadian Centre for Justice Statistics. (Statistics Canada no. 85-002-XIE)*

dental floss must be disposed of after use in the health care area rather than be allowed in the inmate living area. Nurses are not permitted to use metal or hard plastic splints to support a limb because this splint may be fashioned into a weapon. Instead, they use magazines as splints. If an inmate has a food allergy, the nurse must work with correctional officers to ensure that the inmate has immediate access to an Epipen when eating. Usually this is done by taking the inmate to a separate locked area to eat. The food and Epi-pen are given to the inmate. After the meal, the Epi-pen is handed to the officer before the inmate is allowed out of the locked area. Nurses working in a community setting certainly understand the need for innovation; nurses working in the correctional setting require similar "thinking outside the box."

Correctional nurses have to confront their own reactions to inmates' alleged offences. They then must set these reactions aside and proceed to develop therapeutic relationships and provide professional and ethical care to this population. Some correctional nurses have difficulty doing this and prefer to provide care without knowing the nature of the alleged offences.

Opportunities to improve the health status of this population abound. Many inmates have neglected their health and/or have had limited exposure to our health care system. Often a nurse has the inmate's undivided attention. If this time is used to provide individualized care, health promotion, and health education, the inmate may be motivated to make lifestyle changes that would improve overall health status. While doing health assessments, nurses will often identify health problems requiring care and treatment. Finding of such health problems may not have occurred if the inmate were not in custody.

Health Care Status of Inmates

Inmates have many of the same health care needs that the general population has. Some health care problems are more prevalent in this population, while the secure closed environment affects others.

TABLE 18.2
Average numbers of remanded and sentenced inmates per 100 000 population, percentages of females and Aboriginals, and median age of sentenced inmates

Province	Average number of adult inmates (both remanded and sentenced) per 100 000 adult population, 1998/99 to 2000/01	Percentage of sentenced inmates that are female, 2000/01	Percentage of sentenced inmates that are Aboriginal, 2000/01	Median age, 2000/01
Newfoundland and Labrador	69	8	7	-
Prince Edward Island	82	10	1	-
Nova Scotia	47	6	7	30
New Brunswick	48	-	-	-
Quebec	56	10	2	35
Ontario	83	9	9	32
Manitoba	130	6	64	30
Saskatchewan	150	9	76	29
Alberta	85	11	39	31
British Columbia	79	7	20	31
Yukon	609	9	72	31
Northwest Territories	191	5	-	-
Nunavut	434	0	98	-

Source: Statistics Canada. (2002). Adult correctional services in Canada, 2000–2001. *Ottawa, ON: Canadian Centre for Justice Statistics. (Statistics Canada no. 85-211-XIE)*

The correctional system provides care for inmates with all types of acute and chronic illnesses such as acute infections, diabetes, cardiovascular disease, renal disease, physical handicaps, and so on. There are life-stage health care issues for youth, women, and older adults, including first episode psychosis for youth, reproductive issues and family responsibilities for women, and age-related health care needs for older adults. The lifestyle of many inmates includes substance abuse, which gives rise to various drug and alcohol withdrawal syndromes, diverse infectious diseases, and the need for long-term treatment interventions. Crowded living conditions on the street and in correctional facilities result in a higher exposure to infectious diseases than for the ordinary population. Recent changes to the delivery of mental health services have resulted in the arrest of more people with serious mental illnesses. These people are often kept in correctional facilities as the police have nowhere else to take them.

Inmates presenting with acute health care problems are assessed and triaged by the nurse. Any inmate requiring acute emergency care is transferred to the community general hospital for treatment. The nurse and/or the facility doctor manage other less urgent issues. Often, inmates' prior management of their chronic health problems has been poor. The nurse assists them to bring chronic conditions under better control by increasing attention to treatment protocols, assessing for other disabilities resulting from the primary chronic condition, and providing health education for lifestyle changes during custody and after discharge. Community supports for these individuals can be identified and the first contact made while the inmate is still in custody.

Correctional Services Canada (CSC) has recently compiled data on health care needs of offenders over age 50. They were found to have poorer physical, dental, and nutritional health than younger inmates and less depression than younger inmates; however, they committed suicide at a slightly higher rate than would be expected. This study concludes that introduction of palliative care programs and wellness programs (e.g., walking, low-impact exercises, passive recreational activities) will be necessary in the future to meet health care needs of older inmates (Gal, 2003).

Female Inmates Female inmates have unique and special health care needs that are related to social, psychological, and physiological factors. Female inmates continue to be responsible for the emotional maintenance of the family unit even when they are not with the family. This sense of responsibility along with the actual responsibility, with little or no means to meet these responsibilities, may result in increased stress. Lagner, Barton, McDonagh, Noel, and Bouchard (2002) found that 87% of federal female inmates have orders for medication. Of these, 42% had an order for psychotropic medication (antidepressants, neuroleptics, antipsychotics, anxiolytics, antimanics, and antihistamines prescribed specifically for sedation, benzodiazepines, and anti-epileptic medication prescribed for mood stabilization purposes).

Studies indicate that 50–70% of female inmates report physical and/or sexual abuse (Heney & Kristiansen, 2002). Thus, the correctional nurse must assess for continuing effects of this abuse, such as post-traumatic stress disorder, and for further re-victimization.

Reproductive issues require considerable attention. A female inmate may be pregnant. The nurse must support the woman in her decision making about continuing the pregnancy. If delivery occurs while the women is incarcerated, special provisions must be made so the woman has contact with her child and normal mother-child bonding is allowed to occur. The mother may require help with parenting skills and a referral to a community agency for help with these skills on release. If there is a prior history of child abuse, some mothers will lose their child to the Children's Aid Society. These mothers will need to be supported in the grieving process over the loss of their child. Pregnant women who are addicted to opiates and/or are on a methadone maintenance program will need to have this program initiated or continued to prevent damage to the fetus from opiate withdrawal. Female inmates may also require family planning services.

The population of female inmates requires strong advocacy to ensure that services are available in correctional centres to meet their social, psychological, and physiological needs. Nurses in Ontario correctional centres have developed a Prenatal, Birth, and Postpartum Care program and are in the process of developing a mental health program for female inmates. Much more needs to be done.

Youth Youth residing in correctional facilities (age 12–17 since April 1, 2003) have health care needs distinct to this age group. The first episode of schizophrenia may be seen in this age group, so the nurse must consider this when doing a mental health assessment. Often the symptoms of the first episode of schizophrenia are not as overt as those in later episodes. The youth may be withdrawn, display a little abnormal affect, and demonstrate a minor thought disorder. They may not be grossly delusional or have hallucinations. A suicide assessment of every youth is also necessary since studies have found that 11% of non-incarcerated people with a first episode of psychosis have attempted suicide (Tandon & Jibson, 2003).

Youth require life skills and substance abuse programs plus education in prevention of sexually transmitted diseases, family planning, and parenting skills (if necessary). Perhaps the biggest contribution of nurses who provide care to this population is the role model they provide on a daily basis. Some of the behaviours they model are problem solving, commitment to a profession, service to the community, and effective interpersonal communication skills.

Substance Abuse

Approximately 85% of inmates are thought to have substance abuse problems. Substances of abuse include alcohol, nicotine, cocaine, opiates, benzodiazepines, cannabis products, and hallucinogens. The inmate may present with signs of alcohol or drug withdrawal, physical problems such as injection site abscesses, a weakened cardiovascular system due to stimulant use, hepatitis B, hepatitis C, and/or HIV. The severity of withdrawal syndromes varies from inmate to inmate.

The more serious withdrawal syndromes require medical treatment to prevent any further damage to the client such as seizures and delirium tremens.

The nurse is the first health care professional to see inmates after admission. Excellent clinical skills are necessary to do early case finding and to implement monitoring, supportive care, and/or medication administration. This is also an excellent time to promote the idea that the client needs to begin long-term treatment for their substance-abuse problem.

The Ontario correctional system has been completely non-smoking since the year 2000. Inmate and staff pressure for healthy environments helped to move this initiative to implementation. Assaults and riots, which were predicted during implementation, did not occur. In fact, many described the move as a non-event. However, it was a huge public health initiative that was successfully implemented, and it was a step toward more healthy living for inmates as they break their physical dependence on nicotine during their incarceration and possibly for their lifetime.

Methadone maintenance programs are in place in most correctional facilities in Canada. Many correctional staff do not condone or understand this harm-reduction strategy. They see methadone administration as giving the inmate a drug that replaces the illicit drug they were taking prior to arrest and assume that the inmate will remain high during their incarceration. On the other side of this issue is an inmate advocacy group, Prisoner AIDS Support Action Network (PASAN), that presses for increased methadone continuation and initiation for inmates. Methadone is a highly sought-after drug by inmates. There are many inmate attempts to divert the drug and to muscle other inmates for it. A dose of over 70 mg is lethal for a non-tolerant individual. Consequently, the procedure for administration of methadone is tightly supervised and time consuming. Table 18.3 outlines the status of methadone program initiation and continuation according to a recent survey of Canadian correctional jurisdictions.

Inmates with substance abuse problems manifest these problems while in the correctional facility. Nurses have to be alert for drug-seeking attempts and identify inmates who are searching for drugs (as part of their problem) from those who legitimately require medications for health problems. Special precautions, such as crushing medications and talking with inmates after medication administration, help to ensure that inmates who require medications actually receive them. These processes are also methods to prevent stronger inmates from muscling medication from weaker inmates and to prevent sale of medications for various other commodities.

Mental Illness

With the closure of many psychiatric beds in the past decade, there has been an influx of inmates with serious mental illness to correctional facilities. Prior to these bed closures, police would transport a person with bizarre behaviour to a mental health facility; now they take them to a remand centre. In a one-day, snapshot survey completed by the author in the summer of 2001, eight urban Ontario remand centres reported that between 3% and 22% of inmates were suffering from a serious mental illness (primarily schizophrenia and bipolar illness). Konrad (2002) reported that 3.7% of male inmates in Germany had a psychotic illness and 10% had a clinical depression; 4% of female inmates had a psychotic illness and 12% had a clinical depression. These figures indicate a wide variation in actual numbers. However,

TABLE 18.3
Methadone Programs
Initiation and continuance of methadone programs in federal and provincial correctional facilities

Jurisdiction	Methadone Program Continuation	Methadone Program Initiation
Alberta	For 1 month only	No
British Columbia	Available	In some institutions
Federal	Yes	Yes
Manitoba	Yes	No
New Brunswick	Yes	No
Newfoundland & Labrador	No	No
Northwest Territories	Yes	No
Nova Scotia	Yes	No
Nunavut	No	No
Ontario	Yes	Only for pregnant inmates
Prince Edward Island	No	No
Quebec	Yes	Permitted in some cases
Saskatchewan	Yes	Permitted in exceptional circumstances
Yukon	Yes	In some circumstances

Source: Lines, R. (2002). Action on HIV/AIDS in prisons: Too little, too late. A report card. *Ottawa, ON: Canadian HIV/AIDS Legal Network.*

the discrepancy is most likely due to how mentally ill inmates are assessed and labelled. Many Ontario facilities have inmates who are mentally ill but who have not been identified, along with many mentally ill inmates who manage to cope on a regular living unit.

Staff in correctional facilities cannot provide mental health care at the standard that hospitals used to provide; however, that is what the public expects. Every day, several inmates are admitted to remand centres. The nurse must assess each one for the whole range of physical and mental problems. Often, those with a mental illness are withdrawn, non-communicative, and possibly suicidal. The nurse requires highly developed assessment and communication skills to elicit the data necessary to identify mentally ill inmates and ensure their safety. It is very important that inmates with psychosis or those who have decompensated from their mental illness are housed in an area where they can be protected from other inmates. If not so housed, the mentally ill inmate may be victimized and/or physically intimidated for their psychotropic medications.

After mentally ill inmates arrive at a remand centre, they will each require an advocate to ensure that they move through the justice system as quickly as possible and that discharge plans are in place. Being an advocate (who are usually nurses or social workers) is a great opportunity to work with external community-based services to meet the needs of these inmates. The Canadian Mental Health Association, community ACT and case management teams, Community Care Access Centres, and court support and diversion workers are some of the resources found in the community.

Mentally ill inmates are supervised 24 hours per day by correctional staff. Many of the staff have varied backgrounds and education in security procedures. They often have minimal training in mental health theory and practice. The nurse must educate the officers to help them provide appropriate and therapeutic supervision. Education topics include basic psychopathology, basic therapeutic interventions, suicidal ideation assessment, the effects and side effects of psychotropic medications, and provisions of the provincial mental health and consent to treatment acts.

All inmates are assessed for suicidal thoughts and plans on admission and as indicated throughout their incarceration. Suicide may be viewed by inmates as the only way to cope with their charges and/or sentence, family responsibilities that cannot be met, fear of the actions of fellow inmates, and living conditions in a correctional facility. For the mentally ill, severity of current psychotic symptoms is related to current risk of suicide (Tandon & Jibson, 2003). Inmates may be placed on a suicide watch if assessment indicates. These inmates are then assessed by a psychiatrist for pharmacotherapy, other treatments, and/or hospitalization.

When we place these clients in a correctional facility and expect their mental health care to be sufficient, we are depriving these very vulnerable people of the standard available in the community. Generally, the mentally ill in our society do not receive the same level of care we provide to people with physical illnesses. The inmate with a mental illness in a correctional facility is thus doubly deprived of the generally accepted standard of health care. These people need both individual and systemic advocacy in order to obtain specific and general care and support while institutionalized and on their return to the external community.

Infectious Diseases

The most frequent infectious diseases seen in correctional facilities are hepatitis B and C, tuberculosis, and sexually transmitted diseases such as chlamydia, gonorrhea, and HIV. A viral infection such as the 2003 outbreak of severe acute respiratory syndrome (SARS) in Ontario could have had a catastrophic effect on inmates in crowded Ontario facilities.

A CSC study found that in 2000 and 2001, the number of reported infections of hepatitis B in the federal facilities was 13 and 43 respectively. This corresponded to 0.1% of the inmate population in 2000 and 0.3% in 2001. The rate in the general population was estimated to be between 0.5%–1.0% in 2000 (De, 2002). The prevalence of reported hepatitis C infection in federal inmates was 20.1% in 2000 and 23.6% in 2001, compared with a general population prevalence of 0.8% (De). HIV antibody prevalence in provincially held adult female inmates was 1.2% and, in provincially held male inmates, it was 1.0%. The study concluded that over 600 HIV-infected individuals are admitted annually to Ontario remand facilities (Calzavara et al., 1995). Calzavara is currently updating this study.

The HIV infection rate in federal facilities is 1.7% for males and 4.7% for females (CSC, 2003). However, up to 70% of federal inmates may remain unscreened for HIV and hepatitis (CSC). Thus, the above rates could underestimate the true rates. Women have a rate 2.5 times that of men. Is this difference due to an actual higher infection rate, or do the women request testing more often than the men do?

In 2001, 0.18% of federal inmates had genital chlamydia and 0.10% had gonorrhea. The general population rate of chlamydia infection was estimated at 0.15%, and gonorrhea was 0.02% (De, 2002). Condoms, dental dams, and water-based lubricants are provided to inmates who request such products. However, in provincial correctional facilities, sex between inmates is forbidden and can result in a citation for misconduct. Therefore, inmates are ambivalent about requesting these products. On one hand, they are being responsible by using a coping mechanism to prevent spread of disease; on the other hand, by merely requesting these products, they are risking a misconduct. PASAN recommends that condoms, dental dams, and water-based lubricants be freely available to inmates (Lines, 2002). They also recommend that bleach be freely available and that correctional centres introduce a needle-exchange program (Lines). However, many inmates have charges of drug possession and/or trafficking. If governments were to introduce such harm-reduction programs as accessible bleach and needle exchange, they could be seen to be condoning the criminal activity that caused the inmate to be in the correctional facility in the first place, as well as condoning illicit drug use in general. This is another example where health care interventions and correctional methods are in conflict.

The prevalence of tuberculosis infections in previously Mantoux naive or negative provincial inmates was 7.5% for the 11 months ending February 2003. Of these, two inmates were diagnosed with active TB (Ferris, personal communication, 2003).

Nurses are often the first health care providers to assess inmates for infectious disease. This assessment is important in case finding and subsequent medical treatment. Nurses also implement infection-control precautions to prevent subsequent infection of staff and other inmates. Health education for inmates and staff on the prevention of infection transmission is a prime intervention.

When the Ontario government declared a provincial emergency because of SARS, nurses working in Ontario correctional centres saw a potential for massive risk to inmates and staff working in correctional facilities. At that time, not much was known about the disease and its control or treatment. The strategy from the beginning was to prevent an inmate or staff member with SARS from entering the facilities. Inmate visits in the greater Toronto area were stopped where SARS cases had been reported.

A group of senior nurse leaders developed a screening tool to screen all people entering a facility and/or transferring to another facility. Approximately 6000 inmates were screened in the Toronto area in an eight-week period. This tool was later adopted for screening in many other sectors in Ontario (see Table 12.2 in Chapter 12). The tool was adapted as new information became available.

Using this screening tool, Ontario correctional nurses identified several inmates who required voluntary quarantine as directed by the local public health unit. These inmates were isolated in the province's correctional facilities. Several other inmates, identified with SARS-like symptoms, were sent to hospital and returned to the facility once SARS had been ruled out. As well, several staff members were advised to leave work and consult with public health, Telehealth Ontario, or their personal MDs. Ontario correctional nurses worked very closely with nurses in their local public health units to determine who should be in voluntary isolation and what should be done with inmates with SARS-like symptoms. Their efforts were successful in finding symptomatic inmates and in allaying some of the anxiety felt by inmates and staff over this new infectious disease.

CORRECTIONAL STAFF

Correctional staff have direct contact with inmates who may have a variety of health care conditions and infections. Officers receive basic universal precautions training but do not have in-depth knowledge of infections or control measures. They fear what they do not know. Staff often request confidential health care information so they know what they are dealing with. Nurses cannot provide this confidential information; however, they must educate and inform correctional staff of infection control and other health care procedures. Nurses function within a very narrow margin when addressing staff members' need to know and inmates' confidentiality. Most nurses do find a way to provide health education to staff and, in doing so, improve the staff's overall health status and reduce some of their work-related stress. For example, a nurse may:

- review respiratory isolation procedures if an inmate with suspected TB is in the facility;
- remind correctional staff of the need for confidentiality when they escort an inmate with a positive HIV test to a HIV clinic;
- encourage the use of universal precautions at all times; and/or
- instruct officers in suicide assessment, care of inmates with mental illness, or the principles of harm reduction.

The pressure from staff for confidential health care information will continue, as will the need for nurses to protect that confidentiality. Nurses working in correctional facilities must continue to find methods to address both issues.

POLICY CHANGES

Nurses working in correctional facilities have many opportunities for input into policy and for initiating policy changes to improve and or maintain the health status of inmates and staff. For example, nurses played a huge role in initiating and implementing the no-smoking policy in Ontario centres. They also developed the policy and procedures for inmate and staff screenings in the 2003 SARS outbreak. Nurses have advocated for and developed infection control courses at individual facilities, a pre- and postnatal program in facilities with female inmates, and a policy regarding palliative care for inmates. They have also initiated the policy for the introduction of telemedicine and automated external defibrillators in Ontario correctional facilities. Much has been done, but much more needs to be done.

RESEARCH IN CORRECTIONAL NURSING

There is a severe scarcity of research in correctional nursing in Canada and elsewhere. It is possible that researchers have ethical concerns in obtaining consent from those who have lost their freedom. Would consent under these circumstances be given freely or with the expectation of something in return? Canadian Research Box 18.1 highlights a recent Canadian project.

While published research is sparse, some projects are underway. For example, the Ontario Ministry of Community Safety and Correctional Services is proceeding with a program evaluation of nurses providing discharge planning to remanded inmates with mental illness, is developing an operational definition of the discharge-planning program, and will soon start to study the effects of the program on inmates. Other areas for research could include the effects of health teaching to inmates and staff, of control measures to reduce infectious diseases in a prison population, and of nursing interventions to relieve chronic pain or anxiety.

Canadian Research Box 18.1

Schafer, P., & Peternelj-Taylor, C. (2003). Therapeutic relationships and boundary maintenance: The perspective of forensic patients enrolled in a treatment program for violent offenders. *Issues in Mental Health Nursing, 24,* 605–625.

These authors wanted to describe the relationships, as described by the clients, between nurses and clients in a correctional treatment setting. The clients were referred to the treatment program from their parent correctional facilities. Twelve male clients volunteered to participate in the study and each was interviewed at least three times. The data were the verbatim transcripts of the interviews. Themes that emerged from the data were set in the analogy of a house and included:

- adjusting to the house (transition from parent institution);
- knowing the fundamental structures of the house (influential contextual factors);
- evaluating the primary therapist as a guide (is the therapist "for them or against them");
- experiences that promote or hinder the relationship; and
- ways of being with the primary therapist: head, head and heart, heart, and wallet (four types of relationships identified by the clients).

While the authors note that the themes are interrelated, they present them individually, supported by quotes from the data. As the authors state, "This research indicates that therapeutic relationships, gender relations, power, patterns of interacting, and self-awareness are among the essential concepts to guide forensic mental health nurses in establishing therapeutic relationships and maintaining boundaries" (p. 622).

Discussion Questions

1. Inmates are considered a vulnerable population. Are there other vulnerable populations to which this research may apply? Why?
2. How might a nurse use the information gleaned from this study in establishing and maintaining therapeutic relationships with clients?

SUMMARY

Inmates in correctional facilities have many of the same health problems as the general population although the prevalence of some health problems is higher for inmates. Some inmates require specialized care to address their demographic, i.e., youth, women, and elderly.

There is an additional population in correctional facilities: the correctional staff. If this population is also considered a client, nurses can do much in the way of prevention of disease, promotion of health, and health education.

CASE STUDY

An 18-year-old male is admitted to a detention centre, charged with the sexual assault of a child. On assessment you find that he is quiet, has difficulty establishing eye contact, and answers questions in an abbreviated way. His affect does not quite match the topic under discussion. He tells you he has been consuming approximately three cannabis cigarettes per day for the last year. The police call and want to know this inmate's HIV and hepatitis B and C status. The victim's family wants their child treated if there is any risk of these diseases in the inmate.

Discussion Questions

1. How do you feel about the inmate? The child? The family of the child?
2. How will you work through these feelings so you are able to provide health care to the inmate?
3. What would your working diagnosis be for the inmate? What other data would you need to collect on this inmate?
4. How would you respond to the request for the inmate's HIV and hepatitis B and C status?

Nurses working in correctional facilities have a fairly independent practice. They do have to confront and find resolution for ethical issues that caring for this population poses for them. However, correctional nurses are able to make a difference in their clients' health status.

KEY TERMS

provincial correctional centres
federal correctional facilities
Correctional Service Canada (CSC)
methadone maintenance program

INDIVIDUAL CRITICAL THINKING EXERCISES

1. What types of assessment tools would you need to assess inmates for their most prevalent health problems?
2. What information would you give to a correctional officer when asked what an inmate's positive Mantoux test means?

GROUP CRITICAL THINKING EXERCISES

1. Are harm-reduction strategies, such as needle exchanges and accessible bleach, suitable for correctional facilities when the purpose of these facilities is to correct behaviour related to illicit drug use?
2. What advocacy is needed for inmates with mental illness in conflict with the justice system?

REFERENCES

Calzavara, L., Major, C., Myers, T., Schlossberg, J., Millson, M., Wallace, E. et al. (1995). The prevalence of HIV-1 infection among inmates in Ontario, Canada. *Canadian Journal of Public Health, 86*(5), 335–339.

Correctional Service of Canada. (2003). *Infectious diseases prevention and control in Canadian federal penitentiaries 2000–01.* Ottawa, ON: Author.

De, P. (2002). Infectious diseases in Canadian federal penitentiaries. *Forum on Corrections Research, 14*(2), 24–27.

Gal, M. (2002). The physical and mental health of older offenders. *Forum on Corrections Research, 14*(2), 15–19.

Heney, J., & Kristiansen, C. (2002). *Working with women in conflict with the law: A trainers' guide.* Toronto, ON: Ministry of Public Safety and Security.

Konrad, N. (2002). Prisons as new asylums. *Current Opinion Psychiatry, 15*(6), 583–587.

Langer, N., Barton, J., McDonagh, D., Noel, C., & Bouchard, F. (2002). Rates of prescribed medication use by women in prisons. *Forum on Corrections Research, 14*(2), 10–13.

Lines, R. (2002). *Action on HIV/AIDS in prisons: Too little, too late. A report card.* Ottawa, ON: Canadian HIV/AIDS Legal Network.

Robinson, P. (2003). *Juristat.* Ottawa, ON: Canadian Centre for Justice Statistics. (Statistics Canada no. 85-002-XIE)

Statistics Canada. (2002). *Adult correctional services in Canada, 2000–2001.* Ottawa, ON: Canadian Centre for Justice Statistics. (Statistics Canada no. 85-211-XIE)

Tandon, R., & Jibson, M. (2003). Suicidal behaviour in schizophrenia: Diagnosis, neurobiology and treatment implications. *Current Opinion Psychiatry, 16*(2), 193–197.

ADDITIONAL RESOURCES

WEBSITES

College of Nurses of Ontario. (2002). *Professional standards* (rev. ed.):
www.cno.org

Correctional Service Canada:
www.csc-scc.gc.ca

Ministry of Correctional Services Act (Ontario):
www.e-laws.gov.on.ca:81/ISYSquery/IRLF572.tmp/1/doc

Ministry of Community Safety and Correctional Services (Ontario):
www.mpss.jus.gov.on.ca/

National Commission on Correctional Health Care:
www.ncchc.org

Prisoner AIDS Support Action Network:
www.pasan.org

Statistics Canada:
www.statcan.ca

About the Author

Joanne Shaw is the Senior Nursing Consultant, Ministry of Community Safety and Corrections Services, Government of Ontario. Joanne graduated from the Saint John General School of Nursing and the University of New Brunswick. In the early part of her career, she worked as a general duty nurse and an infection control nurse. Later, she worked at the Clinical Institute of the Addiction Research Foundation, Toronto, Ontario and in this position developed the first CIWA (Clinical Institute Withdrawal Assessment) form and protocol. She then moved to the mental health field, working at two large psychiatric hospitals in Ontario. One of these hospitals was the Oak Ridge Division of the Mental Health Centre in Penetanguishene. This facility was a maximum-security facility for the assessment and treatment of men with a serious mental illness that put them in conflict with the justice system.

Joanne worked for two years at the Registered Nurses Association of Ontario where she was the staff resource to the entry-to-practice project. In 1997, Joanne became the coordinator of health care services at a mid-size detention centre in Toronto. She has been in an acting position as Senior Nursing Consultant since January 2002 and was confirmed in this position in July 2003.

Part Four

COMMON COMMUNITY HEALTH ISSUES

CHAPTER 19

Family Violence

Margaret M. Malone

OBJECTIVES

AFTER STUDYING THIS CHAPTER, YOU SHOULD BE ABLE TO:

1. Analyze critically the concept of "family violence."
2. Relate family violence to health implications for women, children, and seniors.
3. Investigate the impact of gender, race, age, class, sexuality, and culture on family violence.
4. Examine how community health nurses can work to eliminate family violence.
5. Explore critical theories and approaches that inform community health nurses' strategies to raise community awareness about family violence and its health impacts.
6. Develop health promoting interventions to address family violence in the community.

INTRODUCTION

Family violence is a major health and social problem in Canada, with devastating effects for women, children, seniors, and families. Societal responses have focused on identification, crisis intervention, and services to individuals and families. Violence in intimate relationships is of special concern to community health nurses (CHNs). CHNs are often the first health care providers to interact with those who have been injured from any form of violence. Furthermore, CHNs are strategically located within communities where health promoting initiatives can be researched, developed, implemented, and evaluated.

In this chapter, we examine recent Canadian statistics and the Canadian Nurses Association's position statement on family violence. We describe theoretical frameworks, including critical social theory and analytical approaches to the interconnections with gender, race, class, ethnicity, sexuality, age, ability, religious belief, and culture. We illustrate how these frameworks inform strategies for earlier identification of family violence, raise critical awareness in communities of its health impacts, and improve prevention and health promoting initiatives.

A CRITICAL ANALYSIS OF FAMILY VIOLENCE AND HEALTH IMPLICATIONS

Most of us cling to a family ideal that includes love between members, shared norms and values, happiness, mutual protection, caring and nurturing relationships, and above all, *safety.* Moreover, we often assume violent acts occur between strangers. But for many women, children, and elders, the home is the single most dangerous place they can be (Kimmel, 2000). In 2001, two-thirds of the reported violent crimes were committed by a spouse or an ex-spouse, and 85% of these victims were female. Among those cases, women aged 25–34 had the highest rates of spousal violence, and girls between 12 and 15 years of age were at greatest risk of sexual assault by a family member. Between 1977 and 1996, three times as many women were killed by their spouses as were men, and the number was slightly higher in 2001 than in 2000 (Health Canada, 2002a; Statistics Canada, 1998; 2003). Health Canada (2002b) reports that "The mortality rate due to violence for Aboriginal women is three times the rate experienced by all other Canadian women. For Aboriginal women in the 25 to 44 age cohort, the rate is five times that for all other Canadian women" (p. 2). These statistics reveal how an individual's social location affects their life experiences and health. Therefore, CHNs must develop an analysis of family violence that encompasses gender, age, class, race, ethnicity, culture, and sexuality.

Family Violence Experienced by Women

Violence against women involves "acts that result, or are likely to result, in physical, sexual, and psychological harm or suffering to a woman, including threats of such an act, coercion or arbitrary deprivation of liberty whether occurring in public or private life" (Health Canada, 2002b, p. 1). The most comprehensive national survey to date of violence against women (Statistics Canada, 1993) reports that:

- one-half of all Canadian women have experienced at least one incident of violence since the age of sixteen,
- almost one-half of women reported violence by men known to them and one-quarter reported violence by strangers,

- one-quarter of all women have experienced violence at the hands of a current or past marital partner (including common-law unions), and
- more than one woman in ten who reported violence in a current marriage have at some point felt their lives were in danger.

Health Canada (2002a) indicates that, "Ignoring violence as a factor in women's health and well-being not only leads to misdiagnosis and inadequate treatment, it also disregards the full extent of the personal and social consequences of violence" (p. 2). Furthermore, it has been estimated that violence against women may cost $4.2 billion annually (Middlesex-London Health Unit, 2000).

Family Violence Experienced by Children

Child abuse occurs when a parent, guardian, or caregiver mistreats or neglects a child, resulting in significant emotional or psychological harm, injury, or serious risk of harm. It entails the betrayal of a caregiver's position of trust and authority over a child (Health Canada, 1997). **Child neglect** involves either emotional or physical harm to a child "that deprives them of any or all of the following basic human needs: human nurturance, food, clothing, shelter, necessary health care, and provisions for safety and medical care" (McAllister, 2000).

Because of under-reporting, we still do not know how many children experience abuse and neglect. However, Health Canada (2002c) figures suggest the extent of child abuse and neglect. In 1998, child welfare agencies investigated an estimated 135 573 child maltreatments in Canada, consisting of physical abuse (31%), sexual abuse (10%), neglect (40%), and emotional maltreatment (19%). Onyskiw (2002) noted that "exposure to family violence has an adverse effect on children's health and use of health services" (p. 416). Moreover, "these children generally fared less favourably on several measures of health than children of non-violent families" (p. 419).

Family Violence Experienced by Older Adults

Elder abuse is "the mistreatment of older people by those in a position of trust, power, or responsibility for their care" (Health Canada, 1999a, p. 1). **Elder neglect** involves "the failure of a caregiver to meet the needs of an older adult who is unable to meet those needs alone. It includes behaviours such as denial of food, water, medication, medical treatment, therapy, nursing services, health aids, clothing, and visitors" (Health Canada, 1999a, p. 1).

Only a small proportion of elder abuse comes to the attention of the health, social service, and justice systems. Abuse and maltreatment of older adults are least likely to be reported (14 times lower than the rate for 18- to 24-year-olds) because of emotional, physical, or financial dependence on the abuser, because of embarrassment (especially if the abuser is an adult child), or because they fear institutionalization (Statistics Canada, 1998; 2003).

Family Violence among Aboriginals

"Eight out of every ten Aboriginal women, and four out of every ten children" have been abused or assaulted (Hare, 1991, p. 79). Attitudinal change is vital in removing the barriers faced by First Nations women and children experiencing family violence. The emotional, psychological, physical, and mental health of Aboriginal women, children, and men must be addressed in a culturally appropriate way. While patriarchal attitudes and gender relations are important considerations, Aboriginal women's experience of violence must also be understood through "the important prisms of racism, colonialism, and classism" (Mandell & Duffy, 2000, p. 308).

Family Violence among Immigrants

Canada is one of the most culturally diverse countries in the world. Yet there is a lack of specific data addressing differential experiences of family violence by race, ethnicity, class, and culture. Fong's (2000) research showed that immigrant "women experienced a great deal of pain and hardship due to their isolation, burden of childcare responsibilities, lack of English skills, unfamiliarity with the new environment and new culture, lack of an adequately paid job, and/or financial dependence on their husbands" (p. iv), in addition to an abusive relationship. Yet these same women "employed a wide range of strategies to resist the abuse and protect themselves from different dangerous situations" (p. iv). Drawing on case studies, reports, and interviews, Agnew (1998) captured similar experiences for immigrant women from Asia, Africa, and the Caribbean who have suffered wife abuse.

Family Violence in Lesbian and Gay Families

Abuse in same-sex couples, with or without children, has important implications for the analysis of family violence. Mandell and Duffy (2000) argue that these occurrences push "feminists to focus on power and control perspectives rather than the interplay of genders" (p. 309). Gochros and Bidwell (1996) outline health risks, interpersonal stresses, and psychological challenges faced by lesbian and gay youth, especially when compounded by family violence and social discrimination. They also challenge health care workers to develop innovative early intervention programs for lesbian and gay youth while acknowledging the formidable barriers to providing these services.

COMMUNITY HEALTH NURSING AND FAMILY VIOLENCE

Brown (1991) asserts that "violence in any society persists because there is a role for it, because it serves a purpose. Violence persists... because people opposed to it have been addressing its manifestations rather that its root causes" (p. 104). Therefore, in relation to community health nursing and family violence, "if we think of health as broadly defined and influenced, we... arrive at the inescapable conclusion that to be concerned about health is to be concerned with the social context" (CNA, 2000, p. 1). Neysmith (1995) argues that woman, child, and elder abuse "occurs within familial relationships because these are sites of power and locations that permit it to happen" (p. 48). The Canadian Nurses Association's position statement on violence to guide nursing practice is outlined in the text box. Moreover, violence in families is difficult to address because of the sensitive issues and strong emotions it raises.

Theoretical Frameworks and Approaches

This section considers approaches that help us advocate for populations vulnerable to violence, abuse, and neglect. We address critical theories; inclusive race, class, and gender analytical frameworks; empowerment and partnership approaches; and critical perspectives on terms and defining characteristics.

Critical Social Theories **Critical social theories** include liberation work against poverty and illiteracy; feminist scholarship on the oppression of women; lesbian and gay liberation studies; and critical perspectives on race and ethnic relations, gender inequalities, and health promotion (Stevens & Hall, 1992). Critical social theories include research methods that examine the lived experiences of women with a view to social change and theories of violence against women, children, youth, elders, older lesbians, and men. In defining a violent society, critical theorists include the social, economic, and political ways individuals and groups are harmed by social institutions and the state (Brown, 1991).

Inclusive Race, Class, and Gender Analytical Frameworks Understanding the interrelationships among races, ethnicities, classes, genders, abilities, sexualities, cultures, ages, and religious beliefs expands our capacity to work effectively against violence in families and communities. CHNs must understand the concerns of the marginalized groups and provide culturally sensitive services to victims of abuse within their ethnic and racial communities. When developing health promotion programs related to violence for newly immigrant women, CHNs must be respectful of the need to maintain culture and tradition, while at the same time working for change (Choudhry et al., 2002). Changing our thinking requires not just assessing data, but also examining our own biases, beliefs, and feelings about these issues. The capacity to reflect on our own experiences is a major principle in CHN practice (Community Health Nurses Association of Canada [CHNAC], 2003).

Empowerment and Partnership Approaches **Empowerment** describes the creation of relationships with greater equity in resources, status, and authority. "Power over" becomes "power with." CHNs must empower themselves and others to use their individual and collective strength to address violence in families by using the continuum of empowerment strategies listed in the text box.

Critical Perspectives on Terms and Defining Characteristics

We do not have adequate definitions to sensitively address what people experience or recognize as violence, abuse, and neglect. Most researchers, critical theorists, and people working with individuals and populations agree that violence is a social act. Here we examine critically concepts found in the literature, statistics, and reports: family violence, victim, abuse, and women abuse in international contexts.

Family Violence The Toronto Child Abuse Centre (2002) states that **family violence** is "the result of an imbalance of power, and its aim is to frighten, intimidate, and gain control" (p. 1). Although often discussed as violence between husband

Canadian Nurses Association's Position Statement on Violence

Violence is recognized as a social act involving a serious abuse of power. Over the past decades, it has become a [community health and] public health concern of epidemic proportion with serious consequences both for those who provide and those who receive health care. CNA defines violence in a broad sense to encompass verbal and emotional abuse, physical violence, and sexual harassment. Violence has many manifestations (e.g., violence against women, spousal/partner violence, dating violence, and abuse or neglect of children and the elderly) and takes place in diverse settings, including homes, schools, and places of work. Violence is deeply rooted in cultural values and traditional social structures that particularly disempower women and children, who are the most common victims. Different cultures may have different interpretations as to what actions are considered violence.

Often the first to interact with individuals affected by violence, and often victims themselves, nurses have critical roles to play in dealing with and eliminating violence. CNA believes nurses have an equally important role to play in advocating the elimination of violence in society. Nurses in all practice settings must take an active role in communicating the fundamental principle that everyone has a right to live a life free from violence. Refusal to accept violence plays a role in changing societal attitudes.

Nurses cannot manage and/or eliminate violence alone. The approach must be multidisciplinary, multisectoral, and multifacted. The public, professionals and workers across sectors, employers, unions, and governments have roles to play that ensure that legislation, education, research, administrative supports, and adequate resources are in place to deal with the impact of violence and to promote changes in societal attitudes.

Source: Adapted from Canadian Nurses Association. (2002). Position statement: Violence. *Retrieved February 28, 2003 from* www.cna-nurses.ca/_frames/policies/policiesmainframe.htm

Empowerment Strategies: A Continuum

Personal empowerment: Organizes individuals around issues and problems unique to the individual

Small group empowerment: Organizes people around issues or problems unique to group members

Community organization: Organizes people around problems or issues that are larger than group members' own immediate concerns

Coalition advocacy: Takes a position on a particular issue that unifies the differing values of member groups; initiates action in a deliberate attempt to influence private and public policy

Political action: Intensifies actions initiated under coalition advocacy

Source: Adapted from Registered Nurses Association of British Columbia. (1992). Determinants of health: Empowering strategies for nursing practice: A background paper. *Ottawa, ON: Health Canada (pp. 9–10).*

and wife, "family violence... does not exist solely in male/female relationships. It is also found in lesbian and gay relationships and in homes where extended families live together. In heterosexual relationships, men are not the only perpetrators. However, statistically, women are most likely to be victimized by family violence and the perpetrator is likely to be her male partner" (p. 1). When "family violence" is used to include elder abuse, we may miss the importance of abuse *and* neglect for the elder population (MacLean & Williams, 1995). Similarly, we must also consider neglect in child abuse cases (McAllister, 2000).

Victim We use the term **victim** cautiously because people are not just victims. MacLean and Williams (1995) state that, "to refer to the person primarily as 'victim' is to overstress the passivity which 'victim' connotes and to undervalue the strength and dignity that he/she retains as an autonomous individual" (p. xi).

Abuse Like the word "victim," **abuse** can also produce negative reactions. Health Canada (1999) states that "whenever someone uses power over another person to try to harm that person, or to exert control that will harm that person... it is abuse" (p. 1).

Physical abuse includes "slapping, punching, kicking, biting, shoving, choking, or using a weapon to threaten or injure. It includes unwanted contact or physical neglect and may result in death" (Health Canada, 1999a, p. 1). **Sexual abuse** includes any forced sexual activity. It can also include "infecting a person with a sexually transmitted disease by engaging in unsafe sexual practices" (Health Canada, 1999a, p. 1).

Psychological and/or **emotional abuse** includes "various forms of intimidation, harassment, excessive jealousy, control, isolation, and threats" (Health Canada, 1999b, p. 1). Emotional abuse also includes "rejecting, degrading, terrorizing, corrupting/exploiting, and denying emotional responsiveness" (Health Canada, 1996, p. 4). **Verbal abuse** includes "constant criticism, blaming, false accusations, name calling, and threats of violence toward a person or the people or things that person cares about" (Health Canada, 1999b, p. 1).

Woman Abuse in International Contexts The United Nations sets woman abuse in the social, economic, and political context with attention to gender relations, culture, and war. Violence against women encompasses, but is not limited to, acts of physical, sexual, and psychological violence in the family and the community. These acts include spousal battering, sexual abuse of female children, dowry-related violence, rape (including marital rape), and traditional practices harmful to women, such as female genital mutilation. They also include non-spousal violence, sexual harassment and intimidation at work and in school, trafficking of women, forced prostitution, and violence perpetrated or condoned by the state, such as rape in war (John Hopkins School of Public Health, 1999). CHNs must non-judgmentally support all victims of family violence and consider the many forms of violence and abuse and how they are interconnected.

COMMUNITY HEALTH NURSING PRACTICE

In this section, we illustrate how assessment at the individual level facilitates critical awareness of the extent of family violence in the community. We make connections between this strategy and community initiatives. The process includes addressing the safety of the person in addition to being critically aware of family violence, indicators of abuse and neglect, the importance of asking about abuse, how to ask about abuse, individual risk factors, routine universal comprehensive screening, community resources, prevention and health promoting strategies, and connecting individual harm with the community context.

First, *safety of the person* is key. Poorly designed and implemented assessment strategies put women, children, and elders in violent, abusive, or neglectful relationships at substantial risk. The environment must make the individuals feel *safe* before they could discuss their experiences. A short form ABCD-ER Mnemonic Tool may be used as a guide in this process (see text box).

Second, CHNs must become more *critically aware* of family violence and abuse and that it cuts across all ages, races, genders, sexualities, cultures, religions, abilities, classes, and other socially organized structures. The London Battered Women's Advocacy Centre developed a Power and Control Wheel (Figure 19.1) that outlines some of the tactics used by the abuser in woman abuse situations.

Third, CHNs need to know *indicators* of emotional abuse and neglect for children, adults, and elders. Some indicators manifest themselves in health effects. Indicators for both children and adults include depression, withdrawal, low self-esteem, severe anxiety, fearfulness, being overly passive or complaint, sleep disturbances, suicide attempts, and other forms of physical abuse present or suspected. Indicators for

Short Form ABCD-ER Mnemonic Tool

Guiding principles for screening:

A: *Attitude* and *Approachability* of health care professionals

B: *Belief* in the woman's account of her own experience of abuse

C: *Confidentiality* is essential for disclosure

D: *Documentation* that is consistent and legible

E: *Education* about the serious health effects of abuse

R: *Respect* for the integrity and authority of each woman's life choices and *Recognition* that the process of dealing with the identified abuse must be done at her pace, directed by her decisions

Source: Reproduced with permission from the Middlesex-London Health Unit, London, Ontario, Canada. (2000). Task force on the health effects of women abuse: Final report *(pp. 34). London, ON: Author. While the information contained in the materials is believed to be accurate and true, no responsibility is assumed by MLHU for its use.*

children include failure to thrive in infancy, emotional instability, physical complaints with no medical basis, over- or underachievement, and inability to trust. Additional indicators for adults include feelings of shame and guilt, substance abuse, discomfort or nervousness around caregiver or relatives, and social isolation (Health Canada, 1996).

Fourth, CHNs must understand the importance of *asking about abuse.* Asking increases the chances of preventing further abuse and is an important signal of support. It lets a woman know she is believed, respected, supported, and heard. Moreover, naming the problem raises awareness and makes it public and political.

Fifth, CHNs need to learn *how* to ask about abuse. Privacy is key. Direct and specific questions are best and should be non-threatening, non-blaming, open-ended, and always preceded by genuinely supportive statements of concern. (See text box, Screening for Woman Abuse: Developing a Personal Style.)

Sixth, CHNs need to understand *individual risk factors* to intervene in the cycle of violence. The social determinants of health, which include income and social status, employment

FIGURE 19.1 Battering in Intimate Relationships: "The Power and Control Wheel"

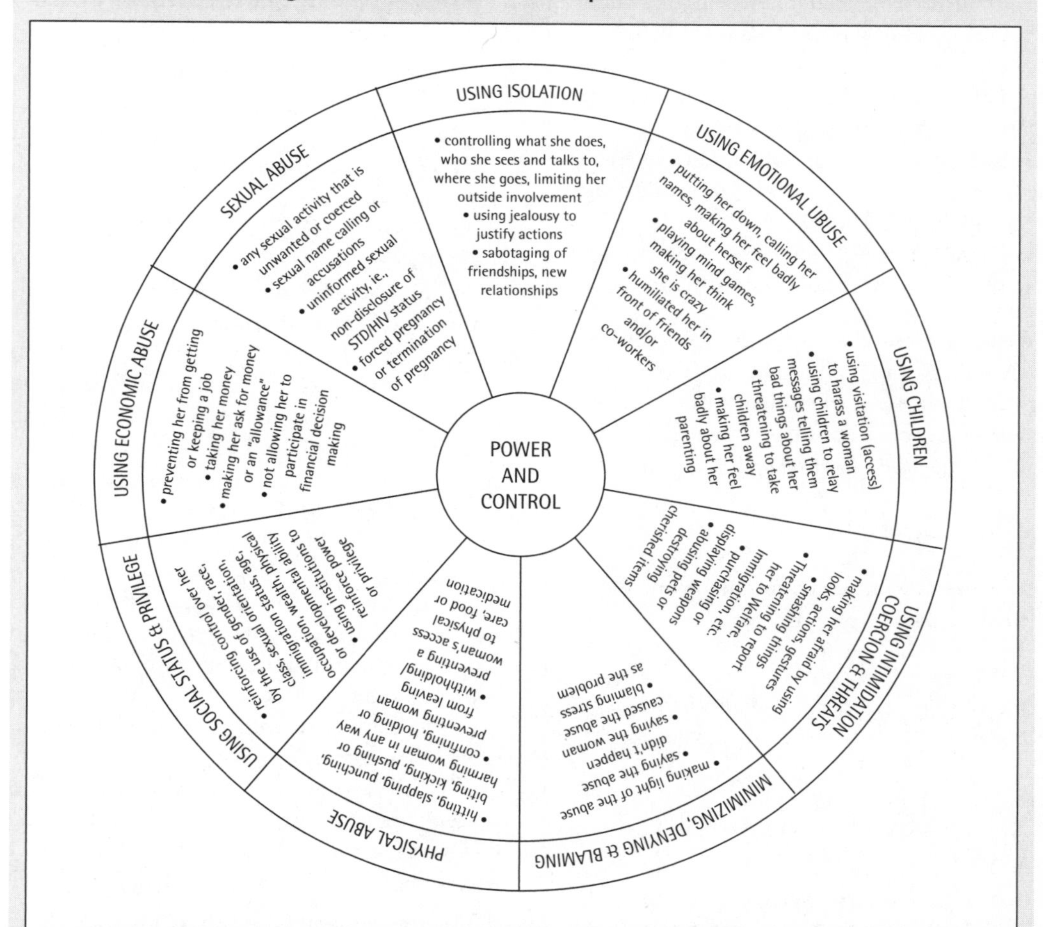

Source: Reproduced with permission from the Middlesex-London Health Unit, London, Ontario, Canada. Originally developed by The Domestic Abuse Intervention Project, Duluth, U.S.A. Further adapted by The London Battered Women's Advocacy Centre. Task force on the health effects of woman abuse: Final report. (2000). London, ON: Author.

and working conditions, personal health, coping skills, gender, race, ethnicity, age, sexuality, religion, culture, and social environment, should be considered when assessing risk factors.

Seventh, through *routine universal comprehensive screening*, CHNs can demonstrate connections between individual harm and social context. The Task Force on Health Effects of Woman Abuse (Middlesex-London Health Unit, 2000) outlines four approaches to screening:

- **Indicator-based diagnosis** means that a health care professional notices one or more indicators that a woman may have been abused, and referring to the indicator(s), asks the woman whether abuse has caused that injury or condition.
- **Routine screening** means that screening is done on a *regular* basis when women come in contact with health care professionals, whether or not indicators of abuse are recognized.
- **Comprehensive screening** means that women are asked by health care professionals whether they have experienced or are currently experiencing any form of physical, sexual, and/or emotional abuse as children, adolescents, or adults.
- **Universal screening** means that "*every* woman over an agreed-upon age is asked about her current or past experience of abuse by health care professionals with whom she comes in contact" (p. 22). For example, the Task Force (Middlesex-London Health Unit) recommends that "every woman over the age of 12 years should be routinely screened for woman abuse" (p. 30) (see Figure 19.2).

Eighth, CHNs must *make appropriate referrals* in their communities to assist abused women, children, seniors, and men. Support services could include "police; shelters; victim assistance and services (police based, court based, other); sexual assault support; women's centres; child advocacy centres; children's aid services; crisis telephone lines (e.g., kids-help lines, distress lines); medical services and health care centres; counselling services for women, children, Aboriginals, immigrants, and seniors; legal assistance (legal aid, lawyer referral services, other); Aboriginal services; immigrant and refugee services; ethnocultural organizations that address abuse issues; child welfare authorities; programs for men that abuse women and for men that have been abused; self-help clearinghouses and networks; community resources centres; and other related services" (Health Canada, 1999b, p. 41).

Ninth, CHNs must work together to *develop broad-based, comprehensive health promoting strategies* in their communities that include primary, secondary, and tertiary prevention approaches to family violence. These should include ethical, research, and evaluative components. CHNs should also address the diversity of their community by attending to gender, race, class, age, ethnicity, ability, sexuality, language, literacy, and culture.

Tenth, when CHNs *connect individual harm with the community context*, it makes violence public and political. Here, CHNs can activate political actions supported by critical theoretical frameworks (Stevens & Hall, 1992). This means:

- *taking a stand.* CHNs have a responsibility to diverse communities that are vulnerable to the oppressive, health-damaging conditions of violence.
- *asking critical questions* to demystify oppressive situations. For example, why has a unified effort to eradicate

Screening for Woman Abuse: Developing a Personal Style

A screening protocol should be flexible so that it can be altered to fit the context of the particular situation. The process may vary depending on the health care or community setting, the relationship of the CHN to the woman, the presenting problem, the woman's history, and the role of the particular CHN in meeting the woman's health needs.

A few suggestions:

- Ask simple, direct questions.
- Maintain a matter-of-fact tone of voice and a relaxed demeanour.
- Be sure your body language, facial expressions, and words all convey the same thing: that you are willing to hear what the woman has to say and are willing to help.
- Emphasize that all women are screened routinely for abuse as part of health care interactions.
- Use the screening process as an opportunity to educate the woman about the prevalence, dynamics, and health effects of abuse.
- Use neutral terms in asking about abuse. (Someone of the same sex may have abused the woman.)

Ways to ask about abuse—some sample questions:

- We know that abuse and violence in the home affect many women and directly affect their health. I wonder if you ever experience abuse or violence at home?
- Have you ever felt unsafe or threatened in your own home?

Physical abuse

- The injuries you have suggest to me that someone may have hit you. Did anyone hit you?

Emotional abuse

- Does anyone close to you call you names, criticize your friends or family, or try to control what you do?

Sexual abuse

- Have you ever been forced to have sex with your partner when you did not want to?

Sources: Adapted from Health Canada. (1999). A handbook for health and social services professionals responding to abuse during pregnancy *(pp. 24). Ottawa, ON: Health Canada, Health Promotion and Services Branch. (Cat. No. H72-21/165-1998E); and Middlesex-London Health Unit. (2000).* Task force on the health effects of women abuse: Final report *(pp. 33–34). London, ON: Author.*

FIGURE 19.2 The Routine Universal Comprehensive Screening (RUCS) Protocol

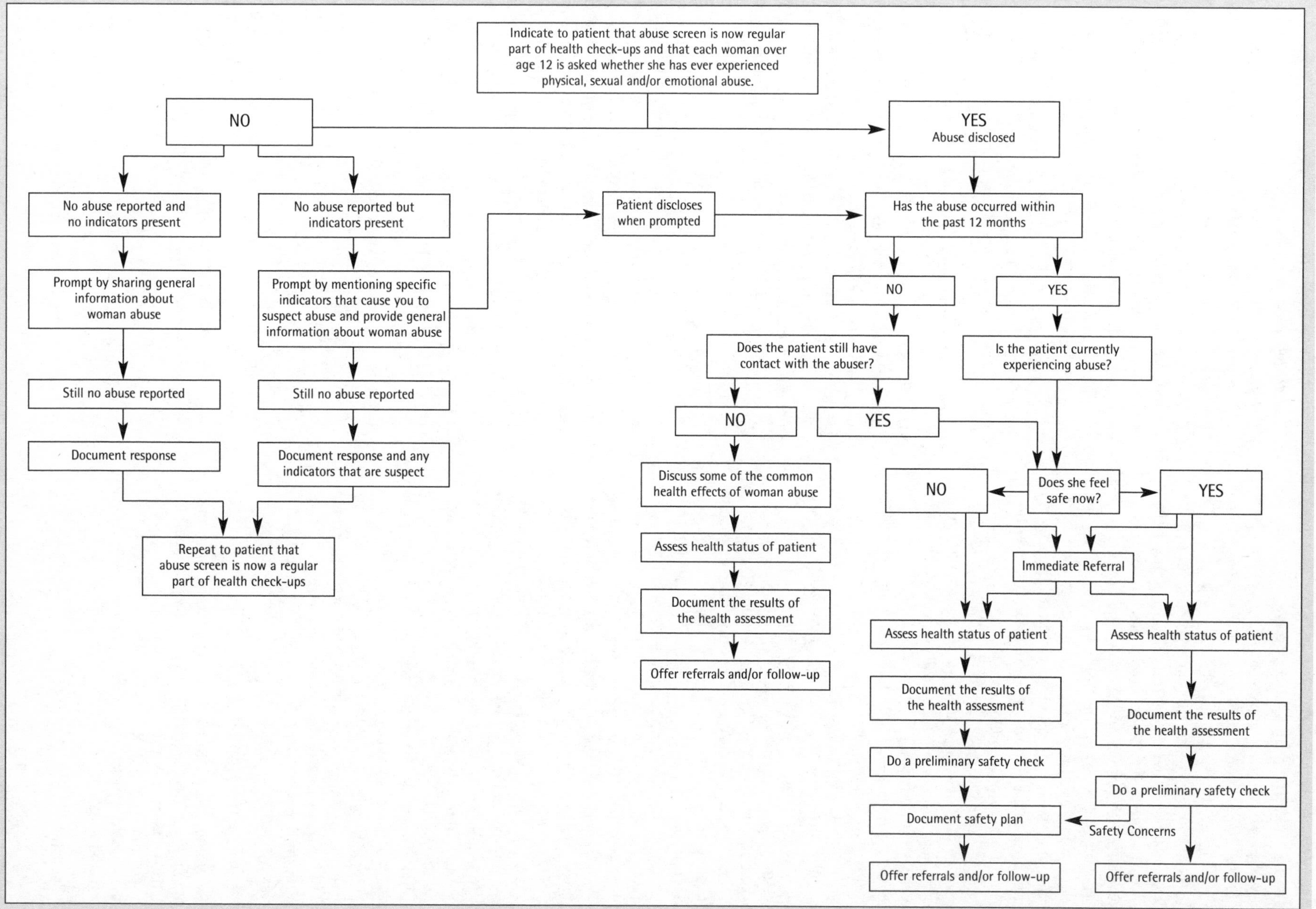

Indicate to patient that abuse screen is now regular part of health check-ups and that each woman over age 12 is asked whether she has ever experienced physical, sexual and/or emotional abuse.

NO

No abuse reported and no indicators present

Prompt by sharing general information about woman abuse

Still no abuse reported

Document response

No abuse reported but indicators present

Prompt by mentioning specific indicators that cause you to suspect abuse and provide general information about woman abuse

Still no abuse reported

Document response and any indicators that are suspect

Repeat to patient that abuse screen is now a regular part of health check-ups

Patient discloses when prompted

YES
Abuse disclosed

Has the abuse occurred within the past 12 months

NO

Does the patient still have contact with the abuser?

NO

Discuss some of the common health effects of woman abuse

Assess health status of patient

Document the results of the health assessment

Offer referrals and/or follow-up

YES

YES

Is the patient currently experiencing abuse?

Does she feel safe now?

NO

Immediate Referral

Assess health status of patient

Document the results of the health assessment

Do a preliminary safety check

Document safety plan

Offer referrals and/or follow-up

YES

Assess health status of patient

Document the results of the health assessment

Do a preliminary safety check

Safety Concerns

Offer referrals and/or follow-up

Source: Reproduced with permission from the Middlesex-London Health Unit, London, Ontario, Canada.

Canadian Research Box 19.1

Wolfe, D. A., & Jaffe, P. G. (1999). Emerging strategies in the prevention of domestic violence. *The Future of Children, 9*(3), 133.

The authors address research that explores innovative domestic violence prevention strategies currently being implemented in North America, together with the results from their evaluation, where available. The authors note that responses to domestic (family) violence have focused on intervention after the problem has been identified and harm has occurred. To date, there is no information available on the total number of prevention programs that address domestic violence. However, in their analysis of the research results, Wolfe and Jaffe highlight some new strategies and prevention programs/models from the public health field, which they argue can serve as models.

The first model involves public (community) health campaigns that identify and address underlying causes. Although identifying the underlying causes of family violence is difficult—experts do not agree on causation, and several theories exist—these theories can serve as a foundation for prevention strategies.

The second model identifies opportunities for domestic violence prevention along a continuum of possible harm: primary prevention to reduce violence before it occurs; secondary prevention to decrease prevalence after early signs of the problem; tertiary prevention to intervene once violence is clearly evident. Primary prevention includes school-based programs that teach students about family violence along with alternative conflict-resolution skills and public education to increase awareness of family violence and available victims' services. Secondary prevention includes home visiting for high-risk families and community-based programs on dating violence for adolescents referred through child protective services (CPS). Tertiary prevention includes targeted intervention programs.

Evaluations of existing prevention programs show promise, but programs remain small, locally based, and scattered throughout North America. A broad-based, comprehensive prevention strategy, supported by sound research and evaluation, receiving adequate public backing, and based on zero tolerance for domestic violence, is needed.

Discussion Questions

1. How would you as a CHN develop a program to raise critical awareness about family violence, including diversity issues, so that elementary school students understand alternatives to family violence? What issues would you address? What strategies would you use to address them?
2. What safety and ethical issues should be considered in your program? How would you implement and evaluate these strategies?

violence in its many forms not occurred? Whose interests are served by violence?

- *working with communities* to solve health problems. Targeting problems people identify, such as violence and abuse, situates CHNs' efforts in communities' struggles.
- *acting collectively.* Forming alliances with community members and groups concerned with violence in families creates solidarity and uses collective strength to work for healthy social change. Sustaining these alliances requires an ongoing commitment supported by sufficient funding.

Learning how to do this work takes time, commitment, and a caring presence. To assist in this endeavour, we have listed useful websites and resources at the end of this chapter. Other resources may be obtained at women's centres, clinics, shelters, and health and social service agencies.

SUMMARY

Family violence occurs in our families and our communities, locally and globally. Violence is a social act that involves a serious abuse of power. It crosses all races, classes, genders, ages, ethnicities, cultures, sexualities, abilities, and religions. Therefore, violence in families needs to be understood in the broader social, economic, cultural, and political contexts.

CASE STUDY

Serena, a 30-year-old Mexican-Canadian woman, has recently given birth to her first child, a small but healthy baby girl. During her short hospital stay, Serena attended all the postnatal classes, including one on breastfeeding, and appeared to be confident in her care of the baby. However, during the discharge planning, when in the presence of her husband, the nurse noted Serena appeared quite nervous.

You do a follow-up home visit as part of the "Healthy Mother, Healthy Baby" program sponsored by the Community Health Department and the hospital. You are welcomed by Serena, who informs you that her husband is out buying groceries. You assess the health of mother and baby and offer support and advise about breastfeeding. You also invite Serena to the local "Mothers and Babies Group." But Serena, who seems quite interested, does not think her husband will let her go. She also mentions that when the baby cried for a while last evening, her husband became angry, telling her to keep the baby quiet because he needed his sleep. Serena appears anxious about her husband's impending return.

Discussion Questions

1. Given her concerns about her husband, what is your first response to Serena?
2. How do you initiate an assessment of her situation?
3. What are your priorities?

Herein lie the roots of political activism. CHNs must make the connections between common problems affecting the people we work with and the larger social issues in which they are immersed if we are to be effective in working together with our allies to eradicate violence. CHNs who guide their practice with critical theories, while working with people where they live, affirm those who are dealing with experiences of violence in families as active, engaged subjects in their own struggle. Simultaneously, CHNs can work to facilitate social changes at the level of individual, family, group, community, and population.

KEY TERMS

physical abuse
sexual abuse
violence against women
child abuse
child neglect
elder abuse
elder neglect
emotional abuse
verbal abuse
critical social theories
empowerment
violence
family violence
victim
abuse
indicator-based diagnosis
routine screening
comprehensive screening
universal screening

INDIVIDUAL CRITICAL THINKING EXERCISES

1. Consider your experiences with people in your practice placements or your community who have experienced violence or abuse. Examine critically your own perspectives, assumptions, and biases, including thinking about where, when, and how you developed these ideas.
2. How is family violence represented in the media? Give two examples. Drawing on the material in this chapter, provide a comparative critical analysis of your examples, addressing the strengths and limitations of each. Include a critical analysis of the implications these media representations have for the community's understanding of family violence, for health and health care, and for CHN theory and practice.

GROUP CRITICAL THINKING EXERCISE

You are a nurse in an urban community health centre serving a mixed-income, ethnically/racially diverse community. A number of women have recently disclosed that they have been victims of "family violence." After reading on this topic and talking with other health care providers, you realize that family violence is much more pervasive than you had imagined. You decide to address this issue within the community.

You and your colleagues begin to think about strategies to stop family violence. Using critical theories and other CHN frameworks and approaches, develop a health promotion program to address this problem.

REFERENCES

Agnew, V. (1998). *In search of a safe place: Abused women and culturally sensitive services.* Toronto, ON: University of Toronto Press.

Brown, R. (1991). Attack violence at its roots. *Canadian Woman Studies/Les Cahiers de la Femme, 12*(1), 12–15.

Canadian Nurses Association. (2000). Nursing is a political act. Nursing now: Issues and trends in Canadian Nursing. Retrieved February 28, 2003 from **http://www.cna-nurses.ca/_frames/issuestrendsframe.htm**

Canadian Nurses Association. (2002). *Position statement: Violence.* Retrieved February 28, 2003 from **www.cna-nurses.ca/_frames/policies/policiesmainframe.htm**

Choudhry, U. K., Jandu, S., Mahal, J., Singh, R., Sohi-Pabla, H., & Mutta, B. (2002). Health promotion and participatory action research with South Asian women. *Journal of Nursing Scholarship, 34*(1), 75–81.

Community Health Nurses Association of Canada (CHNAC). (2003). *Canadian community health nursing standards of practice.* Retrieved December 18, 2003 from **www.communityhealthnursescanada.org**

Fong, J. S. (2000). *Silent no more; How women experienced wife abuse in the local Chinese community.* Unpublished doctoral dissertation, York University, Toronto, Ontario.

Gochros, H., & Bidwell, R. (1996). Lesbian and gay youth in a straight world: Implications for health care workers. *Journal of Gay and Lesbian Social Services, 5*(1), 1–17.

Hare, S. (1991). Breaking free: A proposal for change to Aboriginal family violence. *Canadian Woman Studies/Les Cahiers de la Femme, 11*(4), 79–80.

Health Canada. (1996). *What is emotional abuse?* Retrieved March 10, 2003 from **http://www.hc-sc.gc.ca/nc-cn**

Health Canada. (1997). Child abuse and neglect fact sheet. Retrieved March 10, 2003 from **http://www.hc-sc.gc.ca/nc-cn**

Health Canada. (1999a). *Abuse and neglect of older adults.* Ottawa, ON: National Clearinghouse on Family Violence. Retrieved March 10, 2003 from **www.hc-sc.gc.ca/hppb/familyviolence/index.html**

Health Canada. (1999b). A handbook for health and social services professional responding to abuse during pregnancy. Ottawa, ON: Health Canada, the National Clearinghouse on Family Violence. (Cat. No. H72-21/165-1998E).

Health Canada. (2002a). *The health of Aboriginal women.* Retrieved March 10, 2003 from **www.hc-sc.gc.ca/english/women/facts_issues/facts_aborig.htm**

Health Canada. (2002b). *Violence against women.* Retrieved March 10, 2003 from **www.hc-sc.gc.ca/english/women/facts_issues/facts_violence.htm**

Health Canada. (2002c). *The Canadian incidence study of reported child abuse and neglect.* Retrieved March 10, 2003 from **www.hc-sc.gc.ca/hppb/familyviolence/html/nfntscie_e.html**

Johns Hopkins School of Public Health, & Center for Health and Gender Equity. (1999). Ending violence against women. *Population Reports, 28*(4); *Issues in World Health, Series L* (11). Retrieved December 11, 2003 from **www.infoforhealth.org/pr/l11edsum.shtml**

Kimmel, S. (2000). *The gendered society.* New York: Oxford University Press.

Mandell, N., & Duffy, A. (2000). *Canadian families: Diversity, conflict, and change.* Toronto, ON: Harcourt Brace Canada.

McAllister, M. (2000). Domestic violence: A life-span approach to assessment and intervention [Electronic version]. *Lippincott's Primary Care Practice, 4*(2), 174–189.

MacLean, M. J, & Williams, R. M. (1995). Introduction. In M. J. MacLean (Ed.), *Abuse & neglect of older Canadians: Strategies for change* (pp. ix–xii). Toronto, ON: Thompson Educational.

Middlesex-London Health Unit. (2000). *Task force on the health effects of women abuse: Final report.* London, ON: Author.

Neysmith, S. M. (1995). Power in relationships of trust: A feminist analysis of elder abuse. In M. J. MacLean (Ed.), *Abuse & neglect of older Canadians: Strategies for change* (pp. 43–54). Toronto, ON: Thompson Educational.

Onyskiw, J. E. (2002). Health and the use of health services of children exposed to violence in their families. *Canadian Journal of Public Health, 93*(6), 416–420.

Statistics Canada. (1993). *Violence against women survey.* Ottawa, ON: Author. (Cat. No. 11-001E)

Statistics Canada. (1998). *Family violence in Canada: A statistical profile, 1998.* Ottawa, ON: Author. (Cat. No. 85-224-XPB)

Statistics Canada. (2003). *Family violence in Canada: A statistical profile, 2003.* Ottawa, ON: Author. (Cat. No. 85-224-XIE)

Stevens, P., & Hall, J. (1992). Applying critical theories to nursing in communities. *Public Health Nursing, 9*(1), 2–9.

Toronto Child Abuse Centre. (2002). *What is family violence?* (Information package #14). Retrieved March 11, 2003 from **www.tcac.on.ca/FAQ14.html**

ADDITIONAL RESOURCES

WEBSITES

Health Canada:
www.hc-sc.gc.ca

Health Canada, Women's Health Bureau:
www.hc-sc.gc.ca/english/women/facts_issues/factsandissues.htm

Metropolitan Action Committee on Violence Against Women and Children (METRAC):
www.metrac.org

National Clearinghouse on Family Violence:
www.hc-sc.gc.ca/nc-cn

Toronto Child Abuse Centre:
www.tcac.on.ca

READINGS AND RESOURCES

Ellesberg, M., & Heise, L. (2002). Bearing witness: Ethics in domestic violence research. *Lancet, 359*(9317), 1599.

Geffner, R. A., Jaffe, P. G., & Snudermann, M. (Eds.). (2000). *Children exposed to domestic violence: Current issues in research, intervention, prevention, and policy development.* New York: Haworth Press.

Hoff, L. A. (1995). *Violence issues: An interdisciplinary curriculum guide for health professionals.* Ottawa, ON: National Clearinghouse for Family Violence. (Cat. No. H72-21/129-1995E)

Sev'er, A. (2002). *Fleeing the house of horrors: Women who have left abusive partners.* Toronto, ON: University of Toronto Press.

Woodtli, M. A. (2000). Domestic violence and the nursing curriculum: Tuning in and tuning up. *Journal of Nursing Education, 39*(4), 173–189.

About the Author

Margaret M. Malone, RN (St. Michael's Hospital, Toronto); DPHN (Ottawa); BScN (Ryerson); BA, MA, and PhD (Toronto), is Associate Professor at the School of Nursing, Ryerson University. She was awarded a Ruth Wynn Woodward Postdoctoral Fellowship in Women's Studies at Simon Fraser University. As a nurse sociologist, Margaret Malone taught sociology and women studies at the University of Toronto, Trent University, and Wilfrid Laurier University. Currently, she teaches community health nursing in the four-year degree and the Post-RN programs with a focus of emphasis on research. Her research interests include health promotion, community development, marital separation, divorce, violence against women and children, and the development of a social theory of gender, emotions, and knowledge.

CHAPTER 20

Poverty and Homelessness

Patricia Malloy and
Lynnette Leeseberg Stamler

OBJECTIVES

AFTER STUDYING THIS CHAPTER, YOU SHOULD BE ABLE TO:

1. Describe the multiple definitions of poverty and homelessness and discuss the origins of those definitions.
2. Use the determinants of health framework to assess the influence of poverty and/or homelessness on an individual's or family's health.
3. Describe the community health nurse role in advocating for groups and populations affected by poverty and homelessness.

INTRODUCTION

Homelessness is a growing problem in Canadian cities. Each night, in 11 of Canada's largest cities, approximately 11 000 people sleep in shelters (Murphy, 2000). Homelessness is also a rural problem, but there are no shelter beds for the rural homeless. Many factors contribute to homelessness, poverty being significant. In fact, some authors consider poverty to be the primary contributing factor in homelessness. While there is significant interest in poverty and homelessness in the media and on the internet, it is disheartening to realize that few firm statistics are available that demonstrate the scope of the issue. While the authors did not explore the entire internet, searching the keywords "homeless" and "poverty" in the Statistics Canada and Health Canada websites revealed few hits.

In this chapter, we will consider the scope of poverty and homelessness in Canada and the demographic composition of these populations. Using the Health Canada determinants of health as a framework, we will examine the effects of poverty and homelessness on the health of Canadians and the role of community health nurses (CHNs) who work with these populations.

POVERTY

One difficulty inherent in discussing poverty is the fact that we have no universally accepted definition of poverty. "The measurement of a societal condition (such as poverty) is a fundamental prerequisite to taking corrective policy action. Moreover, it seems that in modern societies, unless a societal condition has some statistical visibility, it is deemed not to exist" (Ross, Scott, & Smith, 2000, p. 38). Ross, Scott, and Smith suggest that at least eight working definitions of poverty are available for Canadian researchers. Four are most commonly used by policy makers; of these, three are government developed.

The "**basic needs**" approach defines **poverty** as lacking food, clothing, and shelter plus other necessities "required to maintain long-term physical well being" (Sarlo, 1996 p. 25). The author of a basic needs measure arbitrarily determines the basic necessities and costs them out. Those who cannot afford these items are, by definition, poor. The **market basket measure** (MBM), created by Human Resources Development Canada, is similar except that the contents of measure include a non-defined category of essentials in addition to food, clothing, and shelter. Thus the MBM looks at needs beyond purely physical needs. In both measures, the reference family includes two adults and two children. Inferences for other family configurations must be drawn by the users of the measure.

The **low-income cut-off measure** (LICO) and **low-income measure** (LIM) are based on family income rather than family costs. The better known of these two measures, the LICO is based on the premise that the average Canadian family spends half its income on food, clothing, and shelter. Researchers at Statistics Canada therefore concluded that any family that had to spend more than 70% of its income on those three items would have little disposable income to spend on other things such as transportation. The LICO measure identifies those persons in Canada who "are substantially worse off than the average" (Fellegi, 1997, p. 2). Although Statistics Canada denies that this is a measure of poverty (Fellegi), it is a commonly used measure to describe that segment of our population that is worst off in economic terms, which some policymakers believe to be synonymous with poverty. "The implication of LICO is the view that poverty has a relative definition rather than an absolute one" (Ross, Scott, & Smith, 2000, p. 16). The LIM is an alternative measure also developed by Statistics Canada. It is based directly on income and is calculated based on what a single person requires, with the assumption that food, clothing, and shelter should account for 50% of the median income for one person. Other family configurations are considered, and the LIM stratifies between adult and child members of a family. LIM rates were last calculated by Statistics Canada in 1997 (Ross, Scott, & Smith).

One of the advantages of the LICO is that it reflects the community of residence and the composition of the family. Table 20.1 illustrates the 2001 LICO levels. This measure assumes that it takes more income to live in a larger centre and to support a larger family. Families with lower incomes than those in Table 20.1 are considered to live in poverty.

The LICO provides a unique view of poverty in Canada by looking at the issue from the local level and then comparing the incomes with those in other centres. Economic growth is not equally divided among the constituents of a country. As the economy grows and communities prosper, the numbers living in poverty also grow, although at different rates. Between 1990 and 1995, metropolitan areas grew by 6.9% overall, while there was a 33.8% increase in the poor population (Lee, 2000).

When you examine Table 20.1 further, you will notice that people who live in small towns need less income to survive than those in bigger centres. Also, people can have working income and still be considered poor. Both Lee (2000) and Ross, Scott, and Smith (2000) note a movement of poverty (as defined by LICOs) into working (middle income) households. Several factors contribute to this movement:

- Recent tax policies have shifted the burden of federal and provincial income taxes onto lower income workers.
- A second tax is the consumption tax, such as the sales tax. The required outlay for basic necessities takes a larger percentage of the poor family's income, thus, they bear a higher burden from consumption taxes.
- Wages, including low-income wages, have only been increasing at or below the rate of inflation.

Thus, relative income is stagnant across all but the higher incomes.

Lee (2000) used data from the 1995 Canada Census to examine many factors that place persons at risk for living in poverty. He found that both youth and elderly were over-represented in poverty populations, and women had higher poverty rates than men in almost every age category. A child's economic status reflects the family income; therefore, childhood poverty is considered family poverty. Lee noted that the type of family a child lives in has a bearing on the risk of poverty—single-parent households had the highest poverty rates. The high poverty rate of youth aged 15–24 may be a reflection of leaving home and decreased educational preparation (or the youth have part-time jobs or short-term employment supplemented by other family income during the post-secondary education years). When examining poverty rates of the elderly, Lee noted that 25% of urban elderly live in poverty despite government income security programs. Aboriginal Canadians living in urban centres were two times more likely to live in poverty than non-Aboriginals. Recent immigrants (in Canada less than ten years) were another population with a high risk of living in poverty, even though they are more likely to have a university degree than Canadian-born citizens. Persons who are members of a visible minority or who have disabilities were also at high risk (Lee, p. 27–44).

Lee (2000) also examined regional differences in the urban poor in Canada. He found that "poverty rates were higher in metropolitan areas than in other urban or rural areas in 1995" (p. 8). Using 1995 census statistics for cities of over 500 000 population, Lee found Montreal to have the most persons living in poverty, as well as the highest poverty rate. Vancouver and Winnipeg had the next highest rates of poverty, while Toronto had the second highest number of poor people. For centres under 500 000 population, communities in Atlantic Canada and Quebec were more likely to have higher poverty rates than other parts of the country. Cape Breton had the highest incidence of poor persons. While some of the numbers may change with the 2000 census, it is clear that Canada is not winning the war on poverty.

HOMELESSNESS

As with poverty, the definitions of homelessness are many and varied. Murphy (2000) chose to define **homelessness** in its

TABLE 20.1
Low-Income Cut-Offs (LICOs), 2001

	Population of Community of Residence				
Family Size	500 000+	100 000–499 999	30 000–99 999	Less than 30 000	Rural
1	$18 841	$16 160	$16 048	$14 933	$13 021
2	$23 551	$20 200	$20 060	$18 666	$16 275
3	$29 290	$25 123	$24 948	$23 214	$20 242
4	$35 455	$30 411	$30 200	$28 101	$24 502
5	$39 633	$33 995	$33 758	$31 412	$27 390
6	$43 811	$37 579	$37 317	$34 722	$30 278
7+	$47 988	$41 163	$40 875	$38 033	$33 166

Source: Canadian Council on Social Development. (2002). Retrieved December 21, 2003 from www.ccsd.ca/factsheets/fs_lic01.htm. *Reprinted with permission.*

narrowest and most limiting terms, which is, "those using emergency shelters and those sleeping in the street" (p. 12). In contrast, the Niagara District Health Council (1997, p. i–ii) identified four categories of homelessness:

- episodic (moves often, has periods of no housing),
- situational (absence of housing due to significant life event such as violence, illness, fire),
- seasonal (able to find housing during winter or other inclement weather), and
- absolute (lives on the street or in shelters for the majority of any given time).

Stearman (1999, p. 5) chose four other categories to describe this population:

- inadequate or inferior housing (lack of basic facilities),
- insecure housing (squatters in buildings or refugee camps),
- houselessness (people who use shelters, institutions, or other short-term accommodation like hotels), and
- rooflessness (living and sleeping outdoors).

Once a definition of homelessness has been chosen, the next step is to ascertain how many people fall into that category. However, this presents significant difficulties. The data are incomplete because most population descriptions are a snapshot of time, and many methodologies are based on the ability to contact the population in order to survey them. In other words, telephone surveys and census surveys assume a fixed address and/or telephone number. Thus the episodic, situational, and seasonal homeless may well be absent in any given counting and the absolute homeless, unless they happen to be in a shelter during census time, may be completely missed. Given these difficulties, it is not surprising that agencies like Statistics Canada are unable or unwilling to publish complete statistics on Canada's homeless population. At best, they can suggest inferences from other data. For example, B.C. Housing (2003) states that it processed an average of 485 new housing applications each month during the fiscal year 2001–2002. Eighty-five percent of those applications were from the Lower Mainland. The agency also provided housing subsidies to "more than 82 000 families, seniors, and individuals with disabilities" during the same year and stated that "as of December 31, 2002, there were 11 380 households on B.C. Housing's applicant registry" (B.C. Housing, p. 1). Of these, the majority (62%) were families. While those numbers are disturbing, they do not include people who have not applied, and the large applicant pool indicates that a significant portion of the population is underserved.

Murphy (2000) contends that this inability to be precise is a grave difficulty because "overestimating (the number of homeless) invites public cynicism, [and] underestimating incurs the wrath of service agencies that rely on public funding" (p. 11). She acknowledges that counting people in shelters misses "Canadians whose incomes force them to live in substandard housing with constant fear of eviction if their meagre incomes should temporarily disappear. Nor does it address the growing number of poor who must spend up to 70% of their incomes on rent, leaving very little for food, nor those doubling up in accommodations" (p. 12–13). She notes that some studies have estimated that for every person in a shelter on a given night, there are 1–2 persons living on the street on the same night. Still, using the narrow definition of "those using emergency shelters and those living on the street" (p. 12), Murphy estimates that 35 000 to 40 000 Canadians are absolutely homeless on any given night.

But what does being homeless really mean? Is it more than not having a roof over one's head? Murray (1990) used Tognoli's (1987) framework to examine the concept of homefullness in light of the homeless population. Tognoli (p. 657–665) suggested that the following aspects are missing in the life of the homeless person:

- centrality, rootedness, and place attachments;
- continuity, unity, and order;
- privacy, refuge, security, and ownership;
- self-identity and gender differences;
- home as a context of social and family relations; and
- home as a sociocultural context.

It is clear that the homeless are missing much more than a roof. Rather, many of the connections in their life that link them to mainstream society are decreased or absent.

Golden, Currie, Greaves, and Latimer (1999, p. v) summarized the causes of homelessness, including

- increased poverty,
- lack of affordable housing,
- deinstitutionalization and lack of discharge planning, and
- social factors.

Morrell-Bellai, Goering, and Boydell (2000) used qualitative methodology to examine how and why persons become and/or remain homeless. They found that both macro (poverty, unemployment, or poor employment) as well as individual (mental health issues, childhood abuse, and/or substance abuse) vulnerabilities contributed to homelessness. Persons who were chronically homeless frequently indicated severe childhood traumas. Goering, Tolomiczenko, Sheldon, Boydell, and Wasylenki (2002) interviewed 300 unaccompanied adult users of homeless shelters. They found fewer differences than similarities between those homeless for the first time and those who had been homeless previous to the study. While they found some indications of childhood homelessness issues as a characteristic of adult homelessness, they concluded that both groups had multiple problem indicators that required immediate intervention. In most of the reports, poverty was listed as a significant factor in homelessness.

Poverty, Homelessness, and the Determinants of Health

Health Canada (2003) has identified 12 key determinants of health. In this chapter, we do not reiterate the data that have produced these determinants; rather, we discuss how poverty and homelessness affect each one.

Income and Social Status Health Canada, Statistics Canada, and the Canadian Institute of Health Information (1999) report that 73% of Canadians in the highest income group rate their health as good or excellent, compared to 47% of Canadians in the lowest income group. Seguin, Xu, Potvin, Zunzunegui, and Frolich (2003) supported that notion when they found that mothers with low incomes perceived their infants to be in poorer health than mothers with higher incomes did. Persons who perceive their health as poor may be less likely or able to overcome barriers to seeking health care.

Social Support Networks Historically, Canadians have looked out for each other. This is evident in the way our health care and social support systems have evolved. However, the poor and the homeless are less able to meet this determinant of health in several ways.

- Many of these networks are not available to them. A poor family's circle of friends and relatives may have exhausted the assistance they are able to give, putting strain on the relationships. This absence may come just at a time when the family needs the support desperately.
- Obtaining money for travel or long-distance communication to continue the relationships may be problematic. Not having a fixed address makes it very difficult to receive mail or other communication from family and friends.
- Establishing new and meaningful relationships in shelters or when frequently moving is difficult.
- Poor persons may perceive they have nothing to offer in a relationship and begin to withdraw, increasing a sense of low self-esteem.

Education and Literacy People who are poorly educated are less likely to qualify for high-paying jobs. As technology increases, literacy requirements for many jobs are increasing. Persons with undiagnosed or untreated learning disabilities are more likely to drop out of school, again decreasing the opportunities available. Even if upgrading classes are subsidized and can be reached with affordable transportation, these people may not be able to afford the simplest of supplies to go to school or the childcare required in order to attend.

Employment/Working Conditions Persons with no fixed address and little or no income have difficulty getting identification papers, applying for jobs, or maintaining employment. The jobs they do get are often transitory, hourly-wage jobs with few benefits, forcing them to choose, for instance, between going to a health professional for a personal or family health problem, and going to work.

Social Environments Poverty can be viewed as a social exclusionary factor (Health Canada, Population and Public Health Branch, Atlantic Region, 2002). Many persons who are poor and/or homeless are victims of violence or have been deinstitutionalized. Thus, social supports previously available may not be in place.

Physical Environments Housing that is affordable to the poor family and is not subsidized is frequently substandard. Further, it is more likely to be in an unsafe neighbourhood. Even if the neighbourhood is safe, it may contain more pollution than other neighbourhoods. Thus, poor children and adults are exposed to more environmental toxins and violence.

Personal Health and Coping Skills The facilities and opportunities available for basic personal hygiene, much less optimal health practices, are more difficult for the poor and the homeless populations. Votta and Manion (2003) found that homeless male youths reported more substance abuse, families that were dysfunctional, difficulties in school, legal problems, and suicide attempts than non-homeless youths. Further, these youth reported less parental support, greater depressive episodes, and increased use of disengagement as a coping style.

Healthy Child Development One of the greatest concerns with poverty and homelessness is their effect on children. In addition to the potential for food insecurity (Health Canada, Office of Nutrition Policy and Promotion, 2002), poor nutrition, poor hygiene, and increased exposure to hazards and violence, families with little or no disposable income have difficulty ensuring their children have access to activities that would enhance their development. Even reading to a child at night becomes problematic when one cannot afford books and is not allowed to take books out of the library due to the lack of fixed address, which results in the refusal of a library card. Constant moving can also interfere with normal progress through public education. Further, poor children who do not dress like other children or have the same type of school supplies may feel more ostracized and victimized by peer bullying.

Biology and Genetic Endowment Mortality rates in poorer neighbourhoods are higher than in the general population. Hwang (2000) found that the mortality rate of men using shelters in Toronto was higher than that of the general population but lower than that of men using shelters in several U.S. cities.

Genetic endowment can influence mortality in all people. However, poverty and homelessness appear to increase that influence. Poor people may delay seeking help due to their inability to pay for medication or other treatment not covered by the health care system. While biology and genetics may account for vision, hearing, and dental problems, poverty may ensure those problems remain untreated.

Health Services Access to services such as immunizations may be decreased for the poor and the homeless. When a poor or homeless person is hospitalized, assumptions may be made about the care that can be delivered after discharge—a challenge even for families with adequate income.

Gender Women generally live longer than men and experience greater incidences of depression, stress overload, and some chronic conditions. They are more likely to be the victims of family violence. As well, they are more likely to be in the lower employment categories and to head single-parent households. In fact, almost 50% of single-parent families headed by women were considered low-income in 1995 (Health Canada et al., 1999). All these factors contribute to inclusion within the populations of poverty and homelessness. When rates of physical activity are included in the equation, risk for chronic illnesses among women increases.

Culture Each person belongs to several different cultures, including ethnic, neighbourhood, work, club (e.g., the Legion), and religious. Part of belonging to any given culture is the desire to meet that culture's expectations. Poverty and homelessness may increase the barriers to meeting one's cultural tasks.

This limited discussion on the effects of poverty and homelessness on the determinants of health demonstrates that both poverty and homelessness increase the barriers to meeting the determinants and reinforces their interrelatedness. A **barrier** is anything that prevents the person or family from accomplishing a health task. Barriers may be actual (lack of address or identification, resulting in refusal of services) or perceived (belief that as a poor or homeless person I have nothing to offer a relationship). In the case of poverty and homelessness, the above discussion has identified multiple barriers to each of the determinants of health. When there is a barrier to one determinant of health, that barrier influences several other determinants as well. In the next section, we will consider specific health issues for these populations.

SPECIFIC HEALTH ISSUES OF THE HOMELESS AND POOR

Health issues of the homeless do not differ from those of the general population. Disease severity is related to a number of factors: poverty, cognitive impairment, delays in seeking treatment, non-adherence to therapy, and the adverse health effects of homelessness itself (Hwang, 2001). Adverse health effects of homelessness include, but are not limited to, skin and foot disorders, poor oral hygiene, respiratory tract infections, and hypertension (Hwang). Foot disorders, for example, can be related to improperly fitted footwear or wearing the same footwear for prolonged periods of time. Shoes are sometimes used as pillows to allow the foot to breathe. Socks also may be worn for extended periods of time. All of these factors can impact the treatment of specific foot disorders such as fungal infections, plantar warts, ulcers, and large calluses.

Diseases and conditions often seen by clinicians whose practice includes homeless individuals reflect environmental factors, lifestyle choices, and the impact of poverty on health. Hypertension, cardiovascular disease, diabetes, asthma, renal disease, mental illness, cancer, HIV infection, AIDS, sexually transmitted diseases, infant mortality, trauma caused by violence, and substance abuse are some of the conditions experienced by people who are homeless. An obvious correlation can be found between some of the diagnoses and life on the street. For example, a person sleeping on heating grates may be burned.

To find the relationships between an adverse health effect and a homeless person, the health care provider needs to assess the lifestyle of the client. Assessment should include sleeping patterns and where sleep is obtained, food, smoking, substance use, support networks, and income. A thorough assessment of the daily routine of the client is important because it may reveal the relationships. A good understanding of the determinants of health and their application is important when doing the assessment. Other relationships or the weight these relationships place on the health of the person may not be so obvious to the novice clinician.

Chronic conditions or the exacerbation of symptoms caused by acute onset can also be influenced by both internal and external barriers to health. External barriers can include fragmented health care and misconceptions, prejudice, and frustration from the health care providers (Plumb, 2000). Poor perception of health problems, competing priorities (shelter, food, safety versus accessing health care), and feelings of prejudice are some of the internal barriers (Plumb). Other barriers can also make the delivery of health care difficult for this population. Once health care is accessed, it can be fragmented if the care is gained at an ER or walk-in clinic. Care in either the ER or a walk-in clinic may be for symptom management with little opportunity to develop a long-term plan of care. If specialist care is needed, access becomes difficult without a valid health card, return phone number to confirm the appointment, and physician to consult with or develop a plan of care.

The challenge in the delivery of health care to this population revolves around clinicians' ability to reduce their own feelings of frustration and comprehend the impact that environment and lifestyle play on a person's health. Also, it is important to be aware that health conditions normally seen in housed 60-year-old people may appear in 40-year-old homeless persons due to the harsher living conditions for the homeless.

Community Health Nurses' Role

By increasing their clinical acumen within this population, CHNs learn or rather take on new roles. One role is that of an advocate through political action. Another is empowering or enabling clients to empower themselves. Cathy Crowe and Ruth Ewert are two examples of CHNs who are committed to this high-risk population. It is fitting that these two CHNs work in the Canadian city with the second highest population of poor, although there are CHNs in most major cities working with this population.

Ms Crowe advocates through strong political action for the rights of the homeless. She is noted for legal action she has brought against the Province of Ontario to increase affordable housing, to reduce the number of deaths related to homelessness, and to be accountable for its policies. The Toronto Disaster Relief Committee made these accomplishments possible through strong lobbying of the municipal, provincial, and federal governments. Ms Crowe and others formed the Toronto Disaster Relief Committee in the mid-1990s. She works closely with this Committee and a community health centre. Her strong commitment to this population has lead to the formation of the federal ministry devoted to Homelessness (Keung, 2002).

"Housing is a prerequisite for health and it is purely and simply the lack of housing that creates the ill health I see every day," Crowe noted. "... Homeless deaths are not simply about freezing to death, just as death by bullet is not the only cause of death in war" (Keung, 2002, p. 1).

Ms Crowe can also be found delivering care to the homeless, carrying the essentials in her backpack. Tent City, a homeless ad hoc city on the shore of Lake Ontario, was part of her practice. Tent City residents were evicted in the fall of 2002 after much discussion with the owners of the property and the city of Toronto.

Ms Crowe received the first-ever Woodsworth Award for Social Advocacy in recognition of her commitment to social advocacy. The award was named after Jean Woodsworth, a social advocate who fought for the universality of old-age pensions (Keung, 2002).

In contrast, Ruth Ewert works in a clinic that she developed under the auspices of the Yonge Street Mission. The Mission provides services to the homeless of downtown Toronto. Ms Ewart's clinic targets youth under the age of 25 years who are underhoused or homeless. Five afternoons a week, Ruth can be found in the clinic performing a diverse variety of tasks: drawing blood, providing counselling, or repairing the toilet. In her work with the youth, Ms Ewert is empowering the individuals to increase control over their lives by assessing their aspirations, needs, and the changes they can make to see their aspirations realized. Like Ms Crowe, Ms Ewert sees the homeless population increasing in Toronto with no increase in resources. She also advocates for this population, focusing on the subject of child protection. The first-ever Florence Nightingale Award was awarded to Ms Ewert in 2002. This is a joint award presented by the *Toronto Star* newspaper and Registered Nurses Association of Ontario.

Canadian Research Box 20.1

Canadian Housing and Mortgage Corporation. (1999). Research report: Documentation of best practices addressing homelessness. Ottawa, ON: Author. Retrieved December 20, 2003 from www.cmhc-schl.gc.ca/publications/en/rh-pr/socio/socio041e.html

Canadian Mortgage and Housing Corporation provided funds to enable a cross section of agencies across Canada that work with the homeless to document their best practice projects. Inclusion criteria for best practice projects were the involvement of homeless persons in developing solutions, empowerment of the individuals to actively pursue the goal of independence, and offering safety and security to the vulnerable (women, children, and youth). Ten projects met the inclusion criteria, each one providing a unique approach to homelessness. In Victoria, Sandy Merriman House is the result of an initiative called the Downtown Women's Project. The intended goal of the project was to train long-term unemployed women in basic carpentry. While working and gaining marketable skills, the women worked on their own personal development to assist in their reintegration into the work force. Projects in Vancouver, Calgary, Winnipeg, Toronto, Ottawa, Montreal, Quebec City, and Halifax have also been identified as having best practices. The projects are as diverse as the cities they represent.

Discussion Questions

1. You are asked to coordinate the development of a program for the homeless in your city. Would this research paper be helpful in that development?
2. Who would you approach to be on the coordinating committee, and why?

Research

Research in the area of homelessness can be difficult for a number of reasons. Not knowing who the homeless people are or where to find them is the most obvious. Other reasons may include, but are not limited to, competing priorities of the client (finding food may take precedence over participation in research), the perception that the endpoint of the research does not make a difference in the daily life of the homeless, and the inability of the researcher to find a funding agency. To overcome some of these barriers, researchers have begun to use the community participation approach to their research. Community participatory research is characterized by using community leaders in partnership with the researchers through the entire research process. That is, the community is involved from the inception, when the gap is identified, to the endpoint of writing the report and disseminating the information. Through this process the community has the opportunity to see a difference in their daily lives as a result of the research process.

Research for these populations is limited. Canadian Research Box 20.1 describes a report of various studies. The highest priority for research is the long-term effects of poverty and homelessness on children since these children are our future. Another high-priority issue is delivery of health care to these populations. As well, Canada must look "upstream" to alleviate the root causes of poverty and homelessness.

SUMMARY

In this chapter we have explored the definitions and scope of poverty and homelessness in Canada. Recognition of the difficulty in defining and describing these populations separately or together has informed the process. Using the determinants of health as a framework, we have explored the effect of poverty and homelessness on the determinants. Specific health issues for these populations and the CHN's role were explored.

The CHN is the health care provider who may have first access to poor or homeless persons through community outreach activities. By initiating communication and making a determined effort to understand their world, the CHN may be able to establish a trusting relationship that enables the nurse and the client to co-create a higher level of health.

CASE STUDY

You are working in a drop-in clinic. A 17-year-old male comes to the clinic with complaints of generalized malaise. Medical history is unremarkable. Current history includes weight loss (10 kilograms), headaches, loss of appetite, difficulty sleeping, night sweats, and cough. He denies alcohol or illicit drug use but smokes about 10 cigarettes per day. Sexually active, he admits to only female partners and uses a condom. He lives in a shelter when beds are available and, if not, on the street. He was born in Costa Rica and came to Canada four years ago without his family. He has not finished high school, speaks in broken English, and works intermittently.

As part of the visit, an HIV serology is drawn, a tuberculin skin test is planted, and other blood work is completed, including hemoglobin, white count with differential, glucose, electrolytes, and VDRL.

He returns three weeks later.

Discussion Questions

1. Identify the determinants of health and explain their effect on attainment of optimum health for this young man.
2. By returning to the clinic three weeks later, what opportunities has he missed?
3. The HIV result is positive. Explain the difficulty in referring this individual to an expert.

KEY TERMS

basic needs
poverty
market basket measure
low-income cut-off measure
low-income measure
homelessness
barrier

INDIVIDUAL CRITICAL THINKING EXERCISES

1. In 1990, the Canadian Public Health Association described the advocacy role of public health nursing as one of helping the socially disadvantaged to become aware of issues relevant to their health and promoting the development of resources that will result in "equal access to health and health-related services." As a nurse working in the community, how would you develop a plan of care for a person living in a shelter? Use the above statement as a guide, paying close attention to accessing health care services.
2. Consider how many times a day you are asked for some form of identification. What activities would you be unable to perform if you did not have this identification? How might this affect your health and health care?

GROUP CRITICAL THINKING EXERCISES

1. "... There is evidence that homeless children have more health problems, more hospitalizations, and more developmental problems than poor children who have never been homeless" (Egan, 2002). Using the determinants of health as your guide in the discussion, comment on this quotation and discuss its validity.
2. "The working poor live on a precipice that can tumble them into homelessness at any time. An illness or an unexpected layoff brings missed paycheques, which leads to skipped utility or rent payments, which snowballs into penalties, which ends in shutoffs or evictions" (Plumb, 2000). Discuss how a CHN would interact with a person in this situation. Consider advocacy measures and possible research questions that would assist this high-risk clientele.

REFERENCES

BC Housing. (2003). *Housing facts.* Retrieved December 11, 2003 from **www.bchousing.org/Research_and_Publications/Housing_Facts.asp**

Canadian Council on Social Development. (2002). *2001 poverty lines.* Ottawa, ON: Author.

Egan, J. (2002 March 24). To be young and homeless. *The New York Times.*

Fellegi, I. P. (1997). *On poverty and low income.* Ottawa, ON: Statistics Canada. Retrieved October 15, 2003 from **www.statcan.ca/english/research/13F0027XIE/13F0027XIE.htm**

Goering, P., Tolomiczenko, G., Sheldon, T., Boydell, K., & Wasylenki, D. (2002). Characteristics of persons who are homeless for the first time. *Psychiatric Services, 53*(11), 1472–1474.

Golden, A., Currie, W. H., Greaves, E., & Latimer, E. J. (1999). *Taking responsibility for homelessness: An action plan for Toronto.* Toronto, ON: Toronto, Mayor's Homelessness Action Task Force.

Health Canada. (2003). *What determines health?* Ottawa, ON: Author. Retrieved October 17, 2003 from **www.hc-sc.gc.cq/hppb/phdd/determinants/index.html**

Health Canada, Statistics Canada, & Canadian Institute of Health Information. (1999). *A statistical report on the health of Canadians.* Ottawa, ON: Authors. Retrieved October 16, 2003 from **www.hc-sc.gc.ca/hppb/phdd/report/stat/index.html**

Health Canada, Office of Nutrition Policy and Promotion. (2002). *Discussion paper on household and individual food insecurity.* Ottawa, ON: Author. Retrieved October 15, 2003 from **www.hc-sc.gc.ca/hpfb-dgpsa/onpp-bppn/food_security_entire_05_e.html**

Health Canada, Population and Public Health Branch, Atlantic Region. (2002). *Poverty as social and economic exclusion.* Halifax, NS: Author. Retrieved October 15, 2003 from **www.hc-sc.gc.ca/hppb/regions/atlantic/work/e_c_1.html**

Hwang, S. W. (2000). Mortality among men using homeless shelters in Toronto, Ontario. *JAMA: Journal of the American Medical Association, 283*(16), 2152–2157.

Hwang, S. W. (2001). Homelessness and health. *Canadian Medical Association Journal, 164*(2), 229–233.

Keung, N. (2002). *Cathy Crowe: Toronto's street nurse.* Retrieved October 20, 2003 from **www.ottawainnercityministries.ca/newsArticlesStats/Cathy_Crowe.htm**

Lee, K. (2000). *Urban poverty in Canada: A statistical profile.* Ottawa, ON: Canadian Council on Social Development.

Morrell-Bellai, T., Goering, P. N., & Boydell, K. M. (2000). Becoming and remaining homeless: A qualitative investigation. *Issues in Mental Health Nursing, 21*(6), 581–604.

Murphy, B. (2000). *On the street: How we created homelessness.* Winnipeg, MB: J. G. Shillingford.

Murray, A. (1990). Homelessness: The people. In G. Fallis & A. Murray (Eds.), *Housing the homeless and poor: New partnerships among the private, public and third sectors.* Toronto, ON: University of Toronto Press.

Niagara District Health Council. (1997). *Report on homelessness in Niagara.* Fonthill, ON: Author.

Plumb, J. D. (2000). Homelessness: Reducing health disparities. *Canadian Medical Association Journal, 163*(2), 172.

Ross, D. P., Scott, K. J., & Smith, P. J. (2000). *The Canadian fact book on poverty.* Ottawa, ON: Canadian Council on Social Development.

Sarlo, C. (1996). *Poverty in Canada* (2nd ed.). Vancouver, BC: Fraser Institute.

Seguin, L., Xu, Q., Potvin, L., Zunzunegui, M., & Frolich, K. (2003). Effects of low income on infant health. *Canadian Medical Association Journal, 168*(12), 1533–1538.

Stearman, K. (1999). *Homelessness.* Austin, TX: Raintree Steck-Vaughn.

Tognoli, J. (1987). Residential environments. In D. Stokols & I. Altman (Eds.), *Handbook of environmental psychology.* New York: Wiley Interscience.

Votta, E., & Manion, I. G. (2003). Factors in the psychological adjustment of homeless adolescent males: The role of coping style. *Journal of the American Academy of Child & Adolescent Psychiatry, 42*(7), 778–785.

ADDITIONAL RESOURCES

Beavis, M. A., Klos, N., Carter, T., & Douchant, C. (1997). *Literature review: Aboriginal peoples and homelessness.* Ottawa, ON: Canada Mortgage and Housing Corporation **www.cmhc-schl.gc.ca/en/imquaf/ho/abpeho_001.cfm**

Cameron, S., & Clarke, P. (1997). *Poverty: A student learning resource.* Vancouver, BC: BC Teachers' Federation **www.bctf.bc.ca/lessonaids/online/la2030.html**

Campaign 2000. (2002). *The UN special session on children: Putting promises into action: A report on a decade of child and family poverty in Canada.* **www.campaign2000.ca/rc/unsscMAY02/MAY02statusreport.pdf**

Canadian Public Health Association. (1997). *Position paper on homelessness and health.* **www.cpha.ca/english/policy/pstatem/homeles/page1.htm**

Edmonton, Homelessness.ca: **www.edmonton-homelessness.ca/index.asp**

Kappel Ramji Consulting Group. (2002). *Common occurrence: The impact of homelessness on women's health: Phase 2, community based action research: Final report: Executive summary.* Toronto, ON: Sistering: A Woman's Place & Toronto Community Care Access Centre **www.sistering.org/issues.html#Anchor-COMMO-369**

Strathdee, S. A., Patrick, D. M., Archibald, C. P., Ofner, M., Craib, K. J. P., Cornelisse, P. G. A. et al. (1996). *Social determinants predict needle-sharing behaviour among injection drug users in Vancouver* **http://cfeweb.hivnet.ubc.ca/vanguard/PAPERS/XI96VIDUS.html**

About the Authors

Patricia Malloy, BSN (Northeastern), MSN (Northeastern), is a Clinical Nurse Specialist/Nurse Practitioner in the Infectious Diseases division at The Hospital for Sick Children. Ms. Malloy's clinical area focuses on tuberculosis in children and children living in homeless or underhoused situations. Ms. Malloy is currently involved in a research project that focuses on the management of homeless/underhoused youth who abuse substances and have mental illness. She has developed, with other experts, the Canadian Nurses' Association handbook on hepatitis C. She has also developed an intake sheet for patients seen in the tuberculosis clinic. Ms Malloy is cross-appointed to the Faculty of Nursing at the University of Toronto.

Lynnette Leeseberg Stamler, RN, PhD, is an Associate Professor and Director of the Nipissing University/Canadore College Collaborative BScN Program. She completed her BSN at St. Olaf College, Minnesota, her MEd at the University of Manitoba, and her PhD in nursing at the University of Cincinnati. Her research interests include patient/health education, breast health, diabetes education, and nursing education. She was a VON nurse for four years prior to her career in nursing education. She has been active in research and professional nursing organizations as well as Sigma Theta Tau International, the Nursing Honor Society.

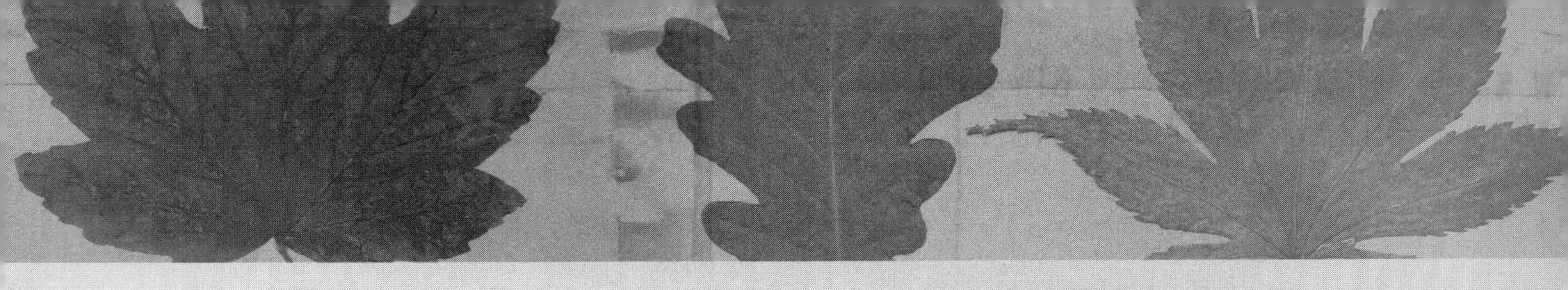

CHAPTER 21

Sexually Transmitted Infections and Blood Borne Pathogens

Janet L. Wayne and
Janet B. Hettler

OBJECTIVES

AFTER STUDYING THIS CHAPTER, YOU SHOULD BE ABLE TO:

1. Review different sexually transmitted infections and the issues surrounding their transmission, testing, treatment, and prevention.
2. Identify the public health issues for special populations surrounding STI/HIV.
3. Recognize the potential impact of STI/HIV by reflecting on the current trends, on rising statistics in Canada (Canadian population surveys), and on the issues raised in the research literature.
4. Identify different ways to use the population health promotion model when developing STI/HIV health promotion and prevention strategies.
5. Describe innovative interventions that have been successful in different areas of Canada.

INTRODUCTION

Traceable back to early times, sexually transmitted infections (STIs) are a significant public health issue. Through the centuries, people with STIs have been stigmatized. This stigma often impedes individuals from seeking testing and treatment. Blood borne viruses such as human immunodeficiency virus (HIV)/acquired immune deficiency syndrome (AIDS) and hepatitis B are often associated with chronic illness or death. This has prompted a societal reaction of intolerance and fear, further marginalizing groups who may already have poor access to health services. CHNs are challenged with promoting healthy behaviour among the general population, but especially with marginalized populations. In this chapter, we discuss the categories of STIs and historical and current challenges regarding policy and prevention. Implications for CHNs working with marginalized populations are discussed. Trends in research are reviewed, and suggestions of how to address STI issues by using the PHP Model are presented. Lastly, examples of innovative programs are provided.

HISTORY OF SEXUALLY TRANSMITTED INFECTIONS AND EFFECT ON HEALTH POLICY

Over the years, STIs have been labelled in different ways, such as **venereal disease (VD)** and **sexually transmitted disease (STD)**. The most recent term used is STI. Prior to the discovery of antibiotics, these infections were not treatable and serious illness was common. Policies were implemented to test men and women for syphilis before marriage and to test women during pregnancy to prevent neonatal infection.

With the advent of antibiotic treatment, new policies were developed. For example, over 100 years ago, silver nitrate eye drops were mandatory for all newborns to prevent blindness from gonorrhea. However, this treatment became controversial when parents expressed concerns about how it decreased neonates' ability to see immediately postpartum, which hampered infant bonding. The policy was revised so less irritating antibiotic eye drops were administered. Recently in some provinces, universal prenatal HIV-testing policies were developed to detect HIV early and offer the pregnant mother antiretroviral drugs to prevent the infant from developing HIV.

Health policies have also been developed in response to community action. For example, the infection of people with HIV through blood transfusions in the late 1980s prompted a national reaction to implement strict blood bank surveillance guidelines. Sexual health policies need to be constantly revisited and updated to assist in protecting the public from the consequences of STI/HIV.

THE SEXUALLY TRANSMITTED INFECTIONS

STIs can be categorized as bacterial, viral, or ectoparasitic infections. Some viral diseases such as HIV and hepatitis B are found in the blood and are spread through contact with infected blood and body fluids, one of those ways being unprotected sex. The following is a summary of the most common STIs in Canada.

Bacterial STIs

The main **bacterial STIs** are chlamydia, gonorrhea, and syphilis. Chlamydia is the most prevalent STI in young adults in Canada. Bacterial STIs are transmitted by unprotected vaginal, anal, or oral sexual activity and from mother to newborn during delivery. Syphilis is also spread by touching infected chancres and during pregnancy.

Symptoms for chlamydia or gonorrhea may include unusual discharge from the penis or vagina and burning or pain when urinating. A sore throat may indicate infection from oral sex, and anal discharge and bloody stools may indicate infection through anal sex. Many women have no symptoms and remain infected for an extended period until a prudent health practitioner does an STI test during an annual physical or the woman experiences pelvic inflammatory disease (PID). Women with PID may experience severe pelvic pain and painful intercourse, and are at high risk for infertility. The signs and symptoms of syphilis are often overlooked because in the early stages it manifests as painless sores with flu-like symptoms. Diagnosis is often delayed until later stages when there is already extensive damage to the central nervous or cardiovascular system, resulting in complications such as paralysis or mental illness.

Many people avoid having STI testing due to the misapprehension of inevitable pain and embarrassment. Fortunately, urine testing for chlamydia is now available. People may also have penile or vaginal/cervical swabs taken to test for chlamydia and gonorrhea. Syphilis is diagnosed through blood tests and clinical symptoms such as chancres and rash. Because most CHNs have never seen syphilis in their careers, the chancres are often misdiagnosed as other conditions such as herpes. Since syphilis infection is re-surfacing in major cities like Vancouver, Toronto, and Calgary, CHNs will have to re-establish their diagnostic abilities. Bacterial infections are relatively simple to treat with antibiotics if they are diagnosed early.

Viral Blood Borne Pathogens

Viral STIs such as HIV and hepatitis B need special consideration as they are not solely transmitted by sexual activity. Transmission can also occur by reusing needles or drug equipment (e.g., spoons) that have traces of infected blood from activities such as tattooing and piercing. HIV can be transmitted through breast milk and from mother to unborn baby. Furthermore, sharing razors or toothbrushes with an infected person can spread hepatitis B.

Many people live with HIV and hepatitis B for many years with no symptoms. Even with treatment, HIV will eventually progress into AIDS. Primary HIV symptoms occur three to six weeks after infection, and 50–70% of people experience flu-like symptoms such as sore throat, fatigue, fever, and nausea. Seroconversion occurs three to six months after infection when the body makes antibodies that become detectable through blood tests. The symptomatic phase occurs when the HIV weakens the immune system and the body exhibits long-term symptoms such as swollen lymph nodes, night sweats, fever, and diarrhea. AIDS is diagnosed when multiple opportunistic infections occur, such as pneumonia, lymphomas, and fungal infections.

The symptoms of hepatitis B often occur 45 to 60 days after exposure and may include fever, nausea, weight loss, yellowing of the skin or whites of the eyes, and joint swelling or pain. Most people infected with hepatitis B recover, but some people become chronic carriers. Most carriers have no symptoms but can infect others and may develop cirrhosis or liver cancer later in life.

HIV and hepatitis B are diagnosed through special blood tests. There is a window period of three months during which HIV antibodies may remain undetectable, requiring the client to return for follow-up testing. Pre- and post-test counselling by CHNs is very important because they can engage the clients, prepare them for the potential impact of test results, and raise awareness of harm-reduction practices such as condom use. Some provinces are thoughtlessly foregoing pre- and post-testing counselling as they believe it is time consuming and not cost effective.

Unfortunately, there is no cure for HIV infection or hepatitis, but there is treatment. A variety of antiretroviral drugs are now available that delay the progression of HIV infection to AIDS. Combination antiviral drugs are available for chronic hepatitis B carriers.

Other Viral Infections Genital herpes and human papilloma virus (HPV) are prevalent among sexually active people. These viruses are easy to spread, more difficult to prevent and detect, and non-traceable. Herpes and HPV are transmitted through vaginal, oral, or anal sexual activity but mostly through skin-to-skin sexual contact. Herpes can also be spread from mother to baby through childbirth and can cause serious complications and possible death of the neonate if it is an initial outbreak.

Many people with herpes and HPV have no symptoms. Herpes often appears as one or a group of painful, itchy, fluid-filled blisters in or around the genitals, buttocks, or thighs. People may experience burning during urination, fever, flu-like symptoms, and swollen glands. After being infected with genital herpes, some people experience only one herpes outbreak while others can have an outbreak every month or so.

There are over 80 strains of HPV. Some cause genital warts while others cause abnormal cell growth on the cervix, which may lead to cervical cancer if untreated. A person can have more than one type of HPV. While cervical abnormalities are typically not noticed, genital warts appear as groups of cauliflower-like growths in the genital area.

Herpes is diagnosed through clinical examination or a culture of the fluid drawn from a sore. There are two types of herpes: type 1 (most commonly found on the mouth) and type 2 (most commonly found on the genitals). Both type 1 and 2 are now being found on the genitals and/or mouth due to the increased occurrence of oral sex. HPV is diagnosed through clinical examination and special testing to visualize the genital warts. Abnormal cervical changes resulting from HPV are only detected through a Pap smear.

There is no cure for herpes or HPV. Herpes outbreaks can be managed through intensive and/or preventive doses of antiviral medication and lifestyle changes, including diet and stress management. Freezing, burning, or laser therapies are used to treat genital warts. Abnormal cervical changes may be monitored by repeat Pap smears, or the client may be referred to the colposcopy clinic for more intensive treatment.

Ectoparasites

Ectoparasites include pubic lice (crabs) and scabies, both of which can be transmitted through sexual activity or direct skin-to-skin contact. Pubic lice are most commonly found in the genital area. The hatched nit and adult louse are dark grey to red-brown in colour.

Scabies are parasites that burrow under the skin, leaving a red track or bumps that cause symptoms of irritation and itchiness. Scabies can be found on any part of the body, preferring warm moist places such as the genital area.

Both conditions can be diagnosed through clinical examination and treated with over-the-counter products such as NIX, Kwellada, and RC. A client should consult with a physician or pharmacist as these products can cause genital irritation.

Vaginal Infections

Vaginal infections include bacterial vaginosis, candidiasis, and trichomoniasis. Not all these infections are transmitted sexually, but they are included in the category of STIs. For more information on these conditions, please refer to the STD guidelines (Health Canada, 1998).

IMPLICATIONS OF SEXUALLY TRANSMITTED INFECTIONS

Health professionals are slowly becoming aware of the large number of people living with incurable, non-traceable STIs such as herpes. Reportable STIs, such as chlamydia and HIV, provide the CHN with an idea of the extent of the problem. If STIs remain inadequately addressed and treated, they can lead to mental health issues, ongoing spread of the disease, infertility, neonatal complications, and more severe health concerns such as pelvic inflammatory disease or even death (Health Canada, 2002b). All STIs have potential implications for a person's relationships, mental health, and coping abilities. STIs have economic implications due to the medical costs associated with medication and with treating the medical complications, such as neonatal infection and infertility, along with social costs such as loss of work productivity.

CHNs are attempting to address not only the medical issues such as treatment, but also the social and economic issues. For example, CHNs must raise awareness in the workplace and community to increase the funding for HIV medication, research, and alternative employment during times of intense treatment. Other groups in Canada are working with clients living with HIV or herpes who wish to pursue loving, sexual relationships with an understanding partner.

Trends and Research

HIV rates remain high among injection drug users, yet the focus is shifting back to increasing rates in heterosexual women, men who have sex with men (MSM), and Aboriginals. According to Health Canada (2002a), in the first half of 2002, 40% of adult HIV infection reported in Canada arose primarily from MSM. In the same time period, females constituted 26.0%, more than double the 11.4% reported before 1996. The social, cultural, and gender issues surrounding these populations are very diverse and require different, innovative health promotion approaches.

Between 1997 and 1998, the number of chlamydia cases increased, with males increasing by 27% and females by 10% (Health Canada, 2000). Women and men aged 15 to 24 appear to be the highest risk group for chlamydia, as well as for HPV and HIV.

To further complicate matters, researchers are starting to investigate the complex relationship between STI and HIV. To date, what is known about "STI and HIV synergy" is that STI and HIV infections often coexist: having an STI likely increases the ease of transmission of HIV and the susceptibility to infection. If one can take precautions to prevent STIs, HIV infection could be reduced (Health Canada, 2000). The statistics are likely higher as STIs and HIV are under-reported—many Canadians do not go for testing or are unaware they are infected.

Prevention

Accurate and consistent use of latex or polyurethane **male condoms** or polyurethane **female condoms** is important to decrease the transmission of STIs. However, condoms may not be 100% effective to protect against herpes or genital warts on the testicles or labia. Abstinence from all types of sexual activity is the only 100% effective method of preventing STIs. Infection by blood borne pathogens, such as HIV and hepatitis B, is prevented by condom use and by using clean needles and equipment for tattooing, piercing, and injecting drugs. Condoms and/or dental dams should always be used for oral sex. Many provinces have committed to the eventual eradication of hepatitis B by investing in hepatitis B vaccination programs for children in Grade 5.

The Canadian health goals (Health Canada, 1997) encourage health professionals to target three main behaviours that contribute to STIs: number of partners, age of first intercourse, and condom use. Presently, condom use is the primary target. Health Canada (1997) encourages health professionals to expand their focus to include age; gender; socioeconomic status; ethnicity; presence, type, and persistence of symptoms; and sex education that normalizes STIs as a concern for *all* sexually active people instead of certain "types of people" who are defined as "high risk."

Interventions such as sexual health education are important, but, to have an impact, they must be timely and relevant to the target population (Hamilton & Bhatti, 1996). It is vital to find innovative ways to promote the use of male condoms, female condoms, and dental dams. CHNs must think upstream and use health promotion approaches that address the issues of their target population. CHNs can reach individuals through street outreach, counselling, and peer mentoring programs. Furthermore, CHNs can explore innovative ways to make these harm reduction measures appealing to groups or communities through poster and media campaigns. CHNs can work with other sectors and multidisciplinary groups to develop healthy public policy to address STI issues. Offering chlamydia urine testing in outreach vans and putting condom machines in schools are examples of healthy public policies.

HIV/AIDS research has identified that many clients who are unwilling or unable to prevent the spread of HIV present with one or more of the following issues (Avants, Warburton, & Margolin, 2001; Carey, Carey, Maisto, Gordon, & Vanable, 2001; John Hopkins AIDS Service, 2002; Semple, Patterson, & Grant, 2000):

- psychiatric deficits (e.g., depression, fetal alcohol syndrome),
- addictions,
- social deficits (e.g., lack of support and housing, involvement in the sex trade), and
- health deficits (e.g., lack of HIV knowledge, deteriorating health).

Researchers believe that the above variables contribute to higher-risk activities (e.g., having sex without a condom) and can impede a person's efficacy at implementing harm-reduction practices.

Canadian researchers, policy analysts, and health activists are initiating discussions on the legal implications and issues facing people who are unable to prevent the spread HIV (Culver, unpublished; Friesen, Paquin, & Smith, 2002; Ontario Advisory Committee on HIV/AIDS, 2002). Health authorities across Canada are addressing this issue in different ways, ranging from implementing comprehensive referral systems to providing comprehensive housing and treatment.

Special Populations

The following is not an exhaustive discussion of all the hard-to-reach or marginalized populations in Canada. However, it is meant to raise awareness of some special groups.

Men Who Have Sex with Men MSM populations in Canada have the highest incidence of HIV/AIDS (Health Canada, 2002a). Through health promotion and education efforts, condom use is being reinforced with this population. A Montreal study investigating cohorts of MSM found that 50% of MSM who reported recent sex with regular partners used a condom on every sexual encounter (Dufour et al., 2000). This is significant because 270–360 potential HIV infections could occur each year in the MSM population in Montreal (Dufour et al.).

New generations of MSM youth claim that prevention efforts are overused and tediously boring. Many are having unprotected sex regardless of the risk; this phenomenon is called **safer sex fatigue** (Canadian Public Health Association & Canadian HIV/AIDS Information Centre, 2001). The younger generations have not witnessed many of their friends dying of AIDS and believe the new advances in AIDS medication will result in longer life.

Even though health education messages addressing condom use are constantly being reinforced, some cohorts of MSM are still not reached with traditional prevention messages. The harm-reduction approach serves to limit the vulnerability of people who engage in high-risk behaviour and improve their health and well-being by increasing access to appropriate education, housing, mental health services, and other supports (Canadian AIDS Society, 2002). CHNs must find innovative ways to implement harm-reduction strategies to address safer sex fatigue.

Sex-Trade Workers, People in the Correctional System, and Injection Drug Users Both sex-trade workers and people in Canadian jails are at risk of contracting STI/HIV because of the barriers to accessing services and harm-reduction resources. Sex-trade workers often report the use of condoms with their customers ("Johns") but not in their private relationships (Maticka-Tyndale, Lewis, Clark, Zubrick, & Young, 1999). Lack of condom use in their private relationships may be due to unequal power, as many boyfriends/pimps do not allow condoms. This places the sex-trade worker at increased risk for contracting STI/HIV. For some, the unequal power relationship extends to their work when "Johns" either refuse to use condoms or offer a higher payback for "condomless" sex.

There is a high rate of HIV infection among injection drug users in Canadian correctional facilities (Calzavara et al., 1995). Most federal jails offer confidential HIV testing, counselling, condoms, lubricants, and HIV education; however, bleaching kits or clean needles/syringes are not offered (Calzavara et al.). The challenge in prisons is providing effective and acceptable programs that do not breach jail regulations. Provincial prison standards vary, and some do not offer any services other than testing and education.

Intravenous drug users living in the community represent a growing concern for CHNs as the craving for "another hit" overrides the importance of using a clean needle to prevent the transmission of HIV or hepatitis B. Some injection drug users may take years to receive appropriate treatment that addresses their addiction issues. Offering better access to condoms and clean needles/drug equipment in jails and the community may help these populations prevent contracting HIV while they search for effective treatment.

New Immigrants Language, culture, socio-economic factors, and education level may deter immigrant populations from seeking medical treatment (Hislop et al., 2003). This includes STI/HIV testing, education, and counselling. New immigrants are overwhelmed with adapting to new culture, language, rules, and health care practices. Many come from countries where HIV, hepatitis, and other STIs are more prevalent and treatment is inaccessible. Many provinces lack

Canadian Research Box 21.1

Maticka-Tyndale, E., Lewis, J., Clark, J. P., Zubrick, J., & Young, S. (1999). Social and cultural vulnerability to sexually transmitted infection: The work of exotic dancers. *Canadian Journal of Public Health, 90*(1), 19–22.

The researchers (non-nurse) in this study examined the social and cultural factors influencing the vulnerability of exotic dancers to STIs. They used qualitative exploratory methods and conducted in-depth interviews with 30 female dancers from 10 clubs in Southern Ontario. The bars and dancers were selected using non-probability purposive sampling. Field teams of two to four people spent 2–3 hours diagramming club layouts and observing the work and interactions of dancers, customers, and other club staff. The interviews were conducted in locations chosen by the dancers and lasted 1–4 hours. Topics of discussion included demographic characteristics, occupational history, work, work environment, interpersonal and sexual relationships, sexual history, substance use, home and leisure, and health concerns.

The results indicated that the social and cultural context in which exotic dancing takes place contributes to sexual harassment and sexual assault. These women are pressured by their economic situations and customers to engage in paid sexual activity. The researchers concluded that the risk of STIs could be reduced amongst exotic dancers if the social and cultural context was altered. CHNs can work with strip club employers to develop policies to decrease the risks of assault and harassment, for example, dancing only in public areas of the club and enforcing "no touch" rules.

Discussion Questions

1. How could a CHN involve strip club employers and employees to develop strategies to decrease STIs among exotic dancers?
2. What determinants of health could be influenced to improve the health of exotic dancers?

services and resources that are translated, culturally sensitive, and accessible to newcomers. Cultural beliefs also often influence a person's motivation to access health services. Some may have learned that HIV is not life threatening and treatment is unnecessary. Others may try a variety of herbs or culturally accepted medications before seeking medical treatment for an STI. Many health centres are developing diversity programs to help address some of these issues.

Planning Interventions with the Population Health Promotion (PHP) Model

The PHP model (Hamilton & Bhatti, 1996) provides a comprehensive tool for CHNs to utilize when planning STI interventions with individuals, groups, and populations. Refer to Chapter 8 for more information on the PHP model.

Innovative Interventions in Canada

Novel and innovative strategies are being implemented across Canada to lower the rates of STIs.

Needle Exchange Programs and Safe-Injection Facilities

Injection drug use is a mounting public health concern in Canada. Individuals who inject drugs pose a number of potential health risks to themselves and others, such as HIV/AIDS and hepatitis B and C (Elliott, Malkin, & Gold, 2002). Some Canadian communities have addressed the drug issue with needle exchange programs, which provide injection drug users with free sterile injecting equipment to reduce their risk of infection. Even though needle exchange programs are controversial, they are widely accepted as a means to control disease (Elliott, Malkin, & Gold). They have helped minimize the harm of blood borne diseases and have provided the opportunity for education.

CASE STUDY

A fictitious community called Realville has a large population of people living with HIV in the community. These people face extraordinary life circumstances that affect their ability to prevent the spread of HIV to others. Several CHNs work in a lower-income sector of the city with immigrant women living with HIV. The CHNs understand, through the research and talking with their clients, that services are lacking for immigrant women with HIV.

Using the PHP model, the CHNs focus on the health determinants of health services and culture. They collaborate with a group of representatives from health, social services, and business sectors to discuss the lack of services for this group. The group conducts an evaluation to determine if there are any gaps in health services for immigrant women in the city. They work together to apply for and secure sustained funding to develop adequate support groups, outreach services, and appropriate treatment services staffed by professionals and peer mentors who are aware of the cultural issues. Culturally appropriate HIV teaching is conducted with these groups to address cultural barriers to accessing and using condoms. This type of intervention uses the comprehensive action strategy of reorienting health services at the sector level.

Discussion Questions

1. Considering population health promotion, what determinants of health should the CHNs be aware of when working with people who live with HIV in extraordinary life circumstances?
2. What strategies can the CHNs and community agencies implement to address the issues of these clients?
3. How can clients be involved in the development of these strategies?

PHOTO 21.1 Calgary Poster

Credit: Calgary Coalition on HIV/AIDS, Prevention and Education Working Group.

Some Canadian cities, such as Vancouver, Montreal, and Toronto, are currently establishing trial safe-injection facilities. These facilities provide a place for drug users to inject their drugs with clean equipment under the supervision of medically trained professionals. But safe-injection facilities are highly controversial. According to Elliott, Malkin, and Gold (2002), concern arises about sending out the "wrong message" that injection drug use is acceptable. However, they suggest that countries such as Australia, Switzerland, Germany, and The Netherlands have shown success in implementing pragmatic, practical, and effective harm-reduction strategies through government operated injection facilities. In other words, the total number of drug users has decreased. These facilities are for people who are entrenched drug users rather than casual or new users. They are intended to reduce fatal overdoses and the spread of blood borne diseases and to refer clients for education, treatment, and rehabilitation. Safe-injection sites are an innovative public health intervention. Nevertheless, they remain controversial in Canada, and, to date, no evaluation studies have been done.

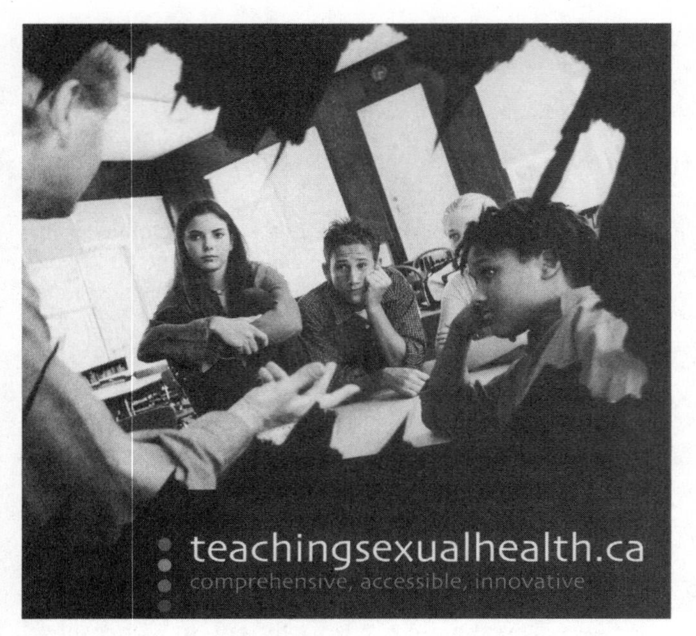

PHOTO 21.2 Website that Promotes Sexual Health

Credit: teachingsexualhealth.ca

Social Marketing Campaigns Poster campaigns in Canada are becoming more innovative, providing more blatant and, at times, provocative messages to different target populations. For example, in 1999, the Calgary Coalition on HIV and AIDS developed a poster to target young adult men and women regarding HIV and STIs. Focus groups were conducted with the target population to ensure that the messages and images were appropriate and impactful. The poster shown in Photo 21.1 was distributed to bars and western venues during the Calgary Stampede, which attracts over a million people. Although the poster produced initial controversy, it was discussed on city radio, in newspapers, and on national television. Controversial media coverage is sometimes an effective approach to promoting harm-reduction messages.

Similarly, the AIDS Committee of Toronto launched a Condom Country campaign targeting gay and bisexual men. Although the campaign encountered some controversy, it provided important information to the target population and has been used across Canada.

Internet Another innovative approach to disseminate STI prevention information is through websites. One example, www.teachingsexualhealth.ca (Photo 21.2), was developed to provide accurate, relevant, community-focused resources for teachers, parents, and students. Health and education administrators, CHNs, and teachers formed a committee, secured funding for the website, and were involved in the planning and development of the website content. The website was based on a theoretical framework, which integrates three well-known models: comprehensive school health, resilience theory, and social learning theory. The website provides teachers with hints on teaching while considering diversity issues, such as ethnicity, or gender issues in the learning environment.

SUMMARY

This chapter has addressed the various STIs that are common in Canada. The history of STIs in Canada and how they have affected healthy public policy were briefly discussed. Marginalized populations present unique challenges and should receive special consideration from CHNs planning action strategies with the PHP model. Research, trends, and other innovative programs were offered as a guide for future public health initiatives. The PHP model provides a strong guide when planning STI promotion and prevention programs in communities.

KEY TERMS

venereal disease (VD)
sexually transmitted disease (STD)
bacterial STIs
viral STIs
male condoms
female condoms
safer sex fatigue

INDIVIDUAL CRITICAL THINKING EXERCISES

1. The rate of HIV infection in pregnant women is rising. Some of the women being diagnosed with HIV are new immigrants. Transmission to the neonate can be reduced from 25% to 8% through the use of antiretroviral drugs during the first trimester, during labour and delivery, and when given orally to the infant for six weeks (Health Canada, 1998). Many women lack the information, support, and income to follow through with treatment regimens, as well as buying infant formula and condoms. How can CHNs work with pregnant immigrant women living with HIV to increase adherence to medication and use of harm-reduction strategies?
2. STI rates are increasing in males 15–24 years old. Health Canada (1997) states that testing and education are important to prevent STIs. Unfortunately, many youth at risk for STIs leave school early and become street involved, thus missing the benefit of sexual health education courses. Examine clinics in your area that offer STI testing and treatment. What determinants of health could be addressed by this sexual health agency to address the issues of street-involved male youth?

GROUP CRITICAL THINKING EXERCISES

1. Gay youth often face rejection from significant support systems such as family and friends when they "come out." Some youth quit school and leave home to live on the street. Some rely on panhandling and prostitution to support themselves and pay for drugs that help them cope. Their high-risk activities and a lack of resources for these youth increase their risk for STIs. How can an STI clinic nurse focus on the determinants of health to care for these individuals and direct them to resources that will assist them in becoming healthier in the future?
2. To address the complications associated with STIs, healthy public policy has been initiated and developed by policymakers and health professionals, but with little input from the public. Refer to the history section in this chapter. How can CHNs use public participation to inform the development of healthy public policy?

REFERENCES

Avants, S. K., Warburton, L., & Margolin, A. (2001). How injection drug users coped with testing HIV-seropositive: Implications for subsequent health-related behaviors. *AIDS Education & Prevention, 13*(3), 207–218.

Calzavera, L. M., Major, C., Myers, T., Schlossberg, J., Millson, M., Wallace, J. et al. (1995). The prevalence of HIV-1 infection among inmates in Ontario, Canada. *Canadian Journal of Public Health, 86*(5), 335–339.

Canadian AIDS Society. (2002). *Health is a human right.* A brief prepared for the Commission on the Future of Health Care in Canada. Retrieved June 18, 2003 from **www.cdnaids.ca/web/backgrnd.nsf/24157c30539cee20852566360044448c/09ebf6326db72c8d85256bf1005fa435?OpenDocument**

Canadian Public Health Association, & Canadian HIV/AIDS Information Centre. (2001). *A discussion of safer sex fatigue.* Ottawa, ON: Author.

Carey, M. P., Carey, K. B., Maisto, S. A., Gordon, C. M., & Vanable, P. A. (2001). Prevalence and correlates of sexual activity and HIV-related risk behavior among psychiatric outpatients. *Journal of Consulting & Clinical Psychology, 69*(5), 846–850.

Culver, K. A. (unpublished). *Concise policy guide to persons unwilling or unable to prevent HIV transmission: A legislative analysis and literature review. Federal/Provincial/Territorial Advisory Committee on AIDS.* Ottawa, ON: Health Canada.

Dufour, A., Alary, M., Otis, R., Remis, B., Turmel, B., Vincelett, J. et al. (2000). Risk behaviours and HIV infection among men having sexual relations with men: Baseline characteristics of participants in the Omega cohort study, Montreal, Quebec, Canada. *Canadian Journal of Public Health, 91*(5), 345–349.

Elliott, R., Malkin, I., & Gold, J. (2002). *Establishing safe injection facilities in Canada: Legal and ethical issues.* Ottawa, ON: Canadian HIV/AIDS Legal Network.

Friesen, B., Paquin, M. J., & Smith, L. A. (2002). *Guide for public health practitioners in Alberta for persons living with a communicable disease who are unwilling or unable to protect themselves and others.* Calgary, AB: Calgary Health Region. Draft.

Hamilton, N., & Bhatti, T. (1996). *Population health promotion: An integrated model of population health and health promotion.* Ottawa, ON: Health Canada, Health Promotion Development Division. Retrieved December 17, 2003 from **www.hc-sc.gc.ca/hppb/healthpromotiondevelopment/pube/php/php.htm**

Health Canada. (2002a). *HIV and AIDS in Canada: Surveillance report to June 30, 2002.* Ottawa, ON: Health Canada, Division of HIV/AIDS Epidemiology and

Surveillance. Retrieved December 20, 2003 from **www.hc-sc.gc.ca/pphb-dgspsp/publicat/aids-sida/haic-vsac0602/index.html**

Health Canada. (2002b). *STD Epi update.* Ottawa, ON: Health Canada, Centre for Infectious Diseases Prevention and Control. Retrieved May 28, 2003 from **www.hc-sc.gc.ca/pphb-dgspsp/publicat/epiu-aepi/std-mts/condom_e.html**

Health Canada. (2000). *1998/1999 Canadian sexually transmitted diseases (STD) surveillance report: Volume 26S6.* Retrieved December 20, 2003 from **www.hc-sc.gc.ca/pphb-dgspsp/publicat/ccdr-rmtc/00vol26/26s6/26s6b_e.html**

Health Canada. (1998). *Canadian STD guidelines.* Ottawa, ON: Author.

Health Canada. (1997). *National goals for the prevention and control of sexually transmitted diseases in Canada: Volume 23S6.* Retrieved May 20, 2003 from **www.hc-sc.gc.ca/pphb-dgspsp/publicat/ccdr-rmtc/97vol23/23s6nat/index.html**

Hislop, T. G., Deschamps, M., The, C., Jackson, C., Tu, S.-P., Yasui, Y. et al. (2003). Facilitators and barriers to cervical cancer screening among Chinese Canadian women. *Canadian Journal of Public Health, 94*(1), 68–73.

Johns Hopkins AIDS Service. (2002). Challenges and barriers to implementation of HIV prevention efforts. Retrieved March 18, 2003 from **www.hopkins-aids.edu/prevention/prevention6.html**

Maticka-Tyndale, E., Lewis, J., Clark, J. P., Zubrick, J., & Young, S. (1999). Social and cultural vulnerability to sexually transmitted infection: The work of exotic dancers. *Canadian Journal of Public Health, 90*(1), 19–22.

Ontario Advisory Committee on HIV/AIDS. (2002). *Reducing HIV transmission by people with HIV who are unwilling or unable to take appropriate precautions: An update.* Toronto, ON: Author.

Semple, S., Patterson, T., & Grant, I. (2000). Psychosocial predictors of unprotected anal intercourse in a sample of HIV positive gay men who volunteer for a sexual risk reduction intervention. *AIDS Education & Prevention, 12*(5), 416–430.

ADDITIONAL RESOURCES

WEBSITES

Canadian AIDS Society:
www.cdnaids.ca

Canadian Health Network. *Sexuality/reproductive health:* **www.canadian-health-network.ca/1sexuality_reproductive_health.html**

Canadian HIV/AIDS Information Centre:
www.clearinghouse.cpha.ca/

Canadian HIV/AIDS Legal Network:
www.aidslaw.ca

Health Canada, Sexual and Reproductive Health Promotion:
www.hc-sc.gc.ca/hppb/srh/

Health Canada, Division of HIV/AIDS Epidemiology and Surveillance:
www.hc-sc.gc.ca/pphb-dgspsp/hast-vsmt/index.html

Health Canada, Population and Public Health Branch. *Canadian STD guidelines:*
www.hc-sc.gc.ca/pphb-dgspsp/publicat/std-mts98/index.html

Planned Parenthood Federation of Canada (see "Beyond the Basics" under Resources and Links):
www.ppfc.ca/home.html

Sex Information and Education Council of Canada:
www.sieccan.org

Sexualityandu.ca:
www.sexualityandu.ca

Teaching Sexual Health Website:
www.teachingsexualhealth.ca

About the Authors

Janet L. Wayne, BScN (University of Alberta), MN (University of Calgary), is currently the Communicable Disease Consultant for the Calgary Health Region. Janet has worked in the area of sexual and reproductive health for over a decade. She has spearheaded and managed a number of large, innovative health promotion and telehealth projects involving community and cross-ministry partners, most recently teachingsexualhealth.ca. Janet has presented these sexual health projects at different conferences across Canada and to university classes in Calgary. Most recently, she taught a Lifespan Sexual Heath Promotion course to a group of multidisciplinary students at the University of Calgary.

Janet B. Hettler, DipN (Kelsey Institute of Applied Arts and Sciences, Saskatoon), BScN (University of Saskatchewan, Saskatoon), MN (University of Calgary), has worked in public health since 1981, initially as a public health nurse in rural Alberta. She has worked in the area of sexual and reproductive health since 1988, first in a rural health unit outside Calgary then with the Calgary Health Region as a Sexual and Reproductive Health Clinical Nurse Specialist. In 2001, she became a Public Health Clinical Nurse Specialist on an interdisciplinary pilot project, "Public Health Services for Children in Government Care," working with marginalized children and their families.

CHAPTER 22

Substance Abuse

Hélène Philbin Wilkinson

OBJECTIVES

AFTER STUDYING THIS CHAPTER, YOU SHOULD BE ABLE TO:

1. Understand and discuss the reasons why people use psychoactive substances.
2. Identify the differences between substance use and abuse, and understand the concept of dependency.
3. Describe the scope of substance use and abuse in Canada.
4. Discuss socio-demographic factors that are commonly associated with substance abuse patterns.
5. Explain the harms associated with substance abuse.
6. Articulate the components of effective substance abuse strategies.
7. Understand and begin to apply the concepts of health promotion, harm reduction, and resiliency theory.
8. Articulate your own values and attitudes toward substance abuse.

INTRODUCTION

Substance abuse is a complex public health issue that can have severe and permanent consequences for individuals, families, and communities. Substance abuse (including alcohol, tobacco, and illicit drugs) was estimated to cost Canadians more than $18.45 billion in 1992 (Single, Robson, Xie, & Rehm, 1996). It is also associated with high rates of diseases and other lifestyle-related causes of death and injury. For example, in 1995 in Canada, substance abuse accounted for 20% of all deaths (through cancer, cardiac and pulmonary disease, as well as overdoses, motor vehicle accidents, and death by fire), 22% of years of potential life lost, and more than 9% of hospitalizations (Single, Rehm, Robson, & Van Truong, 2000.). There are also considerable non-monetary costs to Canadian society, such as the pain, suffering, and bereavement experienced by families, friends, and victims, which can have profound and lasting effects that cannot be measured in dollars.

Just as substance abuse causes poor health, poor health and other socioeconomic disadvantages can contribute to substance abuse (Single, 1999). This socio-environmental perspective has guided the development of holistic substance abuse strategies that recognize the interrelationships between the person, the substance, and the environment. This chapter is intended to introduce the community health nurse (CHN) to the practice of developing comprehensive community-based responses to substance abuse. It is also intended to stimulate further discussion and research about a multifaceted public health issue that you will undoubtedly encounter at some point in your career.

WHY DO PEOPLE USE DRUGS?

People use different drugs for different reasons, and the reasons vary from drug to drug, from person to person, and from circumstance to circumstance. While certain psychoactive drugs may be prescribed to relieve anxiety, tension, stress, or insomnia, some people may self-medicate to improve performance or to resolve physical or emotional discomfort. The mere availability of a drug may cause individuals to be curious enough to experiment. The danger, however, is that experimental use may lead to other reasons for using, which may in turn result in abuse and/or dependence.

Other people may take drugs to boost their self-confidence or to forget about or cope with traumatic life events or situations. Immediate gratification from drugs may make people feel good and/or can quickly reduce or eliminate uncomfortable emotions, albeit temporarily. Social pressures to use drugs can be very strong for both young people and adults. However, children are especially vulnerable as they may imitate and interpret their parents' use as a necessary part of having fun or relaxing. Young people may use drugs to rebel against unhappy situations or because they feel alienated, have an identity crisis, or need to be accepted by their peers. The media is also considered a powerful source of influence. Ads often promote drinking or smoking as a social activity or as a factor in the achievement of success.

TERMINOLOGY

The term **drug** refers to a **psychoactive substance** that affects a person's physiological or psychological state or behaviour. In this chapter, drugs will be referred to as substances consumed for medicinal and non-medicinal purposes, legally or illegally, and will be used interchangeably with the term psychoactive substances.

Most people don't think of **alcohol** as a drug but it is. Ethyl alcohol is present in beer, wine, spirits, and liqueurs, and methyl alcohol is found in solvents, paint removers, antifreeze, and other household and industrial products. At low doses, alcohol acts as a central nervous system depressant, producing relaxation and a release of inhibitions. At higher doses, it can produce intoxication, impaired judgment and coordination, even coma and death.

Tobacco leaves, which are shredded and dried, can be smoked in cigarettes, cigars, or pipes or be chewed or inhaled. More than 4000 chemicals are found in tobacco, including nicotine, the main psychoactive component that stimulates the central nervous system.

Illicit drugs (illegal drugs) include cannabis (marijuana and hashish), phencyclidines (PCP, ketamine), hallucinogens (LSD, mescaline, psilocybin, MDA), stimulants other than caffeine and nicotine (amphetamines, cocaine, crack), depressants (barbiturates, methaqualone, benzodiazepine), and opiates (heroin, morphine, methadone, codeine). **Inhalants**, also known as volatile solvents, are depressant drugs that produce feelings of euphoria, exhilaration, and vivid fantasies. Their use can cause brain damage, asphyxiation, and death. Using inhalants such as gasoline or certain illicit drugs such as PCP can cause immediate and serious problems regardless of how or when they are taken.

Licit drugs (legal drugs) that are used for medicinal purposes are legally available by prescription or sold over the counter and include drugs to relieve pain, control anxiety, or combat insomnia. Licit drugs used for non-medicinal purposes include alcohol and tobacco, either of which can be legally purchased and used by those who are of legal age.

Substance use refers to any consumption of psychoactive drugs, which can result in benefits or harm. **Substance abuse** or misuse refers to drug use that leads to adverse physical or psychological consequences, which may or may not involve **dependence**. Drug dependency is progressive in nature and affects the physiological, cognitive, behavioural, and psychological dimensions of a person's health. It is manifested by continuous use despite the presence of problems that are caused by the pattern of repeated self-administration that results in tolerance, withdrawal, and compulsive substance-taking behaviour (American Psychiatric Association, 1994). Dependence can be physical and/or psychological. **Physical dependence** occurs when an individual's body reacts to the absence of a drug, and **psychological dependence** occurs when drug use becomes central to a person's thoughts and emotions. You may wish to consult your psychiatric nursing text to further explore this topic.

FIGURE 22.1 Use of Alcohol, Tobacco, and Illicit Drugs, Age 15 Years+, Canada, 1994

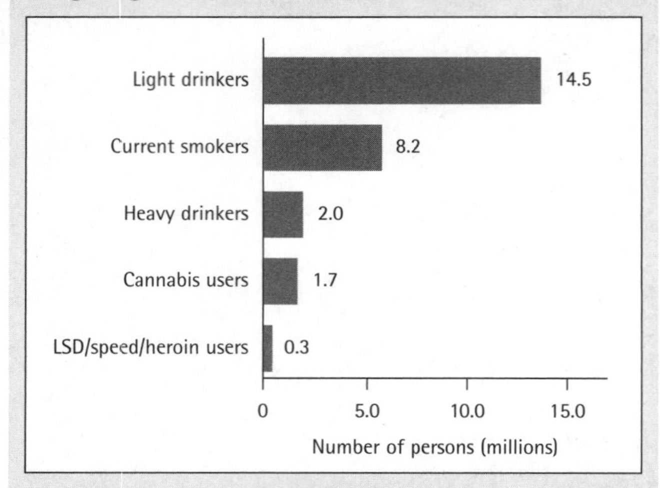

Source: Federal, Provincial, and Territorial Advisory Committee on Population Health. (1999). Statistical report on the health of Canadians. *Ottawa, ON: Author. Reproduced with the permission of the Minister of Public Works and Government Services Canada, 2003.*

THE SCOPE OF SUBSTANCE USE AND ABUSE IN CANADA

Approximately 20 million people in Canada consume psychoactive substances (see Figure 22.1). Despite the fact that overall rates of use have decreased among Canada's general population, the abuse of tobacco and alcohol continue to be leading causes of preventable death and illness (Federal, Provincial, and Territorial Advisory Committee on Population Health [FPTACPH], 1999).

Prevalence patterns of substance use and abuse are influenced by both individual and socio-demographic factors such as age, gender, education, changes in lifestyles, attitudes, and beliefs. For example, researchers have found that men are more likely than women to report alcohol and other drug use, and that use tends to decline with increasing age (Adlaf & Ialomiteanu, 2002). The additional resources at the end of this chapter provide further details about the differences in consumption patterns across Canada and the individual, social, geographical, and historical factors that can influence the use and abuse of substances.

Tobacco

Health Canada (1999) estimates that smoking prematurely kills three times more Canadians than car crashes, suicides, drug abuse, murder, and AIDS combined, and that it accounts for approximately one in six deaths in Canada. Smoking rates continue to be highest among males and young people, but the gender gap is narrowing as young adolescent females are now more likely to smoke than their male peers. Smoking also appears to be strongly related to employment, income, and education: the higher the education and income levels, the lower the percentage of smoking (FPTACPH, 1999).

Alcohol

Approximately 12.7 million Canadians are regular drinkers. Overall, men tend to drink twice as much as women, and high rates of consumption appear more prevalent among Aboriginal

Canadian Research Box 22.1

Chalmers, K., Sequire, M., & Brown, J. (2002). Tobacco use and baccalaureate nursing students: A study of their attitudes and personal behaviours. *Journal of Advanced Nursing, 40*(1), 17–24.

The researchers in this study explored the potential influence nurses can have on shaping public policy and influencing the behaviours of individuals and groups regarding the use of tobacco. A cross-sectional survey was administered to the total population of baccalaureate nursing students in the province of Manitoba. Respondents completed a self-administered questionnaire that included questions about their own smoking, stages of behavioural change, and personal beliefs and attitudes about tobacco. Instruments included the Fagerström Nicotine Tolerance Scale (a tool that assesses the level of nicotine addiction), the Beliefs and Attitudes Questionnaire (a measure that assesses women's beliefs and attitudes toward smoking), and the Health Promotion Lifestyle Profile (a tool that measures health promotion attitudes and behaviours). Data from a total of 272 responses out of 439 were analyzed using both descriptive and analytic procedures.

Approximately 22% of the respondents indicated that they smoked daily or in social situations. Although they demonstrated a low level of nicotine dependence, few were found to be actively involved in smoking cessation. Comparing non-smokers with smokers revealed other interesting findings. Non-smokers reported more health promoting behaviours, including physical activity, nutrition, and stress management. The comparison also revealed that the smokers are less likely to agree that laws prohibiting smoking in public areas are needed to protect the health of communities and that non-smokers considered the role of internal motivation and external supports more important than their smoking counterparts did. The authors concluded that smoking prevention, protection, and cessation strategies can be influenced by nurses' personal attitudes, beliefs, and behaviours. The findings reinforce the importance of addressing these issues in nursing curricula.

Discussion Questions

1. The findings in this study support previously reported research about smokers being less supportive of smoking by-laws. How might you use these findings to support a smoke-free policy or by-law in your workplace or community?
2. How do these findings support or refute what you have observed in your own nursing student cohort?

Canadians, street youth, people who are unemployed, and people who have lower status jobs (FPTACPH, 1999).

Significant social problems caused by the misuse of alcohol in our country include driving under the influence of alcohol and domestic and interpersonal violence. Although impaired driving rates have dropped over the last couple of decades, the largest number of alcohol-related deaths stem from impaired driving accidents, many of which involve young people (Single, Rehm, Robson, & Van Truong, 2000). Canadian researchers report that women whose partners drink heavily are at much higher risk of being assaulted than women whose partners never drink. And women who experience abuse report a more frequent use of substances such as sleeping pills and sedatives than women who have not been abused (Health Canada, National Clearinghouse on Family Violence, 1993).

Illicit Drugs

Cannabis is the most widely used illicit drug in Canada. Other commonly used illicit drugs include LSD, speed, heroin, and cocaine. Although the overall consumption of illicit drugs is relatively low compared with that of alcohol and tobacco, research reports indicate that one-quarter of Canadians use an illicit substance at least once in their lifetime, and approximately 1.7 million Canadians over the age of 15 years use marijuana. Illicit drug use is more common among males and young people, especially among street youth (FPTACPH, 1999).

The prevalence of drug-related disorders in Canada is approximately 82 per 100 000 population (Single, MacLennan, & MacNeil, 1994). Tragically, suicides account for almost half of illicit drug–related deaths. Although mortality resulting from illicit drug use is lower than from alcohol and tobacco, illicit drug–related deaths tend to involve younger people (Single, Robson, Rehm, & Xie, 1999).

Approximately 7% of Canadians use at least one **injectable drug** (cocaine/crack, LSD, amphetamines, heroin, or steroids), and two out of five of these individuals share needles, a known risk for the transmission of HIV, hepatitis B, and other blood borne pathogens (FPTACPH, 1999). AIDS acquired through the use of illicit drugs accounts for approximately 8% of deaths related to the use of illicit drugs.

As for inhalants, fewer than 1% of Canadians use solvents or glue, but children and youth are the highest users (MacNeil & Webster, 1997). For example, some studies involving inmates of detention centres reveal that inhalants were the first drugs ever used by this group. They are often the primary drug used by Aboriginal children under the age of 12 (Single, MacLennan, & MacNeil, 1994). Aboriginal youth appear to have a greater lifetime prevalence of substance abuse, with the rate of solvent use significantly higher than that of the general population (Scott, 1992).

Licit Drugs

Approximately 21% of Canadians use, appropriately and inappropriately, one or more licit drugs, including over-the-counter and prescription pain pills, sleeping pills, tranquilizers, antidepressants, and diet pills. Of the prescription drugs, narcotic pain relievers (e.g., codeine, Demerol, morphine) are the group most commonly used by Canadians, particularly women and people between the ages of 25 and 34 (Single, MacLennan, & MacNeil, 1994). Females also use more tranquilizers, antidepressants, and sleeping pills, and the elderly have the highest use of sleeping pills and antidepressants (MacNeil & Webster, 1997). Of particular concern is the use of medications among older persons since the aging process is frequently accompanied by an increase in chronic or acute illness and an increase in the total number of prescribed drugs.

HARMFUL CONSEQUENCES OF SUBSTANCE ABUSE

All drugs have adverse and undesirable effects. For example, the long-term use of tobacco can cause lung damage; alcohol abuse can cause liver damage; sniffing cocaine can damage nasal passages; people who inject drugs intravenously can become infected with blood borne diseases such as HIV or hepatitis B; and exposure to second-hand smoke among neonates, infants, children, and adults is associated with an increased risk of a number of acute and chronic conditions.

People who use drugs that have been obtained illegally can never really know what they are taking. Some drugs may be laced with other substances and/or chemicals or be contaminated by fungi or moulds. The consequences can be devastating, including severe drug reactions and fatal overdoses. Other associated harms can include an increase in crime and violent acts; strained relationships; workplace and school absenteeism; and health problems such as ulcers, liver and kidney damage, pancreatic diseases, heart disease, cancer, sexual and reproductive issues, and pre- and postnatal complications.

The consumption of alcohol during pregnancy can result in **fetal alcohol syndrome** (FAS) and the less severe **fetal alcohol effect** (FAE), both of which are manifested by developmental, neurological, and behavioural delays in infants and young children. Though the major cause of these conditions is the frequency and volume of an expectant mother's alcohol intake, other contributing factors to consider include genetic predisposition, poor nutrition, age, the lack of prenatal care, and the use of other drugs. Since a safe level of alcohol consumption during pregnancy or while breastfeeding has not been established, public health professionals advise expectant and breastfeeding mothers not to drink alcohol, even in moderation. Consult your maternity and pediatric nursing texts for additional information about the incidence and clinical symptoms of FAS and FAE.

The Response to Substance Abuse

Given the wide range of individual, social, and cultural factors that can influence patterns of drug use, strategies have shifted from the view that substance abuse is not merely caused by individual psychological or moral factors. This shift in perspective has stimulated the development of public health models that combine elements of primary, secondary, and tertiary prevention, which have been described and referred to in previous chapters.

The Risk Continuum The **risk continuum**, initially developed by the Ontario Ministry of Health (1988), is a conceptual framework that has been widely used to design community-based strategies that correspond to the different risks associated with the use and abuse of different substances. Composed of risk categories (see Figure 22.2), the continuum is based on the principle that the degree of risk associated with drug use is related to the amount of the substance being consumed and the conditions under which it is consumed, thus reflecting socio-behavioural and environmental approaches. Strategies are based on this premise but also reflect the nature of the substance. For example, the "low risk" category is not applicable to the use of illicit drugs and inhalants as they are considered harmful even at low doses. Similarly, the concept of "no risk" is not consistent with the use of prescription drugs because there is always some risk of side effects when taking any medication.

The risk continuum illustrates that a comprehensive community-based substance abuse strategy combines activities that are related to both health promotion and health recovery. For example, more and more communities are introducing strategies that combine treatment, prevention, law enforcement, and harm reduction. Depending on the level of risk, activities may include health enhancement, risk avoidance, risk reduction, early identification and intervention, and treatment and rehabilitation, all of which draw from the concepts of primary, secondary, and tertiary prevention.

Planning any of these strategies in the community typically consists of four fundamental steps:

- identify priority population groups;
- establish intermediate and ultimate objectives for each target population group;
- determine existing programs, services, and policies that can address these objectives; and
- identify and involve appropriate groups, agencies, and organizations.

Substance abuse is a multifaceted issue and therefore requires the collaboration of several sectors, including home, schools, workplaces, health care settings, recreational settings, enforcement and justice systems, and so on. Examples of activities that can be implemented in a few of these sectors are provided in Table 22.1.

Health Promotion

Health promotion consists of activities related to health enhancement, risk avoidance, and risk reduction. **Health**

FIGURE 22.2 The Risk Continuum

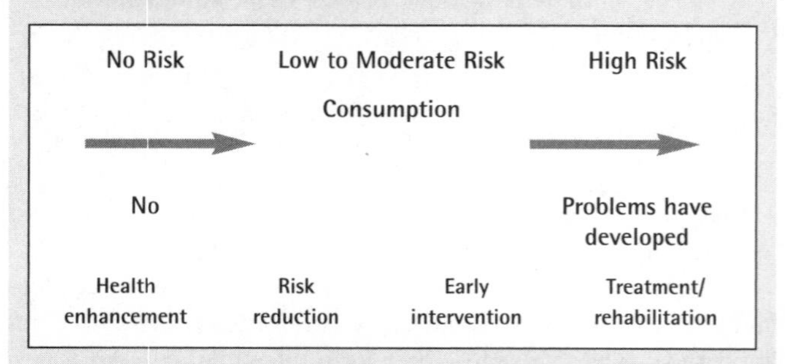

Source: Adapted with permission from Ontario, Ministry of Health. (1988). A framework for the response to alcohol and drug problems in Ontario *(p. 8). Toronto, ON: Author.*

TABLE 22.1
Examples of Substance Abuse Prevention Activities by Sector, Stakeholders, and Target Group

Sector	Stakeholders	Target Group	Activities
Home	Parents, children, local media, mass media, public health, community organizations and groups, health agencies	• Children • Youth • Parents	• Discuss substance use/abuse issues with children and youth. • Provide skill development programs for parents. • Promote educational materials. • Encourage the development of a home drinking policy. • Encourage alternative healthy activities/behaviours.
Elementary and secondary schools	School administration, public health, students, parents, teachers, guidance counsellors, physical education and health consultants, parent teacher group, community alcohol and drug consultants	• Students (K–12) • Staff • Parents • Teachers • Peer leaders	• Develop school policies on alcohol and drugs. • Encourage an integrated drug education curriculum that spans the school years. • Provide ongoing training for those delivering the drug education curriculum. • Hold special events to supplement drug education curriculum. • Organize student interest groups (e.g., students against drunk driving). • Provide early identification and intervention programs in the schools.

Source: Adapted with permission from Ontario, Ministry of Health, Health Promotion Branch. (1991). Ideas for action on alcohol. Community mobilization manual, vol. 4. *(pp. 9)*

enhancement is a strategy involving activities that are designed to increase resilience. The main focus in this strategy is to develop or enhance health rather than reduce substance use or abuse. It combines both behavioural and socio-environmental approaches. For example, abstaining from the consumption of drugs is often promoted and integrated with other healthy lifestyle choices and supported by healthy environments.

Risk avoidance, another socio-environmental approach, reinforces the adoption of low-risk consumption. It is intended to increase the likelihood that drinking (for example) will take place at a level and in a context that has a low association with health and social problems. This approach is intended to reduce drug consumption before health and social problems develop, particularly among people who find themselves in the "moderate risk" category of the continuum.

An effective substance abuse strategy combines education, and policy change and environmental support, and as they are mutually complementary and strengthen the impact of other prevention activities. Education helps people make healthy decisions and participate in health activities by increasing knowledge and motivation, changing attitudes, and increasing the skills that are required to avoid or reduce risk. These activities can consist of programs and services that impart knowledge about substances and help develop refusal skills. Policy changes are intended to create an environment that is conducive to healthy practices by making it easier to adopt healthy behaviours and more difficult to adopt unhealthy practices. Policies such as tobacco by-laws or alcohol legislation can create healthy social and physical environments. **Environmental support** helps to ensure healthy conditions, practices, and policies that make it easier for people to achieve and maintain their health. For example, the presence of recreational activities and self-help groups can provide important environmental supports for a community (Ontario Ministry of Health, Health Promotion Branch, 1991).

Health Recovery Early identification and intervention programs and treatment and rehabilitation programs are strategies designed for people who have started to experience problems related to their substance abuse. The emphasis is on the early identification of signs and symptoms in order to intervene and reduce consumption levels and effectively manage the problems that have developed. Treatment and rehabilitation (health recovery) is intended to assist people with substance abuse problems as their consumption is considered to be "high risk." These individuals should be provided with comprehensive assessments in order to match their recovery needs and their personal circumstances with the appropriate treatment services. Overall, the purpose in health recovery is to prevent further deterioration and reduce the harms that have resulted from a problematic drug-consumption pattern.

Treatment and rehabilitation services in Canada typically include detoxification services, assessment and referral, inpatient and outpatient treatment programs, and aftercare and follow-up. Additionally, special programs have been designed to address the unique needs of certain population groups such as women, youth, Aboriginal people, impaired driving offenders, and inmates of correctional institutions.

Harm Reduction and Resiliency Theory Harm reduction and resiliency theory can be powerful tools to minimize the harms associated with substance abuse. They also offer a wide spectrum of opportunities for the CHN to help strengthen the capacity of individuals and communities experiencing the adverse effects of substance abuse.

Harm reduction is a public health philosophy that has gained popularity in the last two decades; however, some claim that it is a new name for an old concept. It is described as a program or policy designed to reduce drug-related harm without requiring the cessation of drug use (Centre for Addiction and Mental Health, 2002). Examples include alcohol server training programs and impaired driving countermeasures. In the treatment field, the most pre-eminent harm reduction strategies are needle exchanges and methadone maintenance programs, both of which allow the individual to live with a certain level of dependency while minimizing risks and other disruptive effects to the person and the community. For example, in addition to clean needles and syringes, needle exchange programs provide condoms and sexual health counselling as a means of reducing the risk of spreading HIV by sexual activity (Laurie & Green, 2000). It is often said that harm reduction is not what's nice, it's what works. The focus is therefore not on the use or the extent of use, but on the harms that are associated with the use. This approach is characterized by five principles.

- Pragmatism: some level of substance use in society is inevitable, acceptable, and normal. The goal is to reduce more immediate and tangible harms rather than focus on the abstract ideal of a drug-free society.
- Harms: the primary focus is on the reduction of harmful consequences. The extent of an individual's drug use is of secondary importance.
- Prioritization of goals: there is a hierarchy of goals with immediate attention given to the most pressing needs and achievable milestones. While becoming drug free may be the ultimate goal, it is not required from the outset.
- Flexibility: initiatives are flexible and acknowledge individual differences and that goals may change.
- Autonomy: the individual's decision to use is acknowledged as a personal choice for which they take responsibility and become an active participant in managing their addiction. Reintegration into the community is emphasized over stigmatization and social exclusion.

A harm reduction message to the public is somewhat different from other types of prevention messages, for example, *avoid problems when you drink* vs. *drinking less is better* (Single, 2000). As you work through the policy exercise at the end of this chapter, you will learn that many policies, such as the promotion of low-alcohol beverages, are based on a harm reduction approach. Consequently, harm reduction stands in contrast to other models and philosophies such as abstinence-based health promotion initiatives and recovery approaches.

When harm reduction emerged as a public health strategy, it initially involved socially marginal populations such as injection drug users and correctional inmates. It may therefore provoke debate and controversy as an appropriate strategy for some communities or organizations. Consider the progress that has been made, however, since the introduction of clean needle and syringe exchange programs. Strong community stakeholder endorsement is key with this approach in order to prevent a public outcry on its appropriateness, which would inadvertently shift the focus from its intended purpose to a debate about other peripheral social issues. On the other hand, such a dialogue may be crucial given its potential to produce a shift in knowledge, attitudes, and values.

The theory of **resiliency** consists of two fundamental concepts—risk and protective factors—both of which contribute to one's sense of resiliency. Resiliency is described as the capability of individuals, families, groups, and communities to cope successfully in the face of significant adversity or risk (Mangham, McGrath, Reid, & Stewart, 1995). **Risk factors** are considered stresses that challenge individuals, including their own personal and environmental characteristics. When stresses such as substance abuse are greater than one's protective factors, even those who have been resilient in the past may become overwhelmed. **Protective factors** are skills, personality factors, and environmental supports that act as buffers when people are faced with stressful events. Individual protective factors may include literacy and interpersonal skills. Community-based protective factors may consist of shared values and strong volunteer participation.

The application of resiliency in the development of substance abuse strategies is particularly valuable as both risk and protective factors must be examined and analyzed in order to recognize the aspects of an individual's or community's health that can be enhanced or reduced. Using the framework helps

CASE STUDY

A local Junior A hockey team plays in your community's municipally owned arena. Team officials have been selling beer during home games as a means of generating revenue for the team. There have been recent and well-publicized complaints about people becoming intoxicated and creating disturbances during and after games. Community officials and private entrepreneurs are looking for the support of the local police department and your public health unit in order to effectively address this issue and prevent further disturbances. The well-attended hockey games represent the source of entertainment for many families during the long winter season. Your public health board has requested a substance abuse program to explore this issue and develop an appropriate strategy to reduce these emerging alcohol-related problems.

Discussion Questions

1. Discuss the health, social, and legal risks that are commonly associated with the practice of serving alcohol during sports events in municipally owned facilities.
2. Explore various prevention and enforcement strategies that can be adopted to minimize the risks that are associated with the service of alcohol.
3. Identify the various groups of stakeholders that should be targeted as part of these strategies.

FIGURE 22.3 Framework of Community Resilience

Community Risk Factors

Social	Environmental	Behavioural
Economic disadvantage Unemployment Educational disadvantage Cultural barriers	Isolation - geographical - social Disasters	Communal apathy Community anger Low participation in community development

+

Community Protective Factors

Social Support	Empowerment	Community Connectedness	Communal Coping
Communal support Family and friends Volunteers Lay support Community organizations	Communal responsibility and action Retraining Educational services	Shared history and culture Residents "know everyone" Schools and churches	Problem focused Emotion focused

↓

Community (Positive) Resilient Outcomes

Growth	Residents' Health	Community Tone/Outlook	Community Development
New economic and cultural initiatives	Physical health Mental health Healthy behaviours	Hope Optimism Embrace opportunities	Community participation and connectedness Organizations survive Acquire resources

Source: Health Canada (1999). A study on resilience in communities. Office of Alcohol, Drugs and Dependency Issues, Health Canada. Reproduced with the permission of the Minister of Public Works and Government Services Canada, 2003.

to identify predominant risk factors and ensure that responses are anchored in resiliency for a specific situation, as opposed to lifetime resiliency. For example, analyzing factors such as age or social isolation, which may lead to compulsive patterns of drug use, can help generate knowledge and understanding about why some individuals and communities respond differently to this kind of adversity. As illustrated in Figure 22.3, protective factors can influence outcomes, thus making it critical to capitalize on the individual's or community's strengths. The framework is especially useful because it supports the integration of other determinants of health, such as employment, and considers the linkages with a person's or a community's socio-cultural and economic environment.

SUMMARY

In this chapter, we have explored the impact that substance abuse can have on the health of individuals and communities. Three types of drug consumption, including the use and abuse of drugs, and the concept of dependency were briefly presented. The reasons why people use and abuse drugs were discussed, as well as how a maladaptive pattern of substance abuse progresses toward physical and psychological dependence.

The scope of alcohol, tobacco, and illicit and licit drug use and abuse was discussed. Socio-demographic characteristics commonly associated with certain prevalence patterns were examined because it is essential to understand that substance abuse can cause poor health, just as poor health and other social, health, and economic disadvantages can contribute to substance abuse. Although substance abuse affects many Canadians, some populations are particularly vulnerable to its effects, including women, infants and children, adolescents, street youth, and the Aboriginal population. Harms commonly associated with substance abuse were identified, including fetal alcohol syndrome, impaired driving, suicides, and interpersonal violence.

Responding to substance abuse problems in the community requires sound data, a plan grounded in theory, and strong intersectoral collaboration. The public health and substance abuse strategies presented in this chapter reflect both behavioural and socio-environmental frameworks, including health promotion, harm reduction, and the resiliency theory, all of which draw from the models of primary, secondary, and tertiary prevention. The risk continuum is an effective tool to determine strategies that appropriately correspond to the different risks associated with various levels of drug consumption. A community's substance abuse strategy should combine health promotion and health recovery activities, including education, policy, and environmental support. No single activity can be effective on its own; they are mutually complementary and strengthen the overall strategy. The theories of harm reduction and resiliency were presented, both of which can support and enhance other approaches. The application of the conceptual frameworks presented in this chapter can serve to guide the CHN in the development of comprehensive substance abuse strategies linking the individual, the drug, and the environment.

KEY TERMS

drug
psychoactive substance
alcohol
tobacco
illicit drugs
inhalants
licit drugs
substance use
substance abuse
dependence
physical dependence
psychological dependence
injectable drug
fetal alcohol syndrome
fetal alcohol effect
risk continuum
health promotion
health enhancement
risk avoidance
environmental support
harm reduction
resiliency
risk factors
protective factors

INDIVIDUAL CRITICAL THINKING EXERCISES

1. Privately explore the first thing that comes to mind when you read each of the following expressions. Then, explore your reactions to each expression. Do they differ from each other? If so, consider the reasons why. Did any of your reactions surprise you? If yes, think about how your personal values could influence your professional practice.

- Alcoholic
- Needle exchange program
- Abstinence-based treatment
- Problem drinker
- Methadone treatment
- Parent with hangover
- IV drug user
- Crack dealer
- Professor smoking marijuana
- Pregnant speed addict
- Chain (tobacco) smoker
- Female cocaine user
- Drunk driver
- Twenty-year-old buying booze for underage sibling
- Person with HIV
- Gas sniffer
- Underage drunk
- Coffee drinker

2. Read your local newspaper, a magazine, or watch the news, a television program, or a movie. Pay attention to the images and messages about the consumption of alcohol, tobacco, and illicit or licit drugs. Who are these messages aimed at? What are they portraying? Consider the degree of influence that these images have on drug consumption patterns in society.

GROUP CRITICAL THINKING EXERCISES

1. Select a particular issue or harm that is associated with substance abuse in your community (e.g., impaired driving, FAS). What sources of information (local, regional, provincial, and national) can be used to help your group accurately define the problem?
2. For the issue identified in Question 1, have your group map your community's current capacity in terms of substance abuse prevention and treatment (health promotion and health recovery) services and programs. You may use the telephone directory or contact local health and social service agencies. For example, you should highlight how people access general information about the issue and, if appropriate, where people access treatment services. Make note of any gaps your group observes.
3. Using the results of the mapping exercise in Question 2, discuss as a group the risk factors that you believe have contributed to the development of the issue or harm identified in Question 1. Additionally, your group should explore the protective factors that have acted as buffers or that will have the capacity to create positive outcomes for your target population or for the community.

REFERENCES

Adlaf, E. M, & Ialomiteanu, A. (2002). *CAMH monitor e-report: Addiction and mental health indicators among Ontario adults in 2001, and changes since 1997.* CAMH Research Doc. Series No.12. Toronto, ON: Centre for Addiction and Mental Health. Retrieved January 2, 2004 from **www.ocat.org/pdf/CAMH_report_prevalence.pdf**

American Psychiatric Association. (1994). *Diagnostic and statistical manual of mental disorders* (4th ed.). Washington, DC: Author.

Centre for Addiction and Mental Health. (2002). *CAMH position on harm reduction: A background paper on its meaning and applications for substance use issues.* Toronto, ON: Author.

Federal, Provincial, and Territorial Advisory Committee on Population Health. (1999). *Statistical report on the health of Canadians.* Ottawa, ON: Health Canada.

Health Canada. (1999). *Health Canada online-information.* Retrieved December 27, 2003 from **www.hc-sc.gc.ca/english/media/releases/1999/9907ebk6.htm**

Health Canada, National Clearinghouse on Family Violence. (1993). *Fact sheet on family violence and substance abuse.* Ottawa, ON: Author. Retrieved December 11, 2003 from **www.hc-sc.gc.ca/hppb/familyviolence/html/fvsubstance_e.html**

Laurie, M. L., & Green, K. L. (2000). Health risk and opportunities for harm reduction among injection-drug-using clients of Saskatoon's needle exchange program. *Canadian Journal of Public Health, (91)*5, 350.

MacNeil, P., & Webster, I. (1997). *Canada's alcohol and other drugs survey, 1994: A discussion of findings.* Ottawa, ON: Health Canada.

Mangham, C., McGrath, P., Reid, G., & Stewart, M. (1995). *Resiliency: Relevance to health promotion: Discussion paper.* Ottawa, ON: Health Canada.

Ontario Ministry of Health. (1988). *A framework for the response to alcohol and drug problems in Ontario.* Toronto, ON: Author.

Ontario Ministry of Health, Health Promotion Branch. (1991). *A guide for community health promotion planning.* Toronto, ON: Author.

Scott, K. A. (1992). Substance use among indigenous Canadians. In D. McKenzie (Ed.), *Aboriginal substance use: Research issues.* Ottawa, ON: Canadian Centre on Substance Abuse.

Single, E. (1999). *Substance abuse and population health: Workshop on addiction and population health. Edmonton, Alberta, June, 1999.* Ottawa, ON: Canadian Centre on Substance Abuse. Retrieved December 12, 2003, from **www.ccsa.ca/ADH/single.htm**

Single, E. (2000). *The effectiveness of harm reduction and its role in a new framework for drug policy in British Columbia.* Presentation to the National Federal/Provincial/Territorial Meeting on Injection Drug Use, Vancouver, BC. Retrieved February 23, 2003 **from www.ccsa.ca/plweb-cgi/fastweb.exe?getdoc+view1+General+505+0++different%20ap**

Single, E., MacLennan, A., & MacNeil, P. (1994). *Horizons 1994: Alcohol and other drug use in Canada.* Ottawa, ON: Health Canada, Health Promotion Directorate, & Canadian Centre on Substance Abuse.

Single, E., Rehm, J., Robson, L., & Van Truong, M. (2000). The relative risks and etiologic fractions of different causes of death and disease attributable to alcohol, tobacco and illicit drug use in Canada. *Canadian Medical Association Journal, 162*(12), 1669–1675.

Single, E., Robson, L., Rehm, J., & Xie, X. (1999). Morbidity and mortality attributable to substance abuse in Canada. *American Journal of Public Health, 89*(3), 385–390.

Single, E., Robson, L., Xie, X., & Rehm, J. (1996). *The costs of substance abuse in Canada: Highlights from a major study on the health, social and economic costs associated with the use of alcohol, tobacco and illicit drugs.* Ottawa, ON: Canadian Centre on Substance Abuse.

ADDITIONAL RESOURCES

WEBSITES

Against Drunk Driving Canada (ADD):
www.add.ca

Health Canada. (2002). *Canada's drug strategy:*
www.hc-sc.gc.ca/hecs-sesc/cds/index.htm

Canadian Centre for Substance Abuse (CCSA):
www.ccsa.ca

Canadian Community Epidemiology Network on Drug Use:
www.ccsa.ca/ccendu/

Canadian Health Network, Substance Abuse/Addictions:
www.canadian-health-network.ca/1substance_use_addictions.html

Canadian Centre for Ethics in Sport:
www.cces.ca

Canadian Foundation for Drug Policy:
www.cfdp.ca/

Canadian Centre on Substance Abuse. (2002). *Directory of FAS/FAE information and support services in Canada* (4th ed.). Ottawa, ON: Author.
www.ccsa.ca/fasis/fasindex.htm

MADD Canada Mothers Against Drunk Driving:
www.madd.ca

National Native Alcohol and Drug Abuse Program (NNADAP):
www.hc-sc.gc.ca/fnihb/cp/nnadap/index.htm

Alberta Alcohol and Drug Abuse Commission (AADAC):
www.gov.ab.ca/aadac

British Columbia Ministry of Health Services, Addictions Homepage:
www.healthservices.gov.bc.ca/addictions/

Addictions Foundation of Manitoba:
www.afm.mb.ca/

New Brunswick Department of Health and Wellness, Addiction Treatment Services:
www.gnb.ca/0051/0378/index-e.asp

Newfoundland and Labrador Department of Health and Community Services, Addictions Services:
www.gov.nf.ca/youth/ay/old%20site/drugdep2.htm

Government of the Northwest Territories, Department of Health and Social Services:
www.hlthss.gov.nt.ca/default.htm

Nova Scotia Department of Health, Addiction Services:
www.gov.ns.ca/health/

Ontario Centre for Addiction and Mental Health:
www.camh.net

Ontario Ministry of Health and Long-Term Care, Substance Abuse Bureau:
www.gov.on./health

The Substance Abuse Network of Ontario (SANO):
http://sano.camh.net/

Prince Edward Island Department of Health and Social Services, Division of Child, Family and Community Services, Addiction Services:
www.gov.pe.ca/hss/addiction/provservices.php3

Québec Ministère de la Santé et des Services Sociaux. *Alcoolisme et toxicomanie*:
www.msss.gouv.qc.ca/sujets/prob_sociaux/alcool_toxico.html

Saskatchewan Health, Community Care Branch, Alcohol and Drug Services Program Support Unit:
www.health.gov.sk.ca/ps_alcohol_and_drugs.html

Yukon Health and Social Services, Alcohol and Drug Secretariat:
www.hss.gov.yk.ca/prog/ads/index.html

INTERNATIONAL RESOURCES

University of Washington, Alcohol and Drug Abuse Institute:
http://depts.washington.edu/adai/

Alcoholics Anonymous World Services:
www.alcoholics-anonymous.org/

National Council on Alcoholism and Drug Dependence (U.S.):
www.ncadd.org

The Drug Policy Alliance (formerly the Lindesmith Center Drug Policy Foundation):
www.lindesmith.org

About the Author

Hélène Philbin Wilkinson is a senior health planner with the Northern Shores District Health Council where she oversees the addiction, mental health, and French language health services planning portfolios. After spending the early part of her career in hospital and public health, she turned to the community health setting and worked as a consultant with the Addiction Research Foundation (ARF), currently known as the Centre for Addiction and Mental Health (CAMH). In that capacity, she provided leadership in several research and evaluation projects, most of which focused on alcohol and drug policy. She was instrumental in designing "Setting a new direction: A resource guide for alcohol, tobacco and other drug policies for summer camps," which was distributed to residential summer camps across Canada. Hélène has also developed curriculum in the areas of social marketing and program evaluation and worked as a part-time instructor and mentor in nursing and health promotion certificate programs. She holds a BScN from Laurentian University, is presently completing an MN at Athabasca University, and remains keenly interested in policy planning and analysis. She lives in North Bay with her husband and their three sons and has dedicated her chapter to Dave, Jonathan, Zachary, and Paul for their unwavering support.

CHAPTER 23

Adolescent Pregnancy

Ann Malinowski

OBJECTIVES

AFTER STUDYING THIS CHAPTER, YOU SHOULD BE ABLE TO:

1. Describe why adolescent pregnancy is an important societal issue.
2. Discuss issues/factors linked to the increased risk of experiencing an adolescent pregnancy.
3. Recognize developmental aspects and consequences that have the potential to influence the outcomes of a teen pregnancy.
4. Understand the broad tenets central to successful adolescent pregnancy prevention programs.
5. Define general factors inherent in an effective adolescent pregnancy prevention program.
6. Discuss the roles of community health nurses in supporting pregnant adolescents and adolescents who are at risk for pregnancy.

INTRODUCTION

In the last two decades, the teen pregnancy rate in Canada has been declining (Wadhera & Millar, 1997). Nevertheless, in 1998, an estimated 41 588 pregnancies occurred in women aged 15–19 years. Approximately 19 700 of these ended in birth, while 20 800, roughly one-half, ended in abortion (Statistics Canada, 2001). These figures place Canada's teen pregnancy rate in the middle of 22 comparable countries. Germany, Denmark, and Sweden all reported lower rates of teen pregnancy, while England, Iceland, and Australia were slightly higher but comparable to Canada. Hungary and Belarus showed significantly higher rates, while Bulgaria and the United States topping the list (Singh & Darroch, 2000). Clearly, adolescent pregnancy is a relevant issue facing Canada today.

This chapter will provide an overview of factors central to this complex phenomenon with emphasis on aspects pertinent to the work of community health nurses (CHNs) and, particularly, their efforts to decrease the rates of teenage pregnancy and its consequences.

WHY IS ADOLESCENT PREGNANCY A SOCIETAL ISSUE?

Adolescent pregnancy refers to pregnancies occurring in young women 15 to 19 years old. DiClemente, Hansen, and Ponton (1996) proposed that some of the possible outcomes for pregnant adolescent women include:

- school failure or "dropping out,"
- welfare dependence,
- lower wages,
- higher risk of unemployment,
- greater chance of unhappiness in marriage, and
- higher incidence of repeat pregnancies.

They further noted that some negative outcomes for infants might include:

- **premature birth** (less than 37 weeks of gestation);
- **low birth weight** (less than 2500 g or 5.5 lbs);
- increased risk of **sudden infant death syndrome** (sudden death of a child, usually <2 years old, which is unexpected and fails to demonstrate an adequate cause for death at autopsy);
- higher incidence of accidents and trauma; and
- higher incidence of behavioural problems and lower academic achievement.

It may be useful to conceptualize these outcomes in terms of the **determinants of health** (Federal, Provincial, & Territorial Advisory Committee on Population Health, 1994). These determinants consist of the biological, physiological, behavioural, and environmental factors whose interaction results in health or illness. The environmental factors often include income and social status, social support networks, education, employment and working conditions, indoor and outdoor environments, genetics, personal health practices, coping skills, child development, and health services.

Within this context, school failure equates with lower education levels, which are also associated with unstable employment and working conditions, translating to lower income and social status and resulting in a poorer physical environment. Lower education levels also affect personal health practices and coping skills, as well as knowledge of healthy child development and ability to access proper health services. This sequence, in turn, has the potential to negatively influence the health of the fetus and infant and can also account for the higher incidence of accidents and trauma to children of adolescent mothers. Additionally, the possibility of lower academic achievement by the children of teen mothers will potentially continue this cycle. It is quite obvious that these adverse outcomes globally affect the potential for successful endeavours in the future (see Figure 23.1).

Who Is at Risk?

Adolescents who are sexually active are at risk for becoming teen parents. The Canadian Institute of Child Health (1994) and Statistics Canada (1994) reported that sexual activity is occurring at younger ages. Approximately 12% of young women have engaged in sexual intercourse at least once before the age of 15, and 83% of young women aged 15 to 19 report having had one sexual partner in the past year. Approximately 50% of these women did not use contraception. In light of such alarming trends, the Committee on Adolescence (1999) suggested certain predictors of initiation of sexual activity during early adolescence, including:

- early puberty,
- history of sexual abuse,
- lack of a nurturing parental relationship,
- poverty,
- cultural and family models of early sexual activity, and
- lack of educational motivations/goals.

Understanding that the biological, social, and emotional foundation is set during early childhood, a healthy start in life provides the capacity to develop a positive self-image, make healthy choices, establish satisfying relationships, and cope with life challenges, providing the foundation that forms the very base of sexual and reproductive health throughout life (Health Canada, 1999).

The characteristics associated with poor sexual choices represent several of the determinants of health. A parallel could also be drawn between these facets and the negative outcomes of teen pregnancy, the perpetuation of which creates a vicious cycle of disadvantage for all individuals involved. It is thus imperative that CHNs caring for teens become aware of these complexities and become comfortable when addressing the needs of already sexually active, but not yet pregnant, adolescents. Also, while balancing sexuality's essential importance throughout life, opportunities and supports for sexual and reproductive health must be available throughout the life cycle. Furthermore, "mature individuals evolve a flexible way of dealing with conflicts between impulse and norm, where self and others are both acknowledged and then integrated within self-chosen standards. They tend to perceive stress as having the locus of control within the self" (Speier, Melese-D'Hospital, Tschann, Moore, & Alder, 1997, p. 18). Therefore, adolescents who show immature ego development are at risk for inconsistent contraceptive use and are prime candidates for **primary prevention** activities, which are aimed at early prevention of a condition before it occurs or the reduction of the incidence of a condition.

Childhood **maltreatment**, defined as specific parental activities that result in physical, sexual, or emotional injury to the child, neglect of the child, or exposure of the child to family violence is another significant predictor of teenage pregnancy, perhaps because maltreated children often go in search of early sexual intimacy. Moreover, it seems that contact with a variety of maltreatment experiences, rather than any particular type, constitutes a risk for pregnancy (Smith, 1996). Thus, childhood abuse does not necessarily have to be of a sexual nature in order to signal pregnancy risk—psychological, emotional, and physical forms of abuse are also factors. Additionally, parenting styles have a bearing on a teen woman's risk for sexual activity and pregnancy. It appears that demanding and controlling parents, as well as neglectful and permissive parents, are not successful in passing on their values to their children. Conversely, parents who are able to discuss contraception, sexuality, and pregnancy with their children can have a positive influence in delaying sexual initiation and promoting effective birth control use (Stanhope & Lancaster, 2004).

A delay in the initiation of sexual activity and the consistent use of contraception are also recognized as important. This is especially so since although many young women start sexual relations early, they later acknowledge that they were not ready for such encounters and did not comprehend the potential risks (Rosenthal, Burklow, Lewis, Succop, & Biro, 1997). This lack of developmental readiness becomes clearer when confronted with some of the reasons cited for initiation of sexual activity. According to Rosenthal et al., these include physical attraction, romanticism, curiosity, loneliness, feeling too excited to stop, pressure from the partner, feeling grown up, and having friends who are sexually active.

Teenagers are influenced by what they see and read in the media. Sexual unions in the media are often depicted as spontaneous and emotional, initiated by a dominant man and allowed to continue by a woman incapacitated by passion (Marot, 1994). Nowhere in the course of these encounters is there talk of the risk of pregnancy or the use of effective contraception. Thus, the impressionable minds of young people

FIGURE 23.1 Adverse Outcomes of Teen Pregnancy as Reflected by the Determinants of Health

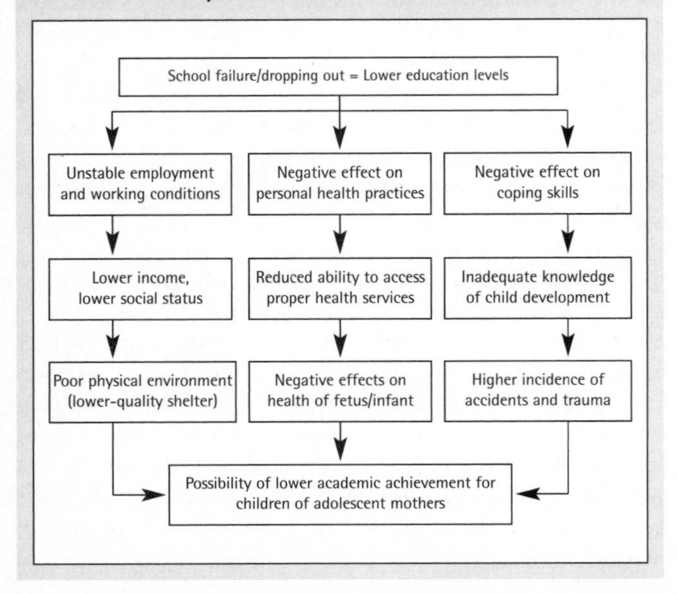

are influenced by romantic notions of sexual activity that do not take into account the realities of the situation.

Accordingly, when initiation of sexual intercourse cannot be delayed, understanding what drives adolescent use or non-use of contraceptive methods becomes a key component of a comprehensive educational strategy. Many adolescents hold myths in relation to fertility. For example, they believe that they are sterile because lack of contraceptive use in the past did not result in pregnancy. Sometimes they think they are too young, have intercourse too infrequently, or have intercourse at a time of month when pregnancy cannot occur (Roth, 1993). One in three adolescent girls holds ambivalent, and sometimes downright positive, views about immediate childbearing. Such visions can interfere with effective and diligent contraceptive use (Stevens-Simon, Kelly, Singer, & Cox, 1996). Furthermore, some of these girls, especially those who come from families plagued by high stress levels, perceive pregnancy as an expected life event based on their family environment. This perception prevents them from protecting themselves against pregnancy (Ravert & Martin, 1997).

What may complicate the educational efforts directed at adolescent females is the attitude toward paternity and contraception held by adolescent males. Males between 15 and 19 years old who come from socioeconomically disadvantaged backgrounds seem to view paternity as a source of self-esteem and, as a result, are more likely to hold the view that fathering a child would make them feel like a real man. This suggests that involving males in intervention strategies would have a beneficial effect on adolescent pregnancy prevention (Marsiglio, 1993).

CHNs must be aware of the salient need to embrace any opportunity that may prevent adolescent pregnancy and break this distressing cycle. Such an opportunity presents itself when a young woman is seen by a health care provider for a pregnancy test, the result of which is negative. This sub-population remains at a high risk of unintended conception in the near future; the majority become pregnant within 18 months of the test (Zabin, Sedivy, & Emerson, 1994). Such findings would suggest that intensive counselling at the time of the negative pregnancy test would be beneficial for this high-risk group. In order to facilitate screening of teens at risk for early pregnancy, the acronym HEADS was developed (Dull & Blythe, 1998):

- H for home life,
- E for education,
- A for activities (hobbies, sports, friends),
- D for drug use, and
- S for sexual behaviour or suicidal thoughts.

Assessing each of these features should alert the health care provider to heightened risk of adolescent pregnancy so that appropriate steps can be taken to try and prevent it.

How Is Development Affected and What Are the Consequences?

Adolescence is a turbulent period characterized by what Erikson (1959) termed a maturational crisis, which culminates in either identity formation or identity diffusion. Adolescents are faced with multiple aspects of reality that compete for integration as part of their identity. They focus their energy on attempting to reconcile what they learned in the context of their culture and family with the norms and expectations of their peer group. These efforts are often hindered by their relative emotional immaturity, perceived invulnerability, evolving self-concept, growing insight into sexuality, and quickly changing body image. In order to attain role identity, teens must experiment with a variety of roles and have the opportunity for positive social support. One risk factor of adolescent parenting is that the teen parent does not resolve her role identity, which leads to role confusion characterized by the inability to differentiate his/her own roles from others' roles. This, in turns, leads to the adolescent taking on another's roles as his/her own or attributing his/her roles to another person. Thus, a mother in role confusion would have a tendency to confuse her child's roles with her own and could experience difficulty viewing other people, including her children, beyond her own needs (Hurlbut, Culp, Jambunathan, & Butler, 1997). Furthermore, when such situations are coupled with powerful feelings of inadequacy and failure in the parental role, they often initiate emotional and physical distancing on the part of the adolescent mother and propagate troubled mother-child relationships (Kaplan, 2001).

Many adolescents are relatively inexperienced with life situations that require prompt adaptation and creative problem solving. This may place them at risk for intense disappointment when faced with the reality of parenting. Trad (1999) presented an intriguing notion that focused on reconciling disparities between the "fantasy" infant anticipated throughout the pregnancy and the "real" infant that presents at birth. This real infant may not resemble the mother's fantasy or may not react as she had envisioned. "While mature mothers are able to 'grieve' the loss of the fantasy child, but fairly rapidly adjust to an acceptance of the real infant, adolescent mothers have greater difficulty with this process" (Trad, p. 229), setting themselves up for disappointment.

The adolescent's ability to control emotions may also be unsound at this time, especially in light of the immense changes in other developmental domains. Because the teen mom is less likely to be able to bring any negative emotions into balance quickly, she can easily become frustrated by her infant's behaviours. Thus it is a possibility that maltreatment of the child will become her coping mechanism. This young mother, lacking the time to devote to her own needs because it is used up while meeting the demands of the infant, may grow to resent her baby, providing a tremendous opportunity for maltreatment to occur (Trad, 1999).

The remarkable changes taking place in the teenaged mother's cognitive development should not be discounted. Erikson (1968) suggested that adolescents develop the potential to "operate on hypothetical propositions and . . . think of possible variables and potential relations—and think of them in thought alone, independent of certain concrete checks previously necessary" (p. 245). This advance in cognitive development makes it possible for adolescents to benefit from practical interventions. It is therefore reasonable to propose that successful pregnancy prevention programs be framed in terms of strategies that can open the door for candid discussions directed at future-oriented hypothetical situations and that address the determinants of health.

PREGNANCY PREVENTION PROGRAMS: WHAT WORKS?

DiCenso, Guyatt, and Willan (1999) provided a systematic review of studies addressing adolescent pregnancy prevention and concluded that interventions focusing solely on abstinence do not delay initiation of sexual intercourse and do not reduce pregnancy rates. They also noted that sex education programs are relatively ineffective. Interestingly, they found a reduction in adolescent pregnancy after the presentation of multifaceted programs that aimed their interventions at the determinants of health. Similarly, Pearlman and Bilodeau (1999) reported on a successful program that was constructed to help its participants develop and accomplish specific goals. Its female and male participants were recruited during Grade 6 and typically came from poor families with under-educated parents. The program's goals were to motivate and equip the students to function successfully in society, to avoid early pregnancy, and to focus on a future that involved ongoing education. The foundation of this highly successful program was the philosophy that connected educational failure and poverty to adolescent pregnancy, and educational success to a positive vision of the future and thus avoidance of pregnancy, all closely linked to the determinants of health.

Also, Allen, Philliber, Herrling, and Kuperminc (1997) detailed their inquiry into Teen Outreach, another effective program that linked volunteer community service with classroom dialogue about life choices. The program did not concentrate on the behaviours it was trying to prevent; instead, it focused on enhancing decision-making skills, cultivating positive peer interactions, and handling emotional reactions.

Likewise, Atwood and Donnelly (1993); Franklin, Grant, Corcoran, O'Dell-Miller, and Bultman (1997); and Montessoro and Blixen (1996) promoted a multifaceted or multi-systemic approach. They described interventions involving development of critical-thinking skills, improvement of educational and employment opportunities, goal setting, and continued motivation for higher aspirations. These authors believed that it is the comprehensive and holistic approach, as opposed to disjointed, narrowly focused strategies, that will eventually lead to reducing teen pregnancy. Furthermore, the strategies used in all these successful programs also addressed the determinants of health. Medora, Goldstein, and von der Hellen (1993) suggested that effective primary prevention programs should include debates on the realities of love, marriage, and parenthood to help teens modify their idealistic visions and adopt more realistic expectations. Further, it is fascinating to note that Medora and von der Hellen (1997) discovered that non-pregnant and non-parenting teens had significantly lower romanticism scores than did pregnant teens and teen mothers. They surmised that the non-pregnant and non-parenting teens have more realistic and pragmatic attitudes toward these issues.

Finally, Unger, Molina, and Teran (2000) proposed that a large number of teenage girls may undertake risky sexual activities because they equate childbearing with significant benefits, thus lacking motivation to avoid pregnancy. They advocated that "pregnancy prevention programs may be more effective if they address adolescents' unrealistic positive illusions about the consequences of teenage childbearing and their perceptions of invulnerability to negative outcomes" (p. 211). Witte (1997) reported that when teen mothers were shown the daily realities and struggles of teen parenthood, the glamour and perceived positive consequences associated with being a teen mother diminished.

A variety of pregnancy prevention programs boast varying degrees of success. A review commissioned by the Effective Programs and Research Task Force of the National Campaign to Prevent Teen Pregnancy ascertained several unifying characteristics inherent in effective programs (Kirby, 1997). Such programs

- focus on reducing risky sexual behaviours;
- incorporate behavioural goals and teaching methods appropriate for the age of the participants;

Canadian Research Box 23.1

Malinowski, A., & Stamler, L. L. (2003). Adolescent girls' personal experience with *Baby Think It Over™*. *MCN: The American Journal of Maternal Child Nursing, 28*(3), 205–211.

The *Baby Think It Over™* (BTIO) is an infant simulator in the form of a life-size newborn that cries at unpredictable intervals over a 24-hour period, necessitating simulation of caregiving behaviours. This qualitative study employed phenomenological methodology to explore adolescent girls' personal experience with the BTIO. Data were collected from nine adolescents from Windsor, Ontario using audiotaped, semi-structured interviews. The themes that emerged from the data included the adolescents' parenting journey, incorporating intellectual, emotive, and physical faculties, and recognition of the illusionary nature of ideas they previously held about parenting an infant.

The new perspectives gained by the participants about parenting a newborn infant differed markedly from the romantic fantasies they had prior to the experience. The teens also initiated new thinking processes related to future consequences of sexual activity. Used for a period of one to two weeks in conjunction with budgeting exercises and provocative small-group discussions, the BTIO shows promise as an effective tool to help modify teen views of adolescent pregnancy and parenting.

Discussion Questions

1. What are the advantages of a program that utilizes the BTIO to help reduce the rate of adolescent pregnancy?
2. How should the BTIO experience be designed in order to make it a worthwhile educational endeavour? Provide time frames, conditions, etc.

- employ theoretical approaches that have been shown to positively influence other health-related risky behaviours;
- provide a reasonable time frame to allow participants to accomplish required activities;
- provide basic information on risks of unprotected intercourse and methods of protection;
- use a variety of teaching approaches;
- include activities that address peer pressure as it relates to sex;
- provide ample opportunity to practise communication, negotiation, and refusal skills; and
- utilize teachers who believe in the program and are committed to its success.

What Can Community Health Nurses Do?

A growing body of literature suggests that nursing agendas that are inconsiderate of adolescents' norms and life contexts contribute to both their estrangement and dependence. Conversely, curriculums that engage adolescents in respectful interaction authenticate their strengths and ambitions (Smith-Battle, 2000). Thus, by using non-judgmental, therapeutic nurse-patient relationships based on trust and mutual understanding, CHNs can bring empowerment to adolescents struggling with tough choices about the future of a pregnancy or about the challenging world of parenting. Since many adolescents experience ambivalence when faced with the reality of pregnancy, CHNs must engage them in conversation that directly addresses their uncertainties and offer to explore viable solutions. Positive and negative thoughts and feelings regarding pregnancy and parenting may be explored with three purposes in mind (Polaneczky & O'Connor, 1999):

- to acquaint the adolescents with the multitude of emotions they will experience,
- to validate the intricacies of these emotions, and
- to allow clinicians to gather context information that is relevant to the decisions these adolescents must make.

CHNs are well positioned to tackle this challenge. Their clinical work often involves primary care responsibilities that place them in direct contact with adolescents and makes possible the development of a strong nurse-patient relationship based on trust and mutual respect. An alliance built on such a strong foundation has the potential to ensure continual contacts with the adolescent who no longer feels intimidated or uncomfortable in approaching the CHN with intimate concerns. In this way, CHNs work to support and build the needed skills in a caring environment appropriate for the clients, allowing them to be accountable and to take responsibility for making choices that are consistent with healthy lifestyle practices (Gillis, 1995).

When helping adolescents who are faced with issues surrounding pregnancy, CHNs offer interventions that span the three stages of prevention: primary, secondary, and tertiary. For primary prevention, nurses provide sexual health education that incorporates counselling on responsible decision making with regard to sexual activity, contraception, and protection against sexually transmitted infections.

When encountering an adolescent female, early identification of whether she is pregnant is paramount. Thus, **secondary prevention** activities, which aim at early identification of individuals with risk factors for a condition, are extremely important in the interventional repertoire of a CHN. These activities can be quite broad in scope depending on the circumstances surrounding the particular teen's situation. When working with a teen who is ambivalent toward the pregnancy, a CHN needs to counsel her (and her partner if the young woman wishes) on the options that are available regarding the future of the pregnancy. Such information must be presented in a factual, caring, and non-judgmental manner. The teen should be aware that her alternatives include continuing the pregnancy and keeping the infant, continuing the pregnancy and placing the infant for adoption, or terminating the pregnancy. Furthermore, she should be assured that services are available in the community regardless of which option she chooses to pursue.

If the adolescent chooses to carry the child to term, the CHN may be instrumental in ensuring that she receives adequate prenatal care and education on the physical and emotional changes of pregnancy. If the teen chooses adoption after the birth, she may need counselling or support when dealing with the conflicting emotions she may experience. If the CHN has established rapport with the adolescent through previous visits, these issues can be addressed much more easily.

CASE STUDY

Sixteen-year-old Maya, who is well known to you, comes to see you at the community health centre because she is two weeks late for her period. She has been taking her birth control pills, but she remembers a day when she forgot them. Her mom is sitting in the waiting room thinking that Maya is seeing you for a series of headaches. You do a pregnancy test and it turns out to be positive. Maya is devastated. She pleads with you not to tell her mom, who is very strict. She fears that her parents will "disown" her. Her 19-year-old partner of six months has told her that if she's pregnant, she should have an abortion because he's too young to have his "life ruined by some kid." Maya is now sobbing in your office. She's hoping that you can provide her with some direction, but asks if she can step out back for a cigarette to calm herself a little.

Discussion Questions

1. What options will you be able to offer Maya?
2. What are your responsibilities with regard to Maya's mom, who is also your client?
3. What are your feelings when faced with the multiple issues in this situation and how will they affect the nurse-patient relationship and your ability to provide appropriate care to Maya?

If the teen wishes to obtain a **therapeutic abortion** (termination of pregnancy, preferably in the first trimester), the CHN can ensure that the teen is capable of making this decision. The pregnant teen must comprehend the risks and consequences of this procedure. Furthermore, the CHN's responsibilities may include referral to an obstetrician/gynecologist, as well as counselling pre- and post-procedure.

CHNs may also provide care in the realm of **tertiary prevention**, which aims at care of established disease, restoration to highest function, minimization of negative effects of a condition, and prevention of condition-related complications. Such care may include support of adolescents who are encountered for the first time in an advanced stage of pregnancy without benefits of prenatal care and/or with a history of drug/alcohol abuse. In these circumstances, CHNs must establish a strong relationship with the teen in order to have enough influence to connect her with health care services that would optimize the outcome of the pregnancy for herself and her child. Additionally, this level of prevention may incorporate education and support relating to infant care and development, counselling around conflicts in the teen's personal relationships resulting from the unexpected and abrupt role changes she faces, or referral to social services if the adolescent needs shelter or other more complex community supports. Moreover, teaching about contraception is also of utmost importance in order to help the teen avoid a second pregnancy.

Services may be more accessible to teens if they are located within the school. However, some adolescents may feel self conscious if they are seen entering the nursing office by their peers or teachers. Other successful venues are health centres that cater solely to teens and offer a wide range of health care services, drop-in centres that offer recreational activities but also employ health care personnel, or public health units, which are present in many cities and may offer a more anonymous and less threatening alternative.

A cautionary note must be made about the prevailing notion that becoming a parent in adolescence ruins young lives (Arenson, 1994). This belief is held by a majority of the population. However, while adolescent childbearing often has negative outcomes, one needs to remain cautious about extending this view to all adolescent parents. Such a stereotype can have extremely detrimental effects on those adolescent mothers who are making great efforts to adjust to their life circumstances and their educational and career needs. Some adolescent mothers "handled the responsibilities of child rearing and managing their lives with surprising fortitude, determination, and resiliency. Hard work, motivation and family and social support are crucial for teen mothers to turn their challenging situations into fulfilling opportunity for growth. Several long-term studies confirm this viewpoint, suggesting that two decades after giving birth many adolescent mothers are not dependent on social assistance, have completed high-school, secured steady employment, and go on to have comfortable and satisfying lives" (Committee on Adolescence, 1999).

SUMMARY

The issues surrounding adolescent pregnancy are complex. Pregnancy prevention is an intricate undertaking requiring intervention from many different perspectives and professions. CHNs must develop therapeutic relationships at the individual, family, and community level with an aim to support the pregnant adolescent and to implement global interventions to prevent teen pregnancy. It is crucial that CHNs work with adolescents to maintain a delicate balance between efforts aimed at preventing pregnancy and endeavours directed at supporting adolescent parents and allowing them to flourish into the capable parents they can become.

KEY TERMS

adolescent pregnancy
premature birth
low birth weight
sudden infant death syndrome
determinants of health
primary prevention
maltreatment
secondary prevention
therapeutic abortion
tertiary prevention

INDIVIDUAL CRITICAL THINKING EXERCISE

Jason and Kate are a teen couple and parents of a 6-month-old infant. They use condoms occasionally. They said they are "always careful," and having this baby "was an accident." Karen and Dave are their good friends. They have recently initiated sexual activity and also use condoms, but only occasionally. They do not use any other form of contraception but have no desire to have a child at present. Using what you know about adolescent development, give two reasons to explain their sexual practices. What could you as a CHN do to change their behaviour?

GROUP CRITICAL THINKING EXERCISE

The media is an important influence on adolescents' worldview. How do the media (television, music, movies, etc.) promote lifestyles and sexual practices that increase the risk of adolescent pregnancy? Is prevention of pregnancy commonly portrayed in the media? Why or why not?

REFERENCES

Allen, J. P., Philliber, S., Herrling, S., & Kuperminc, G. P. (1997). Preventing teen pregnancy and academic failure: Experimental evaluation of a developmentally based approach. *Child Development, 64*(4), 729–742.

Arenson, J. D. (1994). Strengths and self-perceptions of parenting in adolescent mothers. *Journal of Pediatric Nursing, 9*(4), 251–257.

Atwood, J. D., & Donnelly, J. W. (1993). Adolescent pregnancy: Combating the problem from a multi-systemic health perspective. *Journal of Health Education, 24*(4), 219–227.

Canadian Institute of Child Health. (1994). *The health of Canada's children: A CICH profile* (2nd ed.). Ottawa, ON: Canadian Institute of Child Health.

Committee on Adolescence. (1999). Adolescent pregnancy: Current trends and issues. *Pediatrics, 103*(2), 516–520.

DiCenso, A., Guyatt, G., & Willan, A. (1999). *A systematic review of the effectiveness of adolescent pregnancy primary prevention programs.* Hamilton, ON: Region of Hamilton-Wentworth Social and Public Health Services.

DiClemente, R. J., Hansen, W. B., & Ponton, L. E. (Eds.). (1996). *The handbook of adolescent health risk behaviour.* New York: Plenum.

Dull, P., & Blythe, M. J. (1998). Preventing teen pregnancy. *Primary Care Clinics in Office Practice, 25*(1), 111–122.

Erikson, E. H. (1959). *Identity and the life cycle: Selected papers.* New York: International Universities Press.

Erikson, E. H. (1968). *Identity, youth, and crisis.* New York: Norton.

Federal, Provincial, and Territorial Advisory Committee on Population Health. (1994). *Strategies for population health: Investing in the health of Canadians.* Ottawa, ON: Author.

Franklin, C., Grant, D., Corcoran, J., O'Dell-Miller, P., & Bultman, L. (1997). Effectiveness of prevention programs for adolescent pregnancy: A meta-analysis. *Journal of Marriage and the Family, 59*(3), 551–567.

Gillis, A. (1995). Exploring nursing outcomes for health promotion. *Nursing Forum, 30*(2), 5–12.

Health Canada. (1999). *Report from consultations on a framework for sexual and reproductive health.* Ottawa, ON: Health Canada.

Hurlbut, N. L., Culp, A. M., Jambunathan, S., & Butler, P. (1997). Adolescent mothers' self-esteem and role identity and their relationship to parenting skills knowledge. *Adolescence, 32*(127), 638–654.

Kaplan, D. W. (2001). Care of adolescent parents and their children. *Pediatrics, 107*(2), 429–434.

Kirby, D. (1997). *No easy answers: Research findings on programs to reduce teen pregnancy.* Washington, DC: National Campaign to Prevent Teen Pregnancy.

Marot, F. (1994). Teenagers and sex: A suitable case for education. *Professional Care of Mother and Child, 4*(2), 46–49.

Marsiglio, W. (1993). Adolescent males' orientation toward paternity and contraception. *Family Planning Perspectives, 25*(1), 22–31.

Medora, N. P., Goldstein, A., & von der Hellen, C. (1993). Variables related to romanticism and self-esteem in pregnant teenagers. *Adolescence, 28*(109), 158–170.

Medora, N. P., & von der Hellen, C. (1997). Romanticism and self-esteem among teen mothers. *Adolescence, 32*(128), 811–824.

Montessoro, A. C., & Blixen, C. E. (1996). Public policy and adolescent pregnancy: A re-examination of the issues. *Nursing Outlook, 44*(1), 31–36.

Pearlman, S. F., & Bilodeau, R. (1999). Academic-community collaboration in teen pregnancy prevention: New roles for professional psychologists. *Professional Psychology: Research and Practice, 30*(1), 92–98.

Polaneczky, M., & O'Connor, K. (1999). Pregnancy in the adolescent patient: Screening, diagnosis, and initial management. *Pediatric Clinics of North America, 46*(4), 649–670.

Ravert, A. A., & Martin, J. (1997). Family stress, perception of pregnancy, and age of first menarche among pregnant adolescents. *Adolescence, 32*(126), 261–269.

Rosenthal, S. L., Burklow, K. A., Lewis, L. M., Succop, P. A., & Biro, F. M. (1997). Heterosexual romantic relationships and sexual behaviours of young adolescent girls. *Journal of Adolescent Health, 21*(4), 238–243.

Roth, B. (1993). Fertility awareness as a component of sexuality education. *Nurse Practitioner, 18*(3), 42–54.

Singh, S., & Darroch, J. E. (2000). Adolescent pregnancy and childbearing: Levels and trends in developed countries. *Family Planning Perspectives, 32*(1), 14–23.

Smith, C. (1996). The link between childhood maltreatment and teenage pregnancy. *Social Work Research, 20*(3), 131–140.

Smith-Battle, L. (2000). The vulnerabilities of teenage mothers: Challenging prevailing assumptions. *Advances in Nursing Science, 23*(1), 29–40.

Speier, P. L., Melese-D'Hospital, I. A., Tschann, J. M., Moore, P. J., & Adler, N. E. (1997). Predicting contraceptive vigilance in adolescent females: A projective method for assessing ego development. *Journal of Adolescent Health, 20*(1), 14–19.

Stanhope, M, & Lancaster, J. (2004). *Community and public health nursing* (6th ed.). St. Louis, MO: Mosby.

Statistics Canada. (1994). *National population health survey.* Ottawa, ON: Statistics Canada.

Statistics Canada. (2001). Teen pregnancy, by outcome of pregnancy and age group, count and rate per 1,000 women aged 15 to 19, Canada, provinces and territories, 1998. *Health Indicators, 2001*(3). Retrieved December 23, 2003 from **www.statcan.ca/english/freepub/82-221-XIE/01002/tables/pdf/411.pdf**

Stevens-Simon, C., Kelly, L., Singer, D., & Cox, A. (1996). Why pregnant adolescents say they did not use contraceptives prior to conception. *Journal of Adolescent Health, 19*(1), 48–53.

Trad, P. V. (1999). Assessing the patterns that prevent teenage pregnancy. *Adolescence, 34*(133), 221–240.

Unger, J. B., Molina, G. B., & Teran, L. (2000). Perceived consequences of teenage childbearing among adolescent girls in an urban sample. *Journal of Adolescent Health, 26*(3), 205–212.

Wadhera, S., & Millar, W. J. (1997). Teenage pregnancies, 1974 to 1994. *Health Reports, 9*(3), 9–17. (Available from Statistics Canada, Catalogue 82-003)

Witte, K. (1997). Preventing teen pregnancy through persuasive communications: Realities, myths, and the hard-fact truths. *Journal of Community Health, 22*(2), 137–154.

Zabin, L. S., Sedivy, V., & Emerson, M. R. (1994). Subsequent risk of childbearing among adolescents with a negative pregnancy test. *Family Planning Perspectives, 26*(5), 212–217.

ADDITIONAL RESOURCES

Teen Health Centre, Windsor, ON (Health related information for adolescents):
www.teenhealthcentre.com

Hospital for Sick Children, Toronto, ON. Motherisk (Information on use of drugs/medication during pregnancy and breastfeeding):
www.motherisk.org

Health Canada, Population and Public Health Branch. (1999). *Measuring up: A health surveillance update on Canadian children and youth.* Ottawa, ON: Author.
www.hc-sc.gc.ca/pphb-dgspsp/publicat/meas-haut/mu_ee_e. html

Young/Single Parent Support Network of Ottawa-Carleton, Timmins Native Friendship Centre, & Canadian Institute of Child Health. (2002). *A framework for action to reduce the rate of teen pregnancy in Canada.* Ottawa, ON: Health Canada, Division of Childhood and Adolescence.
www.hc-sc.gc.ca/dca-dea/publications/reduce_teen_pregnancy_section_1_e.html

About the Author

Ann Malinowski, BScN, MScN (Windsor), has worked with the adolescent population as a Nurse Educator at the Teen Health Centre in Windsor, Ontario. The focus of her work was in wellness promotion during the perinatal period. Currently, Ann is a medical clerk in the final year of medical school at McMaster University. She hopes to secure a residency position in obstetrics and gynecology. Her research interests include various issues germane to the perinatal period, including promotion of breastfeeding and Kangaroo Care in the NICU and prevention of adolescent pregnancy.

CHAPTER 24

Suicide

Bonnie Myslik

OBJECTIVES

AFTER STUDYING THIS CHAPTER, YOU SHOULD BE ABLE TO:

1. Discuss the historical perspective of suicide, comparing views and societal reaction over the centuries.
2. Recognize the importance of assessment and active intervention when dealing with individuals who may be at risk of suicide.
3. Identify individuals who are at risk of suicide.
4. Apply crisis intervention strategies for suicidal behaviour.
5. Formulate a plan of action in dealing with survivors of suicide.
6. Identify potential roles for community health nurses in the prevention of suicide in their community settings.

INTRODUCTION

As you read these words, one person will have attempted suicide. At some point during their lifetime, one in ten individuals will consider committing suicide (Langlois & Morrison, 2002). **Suicide** is the deliberate act of killing oneself. Regarded as a highly ambivalent act, suicide is committed by an individual who is desperate and is reacting to both external and internal circumstances in an effort to avoid emotional pain (Bonner, 2001). Unfortunately, the subject of suicide is still taboo. Our society continues to attach a stigma to those who commit the act. The cost to society is high. The illness itself reduces the individual's ability to contribute meaningfully to society. The suicide act leaves in its wake the pain of those who survive the individual, including the family and members of the community.

Community health nurses (CHNs) are in an ideal position to assess and intervene not only with individuals, but also with families and entire communities in the prevention of suicide. This chapter explores suicide and the CHN's role in health promotion, prevention, and community interventions.

HISTORICAL PERSPECTIVES

Suicide has been known to man since first recorded history. Generally, in political and religious circles, suicide was regarded as a crime or a sin. In ancient Greece, citizens who committed suicide were denied burial in community graves, and the bodies were often mutilated. In Rome, suicide was accepted in acts of heroism. Groups of people were known to kill themselves to prevent capture by the enemy during war. It was not until the Middle Ages that a more philosophical approach to suicide emerged. Playwrights in the seventeenth to nineteenth centuries, such as Shakespeare, began to write about suicide, connecting the melancholy felt by a character with the eventual suicide (Tondo & Baldessareni, 2001).

While Judaism, Christianity, and Islam have considered suicide to be a sin, self-sacrifice during holy wars has been accepted. Whole groups of people have committed suicide as a result of religious persecution. Christians continued to condemn suicide until 1983. In the Islamic faith, Allah determines the time for death, not the individual. Hinduism has been more tolerant of suicide as there is the belief in reincarnation. Although the practice is rare now, Hindu widows committed suicide to atone for the sins of their husbands and bring honour to their children. Buddhists also believe in the separation of mind and body but feel that destiny plays a role in life, with suicide defeating the purpose of this current life (Tondo & Baldessareni, 2001).

It was not until the twentieth century that suicide was considered the result of social, psychological, and biological effects on the individual. The movement to decriminalize suicide has been slow. Suicide was illegal in England until 1961. In Ireland, suicide remained a crime until 1993. As recently as 1995, Pope John Paul II reinforced the Catholic Church's opposition toward suicide as a crime against life, similar to homicide and genocide. Thus, the stigma attached to suicide has been well rooted in history with generations of negativity making it difficult to change attitudes even today (Tondo & Baldessareni, 2001).

In Canada, suicide has accounted for approximately 2% of all deaths since the 1970s. In 1998, approximately 3700 Canadians committed suicide, a rate of ten per day. Suicide is a leading cause of death of Canadian males and females between adolescence and middle age. Canada's suicide rate is mid-rank of 22 countries that were surveyed (Statistics Canada, 1997). The World Health Organization (cited in Langlois & Morrison, 2002) has estimated that for every successful attempt, 20 are unsuccessful.

Four times more males attempt suicide than females, and they are more likely to die in their first attempt. Suicide is the most common cause of death for males 20–29 and 40–44 years of age; women are more at risk between the ages of 30 and 34. Teenagers aged 15 to 19 have showed an alarming increase, doubling from 7 to 14 per 100 000 population since 1970. It is the second leading cause of death for both sexes between the ages of 10 and 24, surpassed only by motor vehicle accidents. Males tend to choose firearms, hanging, and gas vapours to commit the act, while females choose hanging or ingestion of solid or liquid substances, drugs, or prescription medication (Langlois & Morrison, 2002).

The national suicide rate in Canada is 13 deaths per 100 000. Provincially, Quebec has the highest age-standardized rate at 21 per 100 000. Alberta comes in second with 16 per 100 000. The rates in Ontario, British Columbia, and Newfoundland and Labrador are much lower than the national average, while the Yukon and Northwest Territories report rates of 25 to 26 per 100 000 (Langlois & Morrison, 2002).

Suicide rate is also high among the Aboriginal Canadian population and the inmates in correctional facilities. The Aboriginal population has reported an epidemic of suicidal behaviour, with a suicide risk estimated at 2.5 times that of the general population. Native youths are particularly at risk; their suicide rate is five to six times the rate of non-native teens (Chenier, 1995). Over the last 10 years, there have been 345 suicides in Canadian correctional institutions. More than 35% of deaths in prison are due to suicide (Langlois & Morrison, 2002).

THEORETICAL PERSPECTIVES

There have been a number of approaches to the theoretical study of suicide. More traditional models explored the effects of environment and social support. Others focused on the psychological and personological background of the individual. Durkheim, a sociologist, developed a classic theory of anomie and low social integration to guide sociological risk research. Socio-demographic variables that were studied included sex, race, religion, socioeconomic status, marital status, place of residence, season of the year, time of day, and social contagion. Freud used his classic psychoanalytic theory to hypothesize that suicide was the result of a psychological drive that he called the death instinct. He postulated that individuals who committed suicide turned their hostility for others against themselves. Studies in these areas have not been conclusive and identify inconsistencies in the relationships between personality assessment and suicide risk. Researchers have also postulated that personality assessment could be helpful in identifying personality characteristics that may protect an individual from considering suicide when dealing with a major life stress or crisis (Bonner, 2001).

Over the years, there has been a shift to a more process/continuum approach to suicide risk assessment. This focuses on the maladaptive coping processes that may occur in relation to the influence of the environment or personality. Integration of both streams of thought has been thought to better facilitate suicide risk assessment. It has been suggested that suicide risk assessment profiles should include components of psychological, psychiatric, diagnostic, demographic, historical, self-destructive/self-harm lifestyle, economic, and biologic factors. Thus, when CHNs review the methods of assessing suicidal risk, they might critique these scales or tools and decide whether to include or exclude each component.

Common Myths about Suicide

Although many myths exist about suicide, six will be discussed here.

- The myth that suicides occur with little or no warning is not true. People often communicate in the form of direct statements, emotional reactions, or behavioural cues that they are contemplating suicide.
- Most suicides are not caused by a single, sudden, traumatic event. One single, stressful event is not likely to be the cause of a suicide attempt. Usually, a number of events and feelings over a long period of time culminate in the thought of suicide.
- Some people think that a person should not talk about suicide with someone who might be at risk. However, raising the issue of suicidal thoughts does not increase risk or give the person the idea to commit suicide. Individuals are usually relieved that someone is concerned and wants to talk about their thoughts of suicide.
- Another myth is that suicidal persons want to die and will succeed no matter what you do. **Ambivalence** refers to feelings of uncertainty—conflicts of ideas or attitudes along with opposing views or emotions at the same time. Ambivalence is a key factor in suicidal behaviour. The person may contemplate death to escape the emotional pain they feel, but a part of them wants to live.
- Some people think that they themselves cannot help a person who is suicidal; a specialist is needed to prevent a suicidal act. This is not true. The average person or caregiver can offer immediate support and emergency first aid in the case of a suicide attempt. Helping a suicidal person is no more complicated than showing care and concern for a person who is distressed.
- Another myth is that once the suicide attempt is over, the person will not do this again or need your help. Someone who has attempted suicide is at a greater risk of trying again. Friends and family of this person need to remain vigilant in their care and concern for this individual (Ramsay et al., 1999; Paré, 2000).

Risk Factors

Before people with suicidal intent can be helped, one has to be able to recognize existing risk factors that may predispose the individual to the thought of suicide. Hopelessness is one of the most reliable indicators of suicide risk in the long term (Murphy, Cowan, & Sederer, 2001). Many of these people have few coping resources left and little idea of any meaningful future, increasing the risk of completing the act. They often ask what meaning there is in their lives, express that they have nothing to contribute to the world, feel that they have hurt so many people that there can be no repair, and feel that no one has ever cared or will ever care for them. They are usually very depressed (often, many depressed individuals in primary care practices are not identified as suicidal). Alcohol use can also be a factor. Depression and alcohol/substance abuse are a deadly mix, often leading to suicidal behaviour.

Mental illness, including schizophrenia, depression, personality disorders, and organic brain syndrome, places people at increased risk of suicidal behaviour. **Schizophrenia** is a severe psychiatric disorder with symptoms of detachment from reality, often with delusions and hallucinations. **Depression** is a state of persistent unhappiness and hopelessness. **Personality disorder** is a psychiatric disorder in attitude or behaviour that makes it difficult for an individual to get along with other people and to succeed at work or in social situations. Similarly, **organic brain syndrome** is a psychiatric disorder caused by a permanent or temporary physical change in the brain.

Individuals with mental illness often become so tortured by the voices they hear that they will do anything to escape them. The voices they hear may also tell them to harm themselves, causing them to carry out the final act.

Various life stages bring with them stressors that may seem overwhelming. Teenagers feel great pressure to perform among their peers. Failing a driver's test, not being asked to the prom, or breaking up a relationship can take on more importance to the adolescent than an adult would estimate. Turbulent households, in which growing up is complicated by physical, emotional, or sexual abuse, neglect, and lack of love, can also be a risk factor for teen suicide. Elders also struggle with the psychological pain of growing older. Unemployment can be a key factor, whether it be the sudden loss of a job or the inability to find meaningful work. Physical illness, isolation, homelessness, loneliness, alcohol use, and loss of a spouse or significant other are also major risk factors. As well, physicians, dentists, police, and lawyers have been identified as individuals more likely to commit suicide.

Having a first-degree relative who has committed suicide significantly increases the risk of people committing suicide themselves (Murphy, Cowan, & Sederer, 2001). Being homosexual can also increase the risk of suicidal behaviour. The suicide rate for gay and lesbian individuals is two to three times higher than for heterosexual individuals. Feelings of isolation and discrimination in a society that still struggles to accept this sexual orientation may be an influence (Ramsey et al., 1999). New immigrants may also be at risk as they often suffer from loss of family, friends, previous professional status, and financial affluence. Unfamiliarity with a new culture, language, and climate can seem overwhelming.

A number of secondary risk factors must be also be considered in the assessment of suicide risk. Sleep deprivation, alcohol or drug intoxication, brain neurotransmitter dysfunction, and increased stress levels play a key role in lowering the threshold for committing suicide.

Although we have reviewed many negative factors, a number of positive factors may actually help the individual restrain from the notion of suicide. These include satisfaction with life and career, adequate family/social support, and good health. However, when the negative factors outweigh the positive factors, the likelihood of suicidal ideation and attempt increases. What is interesting to note in reviewing risk factors is that no single stress factor is *the* predictor in estimating suicide risk. In many individuals, it is the slow accumulation of factors that eventually leads the person to believe that there is no hope left (Simmie & Nunnes, 2001).

Assessment

Never be afraid to ask the question, "Are you suicidal?" Most clients, relieved that they have been asked, will be bluntly honest. Ask what the suicidal thoughts include. What is their plan? What is keeping them from doing it? What makes them think about it? Asking these questions will not give the client the idea or the incentive to commit suicide. Many clients will hold back from the act based on loyalty to family, not wanting to feel guilty about hurting loved ones and/or not wanting to leave children behind without a parent. Most clients will be ambivalent about committing the act. The will to survive is usually quite strong.

Risk assessment should include four components, the first of which is the clinical interview of the client. Key aspects include questions about recent stressors. For the average client, stressful events may not create a problem. However, what may seem to be a tolerable event, like the death of a pet, could be the trigger for feelings of despair and hopelessness. The death of a parent or child could cause an overwhelming sense of loss. Anticipated loss can also be a trigger. Fear of failing at school or the loss of a parent through divorce can also cause personal despair and overwhelming sadness. Most clients, if asked, will talk about the stress in their lives. What needs to be determined is what this stress means to them, how they will cope, how distressed they feel about it all, and if they see any hope for resolution of the situation or their feelings.

The second component in identifying suicide risk is to recognize signs and symptoms that may indicate the client may be contemplating suicide. Some people report a decrease in sleep, loss of appetite, decreased libido, loss of interest in usual activities or hobbies, or decreased motivation. The client may be preoccupied or say that the situation is hopeless. Anger, sadness, feelings of loneliness, or lack of optimism for any good outcome from a situation may be crucial signs of possible thoughts of suicide. The use of alcohol and drugs may complicate and intensify the feelings of hopelessness and should be noted in the assessment.

The third component is to determine suicidal thoughts, intents, and plans. People who are contemplating suicide will likely share those thoughts if they feel that they will be safe in divulging this information. However, since suicide is not regarded as acceptable in our culture, it may difficult for them to share this intimate information. If people feel they are able to speak openly about their suicidal thoughts and plans, they often reconsidered. Although it seems difficult to ask about suicidal thoughts, it is often easy to integrate this into the conversation by merely stating to the client that it is not unusual to think about suicide when feeling down. Ask if the client has had any thoughts of suicide. If so, ask if the client has a plan. Will it happen soon? What is the plan? The listener can then make some assumptions about how lethal the plan is and how imminent the act might be (Gliatto & Rai, 1999) (see text box).

Fourthly, and with the client's permission, consult with significant others: family, friends, and/or previous treatment providers. Are they aware of the stressors the client has experienced? Have they noticed any changes in behaviour? Has the client made any uncharacteristic gestures such as giving things away or making plans? What support is available to the person? What can family and friends do to intervene in a stressful time? If risk has been ascertained, removing access to sharp instruments, firearms, prescriptions, and over-the-counter medications reduces the likelihood that the environment could facilitate an attempt (Bonner, 2001).

Over the years, a number of instruments have been introduced that help estimate suicide risk. Motto, Heilbron, and Juster (1985) developed one such tool that assesses the state of suicidal ideation and intention, lethality of the method, mental and mood status, personal and family history of psychiatric illness, stress level, and demographic risk. A total overall score can be derived and used to estimate the level of current suicide risk. More recent models of risk scales have attempted to integrate the concepts of various theoretical frameworks.

Interventions

The approach to treatment of suicidal clients is very individualized. In cases where mental illness, such as depression, has been diagnosed by a physician or psychiatrist, medication therapy may be initiated. CHNs can advocate for keeping only small amounts of medication in the client's home to reduce the risk of overdose. Since medication may take weeks to become effective, close follow-up by the CHN is helpful. If the client is at immediate risk of harm, consider communicating with the physician regarding the potential for hospitalization. Initiate interventions to provide social support, ongoing psychotherapeutic counselling, and home follow-up. Consider removing the means for suicide, such as firearms or prescription medication. Finally, educate the family and client about the illness and about developing coping strategies. Stress management education may also be helpful. Identification of community social supports, including church, service groups, or community suicide prevention programs, is also important for the CHN to explore with the client and family.

Beyond these services, the CHN also has the opportunity to explore community solutions to homelessness, unemployment, financial assistance for single-parent families, daycare, and access to mental health services. Improvement in these social conditions can help reduce the some of the risk factors that are often related to suicide. In this way, primary prevention of suicide could be achieved.

Crisis Intervention

Caring and empathy are pivotal to successful intervention with the suicidal client. One of the basic tenets of **crisis intervention** is the belief that the state of mind of a suicidal client, usually fraught with ambivalence about dying, is temporary and reversible. This ambivalence provides the opportunity to intercede and halt the process. It has been proposed that there

Interviewing a Client about Suicidal Thoughts

People who feel sad and depressed often think about suicide. Have you ever had these thoughts?

- Has any recent stress caused you to think about suicide?
- How often do you think about suicide?
- Do you have a plan?
- If you were thinking of suicide, is there anyone you could call for help?
- What keeps you from killing yourself (e.g., family, religion, children)?
- What makes you think of suicide?
- What makes you stop thinking of suicide?
- Are there guns in your home?
- Are there harmful medications in your home?
- Have you practised your suicide?
- How will people around you react to your death?
- Have you changed your will or life insurance lately?

Canadian Research Box 24.1

Leenaars, A., Cantor, C., Connolly, C., EchoHawk, M., Gailiene, D., Ziong, A. S. et al. (2000). Controlling the environment to prevent suicide: International perspectives. *Canadian Journal of Psychiatry, 45*(9), 639–644.

The researchers discuss the effect of controlling the environment in an effort to decrease suicide and suicidal behaviour. The team was composed of experts from twelve different cultures around the world. Their view is that environmental control has received minimal attention compared with the traditional approaches of clinical treatment and prevention programs for suicidal individuals. Other measures, such as detoxification of domestic gas, detoxification of car emissions, control of availability of toxic substances, and reducing the sensationalism in media reports of suicide, are also identified as tactics for preventing suicide, which have been supported globally in the scientific literature. Laws to regulate access to lethal means such as guns and toxic substances resulted in significant decreases in suicides that used these methods.

Discussion Questions

1. How might the CHN use this information to influence municipal, provincial, and federal legislation or community action?
2. What might be the implications for environmental control in a northern community that relies heavily on firearms for hunting? What might be the alternatives?

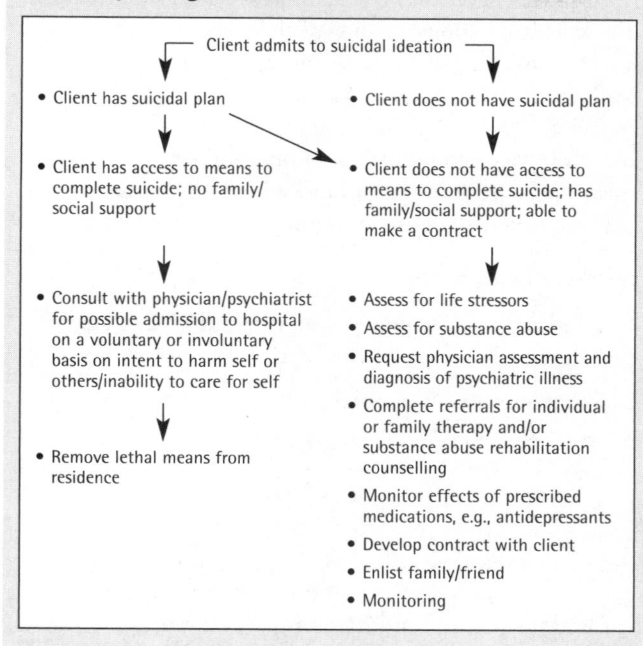

FIGURE 24.1 Nursing Decision Tree for Clients Contemplating Suicide

are four stages to the suicidal experience (Stillion, McDowell, & May, 1989):

- the feelings of being troubled increase;
- negative emotions, which can include guilt, shame, and self-hate, increase;
- the thinking processes become rigid, losing the ability to consider other options; and finally
- the idea of suicide becomes a continuing thought as a means to end the **psychological pain**.

The caregiver, whether it is the CHN, police officer, schoolteacher, parent, spouse, neighbour, or friend, can initiate crisis intervention at any stage of the process. The most important part of any intervention is just being there, both physically and emotionally, for the person in distress. Calm, quiet conversation and slow deliberate attempts to connect with the individual are important. Always remember that suicidal clients are usually extremely ambivalent about committing the act of suicide. They are often hopeful that this is not the only solution to relieve their psychological pain. Often, clients can be given food for thought with questions to reflect on the action they are about to take (Simmie & Nunnes, 2001). Acknowledge the client's pain, attempt to quietly ascertain what is bothering them the most, and determine if the client will consider any other alternatives. Depending on the situation, a client might agree to speak with someone they trust and respect, such as a teacher, lawyer, family member, or minister.

SURVIVORS OF SUICIDE

There are two types of survivors of suicide: the people who survive a suicidal attempt and those who survive an individual who has committed suicide. The resulting pain and distress requires active intervention.

People who attempt suicide but are not successful are most at risk of repeat attempts within the first three months. This risk continues for the next three years. People who do commit suicide leave at least six individuals severely affected by their action (Chance, 1992). Families and friends often suffer profound and sometimes debilitating grief. To complicate matters, suicide still carries the social taboo that may mean that other caregivers or clergy members may be less than helpful, hindered by their own negative attitudes about suicide. The shame and stigma may cause isolation of survivors, increasing the risk of unresolved grieving, depression, and possibly suicide.

Survivors of suicide often feel the double-edged sword of feeling extreme anger toward the family member/friend who has committed suicide. Not only do they feel shame, but they are angry at the person for doing exactly what they tried to talk them out of (Chance, 1992). In some cases, they did not even get the chance to talk it over with the person. There is a feeling of impotence in the whole event because so many questions are left unanswered. It is an unsettling experience. If a note is left (which happens rarely), it can increase the anger if the note is negative, or may increase sadness if it tells of resolvable issues.

How can the CHN intervene in suicide prevention? Reflect on your own attitudes about suicide. Attend training to assist clients and their families as they struggle with bereavement issues. Find the local resources for grief and bereavement counselling. Contact suicide-survivor self-help groups. If none exist, lobby for community funding to initiate a group. Remember that just being present with a survivor is often the most therapeutic action. Assist the family to acknowledge their loss. Help them acknowledge that their fear, anger, and remorse are normal aspects of the grieving process. Explore personal coping methods that have helped them in difficult times before. Help them honour the memory of the loved one who has died.

Survivors also include those health care providers who have been involved in the care of the client. It is a traumatic event, and most caregivers are affected in their reflections of the care that they provided. It is important that caregivers have a professional network to consult with for case review and critical-incident stress counselling. Primary care providers need to realize that while most interventions can successfully intervene in the care of the suicidal person, some clients will commit the suicidal act in spite of all treatment. Although this is a fact, it can still be difficult to accept. It is essential that caregivers look after themselves so that they may continue to work with individuals who are threatening suicide.

COMMUNITY ACTION

The impact of suicide on the community is substantial. The direct costs for every **parasuicide** (a suicide attempt or act of self-injury) are substantial in the use of emergency casualty services and medical and psychiatric services. For individuals who commit suicide in their teenage years, over fifty years of productive life are lost. These indirect costs reflect loss of productivity for lifetime income or suicide-related disability. Similarly, the effect on community members who survive the individual who has successfully committed suicide can be substantial. The loss of productivity and the need for follow-up medical or psychiatric counselling place additional cost on the community (Tondo & Baldessareni, 2001).

SUICIDE IN THE FUTURE

The World Health Organization (1999) estimated that 10 million individuals commit suicide annually. This group has outlined a global strategy to decrease mortality associated with suicidal behaviour. Their objectives include:

- early assessment and elimination of risk factors associated with suicide,
- raising general public awareness about suicide,
- support and treatment of populations at risk for suicide,
- training primary health care workers and other sectors, and
- provision of support/networks for survivors of suicide.

Suicide prevention must focus on three areas: societal conditions, education to improve people's ability to cope with stress, and education specifically directed toward suicide prevention (Stillion, McDowell, & May, 1989). In 1987, the National Task Force on Suicide in Canada (1987) released a report that included specific recommendations for changing social conditions associated with suicide. These recommendations included measures to decrease the stigma associated with mental health problems and to provide assistance for education programs for health care professionals as well as the general population. Working in the community, the CHN has the opportunity to initiate education programs and strategies in a primary care prevention approach.

Early detection may well be the key to prevention of suicide. Early diagnosis of risk or psychiatric illness and medical treatment is essential. Primary health care providers need to recognize the signs of psychiatric disorders and assess suicide risk. This involves education of physicians and nurses. In addition, regular, frequent follow-up of clients who are in high-risk groups may prove helpful in reducing suicidal behaviour. Programs such as the Alberta-based "Living Works Incorporated" promote suicide assessment and intervention skills, benefiting both lay workers and professionals in dealing with suicide prevention (Ramsay et al., 1999).

Further to assessment and education, Leenaar et al. (2000) suggest that controlling the environment may be a key factor in suicide prevention. Decreasing access to lethal means has been found to be a significant factor in decreasing suicide rates. For example, Canada reported the significant use of firearms as a suicide agent. After gun laws were introduced, suicide rates with use of firearms decreased between 1969 and 1985. Other measures to reduce lethal means—detoxification of domestic gas, detoxification of car emissions, control of toxic substance availability, and limiting media reports of suicide—have been found to be significant factors in decreasing suicide rates. CHNs are in a position to join community actions groups and local District Health Councils in lobbying political groups to advocate for ways to control community access to suicidal means, in addition to requesting funding for crisis hotlines, education programs, and support groups.

CHNs need to conduct further research related to the effectiveness of various nursing interventions. Researchable questions need to be generated with regards to screening and intervention in order to provide evidenced-based protocols for action to support individuals at risk of suicide.

CASE STUDY

A CHN has recently been stationed in a northern community with a known high statistical record of adult male suicide. On one particular visit to a 55-year-old male who has lost his wife to cancer, the nurse notes that the client's behaviour has changed. He is more subdued, less talkative, and paying less attention to his home and personal appearance. There are empty beer bottles in the living room. His hunting rifle is standing up against the back door.

Discussion Questions

1. Outline four components of a suicide risk assessment that the CHN would conduct.
2. What interventions might the CHN consider if suicide risk is determined?

SUMMARY

CHNs are in an ideal position to assess individuals in their home settings for the possible risk of suicide. The role facilitates engagement with the entire family and community. This interaction offers a unique opportunity to establish risk and begin early intervention, core elements of the CHN's role in health promotion and prevention of illness. As a profession, nursing enjoys a high level of respect from the community. This places nurses in an enviable position to influence community leaders in our municipalities to consider funding programs that will not only maintain the health of the constituents but also promote good health. Decreasing the financial and emotional community burden associated with suicide is within the realm of the influence of nursing. Using their cumulative nursing knowledge, research, and leadership skills, CHNs can make the difference in leading individuals back from one of the darkest moments in their lives and in building healthier communities.

KEY TERMS

suicide
ambivalence
schizophrenia
depression
personality disorder
organic brain syndrome
risk assessment

crisis intervention
psychological pain
parasuicide

INDIVIDUAL CRITICAL THINKING EXERCISES

1. Describe your own feelings and fears about suicide.
2. Has anyone you know attempted or completed suicide? How did it make you feel? What feelings still linger?
3. Do you have strong feelings about people who contemplate or commit suicide?
4. Do you think it is possible to intervene successfully in suicidal behaviour?

GROUP CRITICAL THINKING EXERCISES

1. Suicidal behaviour in the First Nations population is epidemic. How might one develop a culturally sensitive approach to addressing this problem?
2. Identify a researchable nursing practice question that could be studied to examine the effectiveness of interventions with suicidal ideation or behaviour.
3. The World Health Organization has identified a global strategy for reducing mortality and morbidity from suicide. What steps would need to be taken to incorporate these strategies in your community?
4. What resources exist in your community for a) suicidal individuals, b) family or friends of suicidal individuals, and c) professionals who deal with suicide, including physicians, nurses, firefighters, and police?
5. What role could the CHN play in facilitating programs to assist community members in the prevention of suicide?

REFERENCES

Bonner, R. L. (2001). Moving suicide risk assessment into the next millennium: Lessons from our past. In D. Lester (Ed.), *Suicide prevention: Resources for the millennium* (pp. 83–98). Ann Arbour, MI: Sheridan.

Chance, S. (1992). *Stronger than death: When suicide touches your life.* New York: W. W. Norton.

Chenier, N. M. (1995). *Suicide among Aboriginal people: Royal Commission report.* Ottawa, ON: Library of Parliament, Parliamentary Research Branch. Retrieved July 8, 2002 from **www.parl.gc.ca/information/library/PRBpubs/mr131-e.htm**

Gliatto, M. F., & Rai, A. K. (1999, March 15). Evaluation and treatment of patients with suicidal ideation. *American Family Physician.* Retrieved July 20, 2002 from **www.aafp.org/afp/990315ap/1500.html**

Langlois, S., & Morrison, P. (2002). Suicide deaths and suicide attempts. *Health Reports, 13*(2). Retrieved January 30, 2003 from **www.statcan.ca/english/indepth/82-003/feature/hrab2002013002s0a01.htm**

Leenaars, A., Cantor, C., Connolly, C., EchoHawk, M., Gailiene, D., Ziong, A. S. et al. (2000). Controlling the environment to prevent suicide: International perspectives. *Canadian Journal of Psychiatry, 45*(9), 639–644.

Motto, J. A., Heilbron, D. C., & Juster, R. P. (1985). Development of a clinical instrument to estimate suicide risk. *American Journal of Psychiatry, 142*(6), 680–686.

Murphy, M. J., Cowan, R. L., & Sederer, L. I. (2001). *Blueprints in psychiatry* (2nd ed.). Malden, MA: Blackwell Science.

National Task Force on Suicide in Canada. (1987). *Report of the National Task Force on Suicide in Canada: Suicide in Canada.* Ottawa, ON: Health and Welfare Canada.

Paré, M. (2000). Myths about suicide and the truth. *Just the Berries for Family Physicians.* Retrieved January 27, 2001 from **www.theberries.ca/BOTW_archives/suicide_myths.html**

Ramsay, R. F., Tanney, B. L., Lang, W. A., Tierney, R. J., Kinzel, T., & Turley, B. (1999). *Suicide intervention handbook.* Calgary, AB: LivingWorks Education.

Simmie, S., & Nunes, J. (2001). *The last taboo: A survival guide to mental health care in Canada.* Toronto, ON: McClelland & Stewart.

Statistics Canada. (1997). *Selected leading causes of death by sex* [Table]. Retrieved June 12, 2002 from **www.statcan.ca/english/Pgdb/health36.htm**

Stillion, J. M., McDowell, E. E., & May, J. H. (1989). *Suicide across the life span: Premature exits.* New York: Hemisphere.

Tondo, L., & Baldessareni, R. J. (2001). *Suicide: Historical, descriptive and epidemiological considerations.* Retrieved June 15, 2002 from **www.medscape.com/viewprogram/352**

World Health Organization. (1999). *Figures and facts about suicide.* Retrieved December 26, 2003 from **www.who.int/mental_health/media/en/382.pdf**

ADDITIONAL RESOURCES

Alberta Mental Health Board:
www.amhb.ab.ca

Bereaved Families of Ontario:
www.bereavedfamilies.net

Canadian Association for Suicide Prevention:
www.suicideprevention.ca

Canadian Mental Health Association:
www.cmha.ca

Chenier, N. M. (1995). *Suicide among Aboriginal people: Royal Commission report.* Ottawa, ON: Library of Parliament, Parliamentary Research Branch.
www.parl.gc.ca/information/library/PRBpubs/mr131-e.htm

Community Health Nurses Association of Canada:
www.communityhealthnursescanada.org

Federal, Provincial, and Territorial Advisory Committee on Population Health. (1999). *Statistical report on the health of Canadians.* Ottawa, ON: Health Canada.
www.hc-sc.gc.ca/hppb/phdd/report/stat/index.html

Federal, Provincial, and Territorial Advisory Committee on Population Health. (1999). *Statistical report on the health of Canadians: Errata.*
www.hc-sc.gc.ca/hppb/phdd/pdf/report/stats/Errataen.pdf

Nursing in First Nations Communities:
www.hc-sc.gc.ca/fnihb/ons/nursing/index.htm

Robinson, B. A. (2001). *Suicide among Canada's native people.* Ontario Consultants on Religious Tolerance.
www.religioustolerance.org/sui_nati.htm

Sarnia-Lambton Suicide Prevention Committee. *Suicide in Canada*:
www.sarnia.com/groups/suicideprevention/incanada.html

Suicide Information and Education Centre Website:
www.siec.ca

Teen Survivors of Suicide:
www.teensos.org

Turtle Island Native Network, Healing and Wellness. *Suicide prevention:*
www.turtleisland.org/front/chandler.htm

Vanier Institute of the Family:
www.vifamily.ca

About the Author

Bonnie Myslik, BScN (Windsor), MScN in Administration (Western Ontario), Acute Care Nurse Practitioner (Toronto), Primary Health Care Nurse Practitioner (COUPN), has worked for 20 years in medicine, emergency, intensive care, geriatrics, and rehabilitation. She has worked with Family Medicine and Internal Medicine. She is currently a primary health care nurse practitioner specializing in the care of individuals experiencing severe and persistent mental health issues. In addition, she is active in teaching future nurse practitioners as a tutor with the University of Windsor and also as a course professor with McMaster University.

CHAPTER 25

Hospice and Respite Care

Dauna Crooks

OBJECTIVES

AFTER STUDYING THIS CHAPTER, YOU SHOULD BE ABLE TO:

1. Define and distinguish the definitions and services of palliative, supportive, hospice, and respite care.
2. Describe common models of hospice palliative care.
3. Describe the benefits and barriers of hospice palliative care.
4. Discuss the impact of government health policies, funding, and political action on access and distribution of hospice, palliative, and respite services.
5. Identify the roles of community health nurses and other disciplines and volunteers in hospice palliative and respite care.

INTRODUCTION

While medical techniques and technology save lives, it is clear that medical treatment alone does not address the range of sequelae of life-threatening conditions such as trauma, disease, or premature birth. A different and complementary level of health and social services is required by individuals and their family members or caregivers to meet the range of complex needs. Support for families coping with disability or the late stages of a disease trajectory is found in hospice care, respite care, palliative care, and supportive care. Whether delivered in an institution or in the community, the goal of hospice care is to maintain quality of life until death (National Hospice Organization [NHO], 1989). Hospice care overlaps conceptually and practically with palliative, respite, and supportive care and services. Service combinations vary within and between health care contexts, with differences attributable to medical, economic, political, geographic support and rationale for service.

Community health nursing is central to the excellence of hospice palliative care and respite care. This chapter focuses on the services of hospice and respite care with specific reference to models of care and Canadian literature. This chapter discusses the goals, outcomes, and barriers of hospice and respite care; the interchange with palliative and supportive care; and the roles of health care providers in patient well-being and family support. Readers are encouraged to compare the models of care with models, services, practices, and issues within their own community.

Hospice Care

"Hospice" once meant a place of shelter for travellers on a long and arduous journey. The meaning is appropriate when one considers the journey families and individuals take in the last days of life. **Hospice care** or **hospice palliative care** is defined as active compassionate care directed toward improving the quality of life of those with life-threatening illness, as well as their families, as they are living, dying, or bereaved (Hospice Association of Ontario, 2003), or directed toward improving the quality of life of those not seeking or unlikely to benefit from active life-sustaining treatment (NHO, 1989; Saunders, 1990).

The principles of hospice care include a primary focus on the physical, emotional, social, and spiritual needs of the individual and family. Personal, cultural, and religious beliefs and values inform the decision making, planning of services, and collaboration with the family in order to determine clinical outcomes and evaluate measures for care. A team of health care professionals and volunteers, educated in the palliative, bereavement, and caring process, works with the family unit. In addition, the team treats all active issues, prevents new issues from arising, and promotes opportunities for meaningful experiences that enhance personal and spiritual growth (Hospice Association of Ontario, 2003). The community health nurse (CHN) is very often the leader and coordinator of care.

Hospice services may be provincially funded or sponsored by community-based volunteer organizations, religious orders, or donors. A hospice may be a free-standing institution or a unit within an acute or chronic care facility. Some hospice services have been developed for specific populations (e.g., AIDS patients: Casey House, Toronto; pediatrics: Canuck Place, Vancouver) while others tend to a mixed population of dying patients (e.g., Elizabeth Bruyere, Ottawa). Hospices may provide day services, home care, support services, or a combination of inpatient and community services.

Palliative Care

Palliative care is defined globally as the active total care of patients whose disease is not responsive to curative treatment (World Health Organization, 1990). This definition suggests that despite expectations of no cure, or when curative treatment is no longer a viable option, the various and complex needs of patients will still be met in a planned, comprehensive manner. The choice for medical treatment is not considered to be a barrier to receipt of palliative care, nor is palliative care service a barrier to medical treatment planning.

Palliative care in the Canadian context has been described as a combination of active and compassionate therapies intended to comfort and support individuals and families who are living with a life-threatening illness (Ferris & Cummings, 1995). Palliative care focuses on quality of life, symptom management, and death with dignity and comfort. Care is based on an assessment of needs and issues resulting from treatment, disease, and quality of life as defined from the patient's point of view.

Respite Care

Respite care is a form of daycare, providing recreational and restorative services for individuals with functional limitations. The goal of **respite care** is to relieve the stress on the family and other caregivers for a specified period of time depending on community resources available. Respite for adults or children with physical and mental disabilities may occur in acute care hospitals, continuing care centres, chronic facilities, daycare centres, or in the home. Care is provided by one or more services depending on the complexity of the situation. Homemakers, home care services, registered nursing staff, or personal support workers provide most respite care, with other disciplines providing services to improve physical or cognitive function and living skills. Whether offered in institutions or the home setting, respite care is facilitated by a family physician and processed through available resources in the acute care or community setting. When the family physician is attentive to family needs and is successful in securing resources, the family gains respite.

Supportive Care

Supportive care is a concept designed to meet the social, emotional, psychological, spiritual, informational, and physical needs of families. Supportive care initiatives have been developed based on scientific evidence and patient need. Supportive care encompasses aspects of palliative, hospice, and respite care. It has broad application, from pre-diagnosis to the period of bereavement, in the following areas:

- health promotion and awareness;
- preparatory information designed to enhance knowledge and provide anticipatory guidance;
- psychological support;
- tangible support;
- financial support for transportation, supplies, and equipment; and
- symptom management.

Nurses comfortable with these issues assess the range of needs early in the clinical encounter and follow these through to the final phase of care.

MODELS OF CARE

Canadian palliative care was originally formalized within urban hospital settings, but today much of the care occurs in the local community or in the family home (Critchley et al., 1999). Several models of care are described below. In any model of palliative, hospice, supportive, or respite care, the primary need is for expert and dedicated health professional services, for example:

- hospital-based nurses and CHNs who can assess and manage palliative issues and deliver supportive care in the home, and
- seasoned pain- and symptom-management teams who can assess issues and access resources quickly.

Successful palliative hospice care also requires a flexible interchange between hospital care, primary care, and community care. When one considers the short-term cost against the longer-term benefit for the family, or the cost of hospitalization or nursing home placement, community-based palliative hospice care is efficient, effective, and mandatory for the care of dying patients.

Acute Care Model

In the hospital context, palliative care usually consists of a multidisciplinary team of a physician, a nurse with an interest in or education supporting palliative care, a social worker, and a chaplain. The service, called the **acute care model**, provides comprehensive care to all inpatients identified as palliative. Care may occur across the hospital or only in designated units and is provided to patients with a projected life span of 6–8 weeks. The team works with the referring specialist or family physician to assess and manage symptoms on a daily basis to facilitate ongoing care and/or a peaceful death. The focus of care is primarily on symptom control to allow the patient to return home but may include spiritual, psychological, and social assessment.

The **acute care consultative palliative care team** provides consultation to the attending physician or unit upon request. This team assesses the patient and family needs, suggests treatment for symptom management, and refers to other services as needed. The attending physician retains medical control.

Community-Based Palliative Care

The **community-based palliative care** team, located in the community hospital, provides consultation and assessment and, in some cases, the full range of active and follow-up care. Home care services are used to assess and support the patient after returning home.

Community-based palliative care outreach teams provide palliative and hospice care in the home. Community-based teams consist of family practitioners, CHNs with palliative experience, pain- and symptom-management nursing teams, and home care.

Hospice Programs

Hospice programs are usually volunteer managed services that support people with end-stage disease in their homes. Services include emotional, social, practical, and spiritual support for the client and family. Some hospice programs offer day programs, bereavement support, libraries, hospice and palliative education, and complementary therapies such as tai chi, music therapy, and water therapy.

Residential hospices are usually free-standing, volunteer supported residences that provide comprehensive care for patients with end-stage disease. These hospices may fund nursing and other professional positions or work collaboratively with community-based home care nurses, family physicians, home care services, and volunteer agencies to provide personal care, symptom management, homemaking, and psychosocial support.

Community support centres, of the supportive and educative nature, work with patients and families to build rapport, coping skills, and creative skills and help those with terminal disease find meaning in life (e.g., see Wellwood and Wellspring websites in Additional Resources).

GOALS OF HOSPICE, PALLIATIVE, AND RESPITE SERVICES

While cancer patients constitute the majority of patients referred to hospice palliative care, many others need services for symptom management and monitoring, for example, people with congestive heart failure, end-stage kidney disease, severe heart disease, diabetes, or stroke. Those who benefit from hospice care include people who know their family cannot continue to care for them, who prefer to spare their family the difficulty of caregiving as the disease progresses, or who choose hospice over home (Axelsson & Sjoden, 1998; Cantwell, Turco, & Brenneis, 2000; Karlson & Addington-Hall, 1998; Stajduhar & Davies, 1998). However, studies indicate that patients requiring hospice-level care were often not discharged from hospital to hospice. Young caregivers, married men, and people with good functional ability were more likely to be sent home, and home support for these people is often not adequate (McCarthy, Burns, Davis, & Phillips, 2003).

Considering the issues inherent in end-of-life care, it is difficult to imagine that family members, young or older, have the skills, abilities, competence, or resources to manage the complexity of the care required. Pain, dyspnea, delirium, stertorous breathing, dysphagia, fever, cognitive impairment, and myoclonus are common in the final 48 hours of life (Hall, Schroder, & Weaver, 2002). In addition, lay caregivers must provide personal care until death and are often unprepared for taking on that responsibility (Coristine, Crooks, Grunfeld, Stonebridge, & Christie, 2003).

Criteria for a successful home death include:

- the desire to die at home (Axelsson & Sjoden, 1998; Cantwell et al., 2000; Karlson & Addington-Hall, 1998; McWhinney, Bass, & Orr, 1995; Stajduhar & Davies, 1998);
- the family is willing to have a home death (Cantwell et al.; McWhinney et al.);
- the family receives continuous skilled medical, nursing, and homemaking support (McWhinney et al.); and
- the primary caregiver has a backup, or multiple caregivers are available (Dugeon & Kristjanson, 1995).

Care in the home is enhanced when the family has solid financial support for medical expenses, workplace support for temporary work reorganization or leaves of absence, and coverage for medical care resources (Coristine et al., 2003). While families and patients may prefer a home death, lack of adequate resources or family physician involvement, and the inability to manage disease progression (seizures, bladder or bowel incontinence, brain metastases), cause family caregivers to seek additional help, hospitalization, or hospice care (Bruera et al., 1999; Coristine et al., 2003).

Canadian Research Box 25.1

Coristine, M., Crooks, D., Grunfeld, E., Stonebridge, C., & Christie, A. (2003). Caregiving for women with advanced breast cancer. *Psycho-Oncology, 12*(7), 709–719.

This qualitative study was designed using focus groups to explore issues for caregivers in caring for women with end-stage breast cancer at home in Hamilton and Ottawa, Ontario. The authors explored the issues caregivers perceived as important to their role, the factors that allowed women with breast cancer to be cared for at home or to be hospitalized, and the use of resources.

Eighteen of 30 participated in the focus groups. Caregivers were categorized as spousal caregivers (SCGs) and non-spousal caregivers (NSCGs), who were sisters, close friends, or relatives. Caregivers assume great responsibility for providing care, particularly during the terminal phase. SCGs and their patients managed the care cooperatively and shared care-related decision making for as long as possible. NSCGs were working females who managed multiple life-roles. As the activities of daily living became more impaired and incontinence was common, NSCGs had more difficulties managing care demands than the SCGs did. No help was offered to NSCGs from family physicians or oncologists, and community practitioners focused on the needs and desires of the patient. Female caregivers often carried on alone and without authority in directing the care of their mothers, sisters, or friends. Services were actively sought rather than provided.

Discussion Questions

1. Is there evidence for gender explanation for these findings?
2. What do NSCGs need to do to make their needs known?
3. What services are available in your community for women with end-stage breast cancer?

Benefits of Hospice, Palliative, and Respite Care

Emotional and Psychological Benefits Lay caregivers often combine work, care of their own family, and personal health demands with caregiving, often at personal cost to their own health and work role. Caregivers report feeling inadequate to meet the care demands, exhausted in the face of multiple demands, anxious, unable to sleep due to worry about the patient, and a lack of personal time to recoup their strength and optimism (Steele & Fitch, 1996a; Coristine et al., 2003). Respite care is most beneficial to caregivers with long-term care commitments and those who are in ill health or whose health is failing because of multiple demands.

Hospice palliative care has been shown to improve the quality of life for the patient as well as for family members. When the family is supported by hospice palliative care, a sense of normalcy, control, and security may be better maintained, and the family may function better as a unit. However, social needs may be met more readily in the home where family and friends can gather, engage, withdraw, and support each other and their dying relative or friend (Stajduhar & Davies, 1998). Bereavement has been found to be less painful for those family members and friends involved in a home death (McCorkle, Robinson, Nuamah, Lev, & Benoliel, 1998; Payne, Smith, & Dean, 1999). Patients of hospice daycare found the service comfortable, welcoming, and supportive. When patients were given time to discuss personal and illness experiences, feelings of isolation were decreased and self-esteem and self-worth were improved. They were able to make choices about what to say, share, or do. Hospice daycare provided emotional respite from illness, family turmoil, and illness routines (Flanagan, 2000; Hopkinson & Hallett, 2001; Lofeld, Tschopp, Trevor, Brazil, & Kruger, 2000).

Cost Benefit Home palliative care has been found to be less costly than hospital care in the final two weeks of life when medical factors such as supplies, salaries, bed costs, and equipment were factored (Bruera et al., 1999; Critchley et al., 1999). The costs to families has only begun to be addressed by researchers (Kinsella, Cooper, Picton, & Murtagh, 2000) and has recently become a focus of federal interest (Health Canada, 2002).

Barriers to Hospice, Palliative, and Respite Care

Health professionals' translation of clinical perceptions into viable options for palliative care is a complex process. Patients must first be identified as palliative. The changing nature in disease progression and remission makes realistic appraisal of the clinical outcome extremely difficult. The passage from active treatment to palliation and from palliation to terminal care is not clear-cut. The terminal phase may be regarded as the only time for palliative care (Schou, 1993). Attention to cure may not be in the best interests of patients or family members, and setting realistic treatment goals may be the most humane approach to ongoing care (Lesage & Latimer, 1998).

Access to hospice care is problematic in some regions of Canada (Carline et al., 2003). Remote and isolated regions are poorly serviced, and beds and nursing resources in larger centres are limited. Family physicians are not always accessible to meet changing needs, nor compensated for doing so. Transportation, admission criteria, referrals, and fees have also been found to be barriers to hospice palliative care (Lofeld et al., 2000), as have lack of education of care providers, too few respite beds, inadequate support services for families, too few caregivers, and lack of organized volunteer services (Kelley, Sellick, & Linkewich, 2003). Lack of health-provider education and support, limited application/dissemination of research findings, and changing government funding priorities all impact the amount, quality, and outcomes of services (Health Canada, 2002).

HEALTH POLICY AND IMPACT ON SERVICE PROVISION

The federal government of Canada has been active in creating legislation, research, and programs to increase information and access to services. Health Canada has publicly committed to ensuring compassionate care to a gravely ill or dying child, spouse, or parent without putting family income at risk (Reb, 2003; Salsberg-Blom, Turnestedt, & Johanssen, 1998). A Canadian Directory of Hospice and Palliative Care Services and End-of-Life Care is now available online. The National Action Planning Workshop on End-of-Life Care (Tomlinson, 2002) envisions the following by 2010.

- Palliative services will be available and accessible to all Canadians and will include drug coverage, caregiver coverage for costs incurred, and expanded home care services.
- Standards for care will be implemented across federal and provincial jurisdictions. Capacity building in the health professional and volunteer sectors will include education on standards of competency and outcomes of holistic, interdisciplinary, quality care.
- The public will be educated around ethical decisions (withdrawal of fluids, sedation, dying), enabling cultural practices meaningful to dying, and facilitating the understanding of practice terminology.
- Governments will support the infrastructure for all types of research.
- Governments will sponsor a database of palliative and end-of-life issues.

ROLES OF THE HOSPICE AND PALLIATIVE CARE TEAM

Quality palliative and end-of-life care is delivered by a multidisciplinary team and meets the needs for counselling, physical care, respite care, terminal care and support, family support, and bereavement follow-up. Coordination of care depends on need and availability of resources within the family circle, the hospice, and the community. CHNs play a pivotal role in improving the quality of life for palliative care patients and their families.

The Community Health Nursing Role

CHNs provide continuity in assessment and follow-up and are the link between the patient and family and the health care team(s). They identify service gaps and needs arising that may have medical, social, or spiritual implications. This section discusses some of the key activities that may be led by CHNs.

Sharing appropriate information in the right amount at the right time. CHNs assess the ability of the client and family to attend to and process new information such as medication, dispensing, or symptom management. Anticipatory guidance helps families move through crises and stay calm and focused in care. It is important that information be given from an evidence-based perspective.

Completing emotional assessments such as family needs, role strain, stressors, perceptions, and expectations. Often, families are concerned about the safety of their loved one and may experience difficulty letting go of control when the patient is moved to a service setting. Nurses may refer to clinical specialists or social work if family issues are extensive and not readily managed.

Assessing physical needs. It is important to address patient needs quickly, especially those that impede quality of life. Physical needs include assessment and treatment for pain, fatigue, loss of mobility, inability to swallow, nausea, vomiting, constipation from medications, bowel obstruction, dehydration, orientation, and so on. Nutritional support requires rapid assessment and referral to a dietary specialist.

Assessing meaning, spirituality, and hope. Spirituality, the capacity to transcend self, is reflected in the need for meaning and purpose for and of self. Hope is based on love, trust, forgiveness and the need to imagine and embrace a positive future or work to enhance it (Highfield, 1992). CHNs can inspire hope by helping others to sustain relationships, temporarily relinquish difficulties, and attend to and live in the "now" (Miller, 2000). Hope expands the coping repertoire and helps to locate the reality of the situation. The individual is more able to set goals within that reality and to renew the spiritual self. To calm and control fears, CHNs employ interventions such as guided imagery, distraction, therapeutic storytelling, massage, heat or cold, therapeutic touch or music, and managing unwanted distractions.

Teaching self-care strategies and skills for resilience and encouraging caregivers to attend to their own needs. This includes things such as keeping busy, thinking positively, learning more, and talking about the situation (Steele & Fitch, 1996b).

Helping individuals explore options in decision making. CHNs facilitate discussions about treatments, care plans, and requests in an open and non-judgmental manner. Ethical principles of truth telling, autonomy, and confidentiality must underlie this activity.

CASE STUDY

Alison, 62 years old, has had a recurrence of colorectal cancer and is in considerable pain. She has a colostomy from her first rectal cancer two years ago. She manages the colostomy very well and does not feel that it interferes with her life in any way. When she considered treatment for this recurrence, she was offered options for aggressive surgery, including exenteration and addition of an ileostomy opening, radiation to reduce tumour size, and the likelihood of chemotherapy. She recalled the first cancer and the many post-operatively complications like infection and fistula formation. Alison has made a decision not to have treatment. Her partner Glen thinks this is the wrong decision and is angry that she has been allowed to entertain this option. Alison has sought information about the outcomes of extensive surgery and no treatment at all. She is convinced that she is making the right choice. Alison has no living relatives and Glen is very important to her.

Discussion Questions

1. What do you need to know to understand her point of view?
2. What resources are available for Alison and Glen in your own community?
3. How would you plan with Alison for her future care needs and to prepare herself for death?

Helping individuals prepare for dying and manage grief and bereavement. The connectedness of patients to those around them must be maintained as long as possible. Visiting should be monitored to balance support with the need for rest and private reflection. CHNs can help families make final preparations, create a roll-out system for information and caregiver coverage, and discuss plans for the death experience. Further, nurses can help patients and family members voice concerns, self-reflect, and discover themselves. In doing so, both the clients and the nurse discover growth opportunities (Griffiths, Norton, Wagstaff, & Brunas-Wagstaff, 2002).

Roles of Other Members of the Hospice Palliative Team

Volunteers support individuals and families along the continuum of disease, dying, and bereavement.

Palliative physicians direct the medical symptom management but may provide more holistic care if resources allow. They access support from home care, nursing, dietary, volunteer services, and so on.

Family physicians identify changing needs, access resources, and manage issues in palliation and dying. They enhance care through follow-up of new and ongoing health issues; communication with specialists, hospice, and community care; and advocacy for patients to prevent delays in treatment and referral (Norman, Sisler, Hack, & Harlos, 2001). The coordination role of family physicians is especially important in rural communities where resources are less plentiful (Kelley et al., 2003).

Chaplains deal with family, social, and spiritual issues and serve as a link to the patient's home parish.

Social workers deal with emotional and family issues and play a major role in providing psychological and social assessment, supportive care, and management of resource allocation.

Homemakers provide routine home help such as cleaning and cooking. They shop with, or for, the individual, listen, and provide basic comforts. Depending on the home care services available in the area, homemakers may be the sole provider to the patient and family.

Physiotherapists may be involved to improve ambulation, assess transfers and mobility, and direct or provide active physiotherapy care.

Occupational therapists provide life skills, home, and cognitive assessment and help families to manage care in a safe and efficient manner.

Massage therapists provide pain relief and relaxation through gentle or deep manipulation of the musculature.

Respiratory therapists assess the airway and manage the equipment to maintain efficient breathing. They may teach the family to suction, troubleshoot equipment, and make a sufficient assessment of breathing to know when to call for assistance.

Nutritionists assess dietary requirements and suggest supplements to maximize energy and body repair.

Pharmacists help the nurses and family members understand the effects and interactive effects of medication for pain management, fatigue, and constipation to ensure safe and adequate medication coverage.

Other practitioners may be involved for deep relaxation, therapeutic touch, creative writing, music, therapeutic clowning, artistic expression, guided imagery, Reiki, or chiropractic care. These services depend on availability and may or may not be covered in agency services.

Evaluating Nursing and Patient Care

The outcome of nursing care is to provide the optimal quality of life possible for the patient and often for the family. Various tools, such as The Palliative Performance Scale (Victoria Hospice, 1998) and the Toolkit of Instruments to Measure End-of-Life Care (Brown University, Center for Gerontology and Health Care Research, n.d.), may be used to examine physiological and psychological issues for family members as well as to examine the patient's personal impact of illness, physical symptoms, intake, progression of disease over time, emotional closeness/distance, and ability to focus on social and spiritual relationships or imminent death. The Calgary Family Assessment Model (see Chapter 9) may also be used to determine family strengths and needs.

SUMMARY

In this chapter, we have examined the differences and similarities in hospice, palliative, respite, and supportive care. The leadership of Canadian nurses in initiating and maintaining these types of care has been highlighted. The challenge to nurses in hospitals and community agencies is to further develop services and interventions despite economic and political deterrents. While the federal government is sponsoring activity to move these services forward, provincial governments are not as active.

You are challenged to consider what you, as the primary community health nursing practitioner, need to know to address and access services to support patients and families. You are challenged to consider what you need as an educator to teach your patients about the resources available in hospice palliative and respite care. You are challenged to use and create research of value for these vulnerable populations. Your final challenge as a health care provider is to be the voice for political action to move hospice palliative and respite care forward over the next decade.

KEY TERMS

hospice care
hospice palliative care
palliative care
respite care
supportive care
acute care model
acute care consultative palliative care team
community-based palliative care team
community-based palliative care outreach teams
hospice programs
residential hospices
community support centres

INDIVIDUAL CRITICAL THINKING EXERCISE

Create a tool kit for assessing fatigue in patients cared for at home. What instrument(s) or tool(s) would you select? Why?

GROUP CRITICAL THINKING EXERCISES

1. Design a respite service for parents of autistic children. Develop a position paper and strategy that will convince the government to develop and fund your proposal. What services are available in your community?
2. How do you identify those services needed but not existing?

REFERENCES

Axelsson, B., & Sjoden, P. (1998). Quality of life of cancer patients and their spouses in palliative home care. *Palliative Medicine, 12*, 29–39.

Brown University, Center for Gerontology and Health Care Research. (n.d.). *TIME: Toolkit of instruments to measure end-of-life care.* Retrieved August 19, 2003 from **http://as800.chcr.brown.edu/pcoc**

Bruera, E., Neumann, C., Gagnon, B., Brunneis, C., Kneisler, P., & Selmser, P. (1999). Edmonton Regional Palliative Care Program: Impact on patterns of terminal care. *Canadian Association Medical Journal, 161*, 290–293.

Cantwell, P., Turco, S., & Brenneis, C. (2000). Predictors of home death in palliative care patients. *Journal of Palliative Care, 16*(1), 23–28.

Carline, J., Curtis, J., Wenrich, M., Shannon, S., Ambrzy, D., & Ramson, P. (2003). Physician's interactions with health care teams and systems in the care of dying patients: Perspectives of dying patients, family members, and health care professionals. *Journal of Pain and Symptom Management, 25*(1), 19–28.

Coristine, M., Crooks, D., Grunfeld, E., Stonebridge, C., & Christie, A. (2003). Caregiving for women with advanced breast cancer. *Psycho-Oncology, 12*(7), 709–719.

Critchley, P., Jaddad, A., Taniguchi, A., Woods, A., Stephens, R., & Reyno, L. (1999). Are some palliative care delivery systems more effective and efficient than others? A systematic review of comparative studies. *Journal of Palliative Care, 15*(4), 40–47.

Dugeon, D., & Kristjanson. L. (1995). Home vs. hospital death: Assessment of preferences and challenges. *Canadian Medical Association Journal, 152*, 337–340.

Ferris, F. D., & Cummings, I. (Eds.). (1995). *Palliative care: Toward a consensus in standardized practice.* Ottawa, ON: Canadian Palliative Care Association.

Flanagan, J. (2000). Social perceptions of cancer and their impact: Implications for practice arising from the literature. *Journal of Advanced Nursing, 32*(3), 740–749.

Griffiths, C., Norton, L., Wagstaff, G., & Brunas-Wagstaff, J. (2002). Existential concerns in late stage cancer. *European Journal of Oncology Nursing, 6*(4), 243–246.

Hall, P., Schroder, C., & Weaver, L. (2002). The last 48 hours of life in long term care: A focused chart audit. *Journal of the American Geriatric Society, 23*(2), 334–337.

Health Canada. (2002). Ministers salute National Hospice Palliative Care Week and a year of achievements. Retrieved December 14, 2003 from **www.hc-sc.gc.ca/english/media/releases/2002/2002-33.htm**

Highfield, M. (1992). Spiritual health of oncology patients: Nurse and patient perspectives. *Cancer Nursing, 15*(1), 1–5.

Hopkinson, J., & Hallett, C. (2001). Patients' perceptions of hospice day care: A phenomenological study. *International Journal of Nursing Studies, 38*, 117–125.

Hospice Association of Ontario. (2003). About us. Retrieved August 19, 2003 from **www.hospice.on.ca/About_Us/about_us.htm#HAO's%20Programs%20&%20Services**

Karlsen, S., & Addington-Hall, J. (1998). How do cancer patients who die at home differ from those who die elsewhere? *Palliative Medicine, 12*, 279–286.

Kelley, M., Sellick, S., & Linkewich, B. (2003). Rural no physician perspectives on palliative care services in northwestern Ontario, Canada. *Journal of Rural Health, 19*(1), 55–62.

Kinsella, G., Cooper, B., Picton, C., & Murtagh, D. (2000). A review of the measurement of caregiver and family burden in palliative care. *Journal of Palliative Care, 14*(2), 37–45.

Lesage, P., & Latimer, E. (1998). An approach to ethical issues. In N. MacDonald (Ed.), *Palliative medicine: A case-based manual* (pp. 253–277). Oxford: Oxford University Press.

Lofeld, L., Tschopp, A., Trevor, A., Brazil, K., & Kruger, P. (2000). Assessing the need for and potential role of a day hospice. *Journal of Palliative Care, 16*(4), 5–12.

McCarthy, E., Burns, R., Davis, R., & Phillips, R. (2003). Barriers to hospice care among older patients dying with lung and colorectal cancer. *Journal of Clinical Oncology, 21*(4), 728–735.

McCorkle, R., Robinson, L., Nuamah, I., Lev, E., & Benoliel, J. Q. (1998). The effects of home nursing care for patients during terminal illness on the bereaved psychological distress. *Nursing Research, 47*(1), 2–10.

McWhinney, I., Bass, M., & Orr, V. (1995). Factors associated with location of death of patients transferred to a palliative care team. *Canadian Medical Association Journal, 152*, 361–367.

Miller, J. (2000). *Coping with chronic illness* (3rd ed.). Philadelphia, PA: F. A. Davis.

National Hospice Organization. (1989). *Hospice surveyor operation manual.* Arlington, VA: National Hospice Organization.

Norman, A., Sisler, J., Hack, T., & Harlos, M. (2001). Family physicians and cancer care: Palliative care patients' perceptions. *Canadian Family Physician, 47*, 2009–2012, 2015–2016.

Payne, S., Smith, P., & Dean, S. (1999). Identifying the concerns of informal caregivers in palliative care. *Palliative Medicine, 13*, 37–44.

Reb, A. M. (2003). Palliative and end-of-life care: Policy analysis. *Oncology Nursing Forum, 30*(1), 35–50.

Salberg-Blom, E., Ternestedt, B., & Johanssen, J. (1998). The last month of life, continuity, care site and place of death. *Palliative Medicine, 12*, 287–296.

Saunders, C. (1990). *Hospice and palliative care: An interdisciplinary approach.* London: Edward Arnold.

Schou, K. (1993). Awareness contexts and the construction of dying in the cancer treatment setting: Micro and macro levels in narrative analysis. In D. Clarke (Ed.), *The sociology of death: Theory, culture, practice* (pp. 238–263). Oxford: Blackwell.

Stajduhar, K., & Davies, B. (1998). Death at home: Challenges for families and directions for the future. *Journal of Palliative Care, 14*(3), 6–14.

Steele, R., & Fitch. M. (1996a). Needs of family caregivers of patients receiving home hospice care for cancer. *Oncology Nursing Forum, 23*(5), 823–828.

Steele, R., & Fitch, M. (1996b). Coping strategies of family caregivers of home hospice patients with cancer. *Oncology Nursing Forum, 23*(6), 955–960.

Tomlinson, S. (2002). National action planning workshop on end-of-life care: Workshop report. Ottawa, ON: Health Canada. Retrieved August 19, 2003 **from www.hc-sc.gc.ca/english/care/pallative_workshop.html**

Victoria Hospice Society. (1998). Psychosocial care of the dying. *Medical Care of the Dying* (3rd ed.). Victoria, BC: Victoria Hospice Society.

World Health Organization. (1990). *Cancer pain relief and palliative care.* Geneva, Switzerland: World Health Organization.

ADDITIONAL RESOURCES

Canada's Office of Nursing Policy:
www.hc-sc.gc.ca/onp-bpsi/english/index_e.html

Canadian Association of Psychosocial Oncology (CAPO):
http://capo.ca

Canadian Association of Nurses in Oncology (CANO):
www.cos.ca/cano/

Cancer Care Ontario, Program in Evidence-Based Care:
www.cancercare.on.ca/access_PEBC.htm

Cancer Care Ontario, Program in Evidence-Based Care. (2003). *PEBC practice guidelines & evidence summaries.* Hamilton, ON: Author.
www.cancercare.on.ca/access_358.htm

Carstens, J. (2001). The journey: A palliative care review. *Humane Health Care, 1*(2).
www.humanehealthcare.com/vol12e/journey.htm

Illness: Health care information resources: Palliative care links:
www-hsl.mcmaster.ca/tomflem/palliative.html

Health Canada Secretariat on Palliative and End-of-Life Care:
www.hc-sc.gc.ca/english/care/palliative_secretariat.html

Registered Nurses Association of Ontario (RNAO):
http://rnao.org

Seniors and palliative care [Special issue]. (1998). *Expression: Newsletter of the National Advisory Council on Aging, 1*(3).
www.hc-sc.gc.ca/seniors-aines/naca/expression/11-3/expe11-3.htm

Wellspring:
www.wellspring.ca

Resource Centre of Hamilton, Wellwood:
www.wellwood.on.ca

About the Author

Dauna Crooks, BScN (Toronto), MScN (Western Ontario), DNSc (State University of New York), is Associate Professor at McMaster University, Faculty of Health Sciences, and Associate Chief of Nursing (Education) at The Hospital for Sick Children (HSC). Dr. Crooks' research focuses on supportive care issues for patients with cancer and their caregivers as well as families of children with extremely low birthweight. She has developed educational standards and an advanced nurse practice-role designation for nurse educators and has established an educator orientation program at HSC. She designed a clinical nursing teaching unit to develop and sustain pediatric nursing expertise. Dr. Crooks supervises several graduate students. She is English editor for the Canadian Oncology Nursing Journal.

Part Five
FUTURE DIRECTIONS

CHAPTER 26

Expanding Community Health Nursing Practice

OBJECTIVES

AFTER STUDYING THIS CHAPTER, YOU SHOULD BE ABLE TO:

1. Describe the roles and scope of practice for community-based nurses working as entrepreneurs and nurse practitioners, and in faith community nursing, forensic nursing, and disaster nursing.
2. Describe the challenges faced by community health nurses who practise in these fields.

INTRODUCTION

Community health nursing is a specialty within the practice of nursing. Over the years, community health nurses (CHNs) have gradually defined their different roles in their practice settings. Today, for example, there is a clear distinction between home health nurses and public health nurses (see Chapter 4). There are also other community-based nurses who work with specific individuals, families, aggregates, or communities in health centres, community-based clinics, schools, shelters, churches, the Red Cross, and remote or outpost areas to promote, prevent, and maintain their health. Regardless of the focus and/or setting of their practice, CHNs demonstrate a high level of autonomy and competency that are inherent and specific to their practice. They respond to the changes that result directly or indirectly from our health care system, as well as to technological, environmental, political, and societal influences.

Several nursing specialty areas were chosen to illustrate the expanding community health nursing practice. This chapter consists of five independent sections which describe the roles, historical perspectives, and/or scope of each specialty practice along with the challenges faced by nurses in those practices, namely nurse entrepreneurs, nurse practitioners, faith community nurses, and those who work in disaster nursing and forensic nursing. Nurses from practice and academic settings were invited to describe each community health nursing practice discipline.

I. The Nurse Entrepreneur

Linda Patrick

INTRODUCTION

Nurse entrepreneurs are nurses in independent practice. Being in independent practice requires that the nurse develop business expertise in addition to professional knowledge and skills. The thought of operating a business in nursing may seem a little frightening at first, but many nurses, both hospital and community nurses, find that being in independent practice is exciting and rewarding. In this chapter, you will discover the challenges of being a nurse entrepreneur and the many opportunities for working in non-traditional practice settings and will begin to understand what you need to do to start a business in nursing.

THE NURSE ENTREPRENEUR

Before discussing the opportunities for nurses in independent practice, we need to place this emerging role for nurses within the context of the Canadian health care system. The Canada Health Act of 1984 requires provinces to provide universal coverage only for medically necessary hospital and physicians' services. This means that nurses in independent practice receive private payment for the health care services they provide. Private payment systems limit access to those who can afford to pay or have additional health care coverage. Charging a fee for nursing services is an issue that many nurses, including nurse entrepreneurs, struggle to reconcile. A public health insurance system that includes coverage for nursing services provided by nurses in independent practice would remove the financial barrier, but no such coverage exists at this time.

Nurse entrepreneurs are owners of businesses that offer nursing services to the public. Directly accountable to the client, these nurses may provide the nursing services themselves, form partnerships, or employ others. Carpenito and Neal (1997) define a nurse entrepreneur as "one who organizes, manages, and assumes risks of a business enterprise" (p. 47). They are self-disciplined, self-directed, and goal focused. They work independently and feel comfortable working alone (Rodenberg & Rodenberg, 1998). The roles of a nurse entrepreneur include both clinical and non-clinical. **Clinical roles** include working in advanced practice such as nurse practitioners, clinical nurse specialists, or nurse therapists. **Non-clinical roles** include consulting, educating, editing, or writing (Carpenito & Neal). Nursing services available include advocacy, health promotion, direct care, education, research, administration, or consultation (International Council of Nurses [ICN], 1994). Nurse entrepreneurs can develop their personal practices to focus on patient care delivery and offer cost-effective treatment options such as foot care, therapeutic touch, and counselling (Duffet-Leger, 1995; Wright & Dorsey, 1994). Clients who purchase these services are not limited to individuals, but can include a wide range of people, groups, and organizations (Figure 26.1).

HISTORICAL PERSPECTIVES

Nurses in independent practice are not a new phenomenon. Prior to the Second World War, as many as 60% of all registered nurses in Canada were self-employed in private duty settings (Baumgart & Wheeler, 1992; Canadian Nurses Association [CNA], 1996; Gourlay, 1998). Private duty nurses were employed by individuals and families to provide nursing services for people in their homes. Following the war, "... social, economic, and technological changes resulted in a reorganization of nursing practice, whereby most nurses provided services in hospitals as employees of those institutions" (Gourlay, p. 139). The demand for hospital nurses escalated with the arrival of universal hospital insurance in the late 1950s. By 1989, very few nurses were still working in private duty as almost 85% of all registered nurses found employment in hospital settings (Richardson, 1997).

FIGURE 26.1 Possible Services Offered by Nurse Entrepreneurs

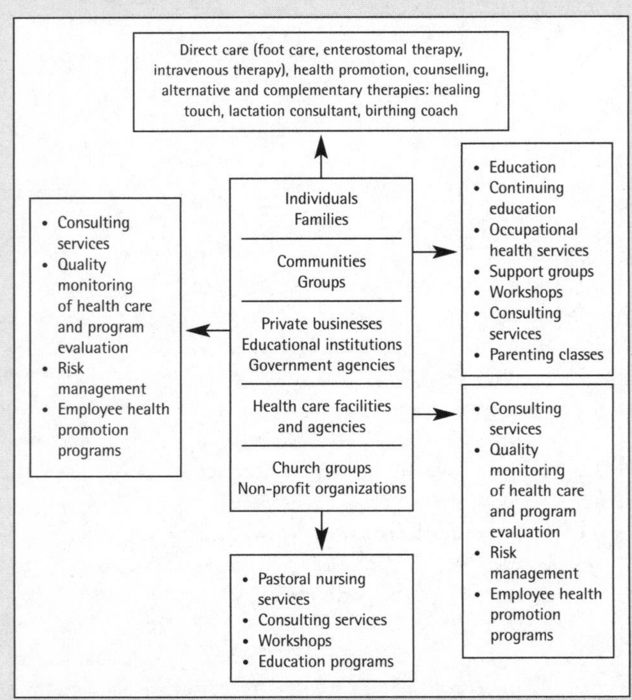

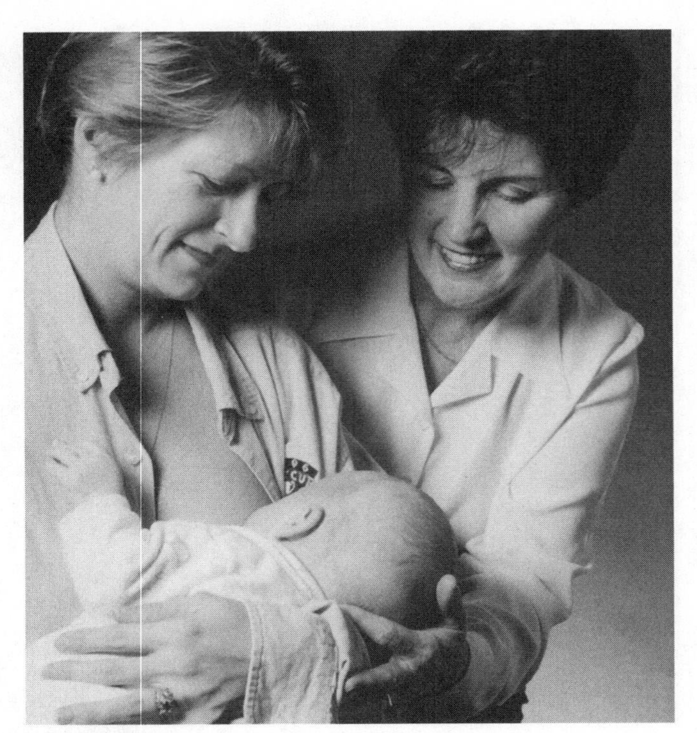

PHOTO 26.1 Lactation Consultant with Mother and Baby

Credit: Reade's Wild Photography

The 1990s, however, saw a resurgence of interest in private practice as nurses became increasingly frustrated with the bureaucracy of large health care institutions (Charbonneau-Smith, 2000). While employment opportunities for Canadian nurses have often been cyclical, the employment climate changed dramatically in the 1990s, particularly in hospital settings. In 1995, the federal government made major reductions in federal cash transfers to the provinces for health care, education, and social services. Nurses in many provinces found themselves unemployed due to the major cuts in provincial health spending that resulted in layoffs and loss of full-time positions. Going into independent practice generated a great deal of interest for unemployed or underemployed nurses. Self-employment offered an alternative during uncertain times. Some nurses viewed independent practice as a way to exert control over an often chaotic and complex environment (White & Bergun, 1998).

BENEFITS OF BECOMING A NURSE ENTREPRENEUR

Today, the search for quality of work life continues to be a key incentive for nurses to look outside traditional places of employment. Independent practice offers opportunities for self-direction and self-control with greater flexibility and freedom (Gourlay, 1998). Tailoring specific nursing skills to meet client needs and practising to their full scope of practice has motivated some nurses to become entrepreneurs. Advancements and changes in nursing education, knowledge, and health care have created new opportunities in health promotion, illness and accident prevention, rehabilitation, and support services (CNA, 1996). In addition, Canadians have become consumers of health care and often wish to choose their own provider (ICN, 1994).

THE CHALLENGES OF INDEPENDENT PRACTICE

Starting a business can be a frightening experience, even for the most experienced nurse. At risk are personal, professional, and financial security, which at first sounds overwhelming. Risks can be minimized, however, with preparation and planning. Gourlay (1998) suggested that learning about potential barriers to success is an essential strategy for managing them later. The barriers identified were "limited education, isolation, dealing with competition, and taking a risk" (p. 140).

Teaching student nurses the management and business skills needed to support independent practice has not been a focus of most undergraduate nursing programs. Nurses seeking this information should talk to other nurses in independent practice and contact their provincial professional organization or the Canadian Nurses Association. Professional nursing organizations across Canada have information, and some provinces have interest groups that provide links for nurses in independent practice. Seek out continuing education courses in business, informatics, computers, and marketing to boost your knowledge and confidence. A search of the internet can provide a great deal of information and be a source of support for nurses who are feeling isolated. Some sites have chat rooms available for sharing stories and ideas. A search of the literature can lead you to articles about nurse entrepreneurship and books written by nurses for other nurses who want to venture into independent practice.

Research Box 26.1

Roggenkamp, S. D., & White, K. R. (1998). Four nurse entrepreneurs: What motivated them to start their own business? *Health Care Management Review, 23*(3), 67–75.

This qualitative study explored the factors that motivate nurse entrepreneurs to go into business, as well as identifying the characteristics of nurse entrepreneurs and the businesses that they operate. Using purposive sampling techniques, it involved one tape-recorded interview and one site visit with each of four nurse entrepreneurs selected to participate. Transcribed interviews, artifacts, and field notes were analyzed for topics. From the most important topics, patterns of relationships were derived. The findings of the study focused on the motivations, behaviours, and attitudes of nurse entrepreneurs.

Three primary factors prompted the four nurses in this study to pursue independent practice: their love of nursing, a belief that they could make a difference, and family influence. The study also identified other factors that either support or impede the success of the business venture, for example, a critical event or something that happens to provide enough incentive for the nurse to jump in and start the business. The primary disabler identified in the study was lack of business training and business skills.

The literature revealed that very little research exists about independent practice and the nurse entrepreneur. This study adds validity to the large volume of anecdotal information that is available on the topic and is a beginning point for future research. No equivalent Canadian studies were located, but some aspects of this study are relevant for all nurses thinking about independent practice.

Discussion Questions

1. What critical event(s) within our Canadian health care system occurred in the 1990s that may have had a strong influence on some nurses in Canada going into independent practice?
2. How can a nurse who would like to go into independent practice overcome the primary disabler identified in this study?

CASE STUDY

L. T. graduated from a Canadian university with a BScN degree in 1990. Following graduation she worked in a variety of clinical settings as a registered nurse, primarily in part-time and casual appointments. In the early years of her nursing career, L. T. experienced employment insecurity. This required her to juggle several jobs to make the equivalent of a full-time paycheque. L. T. became frustrated with her chaotic work schedule and was tempted many times to move out of a nursing career and pursue her other interest of being a teacher. Reluctant to do so, however, L. T. made what she called her "last attempt to make it in nursing" and moved to a large urban centre in 1998. She found a full-time position working as a public health nurse in maternal-child health. The full-time position provided her with enough money to support herself while working in a clinical nursing specialty that she enjoyed. L. T. has also discovered that she has a particular skill in coaching new mothers about breastfeeding. Other nurses often seek her expertise, patience, and skill with challenging cases. A more organized work schedule makes it possible for L. T. to pursue an MScN degree part time. Her career path includes becoming a lactation consultant with her own business.

Discussion Questions

1. Has L. T. chosen the best path of education and clinical experience in her journey to become a lactation consultant? Are there any other credentials she will need?
2. What should L. T. investigate prior to leaving her current position at the health unit to pursue her independent practice as a lactation consultant?

PRELIMINARY STEPS TO BECOMING AN ENTREPRENEUR

Deciding on whether or not independent practice is right for you requires self-assessment. Self-reflection also helps you describe the kind of independent practice that you can offer (CNA, 1996; Gourlay, 1998). Will you offer a service, such as "hands-on care," and who will be your clients? Is any new learning required to be successful and competent in your practice? Being realistic about what you can do and whether or not the service will be competitive and meet the needs in the health care market are very important points to consider. It also helps identify any potential sources of funding and other agencies that might support the services you have chosen to offer (CNA).

Business Issues

Writing a well–thought-out **business plan** is considered a cornerstone of a successful business venture. Starting up a business requires planning, which includes considering how the business will be financed. Small business owners must consider start-up costs, operating costs, and overhead. If the business has employees, employment benefits such as health insurance, pension plans, accident benefits, workers' compensation benefits, and possibly a car allowance must be accounted for. If other registered nurses are employed, a professional practice work environment must be fostered through facilitating access to educational activities and providing support for those nurses to continue their education (CNA, 1998). These professional development opportunities are often partially financed by the employer, shared with the individual nurses, professional nursing organizations, educational institutions, and governments.

Resources available to the nurse entrepreneur include books, seminars, and workshops about the various aspects of owning and operating a business. One important relationship is with a banker or financial advisor—an expert in small business start-up—who can guide the beginning nurse entrepreneur through the potential pitfalls of starting up a business and assist with financial planning for future growth.

Establishing fees for the services provided can be intimidating to a beginning nurse entrepreneur. Fees must cover the direct costs of doing the business and also contribute to overhead and profit. Decisions about fees are influenced by what other nurses who offer similar services are charging and how much consumers are willing to pay (Gourlay, 1998). Doing research upfront and planning the business well in advance of opening the doors will pave the way for a smoother beginning.

Professional Issues

According to the Canadian Nurses Association (1995), "self-employed nurses are legally permitted to offer any service that falls within the practice of nursing and does not infringe on the legislated responsibility or the exclusive practice of another health discipline" (p. 10–12). A nurse who is considering independent practice should begin by reflecting on personal knowledge, skills, experience, and education. It is also imperative that the nurse be familiar with the legislated and legal parameters of the profession, both federally and provincially.

The profession of nursing in Canada requires that its members possess significant education and preparation for practice. The specific standards for each province are monitored to ensure that nursing education programs respond to changes in health care that are due to advances in knowledge and technology (Potter & Perry, 2001). To prepare for independent practice, the nurse must often go beyond this basic education and preparation. A commitment to continuing education is also essential for the nurse entrepreneur. The reasons for this are best captured by the Canadian Nurses Association's policy statement on educational support for competent nursing (see text box).

Canadian Nurses Association Statement on Continuing Education

All Canadian nurses are accountable for providing competent nursing care to their clients. It is a belief of the CNA that in order to provide competent nursing care, a registered nurse must maintain and continuously enhance the knowledge, skills, attitude, and judgment required to meet client needs in an evolving health care system.

Nurses maintain their competence in a variety of ways, and continuing nursing education is one means of maintaining and increasing knowledge and skills. To practise safely and competently, registered nurses must

- comply with professional standards,
- base their practice on relevant knowledge,
- adhere to the Code of Ethics for Registered Nurses, and
- acquire new skills and knowledge in their area of practice on a continuing basis.

Continuing nursing education consists of learning experiences organized by a facility, agency, or educational institution undertaken by registered nurses to enhance their nursing competencies. It is a mechanism for nurses

- to assure that their competencies are relevant to their nursing practice and promote optimal health outcomes in their clients, and
- to advance their knowledge, skills, attitude, and judgment in specific areas of practice.

The responsibility for educational support for competent nursing practice is shared among individual nurses, professional nursing organizations, employers, educational institutions, and governments as they all make decisions that affect the common goal of quality care.

Individual nurses have the primary responsibility for ensuring on a continuing basis that their competencies are relevant and up-to-date.

Source: Adapted with permission from the Canadian Nurses Association. (1998). Educational support for competent nursing practice: CNA policy statement. *Ottawa, ON: Author.*

A critical professional issue is that of liability protection. The Canadian Nurses Protective Society (CNPS) was established in 1988 after commercial professional liability insurance for nurses "became expensive and unreliable" (CNPS, 2002). CNPS was formed as a joint venture by provincial and territorial nurses' professional associations. Membership in CNPS is automatically included in most of these professional associations' yearly dues. The non-profit society is owned and operated by nurses for nurses. The mandate of the CNPS is "to provide, at its discretion, legal and financial assistance to nurses registered with a participating professional association, in the event of a claim made or threatened in connection with the provision of professional nursing services; and to provide legal information and education for the management of risks related to the delivery of nursing services" (CNPS).

In addition to the protection offered by the CNPS, some provincial nursing associations offer additional and optional insurance coverage. For example, the Registered Nurses Association of Ontario (RNAO) offers malpractice and business insurance called NurseInsure. The plan was established to meet the growing number of RNAO members who expressed a need for additional malpractice insurance and business insurance. This group of nurses includes, but is not limited to, nurse practitioners, nurses in independent practice, CHNs, and rehabilitation nurses. The **business insurance** covers physical loss or damage to the practice's buildings, equipment, and contents; extra expenses incurred in the event of a business loss, including associated lost income; theft of money; and employee dishonesty or fraud (RNAO, 1999; 2002).

Additional professional considerations include the management of client records, writing a description of the practice, and accountability (CNA, 1996). As mentioned previously, as members of a self-regulating profession, entrepreneurial nurses are accountable to their clients and their professional regulatory body. In some situations they may also be accountable to a third party who has contracted them to do nursing services. In all cases, nurse entrepreneurs are guided by legislation, provincial/territorial standards of nursing practice, and the CNA Code of Ethics for Nursing (CNA, 1997).

SUMMARY

A career as a nurse entrepreneur may not be for everyone, but for nurses who have a broad knowledge base and an understanding of the community needs and who embrace risk-taking and independence, it can be an exciting opportunity. More nurses are accepting this challenge and becoming entrepreneurs as more opportunities for independent practice emerge. The timing is good as support networks for nurses in independent practice are more abundant today than ever before.

This section on the nurse entrepreneur provides fundamental information about the basic requirements of moving into independent practice. A nurse who is considering this career option should also access the many available books, online internet resources, and guidelines from individual provincial nursing associations and the Canadian Nurses Association.

II. Primary Health Care Nurse Practitioners

Christine Thrasher and Eric Staples

INTRODUCTION

In searching for ways to deal with the challenges of resource allocation, primary health care has evolved as a framework for health service delivery (Schoenhofer, 1995). And to foster the development and advancement of nursing practice, nurse practitioners gradually evolved. Their expanded role in nursing practice combines nursing and medical knowledge with a commitment to client-centred care (Philips & Steele, 1994). A **nurse practitioner** is a registered nurse with advanced knowledge and decision-making skills in assessment, diagnosis, and health care management. This section describes the history of nurse practitioners, their expanded roles, their practice areas, and future directions of their practice. Many nurse practitioners work in primary health care and are called primary health care nurse practitioners (PHC-NPs).

HISTORICAL PERSPECTIVES

In 1967, the first education program for nurse practitioners (NPs) working in northern nursing stations was started at Dalhousie University in Nova Scotia. In 1971, the Boudreau Report made the implementation of the expanded role of the RN a high priority in Canada's health care system. The first university program in Ontario to prepare expanded-role RNs was initiated. In 1973, the CNA/CMA released a joint policy statement on the role of the NPs. In the early 1980s, the first NP initiative ended and the last NP program closed in Ontario due to a perceived physician oversupply, lack of remuneration mechanisms, lack of legislation, lack of public awareness regarding the role of NP, and lack of support from both medicine and nursing. Some 250 NPs continued to function through the 1980s and early 1990s, working mainly in community health centres and in northern nursing stations with a variety of educational preparations and responsibilities. In spite of the failure of the first initiative, the NP role was consistently cited by many provincial health care commissions and task forces as a valuable role in the delivery of health care. As well, a greater emphasis and commitment to disease and injury prevention, health promotion, and community-based care emerged.

In 1993, the Ontario Minister of Health announced a new NP initiative as part of improving access to primary health care while developing a more comprehensive and cost-effective health care system (Ontario Ministry of Health, 1994). The College of Nurses of Ontario approved a new class of registration in the RN category, called the **extended class**, and referred proposed legislation changes to the Health Professionals Regulatory Advisory Council (HPRAC) in April 1995. In June 1996, following extensive hearings from the public and health care professionals, HPRAC released eight recommendations in support of legislative authority for PHC-NPs. Bill 127, the Expanded Nursing Services for

Patients Act, was proclaimed in 1998. The Act gives NPs in Ontario independent authority to communicate a medical diagnosis; prescribe from a range of medications listed in the regulations; and order specific lab tests, x-rays, and diagnostic ultrasounds.

PHC-NPs have advanced education, which permits them to promote health, prevent disease, and monitor and manage stable chronic conditions such as hypertension, diabetes, and asthma. A recent systematic review found that care delivered by NPs in various primary care settings resulted in higher patient satisfaction and quality of care compared with physician care, with no difference in health outcomes (Horrocks, Anderson, & Salisbury, 2002). Other provinces have or are in the process of establishing legislation and credentials through their governments and registering nursing bodies.

The following sections describe the specific practice requirements for NPs as outlined by the College of Nurses of Ontario (2001; 2003). **Primary health care nurse practitioners** (PHC-NPs) are registered nurses who are specialists in primary health care and who provide accessible, comprehensive, and effective care to clients of all ages. They are experienced nurses with additional nursing education that enables them to provide individuals, families, groups, and communities with health services in health promotion, disease and injury prevention, cure, rehabilitation, and support. Whereas NPs are advanced practice nurses functioning within the full scope of nursing practice, they are neither a second-level physician nor a doctor's assistant. NP skills include the ability to:

- provide wellness care, including health screening activities such as Pap smears;
- monitor infant growth and development;
- diagnose and treat minor illnesses such as ear and bladder infections;
- diagnose and treat minor injuries such as sprains and lacerations;
- screen for the presence of chronic disease, such as diabetes; and
- monitor people with stable chronic disease, such as hypertension.

The practice of PHC-NPs is usually regulated through a province's registering body. Standards of practice for advanced practices include:

- practice expectations/competencies,
- expectations for consultation with physicians, and
- standards for prescribing drugs, ordering lab tests, and ordering x-rays and ultrasounds.

ONGOING REGISTRATION

An annual quality assurance reflective practice is usually required for all NPs as are ongoing competency reviews. The reviews focus on the establishment and evaluation of an appropriate network of collaborative consultants from other health professions and the compliance with provincial standards of practice. Currently, many PHC-NPs perform diagnostic and prescribing activities under the authority of a physician, often by means of a medical directive. Registration in an advanced practice category permits the PHC-NP to assume sole accountability for these activities. It is important for clients and colleagues to know whether or not a PHC-NP is registered in an advanced practice category.

Practice Expectations

Several practice expectations are specific to the advanced practice category. Registration is based on the demonstration of competency in each area discussed below.

Health Assessment and Diagnosis The PHC-NP:

- performs a comprehensive health assessment and synthesizes data from multiple sources to make a diagnosis of a disease or disorder within the PHC-NP scope of practice to diagnose.
- completes a comprehensive health assessment, including an appropriate health history and physical examination.
- demonstrates sound clinical judgment and diagnostic reasoning abilities in synthesizing health information in order to identify a health problem or medical diagnosis within the PHC-NP scope of practice.
- modifies assessment techniques according to the client's condition, culture, and stage of development.
- applies the principles of pathophysiology, including etiology, developmental considerations, pathogenesis, and clinical manifestations of commonly encountered acute and chronic illnesses and injuries, in order to diagnose a disease or disorder within the PHC-NP scope of practice.
- determines the need for, appropriately orders from an approved list, and accurately interprets the results of relevant screening and diagnostic laboratory tests in order to diagnose a disease or disorder within the PHC-NP scope of practice and in order to monitor clients who have a previously diagnosed disease or disorder.
- determines the need for, appropriately orders, and interprets reports of chest and limb x-rays and diagnostic ultrasounds to diagnose a disease or disorder within the PHC-NP scope of practice and to monitor clients who have a previously diagnosed disease or disorder.
- effectively communicates health findings and/or the diagnosis of a disease or disorder to the client and discusses the prognosis and options for treatment for those conditions within the PHC-NP scope of practice to treat.

Therapeutics The PHC-NP:

- initiates and manages the care of clients with diseases or disorders within the PHC-NP scope of practice and/or monitors the ongoing therapy of clients with chronic stable illness by providing effective pharmacological, complementary, or counselling interventions.

- critically appraises and applies current, relevant research into clinical practice.
- applies knowledge of pharmacology, including pharmacokinetics and pharmacodynamics, when selecting and prescribing drugs included in the Schedules of the Regulations to treat diseases or disorders within the PHC-NP scope of practice.
- appropriately incorporates or suggests complementary therapies.
- provides effective counselling to individuals, families, or groups.
- determines the need for, and competently sutures tissue in and above the fascia.

The PHC-NP manages the treatment of clients with diseases or disorders within the PHC-NP scope of practice and treats by:

- assisting, supporting, and/or facilitating clients to design, follow, and evaluate recommended therapeutic regimes;
- monitoring the effect of the chosen therapy, making necessary adjustments within the PHC-NP scope of practice; and
- evaluating the effect of selected treatments and interventions using sound diagnostic reasoning skills.

The PHC-NP also manages the treatment of clients with chronic stable diseases or disorders diagnosed by a physician by:

- assisting, supporting, and/or facilitating clients to follow and evaluate recommended therapeutic regimes;
- monitoring the effect of the chosen therapy, making necessary adjustments within the PHC-NP scope of practice; and
- evaluating the effect of selected treatments and interventions using sound diagnostic reasoning skills.

Roles and Responsibilities The PHC-NP:

- practises autonomously, offering the full scope of primary health care NP practice.
- consults with a physician or other health care professional when the client's condition requires care beyond the PHC-NP scope of practice.
- is able to articulate the role of the PHC-NP within the nursing profession and the responsibilities/accountability inherent in autonomous practice and in relation to other health care professionals.
- appropriately consults with a physician in accordance with the Expectations for Consultation with Physicians by Registered Nurses in the Extended Class and/or appropriately refers a client to another health care professional. Consultation or referral can occur at any point in the assessment of the client or when planning, implementing, or evaluating the client's care—whenever the client's condition requires care beyond the scope of practice of the PHC-NP.

Health Promotion and Disease Prevention The PHC-NP:

- implements strategies to promote health and prevent illness with individuals, families, and groups.
- determines the need for and implements health promotion and primary and secondary prevention strategies for individuals, families, and communities or for specific age and cultural groups.
- applies theories of teaching and learning when providing health education to individuals and groups.

Family Health The PHC-NP:

- is proficient in interventions relating to the assessment and care of families.
- synthesizes information from individual clients to identify broader implications for health within the family.
- uses family assessment tools to evaluate family strengths and needs, reinforcing family strengths.
- applies theories of family dynamics, interactions, and role expectations when managing the care of families.

Community Development and Planning The PHC-NP:

- is proficient in interventions relating to community assessment, development, and program planning.
- synthesizes information from individual clients to identify broader implications for health within the community.
- uses community assessment data and knowledge of the determinants of health to identify community needs and resources when developing and implementing age and culturally sensitive community development programs.
- applies principles of epidemiology and demography to clinical practice.

Expectations for Consultation

Consultation with other health professions is the cornerstone of multidisciplinary care. It is expected that PHC-NPs will consult with members of other health professions as appropriate in order to ensure that the overall health care needs of their clients are met. These expectations for consultation focus mainly on the situations that extend beyond PHC-NP practice into medical practice. Although consultation may occur at any time during the nurse-client relationship, it is expected that, as a minimum, all PHC-NPs will consult with a physician when deemed necessary according to these expectations.

The degree to which the physician becomes involved may vary. Consultation may result in the physician providing an opinion and recommendation; an opinion, recommendation, and concurrent intervention; or assuming primary responsibility for the care of the client.

Collaboration Collaboration is a component of all interactions among health care professionals. Collaboration means working together with one or more members of the health care team who each make a unique contribution toward achieving a common goal. Each individual contributes from within the limits of their scope of practice.

Clinical Expectations

The PHC-NP should seek consultation with a physician when the diagnosis and/or treatment plan is unclear or beyond the scope of the PHC-NP to determine, including, but not limited to, any of the following:

- persistent or recurring sign(s) or symptom(s) that cannot be attributed to an identifiable cause;
- report(s) of imaging or laboratory tests that suggest a previously undiagnosed chronic systemic illness;
- symptomatic or laboratory evidence of decreased or decreasing function of any vital organ or system;
- sign(s) of recurrent or persistent infection;
- any atypical presentation of a common illness or unusual response to treatment;
- any sign(s) or symptom(s) of a sexually transmitted disease in a child;
- any sign(s) or symptom(s) of behavioural changes that cannot be attributed to a specific cause;
- any blunt, penetrating, or other wound that may involve damage below the fascia or functional impairment;
- sign(s) or symptom(s) of any fetal or maternal pregnancy risk factor when a client's chronic condition destabilizes, including, but not limited to, symptomatic or laboratory evidence of destabilization and/or unexpected deterioration in the condition of a client who is being managed for a previously diagnosed illness; and
- deviation from normal growth and development in an infant or child in potentially life-threatening situations, including, but not limited to, cases with any of the following present:
    - any sign(s) or symptom(s) of an acute event that is potentially threatening to life, limb, or senses;
    - sign(s) or symptom(s) of obstruction of any system;
    - signs of severe or widespread infection;
    - fever greater than 39°C in a child 3–36 months old with no identifiable focus of infection; and
    - any sign(s) or symptom(s) of illness in a child less than 3 months old.

Scope of Responsibility The PHC-NP may order specific x-rays or ultrasounds to:

- confirm the diagnosis of a short-term, episodic illness or injury as suggested by the client's history and/or physical findings;
- rule out a potential diagnosis that, if present, would require consultation with an appropriate physician for treatment;
- assess/monitor ongoing conditions of clients with stable chronic illnesses; or
- screen for diseases.

PRACTICE SITES

Community Health Centres and Mental Health Clinics

The most common settings for NP/MD collaborative practice are community health centres. NPs can meet many of the primary health care needs in underserviced communities. Although part of the role involves monitoring the response to medications for psychiatric conditions, the main focus is to attend to the primary health care needs for preventive health care, health maintenance, disease prevention, and management of chronic medical conditions. Using a collaborative community team that can involve family, friends, and medical and service providers, NPs strengthen the individual's natural support system.

A mental health problem, on the other hand, is a disruption in the interactions between the individual, the group, and the environment. Such a disruption may result from factors within the individual, including physical or mental illness or inadequate coping skills. It may also spring from external causes such as harsh environmental conditions, unjust social structures, or tensions within the family or community. An effective response to mental health problems must therefore address a broader range of factors. Mental health promotion and education, prevention of mental illness, treatment, and rehabilitation activities should take place alongside one another.

Mental health research indicates that early intervention and support following traumatic life events can prevent serious mental health problems such as depression, suicide, and family violence. While 1% of the population has a chronic or serious mental illness, one in three individuals will require mental health services sometime during their lives. A team approach is embodied in the professional relationships between the PHC-NP and the family physician as well as the psychiatrist. Referrals may originate from the NP to the physician or psychiatrist and, likewise, may return to the NP from the physician or psychiatrist for continued follow-up and management after diagnosis and initial determination of therapy. Physicians who require augmented services for their clients may refer them to the NP for medical follow-up for potential medical complications of prescribed psychiatric medications. Monitoring of weight gain and blood glucose levels, along with health teaching for meal plans and exercise, are examples of shared care between members of the health care team.

Emergency Departments

NPs have recently been introduced into a number of emergency departments (EDs) in Ontario hospitals to attend to patients presenting with primary health care needs. Given the long waiting times in EDs and the large proportion of patients who present with non-emergency, primary health care needs, this initiative has tremendous potential to improve the efficiency and effectiveness of health care delivery in EDs. NPs have been utilized in EDs in the U.S. for a number of years. In many parts of Canada there are not enough physicians to cover emergency room needs.

NPs can diagnose and treat 50–80% of the problems seen in hospital emergency departments. They can assess common episodic illnesses, conditions, and injuries; order certain x-rays and lab tests; prescribe certain medications; and suture lacerations. NPs can also perform initial detailed histories and physical examinations for more urgent health problems.

Community and Home Health Care

NPs can work within community and home health nursing agencies to assess and manage the health needs of clients. Many parts of Canada do not have enough family physicians for primary health care, so people are forced to go to hospitals for all kinds of problems. Too often, Canadians are experiencing unnecessary illness and more serious complications because they lack access to comprehensive primary health care services.

Along with public health nurses, NPs can meet most of the health care needs of individuals, families, and communities through different public health clinics (e.g., sexual health clinics, college and university clinics). They can diagnose, treat, and counsel.

Long-Term Care/Palliative Care

NPs are qualified to provide ongoing primary health care to people with stable chronic illness at home or in institutions. Most residents of long-term care or palliative care facilities have chronic illnesses and disabilities that need to be monitored and managed in order to maintain optimal quality of life. Many communities have difficulty providing primary care to institutionalized residents and must transfer them to hospital emergency departments when they become ill. As our population ages, there will be more and more need for primary care for residents in long-term care settings.

Working with registered nurses, registered practical nurses, and public health nurses, NPs can provide care within a health promotion and disease prevention model that would maintain optimum health and decrease transfers and admissions to hospitals.

FUTURE DIRECTIONS

Challenges/Barriers

Challenges to the full integration of PHC-NPs into the primary care system include the lack of long-term remuneration strategies, and consumer awareness. The fee-for-service funding model is a major barrier to NP employment because most primary health care is provided by physicians. Instead, NPs are paid by salary. Physicians in underserviced communities would like to work with NPs, but, currently, no permanent funding mechanism allows them to do so. There are no government channels through which to make requests for NP positions.

Solutions

Permanent, well-established funding mechanisms through which communities can apply for NP positions must be established, possibly through federal transfer funds and savings from hospital restructuring. Provincial underserviced area programs should be expanded to provide permanent assistance to both physicians and NPs to ensure that primary health care is provided in underserviced communities.

RESEARCH ISSUES AND LEGISLATIVE ISSUES

Recent initiatives to integrate NPs into the health care system provide an excellent opportunity to explore unanswered questions. It is critical that any new health profession introduced into a health care setting be safe, effective, economically efficient, and able to provide a high quality of care. Changes to the system must also contribute to a high level of satisfaction for all stakeholders. The public, employers, and decision makers must be convinced that NPs are effective and efficient providers of primary health care.

Research initiatives should include:

- the evaluation of the impact of NPs on quality primary health care services,
- the development of specific performance indicators for the ongoing evaluation of the quality of care delivered by NPs and other health care providers,
- the examination of the impact of a primary care provider on patient satisfaction,
- the evaluation of the impact of NPs on patient outcomes,
- a comparison of the outcomes for patients randomly assigned to NPs or MDs to the outcomes for patients without a primary care provider,
- the examination of the utilization patterns of NPs, and
- the evaluation of the impact of NPs on health care system utilization.

Further evaluation of outcomes and the processes/practices that lead to positive outcomes are required. Future research will be needed to determine the appropriate cost-effective mix of health care providers and to review reimbursement.

SUMMARY

When carrying out the advanced practice role, NPs must examine if there is a need and explore or assess maximum utilization of current resources. Concerted efforts must be made to continue to define their role. By doing this, NPs will be able to provide safe, effective, and efficient care for their clients.

III. Faith Community Health Nursing

Joanne K. Olson and Lynn J. Anderson

INTRODUCTION

The term faith community nurse is used to convey the broad nature of the concept and to include the rich diversity of faith traditions existing in our multicultural Canadian society (Clark & Olson, 2000). Within some faith traditions there is limited understanding of the terms parish and parish nursing because these terms originate mainly from Christian denominations. In this section, the historical background of faith community nursing will be explored with a vignette to illustrate the role and functions of faith community nurses. Education, the challenges facing practice, and research will be addressed.

WHAT IS FAITH COMMUNITY NURSING?

A **faith community nurse** (FCN) is a registered nurse who is hired or recognized by a faith community to carry out an intentional health promotion ministry (Clark & Olson, 2000). Historically, FCNs have been referred to as parish nurses. The Canadian Association for Parish Nursing Ministry (CAPNM) defines a **parish nurse** as "a registered nurse with specialized knowledge who is called to ministry and affirmed by a faith community to promote health, healing, and wholeness" (Canadian Association for Parish Nursing Ministry, 2000).

The term **faith community** refers to a community of people who share a similar history, values, and beliefs around their relationship with a higher power and with others in the world (Buijs & Olson, 2001). They often gather for purposes of worship and to support one another. **Ministry** refers to one who represents the mission and purposes of a particular faith community, carries out their role in accordance with established standards, and is accountable to the public served rather than working in isolation or carrying out a personal agenda (McBrien, 1987; Olson & Clark, 2000). Specialized knowledge for FCNs is acquired beyond basic nursing preparation. Many FCNs receive such knowledge through additional nursing and theology courses that prepare them for a nursing practice within a unique setting and in relationship with faith community leaders.

Historical Background

Faith community nursing developed from parish nursing, which was founded by Granger Westberg. The idea originated in Chicago, Illinois in the mid-1980s but rapidly grew throughout the United States. Westberg noticed that the professional knowledge and skills of registered nurses made a significant contribution to the health of people within faith communities. Nurses were prepared to address physical, psychosocial, and spiritual needs and often served as translators between the faith community and the health care system (Westberg, 1999).

In the early 1990s, the idea of parish nursing began to develop in Canada, and, by 1996, the first Canadian parish nursing practices were established (Olson, Clark, & Simington, 1999). Since that time, interest in faith community nursing has spread across Canada. By 1998, the CAPNM was established to bring together Canadians interested and/or working in faith community nursing. This organization establishes standards of practice for parish nursing and guidelines for the parish nursing education in Canada.

Faith Community Nursing as a Subset of Community Nursing

Faith community nursing is viewed as a sub-specialty of community health nursing. As such, the core standards of practice for community health nursing relate to faith community nursing. FCNs adhere to these standards within a very specialized setting, a faith community. Increasingly, denominations across Canada are seeing the value of such professionals in faith communities and are taking steps to ensure that these nurses are included as a recognized part of ministry teams.

Each of the standards of practice for community health nursing is examined below in light of the professional nursing roles carried out by FCNs (Clark, 2000a; Community Health Nurses Association of Canada, 2003).

Promoting Health The first standard of practice focuses on the promotion of the health of individuals, families, and communities within and beyond faith communities in order to develop and maintain their personal and communal resources (Clark & Olson, 2000). As a sub-specialty of community health nursing, FCNs also address the socio-political and spiritual issues that influence the health of the populations.

Building Individual and Community Capacity FCNs strive to build individual and community capacity with in-depth community, group, and individual assessments. Community development principles are used to address health-related issues that arise in the lives of individuals and families and within the faith community as a whole. Evaluation of the impact of change on individuals and communities is ongoing.

Connecting and Caring Many Canadian FCNs use the McGill Model of nursing, which involves active collaboration with individuals and communities as they identify their health issues, strengths, and resources (Clark & Olson, 2000). They must maintain professional boundaries within a setting in which social and professional relationships could become confused.

Termination of professional relationships when appropriate is also addressed in this standard. FCNs using the McGill Model to guide practice would terminate with specific individuals and families when goals are achieved but would remain in contact because of the nature of faith communities (Olson, 2000a). Finally, this standard refers to the use by community health nurses of reflective practice as an evaluation strategy. To enhance their ability to conduct reflective practice, many FCNs take clinical pastoral education and/or enroll in courses on theological reflection (Clark, 2000b).

Facilitating Access and Equity This standard speaks of CHNs embracing the philosophy of primary health care, working toward universality and equitable access to available services, and acting to influence the determinants of health. FCNs often work with groups within and beyond the faith community to promote social justice, a faith community term for ideas similar to universality and equitable access.

Demonstrating Professional Responsibility and Accountability Similar to CHNs in general practice, FCNs work with a high degree of independence. Therefore, they are keenly aware of the need for their own accountability for professional practice. They are accountable to their clients, to the faith community, and to the professional body that regulates nursing practice in their province. Professional nursing practice that includes appropriate educational preparation, continuing education, and adherence to professional standards of practice is of utmost importance in this complex and autonomous nursing practice (Olson, 2000c).

ROLE AND FUNCTIONS OF THE FAITH COMMUNITY NURSE

The functions of FCNs include integrator of faith and health, health educator, personal health counsellor, referral agent, trainer of volunteers, developer of support groups, and health advocate. The client situations are often complex and require the FCN to carry out these seven interconnected functions simultaneously. Based on the vignette in the text box, each of these functions will be discussed below.

Vignette

K. M. T. is an FCN serving several small faith communities in a rural community in one of Canada's prairie provinces. The rural community has suffered a severe drought, resulting in several years of difficult financial times for local farmers and area businesses. K. M. T. is concerned about several faith community members who have demonstrated behaviours indicative of depression. Her concerns were increased when a national newspaper carried a story about a farmer who had committed suicide in the context of a similar, seemingly hopeless situation. As well, Ellen, a middle-aged woman, recently stopped attending worship services after many years of being active in the church choir and teaching in the Sunday School. Ellen is going through a very difficult time in her marriage.

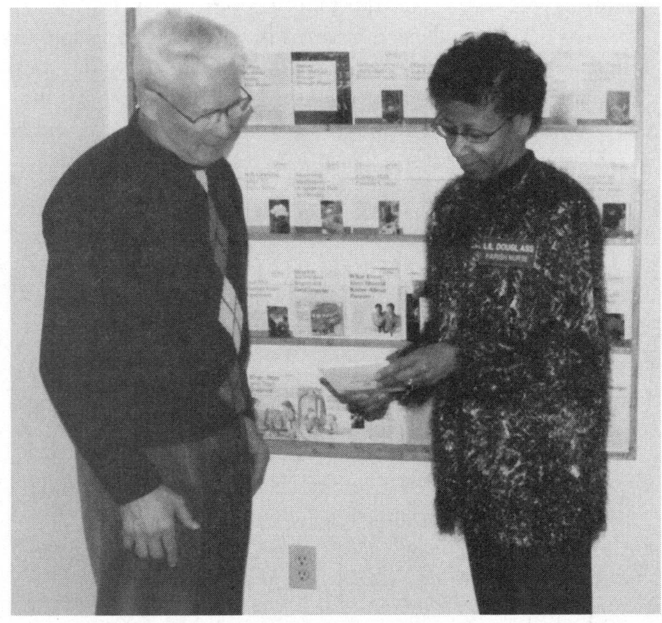

PHOTO 26.2 A Faith Community Nurse in Practice Setting

Credit: Joanne K. Olson

Integrator of Faith and Health

FCNs work to promote dialogue between faith and health, thus assisting people and groups to realize the interconnection. They work with people who are not currently experiencing difficulty to remind them that strengthening their spiritual dimension assists them to remain whole and healthy. When experiencing changes in life situations, people often need help to reflect upon the connection between their faith and health. The FCN may work independently in this area or collaboratively with the faith community leader. FCNs need to be knowledgeable about the human spirit, spirituality, the spiritual dimension, and the commonalities and differences between spirituality and religion. This requires reflection on their own spiritual development and continuous growth related to spiritual health. They need skills in spiritual assessment and intervention, which may include appropriate referral to spiritual resources such as prayer, music, spiritual literature, worship, sacraments, healing touch, healing services, or meditation (Olson, 2000b).

Initially, FCNs may make individual contact with each of the members about whom they are concerned. During an initial assessment, FCNs combine their knowledge and skills about mental health, physical health, and spiritual health. During such visits, questions often emerge that are spiritual in nature: "Why is this happening to me?" "Where is God in my life?" or " Why is God so angry at me?" FCNs must determine whether the individuals need referral or require nursing interventions. In some cases a collaborative approach is required in which both nursing and other ministry personnel become involved. Individual, family, or group intervention may be appropriate. For example, in the vignette, the FCN could refer Ellen to a community group that focuses on supporting people going through marriage difficulties. As well, a support group in the faith community could be established to offer emotional support to local farming families as they share their stories with each other.

Health Educator

Sometimes FCNs carry out health education in formal, planned ways through group work and seminars. At other times, health education occurs spontaneously on an individual basis. In the vignette, the FCN became involved in health education about emotional health in times of stress. K. M. T. knows from her education, research, and previous experience that many people undergoing stress choose to isolate themselves from others, suppress feelings, neglect physical care, and use short-term coping mechanisms. In her professional interactions with these individuals, K. M. T. uses every opportunity to share this important health information.

Personal Health Counsellor

At times, specific individuals and families within a faith community require intense, short-term interaction with an FCN. Using the professional nursing process, FCNs serve in the role of personal health counsellor, meeting regularly with the individual or family around a specific health-related issue. These connections may occur within the faith community, in the home, or during hospital visits. FCNs encourage individuals to express feelings, identify their own health issues, explore possible solutions, and appraise the effectiveness of each solution. While building upon the strengths that already exist within individuals and families, FCNs also introduce new possibilities.

In the vignette, K. M. T. and Ellen determined together that the stress in Ellen's life was contributing to her sleeping difficulties. In an effort to try new ways of dealing with stress, Ellen expressed an interest in yoga. K. M. T. supported Ellen in her interest by discussing the health benefits of yoga and working with Ellen to locate classes being offered in the community. Working with the group of local farmers, K. M. T. learned that they are a group of proud and independent individuals who chose to continue dealing with their issues in their own ways. She respects their choices and offers to remain available should there be an interest later. This way of interacting promotes trust and builds long-term relationships.

Referral Agent

One of the main functions carried out by an FCN is that of referral agent. FCNs are important links between the needs of individuals, families, and groups and the resources available in and beyond the faith community. Through ongoing community assessment, FCNs build relationships within the faith community and with the agencies in the larger community. This helps keep their knowledge of the resources current.

Trainer of Volunteers

FCNs do not carry out their work in isolation. Often they recruit, educate, and support volunteers from within the faith community to assist with the health ministry. Effective use of volunteers can contribute in many ways to the community's health. While volunteers add to the health and well-being of others, the health-promoting benefits of using one's gifts and talents cannot be overlooked. In the vignette, while Ellen was working closely with K. M. T., she experienced the long-term illness and death of her father. The FCN became involved by arranging for volunteers to prepare meals for Ellen and her children several times a week so that Ellen could spend time with her dying father.

Developer of Support Groups

The existing social networks of the faith community provide social support for individuals and families. **Social networks** are the relationships that people have with relatives, peers, coworkers, friends, and others within the faith community. **Social support** refers to the benefits often derived from these ongoing interactions within social networks (Stewart, 1995). Social support can result either spontaneously or with assistance from a professional through the creation of support groups. The results of being socially supported include feelings of belonging and acceptance, being loved, and being valued for oneself (Pender, Murdaugh, & Parsons, 2002).

In the vignette, some of the spouses of local farmers expressed interest in "having a place to talk" about the concerns they are facing. K. M. T. established a support group for interested congregation members. At the first planning meeting, the women selected an appropriate name for the support group, and the nurse offered leadership in stimulating discussion and in bringing several guest speakers in to meet with the women. Several of the women's husbands eventually decided to attend some sessions.

Health Advocate

Health advocacy involves the FCN supporting an individual, family, or group to take action when they are able and stepping in to assist with the action when the individual, family, or group are unable or feel they have no voice. Often this role involves assistance in navigating through the health care system or other social systems. For example, in the vignette, when Ellen decided to seek legal counsel, she asked the FCN for assistance.

CHALLENGES IN PRACTICE, EDUCATION, AND RESEARCH

Faith community nursing is relatively new in Canada. Therefore, many challenges face this evolving type of community health nursing practice, such as:

- the lack of knowledge about the role both within and beyond faith communities,
- the development of a set of standards for nursing practice that are unique to this role,
- the limited funding for these evolving positions,
- the need for some consistency in educational preparation for the role while recognizing individual variation in backgrounds,

Canadian Research Box 26.2

Myers, M. E. (2000). *Parish nursing: A process of authenticating self through holistic theocentric interconnecting.* Unpublished doctoral dissertation, University of Toronto, Toronto, Ontario.

In this study, the meaning of parish nursing was explored with practising parish nurses and the facilitators and supporters associated with parish nursing. A grounded theory approach was used to analyze the data from 22 registered nurses and 19 people who facilitate or support parish nursing. Nurses were asked to clarify what they believed parish nursing to be and to describe past life experiences and their experiences as a parish nurse. Nurses described the process of becoming parish nurses as one in which they established wholeness for themselves through being in authentic relationship with self, others, and the Theo (God).

Discussion Questions:

1. Propose two research questions that could form the basis of further investigation into the practice of faith community nursing in Canada.
2. To whom would the results of this study be of interest, and how might one disseminate the findings appropriately?

- the desire of some denominations to require certain theological preparation in addition to sound nursing education,
- a need for research to demonstrate outcomes of faith community nursing practice when many of the benefits are difficult to measure, and
- a need for funding research in an area where funding for the practice component is not yet fully established.

In Alberta, British Columbia, Manitoba, New Brunswick, Ontario, and Saskatchewan, faith community nursing is becoming well established. Early successes have been largely due to continuing education courses for nurses preparing for these roles, various faith groups embracing the idea of nurses on ministry teams, and health care organizations partnering to provide start-up funding for beginning faith community nursing programs.

SUMMARY

This section has introduced the concept of faith community nursing within the context of community health nursing in Canada. The historical background of faith community nursing was explored and a vignette was discussed in order to describe the functions of an FCN. FCNs play a pivotal role as primary health care providers. The challenges facing practice, education, and research in faith community nursing were also explored. One of the goals of faith community nursing is to extend services to the community at large and to work collaboratively with other partners in the health system.

IV. Forensic Nursing

Sue LeBeau

INTRODUCTION

Forensic nursing is a small but growing field in nursing. Forensic nurses play an important role in the care of survivors of violence, including sexual assault. They work both autonomously and collaboratively with the police to collect physical evidence from the human body in a sensitive and appropriate manner in cases of violence against a person. The survivor who accesses a forensic nurse can expect to obtain health assessment and treatment in addition to forensic data collection in a sensitive, consistent, and organized way. This section describes the prevalence of violence against women in Canada, the role of the forensic nurse in caring for women after sexual assault and violence, and the responsibilities and legal implications required for forensic nursing.

Facts and Statistics on Sexual Assault

Sexual assault, any unwanted sexual act inflicted by a person, is closely linked with family violence. Half of Canadian women (51%) aged 16 and over have experienced a physical or sexual assault at least once in their lifetime (Statistics Canada, 1993). In 2000, 24 049 cases of sexual assault were reported in Canada. Of these cases, nearly 72% involved an assailant known by the survivor (Statistics Canada, 2001). Johnson and Au Coin (2003) noted that in 2001, 25% of all reported violent crimes were related to spousal violence and 85% of the victims were female. Although more victims were willing to contact the police in 2001 than in 1996, of the 1 239 000 victims of spousal violence during this 5-year period, only 27%, or 338 000, spousal violence incidents were reported by either the victims directly (71%) or by others (29%). Of all sexual offences reported to the police, 60% of the victims were children under 18 years of age; and of the 2553 reported family-related sexual assaults, 79% of the victims were girls. More female (53%) than male (26%) victims were harassed by their partner or ex-partner. While all women are at risk, women with disabilities have at least 150% of the risk compared with those without disabilities and of a similar age (Sobsey, 1988). Approximately 83% of women with disabilities will be sexually assaulted during their lifetime (Stimpson & Best, 1991). Although the number of sexual assaults has remained stable following six years of decline (Statistics Canada, 2001), CHNs must understand that sexual assault is an important public health problem in Canada. Sexual assault or violence is preventable. It is also a women's health and gender issue.

EMERGENCE OF FORENSIC NURSING

Only 6% of sexual assaults in Canada were reported to police because of fear of re-victimization, humiliation, or shame (Fassel, 1994; Statistics Canada, 1993). Sexual assault and violence have serious health consequences, including headaches, anxiety, mood swings, depression, eating disorders, substance abuse, sleep changes, or other emotional and psychological reactions in 90% of survivors (Meredith, 1996; Statistics Canada, 1993). The need for nursing intervention to address this public issue and to prevent or mitigate adverse health consequences is inevitable.

In the 1970s, a number of hospitals began to implement certification programs for sexual assault response teams and sexual assault nurse examiners (SANE) as a result of unnecessary delays and repetitive questioning of sexual assault victims in local emergency departments. The **sexual assault response team** can consist of a SANE, a law enforcement investigator, and a rape crisis advocate. **Sexual assault nurse examiners (SANEs)** or **forensic nurses** are registered nurses educated in the nursing field of forensics. They respond specifically to calls relating to sexual assault or domestic violence in the emergency room setting and provide comprehensive care to sexual assault victims (see the Crisis Services of North Alabama website in the Additional Resources). The **SANE certification programs** provide specialized training to experienced nurses with an aim to increase their sensitivity and specialization in caring for sexual assault victims and to improve quality of forensic evidence collection. Calgary's Mount Royal College, the British Columbia Institute of Technology's Forensic Science Technology Department, and Toronto's Sunnybrook and Women's College Hospital offer forensic science courses for nurses. By 2001, more than 300 Ontario nurses had received educational preparation for the nurse examiner role (Ontario Network of Sexual Assault Care and Treatment Centres [ONSACTC], 2002).

SANEs receive a two-part educational preparation prior to working autonomously in the field. In Ontario, for example, the first part is completed before the nurse works with the survivors. The training involves sensitization to issues surrounding sexual assault and domestic violence, including dispelling of myths and recognition of the prevalence of violence in society. Issues surrounding the SANE's responsibilities, services offered by local agencies, the roles of police, history taking, documentation, and correct use of the sexual assault kit are explored. Once a nurse has been part of a sexual assault nurse examiner team for one year and has assisted on a number of cases, the second part of the intensive learning process begins. This includes the specifics of physical assessment findings and documentation in cases of violence, preparation for and appearance in court, the roles of legal and police forensics experts, prophylaxis for infection and pregnancy, and follow-up requirements. This educational path allows SANEs to work to the full scope of their role.

ROLE OF SEXUAL ASSAULT NURSE EXAMINERS

In the past, because the survivors were often medically stable with no visible injuries, they had to wait up to many hours before being seen by emergency room physicians as other more urgent clients had priority status. This added unnecessary emotional trauma to the survivors of violence. The SANE teams were formed to address the specific needs of those survivors of sexual assault and domestic violence at the emergency room immediately following an act of violence. Members of SANE teams are on call 24 hours per day, 7 days per week. The SANE on call responds quickly to calls from the emergency room for survivors triaged as clinically stable but needing assessment, treatment, and possible referral for matters relating to sexual assault or domestic violence. Response time is usually under one hour, often much less.

Forensic data collection is done for legal purposes. It is neither a prerequisite to nor a replacement for health care. The goals of forensic nurses are to provide for health care needs and to collect evidence for police in a way that respects clients' dignity, right to choice, and self-determination. Self-determination is of prime importance, as the survivor of violence has been robbed of control. The SANE therefore aims to return control to survivors very early in the assessment phase of the interaction and strives to maintain a client-led approach throughout the intervention.

The SANE greets the survivor of violence and ensures that communication is facilitated through the use of an interpreter or sign language interpreter if required. The nurse then obtains a brief history and, if sexual assault occurred, determines with the survivor whether or not forensic evidence needs to be collected by using a Sexual Assault Evidence Kit (see Photo 26.3). The **sexual assault evidence kit** typically contains the following tools:

- consent form(s);
- documentation tools for sexual assault nurse examiners and police;
- envelopes for individual pieces of evidence;
- bags for individual pieces of clothing;
- large and small sheets of paper;
- combs;
- tools for collection of fingernails or fingernail scrapings;
- swabs for skin, oral, vaginal, and rectal evidence collection;
- tubes for blood collection (for drug and alcohol testing); and
- urine collection container (for drug testing).

Collection of evidence depends on the wishes of the client and the time elapsed between the assault or violence and presentation to the emergency room. Physical evidence is rapidly destroyed by physiological processes and is rarely useful beyond 72 hours, although, in some cases, it can be helpful even up to one week or more. Adult survivors also have a choice in the matter of evidence collection and must provide informed consent if a sexual assault evidence kit is to be used. Thus an unconscious survivor, or one incapable because of intoxication or mental incapacity, cannot provide consent for use of a sexual assault evidence kit.

Survivors of sexual assault who are capable of providing consent have three options:

- no use of the sexual assault evidence kit,
- use of the kit and immediate reporting to police, or
- use of the kit and secure storage of evidence at the hospital setting for six months. This option allows sur-

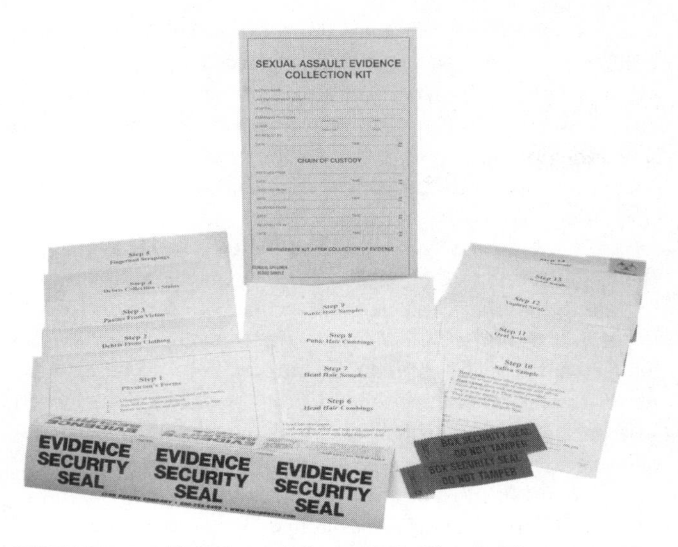

PHOTO 26.3 The Sexual Assault Evidence Kit

Credit: Courtesy of Lynn Peavey Company

vivors to have evidence collected and preserved in case they later decide to report the violence to police.

No matter which option is chosen, the role of the SANE is to explore and describe the possible legal, emotional, physical, and social consequences of each choice for the survivor as well as to provide health assessment and treatment.

Before proceeding with the examination, the SANE uses a documentation tool to elicit history and to guide later activities. Care is taken to allow survivors the time and the sense of confidentiality needed to answer the potentially upsetting and difficult questions in the documentation tool and throughout the examination. The history taking informs the SANE about survivor demographics, allergies, medical history, time and circumstances of assault, number of assailants, type of assault, the specific areas affected (skin, mouth, vagina, rectum, penis), clothes worn during and after the assault, and possible damage inflicted by the survivor to the assailant or vice versa through scratching, kicking, biting, or other methods. Previous pregnancies, menarche, menopause, medication, drug or alcohol use, condom use, and last menstrual period are also identified.

Once history taking is done, the SANE proceeds to the sexual assault evidence kit if the survivor consented to its use. The SANE collects evidence such as hair, soil, or carpet fibres by asking the survivor to undress over a large sheet of paper. Pieces of relevant clothing are placed in individual bags. It is especially important to collect underwear as DNA-rich secretions may accumulate there in the hours following a sexual assault. New clothing is provided upon the survivor's departure from the emergency room.

The SANE also performs a complete physical assessment. All visible injuries are documented thoroughly through the use of body diagrams and occasionally through photographs. All lesions are measured, and their size, colour, characteristics, precise locations, and the survivor's recollection of the mechanisms by which each was sustained are documented.

If a sexual assault evidence kit is used, the nurse then ensures that the client's head and pubic hairs are combed, using separate combs and sheets of paper to collect evidence from both areas. Fingernails or fingernail scrapings are collected in case the survivor has scratched the assailant or has accumulated evidence that could link to the scene of the assault. Dried semen and saliva are collected from relevant areas, and oral swabs can provide DNA evidence from the survivor and sometimes from the assailant. Vaginal and rectal swabs also serve to obtain evidence from the assailant, while urine and blood specimens help determine whether certain drugs or alcohol were ingested near the time of the assault.

Regardless of sexual assault evidence kit use, all survivors are offered testing for pregnancy and sexually transmitted infections such as HIV, hepatitis, syphilis, chlamydia, gonorrhea, and trichomonas. Pregnancy testing is done by urine or serum depending on the resources of the facility at which the survivor presents. Pregnancy prophylaxis is offered for assault that occurred less than 72 hours prior to ER presentation, as is prophylaxis for chlamydia, gonorrhea, and HIV as warranted. Immune globulin is offered for survivors not immunized against hepatitis B.

Survivors also receive counselling relating to community resources, recommended follow-up plans and timing, and normal reactions to domestic violence and sexual assault. Safety planning is done prior to departure, and liaising with shelters, police, and social service agencies is also part of the SANE's role.

The SANE needs to be aware that survivors often have very little, if any, visible injury following sexual assault. Some injuries, particularly those to the posterior fourchette area, are very subtle and require careful examination in order to be detected. The examiner also must be aware that survivors often feel guilty or not credible if no injuries are present and must take the time to explain the normalcy of this: only 11% of survivors of sexual assault sustain physical injury (Statistics Canada, 1993).

Once a sexual assault evidence kit is opened, it must not be left unattended under any circumstances as this would render it useless by breaking the integrity of the chain of evidence. This means that not only the kit, but any specimens collected for it must always be in the SANE's presence or in the presence of police, with no interruptions. If the kit is not given to police immediately, it must be sealed and preserved in a locked environment to protect the evidence.

A large part of the SANE's role involves client-led, client-centred counselling. Therefore, forensic nurses should have experience in basic and advanced short-term counselling approaches and should clearly understand and be able to apply the principles surrounding empathy. Also, the SANE needs to be aware of multicultural issues that may affect reaction to or reporting of sexual assault (ONSACTC, 2002). Stereotypes relating to sexual assault must also be recognized and rejected by the SANE; these can taint the survivor-client encounter by closing doors to communication and by compounding survivor guilt and embarrassment relating to the assault.

A non-judgmental attitude is a prerequisite as domestic violence and sexual assault occur in all cultural, ethnic, and socioeconomic groups at any stage of life (Ontario Women's Directorate, 2002), and emotional reactions to abuse vary from one survivor to another. The SANE who is aware of this will be better equipped to provide empathy and respect to client-survivors. For example, why do survivors of domestic violence often return to the aggressor a number of times before finally leaving permanently? Aggressors in domestic violence situations usually start by gradually wearing down their partner's self-esteem to a point where the survivor feels worthless and at fault for the abuse. Survivors may be lulled into a false sense of security during the "honeymoon," the "good behaviour" phase between assaults. Survivors are often isolated from friends and family by the aggressor, sometimes to the point of loss of contact with them. Financial considerations are also an issue, especially if children are involved; it is very difficult to leave the comfort, familiarity, privacy, and "security" of one's home to go to a shelter. It can also be embarrassing, inconvenient, and daunting to the survivor. The most dangerous time for survivors of abuse is often when they are leaving the abusive relationship (Statistics Canada, 1997).

Heterosexism, the assumption that all relationships are between a female and a male person, is very quickly detectable in a nurse's discourse and, if present, can close doors to communication. The use of words such as "he," "husband," or "girlfriend" when referring to partners reflects heterosexism. The incidence of domestic violence and sexual assault is not limited to male-female dyads; it can and does occur between same-sex persons and is often harder to disclose because of heterosexist attitudes in society. SANEs need to ensure that their vocabulary and approach does not convey heterosexist messages.

Forensic nurses cannot provide objective, client-centred treatment if they have not healed from past abuses to themselves or loved ones. They must give careful consideration to the implications to themselves of taking on the forensic nursing role before they can become involved with survivors of sexual assault or domestic violence as these client encounters can be very emotionally difficult for nurses. Forensic nurses also need mechanisms to help them debrief about client encounters in a confidential and timely manner. This helps relieve stress and provides an opportunity for ongoing learning.

The SANE must be able to explain to survivors the implications of reporting sexual assault or violence as this is frequently a concern of survivors. Candid discussion about factors within and outside a survivor's control and possible consequences of reporting and not reporting incidents can assist the survivor in making informed decisions. The nurse also needs to understand reporting and court procedures in case prosecution does proceed because nurse testimony may be required. Care must be taken to protect evidence, and documentation of assessment findings must be relevant, clear, objective, and, for the physical assessment, detailed.

CASE STUDY

Jana, a sexual assault nurse examiner, receives a pager call from her local emergency room. Calling in for details, she learns that police have arrived with a 23-year-old female survivor of sexual assault that occurred 24 hours ago. Jana arrives to the emergency room 20 minutes later, obtains demographic and triage information from hospital staff, and prepares the examination room. She also ensures that the survivor has been triaged appropriately and is not in need of urgent medical attention. She then greets the survivor and directs her to a confidential room while police wait outside. Jana describes her role and what will occur in the coming hours spent together and obtains informed consent for completion of the sexual assault evidence kit. She approaches the survivor in a non-heterosexist, non-judgmental manner and is sensitive to cultural influences.

Jana proceeds to collect a brief health history and detailed history of the sexual assault. She obtains a urine specimen and splits it into two containers: one for the evidence kit and one for immediate pregnancy testing. Jana establishes that the survivor has been immunized against hepatitis B and does not want HIV prophylaxis. With the survivor, Jana completes the sexual assault evidence kit and physical examination procedures with the assistance of another nurse. She also tests for HIV, syphilis, chlamydia, gonorrhea, trichomonas, and hepatitis B and C. At no time does Jana leave the kit unattended. She again ensures that the survivor is stable and not in need of immediate physician attention.

Once Jana learns that the survivor is not pregnant and has no known allergies, prophylaxis for pregnancy and sexually transmitted infections is offered with counselling related to side effects, risks, benefits, and correct use. She discusses her plan of care with the emergency room physician, following established protocol. Jana and the survivor proceed to safety and follow-up planning. The sealed sexual assault evidence kit is given to the police with copies of the documentation kept for Jana and for the hospital.

Jana files her report for her team supervisor then goes home three hours after being called in. She is aware that she may be called to testify in court about this case and feels confident that her documentation is precise, detailed, and clear enough to help her should this occur. She is also satisfied that she has made a difference in this survivor's life by quickly allowing her to regain control of her situation through facilitation of informed choice and self-determination.

Discussion Questions

1. What is Jana's main priority in this case?
2. Why can't Jana leave the sexual assault nurse examiner kit unattended?
3. What are the advantages of having a SANE collect forensic evidence instead of having a police officer do so?

It is advantageous to the survivor if the SANE has extensive skill in providing physical examinations, especially pelvic examinations. Such skill, which cannot result without knowledge and experience, helps ensure efficiency and speed and minimizes survivor discomfort with an already difficult intervention. The nurse needs to be aware of common injuries secondary to assault in order to assess all relevant areas.

Forensic nurses must understand their scope of practice as well as that of collaborators, such as physicians, emergency room staff, police, attorneys, social workers, and crisis intervention workers, in order to utilize resources effectively. Knowledge of community resources, including referral requirements, costs, and specific services, is also required as the nurse acts as an initial liaison between survivors and these agencies.

The SANE who possesses this knowledge and these skills is more likely to be able to practise confidently and in a way that is reassuring to survivors.

SUMMARY

The forensic nursing role requires confidence, knowledge, and valuing of one's skills and limitations, as well as expert communication and assessment skills. Forensic nursing also requires knowledge relating not only to health assessment and treatment, but also to legal procedures and factors surrounding violence. Forensic nurses can play a key role in violence survivor recovery.

Canadian Research Box 26.3

Canadian research surrounding the role of the SANE or other forensic nursing roles is scant as this field is embryonic compared with other nursing areas. However, there are some current projects that will appear in the literature at a future date.

The departments of Psychiatry, Behavioural Neurosciences, and Pediatrics at McMaster University in Hamilton, Ontario are currently undertaking research to compare indicator-based versus universal screening approaches for early identification of abuse in women in emergency and primary care settings. Various centres throughout the province are involved in the data collection phase of the project. Results will help improve efficiency in screening. The Ontario Network of Sexual Assault Care and Treatment Centres will also be conducting province-wide research relating to HIV post-exposure prophylaxis for survivors of sexual assault. Medication will be offered to survivors at low and moderate risk for contracting HIV following a sexual assault. Outcomes will help identify those who can most benefit from treatment and those most likely to adhere to it.

Discussion Questions

1. How might a CHN use this research when working with adolescents? with adult women?
2. Identify two other research questions for this field of community health nursing.

V. Disaster Nursing

Bonnie Kearns

INTRODUCTION

"As I flew into New York, I wondered where the World Trade Center had been, for I had never seen the twin towers in person. The smoke was still rising off in the distance, so it was quite easy to figure it out. I have taken the Red Cross courses, I've been deployed on several other disasters, and I had been briefed on this one. But nothing I'd done so far in my life prepared me for what I saw and heard (Kearns, 2002; p. 3).

"In the last half of the twentieth century about 250 great natural disasters hit the planet, killing at least 1.4 million people and disrupting the lives of many millions more" (Ryan, Mahoney, Greaves, & Bowyer, 2002, p. 28). Table 26.1 lists a few recent disasters in Canadian history (Health Canada, Population and Public Health Branch, 2003; Jones, 2002; Looker, 2002). It is very possible, considering the increase in the number of incidences and the number of people affected by them, that some CHNs would be asked to respond to a disaster situation. We need to be prepared for that eventuality.

TABLE 26.1
Canadian Disasters and Human Consequences

Date	Disaster	Human Consequences
1917	Halifax Harbour explosion	2000+ dead, 9000 injured
1918	Flu pandemic	Between 30 000 and 50 000 dead in Canada, 18 million dead worldwide
1958	Mining accident, Springhill, NS	75 dead
1965	Avalanche near Stewart, BC	26 dead
1969	Fire in nursing home, Notre-Dame-du-Lac, PQ	54 dead
1985	Terrorist plane crash	329 dead
1986	Train disaster, Hinton, AB	23 dead, 82 injured
1987	Tornado, Edmonton, AB	27 dead, 217 injured
1996	Floods, Saguenay, PQ	10 dead
1998	SwissAir crash, NS	229 passengers and crew dead
1998	Ice storm, ON, PQ, Maritimes	35 dead, 700 injured
1999	Contaminated water supply, Walkerton, ON	7 dead, 65 hospitalized
2000	Tornado, Pine Lake, AB	11 dead, 136 injured
2001	Terrorist attack, New York City	25 Canadians dead
2003	Forest fires in Kelowna, BC	26 000 people evacuated and 248 homes lost
2003	SARS in Canada	A total of 438 cases with 44 dead

WHAT IS A DISASTER?

Nursing in a disaster situation can be exciting, nerve-wracking, boring, rewarding, heartbreaking, scary, frustrating, sad, tiring, and wonderful. CHNs who respond to a disaster situation will learn a great deal about people, nursing, and themselves. Words as simple as "I am a nurse" can quiet fear and provide a sense of hope to someone in distress (see text box). A **disaster** is an event that causes great distress to many people. It usually is sudden, disrupts the local community, depletes resources, and may carry a serious threat to public health. It can bring great loss in terms of lives and property. Disasters can occur naturally, such as pandemic flu, severe acute respiratory syndrome (SARS), weather-related events, and earthquakes. They can also be caused by humans and include the use of chemical, biological, radiation, or nuclear (CBRN) weapons; wars; transportation accidents; explosions; riots; or structure collapses. These events may be intentional or may be caused by misadventure (Garcia, 1985). One common myth is that disasters are random killers. The reality is that when disasters strike, the vulnerable groups—women, children, elderly, and the poor—suffer the most (Pan-American Health Organization, 2001). This warrants the importance for CHNs to understand the special needs of various aggregates and to provide them with appropriate care in their environments.

Emergency Management in Disasters

There are four levels of **emergency management** in a disaster situation. It begins with the individual organization, business, or agency. If the emergency goes beyond their capacity, then the local municipality responds using its resources, including police, fire, and health care personnel. They may also ask for **mutual aid**, that is, reciprocal assistance from nearby communities. When those resources have been exhausted, the head of council declares an emergency and the province assists using its **Emergency Measures Organizations (EMO)** or equivalent. Each province and territory has these organizations available to assist communities during emergency situations and to support relief efforts. If further assistance is required, the federal government provides funding and specialized services such as military support (Millar, 2002). Health Canada's Centre for Emergency Preparedness and Response has a National Emergency Stockpile System, which has mobile hospitals available to be deployed throughout Canada within 24 hours' notice. The hospitals have everything from beds, blankets, and bedpans to laboratories and pharmaceuticals. They also have the capacity to set up first-aid and triage stations to enable responders to quickly identify casualties with urgent and life-threatening conditions.

There are three **phases of a disaster**.

- Before a disaster: this phase is about prevention, mitigation, and preparedness. Plans are developed, people are trained and educated, and the public is informed.
- During a disaster: this phase includes the warning that a disaster is imminent, the actual impact of the disaster, and the response to the disaster.
- After a disaster: this phase is about recovery and rehabilitation. At this time the whole response is evaluated and the plan is improved.

Nursing in a Disaster Situation

An elderly man in an evacuation shelter was found kneeling over a toilet and choking. The nurse never saw his face, but she could see that his neck and hands were pale and that he was diaphoretic. He was conscious but with shallow respirations, and he was unable to speak. She told him she was a nurse, that an ambulance was called, and that she would stay with him. She said, "If you stop breathing, I will help you." For the next thirty minutes she monitored his airway, quietly spoke to him, and kept her hand on his shoulder. The paramedics arrived and she returned to the first-aid station. Days later, the man came into the station and asked for the nurse who helped him. She spoke to him then and he said, "I'd know your voice anywhere. Thank you for saving my life. You were so calm, I knew I was going to be OK." Later, the nurse said to her colleagues, "I didn't save his life. I was just there when he needed someone."

Before a Disaster Local emergency planners, including representatives from police, health, fire, industry, business, agencies, volunteer groups, and the local government, meet regularly to discuss their community plan, which often includes a disaster management plan. This group completes a hazardous risk assessment, determines worst-case scenarios, and considers their available resources. In Sarnia, Ontario, for example, a city with many chemical plants and oil refineries, one of the risks is a hazardous material spill. Salmon Arm, British Columbia has a risk of forest fires. Based on this, they formulate a plan, which must be exercised, evaluated, and constantly improved. It is vital that the public is educated about their community's plan. CHNs can be instrumental in assisting families with personal preparedness plans.

A successful disaster response requires three elements: human resources, material resources, and a process. To respond effectively, CHNs need adequate supplies and a protocol that will help them to use the resources wisely. The protocols must be flexible as every disaster is unique (Garcia 1985). For example, sanitary standards for space allocation for sleeping in group lodging facilities must be followed to prevent or minimize the spread of communicable diseases. The minimum sleeping area per person is 3.5 m^2 and 10 m^3 with a minimum distance of 0.75 m between cots, bunks, or sleeping bags (Canada: Minister of National Health and Welfare, 1994). However, it is very common for families in shelters to push their cots closer together to create family units. Protocols are necessary, but compassion is also important.

During a Disaster This phase starts when the warning is sounded and continues until the disaster impacts. Tornadoes, floods, and hurricanes can be reasonably predicted due to advanced technology. The impact may last only a few minutes or may continue over several days, such as the five-day ice storm that swept through eastern Ontario and southwestern Quebec in January 1998. The impact phase continues until the community is no longer under threat and can begin its recovery efforts. Municipal disaster plans are activated and professional and volunteer relief organizations are deployed. Depending on the severity of the disaster, the community may need one or more of the five social services: food (need to consider religious practices and health restrictions), shelter (may need to shelter people in hotels or community centres), clothing (taking weather into account), personal services (including medications, glasses, baby needs), and family reunification (tracing and reuniting families). The organizations that provide these may include Social Service Departments, the Red Cross, and the Salvation Army.

When CHNs respond to disasters, they must be ready to deal with situations outside their comfort level. CHNs may be asked to work in a **walk-in clinic**, which is a clinic that is open to treat the ill or injured to ease the patient load in emergency departments. They may administer first aid in a field tent, provide health care at an evacuation centre, and work closely with hospitals. During the ice storm of 1998, CHNs managed hundreds of people, admitting some to hospitals and referring others to shelters. In the shelters, they provided crisis intervention, first aid, and medications. They made door-to-door visits and helped care for early discharge patients from the hospitals (Sibbald, 1998a). A forest fire in Salmon Arm, British Columbia, in 1998 required a community evacuation. Some residents were transferred to shelters with their mattresses and were cared for on the floor.

After a Disaster This phase begins when the disaster event is over and people try to make order out of the chaos. For some, it will be a long recovery, especially if there has been a loss of life and/or property. CHNs take part in evaluating the impact of the disaster on the community and coordinating services to help the residents recover. Furthermore, CHNs must also apply epidemiological investigations to ensure that the health of the community is not jeopardized, for example, how to implement infectious control against diseases such as cholera if clean water is lacking after a flood or earthquake. When normalcy resumes, the disaster response plan must be evaluated and improvements made.

PROFESSIONAL NURSING STANDARDS DURING A DISASTER

CHNs have professional standards that provide a framework for their practice. These standards remain constant regardless of where the CHNs are working, be it in a client's home, a hospital, physician's office, or during a disaster. Because of the trust the public holds in nursing knowledge, CHNs may be asked during disasters to take on roles that are beyond their practice domains. Therefore, they must be able to recognize when they have reached the limits of their practice and competency and be clear with themselves and others about what they know and what they do not know (Gebbie & Qureshi, 2002). The four fundamental responsibilities in disaster response, according to the ethical code for Red Cross Nurses, are to promote health, prevent illness, restore health, and alleviate suffering (International Council of Nurses and International Federation of Red Cross and Red Crescent Societies, 1996).

What to Expect when Responding to a Disaster?

This section presents two scenarios to illustrate what nurses should expect when responding to a disaster.

Scenario 1 You are a nurse in the area when a disaster happens. You decide to help. You arrive at the site and see the injured crying, bleeding, and wandering around, obviously in shock. What are your priorities? Many nurses who arrived at the World Trade Center disaster did not have safety equipment or supplies. They worked in unsafe areas. Some worked until they were exhausted and went home; some stayed a few hours and then went home. Few records were kept of who was there, what they did, or if health and safety precautions were taken (Kennedy, Zolot, & Sofer, 2001).

If you arrive at a disaster scene, look for the site manager. Depending on the nature of the incident, either police or fire services will take the lead. The site manager can usually assist you with supplies, information, and updates to the situation. The sorting of casualties to determine priority of need and proper treatment (triaging) is usually done by the paramedics and is either "load and go" or "stay and play." The "stay and play" model is the basis for education in disaster nursing because the "load and go" strategy provides only minimal care before transfer.

When you respond to a disaster, be prepared to look after yourself. Carry safety supplies like gloves, goggles, hard hats, and coveralls. Disaster situations will cause us to be stressed. Dr. Gerry Huot, who was involved in a plane crash in Northern Manitoba, said, "The hardest thing was to keep thinking (clinically) while there was this huge emotional burden" (Sibbald, 1998b, p. 18). There will be less stress for you if you have an action plan, basic assessment skills, first-aid knowledge, and a background in critical or emergency care. Nurses who are educated and trained for disaster situations had far less mental stress at a disaster than nurses without the training (Suserud & Haljamae, 1997).

Scenario 2 In July 1987, a tornado hit Edmonton. One hospital received 54 patients in two hours (Breakey, 1998). You have been asked to report to an emergency department to assist in the care of incoming injured.

During a disaster, those with minor injuries tend to be the first to arrive. During the Oklahoma bombing in 1995, those with minor injuries filled the emergency beds, leaving little space for the critically injured (Hogan, Waeckerle, Dire, & Lillibridge, 1999). The Canadian Council on Health Services Accreditation mandates Canadian hospitals to have emergency response plans (Millar, 2002). These plans include elements such as cancelling elective surgeries and opening day surgery and ambulatory care beds to receive the wounded. In larger disasters, those with minor injuries can be directed to walk-in clinics within the area. In one community, a hazardous material spill sent 34 people to hospital. Each patient went through triage on arrival. A few were sent to emergency, but most were treated and discharged through Ambulatory Care.

TRAINING FOR DISASTER NURSING

Training opportunities are becoming more common since the 9/11 terrorist bombing attack in the United States. Internet-based programs are available. A free disaster-preparedness case study is available through the Sigma Theta Tau International Honor Society of Nursing and the American Red Cross. It discusses the nurse's role and gives examples of clinical decisions a nurse may have to make (Hudson, 2003). Red Cross training can be obtained by volunteering with Disaster Services. Though not nursing based, these courses generally include first aid, family reunification, and assisting with small emergencies and large-scale disasters. The provincial or territorial Emergency Measures Organizations offer basic courses in Emergency Preparedness. This entry-level course is also available on CD-ROM through the Canadian Emergency Preparedness College and is considered a prerequisite for other government-sponsored courses. The Centre for Health Policy at the Columbia University School of Nursing (2001) has created a set of core competencies for emergency response nurses. These competencies include describing the chain of command, demonstrating the use of communication equipment, identifying limits to their own knowledge, creative problem solving, and flexible thinking.

In the United States, rapid-response Disaster Medical Assistant Teams (DMATs) are deployed when needed. They are fully operational and self-sustaining for 72 hours once deployed. In Canada, Health Emergency Response Teams (HERT) are available to provide emergency care during disasters. Local, provincial, and territorial governments work with Health Canada's **Centre for Emergency Preparedness and Response** (CEPR) to help protect the health of Canadians from threats and disasters. Examples of threats and disasters include earthquakes, floods, fires, highly dangerous infectious diseases, and accidents or criminal and terrorist acts involving explosives, chemicals, radioactive substances, or biological threats. The CEPR leads and coordinates the following specialized offices: Emergency Preparedness, Planning and Training, Emergency Services, Laboratory Security, and Public Health Security (Health Canada, 2002).

CHNs must actively search out learning opportunities and experience outside their formal training. Camp nursing offers multifaceted clinical learning opportunities in the care of fractures, lacerations, asthma, bee stings, exhaustion, burns, headaches, fever, colds, diabetic problems, foreign bodies in eyes, and allergic reactions. In New York City during the 9/11 disaster recovery efforts, the nurses dealt with similar injuries in the first-aid stations at Ground Zero, albeit on a larger scale and with higher acuity.

While professional skills are necessary, a sense of humour and the ability to be creative are almost as important. It can be a challenge to meet standards of care in the field, but it can be accomplished with a little ingenuity, adaptability, and a large measure of flexibility. CHNs use these skills every day when they go into a client's home, where a coat hanger becomes an IV pole, and a boiled pot lid becomes the sterile field. One example of creative care occurred when student nurses were volunteering in a remote health clinic. Many people had skin problems, but the students had only one large jar of ointment and no extra containers. They gave the clients cream to take home by dipping their gloved hand into the ointment and pulling the glove off inside out, keeping the cream inside.

During a disaster, about 40 portable toilets were set up near a shelter. The area was without water, so the nurses put hand-sanitizing solution into each of the toilet cubicles. Every time they checked the supplies, someone had taken the hand-sanitizing solution away. The nurses taped them to the wall, tied strings around them, and put them outside on tables, but nothing worked; the bottles kept disappearing. The problem was solved when a nurse removed the lids from the solution bottles. No one took another bottle away.

SUMMARY

We are all challenged to continually be on the alert, to observe what is going on around us, and to be ready. Go beyond increasing your awareness. Become enlightened and then share that knowledge with others. It is up to each of us as citizens to be prepared, but, as CHNs, we are called upon to be prepared on a professional level. The role of the CHN in a disaster is based on the dynamics of the situation and the need at the moment. The tasks may include folding towels in a shelter, treating a client with a fracture, providing education on infection control, or helping to set up a temporary morgue. CHNs must always focus on priorities, that is, deciding what has to be done first and doing or delegating that task. Look at the behaviour of others around you and resolve to be the most composed. Your first priority is your safety. Ask yourself, "Is it safe for me to be here?" If the answer is no, then get out or do something to lower your risk.

Through your nursing education program, you will become proficient at clinical skills and will learn how to use professional judgment and critical thinking to set priorities. Be diligent and watchful and expand your complementary competencies. Seek out opportunities; be tenacious about educating yourself and others. These are the skills that you bring to a disaster situation, and what you take away will be a phenomenal experience.

CHAPTER SUMMARY

Community health nursing is an exciting and expanding practice in the current Canadian health care and political system. This chapter described the diverse roles of community health nurses (CHNs) when caring for individuals, families, groups, populations, or communities in both traditional and non-traditional settings. Their provision of care is community-based and is within the realm of primary health care with a focus on primary, secondary, and tertiary prevention. CHNs enjoy a high level of professional autonomy. They may be entrepreneurs with an independent consulting practice, or they may be nurse practitioners working collaboratively with physicians. Other CHNs, for example, may be parish nurses, forensic nurses, or disaster nurses, caring for clients experiencing crisis.

The high level of professional autonomy also comes with responsibilities. CHNs must go beyond task-oriented activities and position themselves to respond to the changing societal, technological, environmental, and political influences. Most importantly, they must challenge themselves and keep themselves abreast in their practice competency. The health needs of these clients often are related to community problems such as lack of accessibility to health care to family and societal violence or natural disasters as described in this chapter. Analysis of the current health care and political issues and constraints must therefore be an ongoing activity for all CHNs. By doing so, these nurses can devise proactive strategies and find opportunities to effect positive change for their community clients. CHNs must continue to position themselves and to negotiate for their unique and expanding roles as collaborative members of the health care team.

KEY TERMS

nurse entrepreneurs
clinical roles
non-clinical roles
business plan
business insurance
nurse practitioner
extended class
primary health care nurse practitioners (PHC-NPs)
faith community nurse
parish nurse
faith community
ministry
social networks
social support
sexual assault
sexual assault response team
sexual assault nurse examiners (SANEs)
forensic nurses
SANE certification programs
sexual assault evidence kit
disaster
emergency management
mutual aid
Emergency Measures Organization (EMO)
phases of a disaster
walk-in clinic
Centre for Emergency Preparedness and Response

INDIVIDUAL CRITICAL THINKING EXERCISES

1. What qualifications does a nurse need to become a nurse entrepreneur?
2. How should a nurse in independent practice manage client records?
3. Compare and contrast the role of a FCN with a nurse working in an acute care institution and in a government-funded community health agency.
4. Consider the knowledge, attitudes, and skills that are required for effective nursing practice within a faith community.

GROUP CRITICAL THINKING EXERCISES

1. What are the essential components of a business plan?
2. To whom is the nurse in independent practice accountable, and how is this accountability demonstrated?
3. A lack of consensus on the NP's role definition, title, and educational qualifications has resulted in the role being referred to as expanded practice. What does this mean? How is it similar to or different from advanced nursing practice?
4. How can a successful future of the NP role be maintained?
5. Select a health-related condition (e.g., a chronic health issue) and an aggregate or population group (e.g., young adults, aging persons) who might be affected by that condition. Discuss the functions of an FCN in relation to this selected population.
6. You are a newly hired FCN. How would you begin to assess the strengths and needs of the community in which you are practising?
7. Identify some of the stereotypes that surround sexual assault and domestic violence. Discuss the impact these can have on reporting sexual assault and on the social, legal, and health care received from those who believe in these stereotypes.
8. A tornado has just hit your community. The reports indicate that many are dead, with more than 500 injured. Student nurses have been asked to provide first aid in a tent at the site. It will take a few hours to secure the area, but the team must be ready to respond by 1900 hours. The logistics team will provide food, equipment, and supplies, but they will need your lists within the hour. The students will work in teams with a Registered Nurse, providing round-the-clock first-aid services. What is your plan of action and what resources will you need?

REFERENCES

Baumgart, A. J., & Wheeler, M. M. (1992). The nursing workforce in Canada. In A. J. Baumgart & J. Larsen (Eds.), *Canadian nursing faces the future* (pp. 45–69). Scarborough, ON: Mosby-Year Book.

Breakey, P. (1988). Emergency nursing during the Edmonton tornado. *The Canadian Nurse, 84,* 36–38.

Buijs, R., & Olson, J. (2001). Parish nurses influencing determinants of health. *Journal of Community Health Nursing, 18*(1), 13–23.

Canada: Minister of National Health and Welfare. (1994, March). Emergency Lodging. Ministry of Supply and Services Canada. Cat. H34-61/1994E. Retrieved January 4, 2004 from **www.hc-sc.gc.ca/pphb-dgspsp/emergency-urgence/pdf/log_e.pdf**

Canadian Association for Parish Nursing Ministry. (2000). *Canadian Association for Parish Nursing Ministry* [Brochure]. St. Catharines, ON: Author. Retrieved December 15, 2003 from **www.capnm.ca**

Canadian Nurses Association. (1995). *Vision statement: CNA's vision of nursing.* Ottawa, ON: Author.

Canadian Nurses Association. (1996). On your own: The nurse entrepreneur. *Nursing Now: Issues and Trends in Canadian Nursing, 1.* Retrieved December 15, 2003 from **www.cna-nurses.ca/pages/issuestrends/nrgnow/On Your Own Entrepreneur_September 1996.pdf**

Canadian Nurses Association. (1997). *Code of ethics for registered nurses.* Ottawa, ON: Author.

Canadian Nurses Association. (1998). *Educational support for competent nursing practice: CNA policy statement.* Ottawa, ON: Author. Retrieved December 15, 2003 from **www.cna-nurses.ca/pages/policies/educational support for competent nursing practice_march 1998.pdf**

Canadian Nurses Protective Society. (2002). *Canadian nurses protective society: Liability protection for nurses by nurses.* Retrieved December 28, 2003 from **www.cnps.ca/cnps_plus/index_e.html**

Carpenito, L. J., & Neal, M. C. (1997). Nurse entrepreneurs: Who are they, what do they do, and what challenges do they face? In J. C. McCloskey & H. K. Grace (Eds.), *Current issues in nursing* (pp. 45–50). St. Louis, MO: Mosby Year Book.

Charbonneau-Smith, R. (2000). *Nurse entrepreneur: An opportunity for professional fulfilment.* Major Paper. University of Windsor.

Clark, M. (2000a). Characteristics of faith communities. In M. Clark & J. Olson (Eds.), *Nursing within a faith community: Promoting health in times of transition* (pp. 17–30). Thousand Oaks, CA: Sage.

Clark, M. (2000b). The nurse and theological reflection. In M. Clark & J. Olson (Eds.), *Nursing within a faith community: Promoting health in times of transition* (pp. 91–110). Thousand Oaks, CA: Sage.

Clark, M., & Olson, J. (2000). *Nursing within a faith community: Promoting health in times of transition.* Thousand Oaks, CA: Sage.

College of Nurses of Ontario. (2001). *A primer on the primary health care nurse practitioner.* Retrieved October 12, 2003 from **www.cno.org/docs/standards/41030_rnecprimer.html#**

College of Nurses of Ontario. (2003). *Standards of practice for registered nurses in the extended class.* Retrieved October 12, 2003 from **www.cno.org/docs/standards/41038_StrdRnec.pdf**

Columbia University School of Nursing. (2001). *Core public health worker competencies for emergency preparedness and response.* New York: Columbia University School of Nursing, Centre for Health Policy.

Community Health Nurses Association of Canada. (2003). *Canadian community health nursing standards of practice:* Ottawa, ON: Author.

Duffett-Leger, L. (1995). Nursing and entrepreneurship: The opportunities are limitless. *INFO-Nursing, 26*(5), 6–7, 19.

Fassel, M. (1994). *Disclosure of medical and therapeutic records in sexual assault trials: The implications for women's equality.* Unpublished paper presented at the Canadian Institute Conference, Toronto, April 1994. Abstract obtained from Oleskiw, D., & Tellier, N. (1997). *Submissions to the Standing Committee on Bill C-46: An act to amend the criminal code in respect of production of records in sexual offence proceedings* (pp. 9). Ottawa, ON: National Association of Women and the Law.

Garcia, L. M. (1985). *Disaster nursing: Planning, assessment, and intervention.* Rockville, MD: Aspen.

Gebbie, K. M., & Qureshi, K. (2002). Emergency and disaster preparedness. *American Journal of Nursing, 102*(1), 46–51.

Gourlay, B. (1998). Getting into the business of nursing. In G. Donner & M. Wheeler (Eds.), *Taking control of your career and your future: For nurses, by nurses* (pp. 139–154). Ottawa, ON: Canadian Nurses Association.

Health Canada. (2002). *Centre for Emergency Preparedness and Response.* Retrieved on January 4, 2004 from **www.hc-sc.gc.ca/pphb-dgspsp/cepr-cmiu/cepr.html**

Health Canada, Population and Public Health Branch. (2003). *SARS: Severe acute respiratory syndrome.* Retrieved August 15, 2003 from **www.hc-sc.gc.ca/pphb-dgspsp/sars-sras/index.html**

Hogan, D. E., Waeckerie, J. F., Dire, D. J., & Lillibridge, S. R. (1999). Emergency department impact of the Oklahoma City terrorist bombing. *Annals of Emergency Medicine, 34*(2), 160–167.

Horrocks, S., Anderson, E., & Salisbury, C. (2002). Systematic review of whether nurse practitioners working in primary care can provide equivalent care to doctors. *BMJ, 324*(7341), 819–823.

Hudson, J. (2003). Helping nurses respond to disasters. *Registered Nurse Journal, 15*(2), 20.

International Council of Nurses. (1994). *Guidelines on the nurse entrepreneur providing nursing service.* Geneva, Switzerland: Author.

International Council of Nurses, & International Federation of Red Cross and Red Crescent Societies. (1996). *An ethical code for Red Cross and Red Crescent nurses.* Geneva, Switzerland: Authors.

Jones, R. L. (2002). *Canadian disasters: An historical survey.* Retrieved August 14, 2003 from **www.ott.igs.net/~jonesb/DisasterPaper/disasterpaper.html**

Kearns, B. J. (2002). 9/11. *Canadian Red Cross Ontario Zone 2001/2002 Annual Review.* Ottawa, ON: Canadian Red Cross, 3.

Kennedy, M. S., Zolot, J. S., & Sofer, D. (2001). Disaster education and training are sorely needed. *American Journal of Nursing, 101*(11), 18–19.

Looker, J. (2000). *Disaster Canada.* Toronto, ON: Transcontinental.

McBrien, R. P. (1987). *Ministry: A theological, pastoral handbook.* New York: Harper & Row.

Meredith, L. (1996). *Establishing links: Violence against women and substance abuse.* London, ON: Centre for Research on Violence Against Women and Children.

Millar, C. T. (2002). Responding to large-scale emergencies and bio-terrorist threats. *Ontario Hospital Emergency Preparedness Report.* Toronto, ON: Ontario Hospital Association.

Olson, J. (2000a). Components of optimal nursing practice within a faith community: Professionalism, spiritual maturity, and self-care. In M. Clark & J. Olson (Eds.), *Nursing within a faith community: Promoting health in times of transition* (pp. 157–168). Thousand Oaks, CA: Sage.

Olson, J. (2000b). Functions of the nurse as health promoter in a faith community. In M. Clark & J. Olson (Eds.), *Nursing within a faith community: Promoting health in times of transition* (pp. 141–155). Thousand Oaks, CA: Sage.

Olson, J. (2000c). Promoting improved health: Evaluation processes. In M. Clark & J. Olson (Eds.), *Nursing within a faith community: Promoting health in times of transition* (pp. 281–293). Thousand Oaks, CA: Sage.

Olson, J., & Clark, M. (2000). Characteristics of health promoting faith community nurses. In M. Clark & J. Olson (Eds.), *Nursing within a faith community: Promoting health in times of transition* (pp. 125–140). Thousand Oaks, CA: Sage.

Olson, J., Clark, M., & Simington, J. (1999). The Canadian experience. In P. A. Solari-Twadell & M. A. McDermott (Eds.), *Parish nursing: Promoting whole person health within faith communities* (pp. 277–286). Thousand Oaks, CA: Sage.

Ontario Ministry of Health. (1994). *Nurse practitioners in Ontario: A plan for their education and employment.* Toronto, ON: Author.

Ontario Network of Sexual Assault Care and Treatment Centres. (2002). *Sexual assault nurse examiner program (SANE).* Retrieved December 29, 2003 from **www.satcontario.com/sane/**

Ontario Women's Directorate. (2002). *Sexual assault: Dispelling the myths.* **www.gov.on.ca:80/MCZCR/owd/english/publications/sexual-assault/myths.htm**

Pan-American Health Organization. (2001). *Natural disasters: Myths and realities.* Retrieved August 13, 2003 from **www.acdi-cida.gc.ca/cida_ind.nsf/0/642CBC56B02F51EC85256A1D005900CC**

Pender, N., Murdaugh, C., & Parsons, M. A. (2002). *Health promotion in nursing practice* (4th ed.). Upper Saddle River, NJ: Prentice Hall.

Philips, D.L. & Steel, J.E. (1994). Factors influencing scope of practice in nursing centers. *Journal of Professional Nursing, 10*(20), 84–90.

Potter, P. A., & Perry, A. G. (Eds.), Ross-Kerr, J. C., & Wood, M. J. (Canadian Eds.). (2001). *Canadian fundamentals of nursing* (2nd ed.). Toronto, ON: Mosby.

Registered Nurses Association of Ontario, & Ontario Association of Nurses in Independent Practice. (1999). *Joint statement: Practice.* Toronto, ON: Author.

Registered Nurses Association of Ontario. (2002). *What do I get for my membership?* Retrieved December 29, 2003 from **www.rnao.org/html/id_mb_01.htm**

Richardson, S. (1997). Lesson from the past: Entrepreneurial nursing practice in perspective. *AARN (Alberta Association of Registered Nurses) Newsletter, 53*(4), 19, 29.

Rodenberg, J. H., & Rodenberg, H. (1998). Part 1: Can you be self-employed? *Air Medical Journal, 17*(2), 71–72.

Ryan, P., Mahoney, P., Greaves, I., & Bowyer, G. (Eds.). (2002). *Conflict and catastrophe medicine: A practical guide.* London: Springer-Verlag.

Schoenhofer, S. (1995). Rethinking primary care: Connectin to nursing. *Advanced Nursing Science, 17*(4), 12–21.

Sibbald, B. (1998a). RNs unsung heroes during the ice storm '98. *The Canadian Nurse, 94*(4), 18–21.

Sibbald, B. (1998b). Plane crash challenges Northern Manitoba RNs. *The Canadian Nurse, 94*(2), 18–19.

Sobsey, D. (1988). Sexual offences and disabled victims: Research and practical implications. *Vis-à-Vis: A National Newsletter on Family Violence, 6*(4), 1.

Statistics Canada. (1993). *The violence against women survey.* Ottawa, ON: Author.

Statistics Canada. (1997, Autumn). *Canadian social trends.* Ottawa, ON: Author.

Statistics Canada. (2001). Canadian Crime Statistics 2000. Canadian Centre for Justice Statistics. Catalogue No. 85-205-XIE. Retrieved January 4, 2004 from **http://prod.library.utoronto.ca:8090/datalib/codebooks/cstdli/justice/2001/2000_crime_e.pdf**

Stewart, M. J. (1995). Social support, coping and self care: Public participation concepts. In M. J. Stewart (Ed.), *Community nursing* (pp. 98–124). Toronto, ON: Saunders.

Stimpson, L., & Best, M. (1991). *Courage above all: Sexual assault against women with disabilities.* Toronto, ON: DisAbled Women's Network (DAWN).

Suserud, B., & Haljamae, H. (1997). Acting at a disaster site: Experiences expressed by Swedish nurses. *Journal of Advanced Nursing, 25*(1), 155–162.

Westberg, G. (1999). A personal historical perspective of whole person health and the congregation. In P.A. Solari-Twadell & M. A. McDermott (Eds.), *Parish nursing: Promoting whole person health within faith communities* (pp. 35–41). Thousand Oaks, CA: Sage.

White, K. R., & Bergun, J. W. (1998). Nursing entrepreneurship in an era of chaos and complexity. *Nursing Administration Quarterly, 22*(2), 40–47.

Wright, R., & Dorsey, B. (1994). Nurses in independent practice: Is society ready? *Canadian Nurse, 90*(7), 35–37.

ADDITIONAL RESOURCES

WEBSITES

American Academy of Nurse Practitioners:
www.aanp.org

American Nurses Association:
www.nursingworld.org/

British Columbia Institute of Technology. *Forensic science:*
www.newsreleases.bcit.ca/200307/forensicnurse.shtml

Canadian Association for Pastoral Practice and Education:
www.cappe.org

Canadian Association of Advanced Practice Nurses/ Association canadienne des infirmièrs et infirmières de pratique avancée:
www.caapn.com/

Canadian Association of Sexual Assault Treatment Centres (CASAC):
www.casac.ca/enghome.htm

Canadian Emergency Department Triage and Acuity Scale:
www.caep.ca/002.policies/002-docs/ctased16.pdf

Canadian Nurses Association:
www.cna-nurses.ca/_frames/welcome/frameindex.html

Canadian Nurses Protective Society/Société de protection des infirmières du Canada:
www.cnps.ca/index_e.html

Crisis Services of North Alabama. *Sexual assault response team:*
www.csna.org/SANE/SANEProgram.htm

Emergency Management Ontario (EMO):
www.mpss.jus.gov.on.ca/english/pub_security/emo/backgrounders/bg_crit_incident_stress.html

Forensic education and training opportunities. *Forensic Nurse:*
www.forensicnursemag.com/educat.html

International Association of Forensic Nurses:
www.forensicnurse.org/

International Council of Nurses (ICN)/Conseil international des infirmières:
www.icn.ch/

Metropolitan Action Committee on Violence Against Women and Children. *Frequently asked questions about sexual assault*:
www.metrac.org/new/faq_sex.htm

National Association of Independent Nurses:
www.independentrn.com/

Nurse Friendly. *Doing business on the Internet*:
www.nursefriendly.com/nursing/linksections/doingbusiness.htm

Joanne K. Olson, University of Alberta, Edmonton, Alberta:
www.nursing.ualberta.ca/homepage.nsf/faculty/

Online Women's Business Centre:
www.onlinewbc.gov/

Ontario Network of Sexual Assault Care and Treatment Centres. *Sexual assault nurse examiner program (SANE)*:
www.satcontario.com/sane/

Ontario Women's Directorate. *Sexual assault: Dispelling the myths*:
www.gov.on.ca:80/MCZCR/owd/english/publications/sexual-assault/myths.htm

Parish Nursing Institute [Brochure]. McMaster Divinity College, Hamilton, Ontario:
http://divinity.mcmaster.ca/pages/static/publicity/ParishNurse_Brochure_2003.pdf

Sexual Assault Nurse Examiners:
www.csna.org/SANE/SANEProgram.htm

Sigma Theta Tau International Honor Society of Nursing:
www.nursingsociety.org/

Women in Technology International:
www.witi.com/

READINGS

Burkhardt, M. A., & Nagai-Jacobson, M. G. (2002). *Spirituality: Living our connectedness.* Albany, NY: Delmar.

Carson, V., & Koenig, H. G. (2002). *Parish nursing: Stories of service and care.* Radnor, PA: Templeton Foundation Press.

Hanna, J. A. (1995). *Disaster planning for health care facilities.* Ottawa, ON: Canadian Hospital Association Press.

Health Canada. (2001). *Are you prepared in case of DISASTER?* [Brochure]. Ottawa, ON: Author. Retrieved December 15, 2003 from **www.hc-sc.gc.ca/pphb-dgspsp/emergancy-urgence/pdf/disast_e.pdf**

Kim, D. H., Proctor, P. W., & Amos, L. K. (2002). Disaster management and the emergency department: A framework for planning. *Nursing Clinics of North America, 37*(1), 171–188.

Patterson, S. (1994). Becoming an entrepreneur. *Canadian Nurse, 90*(2), 53–54.

Safeguard Program. (2001). *Be prepared not scared: Emergency preparedness starts with you* [Brochure]. Ottawa, ON: Office of Critical Infrastructure Protection and Emergency Preparedness. Retrieved December 15, 2003 from **www.ocipep.gc.ca/info_pro/self_help_ad/pdfs/be_prep_e.pdf**

Solari-Twadell, P. A., & McDermott, M. A. (Eds.). (1999). *Parish nursing: Promoting whole person health within faith communities.* Thousand Oaks, CA: Sage.

Tenner Goodwin, V. (2003). *Disasters nursing and emergency preparedness.* New York: Springer Publishing.

Tutty, L. (1998). Mental health issues of abused women: The perceptions of shelter workers. *Canadian Journal of Community Mental Health, 17*(1), 79-102.

About the Authors

Linda Patrick, RN (Victoria Hospital, London), BScN, MSc (Windsor), MEd (Central Michigan), PhD Candidate (McMaster), is an Assistant Professor at the University of Windsor. Her areas of research are in prevention or delay of type 2 diabetes in women with previous gestational diabetes through lifestyle changes and education, and the promotion of vehicular safety for vulnerable populations, specifically interventions to increase the safe and effective use of child safety restraints. She was a Region One Representative to the Board of Directors for the Registered Nurses Association of Ontario and is a member of the Certification Maintenance Evaluation Committee of the Canadian Diabetes Educator Certification Board.

Christine Thrasher, RN (EC), BScN (University of Windsor), MScN (D'Youville College), Primary Health Care Nurse Practitioner Certificate (Ryerson), PhD Candidate (McMaster University), worked as clinician, administrator, and consultant in community health for St. Elizabeth Health Care for over 15 years. In 1996, Christine joined the Faculty of Nursing at the University of Windsor as an Assistant Professor. She is Chair of the University of Windsor Collaborative Curriculum Committee and Program Coordinator of the Primary Health Care Nurse Practitioner Program. Her dissertation is related to the integration of Nurse Practitioners in Emergency Departments.

Eric Staples, RN (Mohawk College), BAAN (Ryerson University), MScN (D'Youville College), worked as a CNS and ACNP in Oncology at Women's College Hospital and ACNP in Acute Pain Services at St. Michael's Hospital. Eric has also worked as a consultant in pain management. In 1998, Eric joined Dalhousie University and started the Adult NP program. In 2000, he became an Assistant Professor at McMaster University. He is also the Western Ontario Regional Coordinator for the Ontario Primary Health Care NP Program. Eric is completing his Doctor of Nursing degree at Case Western Reserve University in Cleveland. His dissertation is related to the manifestations of pain in PACU patients.

Joanne K. Olson, RN, BSN (Augustana), MS (Minnesota), PhD (Wayne State), is a Professor and Assistant Dean, Graduate Services in the Faculty of Nursing, University of Alberta, Edmonton, Alberta. She also serves as Associate Faculty in the Centre for Health Promotion Studies at the University of Alberta. Her teaching and research interests focus on community health, nursing education, nurse-client interaction, spiritual aspects of nursing care, and faith community nursing. She has served on the Boards of Directors of organizations such as Sigma Theta Tau International Nursing Honor Society and the Canadian Association for Parish Nurse Ministry. Currently she serves on the Academic Senate for St. Stephen's College, a theological institution in Edmonton, Alberta, and co-teaches a graduate level course focusing on spiritual assessment in health promotion.

Lynn J. Anderson, RN, BScN, MN Candidate (Alberta), is the Coordinator of the People in Crisis Program with the Victorian Order of Nurses in Edmonton, Alberta. This unique program provides nursing services to women, men, children, teens, and seniors who have been victims of abuse. She has worked in a variety of areas in nursing over the past 27 years and finds her interest is in community nursing, family violence, parish nursing, and spirituality and nursing. She focused her clinical learning on Faith Community Nursing and will be doing her thesis in the area of spirituality and nursing.

Sue LeBeau, BScN and PHC Practitioner (Laurentian), MScN (Ottawa), was a public health nurse. She now teaches the nurse practitioner program at Laurentian University and the University of Ottawa. Sue was among the first to be accepted in the College of Nurses of Ontario's extended class of practice. She has offered nurse practitioner services in a variety of settings, including Laurentian University student health services, Centre de sant communautaire de Sudbury, and Sudbury Regional Hospital. She also helped create and now coordinates the North Bay Sexual Assault Nurse Examiner Team and the Near North Nurse Practitioner Services, a joint project between two nurse practitioners providing on-site service to clients accessing a medical building, three shelters, an Aboriginal centre, child health agencies, and others. Sue remains politically active and participates actively on the executive of the Nurse Practitioners Association of Ontario.

Bonnie Kearns, RN (Lambton College, Sarnia) BScN (Windsor), has 37 years of nursing experience. She worked at the Sarnia Hospitals for 23 years, first in the Emergency Department and then as an Educator. She is now employed with the Victoria Order of Nurses in Sarnia, Ontario and is a consultant with the College of Nurses of Ontario. Bonnie has been a volunteer with the Canadian Red Cross for eighteen years and teaches other volunteers how to respond during disasters. She has been deployed to several disaster situations, including New York after the terror attack on September 11, 2001. She is one of the visiting staff at Canada's Emergency Preparedness College in Ottawa and coaches students during their disaster simulation exercises. Bonnie received a "Women of Excellence Award" in 1999 and the "Queen's Jubilee Medal" in 2002 for her work in Community Service.

CHAPTER 27

Challenges and Future Directions

Lynnette Leeseberg Stamler and Lucia Yiu

Through reading this book, you have been introduced to the diversity within the practice of community health nursing. Community health nursing has expanded rapidly in the last several decades. In fact, as a specialty, it has burgeoned over the years into many sub-specialties, such as home health nursing and public health nursing, with other community-based nursing such as nurse practitioners, faith community nursing, and forensic nursing. Community health nurses (CHNs) are increasing and moving their practice roles from traditional community settings into a greater number of non-traditional arenas of community nursing practice. From the historical overview in Chapter 1 to the expanding practice settings and roles, the authors have described the internal and external forces that have shaped the evolution of community health nursing into today's reality.

Historically, new areas of community health nursing practice tended to arise from reactions to the needs of a particular group of clients. Through this need identification, CHNs have also acted proactively by identifying what roles and functions would be required to meet those needs successfully. Many of the sub-specialties discussed in this text began in this fashion. Later, educational preparation for continued practice in these roles, such as home health nursing and public health nursing, was developed. Although new arenas of practice in community health nursing continue to develop in response to client needs and the evolving health care system, knowledge about the importance of the determinants of health and health promotion has exploded in the last two decades. These areas of knowledge are critical when defining CHNs' practice. CHNs have an unprecedented opportunity to be proactive in planning for the future and positioning themselves as co-creators of change.

Another area of opportunity lies in influencing the continuing evolution of health care delivery in Canada. While the practice of community health nursing has always been responsive to the needs of its clients, it must also be responsive to the constraints of political and fiscal reality. In the twentieth century, CHNs brought health care to those unable to access it. In the twenty-first century, CHNs will again be instrumental as a primary mechanism for new and creative health delivery with limited health care dollars. It is through both political action and presentation of evidence that CHNs will accomplish this task. Search for new knowledge through identification of health problems and issues for further investigation has become increasingly important. Many of the contributing authors identified large gaps in Canadian nursing research for the topic they were presenting in this book. It is therefore evident that nurses must continue to engage in planning and implementing research with other members of the health care team to identify issues and test interventions. As we learn more about the multifaceted causes/influences on health issues, we expand our opportunities to plan, lead, and participate in multidisciplinary community health research. The evidence gathered in that research can be used to cause social and cultural change within the political and fiscal context.

Realizing the importance of research knowledge and political savvy, it is imperative that community health educators implement curricula that prepare students for the realities of community health practice. Most importantly, they must make every effort to ensure that the curricula will complement and reflect the new standards of community health nursing practice (see Appendix A) (Canadian Health Nurses Association of Canada, 2003; Underwood, 2003). Further, the importance of life-long learning cannot be overstated. Basic nursing education prepares nurses to practise as generalists in both the community and hospital sectors. It is clear that many areas of community health nursing require additional knowledge and skills. The graduate nurse choosing to practise in one of the sub-specialities of community health nursing must explore continuing education opportunities. The required knowledge comes from both the clients in the practice area and the nurse experts working with those clients. Clients are ever more educated and assertive as they strive to lead healthy lives according to *their* personal or cultural definition of health. They frequently possess a wealth of practical knowledge about their health issues and successes that is invaluable to the CHN. Another source of knowledge is the reflection and critical appraisal of one's own practice. While novice or beginning nurses may have the skills to reflect on the practice, experienced CHNs have a responsibility and an opportunity to share their expertise with novice nurses to enhance their practice.

All of these opportunities come complete with corresponding challenges as they emerge in the evolving health care system. The spring of 2003 will be known in some areas as the spring of Severe Acute Respiratory Syndrome (SARS). While many were concerned with the families and co-workers of those who were ill and those who died, for others the economic hardships inflicted on the city of Toronto and other Canadian centres demonstrated a fragile hold on personal economic self-sufficiency. For those of us in health care, SARS once again demonstrated the absolute requirement for a strong infrastructure in nursing, in public health, and in the overall health care system—at all levels and in all settings. With this outbreak, the brevity of time between exposure and illness, coupled with the massive contact tracing and quarantine required in our highly mobile society, contributed to an atmosphere of fear that permeated all nursing practice in the affected geographic areas. CHNs, along with nurses in acute care settings, were at the forefront of calming a fearful population while maintaining their nursing care. In other geographic areas, the identification of a cow with "mad cow" disease resulted in economic and psychological devastation among many farmers and communities already reeling from several years of drought. Here CHNs needed to be knowledgeable about the economic and political impacts on the livelihood of those families in their communities and anticipate health challenges that could arise from these calamities.

Many of the changes in the health care delivery system are in response to societal changes. The demographics in Canada and the Canadian environment are constantly changing, and political realities are both proactive and reactive to those changes. There is much discussion about how we as a society wish our health care to be delivered and how we prioritize our needs and desires. One of the largest challenges in Canada is accessibility to health care. This is linked with primary health care reform that is happening at various levels across the country and around the world. While nurses were at the forefront of the changes to the Canada Health Act, much work remains to be done before accessibility is truly universal.

Each of the authors in this textbook has identified Canadian nursing or health research relevant to their topic. They have also frequently noted the scarcity of Canadian research. Community health nursing is moving forward in terms of evidence-based practice. Many of the chapters have highlighted the challenges of community health nursing research that produces such evidence. Some of these challenges are methodological. For example, the randomized controlled trial may not be the best method for community research; in fact, in some cases it is untenable. Further, as with all research, we must carefully examine the ethics of a particular study. CHNs must demonstrate creativity, rigor, and impeccable skill in designing new methodologies that serve to explore and examine the evidence to answer the research questions we pose.

The curriculum of nursing education is another area of challenge. Nursing is a practice profession, and our basic education curricula must reflect that. Nursing practice is relational, with the nurse-client relationship at the hub of practice. The knowledge and skill requirements for practising as a CHN contributed significantly to the movement of nursing education from the hospitals to educational institutions. Nursing educators in community health nursing are challenged to be creative in designing learning experiences to ensure that student nurses have access to both clients and experienced nurses who will assist them in learning to practise within their profession. Another issue is the rapidly increasing knowledge base. Nursing educators can no longer plan their courses around discrete segments of content, but rather must work to expand the students' repertoire of critical thinking, questioning skills, and expertise in finding the information they need for a particular situation. A further issue is burgeoning technology. The existence of the internet has wildly expanded the opportunities for reaching more people with health education and information. The popularity of using the internet testifies to the desire of consumers to increase their knowledge. The challenges for all include the veracity of the information found and the increased marginalization of segments of the population who are unable to access this information source. The challenges for nursing lie in preparing practitioners to use this source of information wisely and minimize the marginalization.

So what of the future? As each of us gazes into our cloudy crystal ball, a few things are discernable. One is that nurses, including CHNs, have the skills and knowledge to be a political force for the health of Canadians, if we so choose. By supporting our professional organizations, by being proactive in the political process, and by using our knowledge to affect and change healthy public policy, we can contribute significantly to influencing the movement and direction of health care in Canada.

In addition, we know that health challenges such as SARS, hepatitis C, Ebola, and mad cow disease will continue to surface from time to time. CHNs now nurse a global community. As nurses are at the forefront of hospital and community health care in the current eroding nursing administrative structures in which nurses continue to be undervalued (Underwood, 2003), it will be up to us to make a concerted effort to ensure that our voices are heard and that we stand together to protect the health of Canadians. At the same time, we must position ourselves and partner with nurses in other countries to influence and support health care on a global scale. The challenges of preparing practitioners in community health nursing and producing the evidence on which our practice is based will continue to arise. And at the heart of it all will be our nurse-client relationship with a focus to promote and protect the health of the community. What an exciting future to behold!

REFERENCES

Canadian Health Nurses Association of Canada. (2003). Canadian community health nursing standards of practice. Toronto, ON: Author.

Underwood, J. (2003). The value of nurses in the community. Retrieved October 18, 2003 from **http://www.cna-aiic.ca/frames/welcome/frameindex.html**

About the Authors

Lynnette Leeseberg Stamler, RN, PhD, is an Associate Professor and Director of the Nipissing University/ Canadore College Collaborative BScN Program. She completed her BSN at St. Olaf College, Minnesota; her MEd at the University of Manitoba; and her PhD in nursing at the University of Cincinnati. Her research interests include patient/health education, breast health, diabetes education, and nursing education. She was a VON nurse for four years prior to her career in nursing education. She has been active in research and professional nursing organizations as well as Sigma Theta Tau International, the Nursing Honor Society.

Lucia Yiu, BScN, BA (Psychology, Windsor), BSc (Physiology, Toronto), MScN (Administration, Western Ontario), is an Associate Professor in the Faculty of Nursing, University of Windsor, and an Educational and Training Consultant in community nursing. She has published on family and public health nursing. Her practice and research interests include multicultural health, international health, experiential learning, community development, and program planning and evaluation. She has worked overseas and served on various community and social services committees involving local and district health planning.

APPENDIX

The Canadian Community Health Nursing Standards of Practice*

The model in Figure 1 illustrates the dynamic nature of community health nursing practice, embracing the present and projecting into the future. The values and beliefs (shaded) ground practice in the present yet guide the evolution of community health nursing practice over time. The community health nursing process (unshaded) provides the vehicle through which community health nurses work with people, and supports practice that exemplifies the standards of community health nursing. The standards of practice revolve around both the values and beliefs and the nursing process with the energies of community health nursing always being focussed on improving the health of people in the community and facilitating change in systems or society in support of health. Community health nursing practice does not occur in isolation but rather within an environmental context, such as policies within their workplace and the legislative framework applicable to their work.

THE STANDARDS OF PRACTICE

Knowledge of, and adherence to, the following standards is an expectation of every community health nurse working in any of the domains of practice, education, administration or research. These standards serve as a benchmark for novice community health nurses and become basic practice expectations after two years of experience. The practice of expert community health nurses will extend beyond these standards. While each standard is relevant to the practice of both home health nurses and public health nurses, the emphasis in practice on elements of specific standards will vary according to the practice focus.

Standard 1: Promoting Health

Community health nurses view health as a dynamic process of physical, mental, spiritual and social well-being. They believe that individuals and/or communities realize aspirations and satisfy needs within their cultural, social, economical and physical environments. Community health nurses consider health as a resource for everyday life that is influenced by circumstances, beliefs and the determinants of health including social, economic and environmental health determinants: a) income and social status, b) social support networks, c) education, d) employment and working conditions, e) social environments, f) physical environments, g) biology and genetic endowment, h) personal health practices and coping skills, i) healthy child

Reprinted by permission of the Community Health Nurses Association of Canada www.communityhealthnurses.org

development, j) health services, k) gender, and l) culture (Health Canada, 2000). It includes self-determination and a sense of connectedness to the community.

Community health nurses promote health using the following strategies: a) health promotion, b) illness and injury prevention and health protection, and c) health maintenance, restoration, and palliation. It is recognized that it may be relevant to use these strategies in concert with each other when providing care and services. This standard incorporates these strategies by drawing upon the frameworks of primary health care (WHO, 1978), the Ottawa Charter for Health Promotion (WHO, 1986), and the Population Health Promotion Model (Health Canada, 2000).

A) HEALTH PROMOTION

Community health nurses focus on health promotion and the health of populations. Health promotion is a mediating strategy between people and their environments – a positive, dynamic, empowering, and unifying concept that is based in the socio-environmental approach to health. This broad concept is envisioned as bringing together people who recognize that basic resources and prerequisite conditions for health are critical for achieving health. The population's health is closely linked with the health of its constituent members and is often reflected first in individual and family experiences from birth to death. Healthy communities and systems support increased options for well-being in society. Community health nurses consider socio-political issues that may be underlying individual/community problems.

The community health nurse:

1. Collaborates with individual/community and other stakeholders in conducting a holistic assessment of assets and needs of the individual/community.
2. Uses a variety of information sources to access data and research findings related to health at the national, provincial/territorial, regional, and local levels.
3. Identifies and seeks to address root causes of illness and disease.
4. Facilitates planned change with the individual/community/population through the application of the Population Health Promotion Model.
   - Identifies the level of intervention necessary to promote health
   - Identifies which determinants of health require action/change to promote health
   - Utilizes a comprehensive range of strategies to address health-related issues.
5. Demonstrates knowledge of and effectively implements health promotion strategies based on the Ottawa Charter for Health Promotion.
   - Incorporates multiple strategies addressing: a) healthy public policy; b) strengthening community action; c) creating supportive environments; d) developing personal skills, and e) re-orienting the health system
   - Identifies strategies for change that will make it easier for people to make a healthier choice.
6. Collaborates with the individual/community to assist them in taking responsibility for maintaining or improving their health by increasing their knowledge, influence and control over the determinants of health.
7. Understands and uses social marketing and media advocacy strategies to raise consciousness of health issues, place issues on the public agenda, shift social norms, and change behaviours if other enabling factors are present.
8. Assists the individual/community to identify their strengths and available resources and take action to address their needs.
9. Recognizes the broad impact of specific issues such as political climate and will, values and culture, individual/community readiness, and social and systemic structure on health promotion.
10. Evaluates and modifies population health promotion programs in partnership with the individual/community and other stakeholders.

B) PREVENTION AND HEALTH PROTECTION

The community health nurse adopts the principles of prevention and protection and applies a repertoire of activities to minimize the occurrence of diseases or injuries and their consequences to individuals/communities. Health protection strategies often become mandated programs and laws by governments for the larger geo-political entity.

The community health nurse:

1. Recognizes the differences between the levels of prevention (primary, secondary, tertiary).
2. Selects the appropriate level of preventative intervention.
3. Helps individuals/communities make informed choices about protective and preventative health measures such as immunization, birth control, breastfeeding, and palliative care.
4. Assists individuals, groups, families, and communities to identify potential risks to health.
5. Utilizes harm reduction principles to identify, reduce or remove risk factors in a variety of contexts including home, neighbourhood, workplace, school and street.
6. Applies epidemiological principles in using strategies such as screening, surveillance, immunization, communicable disease response and outbreak management and education.
7. Engages collaborative, interdisciplinary and intersectoral partnerships to address risks to the individual, family, community, or population health and to address prevention and protection issues such as communicable disease, injury and chronic disease.
8. Collaborates in developing and using follow-up systems within the practice setting to ensure that the individual/community receives appropriate and effective service.
9. Practices in accordance with legislation relevant to community health practice (e.g. public health legislation, child protection).
10. Evaluates collaborative practice (personal, team, and/or intersectoral) in achieving individual/community

outcomes such as reductions in communicable disease, injury and chronic disease or reducing the impacts of a disease process.

C) HEALTH MAINTENANCE, RESTORATION AND PALLIATION

Community health nurses provide clinical nursing care, health teaching and counselling in health centres, homes, schools and other community based settings to individuals, families, groups, and populations whether they are seeking to maintain their health or dealing with acute, chronic or terminal illness. The community health nurse links people to community resources and co-ordinates/facilitates other care needs and supports. The activities of the community health nurse may range from health screening and care planning at an individual level to the forming of inter-sectoral collaborations and resource development at the community and population level.

The community health nurse:

1. Assesses the individual/family/population's health status and functional competence within the context of their environmental and social supports.
2. Develops a mutually agreed upon plan and priorities for care with the individual/family.
3. Identifies a range of interventions including health promotion, disease prevention and direct clinical care strategies (including those related to palliation), along with short and long term goals and outcomes.
4. Maximizes the ability of an individual/family/community to take responsibility for and manage their health needs according to resources and personal skills available.
5. Supports informed choice and respects the individual/ family/community's specific requests while acknowledging diversity, unique characteristics and abilities.
6. Adapts community health nursing techniques, approaches and procedures as appropriate to the challenges inherent to the particular community situation/ setting.
7. Uses knowledge of the community to link with, refer to or develop appropriate community resources.
8. Recognizes patterns and trends in epidemiological data and service delivery and initiates improvement strategies.
9. Facilitates maintenance of health and the healing process for individuals/families/ communities in response to significant health emergencies or other diverse community situations that negatively impact upon health.
10. Evaluates individual/family/community outcomes systematically and continuously in collaboration with the individuals/families, significant others, other health practitioners and community partners.

Standard 2: Building Individual/Community Capacity

Building capacity is the process of actively involving individuals, groups, organizations and communities in all phases of planned change for the purpose of increasing their skills, knowledge and willingness to take action on their own in the future. The community health nurse works collaboratively both with the individual/community affected by health compromising situations and the people and organizations who control resources. Community health nurses start where the individual/community is at to identify relevant issues and assess resources and strengths. They determine the individual's or community's stage of readiness for change and priorities for action. They take collaborative action by building on identified strengths and facilitate the involvement of key stakeholders: individuals, organizations, community leaders and opinion leaders. They work with people to improve the determinants of health and "make it easier to make the healthier choice". Community health nurses use supportive and empowering strategies to move individuals and communities toward maximum autonomy.

The community health nurse:

1. Works collaboratively with the individual/community, other professionals, agencies and sectors to identify needs, strengths and available resources.
2. Facilitates action in support of the five priorities of the Jakarta Declaration to:
   - Promote social responsibility for health
   - Increase investments for health development
   - Expand partnerships for health promotion
   - Increase individual and community capacity
   - Secure an infrastructure for health promotion.
3. Uses community development principles:
   - Engages the individual/community in a consultative process
   - Recognizes and builds on the group/community readiness for participation
   - Uses empowering strategies such as mutual goal setting, visioning and facilitation
   - Understands group dynamics and effectively uses facilitation skills to support group development
   - Enables the individual/community to participate in the resolution of their issues
   - Assists the group/community to marshal available resources to support taking action on their health issues.
4. Utilizes a comprehensive mix of community/population based strategies such as coalition building, intersectoral partnerships and networking to address issues of concern to groups or populations.
5. Supports the individual/family/community/population in developing skills for self-advocacy.
6. Applies principles of social justice and engages in advocacy in support of those who are as yet unable to take action for themselves.
7. Uses a comprehensive mix of interventions and strategies to customize actions to address unique needs and build individual/community capacity.
8. Supports community action to influence policy change in support of health.

9. Actively works to build capacity for health promotion with health professionals and community partners.
10. Evaluates the impact of change on individual/community control and health outcomes.

Standard 3: Building Relationships

Building relationships within community health nursing is based upon the principles of connecting and caring. Connecting is the establishment and nurturing of a caring relationship and a supportive environment that promotes the maximum participation of the individual/community, and their own self-determination. Caring involves the development of empowering relationships, which preserve, protect, and enhance human dignity. Community health nurses build caring relationships based on mutual respect and on an understanding of the power inherent in their position and its potential impact on relationships and practice.

The community health nurse's most unique challenge is building a network of relationships and partnerships with a variety of relevant groups, communities, and organizations. These relationships occur within a complex, changing, undefined and often ambiguous environment that may present conflicting and unpredictable circumstances.

The community health nurse:

1. Recognizes her/his personal attitudes, beliefs, assumptions, feelings and values about health and their potential effect on interventions with individuals/communities.
2. Identifies the individual/community beliefs, attitudes, feelings and values about health and their potential effect on the relationship and intervention.
3. Is aware of and utilizes culturally relevant communication in building relationships. Communication may be verbal or non-verbal, written or pictorial. It may involve face-to-face, telephone, group facilitation, print or electronic means.
4. Respects and trusts the family's/community's ability to know the issue they are addressing and solve their own problems.
5. Involves the individual/community as an active partner in identifying relevant needs, perspectives and expectations.
6. Establishes connections and collaborative relationships with health professionals, community organizations, businesses, faith communities, volunteer service organizations, and other sectors to address health related issues.
7. Maintains awareness of community resources, values and characteristics.
8. Promotes and facilitates linkages with appropriate community resources when the individual/community is ready to receive them (e.g. hospice/palliative care, parenting groups).
9. Maintains professional boundaries within an often long-term relationship in the home or other community setting where professional and social relationships may become blurred.
10. Negotiates an end to the relationship when appropriate, e.g. when the client assumes self-care, or when the goals for the relationship have been achieved.

Standard 4: Facilitating Access and Equity

Community health nurses embrace the philosophy of primary health care and collaboratively identify and facilitate universal and equitable access to available services. Community health nurses engage in advocacy by analyzing the full range of possibilities for action, acting on affected determinants of health, and influencing other sectors to ensure their policies and programs have a positive impact on health. Community health nurses collaborate with colleagues and with other members of the health care team to promote effective working relationships that contribute to comprehensive client care and the achievement of optimal client care outcomes. Community health nurses use advocacy as a key strategy to meet identified needs and enhance individual and/or community capacity for self-advocacy. They are keenly aware of the impact of the determinants of health on individuals, families, groups, communities and populations. The practice of community health nursing occurs with consideration for the financial resources, geography and culture of the individual/ community.

The community health nurse:

1. Assesses and understands individual and community capacities including norms, values, beliefs, knowledge, resources and power structure.
2. Provides culturally sensitive care in diverse communities and settings.
3. Supports individuals/communities in their choice to access alternate health care options.
4. Advocates for appropriate resource allocation for individuals, groups and populations to facilitate access to conditions for health and health services.
5. Refers, co-ordinates or facilitates access to service within health and other sectors.
6. Adapts practice in response to the changing health needs of the individual/community.
7. Collaborates with individuals and communities to identify and provide programs and delivery methods that are acceptable to them and responsive to their needs across the life span and in different circumstances.
8. Uses strategies such as home visits, outreach and case finding to ensure access to services and health-supporting conditions for potentially vulnerable populations (e.g. persons who are ill, elderly, young, poor, immigrants, isolated, or have communication barriers).
9. Assesses the impact of the determinants of health on the opportunity for health for individuals/families/communities/populations.
10. Advocates for healthy public policy by participating in legislative and policymaking activities that influence health determinants and access to services.
11. Takes action with and for individuals/communities at the organizational, municipal, provincial/territorial and federal levels to address service gaps and accessibility issues.
12. Monitors and evaluates changes/progress in access to the determinants of health and appropriate community services.

Standard 5: Demonstrating Professional Responsibility and Accountability

Community health nurses work with a high degree of autonomy in providing programs and services. They are accountable to strive for excellence, to ensure that their knowledge is evidence-based, current and maintains competence, and for the overall quality of their own practice. Community health nurses are accountable to initiate strategies that will help address the determinants of health and generate a positive impact on people and systems.

Within a complex environment, community health nurses are accountable to a variety of authorities and stakeholders as well as to the individual/community they serve. This places them in a variety of situations with unique ethical dilemmas. These include whether responsibility for an issue lies with the individual/family/community/population, or with the nurse or the nurse's employer, the priority of one individual's rights over another's, individual or societal good, allocation of scarce resources and dealing with issues related to quality versus quantity of life.

The community health nurse:

1. Takes preventive and/or corrective action individually or in partnership with others to protect individuals/communities from unsafe or unethical circumstances.
2. Advocates for societal change in support of health for all.
3. Utilizes nursing informatics (information and communication technology) to generate, manage and process relevant data to support nursing practice.
4. Identifies and takes action on factors which impinge on autonomy of practice and quality of care.
5. Participates in the advancement of community health nursing by mentoring students and novice practitioners.
6. Participates in research and professional activities.
7. Makes decisions using ethical standards/principles, taking into consideration the tension between individual versus societal good and the responsibility to uphold the greater good of all people or the population as a whole.
8. Seeks assistance with problem solving as needed to determine the best course of action in response to ethical dilemmas and risks to human rights and freedoms, new situations, and new knowledge.
9. Identifies and works proactively to address nursing issues that will affect the population through personal advocacy and participation in relevant professional associations.
10. Contributes proactively to the quality of the work environment by identifying needs/issues and solutions, mobilizing colleagues, and actively participating in team and organizational structures and mechanisms.
11. Provides constructive feedback to peers as appropriate to enhance community health nursing practice.
12. Documents community health nursing activities in a timely and thorough manner, including telephone advice and work with communities and groups.
13. Advocates for effective and efficient use of community health nurse resources.
14. Utilizes reflective practice as a means of continually assessing and seeking to improve personal community health nursing practice.
15. Seeks professional development experiences that are consistent with current community health nursing practice, new and emerging issues, the changing needs of the population, the evolving impact of the determinants of health and emerging research.
16. Acts upon legal obligations to report to appropriate authorities situations of unsafe or unethical care provided by family, friends or other individuals to children or vulnerable adults.
17. Uses available resources to systematically evaluate the availability, acceptability, quality, efficiency and effectiveness of community health nursing practice.

Answers to Study Questions

CHAPTER 1

1. The two forms of community health nursing that evolved in Canada in the early twentieth century were public health nursing and visiting/district nursing. PHNs were employed by civic, provincial, or federal health departments to carry out preventive programs in the community. In the later part of the twentieth century, PHNs took on new roles in health promotion and community development.

   Visiting/district nurses offered bedside nursing services in the home. They were most frequently employed by charitable organizations. Visiting nursing is now more commonly referred to as home care nursing.

2. The social gospel movement was one important impetus for the development of community-based social services. It was an ecumenical and evangelical stream within the Protestant churches, which had as its goal the establishment of God's kingdom on earth. Another important social movement was maternal feminism. Maternal feminists had a particular interest in the health and welfare of women and children. The social gospel movement and maternal feminism created an important strategic alliance after World War I, and their efforts are theorized to have had an important influence on the rise of the Canadian welfare state. The last important social movement was the public health movement. Sanitarianism, bacteriology, and health education were all important paradigms within the early public health movement. All contributed to the overarching belief that the application of scientific knowledge would create a healthy nation.

3. Early community health nursing programs focused on women, children, the poor, the working class, and immigrants. There were several interrelated reasons for this emphasis. All these groups were vulnerable within a society where political and economic power was held by elite and middle-class males. Their vulnerability was clearly demonstrated by the higher mortality rates these groups experienced. Another reason for the focus on these groups was the need to create a strong and healthy pool of future citizens to establish Canada's pre-eminence in the twentieth century. Immigrants were an important target group because elite and middle-class reformers believed that they needed to adopt Canadian beliefs and practices rather than retain those of their countries of origin.

4. The earliest public health programs that employed nurses were TB control, school health, and infant welfare. TB was a leading cause of death in early twentieth-century Canada and a particular problem amongst the urban poor. Early efforts to control TB were based on the belief that a reduction in the incidence of this disease would, as well as alleviate suffering, reduce the costs of public welfare and health care programs.

   School health programs were established to identify health problems amongst school-age children. As working-class children entered the public school system, it became apparent that they suffered from many preventable health problems that detracted from their capacity to learn.

   Infant welfare programs were established to reduce infant mortality rates. In the early twentieth century, immigration, industrialization, and urbanization created unprecedented urban squalor.

5. The British North America (BNA) Act reflected nineteenth-century beliefs about the role of the state. In keeping with the philosophy of laissez faire, the state had no role to play in the provision of health care and social welfare for its citizens. These were private matters, which were the responsibility of individuals and families. Those who could not provide for their families were compelled to obtain charitable assistance from local governments or, more likely, voluntary philanthropic agencies. The BNA Act left responsibility for health care in the hands of the provinces, which also took only a limited interest in this area. Enabling legislation for the establishment of health departments was passed by several provinces prior to the end of the nineteenth century, but permanent health departments were not established in most Canadian cities and provinces until the twentieth century. Prior to the end of World War II, local and provincial health departments received no assistance from the federal government. Their capacity to respond to the health needs of the communities for which they were responsible was constrained by their ability to fund programs from local tax revenues.

6. The Canadian welfare state had its origins in the early twentieth century as provincial and municipal departments of health began to provide publicly funded public health programs at the local level. Some provinces, cities, and municipalities, particularly those in Western Canada, were virtually bankrupted by their attempts to respond to widespread unemployment and poverty. They put pressure on the federal government to assist them. However, other provinces, more concerned about maintaining strict divisions between provincial and federal powers, opposed any initiatives that would enable the federal government to intervene into what had previously been provincial responsibilities. Several attempts by the federal government to take a greater role in health and welfare programs were stopped by the Supreme Court, which used the BNA Act as the basis of its decisions. In 1940, the Royal Commission on Dominion-Provincial Relations recommended that the federal government undertake responsibility for old-age pensions and unemployment insurance, but leave responsibility for health with the provinces.

   In the 1940s, 1950s, and 1960s, a series of cost-sharing arrangements enabled the federal government to establish a national health care system by creating incentives for the provinces to spend more money in this area and to extend those services to all citizens regardless of ability to pay. The National Health Grants Program (1948), the National Hospital Insurance and Diagnostic Services Act (1957), and the Medical Care Insurance Act (1968) were key elements in the increased federal role in the provision of health care.

7. First, they often pioneered community health nursing programs, thus demonstrating both the need for and the effectiveness of these programs. Second, they provided community health programs in communities where local governments were either unable or unwilling to do so. Third, they created educational programs to prepare nurses to practise in this area. Fourth, they provided funding to support local initiatives to create community health nursing programs.

CHAPTER 2

1. North America's first universal health insurance program was initially implemented in 1947 at a provincial level in Saskatchewan. In 1957, similar legislation, the Hospital Insurance and Diagnostic Services Act (HIDS), was passed by the federal government. The HIDS provided financial incentives for the provinces to establish hospital insurance plans. In 1962, Saskatchewan led the country again with legislation providing universal, publicly funded medical insurance. In 1966, the federal government followed suit with the passage of the National Medical Care Insurance Act (Medicare). This Act was implemented in 1968, and by 1971, all provinces were fully participating. As a result of the strain on the federal budgets caused by the blanket 50/50 cost-sharing between the federal and provincial/territorial governments, the federal government passed the Established Programs Financing Act (EPF) in 1977. This act changed the federal share of health costs to per capita block grants. In 1984, the Canada Health Act, which banned extra-billing and user fees by physicians, was passed.

2. Practices such as extra-billing by physicians and user fees by provincial institutions rose dramatically once the EPF reduced the federal contribution to health care. Additional factors that contributed to this phenomenon included:
   - the popularity of neo-conservative economics that generally promoted a reduced role for governments and larger role for the private sector,
   - partisan politics with a liberal government at the federal level and conservative governments in 8 of 10 provinces, and
   - wage and price controls, which had included physicians' incomes.

3. The Canadian Nurses Association (CNA) lobbied intensely for the bill's passage into law. In addition, they were successful in amending it. As it was introduced into Parliament in 1983, Bill C-3 identified only physicians as providers of insurable services. The CNA amendment changed the language to include other health care workers as potential providers of insurable services, opening the door for the public to have direct access to nursing care through insured services.

4. Although the 1867 Constitution Act did not explicitly assign responsibility for health policy to either the federal or provincial governments, historically both levels of government have been involved in ensuring the availability of health services for Canadians and in funding those services. Responsibility for hospitals is assigned by the Act exclusively to provinces, and, as a result, health care in Canada has been erroneously interpreted to fall under provincial jurisdiction. The federal government assumes responsibility for delivering a few direct health services, for example, to Aboriginal populations, veterans, and military personnel. Provincial governments are responsible for the delivery of the remainder of health care services, including public health. Funding for health care is another matter, however. The federal government's involvement in funding health care relates both to its mandate to equalize services among provinces and its responsibilities to ensure that provinces are in compliance with the Canada Health Act (CHA).

5. Public health in Canada is funded by a combination of provincial and/or municipal tax dollars, although federal grants may be available for specific initiatives. Without a national public health program, however, provinces are free to make changes in funding mechanisms that can further destabilize the system and deepen disparities among and within provinces.

   In all 13 provinces/territories, the ministries or departments of health and/or social/community services maintain control over home care budgets and funding levels. However, contrary to other forms of health care provided in Canada, home care has retained a significant private sector component. So, while all provincial governments finance home care services to some extent, user fees or co-payments are often required.

6. With respect to stopping the practices of extra-billing and charging user fees, the CHA fulfilled its purpose. However, the issue of provincial/territorial non-compliance with the five criteria of the Act remains to be adequately addressed. The intent of the Act was to relate federal cash contributions not only to insured health services, but also to extended health care services. In that respect, the CHA has not been effective.

   The Act endorsed health promotion but limited its focus to medically necessary hospital and physicians' services. Health promotion services, largely provided by provincial public health, were left unprotected by federal legislation. The resulting variability of health promotion and disease prevention services within and among jurisdictions violates the Act's principle of portability.

CHAPTER 3

1. See text box (Canadian Nursing Association Definitions of Nursing Values).

2. First, feminist bioethics is concerned with the ethical use of power in health care. It examines the broad political and structural dimensions of problems in health care and the day-to-day use of power by health professionals. Second, feminist bioethics tends to suggest that while the ethic of care is a necessary perspective for bioethics, it is not sufficient. An ethic of justice is also needed. Third, feminist bioethics tends to view persons as unique, connected to others, and interdependent, that is, vulnerable and unequal in power. It focuses upon how persons are situated or positioned in society, that is, the entire context of their lives, including culture, history, politics, and socioeconomic status. Fourth, feminist bioethics tends to concern itself not primarily with crisis issues, like euthanasia, but with issues of everyday life.

3. A feminist perspective can facilitate critical thinking about power, gender, and socioeconomic structures, all of which impact significantly upon health. Fundamental to community health nursing is an understanding of the socio-environmental context of health that recognizes that basic resources and prerequisite conditions are necessary to achieve health. Feminism also promotes collaboration with oppressed groups to create social change in a way that is consistent with health promotion strategies. Underlying these strategies is view of health that goes beyond the narrow individual and disease orientation of the medical model.

   Feminist bioethics also has the capacity to focus not only on individuals, but also on entire groups because it goes beyond traditional individual focused caring to include considerations of social justice.

   With respect to home care nursing, feminist bioethics is a highly relevant perspective because it emphasizes the ethical significance of difference, such as gender and race, and makes visible the societal value of caregiving.

   Feminist bioethics is also highly sensitive to context. It can capture the importance of place or setting in health care delivery. Understanding the meaning and impact of various places or settings is central to community health nursing because CHNs deliver nursing services where clients live, work, learn, worship, and play, not in hospitals.

4. - Promoting health: CHNs promote health through a) health promotion; b) illness and injury prevention and health protection; and c) health maintenance, health restoration, and palliation.
   - Building individual/community capacity: CHNs begin where individuals and communities are, helping them to identify relevant health issues and to assess their strengths and resources. CHNs use strategies that involve advocacy and empowerment.
   - Building relationships: CHNs establish and nurture caring relationships with individuals and communities that promote maximum participation and self-determination.
   - Facilitating access and equity: CHNs collaboratively identify and facilitate universal and equitable access to available health care services and the socioeconomic, social, and physical environmental determinants of health.
   - Demonstrating professional responsibility and accountability: CHNs must adhere to federal and provincial professional standards, laws, and codes of ethics and must use resources effectively and efficiently. They have a responsibility to be knowledgeable, competent, and current and must also help others around them, such as colleagues and students, to develop and maintain competence.

5. In order for CHNs to assist clients in making informed choices, at least two elements must be considered: the exchange of information between the client and CHN, and the respect for the client's autonomy. The process of consent includes CHNs disclosing, unasked, whatever the average prudent person in the client's particular position would want to know. CHNs must provide information about the nature of the treatment/procedures they are providing, including benefits and risks, alternative treatments, and consequences if the treatment is not given. The presentation of this information must consider the client's education, language, age, values, culture, disease state, and mental capacity. When clients provide their consent it must be done voluntarily (i.e., without being coerced), and they must have the capacity (i.e., mental competence) to do so. The only times when consent is not required for treatment are in emergency situations and as exempted by law.

6. The four key elements that must be proven to make a finding of negligence are: (a) that there was a relationship between the person bringing the claim (i.e., plaintiff, e.g., client, family) and the person being sued (i.e., defendant, e.g., nurse), (b) that the defendant breached the standard of care, (c) that the plaintiff suffered a harm, and (d) that the harm suffered was caused by the defendant's breach of the standard of care.

CHAPTER 4

1. - Public health nurses work in client homes, schools, workplaces, community centres, clinics, mobile street clinics, within the community on coalitions, and with other partner agencies.
   - Home health nurses provide direct care to clients in homes and schools.
   - Community health centre or outreach nurses provide primary health care in clinic settings or may be involved in mobile clinics.
   - Outpost nurses may work in clinics, clients' homes, or schools, usually in isolated communities.
   - Parish nurses work with members of a congregation in the parish place of worship or in the homes of parishioners.
   - Occupational health nurses work primarily in the workplace, which could range from the industrial shop floor, to corporate offices, to a hospitality industry's casino.
2. - Teacher to individuals and groups
   - Direct care provider to individuals requiring nursing care and interventions in the form of treatment, supportive therapy, or hygiene care
   - Policy advocate for supportive healthy environments
   - Counsellor to supplement the holistic aspect of client care
3. - Through population-based health promotion
   - Public policy support (e.g., smoke-free public places, sidewalk by-laws to encourage active living, alcohol policy for safe serving, safe playgrounds to prevent injuries)
   - Public education through marketing and use of mass media
   - Targeting multiple sites with health education messages
   - Community mobilization to empower communities to gain control over life
   - Skill development, education, and counselling with individuals
4. - Implement holistic strategies that involve the clients in their plan of care.
   - Encourage as much independence as possible.
   - Use collective decision making.
   - Nursing care is enabling, holistic, and as noninvasive as possible.
5. - Degree of influence and autonomy over the practice setting
   - Control over scheduling
   - Rewards for work (i.e., wages, benefits, recognition for specialty knowledge)

- Workloads and care delivery systems that are supported during staff shortages
- Professional development system
- Strong communication systems
- Leadership

CHAPTER 5

1. A discourse is a patterned system of texts, messages, talk, dialogue, or conversations, which can be identified in communications and located in social structures. Key ideas are patterned expressions that can be located within social structures.
2. Primary health care is a balanced combination of medical care, health promotion and prevention, consumer protection, effective health care systems, appropriate technology, and intersectoral cooperation organized to ensure effective action on the determinants of health and to shape environments in support of healthful living and healthy lifestyles.

   A Primary Health Care Model suggests a balanced combination of medical care, health promotion and prevention, consumer protection, effective health care systems, appropriate technology, and intersectoral cooperation (Green & Ottoson, 1999; RNABC, 2002).
3. The difference between these two views originates in how each perspective conceptualizes health. Traditionally, the medical model defines health as the absence of disease, whereas the systems view envisions health as shaped by a myriad of physical, social, environmental, and organizational factors.
4. The challenge to nurses is to be aware of the view of health that dominates in their practice environment and to begin practice from the clients' perspectives on health, working collaboratively within this view in the interest of the client.
5. The Lalonde Report shifted perspectives on health from illness care to health care by suggesting that health is embedded in a web of factors including physical, social, and environmental factors.
6. In the ecological perspective, health is viewed as a consequence of the interdependence between the individual and the family, community, culture, and physical and social environments.
7. In a relational nursing practice, the nurse builds trusting relationships, collaborates with clients to identify and address their health-related issues, fosters clients' strengths, promotes and protects clients' rights, practises in an intersectoral manner to address the determinants of health, and strives for a respectful, integrated, and accessible system of health care delivery.
8. Canadian Research Box 5.1 suggests that the biomedical or mechanistic view of women is located in a discourse in which women's "mechanistic" function is reproduction; thus, when there are "breakdowns" in this function, efforts have to be taken by the medical establishment to "fix" the breakdown so that women can be reproductively "healthy" to best enact their function. A systems discourse of health would see women as more than a reproductive "machine" and would thus conceptualize women's health more broadly.
9. Through the development of a series of charters and frameworks that flesh out the elements of systems views of health, Canada has played a leading role in shaping discourses of health toward a systems view. These works, in combination with the scholarly and advocacy efforts of an army of academics and health advocates, have been fundamental in arguing to maintain a single-payer system for health care in Canada—a system consistent in its philosophy with a systems view of health rather than a biomedical model view of health. Canada's charters and framework of health promotion, population health, and primary health care, along with the related health care system, are models in the international arena for a health care system that advances a systems view of health.
10. The authors invite students to offer their views on the metaphors of nursing practice provided in this chapter by e-mail communication to the first author, Lynne Young, at leyoung@interchange.ubc.ca. The author will model a relational process while facilitating the discussion by ensuring that all voices are heard and all opinions are respected. The facilitator will share her observations and reactions and summarize the discussion.

CHAPTER 6

1. Primary care, defined as the point of first contact with the health care system, generally refers to preventive, curative, and rehabilitative care provided to individuals (Stanhope & Lancaster, 2002). Although practitioners are encouraged to assess social and environmental impacts on health, interventions are often biomedical in focus (Starfield, 1998). Although accessibility to primary care is an essential component of primary health care, primary care is narrower in scope and primarily biomedical in focus. Primary health care is a broader concept and includes primary care. Primary health care focuses on the determinants of health in order to create a more socially just environment in which everyone has equal access to opportunities for socially and economically productive lives.
2. Health promotion is "the process of enabling people to increase their control over and improve their health" (WHO, 1986, p. 1). There is a close relationship between health promotion and primary health care in both philosophy and methods. However, primary health care also involves curative, rehabilitative, and palliative care methods as part of the provision of first-line contact with the community.

   "Population health refers to the health of a population as measured by health status indicators and as influenced by social, economic and physical environments; personal health practices; individual capacity and coping skills; human biology; early childhood development; and health services. As an approach, population health focuses on the interrelated conditions and factors that influence the health of populations over the life course, identifies systematic variations in their patterns of occurrence, and applies the resulting knowledge to develop and implement policies and actions to improve the health and well-being of those populations" (Federal, Provincial and Territorial Advisory Committee on Population Health, 1999, p. 7). Population health's emphasis on the use of political and economic policy interventions (Lavis, 2002; Raphael, 2002) to reduce inequities in health is congruent with the original thinking of primary health care outlined in the Declaration of Alma Ata. Population health's strong orientation to evidence-based interventions (Health Canada, 2001) also highlights an aspect of primary health care articulated in the Declaration.

3. Community health nurses' work has evolved to incorporate interventions at multiple levels of society. In the 1970s and '80s, many community health nursing roles focused primarily on the delivery of services to individuals (e.g., immunizations, postpartum home visits, cardiac rehabilitation) and health teaching in schools and small groups (e.g., prenatal classes). Although prevention and health promotion have always been strongly emphasized, the understanding of the importance of the determinants of health was not evident until the late 1980s and early '90s. The focus on the determinants of health increased CHNs' focus on intersectoral strategies aimed at the determinants of health, such as increasing affordable housing, improving access to nutritious food, and political action to influence development of healthy public policy (e.g., access to transportation, bicycle helmet use). CHNs are an integral part of intersectoral community development initiatives because of their ability to stimulate public participation and input. CHNs play key roles in coalition building and community action.

4.
   - Personal care: one-to-one relationship and interaction with clients, for example, a postnatal visit to a new mother.
   - Small group development: facilitate formation of support or self-help group to encourage mutual aid, for example, a group of post-MI patients and/or their spouses.
   - Community organization: the process of connecting and facilitating communication between organizations and individuals in a community for the purpose of identifying and taking action on health issues, for example, the development and implementation of a latch-key-kids' program involving recreation, local business, health, and school as main partners, as well as parents, kids, and a local senior citizens' group.
   - Coalition advocacy: the process of enabling the formation of a group around a specific issue in order to develop programs, lobby for change, and increase coordination between organizations, for example, coalitions formed to improve heart health.
   - Political action: organization and change efforts aimed at changing policy and pubic opinion to influence policy, for example, lobbying by CHNs and other groups to stop tobacco advertising.

5.
   - Accessibility: the five types of health care (promotive, preventive, curative, rehabilitative, and supportive/palliative) are universally accessible to all clients regardless of geographic location. Clients will receive appropriate care from the appropriate health care professional within a time frame that is appropriate.
   - Public participation: clients are encouraged to participate in making decisions about their own health, identifying the health needs of their community, and considering the merits of alternative approaches to addressing those needs. It ensures respect for diversity, flexible and responsive health care design and delivery, and effective and strategic planning and evaluation of health care services in a community.
   - Health promotion: includes health education, nutrition, sanitation, maternal and child health care, immunization, and prevention and control of endemic disease. The goals of health promotion are to reduce the demands for curative and rehabilitative care and build citizens' understanding of the determinants of health and the skills needed to improve and maintain their health and well-being.
   - Appropriate technology: modes of care are appropriately adapted to the community's social, economic, and cultural development. Alternatives to high-cost, high-tech services must be considered. Developing and testing innovative models of health care and disseminating the results of research related to health care are also important.
   - Intersectoral cooperation: recognizes that health and well-being are linked to both economic and social policy. It is needed to establish national and local health goals, healthy public policy, and the planning and evaluation of health services. It also ensures that different sectors and disciplines collaborate and function interdependently to meet the needs of citizens and communities. It also means that health professionals will participate in government policy formulation and evaluation, as well as the design and delivery of health care services.

6. Interventions for homeless: Micro: counselling and referral to food banks and other supportive organizations, advocacy and support to gain access to health services; Meso: facilitate linkages between organizations serving the homeless population to increase effectiveness of services, education of community health nurses and personnel in emergency departments to increase awareness and decrease judgmental attitudes toward homeless, linkages between local post-secondary training organizations (e.g., dental schools, dental assistant/hygiene programs, nursing schools) to develop some service delivery programs; Macro: coalition formation to develop a public education and lobby campaign to influence more supportive policies (e.g., affordable housing, income programs,) and denormalize homelessness.

CHAPTER 7

1. Any five of:
   - consistency: the same events happen over and over again under the same conditions
   - strength: the greater the exposure, the more likely the problem or event will result
   - specificity: during an outbreak, the people without the disease/problem are different from those with the problem
   - time relationship: there is logic between the time of the stressor and the event problem—the problem does not come before the stressor
   - congruence: the comparable logic between what is already known (e.g., natural history of the disease) and what is being examined
   - sensitivity: is this factor the distinct cause, or could other factors be responsible for the disease/problem
   - biological/medical: the strength of the causal factor combined with the receptiveness/risk of the host
   - plausibility: new information may contradict previously held beliefs, but may be credible
   - experiments and research: new or existing information based on rigorous scientific research will add to credibility of causality
   - analogy factors: refers to transfer of knowledge from a known to an unknown situation

2. Mortality statistics look at the deaths due to specific diseases/conditions; morbidity looks at people who become ill with specific diseases/conditions. Morbidity informs epidemiologists how frequently the illness occurs, and mortality tells them how likely the person is to die from the illness. Both types of data assist in planning future foci for health professionals and health promotion, as well as evaluating the usefulness of interventions.

3. - Cohort: a study in which the researcher examines the individual characteristics of a group of people who manifest a particular disease or health challenge to find out what common factors they share and what differences can be discerned. Example research questions: 1) What factors are common or different in a group of teens who are involved in front-end automobile collisions? 2) What are the dietary habits and hygiene practices of 10-year-olds with no dental caries?
   - Case-control: the individuals in the cohort with a disease or health choice are matched to individuals who are similar in some characteristics (e.g., age, gender, time, geographic residence) but who have not manifested the disease or health choice in question. The health histories or characteristics of the individuals in both groups are then obtained. These data are compared and any common and different factors are identified between the two populations. Example research questions: 1) What are the similarities and differences in maternal age, presence of family support system, education, and level of anxiety between teen mothers who choose to breastfeed and those who do not? 2) What are the differences and similarities between women in province X who have multiple sclerosis and those who do not?
   - Cross-sectional: snapshots of the present that are used to suggest relationships that can be tested in future research. Example research questions: 1) What coping behaviours do nursing students use to manage community clinical practice and what are their anxiety levels? 2) How do stress scores differ between people who exercise regularly three or more times a week and those who do not?

4. - Environment: the context in which the event occurs. Examples of environments are physical, economic, and psychological.
   - Agent: the contagious or noncontagious force that begins or continues a health challenge
   - Host: the human being in which the event occurs

5. Incidence is a measure of the new cases of a particular disease/health condition in a given space of time (usually one year); prevalence is the number of persons in a given population who have a given condition/disease at the current time. If prevalence and incidence are different, the disease may be chronic in nature, with death or recovery frequently experienced a long time after diagnosis, for example, rheumatoid arthritis. If prevalence and incidence are similar, the disease is probably short lived, with recovery or death a short time after diagnosis, for example, the flu or Ebola virus.

6. - Prospective: a study in which individuals are followed for a period of time to see if they acquire the disease in question or to find out what happens to them. Example research questions: 1) What illnesses/injuries are experienced by women working in an automobile-manufacturing plant compared with women working in a food-processing plant over a ten-year period? 2) Is the use of health professionals different over time between women in professional university programs and those who are not?
   - Retrospective: a study in which individuals are grouped in the present relative to a particular issue or disease and then examined for past events or situations that may or may not have influenced their susceptibility to the present issue or disease. Example research questions: 1) What are the common factors in the histories of a group of women who required hysterectomies for non-malignant causes in their third decade? 2) What are common wellness strategies that a group of octogenarians have used over their lifetimes?

CHAPTER 8

1. Answers can be found in Table 8.1.

2. - An umbrella term referring to any activity designed to foster health
   - A synonym for health education
   - The marketing or selling of health
   - A strategy concerned with lifestyle behaviour change
   - Health education plus environmental and legislative measures designed to facilitate the achievement of health and prevention of disease
   - An approach that encompasses a set of values that include concepts of empowerment, equity, and collaboration

   The first four interpretations (but especially the second, third, and fourth) reflect the behavioural approach to health promotion, whereas the latter two reflect the socio-environmental approach.

3. Strengths: first time that a national government had made an official statement regarding the importance of health promotion as a key strategy for improving population health; slightly expanded the interpretation of health to include the notion of increased functional ability and wellness; and challenged the dominant thinking of the time that access to health services was the key to population health.

   Weaknesses: while the framework suggested equal emphasis on all four fields, the report focused on the behaviour/lifestyle field; and underlying assumption is that individuals are responsible for their own health and have equal opportunities for engaging in healthy behaviours.

4. The description of each behavioural strategy is found in Table 8.2. Regulatory measures coincide with healthy public policies used in the socio-environmental approach.

5. - Ideological responses to the behavioural approach: influence of social movements, concern with "social justice," the "common good," social change, and social responsibility for health.
   - Theoretical developments: ecological perspective, which suggested that health is a product of the interdependence between the individual and subsystems of the ecosystem, and belief that the environment sets limits on individual behaviour, but also that behaviour influences environments.
   - Limitations of population-level disease prevention initiatives in changing individual behaviours, and failure to address inequalities in health.

- Epidemiological evidence that the distribution of disease in any given society is the result of the economic, political, and social relationship between individuals and groups in society, not the result of individual behaviours.

6. It was the year that the Ottawa Charter for Health Promotion and Achieving Health for All were published.
7. Empowerment is the central concept. It refers to the process or outcome of individuals, communities, and populations gaining power, knowledge, skills, and/or other resources that allow them to achieve positive change, including increased self-efficacy. Empowerment relates directly to the concept of health promotion as a process of enabling individuals, communities, and populations to increase control over the determinants of health.
8. Health promotion:
   - involves the population as a whole and the context of their everyday lives rather than focusing on people at risk for specific diseases.
   - is directed toward action on the determinants or causes of health.
   - combines diverse, but complementary, methods or approaches.
   - aims particularly at effective and concrete public participation.
   - recognizes that health professionals, particularly those in primary health care, have an important role in nurturing and enabling health promotion.
9. - Historically, clinical nursing practice in the community (and, to a certain extent in the hospital as well) has focused on health teaching.
   - Nursing models and theories used in nursing education have been strongly influenced by concepts and theories from the behavioural sciences in which individual behaviour change is the outcome of interest (e.g., Pender).
   - Other aspects of nursing curricula perpetuate individualistic, behaviour-focused health promotion perspectives among nurses (e.g., focus on behaviours, behaviour change of nursing students themselves, focus on communication, counselling roles of nurses).
10. Barriers originating within CHNs: a lack of well-developed collaborative and other "upstream" skills; anxiety caused by working with uncertainty and a lack of direction; a general preference among CHNs for working directly with individuals or families (probably due to the previous factors); and CHNs' difficulty in giving up control over the agenda and direction of nurse-client interactions (tendency to "do for" rather than "do with").

    Barriers originating within organizations: lack of recognition from colleagues within the health care system (including other nurses) that this approach is a legitimate part of CHNs' role; lack of organizational culture/policies that value and support this type of approach in CHNs' practice settings; a lack of role models in practice settings with experience in community development work and other "upstream" skills; lack of time for involvement in such strategies due to increasing demands for mandatory disease prevention/health protection services such as immunization, communicable diseases follow-up, postpartum referrals, and meeting the immediate needs of individuals or families in crisis—all within the context of cuts to fiscal resources in the community health sector; and conceptual and practical challenges in defining community participation and empowerment and measuring community change.

    Barriers originating within the community: lack of recognition from the public that this approach is a legitimate part of CHNs' role; and resistance from sections of the community (based on ethnic, gender, ideological, or social class differences) to community development/empowerment initiatives that they do not see as being in their best interests.

CHAPTER 9

1. - Balancing work and family life
   - Finances: over one million Canadian children live in low-income families, and low income is most prevalent in lone-parent families headed by women (Statistics Canada, 2003)
   - Lack of time with family members
   - Boomerang kids: children living at home until older, returning home between jobs and school
   - Caring for elderly parents
   - For more information, visit the websites for Statistics Canada and The Vanier Institute of the Family, cited at the end of Chapter 9.
2. - Stay at home longer to save money while attending post-secondary education
   - Move home between jobs to save money
   - Move home between school terms to save money
   - Move home between marriages or relationships
   - Difficulty in finding full-time employment that pays an adequate wage
3. Terms used to describe nurses' work with families: provider of direct care, health promoter, partner/collaborator, advocate, teacher, researcher, leader, and administrator/manager. "Nurses help families prevent and manage illness and provide direct care across the continuum—from health promotion to care in the hospital and community" (Davies, Ogden Burke, Lynam, Ritchie, & Van Daalen, 1998, p. 4).
4. A collaborative relationship with a family would be:
   - a relationship with mutual respect between the nurse and the family for each other's roles, expertise, and responsibilities.
   - a relationship in which joint decision making exists.
   - a relationship which encourages cooperation for shared goals.
5. The family can be defined as "being unique and whomever the person defines as being family. They can include, but are not limited to, parents, children, siblings, neighbours, and significant people in the community" (RNAO, 2002, p. 18). A pet may even be considered a family member (Lepage, Essiembre, & Coutu-Wakulczyk, 1996). A family is "two or more individuals who depend on one another for emotional, physical, and economical support. The members of a family are self-defined" (Hanson, 2001, p. 6).
6. - The whole family is the focus of assessment, diagnosis, planning, and intervention.
   - The structure, function, development, and interactions of the family are assessed. Individual members are in the background.

- Strengths, resources, and limitations of the family as a unit are identified.
- The nurse needs to be familiar with family nursing theories and their conceptual sources.

CHAPTER 10

1. Settings where community health nurses work can be homes, schools, medical clinics, community centres, industry, and so on. The main role of community health nurses is disease prevention, health promotion, and maintenance and rehabilitation. For example, public health nurses use population health strategies to promote community health by focusing on risk identification and the five principles of primary health care, whereas home care nurses focus on health maintenance and rehabilitative care for individuals and families.
2. A community is healthy when its members can experience good health with a high level of life satisfaction and quality of life. There is a strong cohesiveness in the daily activities of the families, and various community services and resources are in place to support/complement the daily needs of the members. All components or subsystems within the community work in collaboration to achieve the community goals. Members of the community are actively involved in mobilizing community resources to respond to threats in the environment and make positive change to better the economy, environment, and equity. They work toward their life goals by achieving their individual and family development tasks, pursuing their goals in higher education and secure careers, and enjoying the accomplishments they achieve in life. There would be a clean and safe physical environment where residents have access to food, shelter, and adequate income. It also provides a responsible government that involves people in making decisions about their own lives.
3. Community health nurses first get to know the community by reviewing the history and existing data on the community, talking to the members of the community and listening to their concerns, working with the community, analyzing community data collected, making plans according to priority actions, empowering the members of the community to take ownership and act on the planned action, and evaluating the outcomes. The key is to think community. Use all basic nursing assessment skills to assess the community's real needs; facilitate community participation; involve many community sectors in the decision-making process from assessment to analysis, planning, priority setting, implementation, and evaluation; seek government commitment; and promote healthy public policy.
4. The assessment components include: community history and perception, population, physical environment, socioeconomic conditions, education, cultural characteristics, religions, recreation, health and service systems, transportation, and community dynamics.
5. Community health nurses will analyze the community data, and identify actual and potential community strengths and needs relevant to the issues in order to improve the existing health services. This community analysis involves categorization, summarization, comparison, and inference elaboration of data, which lead to community nursing diagnoses formulation and planning for intervention and evaluation.
6. Population health builds on the traditional practice of health promotion and public health where the focus is on preventive activities and disease management. In providing population health, the nurse will develop community health promotion, targeting the social, economic, physical environments; personal health practices; individual capacity and coping skills; human biology; early childhood development; and health service. The overall goal of population health is to maintain and improve the health status of the entire population and to reduce inequities in health status between population groups. Community health nurses will identify populations at risk and provide the needed care through a wide range of community participatory strategies.

CHAPTER 11

1. The components of an effective occupational health and safety program are:
   - management commitment;
   - worker involvement;
   - assessing and controlling the work environment;
   - addressing injuries, illnesses, and incidents; and
   - administration of health and safety in the workplace.

   Each of these components includes specific elements that make up an effective program.
2. The occupational health and safety team includes the OHN, occupational physician, occupational hygienist, safety professional, and ergonomist. Other team members can include a counsellor, physiotherapist, or other health safety professionals.
3. The role of occupational physicians is to diagnose and treat occupational injuries and illnesses. Their focus is on workers and worker health. These professionals consider the effects of the work environment on worker health. The focus of occupational hygienists and safety professionals is on worker health and safety as well; however, they focus more directly on the work environment. Occupational hygienists look for, measure, and control hazards. Safety professionals also look for hazards using a loss-control perspective. They also conduct investigations of incidents so that controls can be recommended to minimize future human and economic losses.
4. - Safety: exit doorway that is blocked with supplies
   - Physical: noise
   - Chemical: cold sterilizing solution
   - Biological: hepatitis B
   - Ergonomic: computer workstation not properly set up
   - Psychosocial: heavy workloads and insufficient staff
5. Roles identified by Rogers for OHNs include clinician/practitioner, administrator, educator, researcher, and consultant.
6. The five major competences required by CNA for certification are:
   - provision of occupational health, safety, and environment services;
   - assessment of the work environment, hazard control, and surveillance;
   - employee health assessment, surveillance, and intervention in the workplace;

- assessment and care of injuries and illnesses in the workplace; and
- health, safety, and environment education/promotion in the workplace.

7. The major focus of occupational hygienists is on the work environment. Their specialty is in conducting objective evaluations and measurements of the hazards in the work environment such as noise, temperature extremes, or chemicals. Their work provides the background data necessary to establish relationships between hazard exposure and health effects. The major focus of an OHN is on worker health. Along with the exposure information, the OHN considers signs, symptoms, and the effects of hazards on worker health and considers individual factors such as age and health history that can impact the health effects of work hazards on a particular worker. Both professionals are responsible for minimizing or eliminating hazards to protect worker health and prevent work-related illnesses and injuries.
8. Benefits to employees of having access to an OHN at their workplace are many. OHNs provide services that help workers prevent work-related injuries and illnesses, resulting in a decreased risk of workplace illness and injury. OHNs also provide training and education in health and safety that protects health both on and off the job. Programs in occupational health help to place workers in jobs they can perform safety both on initial hire and after returning to work from injury or illness. All this can lead to more job satisfaction and higher morale.

   Employers have both direct and indirect benefits as well. In addition to the direct human and economic cost savings of fewer injuries, illnesses, and sickness-related absences, employers with OHNs have increased compliance with health and safety legislation. Supervisors and managers still have the functions of maintaining health and safety, but they likely will spend less time and resources in dealing with health and safety issues with which they may be unfamiliar. Effective health and safety programs that are delivered by OHNs result in improved employee morale and productivity, improved labour relations, and an enhanced corporate image. There are also indirect savings related to decreased employee turnover, which reduces the costs of recruiting and training staff.
9. Community and occupational health nursing are similar in that they both emphasize prevention and health promotion for improving health and reducing the risks of illness.
10. - Working alone: safety, possibly psychosocial
    - Hepatitis B: biological
    - Needlesticks: safety
    - Dog bites: safety
    - Cold sterilization solution: chemical

CHAPTER 12

1. Epidemiology is the study of patterns of disease. Communicable diseases are transmitted through a community by various methods. Contact tracing, reporting, and surveillance are ways to help control and manage communicable diseases. The data generated from these activities assist or lay the foundation for epidemiological investigations.
2. Modes of transmission of communicable diseases include contact, droplet, airborne, and indirect (common vehicle and vector borne). Horizontal transmission is between people in the community, while vertical transmission is between generations (parent to child).
3. Control measures would include a barrier method (using a condom for penetration of anus or vagina or for oral sex). Other barrier methods include dental dams for protection during anal stimulation and a female condom. Other control measures include assessment of hepatitis status, review of the results, and then, if necessary, starting hepatitis B vaccinations. Drawing serology for other sexually transmitted infections, providing treatment, collecting names of contacts, and referring to a specialist for further evaluation, if necessary, are other measures to control the transmission of communicable diseases.
4. Biologic factors of age, general health status, sex, genetic make-up, and specific immunity
5. The family or household members of this youth would be the starting point in the contact tracing. The teachers at the school will assist you by providing class schedules of this student. The student can assist by providing contact names not included in class lists, as well as others not in their school. As you work through the contact tracing, it is important to remember what constitutes a contact; that person will need a skin test or other screening measures.
6. You would find the necessary information on the Health Canada, Notifiable Diseases Surveillance-on-line website: www.hc-sc.gc.ca/pphb-dgspsp/dsol-smed/index.html

CHAPTER 13

1. Five pressures in Western society that can influence program planning and evaluation are:
   - Economical constraints: there is increased pressure to get maximum value for monies spent. Funders require a full accounting for monies dispersed for health promotion programs. Funders are also interested in the benefits that the program provides to the community, that is, in the value added by their expenditures.
   - Growing emphasis on individual rights: democratization in society leads individuals to expect to be informed and involved in planning and decision-making processes related to their care, education, and treatment. Legislation on informed consent, bills of rights for patients, and the creation of ombudsman positions have increased people's awareness of individual rights and reinforced their expectations about being informed.
   - Advocacy groups: as people become more aware of their individual rights, they also become aware that other groups in society are vulnerable to the abuse of their human rights. Many associations defend the rights of others and fight for legislative changes and government policies that support individual rights and address human needs. As champions of human rights, advocates have a strong interest in how programs are planned and conducted and in the results of program evaluations.
   - An increased demand by the public for accountability: the public trusts CHNs to conduct themselves responsibly and to be answerable for their actions. However, scepticism has grown about whether public organizations and agencies are truly functioning in the best interests of society. This has led to public pressure for greater openness and transparency about what organizations and agencies do. Many people want to be

informed about how programs function and are interested in learning about the results of program evaluations so they can make informed decisions about whether to continue to support the program.

- Dissemination of information via the internet: both health professionals and consumers have easier access to articles, discussion groups, and research on a wide range of topics through the internet. Health professionals must possess or have access to current information about health matters and be able to discriminate between reliable and unreliable information. They need to be able to respond to consumers' questions and be prepared to help community members identify reliable sources of health information and reputable support groups.

2. See Figure 13.1.

3. - Shared vision (optional in terms of its inclusion in the diagram of the program logic model but necessary for program development): the shared vision is based on identification and agreement regarding the core values, beliefs, and principles that will guide the program. It leads to articulation of the overall goal, objectives, and desired outcomes for the program.
   - Inputs: the resources that need to be invested in a program in order to achieve the desired outcomes. Inputs include staff, time, partnerships, volunteers, money, equipment, materials, and facilities. In addition, the information obtained from a community assessment provides essential information for program development.
   - Processes: may also be referred to as throughputs, methods, or outputs. Processes are the strategies used to deliver the program, including activities such as recruitment, education, advertising, and social marketing. Quantifiable statistical data on these activities provide information on services delivered and contribute to the evaluation of the outcomes.
   - Outcomes: include both short-term changes demonstrated by participants in the program and long-term results observed in the target community. Outcomes are the changes or benefits from delivering the program. Short-term outcomes are often measured in terms of changes in awareness, knowledge, attitudes, skills, opinions, aspirations, and motivations. Long-term outcomes are causally related to the program goal and show the ultimate impact of the program on the target community. Long-term outcomes are directional in nature; that is, there is an increase or a decrease in something or some behaviour.
   - Environmental factors (optional in terms of its inclusion in a diagram of the program logic model but necessary for program development): environmental factors are internal and external forces and constraints that may impact the program's development, implementation, continuation, and potential for expansion. They include factors such as health policies, safety regulations, economic conditions, culture, political climate, geography, changes in program personnel, employment conditions, and changes in funders' requirements and stakeholders' priorities.

4. Outcomes are the changes or benefits for participants resulting from their involvement in the program, such as the adoption of healthier lifestyle behaviours. Outputs refer to program activities, such as the number of clients served or the number or units of service provided.

5. - SEE: this level involves consideration of social, economic, and environmental factors such as mortality rates, household income levels, transportation, water potability, and police and fire services.
   - Practices: this level examines the community's capacity to build on its strengths. Examples of practices are patterns of behaviours or actions that individuals or communities use that influence SEE conditions.
   - KASA (knowledge, attitudes, skills, and aspirations): the KASA level focuses on a determination of the knowledge, attitudes, skills, and aspirations needed by people in the target group to achieve desired outcomes at the SEE level.
   - Reactions: the responses, either positive or negative, by existing or potential participants to the subject matter of the proposed program. Reactions include their acceptance of the program facilitators or leaders or the agency they represent, as well as their response to the methods being used for program delivery.
   - Participation: the involvement of individuals, groups, or communities in program activities.
   - Activities: the various strategies and events used to deliver the program. The methods used can include personal contacts, group education sessions, social marketing, and mass media approaches.
   - Resources: the time, money, staff, materials, transportation, and facilities used to plan, promote, implement, and evaluate programs.

6. Formative evaluations are conducted on an ongoing basis to monitor program activities in order to help shape or modify the program while it is being delivered. They are particularly useful in the early stages of program implementation for identifying operational problems. They may also provide documented evidence of the historical development of various aspects of a program.

   Summative evaluations assess the effectiveness of the program. Summative evaluations examine whether a program has met its stated goals and objectives and whether the outcomes of the program have the intended effect. Summative evaluations are often mandated or conducted as part of policy reviews. These final or summary evaluation findings are particularly valuable when decisions need to be made about the continuation or expansion of a program.

7. Table 13.1 summarizes the difference between conventional and participatory monitoring and evaluation.

8. Common participatory monitoring and evaluation methods are shown in Table 13.2.

9. - Accountability for program delivery is a professional obligation and a public expectation that is addressed by reporting evaluation results.
   - To provide feedback to internal stakeholders—the participants, staff, and volunteers who delivered the program; program managers and other administrators; and any persons or groups who collaborated in designing or delivering the program.
   - Funders want to know how the money was spent and whether the program achieved the desired results. Funders are particularly interested in a cost-benefit analysis.
   - Other parties interested in the evaluation results include public officials who may need to respond to questions

from taxpayers, community residents who are interested in activities in their area and the potential effect on them, other community providers who may be interested in interacting with the program, and the media who inform the public and fulfill a watchdog role.

- Researchers investigating programs and strategies for service delivery in other communities may be interested in the report. They may be interested in replicating the program, identifying useful components that could be adapted to another community, or examining a particular aspect of the program more rigorously.

CHAPTER 14

1. For evidence-based decision making, consider research evidence, patient preferences, nurse skills, and resources available.
2. The most critical attitude for a nurse practising in an evidence-based way is a critical questioning approach to care planning and evaluation.
3. You might:
   - collect data for outcomes of care or for process indicators such as number of visits, hours of care, attendance at a session, or number of sessions delivered.
   - deliver experimental interventions, for example, smoking cessation, sexual health intervention, comprehensive stroke care.
   - work collaboratively to develop an important clinical question and to write a proposal to conduct the research.
4. Individual studies can produce different results, including no significant effect of treatment if the sample size was not large enough. By reading a systematic review, you get a more complete picture of the literature, both published and unpublished, compiled in a way that minimizes bias. This pre-appraised literature will save you time, money, and resources from doing the complete literature review yourself.
5. Factors to consider when planning to implement a clinical practice or policy change:
   - characteristics of the change (or innovation) itself, for example, how different it is from current practice, how will it save time or add to the time needed to give care;
   - characteristics of the people involved in adopting the change, for example, how open they are to change, their attitudes toward research and research utilization, age, time since graduation, and level of education;
   - characteristics of the organization where the change will take place, for example, how research intensive the organization is, its culture of using research and "keeping up to date," and its culture of evaluating care given; and
   - characteristics of the organization's environment, for example, rural or urban, academic setting.

Index

G

H

Q

R

T